T0338285

DECISION ANALYTICS AND OPTIMIZATION IN DISEASE PREVENTION AND TREATMENT

Wiley Series in
Operations Research and Management Science

DECISION ANALYTICS AND OPTIMIZATION IN DISEASE PREVENTION AND TREATMENT

Edited By

NAN KONG
Associate Professor
Weldon School of Biomedical Engineering, Purdue University
West Lafayette, IN, USA

SHENGFAN ZHANG
Assistant Professor
Department of Industrial Engineering, University of Arkansas
Fayetteville, AR, USA

Registered Office(s)
John Wiley & Sons, Inc., 111 River Street, Hoboken, NJ 07030, USA

Editorial Office
111 River Street, Hoboken, NJ 07030, USA

For details of our global editorial offices, customer services, and more information about Wiley products visit us at www.wiley.com.

Wiley also publishes its books in a variety of electronic formats and by print-on-demand. Some content that appears in standard print versions of this book may not be available in other formats.

Library of Congress Cataloging-in-Publication Data

Names: Kong, Nan, editor. | Zhang, Shengfan, editor.
Title: Decision analytics and optimization in disease prevention and treatment / edited by Nan Kong, Shengfan Zhang.
Description: Hoboken, NJ : Wiley, 2018. | Includes bibliographical references and index. |
Identifiers: LCCN 2017037696 (print) | LCCN 2017038531 (ebook) | ISBN 9781118960134 (pdf) | ISBN 9781118960141 (epub) | ISBN 9781118960127 (cloth)
Subjects: | MESH: Preventive Health Services | Communicable Disease Control | Decision Making | Models, Theoretical | Therapeutics
Classification: LCC RA643 (ebook) | LCC RA643 (print) | NLM WA 108 | DDC 616.9–dc23
LC record available at https://lccn.loc.gov/2017037696

Cover design by Wiley
Cover image: (Top right) © deepblue4you/Gettyimages; (Bottom left) © Skomorokh/Gettyimages

Set in 10/12pt Times by SPi Global, Pondicherry, India

Printed in the United States of America

10 9 8 7 6 5 4 3 2 1

CONTENTS

PART 3   TREATMENT TECHNOLOGY AND SYSTEM   **259**

**12   Biological Planning Optimization for High-Dose-Rate Brachytherapy
and its Application to Cervical Cancer Treatment**   **261**

Eva K. Lee, Fan Yuan, Alistair Templeton, Rui Yao, Krystyna Kiel, and James C.H. Chu

**13   Fluence Map Optimization in Intensity-Modulated Radiation
Therapy Treatment Planning**   **285**

Dionne M. Aleman

CONTRIBUTORS

Oguzhan Alagoz, Department of Industrial and Systems Engineering, University of Wisconsin-Madison, Madison, WI, USA

Dionne M. Aleman, Department of Mechanical & Industrial Engineering and Institute for Health Policy, Management & Evaluation, University of Toronto, Toronto, ON, Canada; Guided Therapeutics Core, Techna Institute, Toronto, ON, Canada

Sabina S. Alistar, Department of Management Science and Engineering, Stanford University, Palo Alto, CA, USA

Douglas R. Bish, Grado Department of Industrial and Systems Engineering, Virginia Tech, Blacksburg, VA, USA

Ebru K. Bish, Grado Department of Industrial and Systems Engineering, Virginia Tech, Blacksburg, VA, USA

Margaret L. Brandeau, Department of Management Science and Engineering, Stanford University, Palo Alto, CA, USA

Elizabeth S. Burnside, Department of Radiology, University of Wisconsin School of Medicine and Public Health, Madison, WI, USA

Jagpreet Chhatwal, Institute of Technology Assessment, Massachusetts General Hospital, Harvard Medical School, Boston, MA, USA

James C.H. Chu, Department of Radiation Oncology, Rush University Medical Center, Chicago, IL, USA

Ted Cohen, Department of Epidemiology and Microbial Disease, Yale School of Public Health, New Haven, CT, USA

David Craft, Radiation Oncology, Department of Physics, Harvard Medical School, Boston, MA, USA

Brian T. Denton, Department of Industrial and Operations Engineering, University of Michigan, Ann Arbor, MI, USA

Hadi El-Amine, Systems Engineering and Operations Research Department, George Mason University, Fairfax, VA, USA

Tarek Halabi, Radiation Oncology, Department of Physics, Harvard Medical School, Boston, MA, USA

Julia L. Higle, Daniel J. Epstein Department of Industrial and Systems Engineering, University of Southern California, Los Angeles, CA, USA

Krystyna Kiel, Department of Radiation Oncology, Rush University Medical Center, Chicago, IL, USA

Nan Kong, Weldon School of Biomedical Engineering, Purdue University, West Lafayette, IN, USA

Mark A. Lawley, Department of Industrial and Systems Engineering, Texas A&M University, College Station, TX, USA; Department of Biomedical Engineering, Texas A&M University, College Station, TX, USA

Eva K. Lee, NSF-Whitaker Center for Operations Research in Medicine and HealthCare, Georgia Institute of Technology, Atlanta, GA, USA; School of Industrial and Systems Engineering, Georgia Institute of Technology, Atlanta, GA, USA; NSF I/UCRC Center for Health Organization Transformation, Arlington, VA, USA

Adriana Ley-Chavez, Department of Industrial and Mechanical Engineering, Universidad de las Américas Puebla, Puebla, Mexico

Yan Li, Center for Health Innovation, The New York Academy of Medicine, New York, NY, USA; Department of Population Health Science and Policy, Icahn School of Medicine at Mount Sinai, New York, NY, USA

Shan Liu, Department of Industrial and Systems Engineering, University of Washington, Seattle, WA, USA

Jennifer Mason Lobo, Department of Public Health Sciences, University of Virginia, Charlottesville, VA, USA

Mahboubeh Madadi, Department of Industrial Engineering, Louisiana Tech University, Ruston, LA, USA

George Miller, Center for Value in Health Care, Altarum, Ann Arbor, MI, USA

José A. Pagán, Center for Health Innovation, The New York Academy of Medicine, New York, NY, USA; Department of Public Health Policy and Management, College of Global Public Health, New York University, New York, NY, USA; Leonard Davis Institute of Health Economics, University of Pennsylvania, Philadelphia, PA, USA

Anthony D. Slonim, University of Nevada School of Medicine and Renown Health, Reno, NV, USA

Susan L. Stramer, Scientific Affairs, American Red Cross, Gaithersburg, MD, USA

Sze-chuan Suen, Daniel J. Epstein Department of Industrial and Systems Engineering, University of Southern California, Los Angeles, CA, USA

Alistair Templeton, Department of Radiation Oncology, Rush University Medical Center, Chicago, IL, USA

Yu Teng, Avenir Health, Glastonbury, CT, USA

Wanzhu Tu, Department of Biostatistics, Indiana University Medical School, Indianapolis, IN, USA

Sait Tunc, Department of Industrial and Systems Engineering, University of Wisconsin-Madison, Madison, WI, USA

Reza Yaesoubi, Department of Health Policy and Management, Yale School of Public Health, New Haven, CT, USA

Rui Yao, Department of Radiation Oncology, Rush University Medical Center, Chicago, IL, USA

Fan Yuan, NSF-Whitaker Center for Operations Research in Medicine and HealthCare, Georgia Institute of Technology, Atlanta, GA, USA; School of Industrial and Systems Engineering, Georgia Institute of Technology, Atlanta, GA, USA; NSF I/UCRC Center for Health Organization Transformation, Arlington, VA, USA

Shengfan Zhang, Department of Industrial Engineering, University of Arkansas, Fayetteville, AR, USA

Jingyu Zhang, Enterprise Model Risk Management, Bank of America, Wilmington, DE, USA

PREFACE

Advances in disease prevention and treatment have greatly improved the quality of life of patients and the general population. However, it is challenging to truly harness these advances in patient-centered medical decision-making for the uncertainty associated with disease risks and care outcomes, as well as the complexity of the technologies. This book contains a collection of cutting-edge research studies that apply decision analytics and optimization tools in disease prevention and treatment. Specifically, the book comprises the following three main parts.

Part 1: Infectious Disease Control and Management. Common infectious diseases are considered in this part, including tuberculosis (Chapter 1), HIV infection (Chapter 2), influenza (Chapter 3), chlamydia infection (Chapter 4), and hepatitis C (Chapter 6). Although not focusing on a specific type of infectious disease, Chapter 5 deals with the costs and efficacy of detecting infectious agents in donated blood. Controls and decisions investigated in this part include budget allocation (Chapter 2), school closure or children vaccination (Chapter 3), screening scheme design (Chapters 4 and 5), and a whole set of interventions (Chapter 6) such as behavior and public health interventions. Disease modeling techniques introduced in this part include microsimulation (Chapter 1), stochastic transmission dynamic model (Chapter 3), compartmental model (Chapter 4), and Markov-based model (Chapter 6).

In this part, Chapters 1 and 6 provide excellent overviews of decision-analytic modeling research in developing policy guidelines. Between the two chapters, the former focuses more on the disease modeling, whereas the latter focuses more on the analysis with a holistic view covering screening, monitoring, and treatment. In addition, Chapter 6 deals with long-term management of an infectious disease, which helps make the transition to the second part of the book.

Part 2: Noncommunicable Disease Prevention. This part starts with Chapter 7, which examines screening strategies for the prevention of cervical cancers, which are mainly caused by human papillomavirus (HPV) infection. Chapter 7 concerns disease progression from the viewpoint of HPV infection rather than the infectious disease itself. The chapter provides a good connection with the first part of the book. Other prevalent noncommunicable diseases considered in this part include breast cancer (Chapters 8 and 10), prostate cancer (Chapter 9), and cardiovascular diseases (Chapter 11). Methodologies introduced in this part cover simulation with model-based analyses for screening strategies (Chapter 7), Markov decision process (Chapter 8), partially observable Markov decision process (Chapter 9), cost-effectiveness analysis under a partially observable Markov chain model (Chapter 10), and agent-based modeling (Chapter 11).

Part 3: Treatment Technology and System. In this part, optimization studies of several treatment decisions and technologies are reported, including high-dose-rate brachytherapy (Chapter 12), intensity-modulated radiation therapy (Chapters 13 and 14), volumetric modulated arc therapy (Chapter 14), cardiovascular disease prevention and treatment (Chapter 15), and various treatment decisions for type II diabetes (Chapter 16). Methodologies introduced comprise multiobjective, nonlinear, mixed-integer programming model (Chapter 12), fluence map optimization (Chapter 13), sliding window optimization (Chapter 14), Markov modeling (Chapter 15), and Markov decision process (Chapter 16).

The book concludes with Chapter 17, which uniquely presents optimization-based classification models for early detection of disease, risk prediction, and treatment design and outcome prediction. This chapter is expected to showcase extended potentials of optimization techniques and motivate more operations researchers to study biomedical data mining problems.

We believe this book can serve well as a handbook for researchers in the field of medical decision modeling, analysis, and optimization, a textbook for graduate-level courses on OR applications in healthcare, and a reference for medical practitioners and public health policymakers with interest in health analytics.

Lastly, we would like to express our sincere gratitude to the following reviewers for taking their time to review book chapters and provide valuable feedback for our contributors in the blind-review process: Turgay Ayer, Christine Barnett, Bjorn Berg, Margaret Brandeau, Brian Denton, Jeremy Goldhaber-Fiebert, Shadi Hassani Goodarzi, Karen Hicklin, Julie Ivy, Amin Khademi, Anahita Khojandi, Yan Li, Jennifer Lobo, Maria Mayorga, Nisha Nataraj, Ehsan Salari, Burhan Sandikci, Joyatee Sarker, Carolina Vivas, Fan Wang, Xiaolei Xie, Yiwen Xu, and Yuanhui Zhang. We would also like to acknowledge the great support we received from Wiley editors, Sumathi Elangovan, Jon Gurstelle, Vishnu Narayanan, Kathleen Pagliaro, Vishnu Priya. R and former editor Susanne Steitz-Filler.

PART 1

INFECTIOUS DISEASE CONTROL AND MANAGEMENT

1

OPTIMIZATION IN INFECTIOUS DISEASE CONTROL AND PREVENTION: TUBERCULOSIS MODELING USING MICROSIMULATION

SZE-CHUAN SUEN

Daniel J. Epstein Department of Industrial and Systems Engineering, University of Southern California, Los Angeles, CA, USA

Compared with many other optimization problems, optimization of treatments for national infectious disease control often involves a relatively small set of feasible interventions. The challenge is in accurately forecasting the costs and benefits of an intervention; once that can be evaluated for the limited set of interventions, the best one can be easily identified. Predicting the outcome of an intervention can be difficult due to the complexity of the disease natural history, the interactions between individuals that influence transmission, and the lack of data. It is therefore important to understand how a particular disease affects patients, spreads, and is treated in order to design effective control policies against it.

One such complex disease is tuberculosis (TB), which kills millions of people every year. It is transmitted through respiratory contacts, has a latent stage, and is difficult to diagnose and cure in resource-constrained settings, and treatment success varies by

Decision Analytics and Optimization in Disease Prevention and Treatment, First Edition.
Edited by Nan Kong and Shengfan Zhang.
© 2018 John Wiley & Sons, Inc. Published 2018 by John Wiley & Sons, Inc.

demographic factors like age and sex. Moreover, the mechanisms of disease transmission are not fully known, making modeling of transmission difficult, and it is particularly prevalent in areas of the world where reliable disease statistics are hard to find. All of these characteristics make TB a difficult disease to model in the settings where choosing an optimal control policy is most important. Traditional compartmental disease models may become intractable if all relevant demographic and treatment stratifications are specified (state space explosion), so a microsimulation may be a good alternative for modeling TB dynamics. In a microsimulation, individual health and treatment states are probabilistically simulated over time and averaged together to form population statistics. This allows for greater modeling flexibility and a more tractable model but may also result in problems of model stochasticity.

In this chapter, we first discuss the epidemiology of the disease, illustrating why TB modeling is necessary and highlighting challenging aspects of this disease. In the second section, we provide a brief overview of simulation and then discuss in depth a microsimulation model of TB to illustrate subtleties of using microsimulation to evaluate policies in infectious disease control.

1.1 TUBERCULOSIS EPIDEMIOLOGY AND BACKGROUND

In order to understand how to pick a model framework and implement a useful model, it is important first to understand the epidemiological characteristics and background of the disease. TB is caused by the bacteria *Mycobacterium tuberculosis*, which can attack the lungs (pulmonary TB) or other parts of the body (extrapulmonary TB). TB is a respiratory disease and transmitted through the air by coughing or sneezing. It has been declared a global public health emergency, killing 1.3 million people in 2012, while 8.6 million people developed the disease. The majority of cases were in Southeast Asia, African, or Western Pacific regions (Zumla et al. 2013). However, the disease varies by region and cannot be treated identically in all areas—for example, many African cases are concurrent with HIV, while in other regions, like India, HIV prevalence is low although TB prevalence is high (World Health Organization 2013). This means that models for one country may not be easily adapted to another, since comorbidities and the driving factors of the epidemic may be quite different.

Once contracted, TB may stay latent for many years and only activates in about 10% of cases. Latent TB is asymptomatic and cannot be transmitted. Activation rates depend on immunological health and have been observed to vary by demographic factors, like age (Horsburgh 2004; Vynnycky and Fine 1997), and behavioral factors, like smoking (Lin et al. 2007). Transmission of TB, which occurs through respiratory contact, may vary by age (Horby et al. 2011; Mossong et al. 2008), demographic patterns, and cultural trends but is poorly documented or understood.

Nondrug-resistant strains of TB, whether latent or active, are treatable using antibiotics, but misuse of first-line antibiotic regimens may lead to drug-resistant or multidrug-resistant (MDR) TB, defined as strains that are resistant to at least isoniazid and rifampin, two first-line TB drugs. Premature treatment default or failure can result in the development of drug resistance, and drug-resistant strains may then be transmitted to other individuals. Drug-resistant TB can be treatable, depending on the level of drug resistance (pan-resistant TB strains have emerged), but require more expensive second-line antibiotic regimens of longer duration (drugs need to be taken many times a week for up to 2 years) with higher toxicity rates and lower cure rates. Therefore optimization of treatment policies needs to take imperfect treatment behavior and potential drug resistance into account. Drug-resistant TB prevalence varies by region, and this also contributes to the necessity of geographical specificity when evaluating potential TB control mechanisms.

Latent and active TB can be detected through a variety of different tests of varying sensitivity and specificity, and different tests may be preferred in different regions. For instance, Mantoux tuberculin skin test (TST) or interferon-gamma release assay (IGRA) blood test are used to detect TB infection in many areas with low TB prevalence, whereas sputum smear microscopy tests are commonly used to identify active TB cases in areas of high prevalence (Global Health Education 2014). While sputum smear tests have fast turnaround times and low costs, sputum smear tests have low sensitivity and active TB cases may be overlooked. Bacteriological culture may take up to several weeks but is a more accurate diagnosis method and can be used for drug susceptibility testing (it can be used to identify drug-resistant samples from susceptible TB samples). Initial diagnosis can also be passive (patients self-present at local clinics) or targeted (active case finding, contact tracing, etc.). After entering treatment, patients may undergo different tests sequentially to monitor treatment efficacy and determine if second-line treatment is necessary. The cost and the effectiveness of various screening policies vary by patient behavior, latent and active TB prevalence, and what treatment options are available. Identifying optimal region-specific timing and type of diagnosis is an area of active research (Acuna-Villaorduna et al. 2008; Winetsky et al. 2012).

TB infection and disease may be complicated by comorbidities. TB is often observed along with HIV, which can change the natural history of disease and complicate TB diagnosis and treatment. In 2012, 1.1 million of the 8.6 million new cases of TB were among people living with HIV (World Health Organization 2013). HIV patients have a higher risk of developing TB due to immune system compromise. Diabetes is another comorbidity that can change TB activation rates (World Health Organization 2011). While helping patients with multiple chronic diseases is an increasingly important part of TB control, modeling multiple diseases is challenging since the diseases interact and data to inform joint distributions on risks and rates may be scarce.

1.1.1 TB in India

India is the country with the largest number of TB cases—roughly 23% of the global total—despite large gains in the last few decades in decreasing TB mortality, incidence, and prevalence through TB treatment and diagnosis (World Health Organization 2015).

India has a federally funded TB treatment program called the Revised National Tuberculosis Control Program (RNTCP). This program offers the approved antibacterial drug regimens for treating TB, called Directly Observed Treatment, Short Course (DOTS), where health workers help patients administer their drugs to help ensure that they are taken correctly. These regimens require treatment for at least 6 months of treatment and may be longer for those patients who have previously been treated for TB (RNTCP 2010).

Despite this federally funded program, and unlike in many other countries with high TB burdens, many TB patients in India seek care in private sector clinics. Since the symptoms of TB can easily be mistaken for routine respiratory illnesses, many patients tend to first seek care from retail chemists or informal health providers in the private healthcare market. These private clinics may not have health practitioners trained in identifying and treating TB (Tu et al. 2010; Uplekar and Shepard 1991; Vandan et al. 2009), and patients using private clinics may use multiple clinics as they attain temporary relief from symptoms that then recur (Kapoor et al. 2012). This delay to getting appropriate TB care means that patients begin effective treatment at a later stage of their disease, may have infected others with TB, and may have been exposed to anti-TB drugs that can select for drug resistance.

Combating drug-resistant TB is a continuing challenge for India. More than half of the MDR-TB cases notified in 2014 occurred in India, China, and the Russian Federation (World Health Organization 2015). India started the federally funded DOTS-Plus MDR-TB treatment program in 2007, where MDR-TB patients can get access to the necessary 18–24 months of second-line TB antibiotics. However, the long treatment duration and drug toxicity make treating MDR-TB difficult, and patients may default from treatment, potentially generating more resistant disease strains. Cases of extensively drug-resistant TB (XDR-TB), where the MDR-TB strain is additionally resistant to fluoroquinolone and a second-line injectable antibiotic, have also been documented in India (Michael and John 2012).

While comorbidities can often complicate TB treatment, HIV comorbidity is relatively less common in India as in some other countries with high TB burdens: 4% of TB patients are HIV positive in India (as opposed to 61% in South Africa). For this reason we will be considering a simulation model of TB for India that does not specifically consider any comorbidities. We turn to simulations for disease control in the next section.

1.2 MICROSIMULATIONS FOR DISEASE CONTROL

A variety of model types can be used to model the diversity of issues in TB control and prevention. However, while natural disease dynamics and treatment policies can be approximated using difference equations, these may be difficult to solve analytically and require simulation to arrive at numerical answers. Simulations imitate the real system using a probability distribution to generate random events and obtain statistical observations of system performance. Simulations can provide not only the epidemiological trends or costs of each treatment arm being considered but also disease trajectories over time.

One common disease modeling method is to use a compartmental model, where states are formed using health, treatment, or demographic status, depending on the complexity of the model. State transition probabilities can be estimated from the published literature or estimated from survey data, and the probability of an individual or population acquiring disease, incurring treatment costs, or any other outcome of interest, can be estimated by starting the model in one state and applying transition probabilities as time advances. The model would then provide the mean performance outcome at every time period. These models can be very useful and may be applicable for a variety of problems. They are discussed in detail in another chapter of this book.

Unfortunately, these models can quickly become intractable if the state space becomes too large, as can happen if a large number of stratifications are required. To illustrate this, suppose a hypothetical TB model included different transition probabilities for individuals of different ages (age 0–15, 16–45, 46–60, and 60+), sexes (male or female), and TB status (healthy, infected, or active disease). It would have $4 \times 2 \times 3 = 24$ states, and the modeler needs to specify transition probabilities to each of the other states. One can easily see that the number of states would quickly become very large if the model wished to use a finer age stratification (i.e., 1 year age bins) and include demographic characteristics about treatment status, TB strain (i.e., different strains of TB by drug resistance), and past treatment status. The model would potentially become difficult to work with. However, these patient characteristics may be important to capture to accurately reflect TB dynamics.

A microsimulation overcomes this issue by simulating an individual unit (in this case, an individual) over time instead of estimating the mean outcomes for a population. This allows the modeler to specify behavioral characteristics at a very detailed level if necessary—probabilities of disease progression or treatment can depend on the individuals' demographic characteristics and history. Using a random number generator, outcomes for each individual can then be probabilistically determined and recorded at each time period; a population of individuals of sufficient size should then generate the same average outcomes as those estimated in the compartmental model. However, in addition to providing the mean outcome measures of interest, the microsimulation can also provide the distribution of the measures of interest since every individual's heath and treatment state is estimated at every time period. We will illustrate this in the second section of this chapter, in which we will describe in detail a microsimulation of TB in India.

However, before delving into that example, it may be useful to discuss and summarize the advantages and disadvantages of simulation and microsimulation in particular. Simulation methods are powerful and can help us find numerical estimates for outcomes that are analytically intractable. Unlike some analytical models, they easily allow the modeler to examine transient effects, not just model outcomes in steady state. Microsimulation also allows for a great deal of modeling flexibility, since the modeler can easily add characteristics to individuals without specifying another set of states. Organizational structure in a microsimulation is more robust than a compartmental state transition model, since the modeled population can have as many characteristics as a modeler needs without the number of compartments becoming intractably large. However, the modeler also needs to be careful about stochastic fade-out, when no individuals have a certain characteristic just due to chance alone. For instance, since the number of individuals with TB compared with the total population of a country is small, it is likely that no individuals in the simulation will have TB if the total simulation population is too small. For example, consider a country where the TB prevalence is 0.1%; if the simulation only models 1000 individuals, and the individual with TB dies before transmitting the disease, it would look as if TB had been eradicated! Now imagine an analogous case where the modeler cared about TB in different subgroups of the population—then the number of individuals in these subgroups could be small, and the corresponding number of individuals with TB in that group would be even smaller. Therefore the larger the number of characteristics, the larger the modeled population is necessary so that individuals of all characteristics will be represented. If the number of individual characteristics is large, this may mean long computation times (if the simulation population is large) or noisy outcome measurements (if the simulated population is too small).

1.3 A MICROSIMULATION FOR TUBERCULOSIS CONTROL IN INDIA

To illustrate how microsimulation can be used for disease control and prevention, we are going to discuss in detail a microsimulation of the TB epidemic in India (Suen et al. 2014, 2015). This simulation was used to evaluate the impact of TB transmission prevention versus improving treatment as well as to evaluate the cost-effectiveness of treatment policies. The model uses a dynamic transmission model of TB that was calibrated to Indian demography and TB epidemiology from 1996 to 2010 and then projected into the future (until 2038 in the case of the transmission prevention analysis and until 2025 in the cost-effectiveness analysis) and includes health and treatment characteristics for nondrug-resistant and drug-resistant latent and active TB. Since TB dynamics and treatment trajectories can depend on age and sex, among other demographic factors, the model stratifies individuals these characteristics. This means that probabilities of mortality, transmission, activation, and treatment uptake and effectiveness vary by age and sex in the model. This level of detail precluded the model from using the more common compartmental model structure due to the large state space; it makes more sense as a microsimulation. Inclusion of these stratifications allows treatment policies to differentially influence different demographics, which may be of particular interest if there are particular demographics a modeler is interested in (i.e., the elderly, school-aged children, etc.). Treatment availability and effectiveness were also included to estimate the effect of treatment policies that were already in effect. Since not all TB dynamics parameters were known with certainty, this model was calibrated by changing activation and treatment uptake parameters until TB prevalence, incidence, and a variety of treatment demographic characteristics matched values from the literature. After validation, the model was used to estimate incidence, prevalence, and mortality from drug-resistant and nondrug-resistant strains of TB for projection into the future for scenarios where either treatment or diagnosis policies were improved. These estimates could then be used to provide insight on the effectiveness of intervention policies and the cost delaying such efforts. With this information, one could better optimize treatment versus prevention policies for controlling TB in India. We will discuss the model building and analysis process, from population inputs to calibration to treatment, in detail in the next sections.

1.3.1 Population Dynamics

In this microsimulation, individuals are simulated from birth to death as they pass through various health and treatment states. To accurately recreate the Indian population dynamics, the population growth rate in the microsimulation matches historic and projected trends. Non-TB mortality probabilities were calculated using World Health Organization (WHO) life tables for 1990, 2000, and 2009 (World Health Organization 2010a). All individuals in the microsimulation are exposed to age- and sex-specific background mortality, and those with active TB have an additional disease-specific risk of death. The resulting age structure in the model stabilizes during the "burn-in" period and shows population aging thereafter, especially over 2013–2038, as in reality. The "burn-in" period is where the model is run until population demographics and disease prevalence levels stabilize to steady-state levels that match observed pretreatment levels in India. This ensures that treatment policies implemented during the analysis period are due to the treatment arms of interest and not population dynamics effects.

The model uses a simulated population of 6.5 million people in 1996 that grows to 10 million by 2038. Because the model considers a lesser number of simulated individuals than in India in reality, these numbers were ultimately scaled to the total Indian population size to consider impacts on disease burden (thus, proportions of the modeled population are multiplied by the corresponding actual Indian population in a given year).

1.3.2 Dynamics of TB in India

After general population dynamics matched observed trends, the model needed to incorporate TB natural history. To do this, the model simulates individuals acquiring disease with some risk, activating from latent to active TB with some risk, and entering, defaulting, or failing treatment with some risk. Each of these probabilities is age and sex dependent to reflect medical and demographic data.

There are many ways to simulate different mixing patterns for disease transmission. It is common to assume homogeneous mixing, where all patients capable of transmission have equal probability of meeting, and infecting, a susceptible individual, as in classic susceptible–infected–susceptible (SIS) or susceptible–infected–recovered (SIR) models of infectious disease (Kermack and McKendrick 1927). In such models, individuals transition between disease-susceptible and infected (and in the case of SIR models, recovered) health states according to a set of differential equations. The probability of acquiring TB for a susceptible individual is calculated using the proportion of transmitting individuals multiplied by the proportion of susceptible individuals, scaled by a transmission factor.

With a microsimulation, however, we can add a more detailed representation of transmission as needed. If the data is available, individuals can have higher or lower risks of infection if an infected individual is in their family group or community, or vary by age, if individuals of certain ages are more social or susceptible to acquiring infection. Complex infection dynamics can be easily simulated—the only difficulty is to ensure that the parameters reasonably reflect reality. Since data is often scarce and simple models should be preferred to complex models, the most general modeling approach that still captures the relevant disease dynamics should be used. In this microsimulation example, the model used a "who-mixes-with-whom" transmission matrix to allow the probability of acquiring disease to vary by age while still assuming homogeneous mixing within age groups.

Figure 1.1 visually represents this matrix, where the colors represent the frequency of contacts of susceptible individuals across different ages (0–5, 6–10, etc.). Therefore the product of this matrix with the proportion of infectious individuals in each age group, multiplied by the per-contact probability of acquiring TB, should give a vector of probabilities of acquiring disease for susceptible of different age groups (the matrix need not be square, if different age brackets were used for infected and susceptible populations). During implementation, the microsimulation counts up the number of infected individuals in the population, calculates proportions, and applies this matrix to get the probability of infection and the number of newly infected individuals in this time period.

It is important to note that data should support the modeling assumptions made. In this case, the data about age-specific mixing was calculated from the published literature on respiratory contacts, and the per-contact infection probability, a scalar, was calibrated (Mossong et al. 2008). We discuss model calibration and validation further in the chapter.

1.3.3 Activation

Once an individual is infected with TB, TB may stay latent within the individual for years, or may never activate. Activation rates change over time from infection (Horsburgh 2004; Vynnycky and Fine 1997) and other factors like immune system

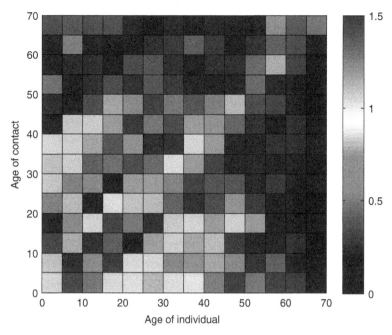

Figure 1.1 Who-mixes-with-whom matrix for a microsimulation. Source: Suen et al. (2014). http://journals.plos.org/plosone/article?id=10.1371/journal.pone.0089822 Attribution 4.0 International (CC BY 4.0) https://creativecommons.org/licenses/by/4.0/.

compromise (as with HIV) or exposure to smoke (such as through smoking or cook fires (Lin et al. 2007)). Unlike active TB, latent TB cannot be transmitted and does not cause decreased quality of life, so accurate modeling of activation rates is important for capturing disease dynamics.

In the case of this microsimulation, activation rates varied over age as well as time from infection according to data from the literature (Horsburgh 2004). Generally, TB activation tends to be higher in the years right after infection and then declines (Horsburgh 2004; Vynnycky and Fine 1997), and this was reflected in the microsimulation activation rates. Since the simulation used data from a published medical study not conducted in India, the overall activation rate was calibrated in order to reflect the average activation rates in the country of interest (more on that in the calibration section).

1.3.4 TB Treatment

Before modeling treatment policies of interest, baseline treatment trends must be accurately captured—if treatment programs are already in effect, additional treatment policies must be evaluated compared with a baseline where these existent programs continue to act or risk overestimating the treatment policy. In India, a federal program

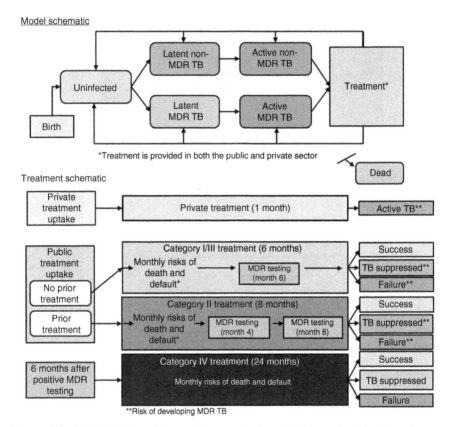

Figure 1.2   Heath state transitions and treatment schematic for a microsimulation. Source: Suen et al. (2014). http://journals.plos.org/plosone/article?id=10.1371/journal.pone.0089822 Attribution 4.0 International (CC BY 4.0) https://creativecommons.org/licenses/by/4.0/.

that scaled up in the 1990s and 2000s is already in place. Since this microsimulation used 1990–2000 as its calibration period, it needed to simulate access to care, treatment uptake, treatment success, and default rates. In this case, since a key outcome parameter was MDR-TB prevalence and incidence, which can be caused by imperfect treatment adherence, these parameters were very important to model accurately. Therefore the microsimulation uses detailed representations of different treatment regimens used in India, shown in Figure 1.2, which vary by prior treatment status and whether the patient has tested positive for MDR-TB. Monthly default and death rates, which vary over treatment regimen, were calculated from survey data from Bihar. These regimens were incorporated in the model by exposing patients on TB treatment to the appropriate death, default, and cure rates for their treatment regimen for the appropriate duration. A schematic of the treatment module for the microsimulation is shown in Figure 1.2.

1.3.5　Probability Conversions

Clearly, the microsimulation relies heavily on the probabilities it uses—whether they describe activation, treatment default, or death, accurate measures are needed to get a valid estimation of disease measures. These probabilities can be calculated from data in the published literature or survey data, but often they will not be presented in a way that can be used directly. When calculating these probabilities, it is important to distinguish rates from probabilities and risk ratios from odds ratios.

Probabilities must lie between 0 and 1, and mutually exclusive, exhaustive events must sum to 1. They describe the possibility of an event occurring over a set time period. Rates, on the other hand, can be larger than 1 and are not associated with a time period—they are formally instantaneous rates. Usually rates are assumed to be constant over particular time periods (as in mortality tables, e.g., where death rates assumed to be constant for individuals between the ages of 0 and 1, 1–2, etc.)

Rates can be converted into probabilities using the following equation, where r is the instantaneous rate, p is the probability, and t is the time period. For instance, if one is converting an annual rate into a monthly probability, t would be $1/12$:

$$p = 1 - \exp(-rt)$$

The microsimulation uses probabilities, not rates, and they should be scaled to the correct duration. Scaling should be done on rates, not probabilities (this is easy to remember if one tries to double a probability larger than 50%—it becomes larger than 1, which cannot be a valid probability).

The literature will often also report relative risk ratios and odds ratios, which also need to be converted into probabilities. A relative risk is a ratio of probabilities—the probability of an event happening to one group divided by the probability of that even happening to another group. An odds ratio, on the other hand, is a ratio of odds—the odds of an event happening to one group divided by the odds of it happening to another group, where odds are equal to the probability of the event happening divided by the probability of it not happening (a 2-to-1 odds of something happening, for instance, means 2/3 probability it will happen and 1/3 it won't). Relative risks and odds ratios cannot be converted into absolute probabilities in isolation, and a modeler will have to find the probability of that event happening to one of the groups and then solve for the probability of the event happening to the other group. To illustrate, if the relative risk of dying from TB for smokers to nonsmokers is 1.5, and the average probability of death for nonsmokers with active TB is 20%, then the probability of death is 1.5 times higher for smokers than nonsmokers (30%). In general, collecting and converting probabilities for all the demographics of interest may be a challenging task, so it is important to do carefully.

In our example microsimulation, the authors needed the probabilities of death, default, and failure stratified by age and sex. To do this, they used data from the literature that provided the odds ratio of male to female defaults, the proportion of males in treatment, the overall default probability, and the total number of people in treatment.

They then solved a system of equations using the definition of odds ratio to find the age- and sex-specific probabilities of death and default. The system of equations for stratifying default by age is shown as follows, where the unknowns to solve for were A, B, C, and D (taken from Suen et al. 2014):

$$\text{Odds ratio of male to female defaults} = (A/B)/(C/D)$$
$$\text{Proportion of males in treatment} = (A+B)/(A+B+C+D)$$
$$\text{Overall default probability} = (A+C)/(A+B+C+D)$$
$$\text{Total number of people} = A+B+C+D$$

where

A = number of males defaulting
B = number of males not defaulting
C = number of females defaulting
D = number of females not defaulting

1.3.6 Calibration and Validation

Some probabilities may not be known, however, and that is where calibration comes in. In our example microsimulation, the overall transmission probability and the activation rate as well as overall treatment uptake probabilities were calibrated since little is known about these parameters in the published literature. Calibration involves identifying model parameters that allow model outputs to best fit certain output targets, aptly called calibration targets. Models may also do this for parameters that are known but have wide uncertainty ranges. In this microsimulation, the calibration targets were WHO estimations of incidence and prevalence over the 1990–2010 period.

There are many methods to go about calibrating a model. Essentially, this is just an optimization problem where the modeler tries to minimize some measure of distance between the calibration targets and model outputs by varying the uncertain or unknown model parameters over reasonable ranges. Since microsimulations are generally complex, it is usually not possible to represent this as an analytical problem. However, traditional algorithms for searching over the feasible space can be used (i.e., Nelder–Mead, etc.). In our example microsimulation, the modelers used a grid search to explore the feasible space since the feasible space was small and could be reasonably explored using this method. It was also relatively easy to implement and performed well (see Figure 1.3).

In the microsimulation, the calibration process was used to find two parameters related to overall TB and one parameter related to treatment seeking behavior. The parameters were (i) an activation rate, which determines the average time to activation for individuals with latent TB infections; (ii) the effective contact rate, a parameter that determines the average probability of TB transmission given a

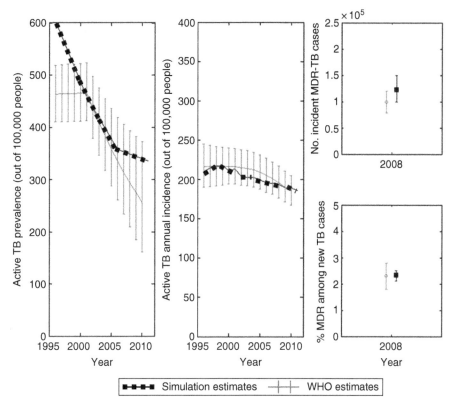

Figure 1.3 Calibration targets for microsimulation model of TB. WHO estimates are compared against model outputs. Source: Suen et al. (2014). http://journals.plos.org/plosone/article?id=10.1371/journal.pone.0089822 Attribution 4.0 International (CC BY 4.0) https://creativecommons.org/licenses/by/4.0/.

contact between a susceptible and infectious individual; and (iii) the average probability of undergoing TB testing among individuals.

Figure 1.3 provides a visual representation of how a microsimulation model outputs' might look compared with empirical data. In this case, the model outputs were calibrated to WHO data for Indian TB prevalence and incidence over the 1995–2010 period and measures drug resistance in 2008. During the calibration period, the model includes treatment present during that period, such as the federal treatment program. This is what drives the decrease in disease prevalence in Figure 1.3 (leftmost panel), as the federal treatment program was scaled up over that period.

While a model cannot exactly match all empirical statistics of the population of interest—and attempting to do so would result in an overly complex model—it is important that the model behaves realistically enough to provide reasonable and useful projections of the future. After calibration, it is important that the model is validated against external epidemiological and demographic measures to confirm that the population and disease dynamics are consistent with reality. These are measures that were not calibrated to (which is why they are called external validation measures). The model should be validated against epidemiological measures that are important for the analysis (ensure that baseline prevalence is consistent with the literature, if the main outcome measure is prevalence, for instance).

Table 1.1 provides validation measures for the microsimulation. These include demographic measures such as life expectancy, for males and females, as well as disease and treatment metrics. These values depend on the rate of transmission and activation, so validating that they match observed values provides evidence that the calibration was reasonable.

1.3.7   Intervention Policies and Analysis

After the model is validated, we can finally begin our policy analysis. The treatment policies considered must first be translated into changes in model parameters—this is one reason that it is important to have clear treatment policies at the beginning, so the model can be built to capture pertinent treatment characteristics.

Microsimulations offer more flexibility than other types of models since there is no assumption of analytical form and individuals can behave differently. This can be particularly useful for examining subgroups (e.g., incidence of MDR-TB in children). In the case of our example microsimulation, the authors were interested in examining prevalence of transmitted versus acquired drug-resistant TB (Suen et al. 2014), and this could be done by counting the number of individuals activating with transmitted or acquired drug-resistant TB without adding a separate compartment to stratify these populations (as would be needed in a compartmental model).

The microsimulation was used to evaluate the cost-effectiveness of several policies that might improve diagnosis and treatment quality in India. The WHO approved Cepheid GeneXpert diagnostic systems (Cepheid, Sunnyvale, CA, USA) for TB in 2010, but while these systems may be able to provide faster and more accurate TB diagnoses, it was unclear at the time of the analysis that these expensive systems should be implemented in resource-constrained settings like India. Using scarce public health treatment funds for improvements in diagnosis could trade off with other polices to combat TB, like improving the quality of care. For instance, since clinic quality in India may vary widely, pilot programs have been testing whether it would be effective to refer patients in low-quality private clinics to federally sponsored clinics. However, at the time of the analysis, it was unclear such a public-private mix (PPM) program would be cost-effective at a national level.

The simulation was therefore used to evaluate the cost-effectiveness of PPM, whether GeneXpert diagnostic systems should be used for all TB diagnosis or only for diagnosis of MDR-TB ("drug sensitivity testing" (DST)), or whether GeneXpert and PPM should be used in combination. The six interventions evaluated were then (i) the status quo, (ii) GeneXpert for all TB diagnoses, (iii) GeneXpert for DST,

TABLE 1.1 Example Simulation Validation Measures

	Empirical Estimate (95% CI, If Available)	Simulation Estimate (95% CI)	Source
Demographics			
Male life expectancy, 1990 (years)	57.2	55.9 (55.6–56.2)	World Health Organization (2010a)
Female life expectancy, 1990 (years)	57.9	55.7 (54.3–57.1)	World Health Organization (2010a)
Tuberculosis			
Life expectancy post TB activation without treatment (years)	~3 years	3.11 (2.95–3.28)	Tiemersma et al. (2011)
Lifetime fraction of latent infections that activate	0.10–0.20	0.17 (0.15–0.18)	Horsburgh (2004)
Treatment			
Average delay from symptom onset to RNTCP treatment (months)	2–7	6.1 (5.63–6.57)	Kapoor et al. (2012), Pantoja et al. (2009), Rajeswari et al. (2002), Selvam et al. (2007), Tobgay et al. (2006)
Median delay from symptom onset to RNTCP treatment (months)	2–7	3.9 (3.72–4.08)	Central TB Division, Directorate General of Health Services, and Ministry of Health and Family Welfare (2010)
Default rates			
Category I	0.06	0.054 (0.047–0.061)	Central TB Division, Directorate General of Health Services, and Ministry of Health and Family Welfare (2010)
Category II	0.14	0.151 (0.119–0.183)	
MDR-TB Incidence in 2008 Using WHO Calculation Methods			
% MDR among new TB cases	2.3 (1.8–2.8)	2.3 (2.1–2.5)	World Health Organization (2010b)
Number of MDR-TB among incident new and relapse TB cases	55,000 (40,000–74,000)	52,000 (47,000–56,000)	
Number of incident acquired MDR-TB cases	43,000 (33,000–56,000)	73,000 (52,000–94,000)	
Number of MDR-TB among incident total TB cases	99,000 (79,000–120,000)	124,000 (99,000–150,000)	

(iv) PPM, (v) PPM combined with GeneXpert for all diagnoses, and (vi) PPM combined with GeneXpert for DST.

These interventions were modeled in the simulation by changing input parameters (ex., using GeneXpert for diagnosis would increase diagnosis accuracy, so the probability of being correctly diagnosed in the simulation was increased to the appropriate level). The simulation was then run with these modified parameters in order to generate outcome measures associated with each intervention. In the next sections we discuss the outcome metrics of the simulation and how cost-effectiveness was evaluated.

1.3.8   Time Horizons and Discounting

Common treatment measures are deaths averted, life years gained, QALYs or DALYs gained, and epidemiological measures like prevalence and incidence. A QALY is a life year adjusted for quality of life, such that a year of perfect health is worth one QALY and a year living with some health compromise is worth less (Weinstein et al. 2009). A DALY is similar but measures life years lost (World Health Organization 2014a).

While epidemiological measures are commonly reported in number of cases per population of 100,000, QALYs/DALYs or treatment costs are often discounted and aggregated to values accumulated per lifetime. In a hypothetical case, a study looking at the effect of mammography screening may report that a particular screening strategy increases a 40-year-old woman's lifetime discounted QALYs by 0.2, indicating that the model follows the individual for their entire life span, counts the QALYs accumulated during that time, and discounts them to the net present value using a discount factor (conventionally 3%).

While the treatment period may be defined (say, at 10 or 25 years), the benefits of that policy may last much longer than that, particularly in the case of a transmissible disease. For instance, suppose a treatment policy increased cure of TB, which has the immediate benefits of reducing mortality and also preventing onward transmission. The policy has then also potentially saved the lives of those who would have been infected by that individual and the lives of those who would have been infected by *those* individuals even later on. Therefore each prevented transmission may have benefits far in the future, and it is important to capture those in the analysis. Perhaps it is easier to see why in handwashing, for instance, clearly, those who have the flu already are not benefited by washing their hands, but their friends are certainty happy that they did so when they themselves are not running a fever a few days after seeing them! In this example, only considering the immediate effects (inconvenience of handwashing) is outweighed by the future benefits (friends not getting sick later), and as a forward-looking society, we should promote handwashing to prevent disease transmission.

But in a dynamic transmission model of an entire population, as in our example microsimulation of TB in India, there is no clear period after which to stop counting benefits and costs. Since the entire population of India is modeled, there is no clear "lifetime" at which to stop counting the QALYs accumulated. One method is to run the microsimulation until the costs and benefits are so far in the future that their net present value is negligible—mathematically saying that we don't care about those effects since they are so far away. Depending on the discount factor and the magnitude of costs and benefits, this may take different amounts of time. However, if discount factors are low and benefits and costs are large, this approach may be unfeasible because it would require too much computation time or undesirable because it is unreasonable to expect that the disease/treatment behaves as we modeled so far into the future (since the model cannot take into account unexpected technological breakthroughs). Another approach is to stop the simulation at the end of the analysis period and ignore all costs and benefits accrued afterward. This may incur those disadvantages discussed earlier to different degrees depending on the length of the analysis duration. One could also take an intermediate approach, where transmission is not considered after a certain period, or the simulation considers only a certain cohort after some time. The necessity of these approaches depends on the computational intensity of the microsimulation, disease dynamics, and the magnitude of the treatment policy affects.

In our example cost-effectiveness analysis, the modelers used such an intermediate approach, where they used a time horizon of 10 years from when the analysis was conducted in 2015, and then considered the lifetime costs and QALYs associated with those still alive at the end of those 10 years without further disease transmission. This approach reduces computational time and does not make assumptions unrealistically far into the future (compared with running the simulation until the discount factor reduces costs and QALYs to essentially zero) and still captures some of the long-term costs and QALYs generated by the intervention (unlike the approach where all costs and QALYs after the time horizon are not considered).

1.3.9 Incremental Cost-Effectiveness Ratios and Net Monetary Benefits

Once calculated, the costs and benefits for each intervention are usually plotted on a cost–benefit plane, and the incremental cost-effectiveness ratio (ICER) is calculated for each strategy. This is given as the incremental cost divided by the incremental benefits of each strategy between it and the next cheapest strategy. In essence, this provides the marginal cost to gain the marginal benefit and has units of dollars per QALY gained (or life year gained or DALY averted). A policy is generally said to be "cost-effective" if it costs less than three times the GDP per capita to gain one QALY and is "very cost-effective" if it costs less than the GDP per capita (R. Hutubessy et al. 2003).

The efficient frontier in Figure 1.4 (interventions on the blue line) highlights policies that are cost-effective (those labeled in white boxes with ICER). Dominated policies are shown off the efficient frontier and labeled with gray boxes. Monte Carlo simulation sampling uncertainty for the costs and QALYs of each strategy is depicted

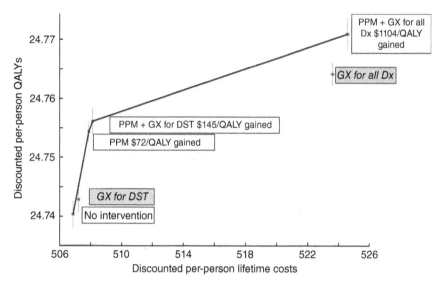

Figure 1.4 Cost-effectiveness frontier. Dx, diagnosis; GX, GeneXpert (Suen et al. 2015). Source: Reprinted with permission of the International Union Against Tuberculosis and Lung Disease. Copyright The Union.

as red 95% confidence intervals. In this analysis, even the most expensive policy, PPM with GeneXpert for all diagnosis, is cost-effective. It has an expected cost of $1103.58 per QALY gained, which is less than one GDP per capita in India ($1450). Even with sampling noise, this finding occurs with 99% probability.

Since it is often more intuitive to compare values in dollar units, the net monetary benefit is another way to represent intervention costs and benefits. It converts the total discounted lifetime benefits and costs into a single scalar value. It is calculated as the willingness-to-pay threshold times the total benefits minus the total costs. This willingness-to-pay threshold can therefore be thought of as the conversion factor between benefits (in units of QALYs or DALYs) to dollars; since there is no agreed-upon value for this conversion factor, the NMB can be calculated for a variety of willingness-to-pay thresholds. This can be useful for succinctly displaying uncertainty in total costs and QALYs; often probabilistic sensitivity analyses will report the probability of a strategy having the highest net monetary benefit for as a measure of how cost-effective it is.

While there is not a set number of microsimulation runs required for every simulation, the number of simulation runs should be large enough that the simulation outcomes are not obscured by Monte Carlo noise. This may vary by the number of individuals in the microsimulation—a larger number of simulated individuals may generate more robust outcome estimates as each individual's outcomes are averaged over a larger population. In the case of this model, the population size was large (6.5 million in the case of the cost-effectiveness results), and only 10 runs were needed to reduce Monte Carlo noise to levels where the results were clear (see error bars on Figure 1.5).

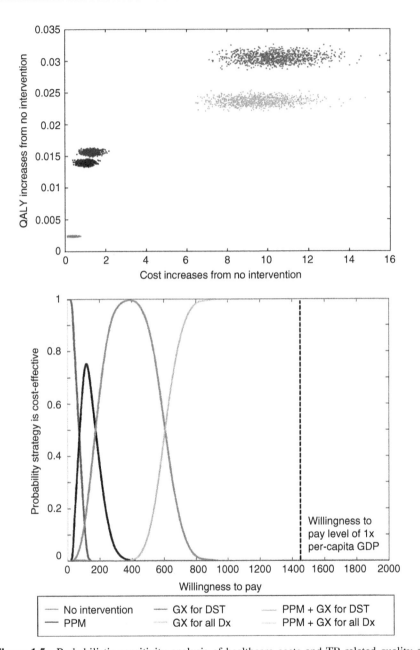

Figure 1.5 Probabilistic sensitivity analysis of healthcare costs and TB-related quality of life. At a willingness-to-pay threshold of India's per capita GDP ($1450), PPM with GeneXpert for all diagnosis is most likely cost-effective. Dx, diagnosis; GX, GeneXpert (Suen et al. 2015). Source: Reprinted with permission of the International Union Against Tuberculosis and Lung Disease. Copyright The Union.

1.3.10   Sensitivity Analysis

It is important to note that a microsimulation will be subject to sampling uncertainty or Monte Carlo noise if the simulated population is not large enough, and this uncertainty will further increase the uncertainty of cost and QALY outcomes of the modeled interventions. This type of uncertainty is due to the model itself and can therefore be reduced by increasing the number of individuals in the simulation or running additional simulation runs and averaging across runs to form an estimate of the average costs and benefits for each intervention. Estimates of the uncertainty of the mean costs and benefits can then be formed using a bootstrapping method over the multiple simulation runs—because cost and benefits cannot be assumed to be Gaussian, the modeler can empirically determine the distribution of mean costs and benefits by sampling from the simulation runs (with replacement) and calculating the average cost and benefits for each sample. Multiple resamples will generate a distribution of the costs and benefits, allowing the modeler to observe the distribution of average costs and benefits and quantify 95% confidence intervals (or other distribution characteristics) to describe the uncertainty due to Monte Carlo noise.

In contrast, parameter uncertainty reflects uncertainty in the outputs due to uncertainty in the input parameters and reflects unknowns about the true state of the world. The only way to reduce this type of uncertainty is to gather more information (incorporate additional study from the literature, run more clinical trials, interview more patients, etc.) and incorporate that information into the model. Accurate portrayal of this type of uncertainty in the model outputs allows decision makers to make informed decisions about how confident they should be in the model results.

We illustrate this with the example of uncertainty around the costs and QALY inputs. In Figure 1.5, the simulation has been run multiple times, each time sampling a costs and QALY input from their distributions (instead of treating them as point estimates, as in Figure 1.4). Each run then generates a different output, and this is reflected in the dispersion of points for each intervention—each point in Figure 1.5 panel a represents one simulation run. The results can be presented in a more compact form (panel b), which gives the probability the strategy is cost-effective over different willingness-to-pay levels. In this example, the strategy PPM + GeneXpert for all diagnosis is likely to be cost-effective even at very cost-effective willingness-to-pay levels (one GDP per capita).

1.4   CONCLUSION

Microsimulation can be a useful tool for evaluating the optimality of disease control policies within a set of intervention options, particularly for infectious diseases, where transmission dynamics and individual behavior may make disease dynamics difficult to represent analytically or in compartmental simulations. Microsimulations are flexible and can accommodate a high level of stratification, which may be important when modeling a disease with a complex natural history that is influenced by demographic and behavioral factors. However, more stratifications make the model more complex, and joint distributions of risks may be unknown or uncertain. These aspects of the model may make communication of the analysis more difficult. Even so, microsimulations are an important tool for modeling infectious diseases, particularly when individual level or subgroup level analyses are desired. Once completed, they can be easily modified to include additional subgroups or treatment policies, provided the transition probability data is available. The output of these analyses can help policy makers assess the impact of different treatment programs on select subpopulations and help articulate the impact of difficult-to-predict behavioral changes on treatment effects. Used effectively, they may be an important tool in the fight against infectious disease.

REFERENCES

C. Acuna-Villaorduna et al., "Cost-effectiveness analysis of introduction of rapid, alternative methods to identify multidrug-resistant tuberculosis in middle-income countries," *Clin. Infect. Dis.*, vol. 47, no. 4, pp. 487–495, 2008.

Central TB Division, Directorate General of Health Services, and Ministry of Health and Family Welfare, "RNTCP performance report, India: Third quarter, 2010," New Delhi, India, 2010.

Global Health Education, "TB tests: Skin test, sputum & other types of TB test serological tests for TB," 2014. [Online]. Available: https://www.tbfacts.org/tb-tests/. Accessed on October 2014.

P. Horby et al., "Social contact patterns in Vietnam and implications for the control of infectious diseases," *PLoS One*, vol. 6, no. 2, p. e16965, 2011.

R. Horsburgh, "Priorities for the treatment of latent tuberculosis infection in the United States," *N. Engl. J. Med.*, vol. 350, no. 20, pp. 2060–2067, 2004.

R. Hutubessy, D. Chisholm, and T.T. Edejer, "Generalized cost-effectiveness analysis for national-level priority-setting in the health sector," *Cost Eff. Resour. Alloc.*, vol. 1, no. (1), p. 8, 2003.

S. K. Kapoor, A. V. Raman, K. S. Sachdeva, and S. Satyanarayana, "How did the TB patients reach DOTS services in Delhi? A study of patient treatment seeking behavior," *PLoS One*, vol. 7, no. 8, p. e42458, 2012.

W. Kermack and A. McKendrick, "A contribution to the mathematical theory of epidemics," *Proc. R. Soc. Lond., Ser. A*, vol. 115, no. 772, pp. 700–721, 1927.

H.-H. Lin, M. Ezzati, and M. Murray, "Tobacco smoke, indoor air pollution and tuberculosis: A systematic review and meta-analysis," *PLoS Med.*, vol. 4, no. 1, p. e20, 2007.

J. S. Michael and T. J. John, "Extensively drug-resistant tuberculosis in India: A review," *Indian J. Med. Res.*, vol. 136, no. 4, pp. 599–604, 2012.

J. Mossong et al., "Social contacts and mixing patterns relevant to the spread of infectious diseases," *PLoS Med.*, vol. 5, no. 3, p. e74, 2008.

A. Pantoja et al., "Economic evaluation of public-private mix for tuberculosis care and control, India. Part I. Socio-economic profile and costs among tuberculosis patients," *Int. J. Tuberc. Lung Dis.*, vol. 13, no. 6, pp. 698–704, 2009.

R. Rajeswari, V. Chandrasekaran, M. Suhadev, S. Sivasubramaniam, G. Sudha, and G. Renu, "Factors associated with patient and health system delays in the diagnosis of tuberculosis in South India," *Int. J. Tuberc. Lung Dis.*, vol. 6, no. 9, pp. 789–795, 2002.

Revised National Tuberculosis Control Programme (RNTCP), "Training module for medical practitioners," New Delhi, India, 2010.

J. M. Selvam et al., "Health-seeking behaviour of new smear-positive TB patients under a DOTS programme in Tamil Nadu, India, 2003," *Int. J. Tuberc. Lung Dis.*, vol. 11, no. 2, pp. 161–167, 2007.

S. Suen, E. Bendavid, and J. D. Goldhaber-Fiebert, "Disease control implications of India's changing multi-drug resistant tuberculosis epidemic," *PLoS One*, vol. 9, no. 3, p. e89822, 2014.

S. Suen, E. Bendavid, and J. Goldhaber-Fiebert, "Cost-effectiveness of improvements in diagnosis and treatment accessibility for tuberculosis control in India," *Int. J. Tuberc. Lung Dis.*, vol. 19, no. (9), pp. 1115–1124, 2015.

E. W. Tiemersma, M. J. van der Werf, M. W. Borgdorff, B. G. Williams, and N. J. D. Nagelkerke, "Natural history of tuberculosis: Duration and fatality of untreated pulmonary tuberculosis in HIV negative patients: A systematic review," *PLoS One*, vol. 6, no. 4, p. e17601, 2011.

K. Tobgay, K. J. Sarma, and P.S. Thankappan, "Predictors of treatment delays for tuberculosis in Sikkim," *Natl. Med. J. India*, vol. 19e, no. 2, pp. 60–63, 2006.

Z. F. Tu, L. M. Pinto, and M. W. Uplekar, "Tuberculosis management by private practitioners in Mumbai, India: Has anything changed in two decades?" *PLoS One*, vol. 5, no. 8, p. e12023, 2010.

M. W. Uplekar and D. S. Shepard, "Treatment of tuberculosis by private general practitioners in India," *Tubercle*, vol. 72, no. 4, pp. 284–290, 1991.

N. Vandan, M. Ali, R. Prasad, and C. Kuroiwa, "Assessment of doctors' knowledge regarding tuberculosis management in Lucknow, India: A public-private sector comparison," *Public Health*, vol. 123, no. 7, pp. 484–489, 2009.

E. Vynnycky and P. E. Fine, "The natural history of tuberculosis: The implications of age-dependent risks of disease and the role of reinfection," *Epidemiol. Infect.*, vol. 119, no. 2, pp. 183–201, 1997.

M. C. Weinstein, G. Torrance, and A. McGuire, "QALYs: The basics," *Value Health*, vol. 12 no. Suppl 1, pp. S5–S9, 2009.

D. E. Winetsky et al., "Screening and rapid molecular diagnosis of tuberculosis in prisons in Russia and Eastern Europe: A cost-effectiveness analysis," *PLoS Med.*, vol. 9, no. 11, p. e1001348, 2012.

World Health Organization, "WHO lifetables for India," Geneva, Switzerland, 2010a.

World Health Organization, "Multidrug and extensively drug-resistant TB (M/XDR-TB): 2010 global report on surveillance and response," Geneva, Switzerland, 2010b.

World Health Organization, "Collaborative framework for care and control of tuberculosis and diabetes," Geneva, Switzerland, 2011.

World Health Organization, "Global tuberculosis report 2013," Geneva, Switzerland, 2013.

World Health Organization, "Health statistics and information systems metrics: Disability-adjusted life year," 2014a. [Online]. Available: http://www.who.int/healthinfo/global_burden_disease/metrics_daly/en/. Accessed on August 10, 2017.

World Health Organization, "Global tuberculosis report 2015," Geneva, Switzerland, 2015.

A. Zumla, M. Raviglione, R. Hafner, and C. F. von Reyn, "Tuberculosis," *N. Engl. J. Med.*, vol. 368, no. 8, pp. 745–755, 2013.

2

SAVING LIVES WITH OPERATIONS RESEARCH: MODELS TO IMPROVE HIV RESOURCE ALLOCATION

SABINA S. ALISTAR AND MARGARET L. BRANDEAU

Department of Management Science and Engineering, Stanford University, Stanford, Palo Alto, CA, USA

2.1 INTRODUCTION

2.1.1 Background

The sixth United Nations Millennium Development Goal (United Nations 2009) called for universal access to antiretroviral therapy (ART) for all eligible HIV-infected individuals by 2010 and zero new HIV infections by 2015, but progress toward achieving this goal has lagged. Although HIV incidence has slowed by approximately one-third in the last decade (Joint United Nations Programme on HIV/AIDS 2013), and ART has extended the lives of millions of HIV-infected people, the epidemic continues to spread. Currently some 35 million people worldwide are living with HIV, and in 2013 an estimated 2.1 million people became newly infected (Joint United Nations Programme on HIV/AIDS 2015). This corresponds to more than 5500 new infections per day.

Recently, the Joint United Nations Programme on HIV/AIDS (2013) set forth a number of ambitious goals for controlling HIV. These include goals to accomplish the following by 2015: halve sexual transmission of HIV and transmission of HIV among people who inject drugs; eliminate HIV infections among children; reduce

Decision Analytics and Optimization in Disease Prevention and Treatment, First Edition.
Edited by Nan Kong and Shengfan Zhang.
© 2018 John Wiley & Sons, Inc. Published 2018 by John Wiley & Sons, Inc.

maternal deaths from HIV; enroll an additional 15 million people living with HIV in ART; and halve tuberculosis (TB) deaths among people living with HIV.

Additionally, recently issued World Health Organization guidelines call for earlier initiation of ART for HIV-infected individuals, starting immediately upon diagnosis with HIV infection, rather than at a CD4 count of 500 cells/mm^3 (World Health Organization 2015). This has increased by millions the number of HIV-infected individuals who should receive ART.

Traditionally, HIV control in developing countries—where most of the world's HIV infections occur—has relied on donations from foundations and governments in developed countries. However, in recent years, the global economic downturn combined with "donor fatigue" (donors have shown less willingness to donate as the HIV epidemic enters its fourth decade with no end in sight) has led to an ongoing shortfall in funding for HIV programs (Schwartlander et al. 2011; Wei 2012). This has created increasing pressure for health ministries and other decision makers to use existing HIV prevention and treatment funds as efficiently as possible.

However, allocating HIV control resources is complicated by several factors. First, a program that is effective in one setting may not yield similar results in a different setting since the epidemic drivers and characteristics (e.g., prevalence, incidence, risk groups) can vary significantly from region to region. For example, the HIV epidemics in sub-Saharan Africa are typically slow growing, have high disease prevalence, and are driven by heterosexual transmission, whereas in Eastern Europe the lower prevalence, fast-growing epidemics are driven by injection equipment sharing among injection drug users (IDUs). Second, as the epidemic evolves, previously effective control programs may become insufficient, since epidemic dynamics are nonlinear. For example, prevention programs targeted to key populations may be most appropriate in the early stages of an epidemic, whereas in the later stages of an epidemic, treatment and more broadly targeted prevention programs are likely to be part of an optimal response. Third, additional investments in HIV control programs may not yield the expected incremental results since there is often a nonlinear relationship between investment and program effectiveness. For example, programs that aim to change risk behaviors may first reach individuals who are most likely to change behavior and then, with additional investment, may be reaching individuals who are less likely to change. Fourth, individual behaviors shape epidemic dynamics, and behavior may change in response to epidemic status or control programs (so-called elasticity of risk behavior). For example, efforts to educate the public about how HIV is transmitted may initially reduce risky behaviors, but as treatment programs are scaled up and become more widely available, people may engage in more risky behaviors since the disease is perceived as treatable. Conversely, as HIV prevalence in a population increases, people may reduce their level of risky behaviors to avoid infection.

To effectively control epidemic spread, decision makers need to choose the right set of prevention programs, balancing scarce resources between different programs and risk groups and determining the appropriate level of funding for each.

Moreover, decision makers need to find the appropriate balance between investments in prevention versus treatment. In many places, this balance has likely not been achieved: for every person recently enrolled in HIV treatment worldwide, an estimated two more people have become infected (Joint United Nations Programme on HIV/AIDS 2010). Political considerations can add a layer of complexity to these investment decisions, since the impact of treatment programs (infected persons receiving life-saving medications) is easy to demonstrate, whereas future negative consequences avoided via prevention programs (persons who do not become infected) are not as easy to demonstrate. In consequence, the tendency has been to spend incremental funds to treat those individuals who are already HIV infected rather than to invest more to prevent others from becoming infected.

2.1.2 Modeling Approaches

In this section we provide a brief description of approaches to modeling the HIV resource allocation problem. More comprehensive reviews of models of resource allocation for epidemic control are available elsewhere (Zaric 2003; Brandeau 2004).

In previous work we identified three main types of models used to support decisions regarding allocation of HIV control resources (Alistar and Brandeau 2012). These include linear models, dynamic epidemic models, and simulation models.

Linear models assume that the epidemic trajectory will be linear (e.g., Kaplan 1998; Kaplan and Pollack 1998; Ruiz et al. 2001; Kaplan and Merson 2002). Such models may or may not account for nonlinearities in the relationship between intervention costs and effects as programs are scaled up. For example, Ruiz et al. (2001) considered a fixed prevention budget B that is to be allocated across risk groups and geographic regions. The decision variable is x_{ij}, which is the amount of funds allocated to programs targeting risk group j in geographic region i. In risk group j in geographic region i, there are n_{ij} people and r_{ij} new infections annually (constant incidence). The cost per program participant in programs targeted to risk group j is c_j. The maximum percentage of the population in risk group j that is reachable by interventions is f_j, and e_j is the percentage reduction in the rate of new HIV infections for those people in programs targeted to risk group j. With this notation, the resource allocation problem is written as

$$\max_{x_{ij}} \sum_i \sum_j \left[\frac{x_{ij}}{c_j} \times \frac{r_{ij}}{n_{ij}} \times e_j \right]$$

$$\text{s.t.} \quad \frac{x_{ij}}{c_j} \leq f_j n_{ij} \quad \text{for all } i, j$$

$$\max \sum_i \sum_j x_{ij} \leq B$$

$$x_{ij} \geq 0 \quad \text{for all } i, j$$

The goal is to maximize the expected number of new infections averted in 1 year, subject to the budget constraint and constraints on the maximum fraction of each risk group that can be reached.

Dynamic epidemic models account for the nonlinearity of epidemic growth and the impact of interventions on population outcomes, thus providing a more sophisticated perspective on choices in epidemic control (e.g., Paltiel 1994; Kahn 1996; Richter et al. 1999). For example, Richter et al. (1999) considered two independent populations, each described by a susceptible–infected (SI) epidemic model with entry and exit. Let $S_i(t)$ and $I_i(t)$ denote the number of susceptible and infected individuals in population i at time t ($i = 1, 2$). Entry into the susceptible population occurs at rate δ_i. Exit from the susceptible and infected compartments in population i occurs at rate μ_{i1} and μ_{i2}, respectively. The rate of contact sufficient to transmit infection in population i is λ_i. The parameter λ_i is a function of the number of contacts per unit time between susceptible and infected individuals and the risk of infection transmission per contact. Given these definitions, the equations of the epidemic model for each population i can be written as

$$\frac{dS_i(t)}{dt} = \delta_i - \mu_{i1} S_i(t) - \lambda_i S_i(t) I_i(t)$$

$$\frac{dI_i(t)}{dt} = \lambda_i S_i(t) I_i(t) - \mu_{i2} I_i(t)$$

For this epidemic model, a closed-form expression can be derived for the cumulative number of people infected in population i over a given time horizon, a quantity denoted by $H_i(\lambda_i)$. The decision variable x_i is the expenditure on prevention in population i. The total available budget is B. Investment in prevention for population i reduces the sufficient contact rate λ_i, so the contact rate after investment is $\lambda_i(x_i)$. It is assumed that the initial sufficient contact rate in population i is λ_{0i} and the contact rate cannot be reduced below a_i. There are N_i people in population i. The resource allocation problem is written as

$$\min_{x_1, x_2} \left[N_1 H_1 \left(\lambda_1(x_1) \right) + N_2 H_2 \left(\lambda_2(x_2) \right) \right]$$

$$\text{s.t.} \quad x_1 + x_2 \leq B$$

$$a_1 \leq \lambda_1 \leq \lambda_{01}$$

$$a_2 \leq \lambda_2 \leq \lambda_{02}$$

The goal is to minimize the number of new infections that occur over a given time horizon, subject to the budget constraint and constraints on the maximum attainable risk reduction in each population. The functions $H_i(\lambda_i(x_i))$ are nonlinear functions of x_i, reflecting the nonlinear epidemic dynamics.

A third category of HIV resource allocation models uses simulation (e.g., micro-simulation) to create projections of the epidemic under a variety of intervention implementation scenarios (e.g., Hogan et al. 2005; Anderson et al. 2014). Such models allow for a greater level of detail around individual behaviors, demographic dynamics, and other sexually transmitted diseases that may be present in the population. For example, individuals with riskier behaviors might be more likely to not use a condom in sexual contacts, share needles if injecting drugs, have lower adherence to treatment regimens, or quit treatment altogether; such characteristics can be granularly defined in a simulation-based model.

Models also differ in the scope of their intended use, which can range from simplified theoretical analyses designed to provide broad insights to models designed for practical use by decision makers.

One body of work uses simplified models for epidemic projections (e.g., grouping individuals into susceptible, infected, or treated compartments) or makes simplifying assumptions about time horizons to ensure tractability and allow deduction of general insights. For example, Zaric and Brandeau (2001b) investigated the optimal resource allocation to control epidemic growth over short time horizons, as well as the optimal way to invest a limited budget allocated over multiple time periods and across several independent populations (Zaric and Brandeau 2002). Zaric and Brandeau (2007) and Lasry et al. (2007) focused on determining the optimal HIV resource allocation when decisions can be made at multiple levels (e.g., first at the country level and then at regional levels) and included considerations of equity when determining optimal choices. Brandeau et al. (2003) characterized the optimal solution (in certain situations) for controlling epidemics in multiple independent populations, each modeled with a simple SI structure (an SI model), using general cost functions to describe the relationship between program costs and benefits.

Another stream of work has used simulation to assess the effects of investment in different portfolios of available HIV prevention and treatment interventions for specific settings. For example, Hogan et al. (2005) compared the relative costs and benefits of a broad range of interventions (e.g., mass media campaigns, education delivered to several population groups, voluntary counseling and testing, and HIV treatment) in sub-Saharan Africa and Southeast Asia and identified the best options for epidemic control in those regions. Zaric and Brandeau (2001a) analyzed the optimal portfolio of interventions to control the spread of HIV in a US population that included IDUs and nonusers. Anderson et al. (2014) used a dynamic mathematical model that included geographic information about epidemic characteristics to compare the relative outcomes of a portfolio of HIV prevention interventions (male circumcision, behavior change communication, early ART and pre-exposure prophylaxis (PrEP)) in Kenya with a budget allocated uniformly across geographic regions versus a portfolio that allows for a more tailored approach.

Finally, several researchers have created models intended for use by decision makers to inform practical decisions about allocating resources among HIV control programs. For example, the Goals model aims to estimate the impact of different allocations of HIV control resources and to show how such allocations affect the achievement of national goals such as reducing HIV prevalence and expanding HIV care and support (Stover et al. 2003; Futures Group 2011). S4HARA is a spreadsheet-based model designed to provide near-optimal resource allocations that take into account influencing factors (barriers or facilitators, such as political power, ethics, culture, or religion) encountered in practice (Lasry et al. 2008). An influence diagram is used to show the impact—favorable or unfavorable to the allocation of resources for each program—of bodies or groups that influence the decision-making process for HIV/AIDS resource allocation in low-income settings (e.g., donors, advocacy groups, nongovernmental organizations (NGOs), government, communities, media).

Researchers at the US Centers for Disease Control and Prevention have developed several mathematical models to inform decision making, facilitate choices among various epidemic control programs, and improve effectiveness of HIV prevention efforts (Lasry et al. 2008, 2011). Other researchers have developed HIV resource allocation models to support decision makers at the state and county level (Earnshaw et al. 2007; Richter et al. 2008). One study analyzed the sources of inefficiency in practical resource allocation settings and found that the efficiency of HIV prevention program portfolios was affected by the set of prevention programs selected and the targeted population groups, as well as the technical efficiency of each prevention program (Bautista-Arredondo et al. 2008).

Creating HIV resource allocation models that are useful in practical situations can be particularly challenging for a variety of reasons (Lasry et al. 2009). For example, complexities of epidemic dynamics, individual risk behavior, and the effects of control programs must be modeled in a manageable way. Needed data may be missing or unreliable. Additionally, political and ethical considerations may impose nonquantitative constraints on allowable investments, and funding sources may be unreliable.

In prior work, we identified several elements that are typically missing in HIV resource allocation studies and that limit their practical use (Alistar and Brandeau 2012). Model results are often not applicable across different settings. Models may not accurately reflect the changing relationship between intervention costs and effects as programs are scaled up. Resource allocation models often do not allow for both treatment and prevention interventions. Additionally, HIV resource allocation models often do not evaluate the broader resource needs for the healthcare system, such as human capital, infrastructure, and supplies. We found that to be useful in practice, models for HIV resource allocation need to include key features organized along three dimensions: input flexibility (capability for parameter customization and incorporation of uncertainty), technical capabilities (the ability to capture epidemic effects, production functions, and effects of combined interventions; incorporation of key constraints; optimization capability; and estimation of overall health and economic impact), and usability (user-friendly design and structure, accessibility). Full descriptions of these features are provided in our prior work (Alistar and Brandeau 2012).

2.1.3 Chapter Overview

Our research on allocation of HIV control resources aims to bridge the gap between theory and practice. Toward this end, our work has focused on developing theory, performing practical analyses, and empowering decision makers. This chapter summarizes our recent work in each of these areas. Specifically, we describe our work on the development of theory that can generate insight into appropriate HIV resource allocations (Section 2.2), practical analyses to address relevant HIV resource allocation problems in a timely fashion (Section 2.3), and a planning tool for use by decision makers who must allocate HIV prevention and treatment resources (Section 2.4). The studies we describe are summarized in Table 2.1. We conclude in Section 2.5 with discussion of the broader decision-making context and key areas for further research.

2.2 HIV RESOURCE ALLOCATION: THEORETICAL ANALYSES

2.2.1 Defining the Resource Allocation Problem

We define the HIV resource allocation problem as follows: determine the optimal investment in available HIV control programs, subject to epidemic dynamics, budget constraints, and other constraints (e.g., equity constraints), where "optimal" is defined by some metric of epidemic control.

We can write the resource problem mathematically. We define a decision variable $\mathbf{x} = (x_1, x_2, \ldots, x_n)$ as the level of investment in a set of available interventions 1, 2, …, n. Without loss of generality, assume that there is a lower and upper limit on investment in each intervention i, denoted by $x_i^{\min}$ and $x_i^{\max}$, respectively. Assume that a budget B is available. The goal is to maximize a health objective that depends on investment, which we denote by $H(\mathbf{x})$. With this notation, the resource allocation problem can be written as

$$\max_{\mathbf{x}} H(\mathbf{x})$$

$$\text{s.t.} \quad \sum_{i=1}^{n} x_i \leq B$$

$$x_i^{\min} \leq x_i \leq x_i^{\max}, \quad i = 1, \ldots, n$$

In general, the objective function depends on the investment in the interventions as well as epidemic dynamics. Different objectives may be appropriate. The objective might be, for example, to minimize the number of new HIV infections that occur or to maximize the number of quality-adjusted life years (QALYs) experienced in the population, over some specified time horizon. Another potential objective is to minimize the reproductive rate R_0, a standard epidemiological measure defined as the

TABLE 2.1 Summary of Models Reviewed

Study	Purpose	Model Type	Objective	Key Findings
Resource Allocation				
Brandeau and Zaric (2009)	Determine the optimal level of spending for an HIV prevention program targeted to a single population, incorporating production functions that relate investment in a prevention program with program effectiveness	Analytical optimization based on an SI epidemic model	Find the level of spending such that cost per HIV infection averted equals willingness to pay per infection averted	The optimal level of investment depends on the shape of the production function and the marginal cost of an averted HIV infection. For decreasing marginal cost, an all-or-nothing solution is optimal. For increasing marginal cost, it may be optimal to spend only a portion of the budget.
Brandeau et al. (2005)	Investigate the effect of knowledge of production functions (which relate investment in a prevention program with program effectiveness) on HIV resource allocation and subsequent health benefits	SI epidemic models, simulated	Minimize the number of new HIV infections that occur, subject to a budget constraint	Even incomplete knowledge of production functions can lead to better investment decisions than simple models that assume the relationship between prevention program expenditure and effect is linear.
Alistar et al. (2014b)	Determine the optimal allocation of a fixed budget between HIV prevention and treatment in multiple interacting populations	Analytical optimization based on an SIT epidemic model	Minimize R_0, the reproductive rate	Analytical conditions derived that show when it is optimal to invest in different programs and populations based on epidemic characteristics in each population and shapes of the production functions.
Juusola and Brandeau (2016)	Determine the optimal mix of investment in HIV treatment and prevention, given a fixed budget	Analytical optimization based on linear approximation of	Minimize number of new HIV infections or maximize QALYs gained	The model provides a simple yet accurate means of determining optimal investment in HIV prevention and treatment.

Portfolio Analysis

Alistar et al. (2011)	Estimate the effectiveness and cost-effectiveness of strategies for expanding OST programs and ART in mixed HIV epidemics, using Ukraine as a case study	Compartmental epidemic model, simulated	Estimate cost per QALY gained	Scaling up OST is the most cost-effective investment. Scaling up ART in addition to OST is also cost-effective, averting significantly more infections than just scaling up OST. Addressing key epidemic drivers is essential when allocating scarce resources.
Alistar et al. (2014c)	Estimate the effectiveness and cost-effectiveness of strategies for using oral PrEP in various combinations with MMT and ART, using Ukraine as a case study	Compartmental epidemic model, simulated	Estimate cost per QALY gained	Oral PrEP for IDUs can be part of an effective and cost-effective strategy to control HIV in regions where injection drug use is a significant driver of the epidemic. Where budgets are limited, focusing on MMT and ART access should be the priority, unless PrEP has low cost.
Alistar et al. (2014a)	Estimate the effectiveness and cost-effectiveness of strategies for oral PrEP and ART in South Africa	Compartmental epidemic model, simulated	Estimate cost per QALY gained	Scaling up ART is more cost-effective than scaling up untargeted PrEP. ART scale-up efforts will be most efficient if delivered to individuals in earlier disease stages in addition to those with more advanced HIV. If targeted to high-risk individuals, PrEP could be cost-effective or even cost saving.

(Continued)

TABLE 2.1 (Continued)

Study	Purpose	Model Type	Objective	Key Findings
Decision Support Tool				
Alistar et al. (2013)	Planning tool for use by regional and country-level decision makers in evaluating potential HIV resource allocations	Compartmental epidemic model, simulated; also, optimization	Estimate a variety of health outcomes for a given allocation of resources; can also determine an optimal allocation	The optimal allocation of funds depends on the objective considered (minimize new HIV infections or maximize QALYs), the time horizon considered, and the available budget for HIV control.

ART, antiretroviral therapy; HIV, human immunodeficiency virus; IDU, injection drug user; MMT, methadone maintenance therapy; OST, opiate substitution therapy; PrEP, HIV pre-exposure prophylaxis; QALY, quality-adjusted life year; SI, susceptible–infected (epidemic model); SIT, susceptible–infected–treated (epidemic model).

number of new infections caused by an infected individual in a fully susceptible population (Anderson and May 1991). The choice of objective and time horizon will affect the optimal solution.

Investment is assumed to be limited by a fixed budget constraint, reflecting the availability of resources for HIV control. Decisions about fund allocation can be made one time at the beginning of the time horizon or reevaluated periodically to adjust for changes in epidemic dynamics.

Resources can be invested in a variety of epidemic control programs, including both prevention and treatment programs, which often reach different population subgroups. For example, needle exchange programs are targeted to IDUs, whereas HIV treatment scale-up could be offered to all eligible individuals or could be targeted to specific population groups (e.g., women of childbearing age). Programs will also vary in how they affect the epidemic dynamics. For example, a program that aims to change risky sexual behavior will lower the rate at which uninfected people acquire HIV via sexual contact, whereas HIV treatment will extend the lives of individuals who receive it and will lower their infectiousness, thus reducing the chance that they transmit HIV to others. In addition, changes in individual behaviors in response to lesser or greater availability of certain interventions can modify the effects of programs.

To model disease transmission in the population, researchers have typically used simple approaches such as dividing the population into susceptible and infected compartments (SI models) with differential equations expressing the evolution of the epidemic over time (e.g., Richter et al. 1999). The number of individuals in each compartment changes over time based on parameters that model disease transmission (e.g., rate of risky contacts), demographic changes (entry and death rates), and the impact of disease control programs. More sophisticated models may include multiple populations (e.g., IDUs and the general population) or more fine-grained disease modeling, including compartments for individuals receiving treatment or individuals in intermediate disease stages with varying rates of infectiousness. Anderson and May (1991) provide a comprehensive exposition of epidemic models.

2.2.2 Production Functions for Prevention and Treatment Programs

One crucial relationship to model is the effect of investing additional resources on a program's effectiveness. We refer to this as a "production function." A standard assumption is that the "return on investment" for each incremental unit of resources invested is constant: for example, for each additional $5000 invested in an opiate substitution therapy (OST) program, it is assumed to be possible to treat one more IDU for 1 year. However, depending on the nature of the program, the relationship may be nonlinear, thus affecting the optimal resource allocation. For example, programs that aim to change behaviors (e.g., programs that aim to increase the rate of condom use) may exhibit decreasing returns to scale, since initial funds invested may reach individuals who are most likely to modify their behavior in the desired way, whereas additional funds invested will need to be used to identify and reach individuals whose behavior is more difficult to change. Conversely, one can think of this relationship in terms of cost: it will cost more to get the same number of people to change their behaviors, as programs expand to include individuals who require additional expenditures to reach and/or whose behaviors are more challenging to change. In this case, the marginal cost to reach each additional person is increasing.

Brandeau and Zaric (2009) used production functions in a model to determine the optimal level of spending for an HIV prevention program targeted to a single population, with the goal of maximizing HIV infections averted. They assumed that the prevention program reduces the sufficient contact rate for disease transmission. Examples of such programs include interventions that promote higher rates of condom use and thus reduce sexual transmission of HIV, or needle exchange programs, which lower the rates of needle sharing and thus reduce the rate of needle-based HIV transmission.

The authors considered several shapes for the prevention program's production function, including constant, increasing or decreasing returns to scale, as well as a combined "S-shape," in which a program incurs some initial start-up costs, then exhibits increasing returns to scale, and finally exhibits diminishing returns for a large enough program. They found that the optimal level of investment depends on the shape of the production function and the marginal cost of an averted infection. For decreasing marginal cost, the optimal solution is to either spend the entire budget or nothing at all, whereas for increasing marginal cost, there may be situations where it is optimal to spend only a portion of the budget.

Interestingly, numerical illustrations using an SI model with replacement (i.e., an SI model with individuals entering and leaving the population at the same rate) showed that under a broad range of epidemic assumptions—fast versus slow growing, short versus long time horizons, low versus high prevalence—it is the shape of the production function that determines the shape of change in the sufficient contact rate as a function of investment rather than the epidemic characteristics. However, knowledge of the epidemic characteristics is needed to determine the optimal level of investment. The paper demonstrated the importance of production functions in determining optimal uses of funds for HIV control.

Further illustrating the impact of production functions, Brandeau et al. (2005) quantified the potential losses caused by ineffective use of funds for the case of resources allocated between two prevention programs for two noninteracting populations. The authors assumed an SI epidemic dynamic for each population and prevention program production functions with an initial fixed start-up cost and exponentially decreasing returns to scale as the programs get larger. The model was populated with HIV epidemic data from California, with men who have sex with men (MSM) and IDUs as the two independent populations. The prevention program production functions for each population were estimated based on published literature.

The authors evaluated the impact—quantified in terms of infections averted—of different allocations of HIV control resources between the two populations, assuming the decision maker has no, incomplete, or complete knowledge about the shape of the production functions. The analysis showed that even incomplete knowledge of production functions—for example, an assumption of decreasing returns to scale (either linear or exponential)—can yield better results than the simple heuristics typically used in practice, such as allocating funds proportional to estimated HIV incidence in each population. Use of the linear and exponential production functions led to a different allocation of funds between populations (100% of funds allocated to MSM for both production function shapes) than the heuristic (83% to MSM, 17% to IDUs) and averted more than three times as many HIV infections.

Surprisingly, complete or even partial knowledge of production functions that included the fixed program cost yielded a different, improved resource allocation (100% to IDUs), averting more than twice as many infections as when fixed cost was not considered in the production function. The authors suggested that even simple assumptions about production functions—in particular, an estimate of program fixed cost along with one point for estimated risk reduction obtained for additional investment—can significantly improve resource allocations for HIV control programs, particularly in settings where fixed program costs are high and budgets are tightly constrained.

2.2.3 Allocating Resources among Prevention and Treatment Programs

Recent work by Alistar et al. (2014b) considered the broader problem of allocating resources between HIV prevention and treatment. The authors examined the optimal allocation of resources between multiple interacting populations. To model epidemic dynamics, they used a susceptible-infected-treated framework (an SIT model) for each population and included the effects of both prevention programs, which lower sufficient contact rates for disease transmission, and treatment programs, which increase the rate at which individuals enter the "treated" compartment, thus gaining benefits to life span and to reduced infectivity. Each program was characterized by production functions (linear or exponential) that reflected typical patterns seen in practice. The authors considered the objective of minimizing R_0 (the reproductive rate of infection) and also investigated how results would change with other choices of objective function (QALYs gained or HIV infections averted).

The work characterized the optimal resource allocation under different conditions, showing when it is optimal to invest in different programs and populations based on epidemic characteristics in each population and the shapes of the production functions. In broad terms, the conditions for choosing either treatment or prevention compared the marginal benefit from investing additional funds in each program. In addition, since treatment extends the life of infected individuals, the optimal solution involves treatment only if the extension is life expectancy is outweighed by the reduction in infectivity caused by taking ART. Since ART reduces infectivity by a factor of approximately 10, but extends life by a factor less than 10, this condition holds.

Importantly, to instantiate the model, the authors developed an innovative technique for estimating production functions based on empirical data about intervention levels and HIV prevalence. To estimate the production functions, a functional form is assumed, and then, using the epidemic model and data on previous intervention levels, production function parameter values are estimated via least-squares estimation comparing model-projected HIV prevalence (as calculated with the assumed production functions) with actual HIV prevalence.

The authors populated the model with data from Uganda, which has a generalized heterosexual epidemic, and Russia, where the epidemic is concentrated in IDUs. Using historical data on epidemic evolution and the scale of treatment and prevention programs in each country, the authors estimated the shapes of production functions for each intervention and then evaluated the impact of alternative investment choices on R_0. Model results indicated that for Uganda, increased investment in condom promotion programs should be a priority, either alone or in combination with treatment programs. For Russia, continuing to invest funds per the status quo is a suboptimal use of resources: the optimal solution allocates significantly more HIV control funds to programs targeting IDUs. The optimal solution averts more than seven times as many infections as the status quo would and has a significantly greater impact on diminishing the HIV epidemic.

Juusola and Brandeau (2016) also considered the problem of allocating resources between HIV prevention and treatment. The goal is to maximize health benefits, either QALYs gained or HIV infections averted (an indirect measure of health benefits), subject to investment constraints. Rather than using a nonlinear epidemic model, they developed a simpler model that approximates health benefits using linear functions. The linear estimate of health effects accounts for both primary health benefits accruing to individuals who receive prevention or treatment and secondary health benefits accruing to other individuals who therefore avoid infection. Other studies have used a similar means of estimating health benefits, but not as part of a resource allocation model. The authors considered production functions that are linear or that have diminishing returns. Additionally, they explicitly modeled the effect of overlapping interventions to capture potential subadditivity in program benefits; because the same infection cannot be prevented twice, it is likely that at a high enough level of investment, the health benefits of two HIV control programs implemented simultaneously will be less than the sum of health benefits if the programs were implemented alone. The linear model has relatively simple data needs, and decision makers could easily solve the model in a spreadsheet after collecting and estimating model inputs.

To illustrate the approach, the authors analyzed the impact of three interventions—community-based education, ART, and PrEP—on the HIV epidemic among MSM in the United States. The analysis showed that education is a priority intervention as it is relatively inexpensive and effective, followed by ART and then followed by PrEP. For this particular epidemic and set of interventions, intervention overlap effects were small when programs were implemented at a limited scale.

These theoretical analyses expand the body of work that explores the resource allocation problem for epidemic control generally and for HIV in particular. We now describe our recent work on evaluating alternative portfolios of investment in HIV control programs in specific settings.

2.3   HIV RESOURCE ALLOCATION: PORTFOLIO ANALYSES

2.3.1   Portfolio Analysis

Portfolio analyses aim to compare the relative results of investing epidemic control funds across two or more interventions. The goal of portfolio analysis is not necessarily to determine the optimal level of investment in each program, as in the resource allocation problems described in the previous section. Instead, the goal is to compare the impact of several possible HIV control strategies implemented singly or in combination and with varying levels of scale, thus identifying the best choice of control measures from a discrete set.

In such analyses, portfolios of interventions are evaluated using a common metric that captures the consequent health benefits. For portfolios that include only prevention programs, HIV infections averted could be selected as the outcome metric, whereas for portfolios that also include HIV treatment, QALYs gained is a more appropriate outcome measure. Analyses that compare only the relative benefits of programs are referred to as "effectiveness analyses"; analyses that additionally include costs are referred to as "cost-effectiveness analyses."

Methods used to analyze the relative cost-effectiveness of portfolios of interventions are similar to those typically used in cost-effectiveness analysis of single HIV interventions but modified to account for multiple interventions implemented simultaneously. An epidemic model is used to project HIV epidemic dynamics over time, and consequent costs and health outcomes are measured. Model parameters are adjusted to reflect the impact of the programs considered in each portfolio. For example, in the case of a condom availability program combined with ART scale-up, parameters reflecting riskiness of sexual behavior would change, as would parameters reflecting length of life and infectivity of infected individuals. The time horizon considered must be long enough to capture the benefits (and costs) of all interventions considered. The results of the various strategies are compared with the status quo, which refers to the results that could be obtained by continuing to implement the interventions already in place at the same scale.

To facilitate the comparison of the different strategies, they are typically mapped on a standard cost-effectiveness plane, which is an $X–Y$ graph with the status quo at the origin and the two axes representing costs and health benefits (Gold et al. 1996). Portfolios of interventions can fall into four categories. Those with lower costs and higher benefits than the status quo should always be considered for implementation. Those with higher costs and lower benefits should never be considered.

Portfolios that are cheaper but also offer fewer health benefits may be considered by some decision makers, depending on the local circumstances. Portfolios with higher costs and higher benefits are selected based on their ratio of costs to benefits, which may or may not meet a maximum threshold defined by the decision maker (known as "willingness to pay" (WTP)). One would first select the program with the lowest cost-effectiveness ratio, verify that it meets the decision maker's WTP, then use that point as the new reference point, and consider the best program to implement next. At each step, strategies with lower costs and benefits than the current "best" are eliminated from consideration. The process is repeated until there are no more strategies to consider or the decision maker's WTP has been exceeded. The World Health Organization suggests that programs that cost less than three times a country's GDP per capita per QALY gained are cost-effective and could be considered for investment, and programs that cost less than a country's GDP per capita are very cost-effective (Murray and Lopez 2002).

We now describe several recent portfolio analyses that we have carried out: two analyses for Ukraine (intended to be representative of Eastern Europe more broadly) and one analysis for South Africa.

2.3.2   Opiate Substitution Therapy and ART in Ukraine

Ukraine has one of the fastest-growing HIV epidemics in the world (Joint United Nations Programme on HIV/AIDS 2008). The epidemic has been primarily driven by injection drug use, but over time an increasing level of heterosexual transmission has occurred, creating a mixed HIV epidemic where both needle-based and heterosexual transmission cause a significant proportion of new infections. Both ART and OST using methadone have been under consideration for scale-up, but scarce resources have not allowed implementation at scale for both programs.

The overall impact of each program, as well as the impact of a portfolio that combines them, is difficult to evaluate in the absence of a mathematical model, since the epidemic involves multiple population groups, and each program affects the epidemic in several ways. ART extends the life of infected individuals (either IDUs or non-IDUs) and reduces their infectivity, thus reducing the chance that they transmit HIV to others. OST lowers the likelihood of needle sharing and other risky behaviors among IDUs, thus reducing needle-based transmission among IDUs as well as sexual transmission to IDUs and non-IDUs.

Alistar et al. (2011) considered portfolios of HIV control measures for Ukraine consisting of OST for IDUs and ART scale-up for IDUs or non-IDUs. They used a dynamic epidemic model that includes IDUs and non-IDUs, with compartments that allow modeling different risk behaviors for IDUs who receive OST versus IDUs who do not. The model also includes compartments that reflect the stages of HIV disease progression according to a standard metric (CD4 cell count) and allows treatment initiation at the appropriate CD4 cell count. Disease transmission occurs through risky sexual or needle-sharing encounters among IDUs and risky sexual behavior involving IDUs, non-IDUs, or both. The authors considered strategies for implementing OST alone or in combination with ART, at various levels of scale-up: up to 25% of IDUs in OST and up to 80% of eligible individuals receiving ART. Given the stigma associated with drug usage and the occasional political reluctance in the region to invest in programs that are mainly intended for drug users, the analysis included strategies that limit the number of OST slots available to approximately 3% of IDUs and strategies where ART scale-up for IDUs is limited when compared with non-IDUs (10% vs. 80%). The authors used the model to estimate the costs and benefits of each strategy over 20 years, comparing them to the status quo in which no OST is available and ART scale-up is limited.

The analysis yielded several key insights. First, scaling up OST is likely to be the most cost-effective investment. Scaling up OST to 25% of IDUs cost $530/QALY gained, far lower than Ukraine's GDP per capita of approximately $7000, and reduced HIV prevalence significantly, averting infections in both IDUs (65% of averted infections) and non-IDUs (35% of averted infections). This is because in a mixed HIV epidemic of the type occurring in Ukraine, a sizeable proportion of infections occurs via sexual transmission from the small, high-prevalence IDU population to the large, low-prevalence non-IDU population. Hence a program that reduces disease transmission among IDUs will have sizeable secondary effects in the non-IDU population. The dynamic compartmental model used in this work is able to capture these effects, and the analysis provides a strong argument in favor of OST programs.

Second, scaling up ART in addition to OST (OST at 25% scale, ART at 80% scale) was also cost-effective, averting significantly more infections than just scaling up OST (OST at 25% scale). At a cost of $1120/QALY gained, ART scale-up is still considered highly cost-effective when compared with Ukraine's GDP per capita. We note that the dynamic epidemic model captured the effects of overlapping interventions: the infections averted by the combined OST and ART programs were slightly lower than the sum of the infections averted by individual programs. This is because the same infection cannot be prevented twice.

Finally, the analysis highlighted the losses (in terms of health benefits that could potentially be achieved) from implementing programs that exclude IDUs. A strategy to scale up ART to 80% of eligible non-IDUs but only 10% of IDUs yielded less than half the benefits of a full ART scale-up to 80% of all eligible individuals. Moreover, the limited ART scale-up strategy reduced health benefits for both IDUs and non-IDUs.

This work sheds light on the interactions of ART and OST programs in a mixed HIV epidemic and demonstrates the importance of addressing key epidemic drivers (in this case, needle-based transmission) when allocating scarce resources. In the recently challenging political environment, Ukraine is struggling to maintain its OST programs, with the lack of access renewing the risk of explosive epidemic growth (Humphreys 2013; Holt 2014).

2.3.3 Pre-exposure Prophylaxis and ART

2.3.3.1 Pre-exposure Prophylaxis and ART in Ukraine Models are particularly useful for evaluating the potential impact of new epidemic control interventions when only limited information is available about their effects over time and when such interventions are used in conjunction with other epidemic control programs. Oral PrEP is a recently introduced intervention in which healthy individuals receive a daily dose of antiretroviral medication so as to reduce their chance of acquiring HIV in risky sexual or needle-sharing contacts. Recent clinical trials have demonstrated reductions of up to 75% in HIV acquisition for heterosexual adults (Baeten et al. 2012; Thigpen et al. 2012) and up to 49% for IDUs (Choopanya et al. 2013), but little is known about the potential large-scale impact of such programs, with cost being particularly uncertain.

Alistar et al. (2014c) modeled a portfolio of HIV control interventions for Ukraine that included OST, ART, and oral PrEP. They extended their previously developed dynamic compartmental model (Alistar et al. 2011) to include compartments for IDUs receiving PrEP. Individuals who receive PrEP have a reduced chance of acquiring HIV and an increased chance of early detection of HIV infection status if they do become infected. The authors considered strategies that scale up PrEP for up to 50% of uninfected IDUs, OST for up to 25% of IDUs, and ART for up to 80% of eligible individuals. They compared various portfolios combining the three interventions, estimating effectiveness (infections averted vs. status quo) and cost-effectiveness (cost/QALY gained vs. status quo) over a 20-year time horizon.

Model results indicated that at a lower scale (25% of IDUs), PrEP averted fewer infections than either OST or ART scale-up; but when reaching 50% of IDUs, PrEP averted more infections than the alternatives. Furthermore, when added to large-scale OST or ART programs, PrEP averted a significant number of additional infections and hence could be an effective part of a portfolio of interventions to control mixed HIV epidemics. As is the case for other HIV control interventions directed to IDUs, a sizeable proportion of the infections averted were in non-IDUs, due to averted heterosexual transmission from IDUs to non-IDUs.

A key consideration when analyzing portfolios containing PrEP is the annual cost per person, which is currently high (e.g., on the order of $25 per person per day in the United States (Paltiel et al. 2009)), but could be significantly lower if PrEP is implemented at scale. The analysis showed that if PrEP cost is comparable with ART cost, then it is more affordable to first scale up OST and then ART, and only after that consider scaling up PrEP, which is still considered cost-effective. Sensitivity analyses showed that when PrEP cost drops to two-thirds the cost of ART, then it is more cost-effective to scale up PrEP first and that PrEP has the potential to be cost saving if its cost drops below half that of ART.

The mathematical model developed in this work allowed for exploration of the potential of a new HIV control intervention and its role as part of portfolios of interventions for HIV control. The insights into intervention attractiveness based on the relative cost of PrEP compared with ART are useful to decision makers who are looking to understand how best to prioritize interventions when resources are scarce.

2.3.3.2 Pre-exposure Prophylaxis and ART in South Africa As medical research advances and guidelines for medical practice change, decisions about investment in HIV prevention and treatment programs need to be revisited, in particular when looking to find the best portfolio of interventions for a specific setting.

Until recently, World Health Organization guidelines recommended ART initiation when an infected individual's CD4 cell count is at or below 350 cells/mm³. This recommendation was changed in 2013 to 500 cells/mm³ after clinical trials demonstrated health benefits to infected individuals and significant reductions in their infectivity (World Health Organization 2013a). In high-prevalence countries such as South Africa, where approximately one-fifth of adults aged 15–49 are infected (Joint United Nations Programme on HIV/AIDS 2010), implementation of the revised treatment guidelines will lead to significant numbers of people newly enrolled in ART. An alternative use of antiretroviral medication, PrEP for uninfected individuals, has recently been suggested as a promising new intervention for controlling HIV in a variety of settings, including high-prevalence settings such as South Africa.

Alistar et al. (2014a) recently analyzed the impact of different strategies for investing in PrEP and expanding ART access to individuals in earlier stages of HIV, consistent with the new World Health Organization guidelines. The authors created a model of the HIV epidemic in South Africa that included heterosexual HIV transmission and allowed for treatment initiation at different disease stages. They considered two approaches for ART scale-up at various levels ("guidelines" or "universal") and two approaches for PrEP scale-up ("general" or "focused"), as well as their combinations. Under the "guidelines" scenario, ART scale-up continues per South Africa's most recent guidelines (Republic of South Africa National Department of Health 2013), which still reflect the old World Health Organization standards. Under the "universal" scenario, ART is scaled up according to the new World Health Organization guidelines. The "general" scenario entails the provision of PrEP broadly in the population, while "focused" PrEP is targeted toward individuals at higher risk of HIV acquisition due to lower rates of condom use and higher number of partners. In each scenario, it was assumed up to 100% of eligible individuals could be reached with the program.

The authors estimated the costs and health benefits of each scale-up strategy over 20 years (here "strategy" refers to a single scenario or a combination of scenarios) and, for the case of full program scale-up, established the maximum health benefits that could be obtained.

The analysis generated several key insights regarding choices for HIV control portfolios in South Africa. First, scaling up ART, either according to current guidelines or with universal treatment, is more cost-effective than scaling up untargeted PrEP. Second, "universal" ART is cheaper and more effective than "guidelines" ART.

Hence ART scale-up efforts will be most efficient if delivered to individuals in earlier disease stages in addition to those with more advanced HIV. At a cost of $160–$220/QALY gained (depending on the scale of the program), "universal" ART is likely to be highly cost-effective in South Africa. Third, untargeted ("general") PrEP is likely to be expensive (at $7680/QALY) and to generate limited incremental benefits when added to ART. However, if PrEP can be accurately targeted to reach individuals at higher risk of HIV acquisition, then the intervention becomes a much better use of scarce resources and could even be cost saving. This result demonstrates the importance of tailoring epidemic control efforts to the specific challenges of each setting and matching the investment to curb the behaviors that drive increased HIV transmission.

2.4 HIV RESOURCE ALLOCATION: A TOOL FOR DECISION MAKERS

The range of interventions available for HIV control and the complexities of the epidemic dynamics make it challenging for decision makers with limited budgets to select the optimal portfolio of interventions for their setting and to determine the best level of investment in each intervention. Our previous work describes in detail some of these challenges (Alistar and Brandeau 2012). In the absence of mathematical approaches that are easy to use and that can be tailored to their specific settings, decision makers rely on political interests, personal values, historical patterns, and their own professional experience to guide their resource allocation process. Employing simple heuristics, such as allocating funds in proportion to past prevalence or incidence, can often lead to mismatches between where resources are allocated and the current state of the epidemic and can even reward settings that are less efficient in managing resources (Ruiz et al. 2001).

Thus, there is a need for decision support tools that are based on mathematical projections of the epidemic in a given setting and that can inform resource allocation decisions from a data-driven perspective.

2.4.1 REACH Model Overview

We designed the **Re**source **A**llocation for **C**ontrol of **H**IV (REACH) model to be a flexible tool for use by decision makers in a variety of settings (e.g., governments, NGOs) to better understand the costs and benefits of various portfolios of HIV control interventions (Alistar et al. 2013). The model is easily accessible since it is implemented in Microsoft Excel, a software available in most settings. REACH is designed to answer broad policy questions about resource allocation among interventions and populations and can be customized to specific settings based on epidemic, demographic, and economic parameters. The model captures the dynamics of the epidemic and accounts for intervention overlap, as well as scale-up effects in terms of both costs and benefits, as described in our discussion of production functions in Section 2.2.2. In addition to the general population, the model can incorporate several key populations: MSM, IDUs and sex workers (SWs). The model allows for scale-up of both treatment and prevention interventions (e.g., condom promotion, OST, PrEP, ART) and identifies the optimal mix of interventions by evaluating costs and health benefits (HIV infections averted, life years gained, QALYs gained) over several time horizons (5, 10, or 20 years). In finding the optimal solution, the model takes into account any constraints imposed in the particular setting in terms of how much funds any particular program can receive. In addition to determining optimal investment, the model can also be used to analyze the costs and health benefits accruing from any investment portfolio specified by the user.

To illustrate the capabilities of the model, we have populated it with data from several countries: Uganda, Ukraine, Brazil, and Thailand. Insights gained from applying the model to Uganda and Ukraine are described elsewhere (Alistar et al. 2013). We present results from analyses for Brazil and Thailand in the next two sections.

2.4.2 Example Analysis: Brazil

Brazil has a stable epidemic that is concentrated in MSM: overall prevalence in the population is estimated to be 0.6%, whereas prevalence among MSM is estimated to be approximately 10.5% (Brazilian Ministry of Health 2012). The country has made significant efforts to scale up HIV treatment, providing ART for free to all individuals in need. Currently in Brazil some 80% of eligible HIV-infected individuals in the general population and 60% of eligible HIV-infected MSM receive ART (World Health Organization 2013b).

We estimated that Brazil spends $310.0 million per year on HIV treatment under the status quo. One new prevention program proposed for uninfected MSM is PrEP, which has been shown to reduce the chance of acquiring HIV from an infected partner by approximately 70% among MSM (Grant et al. 2010). We considered a 10% increase in the current budget, corresponding to incremental funds of $31.0 million, which could be used for ART for MSM or other individuals in the population, as well as for PrEP for MSM. We estimated that the annual cost of ART in Brazil for one person is $1650 (World Health Organization 2013b) and that the annual cost of PrEP would be $3000 (Alistar et al. 2014c).

We populated the model using recent data from Brazil. Selected outputs from the analyses are shown in Table 2.2, which shows life years gained and HIV infections averted over 5 years and over 20 years for each of the budget allocations we considered.

If the new funds are invested proportionally to the current allocation—that is, no money is spent on PrEP for MSM, and all of the incremental funds are spent on ART, with 75.5% spent on ART for the general population and 24.5% spent on ART for MSM—then 26,700 life years are gained and 4,100 HIV infections are averted over 5 years and 186,700 life years are gained and 14,300 HIV infections are averted over 20 years.

TABLE 2.2 REACH Model Results: Brazil

	Status Quo	10% Budget Increase	Optimal: Maximize Life Years Gained (5 Years)	Optimal: Maximize Infections Averted (5 Years)	Optimal: Maximize Life Years Gained (20 Years)	Optimal: Maximize Infections Averted (20 Years)
Resources Allocated						
Treatment	$310.0M	$341.0M	$341.0M	$341.0M	$341.0M	$341.0M
% to general population	75.5%	75.5%	65.0%	65.0%	65.0%	60.0%
% to MSM	24.5%	24.5%	35.0%	35.0%	35.0%	40.0%
Prevention—oral PrEP	$0M	$0M	$0M	$0M	$0M	$0M
Life years gained (5 years)	—	26,700	33,100	33,100	33,100	23,900
Life years gained (20 years)	—	186,700	314,000	314,000	314,000	270,000
Infections averted (5 years)	—	4,100	8,900	8,900	8,900	8,500
Infections averted (20 years)	—	14,300	41,500	41,500	41,500	42,800

We used the optimization capability of the model to determine the investment that maximizes the number of life years gained over 5 years. In this case, it is best to continue to invest only in ART and not in PrEP for MSM, but a larger fraction of treatment funds are allocated to MSM than in the current allocation (35.0% vs. 24.5%). This leads to 24% more life years gained than in the proportional allocation (33,100 vs. 26,700) and more than twice as many HIV infections averted (8,900 vs. 4,100) over 5 years. This occurs because of the transmission benefits achieved by ART. Infected MSM are at higher risk of transmitting HIV than infected individuals in the general population. By putting relatively more MSM on treatment than in the status quo, more HIV infections are averted, which causes a gain of life years in the population. For a time horizon of 20 years, the life year-maximizing solution is the same as that for the 5-year time horizon.

We also determined the allocations that maximize infections averted over 5 years and over 20 years. For a 5-year time horizon, the allocation that maximizes infections averted is the same as the allocation that maximizes life years gained. For a 20-year time horizon, the allocation that maximizes infections averted still allocates all incremental funds to ART (and none to PrEP) but allocates a slightly higher fraction of treatment funds to MSM than when the time horizon is 5 years (40.0% vs. 35.0%). For this allocation, 3% more HIV infections are averted over 20 years than for the allocation that maximizes HIV infections over 5 years and maximizes life years over 5 and 20 years (42,800 vs. 41,500), but 14% fewer life years are gained (270,000 vs. 314,000). The small change in the allocation of ART funds that occurs when maximizing HIV infections averted (allocating 40.0% of treatment funds to MSM rather than 35.0%) increases the number of HIV infections averted but decreases the number of life years gained. The information provided by the model allows the decision maker to evaluate these and other trade-offs when considering different potential portfolios of investment.

We note that unlike other countries such as Ukraine where the key population (IDUs) is responsible for a significant amount of HIV transmission to the general population, in Brazil the key population (MSM) does not spread HIV as significantly to the general population. For the case of Ukraine (described in Alistar et al. (2013)), when the time horizon increases from 5 to 20 years, it is best to increase the level of treatment funds devoted to the general population because of the spread of HIV from IDUs to the rest of the population; but for the case of Brazil, when the time horizon increases, it is best to slightly decrease the level of treatment funds devoted to the general population.

For this example, reallocating ART funds between the general population and MSM yields more health benefit than investing in PrEP for MSM. At current costs, ART is a better use of the limited available funds than PrEP. To achieve epidemic control goals, decision makers must make sure that the resource allocations they choose address the key populations most at risk of acquiring HIV. The appropriate level of investment in the available interventions is likely not obvious *a priori*, but can be determined using the model. Additionally, the model allows a decision maker to evaluate trade-offs between HIV infections averted versus life years gained for different allocations of the same budget.

2.4.3   Example Analysis: Thailand

Thailand has a large population of SWs—an estimated 125,000 individuals—who are considered to be one of the main drivers of the country's HIV epidemic (Joint United Nations Programme on HIV/AIDS 2014). HIV prevalence among female SWs in Thailand is approximately 3.2% and is approximately 1.1% in the general population (Joint United Nations Programme on HIV/AIDS 2014). A strong condom promotion program in the 1990s helped keep HIV prevalence among SWs relatively low, but further progress is needed. The use of a method by which SWs could actively protect themselves, rather than relying on condom use by their male partners, has been proposed. One such method, currently being examined in a number of clinical trials, is topical PrEP, a vaginal gel containing HIV antiviral drugs (Lusti-Narasimhan et al. 2014). It is estimated that topical PrEP could reduce the chance of a woman acquiring HIV by approximately 40% (Abdool Karim et al. 2010; Celum and Baeten 2012).

ART access in the country is relatively high compared with other countries in the region: currently about 56% of eligible HIV-infected individuals in the general population (Joint United Nations Programme on HIV/AIDS 2014) and an estimated 25% of eligible HIV-infected SWs receive ART (Kim et al. 2013).

Under the status quo, $45.9M is spent on ART annually, with the majority of ART focused on the general population. We considered a budget increase of approximately 20%, corresponding to $9.9M in incremental funding. We assumed that the incremental funds could be spent on ART for SWs and the general public and on topical PrEP for SWs. We estimated that the annual per person cost of ART in Thailand is $500 (World Health Organization 2013b) and the annual per person cost of topical PrEP for SWs is $600 (Terris-Prestholt et al. 2014).

We populated the model with recent epidemic information for Thailand. Table 2.3 shows selected outputs from our analyses, including HIV infections averted and life years gained over 5 and 20 years for each of the budget allocations we considered.

Using the portfolio analysis capability of the REACH model, we evaluated a proportional increase in the current budget, where all of the incremental funds are spent on ART and none is spent on topical PrEP for SWs. This allocation averts 5,600 new HIV infections and gains 31,500 life years over 5 years compared with the status quo.

Using the optimization capability of the model, we determined the allocation that maximizes life years gained over 5 years. In this case, it is optimal to invest all incremental funds in ART. The split of ART expenditure is different from the status quo, with 1% of ART funds spent on SWs versus 0.4% in the status quo. This allocation averts nearly 50% more HIV infections than the proportional allocation (8,300 vs. 5,600 over 5 years) and gains 7% more life years (33,800 vs. 31,500 over 5 years), attesting to the importance of SWs in propagating the epidemic. By reducing the infectivity of SWs with ART, significant numbers of HIV infections can be averted and many life years can be gained. Notably, topical PrEP is not part of the optimal solution, due to its relatively low effectiveness when compared with ART (40% vs. 90% effectiveness, for similar annual cost).

TABLE 2.3 REACH Model Results: Thailand

	Status Quo	20% Budget Increase	Optimal: Maximize Life Years Gained (5 Years)	Optimal: Maximize Infections Averted (5 Years)	Optimal: Maximize Life Years Gained (20 Years)	Optimal: Maximize Infections Averted (20 Years)
Resources Allocated						
Treatment	$49.5M	$59.4M	$59.4M	$59.4M	$59.4M	$59.4M
% to general population	99.6%	99.6%	99.0%	98.0%	98.0%	98.0%
% to SW	0.4%	0.4%	1.0%	2.0%	2.0%	2.0%
Prevention—topical PrEP	$0M	$0M	$0M	$0M	$0M	$0M
Life years gained (5 years)	—	31,500	33,800	33,400	33,400	33,400
Life years gained (20 years)	—	242,700	328,300	350,000	350,000	350,000
Infections averted (5 years)	—	5,600	8,300	9,000	9,000	9,000
Infections averted (20 years)	—	37,500	79,100	92,100	92,100	92,100

If the goal is to maximize life years gained over 20 years, then the optimal allocation is to spend all of the incremental funds on ART, with a higher percentage of ART funds (2.0%) targeted to SWs as compared with 0.4% in the status quo and 1.0% in the optimal 5-year allocation. Over 20 years this allocation gains 11% more life years than the allocation that maximizes life years over 5 years (350,000 vs. 328,300) and averts 12% more HIV infections (92,100 vs. 79,100). The same allocation is optimal if the goal is to maximize infections averted over 5 or 20 years. A decision maker could use this information to understand the trade-offs between maximizing HIV infections averted versus life years gained and to pick an appropriate portfolio of investments for his setting.

We note that the optimal allocations yield significantly greater health benefits (life years gained, HIV infections averted) than the proportional budget allocation because they devote more resources to SWs.

As was illustrated in the Brazil example earlier, in order to achieve epidemic control, it is important to address the key population groups. For Thailand, significantly higher health benefits can be achieved by increasing the investment in the most effective programs that reach SWs rather than investments targeted to the general population. Additionally, a greater fraction of funding may be allocated to treatment of key populations if the objective function (maximization of life years gained or HIV infections averted) is considered over a longer period of time.

2.5   DISCUSSION AND FURTHER RESEARCH

We have described a body of work that employs a variety of mathematical modeling techniques to understand how best to allocate HIV prevention and treatment funds. Although progress has been made in slowing the epidemic, millions of individuals continue to acquire HIV infection each year, so HIV control efforts will be needed for decades into the future. Millions of individuals will continue to need treatment, and prevention efforts must also be sustained. The model-based work we have described can inform good decisions about investment of limited resources for HIV control.

A number of key areas for further work remain.

HIV resource allocation decisions are typically made in the face of significant uncertainty about epidemic characteristics, risk behaviors, and the potential impact of interventions. While established procedures exist for measuring standard epidemiological parameters such as HIV incidence or prevalence, in many regions of the world, the data that is collected may be incomplete and/or highly uncertain. It is even more difficult to obtain accurate demographic and behavioral data about key populations, as such populations tend to be marginalized, though these populations are integral to epidemic spread. Additionally, until an HIV control program is implemented in a given setting, the true cost and impact of the program cannot be known with certainty. Thus, extension of existing HIV resource allocation models to allow for systematic exploration of uncertainty is an important area for additional work. This should include, at the minimum, one-way, multi-way, and stochastic sensitivity analysis of uncertain parameters. For some models, sensitivity analysis on model structure and key assumptions is also important. For example, recent work by Suen et al. (2017) demonstrates that the choice of how to discretize risk in compartmental epidemic models (e.g., division of a population into high-risk and low-risk groups) can influence predicted effectiveness of interventions. For such models, sensitivity analysis on choice of risk stratification is important. Model-based analyses that include extended capabilities for sensitivity analyses can help quantify the impact of uncertainty and identify the uncertain parameters and key assumptions that have the greatest impact on potential decisions.

Many resource allocation studies are specific to a particular setting at a particular time. As the epidemic evolves in a given setting, resource allocation decisions need to be revisited periodically to ensure that funds are being put to the best available use. While most mathematical models account for impact of programs over time, it is less common to incorporate dynamic decision making and determine the optimal investment decisions over time. As the epidemic evolves, and parameters such as demographics, behavior, and costs change, the best investment in particular population groups or programs may change. A portfolio of HIV control programs that was previously optimal may no longer be the best means of achieving epidemic control. However, there are significant practical costs to revising an established course of action, and policies cannot be changed as often as would be optimal. Additional research is necessary to establish the frequency with which model results should be reevaluated. Based on such research, it may be possible to incorporate model functionality that suggests the appropriate time interval for policy revisions based on local circumstances.

Another question for future research is to explore the analytical basis for determining when it is reasonable to apply investment findings from one setting to another. The HIV epidemic varies widely among settings. Even among settings with similar HIV epidemics (e.g., certain countries in sub-Saharan Africa where the HIV epidemic is generalized in the adult population and the main mode of transmission is heterosexual contact), a course of action that is optimal in one country may not be immediately applicable in another country due to slightly different demographic, economic, and epidemic parameters. While sensitivity analysis built into current models can help narrow down which parameters are critical to the evolution of the epidemic, systematic analyses of "how different is different enough" to warrant a full reevaluation of results for a new setting are needed.

It has been said that "the era of AIDS exceptionalism is over" (Stolberg 1997; England 2008). Increasingly, governments and NGOs are also focusing on the control of other diseases (both communicable and noncommunicable) such as TB, malaria, and diarrheal diseases; on social conditions that influence health such as nutrition, sanitation, and education; and on the development of health infrastructure that is not focused solely on HIV prevention, care, and treatment. As we describe in the following text, future work on HIV resource allocation could support informed policies by taking into account relevant co-epidemic diseases, synergies with other parts of the healthcare delivery system, and allocation of resources across multiple diseases and perhaps other public investments.

The spread of HIV in different parts of the world has increased the spread of certain other communicable diseases, particularly TB and hepatitis C (HCV), as well as hepatitis B (HBV), malaria, and other diseases. In these co-epidemics, the spread of HIV increases the transmission and progression of the other disease and vice versa. For example, in parts of Africa, India, and Eastern Europe, HIV is co-epidemic with TB. Individuals who are HIV infected are more likely to develop active TB, and HIV infection progresses rapidly in individuals who have TB. In some parts of Africa and Asia, HIV is co-epidemic with HBV. Among IDUs, HIV and HCV frequently co-occur. Dynamic epidemic models of the type described in this chapter can be used to model the spread of such co-epidemics and to evaluate the effectiveness and cost-effectiveness of potential control measures. Researchers have increasingly recognized the importance of co-epidemics when evaluating HIV control measures, and some work in this area has appeared, particularly in the areas of HIV–TB and HIV– HCV coinfection (e.g., Currie et al. 2005; Long et al. 2008; Cipriano et al. 2012; Schackman et al. 2015). Further work is needed to evaluate the control of the HIV– HCV and HIV–TB co-epidemics in different settings, as well as other HIV-related co-epidemics such as HIV–HBV and HIV–malaria. Models that reflect the complex dynamics and interactions of these epidemics will need to include detailed disease projections, as well as functionality to explore the allocation of resources across control programs that significantly differ in nature (e.g., HIV medication must be taken for life, and the person cannot get reinfected, whereas TB medication requires a short timeframe and the patient can recontract the disease).

Additionally, there is increasing recognition that HIV needs to be addressed in the broader healthcare context of each country, particularly in the developing world. For example, efficient and effective delivery of HIV care services (e.g., programs for preventing mother-to-child transmission) requires integration with other healthcare services (e.g., programs for prenatal care) as well as a broad understanding of local conditions (e.g., nutrition, access to clean water, sanitation) (Kim et al. 2013). A variety of important operational problems arise in this context, and these problems are well suited to OR-based analysis. HIV resource allocation models could perhaps be extended to consider integration of HIV prevention and treatment programs into existing or planned healthcare delivery systems.

Finally, investment in HIV control can be considered in the broader context of investment in other disease control programs, other health programs, and other investments of public funds for social welfare. As described earlier, resource allocation models that consider investment in HIV and related co-epidemic diseases could be developed. More broadly, resource allocation models could be developed to determine the allocation of funds across programs to control communicable diseases (including HIV) and noncommunicable diseases. At a higher level, it would be useful to develop a model for determining the appropriate allocation of funds across programs in health, education, and social services and to use such a model to analyze the potential trade-offs at a portfolio level. Establishing the theoretical basis for quantifying such trade-offs (i.e., developing methodology to compare benefits and costs across diverse investments) is an additional direction for further research.

By considering investments more broadly than just those targeted to HIV, planners can coordinate health efforts, thus helping to avoid duplication of services. Additionally, use of a broader investment framework enables planners to consider potential synergies or anergies between investments. Synergies might occur, for example, when investment in one disease control program also has the effect of helping to control another disease. For instance, efforts to reduce the spread of HIV may also reduce the spread of TB, as the two diseases are often co-epidemic. Similarly, investment in the control of HIV may also reduce the spread of other sexually transmitted infections (STIs). Synergies between multiple investments could also occur. For example, investment in a health screening program along with increased funding for treatment of HIV and other STIs could yield greater benefit than the sum of such interventions if implemented in isolation. Anergies between investments—when investment in two interventions yields a lesser health benefit than the sum of benefits if the interventions were implemented in isolation—could also occur. For example, two different HIV prevention programs may yield fewer HIV infections averted than the sum of infections averted if the programs were implemented in isolation. Consideration of potential interactions between investments is essential to the development of appropriate resource allocation models, both for investment in HIV prevention programs and for investment in health interventions more broadly.

According to UNAIDS Executive Director Michel Sidibé, "the persistent burden associated with communicable diseases undermines efforts to reduce poverty, prevent hunger and preserve human potential in the world's most resource-limited settings" (Joint United Nations Programme on HIV/AIDS 2013). More efficient allocation of the limited disease control funds available can help countries achieve these goals and can lead to millions of lives saved.

ACKNOWLEDGMENT

This work was supported by grant number DA15612 from the National Institute on Drug Abuse.

REFERENCES

Abdool Karim Q, Abdool Karim SS, Frohlich JA, Grobler AC, Baxter C, Mansoor LE, et al. (2010) Effectiveness and safety of tenofovir gel, an antiretroviral microbicide, for the prevention of HIV infection in women. *Science* 329(5996):1168–1174.

Alistar SS, Brandeau ML (2012) Decision making for HIV prevention and treatment scale up: Bridging the gap between theory and practice. *Med. Decis. Making* 32(1):105–117.

Alistar SS, Owens DK, Brandeau ML (2011) Effectiveness and cost effectiveness of expanding harm reduction and antiretroviral therapy in a mixed HIV epidemic: A modeling analysis for Ukraine. *PLoS Med.* 8(3):e1000423.

Alistar SS, Brandeau ML, Beck EJ (2013) REACH (Resource Allocation for Control of HIV): A practical HIV resource allocation tool for decision makers. Zaric GS, Ed. *Operations Research and Health Care Policy* (Springer, New York), pp. 201–224.

Alistar SS, Grant PM, Bendavid E (2014a) Comparative effectiveness and cost-effectiveness of antiretroviral therapy and pre-exposure prophylaxis for HIV prevention in South Africa. *BMC Med.* 12:46.

Alistar SS, Long EF, Brandeau ML, Beck EJ (2014b) HIV epidemic control: A model for optimal allocation of prevention and treatment resources. *Health Care Manage. Sci.* 17(2):162–181.

Alistar SS, Owens DK, Brandeau ML (2014c) Effectiveness and cost effectiveness of oral pre-exposure prophylaxis in a portfolio of prevention programs for injection drug users in mixed HIV epidemics. *PLoS One* 9(1):e86584.

Anderson RM, May RM (1991) *Infectious Diseases of Humans: Dynamics and Control* (Oxford University Press, New York).

Anderson SJ, Cherutich P, Kilonzo N, Cremin I, Fecht D, Kimanga D, et al. (2014) Maximising the effect of combination HIV prevention through prioritisation of the people and places in greatest need: A modelling study. *Lancet* 384(9939):249–256.

Baeten JM, Donnell D, Ndase P, Mugo NR, Campbell JD, Wangisi J, et al. (2012) Antiretroviral prophylaxis for HIV prevention in heterosexual men and women. *N. Engl. J. Med.* 367(5):399–410.

Bautista-Arredondo S, Gadsden P, Harris JE, Bertozzi SM (2008) Optimizing resource allocation for HIV/AIDS prevention programmes: An analytical framework. *AIDS* 22(Suppl 1):S67–S74.

Brandeau ML (2004) Allocating resources to control infectious diseases. Brandeau ML, Sainfort F, Pierskalla WP, Eds. *Operations Research and Health Care: Methods and Applications* (Kluwer Academic Publishers, Norwell, MA), pp. 443–464.

Brandeau ML, Zaric GS (2009) Optimal investment in HIV prevention programs: More is not always better. *Health Care Manage. Sci.* 12(1):27–37.

Brandeau ML, Zaric GS, Richter A (2003) Resource allocation for control of infectious diseases in multiple independent populations: Beyond cost-effectiveness analysis. *J. Health Econ.* 22(4):575–598.

Brandeau ML, Zaric GS, De Angelis V (2005) Improved allocation of HIV prevention resources: Using information about prevention program production functions. *Health Care Manage. Sci.* 8(1):19–28.

Brazilian Ministry of Health (2012). Progress Report on the Brazilian Response to HIV/AIDS (2010–2011). Available at http://search.unaids.org/search.asp?lg=en&search=HIV%20 Brazil. Accessed on August 10, 2017.

Celum C, Baeten JM (2012) Tenofovir-based pre-exposure prophylaxis for HIV prevention: Evolving evidence. *Curr. Opin. Infect. Dis.* 25(1):51–57.

Choopanya K, Martin M, Suntharasamai P, Sangkum U, Mock PA, Leethochawalit M, et al. (2013) Antiretroviral prophylaxis for HIV infection among people who inject drugs in Bangkok, Thailand: A randomized, double-blind, placebo-controlled trial. *Lancet* 381(9883):2083–2090.

Cipriano LE, Zaric GS, Holodniy M, Bendavid E, Owens DK, Brandeau ML (2012) Cost effectiveness of screening strategies for early identification of HIV and HCV in injection drug users. *PLoS One* 7(9):e45176.

Currie CS, Floyd K, Williams BG, Dye C (2005) Cost, affordability and cost-effectiveness of strategies to control tuberculosis in countries with high HIV prevalence. *BMC Public Health* 5:130.

Earnshaw SR, Hicks K, Richter A, Honeycutt A (2007) A linear programming model for allocating HIV prevention funds with state agencies: A pilot study. *Health Care Manage. Sci.* 10(3):239–252.

England R (2008) The writing is on the wall for UNAIDS. *BMJ* 336(7652):1072.

Futures Group (2011). Goals Model. Available at http://futuresgroup.com/resources/software_models. Accessed on August 10, 2017.

Gold MR, Siegel JE, Russell LB, Weinstein MC, Eds. (1996) *Cost-Effectiveness in Health and Medicine* (Oxford University Press, New York).

Grant RM, Lama JR, Anderson PL, McMahan V, Liu AY, Vargas L, et al. (2010) Preexposure chemoprophylaxis for HIV prevention in men who have sex with men. *N. Engl. J. Med.* 363(27):2587–2599.

Hogan DR, Baltussen R, Hayashi C, Lauer JA, Salomon JA (2005) Cost effectiveness analysis of strategies to combat HIV/AIDS in developing countries. *BMJ* 331(7530):1431–1437.

Holt E (2014) Fears over future of opioid substitution therapy in Crimea. *Lancet* 383(9923):1113.

Humphreys G (2013) Opioid treatment in Ukraine risks losing momentum. *Bull. World Health Organ.* 91(2):87–88.

Joint United Nations Programme on HIV/AIDS (2008) Ukraine—National Report on Monitoring Progress Towards the UNGASS Declaration of Commitment on HIV/AIDS. United Nations, Geneva, Switzerland.

Joint United Nations Programme on HIV/AIDS (2010) UNAIDS Report on the Global AIDS Epidemic 2010. UNAIDS, Geneva, Switzerland.

Joint United Nations Programme on HIV/AIDS (2013) UNAIDS Report on the Global AIDS Epidemic 2013. UNAIDS, Geneva, Switzerland.

Joint United Nations Programme on HIV/AIDS (2014) The Gap Report. UNAIDS, Geneva, Switzerland.

Joint United Nations Programme on HIV/AIDS (2015). Fact Sheet 2014, HIV Global Statistics. Available at http://www.unaids.org/sites/default/files/documents/20141118_FS_WADreport_en.pdf. Accessed on August 10, 2017.

Juusola JJ, Brandeau ML (2016) HIV treatment and prevention: A simple model to determine optimal investment. *Med. Decis. Making* 36(2), 391–406.

Kahn JG (1996) The cost-effectiveness of HIV prevention targeting: How much more bang for the buck? *Am. J. Public Health* 86(12):1709–1712.

Kaplan EH (1998) Economic evaluation and HIV prevention community planning: A policy analyst's perspective. Holtgrave DR, Ed. *Handbook of Economic Evaluation of HIV Prevention Programs* (Plenum Press, New York).

Kaplan EH, Merson MH (2002) Allocating HIV-prevention resources: Balancing efficiency and equity. *Am. J. Public Health* 92(12):1905–1907.

Kaplan EH, Pollack H (1998) Allocating HIV prevention resources. *Socio-Econ. Plann. Sci.* 32(4):257–263.

Kim JY, Farmer P, Porter ME (2013) Redefining global health-care delivery. *Lancet* 382(9897):1060–1069.

Lasry A, Zaric GS, Carter MW (2007) Multi-level resource allocation for HIV prevention: A model for developing countries. *Eur. J. Oper. Res.* 180(2):786–799.

Lasry A, Carter MW, Zaric GS (2008) S4HARA: System for HIV/AIDS resource allocation. *Cost Eff. Resour. Alloc.* 6:7.

Lasry A, Richter A, Lutscher F (2009) Recommendations for increasing the use of HIV/AIDS resource allocation models. *BMC Public Health* 9(Suppl 1):S8.

Lasry A, Sansom S, Hicks K, Uzunangelov V (2011) A model for allocating CDC's HIV prevention resources in the United States. *Health Care Manage. Sci.* 14(1):115–124.

Long EF, Vaidya N, Brandeau ML (2008) Controlling co-epidemics: Analysis of HIV and tuberculosis infection dynamics. *Oper. Res.* 56(6):1366–1381.

Lusti-Narasimhan M, Khosla R, Baggaley R, Temmerman M, McGrory E, Farley T (2014) WHO guidance grounded in a comprehensive approach to sexual and reproductive health and human rights: Topical pre-exposure prophylaxis. *J. Int. AIDS Soc.* 17(3 Suppl 2): 19279.

Murray CJ, Lopez A (2002) World Health Report 2002: Reducing Risks, Promoting Healthy Life. World Health Organization, Geneva, Switzerland, p. 186.

Paltiel D (1994) Timing is of the essence—Matching AIDS policy to the epidemic life cycle. Kaplan EH, Brandeau ML, Eds. *Modeling the AIDS Epidemic: Planning, Policy, and Prediction* (Raven Press, Ltd., New York).

Paltiel AD, Freedberg KA, Scott CA, Schackman BR, Losina E, Wang B, et al. (2009) HIV preexposure prophylaxis in the United States: Impact on lifetime infection risk, clinical outcomes, and cost-effectiveness. *Clin. Infect. Dis.* 48(6):806–815.

Republic of South Africa National Department of Health (2013) *The South African Antiretroviral Treatment Guidelines* (National Department of Health, Pretoria, South Africa).

Richter A, Brandeau ML, Owens DK (1999) An analysis of optimal resource allocation for prevention of infection with human immunodeficiency virus (HIV) in injection drug users and non-users. *Med. Decis. Making* 19(2):167–179.

Richter A, Hicks KA, Earnshaw SR, Honeycutt AA (2008) Allocating HIV prevention resources: A tool for state and local decision making. *Health Policy* 87(3):342–349.

Ruiz M, Gable A, Kaplan EH, Stoto M, Fineberg H, Trussell J, Eds. (2001) *No Time to Lose: Getting More from HIV Prevention* (National Academy Press, Washington, DC).

Schackman BR, Leff JA, Barter DM, DiLorenzo MA, Feaster DJ, Metsch LR, et al. (2015) Cost-effectiveness of rapid HCV testing and simultaneous rapid HCV and HIV testing in substance abuse treatment programs. *Addiction* 110(1):129–143.

Schwartlander B, Stover J, Hallett T, Atun R, Avila C, Gouws E, et al. (2011) Towards an improved investment approach for an effective response to HIV/AIDS. *Lancet* 377(9782):2031–2041.

Stolberg SG (November 12, 1997) New challenge to idea that 'AIDS is special'. *New York Times*, p. A1.

Stover J, Bollinger L, Cooper-Arnold K (2003) *GOALS Model for Estimating the Effects of Resource Allocation Decisions on the Achievement of the Goals of the HIV/AIDS Strategic Plan* (The Futures Group International, Washington, DC).

Suen SC, Goldhaber-Fiebert JD, Brandeau ML (2017) Distinguishing high-risk versus low-risk subgroups in compartmental epidemic models: Where to draw the line?. *J. Theor. Biol.*, 428:1–17.

Terris-Prestholt F, Foss AM, Cox AP, Heise L, Meyer-Rath G, Delany-Moretlwe S, et al. (2014) Cost-effectiveness of tenofovir gel in urban South Africa: Model projections of HIV impact and threshold product prices. *BMC Infect. Dis.* 14:14.

Thigpen MC, Kebaabetswe PM, Paxton LA, Smith DK, Rose CE, Segolodi TM, et al. (2012) Antiretroviral preexposure prophylaxis for heterosexual HIV transmission in Botswana. *N. Engl. J. Med.* 367(5):423–434.

United Nations (2009) The Millennium Development Goals Report 2009. United Nations, New York.

Wei TL (February 8, 2012) Funding Squeeze, Apathy Risk Another Half Century of AIDS— UN Expert. Thompson Reuters Foundation.

World Health Organization (2013a) Consolidated Guidelines on the Use of Antiretroviral Drugs for Treating and Preventing HIV Infection: Recommendations for a Public Health Approach. World Health Organization, Geneva, Switzerland.

World Health Organization (2013b). Global Update on HIV Treatment 2013: Results, Impact and Opportunities. Available at http://search.unaids.org/search.asp?lg=en&search=global%20 update%20on%20HIV%20treatment%202013. Accessed on August 24, 2017.

World Health Organization (2015). Guideline on When to Start Antiretroviral Therapy and on Pre-exposure Prophylaxis for HIV. Available at http://www.who.int/hiv/pub/guidelines/ earlyrelease-arv/en/. Accessed on August 24, 2017.

Zaric GS (2003) Resource allocation for control of infectious disease epidemics. *Comments Theor. Biol.* 8:475–496.

Zaric GS, Brandeau ML (2001a) Optimal investment in a portfolio of HIV prevention programs. *Med. Decis. Making* 21(5):391–408.

Zaric GS, Brandeau ML (2001b) Resource allocation for epidemic control over short time horizons. *Math. Biosci.* 171(1):33–58.

Zaric GS, Brandeau ML (2002) Dynamic resource allocation for epidemic control in multiple populations. *Math. Med. Biol.* 19(4):235–255.

Zaric GS, Brandeau ML (2007) A little planning goes a long way: Multi-level allocation of HIV prevention resources. *Med. Decis. Making* 27(1):71–81.

3

ADAPTIVE DECISION-MAKING DURING EPIDEMICS

REZA YAESOUBI[1] AND TED COHEN[2]

[1] *Department of Health Policy and Management, Yale School of Public Health, New Haven, CT, USA*
[2] *Department of Epidemiology and Microbial Disease, Yale School of Public Health, New Haven, CT, USA*

3.1 INTRODUCTION

The persistent threat of the emergence of novel viral pathogens (e.g., Ebola, SARS, H1N1, and H5N1 influenza) has generated public concern and triggered extensive efforts to develop better strategic plans to mitigate the health and economic impact of pandemics (Ferguson et al. 2005, 2006; Flahault et al. 2006; Germann et al. 2006; Lipsitch et al. 2003; Yang et al. 2009). The timely deployment of effective interventions plays a central role in controlling epidemics. Recent successes in limiting the spread or delaying the emergence of pathogens have relied on the availability of surveillance data, and, increasingly, national and international public health organizations have encouraged and invested in the development of more robust surveillance systems that can be used to guide the rational use of interventions (Henning 2004; Mandl et al. 2004).

These novel sources of health data offer new opportunities to actively monitor the emergence and spread of infectious disease and to inform more effective selection of interventional strategies. To harness this potential, an integrated framework is required to translate real-time surveillance data into deployable health policy

Decision Analytics and Optimization in Disease Prevention and Treatment, First Edition.
Edited by Nan Kong and Shengfan Zhang.
© 2018 John Wiley & Sons, Inc. Published 2018 by John Wiley & Sons, Inc.

recommendations. The optimality of such health policies should be determined by their ability to reduce disease-related morbidity and mortality while respecting constraints on the availability of resources (e.g., budget, personnel, and supplies).

Utilizing accumulating epidemic data to inform cost-effective decisions during epidemics requires a framework that integrates three main steps (see Figure 3.1). First, a transmission dynamic model must be developed based on domain-specific expertise to describe the natural history and the transmission route of an infectious disease (Step 1, Figure 3.1). This model will be utilized to evaluate and compare the performance of different policies as well as to predict the future behavior of the epidemic. Next, the model must then be calibrated so that it captures the past trends and projects the future behavior of the epidemic within an acceptable degree of accuracy (Step 2, Figure 3.1). Finally, an optimizer is coupled to the calibrated model that identifies the optimal policy, specifying conditions where specific interventions should be employed (Step 3, Figure 3.1). The optimizer considers the available resources (e.g., budget, vaccine doses) as constraints and seeks to find a health policy that maximizes the expected population health while satisfying these resource constraints.

To illustrate the development and employment of adaptive health policies, we consider the spread of a novel viral pathogen (e.g., SARS, H1N1 and H5N1 influenza) in a fully susceptible population. While vaccination remains the most effective intervention to mitigate the impact of epidemics (Germann et al. 2006), vaccines against novel pathogens usually become available only in limited supply and with significant delay (Centers for Disease Control and Prevention 2009). In these circumstances, "transmission-reducing" interventions, such as school or public place closure, are commonly considered as part of national and international pandemic mitigation protocols (Centers for Disease Control and Prevention 2007; Stern and Markel 2009; World Health Organization 2005). For example, closing schools aims to reduce contacts among school-age children, who often play an important role in transmission, and consequently to interrupt or decrease the speed and extent of transmission in the population (Cauchemez et al. 2009; Jackson et al. 2014).

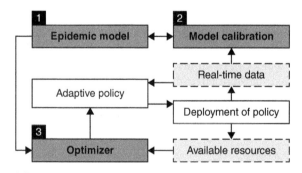

Figure 3.1 A framework for adaptive decision-making during epidemics.

Despite these potential health benefits, the high social and economic costs associated with school or public place closure makes them an expensive control measure to be implemented only when the yield is high enough to offset the cost (Brown et al. 2011; Chen et al. 2011; Sander et al. 2009). If, for example, public place closure were implemented too late in the epidemic, it would fail to have any meaningful mitigating effect while triggering the intervention too soon would incur unnecessary social and economic costs. Of equal importance is the decision about when to reopen schools. Lifting the intervention prematurely may result in a second epidemic peak and erosion of the accumulated benefit (Cauchemez et al. 2009). Here we consider the question about when we should employ and lift a transmission-reducing intervention, such as school or workplace closure, as the pathogen is spreading in the population.

3.2 PROBLEM FORMULATION

The spread of an infectious disease in a population triggers specific events that may result in observations, incur costs, affect population health status, and change resource availability. Examples of such events include incident infections, hospitalizations, or deaths of infectious individuals. We use the random variable X_k to denote events that may occur during the decision period $[k, k+1]$, $k \in \{1,2,3,...\}$. While deterministic epidemic models (Anderson and May 1991; Hethcote 2000) have been widely used to analyze the spread of infectious diseases, these models produce epidemics with deterministic trajectories; if the epidemic trajectory was actually deterministic, it would be possible to identify an optimal series of interventions at the very beginning of an epidemic. We note that the future behavior of an epidemic is never known with certainty, and thus, in order to develop a framework that can provide adaptive decision support over the course of an epidemic, stochastic models are required. Several modeling approaches can be used to describe the random variable X_k to produce stochastic epidemic trajectories including stochastic compartmental models (Daley and Gani 1999; Yaesoubi and Cohen 2011) and agent-based simulation models (Bonabeau 2002; Epstein 2009; Germann et al. 2006) (see Section 3.3.2 for an illustration).

Let $\mathcal{A}$ be the set of available control interventions (e.g. $\mathcal{A} = \{$School closure, Vaccinating children$\}$) and $a_k \in 2^{\mathcal{A}}$ denote the set of control interventions in effect during the decision period $[k, k+1]$, where $2^{\mathcal{A}}$ is the power set of $\mathcal{A}$. Clearly, the interventions in effect during period $[k, k+1]$ will influence the set of epidemic events that may occur over this period. When this dependency should be made explicit, we use $X_k(a_k)$ instead of X_k. An epidemic trajectory is defined as a realization of the stochastic process $\mathbf{X} = \{X_k(a_k), k \geq 1\}$, which we denote by $\chi = \{\chi_k, k \geq 1\}$ (see Figure 3.2).

The stochastic process $\mathbf{X} = \{X_k(a_k), k \geq 1\}$ is not fully observable and neither is the epidemic trajectory $\chi = \{\chi_k, k \geq 1\}$. However, during decision periods, the policy

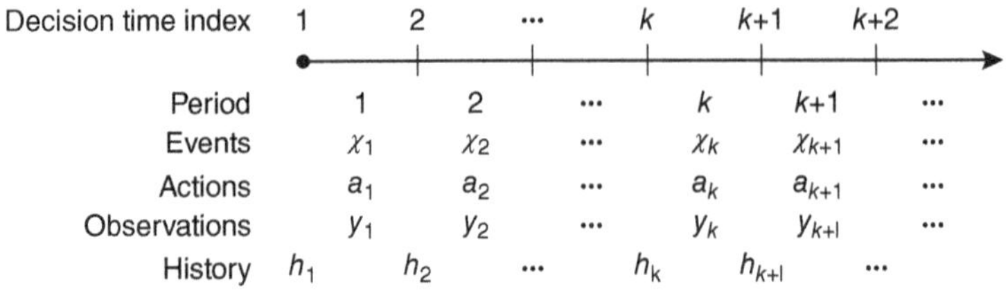

Decision time index	1	2	⋯	k	k+1	k+2
Period	1	2	⋯	k	k+1	⋯
Events	χ_1	χ_2	⋯	χ_k	χ_{k+1}	⋯
Actions	a_1	a_2	⋯	a_k	a_{k+1}	⋯
Observations	y_1	y_2	⋯	y_k	y_{k+l}	⋯
History	h_1	h_2	⋯	h_k	h_{k+l}	⋯

Figure 3.2   Sequence of events, actions, and observations during an epidemic.

maker may obtain observations on different epidemic measures, such as the number of disease-related hospitalizations or deaths (triggered by realized events χ_k). Let y_k denote the vector of observations made during the period $[k, k+1]$ and h_k denote the history of the epidemic at decision point k defined as the sequence of past actions and observations up to the time point k. The history h_k is updated recursively according to $h_k = \{h_{k-1}, a_{k-1}, y_{k-1}\}, k \geq 1$, where h_1, the observed history at the first decision time point, is an empty set.

For a realized trajectory $\chi = \{\chi_k, k \geq 1\}$, we measure the overall outcome of the epidemic as the total discounted population's net health benefit (NHB) (Briggs et al. 2006):

$$\sum_{k=1}^{K} \gamma^{k-1} r(a_k, \chi_k), \tag{3.1}$$

where $r(a_k, \chi_k)$ is the population's NHB during the decision period $[k, k+1]$ if action $a_k \in 2^A$ is in effect, and the events χ_k occur, and $\gamma \in (0,1]$ is the discount factor. In Equation 3.1, the decision horizon K can be a constant predetermined by the decision-maker (e.g., 2 years) or can be a random variable representing the time when the disease is eradicated or some other stopping condition is met.

For a given epidemic trajectory $\chi = \{\chi_k, k \geq 1\}$, our goal is to maximize the objective function (3.1). To this end, we propose an analytical framework that consists of three main steps: (i) the development of a transmission dynamic *simulation model* that describes the natural history and the transmission of the viral pathogen that allows us to project epidemic behavior over time and in response to interventions, (ii) the *calibration* of the transmission dynamic model to available surveillance data, and finally (iii) the employment of a *policy optimization* procedure that efficiently searches over the space of available strategies to identify a policy that maximizes the population's expected total discounted NMB by specifying the epidemic and resource availability conditions, which should trigger the employment or removal of specific control interventions.

When a pathogen first emerges in a population, many pathogen-related parameters will not be known. For example, the transmissibility of the pathogen (i.e., the probability that infection results from a relevant contact between an infectious individual and a susceptible individual) may be especially challenging to estimate based on limited data. We use $\theta = (\theta_1, \theta_2, \ldots, \theta_P)$ to denote the set of parameters that are not observable, but affect the epidemic random events X_k. To predict the behavior of the epidemic, we use the transmission dynamic model $\tilde{\mathbf{X}} = \{\tilde{X}_k(a_k), k \geq 1\}$, where $\tilde{X}_k(a_k)$ is the set of random epidemic events that the model projects for period $[k, k+1]$ given the action a_k. In Section 3.3.2, we detail the development of such model for a novel pathogen epidemic.

We denote the input parameters of this simulation model with the vector $\tilde{\theta}$ that contains estimates for the true epidemic parameter values θ. As the true value of important epidemic parameters are often unknown, the goal of model calibration is to identify values of the vector $\tilde{\theta}$ such that the trajectories generated by the simulation model $\tilde{\mathbf{X}}$ is "sufficiently close" to the observed data from the epidemic.

Let H denote the set of all possible values that the history h_k can take. A policy $\pi: \mathcal{H} \rightarrow 2^{\mathcal{A}}$ specifies the set of interventions to implement during a given decision interval $[k, k+1]$ based on the epidemic history h_k observed at the decision point k. The goal of policy optimization procedure at the decision point $\kappa \in \{1, 2, \ldots\}$ is to find a policy that maximizes the population's expected total discounted NMB from the decision point κ onward:

$$E_{\tilde{\mathbf{X}}}\left[\sum_{k=\kappa}^{\infty} \gamma^{k-\kappa} r\left(\pi\left(\tilde{h}_k\right), \tilde{X}_k\right)\right]. \quad (3.2)$$

The expectation in Equation 3.2 is with respect to the stochastic process $\tilde{\mathbf{X}} = \{\tilde{X}_k(\tilde{a}_k), k \geq \kappa\}$, which models the future events that may occur throughout the epidemic given the future actions $\tilde{a}_k = \pi(\tilde{h}_k)$, $k \in \{\kappa, \kappa+1, \ldots\}$. Here, h_k denotes the history at decision point k generated by the simulation model $\tilde{\mathbf{X}}$. In Section 3.3.4, we develop an approximate policy iteration algorithm to approximate the optimal policy π^* that maximizes the objective function (3.2).

3.3 METHODS

3.3.1 The 1918 Influenza Pandemic in San Francisco, CA

The 1918 influenza pandemic, better known as the "Spanish flu," was caused by an influenza A virus (H1N1). In San Francisco, California, which had an approximate population of 550,000 in that year, 28,310 cases of the Spanish flu were reported during the autumn wave (September–November) (Crosby et al. 2003). During this period, neither an influenza vaccine nor antiviral drugs were available, and the control strategies relied on social distancing and hygienic measures such as isolation, prohibition of public events, and use of face masks. We use the daily number of cases reported during the autumn wave of the 1918 influenza pandemic in the city of San Francisco, California (see Figure 3.3), to calibrate a simple transmission dynamic model that can be used to evaluate and optimize the performance of different control policies.

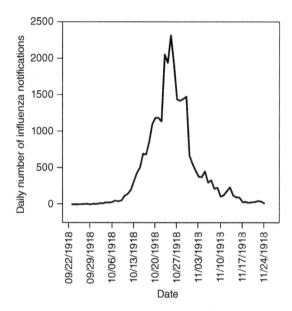

Figure 3.3 Daily number of influenza notifications in San Francisco, CA, during the autumn wave of the 1918 influenza pandemic. Source: Chowell et al. (2007). Reproduced with permission of Interface.

In the following subsections, we first describe the development of transmission dynamic models that can capture the outbreak of a novel viral pathogen. We then propose a calibration method to fit these epidemic models to the daily number of reported cases shown in Figure 3.3. We finally describe a dynamic decision model that can utilize the calibrated epidemic model to generate real-time recommendations.

3.3.2 Stochastic Transmission Dynamic Models

In this section, we develop a simple stochastic compartmental model for describing the spread of a novel viral pathogen such as H1N1 influenza that caused the 1918 pandemic. While the calibration and policy optimization methods that we will describe in the later sections can work with any other modeling framework (such as agent-based models), we chose to use a simple epidemic model to maintain the current focus on presenting the proposed calibration and policy optimization methods.

In this simplified transmission dynamic model (shown in Figure 3.4), population members are fully susceptible to the novel pathogen. A susceptible individual may become infected upon contract with an infectious individual. An infected individual is initially asymptomatic, but is nonetheless infectious. We assume that once an infectious individual becomes symptomatic, the severity of symptoms leads to their

Figure 3.4 A simple model for the outbreak of a novel viral pathogen.

immediate diagnosis, and effective inpatient treatment will start soon after. Once treatment is initiated, the patient is no longer infectious. Individuals recovered from infection are assumed to acquire permanent immunity to the current viral strain. We note that this epidemic model is highly simplified and does not accurately reflect the natural history of influenza, in which most infections are not associated with symptoms and most affected individuals never will receive inpatient treatment. Our model also ignores disease-related mortality. However, for the purposes of this illustrative example, this is a convenient structure. We show later how the proposed modeling framework is readily extended to models with more complicated natural history or to other modeling approaches (e.g., network models or agent-based models).

Let $Z_S(t)$ denote the number of susceptible individuals, $Z_I(t)$ denote the number of infectious individuals, $Z_T(t)$ denote the number of individuals receiving treatment, and $Z_R(t)$ denote the number of recovered individuals at time t. Since influenza epidemics usually last for several months and the number of deaths is generally small relative to population size, it is reasonable to assume that the population size N does not change over the course of epidemic. For a population of a fixed size N, the state of the disease spread at any given time t can be identified by $s_t = \left(Z_S(t), Z_I(t), Z_T(t) \right)$.

Let $\beta(t)$ denote the probability that the next contact of a random susceptible individual is with an infectious person. We assume that a random susceptible individual will contact other population members at rate λ. When transmission-reducing interventions (e.g., school closure) are not used and mixing is homogenous, $\beta(t)$ is equal to $\beta(t) = Z_I(t)/N$. Let $\varphi(t)$ denote overall probability that a susceptible person becomes infected. This probability can be calculated as (Yaesoubi and Cohen 2011):

$$\varphi\left(t \right) = 1 - e^{\lambda \eta \Delta t \beta(t)} = 1 - e^{\lambda \eta \Delta t Z_I(t)/N}, \tag{3.3}$$

where η denotes the probability that a susceptible individual becomes infected upon contact with an infectious person. Variable η may be modified by "hygienic interventions" (reducing the chance of transmission given contact between infectious and susceptible individuals) and variable λ by "social distancing" (reducing the likelihood of contact between susceptible and infectious individuals). We assume that if either of these interventions is in effect during the interval $[t, t + \Delta t]$, the probability $\varphi(t)$ in Equation 3.3 will be reduced to $\varphi(t) = 1 - e^{(1-\sigma)\lambda \eta \Delta t Z_I(t)/N}$, where $\sigma \in [0,1]$ is the fractional reduction in the infection transmission rate. We refer to the parameter σ as effectiveness of the transmission-reducing intervention. Given the state of the epidemic at time t, that is, $s_t = \left(Z_S(t), Z_I(t), Z_T(t) \right)$, the number of new infections during the interval $[t, t + \Delta t]$ will have a binomial distribution with parameters $(Z_S(t), \varphi(t))$ (Yaesoubi and Cohen 2011).

We assume that an infected individual will get hospitalized at a rate μ and will recover at a rate η once treatment is initiated (though we assume that they are not infectious as soon as the treatment starts). Therefore, given the state of the epidemic at time t, the number of newly hospitalized patients and the number of patients who will recover from the infection during the interval $[t, t + \Delta t]$ will have binomial distributions with parameters $\left(Z_I(t), 1 - e^{\mu \Delta t} \right)$ and $\left(Z_T(t), 1 - e^{\tau \Delta t} \right)$, respectively.

To generate trajectories for this epidemic model, we use Monte Carlo simulation to sample from the Markov chain $\left\{ \left(Z_S(t), Z_I(t), Z_T(t) \right): t = 0, \Delta t, 2\Delta t, 3\Delta t, \ldots \right\}$. The random events that govern the evolution of this Markov chain are (i) the infection of a susceptible individual, (ii) the hospitalization of an infectious individual, and (iii) the recovery of a hospitalized individual. The probability distributions of these events are described previously. Therefore, in this epidemic model, the random variable $X_k(a_k)$ (see Section 3.2) is a three-dimensional vector representing the number of newly infected cases (change in health status), the number of newly diagnosed cases (triggering observations, incurring treatment costs, and change in health status), and the number of patients recovered from infection (change in health status).

3.3.3 Calibration

The goal of model calibration is to use the observations gathered throughout the epidemic to reduce the uncertainty around model input parameters (Alkema et al. 2011; Birrell et al. 2011; Cauchemez et al. 2006a, b; Elderd et al. 2006; Wallinga and Teunis 2004). To decide which calibration method to use for the purpose of adaptive decision-making, we note that the simulation model tuned by the calibration procedure will be used later in policy optimization. If the calibration procedure identifies only the "best fit" to the observed data, the performance of the resultant control policies will be extremely sensitive to the observed epidemic data. Therefore, in order to improve the robustness of control policies, rather than trying to find parameter estimates that yield the best fit to the observed data, we characterize a probability distribution for parameter values for a *set* of trajectories that are "sufficiently close" to the observed data. This set of trajectories will be later used in the optimization phase to evaluate performance of different control policies.

To describe the calibration procedure proposed here, we fit the epidemic model of Section 3.3.2 to the data gathered during the first 3 weeks of the Spanish flu in San Francisco (the first 21 data points in Figure 3.3). During the early stage of this pandemic, no particular control interventions were employed and the population's reaction to the pandemic was apparently minimal. To calibrate the epidemic model of Section 3.3.2, we first note that, in this model, parameters λ and η occur as a multiplicative term (see Equation 3.3), and hence only one of them can be identified through calibration. We therefore fixed the value of $\lambda = 10$ effective contacts per day and will try to estimate the pathogen infectivity, η, and the mean of infectious period, $1/\mu$.

Let $\mathcal{P}_{\Theta}(\cdot)$ denote the joint *prior* probability function of the true epidemic parameters $\theta = (\theta_1, \theta_2, \ldots, \theta_P)$, perceived by the policy maker at the beginning of the epidemic. This prior distribution can be characterized using the estimates from similar epidemics that have occurred before. To form a prior distribution for the parameters of our epidemic model, we note that for this model the basic reproduction number, R_0, defined as the average number of secondary cases generated by a primary infectious case in a completely susceptible population, can be calculated as $R_0 = \lambda\eta/\mu$. We chose uniform prior distributions for R_0 and $1/\mu$: $R_0 \sim \mathcal{U}[1.1,3]$ and $1/\mu \sim \mathcal{U}[1,8]$.

Figure 3.5a compares the total number of cases by the end of day 21 observed during the Spanish flu in San Francisco, CA, with the histogram of the total number of cases estimated using our epidemic models. To obtain this probability function, we used 1000 simulation runs for which R_0 and $1/\mu$ were randomly drawn from uniform distributions $\mathcal{U}[1.1,3]$ and $\mathcal{U}[1,8]$, respectively, and η was set to $\eta = R_0\mu/\lambda$. Figure 3.5a demonstrates that the selected prior distributions for R_0 and $1/\mu$ fail to produce epidemic trajectories that capture the accumulating data during the first 21 days of the Spanish flu in San Francisco, CA. In this subsection, we describe an algorithm to identify parameter sets that produce a set of epidemic trajectories that are sufficiently close to the observed epidemic data. This algorithm will also provide a mechanism for sampling from these trajectories. These sampled trajectories can then be used for projection and policy evaluation (see Section 3.3.4).

The proposed algorithm relies on the use of common random numbers (Clark 1990; Murphy et al. 2013) to simulate epidemic trajectories. This variance reduction technique is often used to improve the accuracy of the comparison between two or more alternative configurations by using the same streams of uniform random variates in simulating these alternatives. This approach allows us to retrieve any desired

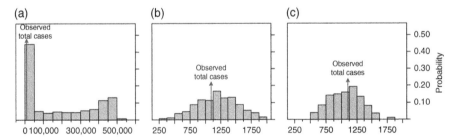

Figure 3.5 Comparison of the total number of cases observed at day 21 during the autumn wave the Spanish flu in San Francisco, CA, with the prediction from the epidemic model. Histogram in (a) is created using 1000 simulation runs for which R_0 and $1/\mu$ are randomly drawn from prior distributions $\mathcal{U}[1.1,3]$ and $\mathcal{U}[1,8]$, respectively. To construct histograms in (b) and (c), first, $N_0 = 25,000$ simulation runs are obtained and then to decide which trajectories to keep, $\alpha = 0.02$ (for b) and $\alpha = 0.01$ (for c) are used. The remaining trajectories are resampled 1000 times according to the mass probability function Π_z returned by the calibration procedure in Table 3.1.

simulated trajectory when evaluating the performance of various control policies in the policy optimization step. In this method, to obtain one simulated epidemic trajectory, we first specify the seed of the simulation's random number generator (RNG) object. The simulator will then use the RNG object to generate a unique stream of random numbers that will be used to both draw a sample for epidemic parameters and generate one simulated trajectory. This approach will enable us to regenerate any desired trajectory by knowing the corresponding RNG seeds.

At a decision point $\kappa \in \{1,2,...\}$, we use the observed epidemic history h_κ to construct the observation matrix $Y_\kappa = (y_1, y_2,...,y_\kappa)$ and the sequence of past actions $A_\kappa = (a_1, a_2,...,a_{\kappa-1})$. Let $\hat{Y}_\kappa^z = (\hat{y}_1^z, \hat{y}_2^z,...,\hat{y}_\kappa^z)$ denote the observation matrix generated by the simulation model $\tilde{X} = \{\tilde{X}_k(a_k), 1 \le k \le \kappa - 1\}$, in which actions over decision periods $\{1,2,...,\kappa-1\}$ are set equal to the actions $A_\kappa = (a_1, a_2,...,a_{\kappa-1})$ taken during the epidemic, and $z \in \mathbb{N}$ is the seed of the simulation RNG object.

To measure the fit of a model to accumulated observations, a popular approach is to use likelihood functions (Alkema et al. 2011; Birrell et al. 2011; Elderd et al. 2006). Let θ denote the model parameters (R_0 and μ in this illustration). The likelihood of observations $Y_\kappa = (y_1, y_2,...,y_\kappa)$ is defined as

$$L(Y_\kappa; \theta) = L(y_1, y_2,...,y_\kappa; \theta) = \prod_{k=1}^{\kappa} \mathcal{P}(y_k | y_1, y_2,...,y_{k-1}; \theta), \qquad (3.4)$$

where $\mathcal{P}(y_k | y_1, y_2,...,y_{k-1}; \theta)$ is the probability of observing y_k given the previous observations $(y_1, y_2,...,y_{k-1})$ and the model parameters θ. Calculating the exact likelihood function (3.4) for stochastic epidemic models is often not possible, so the likelihood function must be approximated (Bettencourt and Ribeiro 2008; Riley et al. 2003). Here, we use an alternative approach to calculate the fit of a simulated trajectory. To measure the distance between the matrices Y_κ and $\hat{Y}_\kappa^z$, we first construct the matrix of relative errors:

$$d(\hat{Y}_\kappa^z, Y_\kappa) = \frac{|\hat{Y}_\kappa^z - Y_\kappa|}{Y_\kappa + E}, \qquad (3.5)$$

where the division is element wise and the matrix E has the same size as Y_κ with all elements set to 1. The matrix E is added to ensure that the denominator in Equation 3.5 is always greater than zero. Now, we use the Frobenius norm of the matrix $d(\hat{Y}_\kappa^z, Y_\kappa)$ to measure the distance between the matrices Y_κ and $\hat{Y}_\kappa^z$. The Frobenius norm of a matrix M is defined as $\|M\|_F = \sqrt{\sum_{i,j}(m_{ij})^2}$, where m_{ij} is the (i,j) element of the matrix M (Golub 2013).

To decide if the epidemic trajectory corresponding to an RNG seed is considered "sufficiently close" to the observed data, we use the following approach. Let $\alpha \in (0,1]$ be a coverage ratio to represent the policy maker's preference over different sets of simulated trajectories; smaller values of α implies the policy maker's preference to identify simulated trajectories that are close to the observed data, whereas larger values of α implies the policy maker's preference to find trajectories that cover a larger neighborhood around the observed data. For example, in Figure 3.5b and c, $\alpha = 0.02$ and $\alpha = 0.01$, respectively. Therefore, the simulated trajectories selected by the proposed calibration procedure are gathered more closely around the observed data (i.e., total number of cases at end of day 21) in Figure 3.5c compared with those in Figure 3.5b.

To build a set of trajectories that are considered sufficiently close to the observed epidemic data, the proposed algorithm first obtains N_0 epidemic trajectories that are not eradicated by the decision point κ. Let the set R_κ contain the RNG seeds used to generate these N_0 epidemic trajectories. We construct the set $\tilde{R}_\kappa \subset R_\kappa$ by selecting $\lfloor \alpha N_0 \rfloor$ seeds from the set R_κ that have resulted in trajectories with the smallest values of $\left\| d\left(\hat{Y}_\kappa^z, Y_\kappa\right) \right\|_F$ among the N_0 simulated trajectories. Now to generate epidemic trajectories for prediction or for evaluating control policies, at each simulation iteration, we select a random number $z \in \tilde{R}_\kappa$ with the probability $\Pi_z = p_z \Big/ \sum_{z \in \tilde{R}_\kappa} p_z$, where $p_z = 1 \Big/ \left\| d\left(\hat{Y}_\kappa^z, Y_\kappa\right) \right\|_F$. Table 3.1 summarizes the steps of the calibration procedure proposed here.

This calibration procedure can also be used to estimate the epidemic parameters. Figure 3.6 shows the estimated values of the basic reproductive number (R_0) and the mean of the infectiousness period $(1/\mu)$ using the first 21 days of observations during the Spanish flu epidemic in San Francisco. To produce these estimates, we first employed the calibration procedure in Table 3.1 with $N_0 = 25,000$ and $\alpha = 0.01$ to find RNG set $\tilde{R}_\kappa$ and the probability mass function $\Pi_z, z \in \tilde{R}_\kappa$ (here, $\kappa = 21$ days). We then formed the histograms in Figure 3.6 by obtaining 1000 samples from the parameter values corresponding to the RNG seeds in the set $\tilde{R}_\kappa$ according to the probability mass function $\Pi_z, z \in \tilde{R}_\kappa$. The estimates shown in Figure 3.6 are consistent with the results from previous studies (Chowell et al. 2007; Mills et al. 2004).

3.3.4 Optimizing Dynamic Health Policies

Classical approaches for identifying optimal strategies for infectious disease control use mathematical or simulation models of disease spread to evaluate the performance of a limited number of *predetermined* health strategies (Dushoff et al. 2007; Ferguson et al. 2005, 2006; Flahault et al. 2006; Germann et al. 2006; Halloran et al. 2008; Patel et al. 2005). Examples of predetermined health strategies might include, "Close schools for a duration of two weeks beginning from the fourth week after the first case of influenza" or "Do contact tracing during the first two weeks of an influenza outbreak." Although these approaches can provide insight into the comparative performance of each strategy, they are usually not structured to assist real-time decision-making as new data become available over the course of epidemic.

To address this shortcoming, we use dynamic optimization methods (Bertsekas 2005; Puterman 1994) to define and optimize policies that inform health recommendations based on the latest epidemiological data. At the epidemic decision point

TABLE 3.1 **Calibration Procedure at the Epidemic Decision Point** $\kappa \in \{1, 2, ...\}$

Step 0:	Initialization
Step 0a.	Specify the joint prior probability distribution of the epidemic parameters, $\mathcal{P}_\Theta(\cdot)$.
Step 0b.	Set the coverage ratio $\alpha \in (0, 1]$.
Step 0c.	Use the observed epidemic history h_κ to construct the observation matrix $Y_\kappa = (y_1, y_2, ..., y_\kappa)$ and the sequence of past actions $A_\kappa = (a_1, a_2, ..., a_{\kappa-1})$.
Step 0d.	Set N_0, the number of the simulated trajectories to initialize the algorithm.
Step 0e.	Set (the set of RNG seeds generating epidemic trajectories that are not eradicated by the decision point κ).
Step 0f.	Set (the set of RNG seeds generating epidemic trajectories which are considered "sufficiently close" to the epidemic data).
Step 1:	
	Reset the seed of the random number generator ($z = 1$);
	While $|\mathcal{R}_\kappa| \leq N_0$:
	Simulate: Generate one simulated trajectory using the simulation model $\tilde{X} = \{\tilde{X}_k(a_k), 1 \leq k \leq \kappa - 1\}$, with the RNG seed z, where actions over decision periods $\{1, 2, ..., \kappa - 1\}$ are set equal to the actions $A_\kappa = (a_1, a_2, ..., a_{\kappa-1})$ taken during the epidemic.
	If the simulated trajectory is not eradicated by decision time κ, then $\mathcal{R}_\kappa \leftarrow \mathcal{R}_\kappa \cup \{z\}$.
	$z \leftarrow z + 1$.
Step 2:	
	Construct the set $\tilde{\mathcal{R}}_\kappa$ by selecting $\lfloor \alpha N \rfloor$ seeds from the set R_κ that have resulted in trajectories with the smallest values of $d \left\| \left(\hat{Y}_\kappa^z, Y_\kappa \right) \right\|_F$ among the N_0 simulated.
	For each $z \in \tilde{\mathcal{R}}_\kappa$, calculate the probability $\Pi_z = p_z / \sum_{z \in \tilde{\mathcal{R}}_\kappa} p_z$, where $p_z = 1/d \left\| \left(\hat{Y}_\kappa^z, Y_\kappa \right) \right\|_F$.
Step 3:	
	Return the set and the probability mass function $\Pi_z, z \in \tilde{\mathcal{R}}_\kappa$.

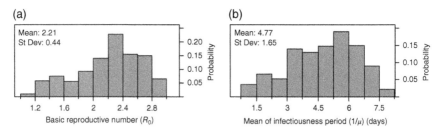

(a)

Mean: 2.21
St Dev: 0.44

Basic reproductive number (R_0)

(b)

Mean: 4.77
St Dev: 1.65

Mean of infectiousness period ($1/\mu$) (days)

Figure 3.6 Estimates for the basic reproductive number (a) and the mean of infectiousness period (b) using the first 21 observations during the Spanish flu in San Francisco, CA.

$\kappa \in \{1,2,...\}$, the optimality equations to maximize the objective function (3.2) can be written as (White 1991)

$$v^*\left(\tilde{h}_k\right) = \max_{a_k \in 2^A}\left\{E_{\tilde{x}}\left[r\left(a_k, \tilde{\chi}_k\right) + \gamma v^*\left(\tilde{h}_{k+1}\right)\middle|\tilde{h}_k, a_k\right]\right\}, \quad \text{for } \tilde{h}_k \in \mathcal{H}, k \geq \kappa, \quad (3.6)$$

where $v^*(\tilde{h}_k)$ is the optimal expected total discounted reward to be accrued from time index k onward, given the history $\tilde{h}_k$. If we solve Equation 3.6 for $v^*(\cdot)$, then the optimal choice at a given decision point k can be found by

$$a^*\left(\tilde{h}_k\right) = \arg\max_{a_k \in 2^A}\left\{E_{\tilde{x}}\left[r\left(a_k, \tilde{\chi}_k\right) + \gamma v^*\left(\tilde{h}_{k+1}\right)\middle|\tilde{h}_k, a_k\right]\right\}, \quad \text{for } \tilde{h}_k \in \mathcal{H}, k \geq \kappa. \quad (3.7)$$

We define the optimal Q-values $Q^*\left(\tilde{h}_k, a_k\right)$ for the pair $\left(\tilde{h}_k, a_k\right) \in \mathcal{H} \times 2^A$ as

$$Q^*\left(\tilde{h}_k, a_k\right) = E_{\tilde{x}}\left[r\left(a_k, \tilde{\chi}_k\right) + \gamma v^*\left(\tilde{h}_{k+1}\right)\middle|\tilde{h}_k, a_k\right]. \quad (3.8)$$

And now, an optimal action given observing the epidemic history $\tilde{h}_k$ at the decision point k can be determined by

$$a^*\left(\tilde{h}_k\right) = \arg\max_{a_k \in 2^A}Q^*\left(\tilde{h}_k, a_k\right), \quad \text{for } \tilde{h}_k \in \mathcal{H}, k \geq \kappa. \quad (3.9)$$

Finding the optimal Q-values $Q^*\left(\tilde{h}_k, a_k\right)$ for each pair $\left(\tilde{h}_k, a_k\right)$ is not computationally feasible because the history space $\mathcal{H}$ can be an enormous and potentially unbounded set. We therefore approximate the optimal Q-values using regression models that will be tuned through an iterative procedure. To approximate the optimal Q-values, we use an *approximate policy iteration* algorithm. The details of this procedure, which is motivated by Lagoudakis and Parr's approach (Lagoudakis and Parr 2004) and is modified for systems where states are only partially observable, are provided elsewhere (Yaesoubi and Cohen 2016).

To approximate the optimal Q-values, this approach uses regression models $\tilde{Q}(\cdot)$ where regressors are simple statistics defined on the epidemic history such as "total number of cases observed so far" or "number of cases observed during the past week." These statistics are usually referred to as *features*, and their role is to extract useful information from the epidemic history such that, for a given history-action pair, the expected future reward can be well approximated by a regression model that is a function of these features. We use $\mathcal{F}(\cdot)$ to denote the *feature extraction* function that takes the epidemic history and calculates the value of defined features. As an example, suppose that schools have been open during the first 3 weeks of an epidemic and 2, 5, and 9 hospitalized cases have been recorded during weeks 1, 2, and 3, respectively. For this scenario, the epidemic history at the beginning of week 4 can be denoted by $\tilde{h}_4 = \{\text{Open},2,\text{Open},5,\text{Open},9\}$. Now, if the feature extraction function $\mathcal{F}(\cdot)$ is defined to return the "total number of hospitalizations thus far" and "number of weeks schools have already been closed," then $\mathcal{F}(\tilde{h}_4) = (\mathcal{F}_1(\tilde{h}_4), \mathcal{F}_2(\tilde{h}_4)) = (16,0)$. We will discuss later how to define the feature extraction function $\mathcal{F}(\cdot)$ for different epidemics.

The approach proposed in Yaesoubi and Cohen (2016) approximates the optimal Q-values $Q^*(\tilde{h},a)$ with a regression model $\tilde{Q}(\mathcal{F}(\tilde{h}),a)$, where $\mathcal{F}(\tilde{h})$ returns the values of features for the history $\tilde{h}$. Now, having observed the history $\tilde{h}_k$ at the decision point k, the control interventions to implement during the next decision period is determined by

$$\tilde{a}\left(\tilde{h}_k\right) = \underset{a_k \in 2^A}{\arg\max}\, \tilde{Q}\left(\mathcal{F}\left(\tilde{h}_k\right), a_k\right). \tag{3.10}$$

To define the feature extraction function, we note that the core goal of feature selection is to identify statistics defined within the historical observations of disease spread that can be used to accurately differentiate the current trajectory from the infinite set of possible trajectories. Based on our experience with applying the proposed algorithm to epidemics with different characteristics, we make the following recommendations for selecting these features (see Yaesoubi and Cohen 2016) for additional details about how the choice of features would impact the performance of dynamic policies).

Policy makers are usually able to observe at least some fraction of incident cases of disease. For example, the number of individuals self-presenting to the healthcare facility can be potentially observable. Several statistics can be defined based on these observations such as the number of new cases during the past week, the average or trend in the number of new notified cases during the past month, or the cumulative number of new notified cases since the beginning of the epidemic. Depending on the nature of the epidemic, some subset of these measures can be chosen as features.

When there is substantial stochasticity in the pattern of disease spread (a situation that is not unusual, especially during emergence of a novel pathogen), the number of new members appearing in observable compartments (e.g., diagnosed cases of disease) may not be a very strong feature; in these cases, the *average* or the *total* number of new members during the past few periods may be a more attractive feature to select. If the epidemic has an absorbing compartment, such as the "recovered" compartment in our model, the total number of members who enter into this compartment (perhaps defined through a serological survey to determine the fraction of the population with evidence of previous infection) can be a strong feature as well.

It is important to note that the process that generates observations during a given decision interval may be strongly influenced by the interventions that are being used. For example, during a tuberculosis (TB) epidemic, after switching from passive case finding to active (i.e., more vigorous) case finding, we would expect to observe a surge in TB case notification (Yaesoubi and Cohen 2013). Hence, it will be important in this setting to use information about which interventions were employed during the period over which observations have been gathered as features as well. Additionally, levels of available resources can also be important features. For example, for influenza epidemics, the number of available antiviral doses at each decision time can be a strong feature.

Finally, when determining which features to include in the regression model for approximating the Q-values, one should also ensure that features have reasonably low multicollinearity. Correlation among features leads to unstable approximation and divergence of the proposed algorithm. In many situations, we would expect substantial correlation among the observations gathered during epidemics. For example, for most epidemics, case notifications will be correlated with the number of the infection-associated deaths, and hence including both of these features leads to divergence of the proposed algorithm. This property may actually be advantageous in generating policies that are convenient to implement in practice since the policy maker needs only to gather data about features with the strongest predictive power and the least correlation with other potential features. For example, it is usually not practical to gather real-time data on the number of TB deaths given the limited quality of vital registration systems in many countries, and therefore health policies may be generated using real-time data on TB case notifications, since TB deaths are expected to be highly correlated with this more easily gathered measure.

3.4   NUMERICAL RESULTS

In this section, we demonstrate how the framework proposed here can be employed to support adaptive decision-making over a course of an epidemic. To this end, we use the epidemic model developed in Section 3.3.2 and calibrated in Section 3.3.3 to evaluate the performance of control policies. We assume that the effectiveness of the transmission-reducing intervention is 20% (i.e., $\sigma = 0.2$). This implies that when this intervention is in effect, either the probability of infection transmission or the contact rate among population members is decreased by 20%. We have not attempted to do a sophisticated costing of the transmission-reducing intervention in this analysis, but to demonstrate the ability of the model framework to identify the cost-effectiveness of such policies, we assume that the daily cost of employing this intervention is $50 per week per capita. This weekly cost is motivated by previous studies of the societal and economic costs of school closure (Chen et al. 2011; Sadique et al. 2008; Sander et al. 2009).

A dynamic policy to inform the employment of transmission-reducing intervention consists of two figures: an affordability curve and a decision rule. The affordability curve (e.g., Figure 3.7a) returns the expected total costs as a function of the policy maker's willingness to pay (WTP) for one additional case averted, while the decision rule (e.g., Figure 3.7b) specifies which intervention to employ during the next decision period given the value of selected features. To use the policy depicted in Figure 3.7, the policy maker must first select a level of WTP for health that satisfies existing budget constraints. For example, for a budget of US$300 million, the policy maker may choose the WTP of $5000 per case averted from Figure 3.7a. Given the selected WTP, the policy maker can then generate decision rules similar to

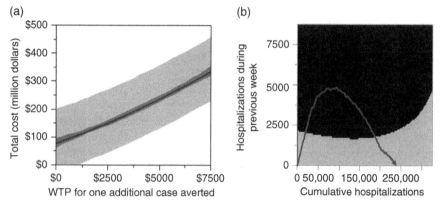

Figure 3.7 A dynamic control policy to inform decisions about the employment of a transmission-reducing intervention (e.g., school or public place closure). (a) Affordability curve returns the expected total cost if dynamic policies with different values of WTP for health is chosen to be implemented. The dark gray area represents the 95% confidence interval for the expected cost, while the light gray area represents the 95% confidence interval for the predicted total cost. (b) Decision rule for WTP=$5000 for one additional case averted. The black and gray areas represents, respectively, the region where the transmission-reducing intervention is recommended to be employed or lifted. The curve corresponds to one simulated epidemic trajectory.

those in the chart in Figure 3.7b to guide real-time decision-making throughout the epidemic based on the number of notified cases during the previous week and the cumulative notified cases thus far.

To illustrate how the decision rule in Figure 3.7b can be used, we overlay one epidemic trajectory (represented by the curve) on this decision rule. For the depicted trajectory, the dynamic policy recommends using the transmission-reducing intervention when the epidemic enters into the black region and recommends lifting the intervention when the epidemic trajectory enters into the gray region.

Using cost-effectiveness planes (Briggs et al. 2006) (e.g., Figure 3.8), we compare the performance of dynamic policies with that of static policies that only specify an interval during which the transmission-reducing intervention should be employed. In these figures the incremental costs (displayed on horizontal axes) and additional influenza cases averted (displayed on vertical axes) are calculated with respect to the baseline scenario where the transmission-reducing intervention is never used during the epidemic. Figure 3.8 reveals that the cost-effectiveness frontiers corresponding to dynamic policies dominate the cost-effectiveness frontiers corresponding to static policies. This implies that for any given budget, the expected health gain by following the appropriate dynamic policy is greater than the expected health gain from the static policy that satisfied the same budget limit.

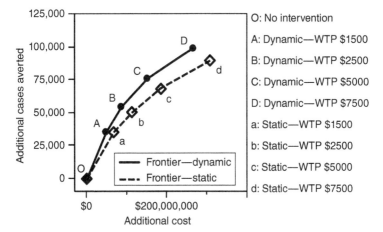

Figure 3.8 Cost-effectiveness plane comparing the performance of static versus dynamic transmission-reducing (TR) policies. Each cost-effectiveness frontier is obtained by optimizing the corresponding policy for different values of willingness to pay (WTP) for health.

3.5 CONCLUSION

The emergence of novel pathogens (e.g., Ebola, HIV, SARS, H1N1 and H5N1 strains of influenza) and the persistence of others (e.g., malaria, TB) along with their devastating health and financial consequences on affected populations have highlighted the need for developing plans to confront new and existing infectious threats in a timely and efficient way. In this chapter, we proposed a mathematical framework to inform adaptive control policies that make recommendations based on accumulated real-time data on disease occurrence and resource availability during an epidemic. The framework seeks to optimize a measure of population's health (e.g., total infection cases or total expected quality-adjusted life years) while satisfying resource constraints (e.g., budget or vaccine limitations) at each decision point.

The decision model proposed here is generalizable and can be used to identify dynamic health policies for various epidemics with very different characteristics, and hence a broad range of pharmaceutical and nonpharmaceutical interventions and their attendant logistical constraints can be incorporated into the underlying epidemic model. Furthermore, the calibration and the policy optimization procedures proposed here do not restrict the type of epidemic model, and hence various modeling frameworks, including Markov chain (Daley and Gani 1999; Yaesoubi and Cohen 2011), agent-based (Bonabeau 2002; Epstein 2009; Germann et al. 2006), or contact network (Meyers 2007; Reis et al. 2007) models may be used to describe the disease spread. We note, however, that computationally intensive epidemic models may fail to inform decisions in a timely fashion since generating epidemic trajectories to be used in calibration and optimization steps (Figure 3.1) can be substantially time-consuming.

To simplify the description of the method to identify dynamic policies, we assumed that each intervention in the set $\mathcal{A}$ can be either on or off. Policies to inform the use of interventions that can be employed at different levels of intensity can be modeled in the same fashion. For example, to decide which age groups {<1, 1–5, 6–18, 19–24, 25+} should be considered for vaccination, we can use five switches to denote or describe which age groups are considered for vaccination. Now, vaccination age group {<1, 6–18} is modeled by turning the first and third switches on while keeping the remaining switches off.

A limitation of the proposed framework is the fact that the specific choice of features and the approximation functions affect the optimality and stability of the generated policies. If these optimization settings are not appropriately selected the algorithm may converge to a suboptimal and/or oscillating solution. This problem can be mitigated to some degree through careful experimental design. The epidemic model described in this book chapter is very simple and not intended to realistically model disease spread or be used directly to guide the selection of interventions. We also have made crude assumptions about the costs of interventions. Accordingly, we do not intend for the actual costs of the interventions to reflect reality, but instead have elected to report these estimates to facilitate comparison of the relative cost and cost-effectiveness across interventions.

As a final note, the successful implementation of the proposed framework to adaptively make decisions during epidemics rely on the ability to continuously examine the accuracy of the underlying epidemic model using accumulating real-time surveillance data. If new observations imply that the model needs to be recalibrated, this can be achieved by a broad range of calibration methods including the one described in this chapter. Clearly, inaccuracies in the surveillance and reporting system may result in suboptimal decisions, further stressing the tremendous importance of public health surveillance for the effective management of epidemics.

ACKNOWLEDGMENTS

The project described was supported by Award U54GM088558 from the National Institute of Health and Award U38PS004644 from the US Center for Disease Control and Prevention. The content is solely the responsibility of the authors and does not necessarily represent the official views of the National Institutes of Health or the Center for Disease Control and Prevention.

REFERENCES

Alkema L, Raftery AE, Gerland P, Clark SJ, Pelletier F, Buettner T, et al. Probabilistic projections of the total fertility rate for all countries. *Demography*. 2011;48(3):815–839.

Anderson RM, May RM. *Infectious Diseases of Humans: Dynamics and Control*. Oxford, U.K./New York: Oxford University Press; 1991. p. viii, 757pp.

Bertsekas DP. *Dynamic Programming and Optimal Control.* 3rd ed. Belmont, MA: Athena Scientific; 2005.

Bettencourt LM, Ribeiro RM. Real time Bayesian estimation of the epidemic potential of emerging infectious diseases. *PLoS One.* 2008;3(5):e2185.

Birrell PJ, Ketsetzis G, Gay NJ, Cooper BS, Presanis AM, Harris RJ, et al. Bayesian modeling to unmask and predict influenza A/H1N1pdm dynamics in London. *Proc Natl Acad Sci U S A.* 2011;108(45):18238–18243.

Bonabeau E. Agent-based modeling: Methods and techniques for simulating human systems. *Proc Natl Acad Sci U S A.* 2002;99(Suppl 3):7280–7287.

Briggs AH, Claxton K, Sculpher MJ. *Decision Modelling for Health Economic Evaluation.* Oxford, U.K.: Oxford University Press; 2006, p. x, 237pp.

Brown ST, Tai JH, Bailey RR, Cooley PC, Wheaton WD, Potter MA, et al. Would school closure for the 2009 H1N1 influenza epidemic have been worth the cost?: A computational simulation of Pennsylvania. *BMC Public Health.* 2011;11:353.

Cauchemez S, Boelle PY, Donnelly CA, Ferguson NM, Thomas G, Leung GM, et al. Real-time estimates in early detection of SARS. *Emerg Infect Dis.* 2006;12(1):110–113.

Cauchemez S, Boelle PY, Thomas G, Valleron AJ. Estimating in real time the efficacy of measures to control emerging communicable diseases. *Am J Epidemiol.* 2006;164(6):591–597.

Cauchemez S, Ferguson NM, Wachtel C, Tegnell A, Saour G, Duncan B, et al. Closure of schools during an influenza pandemic. *Lancet Infect Dis.* 2009;9(8):473–481.

Centers for Disease Control and Prevention. Interim Pre-pandemic Planning Guidance: Community Strategy for Pandemic Influenza Mitigation in the United States. Atlanta, GA: Government Printing Press; 2007.

Centers for Disease Control and Prevention. The 2009 H1N1 Pandemic: Summary Highlights, April 2009–April 2010. Atlanta, GA: Centers for Disease Control and Prevention; 2009.

Chen WC, Huang AS, Chuang JH, Chiu CC, Kuo HS. Social and economic impact of school closure resulting from pandemic influenza A/H1N1. *J Infect.* 2011;62(3):200–203.

Chowell G, Nishiura H, Bettencourt LM. Comparative estimation of the reproduction number for pandemic influenza from daily case notification data. *J R Soc Interface.* 2007;4(12):155–166.

Clark GM, editor. Use of common random numbers in comparing alternatives. *Proceedings of the 22nd Conference on Winter Simulation*, New Orleans, LA. Piscataway, NJ: IEEE Press; 1990.

Crosby AW, ACLS Humanities E-Book (Organization), American Council of Learned Societies. *America's Forgotten Pandemic the Influenza of 1918.* Cambridge, U.K./New York: Cambridge University Press; 2003. Available at: http://hdl.handle.net/2027/heb.03212. Accessed on August 24, 2017.

Daley DJ, Gani JM. *Epidemic Modelling: An Introduction.* Cambridge, U.K./New York: Cambridge University Press; 1999, p. xii, 213pp.

Dushoff J, Plotkin JB, Viboud C, Simonsen L, Miller M, Loeb M, et al. Vaccinating to protect a vulnerable subpopulation. *PLoS Med.* 2007;4(5):e174.

Elderd BD, Dukic VM, Dwyer G. Uncertainty in predictions of disease spread and public health responses to bioterrorism and emerging diseases. *Proc Natl Acad Sci U S A.* 2006;103(42):15693–15697.

Epstein JM. Modelling to contain pandemics. *Nature*. 2009;460(7256):687.

Ferguson NM, Cummings DA, Cauchemez S, Fraser C, Riley S, Meeyai A, et al. Strategies for containing an emerging influenza pandemic in Southeast Asia. *Nature*. 2005;437(7056):209–214.

Ferguson NM, Cummings DA, Fraser C, Cajka JC, Cooley PC, Burke DS. Strategies for mitigating an influenza pandemic. *Nature*. 2006;442(7101):448–452.

Flahault A, Vergu E, Coudeville L, Grais RF. Strategies for containing a global influenza pandemic. *Vaccine*. 2006;24(44–46):6751–6755.

Germann TC, Kadau K, Longini IM, Jr., Macken CA. Mitigation strategies for pandemic influenza in the United States. *Proc Natl Acad Sci U S A*. 2006;103(15):5935–5940.

Golub GH. *Matrix Computations*. 4th ed. Baltimore, MD: Johns Hopkins University Press; 2013, p. xxi, 756pp.

Halloran ME, Ferguson NM, Eubank S, Longini IM, Jr., Cummings DA, Lewis B, et al. Modeling targeted layered containment of an influenza pandemic in the United States. *Proc Natl Acad Sci U S A*. 2008;105(12):4639–4644.

Henning KJ. What is syndromic surveillance? *MMWR Suppl*. 2004;53:5–11.

Hethcote HW. The mathematics of infectious diseases. *Siam Rev*. 2000;42(4):599–653.

Jackson C, Mangtani P, Hawker J, Olowokure B, Vynnycky E. The effects of school closures on influenza outbreaks and pandemics: Systematic review of simulation studies. *PloS One*. 2014;9(5):e97297.

Lagoudakis MG, Parr R. Least-squares policy iteration. *J Mach Learn Res*. 2004;4(6):1107–1149.

Lipsitch M, Cohen T, Cooper B, Robins JM, Ma S, James L, et al. Transmission dynamics and control of severe acute respiratory syndrome. *Science*. 2003;300(5627):1966–1970.

Mandl KD, Overhage JM, Wagner MM, Lober WB, Sebastiani P, Mostashari F, et al. Implementing syndromic surveillance: A practical guide informed by the early experience. *J Am Med Inform Assoc*. 2004;11(2):141–150.

Meyers LA. Contact network epidemiology: Bond percolation applied to infectious disease prediction and control. *Bull Am Math Soc*. 2007;44(1):63–86.

Mills CE, Robins JM, Lipsitch M. Transmissibility of 1918 pandemic influenza. *Nature*. 2004;432(7019):904–906.

Murphy DR, Klein RW, Smolen LJ, Klein TM, Roberts SD. Using common random numbers in health care cost-effectiveness simulation modeling. *Health Serv Res*. 2013;48(4):1508–1525.

Patel R, Longini IM, Halloran ME. Finding optimal vaccination strategies for pandemic influenza using genetic algorithms. *J Theor Biol*. 2005;234(2):201–212.

Puterman ML. *Markov Decision Processes: Discrete Stochastic Dynamic Programming*. Hoboken, NJ/Great Britain: Wiley-Interscience; 1994, p. xvii, 649pp.

Reis BY, Kohane IS, Mandl KD. An epidemiological network model for disease outbreak detection. *PLoS Med*. 2007;4(6):e210.

Riley S, Fraser C, Donnelly CA, Ghani AC, Abu-Raddad LJ, Hedley AJ, et al. Transmission dynamics of the etiological agent of SARS in Hong Kong: Impact of public health interventions. *Science*. 2003;300(5627):1961–1966.

Sadique MZ, Adams EJ, Edmunds WJ. Estimating the costs of school closure for mitigating an influenza pandemic. *BMC Public Health*. 2008;8:135.

Sander B, Nizam A, Garrison LP, Jr., Postma MJ, Halloran ME, Longini IM, Jr. Economic evaluation of influenza pandemic mitigation strategies in the United States using a stochastic microsimulation transmission model. *Value Health.* 2009;12(2):226–233.

Stern AM, Markel H. What Mexico taught the world about pandemic influenza preparedness and community mitigation strategies. *JAMA.* 2009;302(11):1221–1222.

Wallinga J, Teunis P. Different epidemic curves for severe acute respiratory syndrome reveal similar impacts of control measures. *Am J Epidemiol.* 2004;160(6):509–516.

White III CC. A survey of solution techniques for the partially observed Markov decision process. *Ann Oper Res.* 1991;32(1):215–230.

World Health Organization. WHO Global Influenza Preparedness Plan—The Role of WHO and Recommendations for National Measures before and during Pandemics, Report No. WHO/CDS/CSR/GIP/2005.5. 2005, Geneva, Switzerland.

Yaesoubi R, Cohen T. Generalized Markov models of infectious disease spread: A novel framework for developing dynamic health policies. *Eur J Oper Res.* 2011;215(3):679–687.

Yaesoubi R, Cohen T. Identifying dynamic tuberculosis case-finding policies for HIV/TB coepidemics. *Proc Natl Acad Sci U S A.* 2013;110(23):9457–9462.

Yaesoubi R, Cohen T. Identifying cost-effective dynamic policies to control epidemics. *Stat Med.* 2016;35(28):5189–5209.

Yang Y, Sugimoto JD, Halloran ME, Basta NE, Chao DL, Matrajt L, et al. The transmissibility and control of pandemic influenza A (H1N1) virus. *Science.* 2009;326(5953):729–733.

4

ASSESSING REGISTER-BASED CHLAMYDIA INFECTION SCREENING STRATEGIES: A COST-EFFECTIVENESS ANALYSIS ON SCREENING START/END AGE AND FREQUENCY

Yu Teng[1], Nan Kong[2], and Wanzhu Tu[3]

[1] Avenir Health, Glastonbury, CT, USA
[2] Weldon School of Biomedical Engineering, Purdue University, West Lafayette, IN, USA
[3] Department of Biostatistics, Indiana University Medical School, Indianapolis, IN, USA

4.1 INTRODUCTION

Infection with bacterium *Chlamydia trachomatis*, known in short as CT infection, is among the most commonly reported sexually transmitted diseases (STDs) in many developed countries. It inflicts significant human and economic costs (CDC 2016). CT prevalence is estimated to be above 4% in the United States, and a large portion of these more than one million individuals do not know they are infected. Teenage girls and young women are at particularly high risk of infection if they are sexually active.

The majority of CT infections have no symptoms and thus often remain undiagnosed until the infection requires acute care. As a result, CT in women may lead to

Decision Analytics and Optimization in Disease Prevention and Treatment, First Edition.
Edited by Nan Kong and Shengfan Zhang.
© 2018 John Wiley & Sons, Inc. Published 2018 by John Wiley & Sons, Inc.

major morbidities including acute pelvic inflammatory disease (PID), chronic pelvic pain, ectopic pregnancy, and infertility. Some of these morbidities may only be identified many years after the infection or during pregnancy. Although CT generally does not have serious negative consequences in men, sexually active men, if infected but undetected, may infect many women. At present, CT can be accurately diagnosed and can be easily treated when diagnosed early. Therefore, it is critical to conduct CT screening at the population level to identify infected but asymptomatic individuals. The CT screening strategy is currently recommended by the Centers for Disease Control (CDC 2016). From cost minimization viewpoint, the cost of screening a general population for CT may still offset the cost of few individuals needing treatment for the consequent acute and chronic diseases. Several economic studies have found CT screening to be cost-effective and even cost saving (e.g., Howell et al. 1998; Welte et al. 2000; Kretzschmar et al. 2001; Hu et al. 2004, 2006). For literature reviews on economic studies, see Roberts et al. (2006) and Low et al. (2007, 2009).

In this chapter, we conduct a model-based economic study of an average-risk female adolescent population in the United States with the objective of making more detailed screening recommendations about screening age range and frequency. Currently, annual CT screening is recommended for women aged 25 or younger because they are generally at high risk. In addition, CT screening is recommended for older women with a new sex partner or multiple sex partners. However, it is unclear from a cost-effectiveness viewpoint what an initial screening age should be: whether the same screening frequency should be applied to young women of all ages and whether CT screening of the general female population should end at age 25. Increasing evidence suggests that the CT infection rate among young women decreases with age (e.g., Arno et al. 1994; Datta et al. 2007; Teng et al. 2014) possibly due to more stabilized sexual partnership and increased immunological response to CT as women age. Hence, one would expect an optimal screening strategy to be age dependent.

In this chapter, we incorporate the age-dependent CT infection rate into a partial differential equation (PDE)-based compartmental epidemic model. We simulate a large number of screening initiation and termination ages and candidate screening frequencies to compare their costs and effectiveness. To the best of our knowledge, few economic studies have taken into account the age dependency of CT infection risk among young women. Hu et al. (2004, 2006) assumed a constant annual CT incidence in women from 15 to 19 years of age (Shafer et al. 1999; Chlamydia Surveillance Data 2011) and a constant annual reduction in the incidence starting at age 20 (Halvorsen et al. 1988; Buhaug et al. 1989, 1990). However, limited screening strategies were assessed in their economic studies. We test more screening strategies and conduct sensitivity analysis to assess the impact of various cost and utility parameters.

The remainder of the chapter is organized as follows. In Section 4.2, we provide more background on CT biology and its screening. We also provide a literature review on computational modeling of CT transmission and control. In Section 4.3, we develop an age-structured compartmental model that captures CT epidemiology. We also present a PDE-based compartmental model and report the model validation results. In Section 4.4, we present cost-effectiveness analyses on a set of screening strategies differing in screening initiation and termination ages and screening frequency. Finally, we draw conclusions and outline future research in Section 4.5.

4.2 BACKGROUND LITERATURE REVIEW

In this section, we describe the literature on the clinical background of CT infection, current CT screening programs, and modeling approaches to investigate CT and other STD intervention strategies. The modeling approaches reviewed include ODE/PDE-based compartmental models and stochastic network simulation models. ODE stands for ordinary differential equation; PDE stands for partial differential equation.

4.2.1 Clinical Background on CT Infection and Control

CT infection is an STD that can damage a woman's reproductive organs (Chlamydia Surveillance Data 2011). It is one of the most commonly reported STDs in the United States (CDC 2016) and in many other developed countries (World Health Organization 2001). CT can be transmitted during vaginal, anal, or oral sex. It can also be passed from an infected mother to her baby during vaginal childbirth. The infection risk increases as the number of sex partners increases. Teenage girls and young women are at particularly high risk for infection if they are sexually active. As a bacterial infection, CT infection is not known to produce host immunity and thus reinfection is common.

The prevalence of CT infection is high in the general US population. Among young adults (aged 18–26 years) who participated in a nationally representative longitudinal study on adolescent health during 2001–2002, CT prevalence was estimated to be 4.2% (Miller et al. 2004). Figure 4.1 demonstrates the increasing trend in reported CT infections during the last 20 years. Figure 4.2 suggests that young women (age 15–24) have the highest infection risk among different age groups and between the two genders.

CT is often referred to as a "silent" disease as the majority of infected people have no symptoms. Even though CT screening activities have been expanded and more accurate diagnostic tests have been used over the years, a large portion of infected women are still not being identified (CDC 2016). Without prompt diagnosis of the disease, it can progress to serious health problems with both short- and long-term consequences, including PID, chronic pelvic pain, ectopic pregnancy, and infertility (Cates and Wasserheit 1991). Fortunately, CT can be accurately diagnosed through a nucleic acid amplification test (NAAT) (Van Der Pol et al. 2006) and can be easily treated and cured with antibiotics. Figure 4.3 illustrates the disease progression for CT in women. Recent research on CT transmission dynamics addresses a variety of topics, including the long asymptomatic period and its duration (Molano et al. 2005; Althaus et al. 2010), the fraction of infections that are symptomatic and

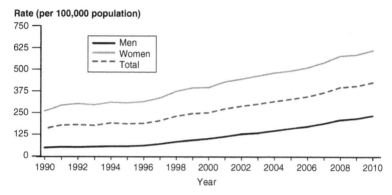

Figure 4.1 Reported CT infection rates by year in the United States, 1990–2010 (Chlamydia Surveillance Data 2011).

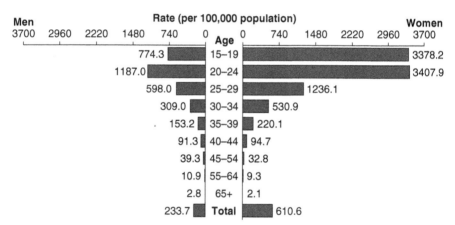

Figure 4.2 Reported CT infection rate by age and gender in the United States, 2010 (Chlamydia Surveillance Data 2011).

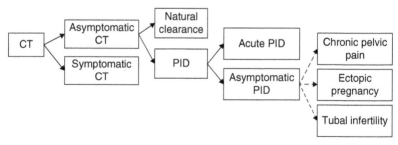

Figure 4.3 Disease progression tree for CT.

that will prompt treatment-seeking behavior (Korenromp et al. 2002), and whether natural clearance is followed by a period of temporary immunity (Brunham and Rey-Ladino 2005).

4.2.2   CT Screening Programs

A screening program refers to a continuing public health service that delivers screening at sufficiently regular intervals to a proportion of the target population to achieve a defined level of benefit at the population level while minimizing harm (Low 2007). Based on the way in which the screening services are organized and delivered, screening programs can be categorized into two main groups, register-based screening and opportunistic screening. Register-based screening (also known as population-based, proactive, cyclical, or systematic screening) keeps an up-to-date register of the target population to send invitations or reminders for screening repeatedly at appropriate intervals (Holland and Steward 2005). With opportunistic screening, healthcare professionals offer screening tests to patients attending care or other defined settings for any reason. Individuals who do not attend relevant health services will not get the screening service (Holland and Steward 2005). The screening programs being piloted in three regions of the Netherlands (Sheldon 2007) can be categorized as register-based CT screening, whereas the National Chlamydia Screening Programme in England (NCSSG 2006) and the regional Infertility Prevention Programs in the United States (CDC 2010) can be categorized as opportunistic screening. Salisbury et al. (2006) suggested that a CT intervention program that combines the advantages of both register-based and opportunistic approaches might achieve higher coverage than either approach alone. For a systematic review of chlamydia screening programs, see Low et al. (2009). The Centers for Disease Control and Prevention and the US Preventive Services Task Force jointly recommend a screening strategy (CDC 2010) that suggests yearly CT testing among sexually active women aged 25 or younger, older women with risk factors for CT (e.g., those with a new sex partner or multiple sex partners), and pregnant women. However, there are only a few economic studies that have assessed the optimality of the recommended screening strategy.

4.2.3   Computational Modeling on CT Transmission and Control

Computational models have been used extensively in economic studies of CT control strategies, including population-based screening programs. These models can be categorized into two classes: (i) ODE/PDE-based compartmental models and (ii) individual-based stochastic network simulation models.

4.2.3.1   *ODE/PDE-Based Compartmental Models*   Althaus et al. (2010) developed an SEIRS (susceptible–exposed–infected–recovered–susceptible) model to analyze CT incidence and the impact of a screening program. The SEIRS model captures

the population dynamics among the five distinct groups. The authors considered yearly screening strategies with different screening rates (5%, 25%, or 50% of the population) and different durations (5 years, 10 years, or long term). A sensitivity analysis shows that (i) varying the fraction of infections that are symptomatic and the duration of the symptomatic period within the range of previously used parameter estimates has little effect on the transmission dynamics and (ii) uncertainties in the duration of temporary immunity and the asymptomatic period can result in large deviations on the predicted impact of a screening program. The authors concluded that (i) the impact of a screening program is more pronounced if the duration of the asymptomatic period is longer and (ii), after screening the cohort for a long enough time, more reduction in disease prevalence would only occur with a longer duration of the asymptomatic period.

Regan et al. (2010) developed a variant of the SEIRS model. A unique feature of the model is that it differentiates symptomatic and asymptomatic infections and their subsequent treatment and recovery rates. The model was populated with Australian sexual behavior and epidemiology data and stratified by age and gender. The authors used the model to evaluate a variety of annual screening strategies with different target age groups (15–19, 20–24, and 25–29), screening coverage levels (20%–80% in 10% incremental), and female-to-male ratios (1:0, 1:1, 4:1, and 0:1). The results show that (i) routine annual screening can significantly reduce CT prevalence within 10 years, given adequate screening coverage, and (ii) the most effective screening strategies target the age group of 20–24 years old women. Heijne et al. (2010) developed a paired SIRS (susceptible–infected–recovered–susceptible) model that captures sexual partnership duration and reinfection. Ongoing sexual partnership may cause repeated CT infection after treatment. The paired model predicts a weaker impact of screening on reducing CT prevalence when compared directly with a single SIRS model that does not accommodate sexual partnerships explicitly. The study suggests that effective management of sex partners to prevent CT infection may need to be considered. Several other studies (e.g., Martin et al. 1996; Brunham et al. 2005; Sharomi and Gumel 2009) performed rigorous mathematical analysis of compartmental models to gain insights into CT transmission dynamics.

There are also studies on the effectiveness and cost-effectiveness of screening and intervention for other STDs. For example, Müller et al. (2000) and Huerta and Tsimring (2002) developed theoretical models to evaluate the effectiveness of contact tracing. Armbruster and Brandeau (2007a, 2010) investigated the cost and cost-effectiveness of mixing screening and contact tracing. Other studies include (i) dynamics of co-infection (Porco et al. 2001; Long et al. 2008), (ii) resource allocation across an array of possible interventions (Zaric and Brandeau 2001, 2002; Brandeau et al. 2003; Zaric 2003), and (iii) behavior change interventions (Velasco-Hernndez et al. 1996).

Age often has a strong influence on disease spread in a population. Increasing number of evidence has shown that the CT infection rate decreases with age

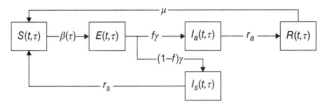

Figure 4.4   Age-structured compartmental model for CT transmission and treatment.

TABLE 4.1   Notation in the Age-Structured Compartmental Model for CT Transmission and Intervention

$S(t, \tau)$	Susceptible	f	Fraction of asymptomatic infection
$E(t, \tau)$	Exposed	$1/\gamma$	Incubation time
$I_a(t, \tau)$	Asymptomatically infected	r_a	Transition rate incurred by temporary immunity
$I_s(t, \tau)$	Symptomatically infected	$1/r_s$	Duration of the symptomatic period
$R(t, \tau)$	Recovered	$1/\mu$	Duration of temporary immunity
$\beta(\tau)$	Age-dependent infection rate		after natural clearance of asymptomatic infection

(e.g., Arno et al. 1994; Datta et al. 2007; Teng et al. 2014). Age-structured models have been used to study the transmission and intervention of infectious diseases with age-dependent infection risk. These models are typically described mathematically with sets of PDEs (e.g., Castillo-Chavez and Feng 1998; Feng et al. 2000; Zhao et al. 2000; Nelson et al. 2004; Huang and Rohani 2006), with derivatives taken in terms of both time and age.

In the remainder of this subsection, we present an age-structured compartmental model for CT transmission, treatment, and natural clearance, as illustrated in Figure 4.4. The solid lines indicate disease transmission and progression. The main notation in the model is described in Table 4.1. Let t and τ be the time and age indices, respectively. At any time $t \in [0, T]$, each population of age $\tau \in [0, \mathcal{T}]$ is divided into five subgroups as follows. Susceptible people ($S(t, \tau)$) get infected at an age-dependent per capita rate of $\beta(\tau) > 0$. They then move through an incubation period ($E(t, \tau)$) at a rate $\gamma > 0$ to become either asymptomatically infected ($I_a(t, \tau)$) or symptomatically infected ($I_s(t, \tau)$). We denote $f \in (0, 1)$ as the fraction of infections that become asymptomatic. Asymptomatically infected people recover through natural clearance at a rate $r_a > 0$ and develop temporary immunity to reinfection ($R(t, \tau)$) for a duration of $1/\mu$ time units. In the absence of screening, symptomatically infected people clear the infection at a rate $r_s > 0$, which can be interpreted as treating the infection with symptom onset and subsequently curing the disease. We assume that the treatment is sought immediately after symptom onset. We also assume that the aforementioned treatment and infection clearance follow Poisson processes. The system dynamics are as follows:

$$\left(\frac{\partial}{\partial t}+\frac{\partial}{\partial \tau}\right)S(t,\tau) = -\beta(\tau)S(t,\tau)+r_s I_s(t,\tau)+\mu R(t,\tau),$$

$$\left(\frac{\partial}{\partial t}+\frac{\partial}{\partial \tau}\right)E(t,\tau) = \beta(\tau)S(t,\tau)-\gamma E(t,\tau),$$

$$\left(\frac{\partial}{\partial t}+\frac{\partial}{\partial \tau}\right)I_a(t,\tau) = f\gamma E(t,\tau)-r_a I_a(t,\tau),$$

$$\left(\frac{\partial}{\partial t}+\frac{\partial}{\partial \tau}\right)I_s(t,\tau) = (1-f)\gamma E(t,\tau)-r_s I_s(t,\tau),$$

$$\left(\frac{\partial}{\partial t}+\frac{\partial}{\partial \tau}\right)R(t,\tau) = r_a I_a(t,\tau)-\mu R(t,\tau).$$

It is also seen in the literature that the age-structured dynamics is described by integro-differential equations, which are equations that involve both integral and derivative of a function. In our context, the integral captures the total number of infected people over the age range, and the infection in the model is dependent upon the number of both susceptible and infected people. Note that the SEIRS model in Althaus et al. (2010) considers the interaction with the cross-term *SI*, and thus its straightforward age-structured modeling extension would be described with a set of integro-differential equations.

4.2.3.2 Stochastic Network Simulation Models   Unlike compartmental models that capture the aggregate system phenomena over the studied cohort, individual-based simulation can efficiently track individuals' behavior and record their contact histories with sex partners. Simulation models (Kretzschmar et al. 1996, 2001, 2009; Welte et al. 2000; Turner et al. 2006; Low et al. 2007) have been developed for economic studies of CT. These models often consider an age-structured population and a dynamic sexual partner network. They update individual characteristics on a daily basis or whenever necessary. These models are often referred to as individual-based stochastic network simulation.

Such simulation models have been developed by different research groups to evaluate CT screening strategies implemented in various European countries: (i) the RIVM model (Kretzschmar et al. 1996), developed at the Dutch National Institute for Public Health and the Environment (RIVM are the initials of the institute in Dutch); (ii) the Chlamydia Screening Studies (ClaSS) model (Low et al. 2007), developed to evaluate population-based screening using home-collected specimens in the United Kingdom; and (iii) the Health Protection Agency (HPA) London model (Turner et al. 2006), developed to inform the National Chlamydia Screening Programme in England. These three models all have an SIS model structure. Kretzschmar et al. (2009) presented a comparison of the three models. For viral infectious diseases (e.g., HIV and influenza), simulation models have been developed in the United States to study the effect of contact tracing (Armbruster and Brandeau 2007b), concurrent partnerships (Morris and Kretzschmar 1997), and combination of treatment and nonpharmaceutical interventions (Halloran et al. 2008).

Stochastic network simulation has also been applied to modeling the spatial spread of infectious disease (Colizza et al. 2006, 2007a, b; Ajelli et al. 2010; Balcan et al. 2009). Infected travelers leaving an infected area can bring the disease to another area not yet infected, which may cause a new outbreak. This mechanism is used to explain the rapid global spread of certain viral infectious diseases (e.g., H1N1 and SARS). Balcan et al. (2010) developed the Global Epidemic model (GLEaM) (www.gleamviz.org/simulator), a discrete stochastic model that integrates sociode-mographic and population mobility data into a spatially structured disease dynamic model to simulate the spread of epidemics worldwide. In the model, the world is defined as a network connecting various geographic census areas with human travel fluxes based on transportation infrastructures and mobility patterns.

Finally, the dynamic network theory has been applied to modeling infectious disease transmission dynamics. Colizza et al. (2007c) modeled the spread of an SIS-type infectious disease in a homogeneous human contact network as a reaction–diffusion process in a scale-free network. The authors showed that the network topology could affect the system's phase diagram (e.g., shift in the critical point for an epidemic outbreak). Gmez-Gardenes et al. (2008) extended the SIS model to incorporate the effect of gender on the disease spread. The authors showed that an epidemic outbreak requires greater disease spread rates when considering the bipartite nature of the human contact network. They argued that gender should be taken into account when designing efficient STD screening and treatment strategies. Hooyberghs et al. (2010) suggested that when modeling STD transmission dynamics in a heterosexual contact network, the network can be modeled as a bipartite scale-free network. General references in this area include an introduction to communication network theory by Monge and Contractor (2003) and a review of scale-free network modeling for biological systems (Ramezanpour 2004).

4.3   MATHEMATICAL MODELING

In this section, we present an age-structured model that incorporates CT screening as well as a few additional features to reflect the stochastic nature of screening and treatment. We first describe the model and present the formulas for computing various system outcomes. We then discuss the model parameterization and validation.

4.3.1   An Age-Structured Compartmental Model

We present an age-structured compartmental model for CT epidemiology, including transmission, screening, acute treatment, natural clearance, and PID sequelae. The model extends both the model in Figure 4.4 and the SEIRS model (Althaus et al. 2010). We introduce two additional compartments to differentiate people who have developed PID. The difference between the two compartments is that the subpopulation in one compartment has had PID symptom onset and the other has not. We use $P_s(t, \tau)$ and $P_a(t, \tau)$ to denote the populations in the two compartments, respectively. Similar to f, we use $f' \in [0, 1]$ to denote the probability that an infected individual with PID remains asymptomatic. Similar to γ, we use r_{PID} to denote the rate of developing acute PID from asymptomatic CT infection. Acute PID indicates that the disease has reached its symptomatic stage, thus getting clear attention from the patient. We introduce $\lambda(\tau)$ to denote the proportion of the entire population that is screened at age τ (i.e., each individual is screened on average within $1/\lambda(\tau)$ years).

Additional considerations in the model are (i) sensitivity of diagnosing CT infection via NAAT, (ii) sensitivity of diagnosing acute PID, (iii) compliance of taking antibiotic medication once the CT test result is positive, (iv) effectiveness of treating CT infection with antibiotics, and (v) effectiveness of treating PID. The underlying assumptions for the aforementioned additions are that (i) likelihood of getting a positive response (i.e., correctly diagnosed for CT infection, denoted by p_{sen}; correctly diagnosed for acute PID, denoted by p'_{sen}; immediate seeking CT treatment and adherence to the medication, denoted by p_{com}; effectiveness of CT antibiotic medication, denoted by p_{CT}; and effectiveness of acute PID treatment, denoted by p_{PID}) is constant among individuals in the studied cohort and over the screening program duration, (ii) these five likelihoods are independent for each individual in the cohort, and (iii) there is no state change for those individuals who get negative response from any of the five aforementioned dichotomies. With these assumptions, we essentially couple five independent Bernoulli random processes with the underlying stochastic processes depicting CT epidemiology. We can adjust the transition rates in the age-structured model accordingly. For example, there are two competing transitions from I_s to S. One transition models the process of curing CT infection among those asymptomatically infected individuals whose infections are detected through screening. To determine the rate of this transition, we consider the sensitivity of detecting CT infection, the probability of seeking CT treatment once the test result is positive, and the probability of completely curing the infection. With the independence assumption, we have $p_{CT}p_{com}p_{sen}\lambda(\tau)$.

The other transition models the process of curing CT infection among those asymptomatically infected individuals who develop symptoms. To determine this transition rate, we consider the rate at which individuals' infections become symptomatic as well as the probability of curing the infection. We thus have $p_{CT}r_s$. In Table 4.2, we summarize the additional notation in the model.

The system dynamics is described with the following PDEs (Figure 4.5):

$$\left(\frac{\partial}{\partial t} + \frac{\partial}{\partial \tau}\right)S(t,\tau) = -\beta(\tau)S(t,\tau) + p_{CT}p_{com}p_{sen}\lambda(\tau)I_a(t,\tau) + p_{PID}p'_{sen}\lambda(\tau)P_a(t,\tau)$$
$$+ \left(p_{CT}r_s + p_{CT}p_{com}p_{sen}\lambda(\tau)\right)I_s(t,\tau) + p_{PID}r'_s P_s(t,\tau) + \mu R(t,\tau),$$

$$\left(\frac{\partial}{\partial t} + \frac{\partial}{\partial \tau}\right)E(t,\tau) = \beta(\tau)S(t,\tau) - \gamma E(t,\tau),$$

$$\left(\frac{\partial}{\partial t} + \frac{\partial}{\partial \tau}\right)I_a(t,\tau) = f\gamma E(t,\tau) - \left(r_{PID} + r_a + p_{CT}p_{com}p_{sen}\lambda(\tau)\right)I_a(t,\tau),$$

TABLE 4.2   Additional Notation in the Model

$\lambda(\tau)$	Age-dependent screening rate
$P_a(t, \tau)$	Acute PID without symptom onset
$P_s(t, \tau)$	Acute PID with symptom onset
r_{PID}	Rate of developing acute PID development from asymptomatic CT
$1/r_s'$	Duration of the symptomatic period of acute PID (i.e., from diagnosis with symptom onset to recovery)
f	Probability that someone's CT infection progresses to PID without symptom
p_{sen}	Probability that someone with CT infection is correctly diagnosed via NAAT testing
p_{sen}'	Probability that someone with asymptomatic acute PID is correctly diagnosed
p_{spe}	Probability that someone without CT infection is correctly labeled via the testing
p_{com}	Probability that someone with a positive CT test result takes CT medication
p_{sid}	Probability of developing medication-related side effects
p_{CT}	Probability that CT infection is completely cured
p_{PID}	Probability that acute PID is completely cured

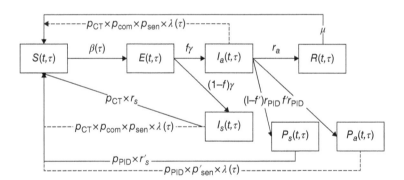

Figure 4.5   Age-structured compartmental model for CT infection.

$$\left(\frac{\partial}{\partial t}+\frac{\partial}{\partial \tau}\right)I_s(t,\tau)=(1-f)\gamma E(t,\tau)-\left(p_{CT}r_s+p_{CT}p_{com}p_{sen}\lambda(\tau)\right)I_s(t,\tau),$$

$$\left(\frac{\partial}{\partial t}+\frac{\partial}{\partial \tau}\right)P_a(t,\tau)=f'r_{PID}I_a(t,\tau)-p_{PID}p_{sen}'\lambda(\tau)P_a(t,\tau),$$

$$\left(\frac{\partial}{\partial t}+\frac{\partial}{\partial \tau}\right)P_s(t,\tau)=(1-f')r_{PID}I_a(t,\tau)-p_{PID}r_s'\,P_s(t,\tau),$$

$$\left(\frac{\partial}{\partial t}+\frac{\partial}{\partial \tau}\right)R(t,\tau)=r_aI_a(t,\tau)-\mu R(t,\tau),$$

In practice, a screening program typically estimates in advance the size of the cohort that can be screened based on its capacity and then keeps its size relatively constant by synchronizing the recruitment and exit processes. Without loss of generality, we set the cohort size to be 1 at any time point, that is, $\int_0^T \left(S(t,\tau) + E(t,\tau) + I_a(t,\tau) + I_s(t,\tau) + R(t,\tau) \right) d\tau = 1$, $\forall t$. This specification simplifies the later computation of per capita care spending. Furthermore, a screening program often only targets those of age 0 (i.e., the smallest age to be considered for CT infection) for recruitment and terminates CT screening for those who reach T (i.e., the largest age to be considered for CT infection). We assume that the number of women with CT at the lowest screening age is negligible. That is, for any t, we have the boundary condition $S(t, 0) = \Lambda$, where Λ is denoted as the rate at which new recruits join the cohort and $E(t, 0) = I_a(t, 0) = I_s(t, 0) = P_a(t, 0) = P_s(t, 0) = R(t, 0) = 0$. We introduce additional notation to set up the initial conditions, that is, $S(0, \tau) = S_0(\tau)$, $E(0, \tau) = E_0(\tau)$, $I_a(0, \tau) = I_{a0}(\tau)$, $I_s(0, \tau) = I_{s0}(\tau)$, $P_a(0, \tau) = P_{a0}(t)$, $P_s(0, \tau) = P_{s0}(\tau)$, and $R(0, \tau) = R_0(\tau)$. In our cost-effectiveness assessment of the screening strategies, we numerically specified the boundary conditions with the assumption that the system is in the steady state under the no-screening scenario.

Given a screening profile $\lambda(\cdot)$ as well as the initial and boundary conditions, the state of the system $(S, I_a, I_s, P_a, P_s, R)$ can be determined for any time point with the PDEs. The screening and treatment costs are accumulated accordingly over the program duration. Let c_s denote the unit time per capita cost of screening for CT infection, c_t denote the unit time per capita cost of treating CT infection with antibiotics, c_{sid} denote the unit time per capita cost of having side effects when treating CT, and c_{PID} denote the unit time per capita cost of treating acute PID and its sequelae. We consider three types of per capita cumulative cost over a screening period T as

- CT screening cost:

$$C_s\left(\lambda(\tau)\right) = c_s \int_0^T \int_0^T \lambda(\tau)\left(S(t,\tau) + E(t,\tau) + I_a(t,\tau) + I_s(t,\tau) + P_a(t,\tau) + R(t,\tau)\right) d\tau dt$$

$$= c_s \int_0^T \int_0^T \lambda(\tau)\left(1 - R_s(t,\tau)\right) d\tau dt;$$

- CT treatment cost:

$$C_t\left(\lambda(\tau)\right) = \int_0^T \int_0^T \left\{ \left(c_t + p_{sid}c_{sid}\right)\left[\left(r_s + p_{com}p_{sen}\lambda(\tau)\right)I_s(t,\tau) + p_{com}p_{sen}\lambda(\tau)\right]I_a(t,\tau) \right.$$

$$\left. + c_t p_{com}\left(1 - p_{spe}\right)\left(S(t,\tau) + E(t,\tau) + R(t,\tau)\right)\right\} d\tau dt$$

- Acute PID and chronic sequelae treatment cost:

$$C_{PID}\left(\lambda(\tau)\right) = \int_0^T \int_0^T c_{PID}\left(r_s' \, P_s(t,\tau) + p_{sen}'\lambda(\tau)P_a(t,\tau)\right) d\tau dt.$$

When computing the cumulative CT screening cost, we exclude individuals with symptomatic PID as the symptoms are clear and thus initiate the acute care. When computing the cumulative CT treatment cost, we consider two possible cases: with and without side effects. The expected cost when considering both cases is $c_t + p_{sid} c_{sid}$. We do not consider any side effects caused by mistakenly receiving CT treatment due to false positive diagnoses. We specify the total cumulative cost as $C_{tot}(\lambda(\tau)) = C_s(\lambda(\tau)) + C_t(\lambda(\tau)) + C_{PID}(\lambda(\tau))$. *In this chapter, we conduct a comparative cost-effectiveness assessment on various screening strategies.* We introduce the following effectiveness measure. We denote $E_{PIDinc}(\lambda(\tau))$ to be the cumulative PID incidence over the screening program duration and screening age range. Thus we have $E_{PIDinc}(\lambda(\tau)) = \int_0^T \int_0^T r_{PID} I_a(t, \tau) d\tau dt$.

Alternatively, we can formulate an optimization problem as $\min_{\lambda(\tau)} C_{tot}(\lambda(\tau))$ subject to the PDEs as well as the boundary and initial conditions introduced earlier. To solve this parameter optimization problem, we can discretize it to a finite-dimensional linear program subject to a set of first-order difference equations and solve it with standard linear programming solvers. Note that the discretization does not significantly affect the solution quality given that (i) many model parameters, for example, $\beta(\tau)$, have only age-dependent point estimates and (ii) it is not plausible to implement a screening strategy with continuously varying screening rate. For more information on the numerical optimization, see Teng (2012).

4.3.2 Model Parameterization and Validation

For the model parameterization, we examined several sources including MEDLINE, EMBASE, and EconLit. We carefully reviewed a few seminal papers on economic studies of CT screening to specify the parameter baseline values and ranges. We categorized the parameters into categories of clinical, screening, treatment, and associated costs. We present the parameter names, baseline values, plausible ranges, and references in Table 4.3. All cost parameters listed in the table were inflated to 2010 US dollars using the medical care component of the consumer price index (Bureau of Labor Statistics 2017).

Many of the parameters listed in Table 4.3 are directly used in the model. Their base-case values are $\gamma = 1/(14 \, days)$, $f = 0.625$, $r_a = 1/(433 \, days)$, $r_s = 1/(35 \, days)$, $\mu = 1/(90 \, days)$, $p_{sen} = 0.9$, $p_{spe} = 0.99$, $p_{CT} = 0.96$, $p_{com} = 0.8$, $p_{sid} = 0.05$, $p_{PID} = 0.6$, $c_s = \$16.5$, and $c_{sid} = \$62.1$. For those parameters not listed in Table 4.3, we first made additional assumptions on the model parameters whose values we could not acquire from the literature. Women who have symptomatic acute PID, typically, no longer need CT screening for the acute PID diagnosis. We assumed that these women seek medical care relatively promptly but may take longer to receive acute PID treatment after the onset of symptoms. We thus assumed $r_s' = r_s$. For women with asymptomatic acute PID, their infection would still need to be detected via NAAT. We assumed that the probability of correctly diagnosing this condition is

TABLE 4.3 Model Parameter Values Extracted from the Literature

Parameter	Base Case	Plausible Range	References
Clinical			
CT infection			
CT incubation time	14 d	[0,28] d	Althaus et al. (2010), Brunham et al. (2005), Kretzschmar et al. (1996), and Turner et al. (2006)
Fraction of asymptomatic CT	0.625	[0.25,1]	Althaus et al. (2010), Brunham et al. (2005), Kretzschmar et al. (1996), and Turner et al. (2006)
Duration of asymptomatic period	433 d	[180,420] d	Althaus et al. (2010), Brunham et al. (2005), Kretzschmar et al. (1996), and Turner et al. (2006)
Duration of symptomatic period	35 d	[30,40] d	Althaus et al. (2010), Brunham et al. (2005), Kretzschmar et al. (1996), and Turner et al. (2006)
Duration of temporary immunity after natural clearance	90 d	[0, ∞)d	Althaus et al. (2010), Brunham et al. (2005), Kretzschmar et al. (1996), and Turner et al. (2006)
Acute PID transition from CT after 6 months			
Incidence rate	0.3	[0.0043,0.4]	CDC (2001). Scholes et al. (1996), and Stamm et al. (1984)
Probability of symptomatic condition occurrence	0.4	[0.15,0.40]	Stamm et al. (1984), Paavonen et al. (1985), and Weström et al. (1992)
PID sequelae			
Probability of developing chronic pelvic pain	0.18	[0.15,0.20]	CDC (2010). Weström et al. (1992), Ness et al. (2002), and Weström (1980)
Probability of developing ectopic pregnancy	0.09	[0.05,0.10]	CDC (2010). Weström et al. (1992) and Weström (1980, 1994)
Probability of developing tubal infertility	0.20	[0.10,0.23]	CDC (2010). Weström et al. (1992), Ness et al. (2002), and Weström (1980)
Screening and Treatment			
Urine nucleic acid amplification test			
Sensitivity	0.9	[0.65,0.96]	Black et al. (2002) and Watson et al. (2002)
Specificity	0.99	[0.99,1]	Black et al. (2002) and Watson et al. (2002)

Effectiveness of treatment for CT infection	0.96	[0.94,1]	Lau and Qureshi (2002)
Probability of adhering to the antibiotics	0.8	[0.75,0.9]	Katz et al. (1988) and Schwebke et al. (1997)
Probability of developing antibiotics-related side effects	0.05	[0.01,0.10]	Lau and Qureshi (2002) and Magid et al. (1996)
Effectiveness of treatment for acute PID	0.6	N/A	Brihmer et al. (1989), Teisala et al. (1987), and Wølner-Hansen and Weström (1983)
Direct Medical Costs, in 2010 $			
NAAT	16.5	[8.9,50.7]	Dean et al. (1998), Gift et al. (2002), and Steece (1997)
Treatment for acute urogenital CT infection			
1 g Azithromycin	12.7	[12.7,38.0]	Cardinale (1998) and Tao et al. (2002)
Short clinic visit	32.9	[13.9,55.7]	Health Care Financing Administration (2000)
Treatment for azithromycin-related side effects	62.1	N/A	Magid et al. (1996) and Health Care Financing Administration (2000)
Treatment for acute PID			
Outpatient	620	[304,620]	Stratton et al. (2000), Rein et al. (2000), Washington et al. (1986), Washington and Katz (1991), and Yeh et al. (2003)
Inpatient	5970	[5970,18740]	Stratton et al. (2000), Rein et al. (2000), Washington et al. (1986), Washington and Katz (1991), and Yeh et al. (2003)
Treatment for PID sequelae			
Chronic pelvic pain	1450	[600,19000]	Stratton et al. (2000), Rein et al. (2000), Washington et al. (1986), Washington and Katz (1991), and Yeh et al. (2003)
Ectopic pregnancy	5490	[1650,18100]	Stratton et al. (2000), Rein et al. (2000), Washington et al. (1986), Washington and Katz (1991), and Yeh et al. (2003)
Tubal infertility	6330	[6330,10765]	Stratton et al. (2000), Rein et al. (2000), Washington et al. (1986), Washington and Katz (1991), and Yeh et al. (2003)
Time Costs, in 2010 $		*Net Work Days Lost*	
Acute urogenital CT infection	45.6	0.5 d	Welte et al. (2000), U.S. Department of Labor Bureau of Labor Statistics (2001), and SIG Health Care Information Netherlands (1994)

(Continued)

TABLE 4.3 (Continued)

Parameter	Base Case	Plausible Range	References
Acute PID			
Outpatient	650	7.1 d	Welte et al. (2000), Washington et al. (1986), U.S. Department of Labor Bureau of Labor Statistics (2001), and SIG Health Care Information Netherlands (1994)
Inpatient	1373	15.0 d	Welte et al. (2000), Washington et al. (1986), U.S. Department of Labor Bureau of Labor Statistics (2001), and SIG Health Care Information Netherlands (1994)
PID sequelae			
Chronic pelvic pain	866	9.5 d	Welte et al. (2000), Rein et al. (2000), Washington and Katz (1991), and U.S. Department of Labor Bureau of Labor Statistics (2001)
Ectopic pregnancy	1830	20 d	Welte et al. (2000), Rein et al. (2000), Washington and Katz (1991), and U.S. Department of Labor Bureau of Labor Statistics (2001)
Tubal infertility	406	4.5 d	Welte et al. (2000), Rein et al. (2000), Washington and Katz (1991), and U.S. Department of Labor Bureau of Labor Statistics (2001)

the same as for women with asymptomatic CT. That is, $p'_{sen} = p_{sen}$. In summary, we had $r'_s = 1/(35\,\text{days})$; $p'_{sen} = 0.9$. Second, we specified f' to be 1 minus the probability of developing symptomatic acute PID, that is, $f' = 0.6$. Third, we knew the probability of developing acute PID from CT after 6 months is 0.3. Then we computed the daily probability of developing acute PID. Given the 30% chance of the PID being asymptomatic, we computed the daily probability of developing asymptomatic acute PID, that is, $r_{PID} = 0.3 \times (1 - e^{(-1/180)})$. Thus, $1/r_{PID} \approx 600\,\text{days}$. Next, we computed c_t to be the sum of the direct medical cost for the CT infection treatment (i.e., a combination of the costs incurred by 1 g of azithromycin, the antibiotics, and short clinic visit) and the associated time cost. Thus, $c_t = \$12.7 + \$32.9 + \$45.6 = \$91.2$. Lastly, we computed c_{PID} to be the sum of the acute PID treatment costs (both inpatient and outpatient) and the costs of treating the three potential sequelae, that is, chronic pelvic pain, ectopic pregnancy, and tubal infertility. Thus, $c_{PID} = \$3500$. Similarly, we computed the upper and lower bounds for the plausible ranges.

As for $\beta(\tau)$, we followed the assumption made in Hu et al. (2004). That is, we assumed a constant annual incidence of 6% in women 15–19 years of age (Shafer et al. 1999; Chlamydia Surveillance Data 2011) with incidence decreasing by 13% per year beginning at age 20 (Halvorsen et al. 1988, Buhaug et al. 1989, 1990). For our numerical study, we performed discretization with 5 days as the minimum interval and took $\beta(\tau)$ values at corresponding discrete time points.

For the model validation, we considered the case where the CDC screening recommendation has been implemented and the underlying cohort is the overall average-risk US female adolescent population with approximately 4% CT prevalence. We computed the sum of equilibrium CT prevalence and acute PID prevalence for given age groups $[\tau_1, \tau_2]$, that is, $\sum_{\tau=\tau_1}^{\tau_2} \left(I_a(t,\tau) + I_s(t,\tau) + P_a(t,\tau) \right)$ when t is sufficiently large so the system reaches a steady state. For this outcome, we obtained the statewide CT infection test positive results for all 50 states (Chlamydia Surveillance Data 2011). Since we were unable to know the number of tested people in each state, we considered the minimum and maximum over the states. See Table 4.4 for the comparison. The table shows that the simulated results fall within the ranges of the respective age groups. Moreover, we were able to replicate the age-dependent trend. We thus gained confidence to use the proposed model for the cost-effectiveness analyses.

TABLE 4.4   Model Validation with Respect to CT Infection Prevalence

Age group	15–19	20–24	25–29
Simulated outcome (%)	4.7	4.2	3.8
Statewide Test Positive (%)			
Minimum	4.0	3.0	2.0
Maximum	16.5	13.0	7.5

4.4   STRATEGY ASSESSMENT

We focused our cost-effectiveness analysis on strategies that differ by their start and end ages as well as screening frequency. We first parameterized the PDE model and the mathematical expressions of two systems outcomes, with base-case values listed earlier. We then identified cost-effective and cost-saving strategies. Finally, we conducted sensitivity analyses on one cost-effective strategy to investigate its robustness with respect to several model parameters.

4.4.1   Base-Case Assessment

We evaluated a total of 36 strategies with screening start age at 15, 16, and 17; end age at 23, 24, and 25; and screening frequency ranging from yearly to quarterly. See Table 4.5 for the set of strategies tested. The reference strategy, indexed by no. 11, resembles the CDC-recommended screening guideline, with annual screening from 15 to 25. Our selections are practically meaningful and some of them have been evaluated in the literature. Our assessment results are presented in Figure 4.6. On the X-axis, we present the increase on the per capita public health spending for each tested strategy as opposed to the recommended strategy. Various components of the total societal spending (C_{tot}) are described earlier. On the Y-axis, we present the decrease on the PID incidence (i.e., E_{PIDinc} as introduced earlier). This quantity reflects the number of PID cases averted, which measures the effectiveness. We next describe the results we obtained.

First, our results show that 27 of the 35 strategies increase the number of PID cases averted, and at an affordable cost, compared with the current CDC recommendation. Of these, two are also cost saving and we call the other 25 strategies cost-effective strategies whose average incremental cost-effectiveness ratio is slightly above $5000 per PID case averted. Note that the expected cost of treating acute PID and its sequelae is nearly $3500. Considering potential social stigma to people with acute PID and emotional devastation of those with PID sequelae, it is quite beneficial to avert these additional negative consequences with merely $1500.

Among the tested strategies, more tests each year, earlier screening start age, and later screening end stage would lead to lower PID incidence, but higher total spending. Later screening end age would lead to more cost increasing or less cost saving; earlier screening start age would generate the same effect although the effect is not as pronounced as moving the screening start age earlier. Among the 25 cost-effective strategies, none of them recommends annual screening unlike the remaining cost-saving strategies. Only two cost-saving strategies also lead to more PID cases averted. These two strategies are similar. They have the same screening end age at 23 and same screening frequency of biannual, though the screening start ages are 17 and 16, respectively.

Additionally, our results suggest that more frequent screening over a wider age range would avert more PID cases with a more affordable cost. For example, if we followed the CDC screening guideline but increased the screening frequency to

TABLE 4.5   Screening Strategies Tested

No.	Start Age	End Age	Number of Tests per Year
1	15	23	1
2	15	23	2
3	15	23	3
4	15	23	4
5	15	24	1
6	15	24	2
7	15	24	3
8	15	24	4
9	15	25	1
10	15	25	2
11	15	25	3
12	15	25	4
13	16	23	1
14	16	23	2
15	16	23	3
16	16	23	4
17	16	24	1
18	16	24	2
19	16	24	3
20	16	24	4
21	16	25	1
22	16	25	2
23	16	25	3
24	16	25	4
25	17	23	1
26	17	23	2
27	17	23	3
28	17	23	4
29	17	24	1
30	17	24	2
31	17	24	3
32	17	24	4
33	17	25	1
34	17	25	2
35	17	25	3
36	17	25	4

quarterly, we would spend the least amount, $556, for each PID case averted. Furthermore, the results suggest that delayed screening coupled with high screening frequency may be beneficial from an effectiveness viewpoint. For example, among the 25 cost-effective strategies, the strategy of quarterly screening from age 17 to 25 yielded the largest PID incidence reduction. This can be understood that delaying screening start age would better coincide with the trend of age-dependent CT

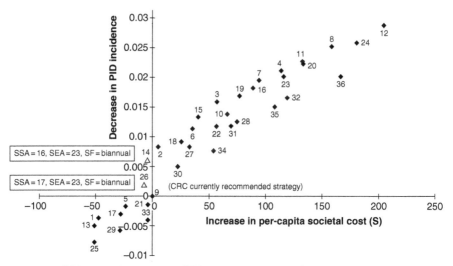

SSA: screening start age, SEA: screening end age, SF: screening frequency

Figure 4.6   Cost-effectiveness analysis results.

infection risk. The results also suggest that early termination of screening would lead to increased PID incidence with less money spent. In fact, both cost-saving strategies do biannual screening with the same end age at 23.

We conclude that a register-based screening program should screen women in a wider age range and more frequently than recommended by the CDC. On the other hand, a smaller age range with modest screening frequency may be preferred because it is cost saving. If PID incidence reduction is emphasized, it is beneficial to keep the frequency high but delay both screening start and end ages for a female adolescent population.

4.4.2   Sensitivity Analysis

In this section, we present a small-scale sensitivity analysis for the purpose of illustration. We selected the strategy that starts biannual screening at age 15 and ends it at age 23. We used the no-screening strategy as the reference. With this reference strategy, the cost-effectiveness ratio is $7062 per PID case averted. We conducted several one-way sensitivity analyses that varied p_{sen}, p_{spe}, p_{com}, p_{sid}, p_{PID}, c_s, c_t, and c_{PID}, respectively. The value ranges for the four probability parameters and the CT screening cost parameter are given directly in Table 4.3. For c_t, the CT treatment cost parameter, we varied the costs of the CT medication and a short clinic visit separately. We considered four extreme cases (i.e., two from varying the medication cost and two from varying the clinic visit charge) and selected the minimum and maximum cost-effectiveness ratios among the four cases. For c_{PID}, we varied five relevant cost parameters in the same way.

TABLE 4.6   One-Way Sensitivity Analysis Results

Parameter	Base-Case Value (Plausible Range)	Minimum CER[a]	Maximum CER[a]
p_{sen}	0.9 (0.65–0.96)	6,713	9,067
p_{spe}	0.99 (0.99–1)	6,855	7,062
p_{com}	0.8 (0.75–0.9)	6,460	7,395
p_{sid}	0.09 (0.01–0.1)	7,017	7,067
p_{PID}	0.96 (0.94–1)	6,775	7,212
c_s	16.46 (8.86–50.65)	4,979	16,431
c_t	91.2 (72.2–116.5)	6,892	7,288
c_{PID}	3497 (3315–7145)	6,454	19,324

[a] CER, Cost-effectiveness ratio; unit: 2010 USD per PID averted.

Table 4.6 suggests that the incremental cost-effectiveness ratio is more sensitive to the cost of treating PID and its sequelae. Note that here we only varied one cost parameter attributing to this treatment cost at a time. It is likely in reality that these costs are positively correlated. So we expect that even wider ranges would be yielded when conducting n-way sensitivity analyses. In addition, the result may be sensitive to the CT screening cost. Among the probability parameters, the CT screening sensitivity seems to be the parameter that impacts the result the most.

4.5   CONCLUSIONS AND FUTURE RESEARCH

In this chapter, we present an age-structured compartmental model to investigate the cost-effectiveness of register-based chlamydia infection screening strategies. Our model incorporates compartments to capture the transitions to PID and several dichotomous likelihoods to capture screening and treatment ineffectiveness as well as individual differences in medication compliance. Our analyses suggest that more frequent screening over a wider age range is cost-effective when compared with the CDC's recommended strategy of annual screening from age 15 to 25. Our assessment also offers quantitative insights into strategies that lead to lowered incidence of acute conditions and long-term sequelae and strategies that are cost saving.

Our work has several limitations. First, our model does not account for different patterns in ongoing sexual partnerships and, more generally, the differences among various sexual networks. In addition, the model does not incorporate immunological and behavioral changes after the initial CT infection. It is evident that the average reinfection risk differs noticeably from the average first-time infection risk (Katz et al. 1987; Batteiger et al. 2010; Teng et al. 2014). Additionally, we assume that screening and treatment effectiveness and medication compliance do not vary overtime. Hu et al. (2004) provided rough estimates on the durations of several conditions related to CT epidemiology. Additionally, model parameterization is critical to establish the validity of the age-structured models (Deriso 1980; Dimitriu 2003;

Ackleh et al. 2005) and, subsequently, the practical relevance of recommended strategies from the assessment. Although we conducted a comprehensive literature review to determine the value of most parameters, we did not have accurate estimates for all parameters. Finally, further work is needed in strategy assessment and sensitivity analysis. For example, it would be useful to incorporate quality-of-life parameters in the cost-effectiveness analysis. Several quality weights are available in Hu et al. (2004). In addition, probabilistic sensitivity analyses could be performed to further explore the joint effects of uncertainty sources; for example, it is more desirable by simultaneously studying parameters that are known to be correlated (e.g., those constituting the direct medical cost). Our future research plan will be centered on dealing with these limitations, with emphasis on the sexual network modeling.

REFERENCES

A. S. Ackleh, H. T. Banks, K. Deng, and S. Hu, "Parameter estimation in a coupled system of nonlinear size-structured populations," *Math Biosci Eng*, 2(2), 289–315 (2005).

M. Ajelli, B. Goncalves, D. Balcan, V. Colizza, H. Hu, J. Ramasco, S. Merler, and A. Vespignani, "Comparing large-scale computational approaches to epidemic modeling: Agent-based versus structured metapopulation models," *BMC Infect Dis*, 10, 190 (2010).

C. L. Althaus, J. C. Heijne, A. Roellin, and N. Low, "Transmission dynamics of *Chlamydia trachomatis* affect the impact of screening programs," *Epidemics*, 2(3), 123–131 (2010).

B. Armbruster and M. L. Brandeau, "Optimal mix of screening and contact tracing for endemic diseases," *Math Biosci*, 209(2), 386–402 (2007a).

B. Armbruster and M. L. Brandeau, "Contact tracing to control infectious disease: When enough is enough," *Health Care Manag Sci*, 10(4), 341–355 (2007b).

B. Armbruster and M. L. Brandeau, "Cost-effective control of chronic viral diseases: Finding the optimal level of screening and contact tracing," *Math Biosci*, 224(1), 35–42 (2010).

J. N. Arno, B. P. Katz, R. McBride, G. A. Carty, B. E. Batteiger, V. A. Caine, and R. B. Jones, "Age and clinical immunity to infections with *Chlamydia trachomatis*," *Sex Transm Dis*, 21(1), 47–52 (1994).

D. Balcan, V. Colizza, B. Gonalves, H. Hu, J. J. Ramasco, and A. Vespignani, "Multiscale mobility networks and the spatial spreading of infectious diseases," *Proc Natl Acad Sci U S A*, 106(51), 21484–21489 (2009).

D. Balcan, B. Gonalves, H. Hu, J. J. Ramasco, V. Colizza, and A. Vespignani, "Modeling the spatial spread of infectious diseases: The GLobal Epidemic and Mobility computational model," *J Comput Sci*, 1(3), 132–145 (2010).

B. E. Batteiger, F. Xu, R. E. Johnson, and M. L. Rekart, "Protective immunity to *Chlamydia trachomatis* genital infection: Evidence from human studies," *J Infect Dis*, 201(S2), S178–S189 (2010).

C. M. Black, J. Marrazzo, R. E. Johnson, E. W. Hook 3rd, R. B. Jones, T. A. Green, J. Schachter, W. E. Stamm, G. Bolan, M. E. St. Louis, and D. H. Martin, "Head-to-head multicenter comparison of DNA probe and nucleic acid amplification tests for *Chlamydia trachomatis* infection in women performed with an improved reference standard," *J Clin Microbiol*, 40(10), 3757–3763 (2002).

M. L. Brandeau, G. S. Zaric, and A. Richter, "Resource allocation for control of infectious diseases in multiple independent populations: Beyond cost-effectiveness analysis," *J Health Econ*, 22(4), 575–598 (2003).

C. Brihmer, I. Kallings, C. E. Nord, and J. Brundin, "Second look laparoscopy; evaluation of two different antibiotic regimens after treatment of acute salpingitis," *Eur J Obstet Gynecol Reprod Biol*, 30(3), 263–274 (1989).

R. C. Brunham and J. Rey-Ladino, "Immunology of *Chlamydia* infection: Implications for a *Chlamydia trachomatis* vaccine," *Nat Rev Immunol*, 5(2), 149–161 (2005).

R. C. Brunham, B. Pourbohloul, S. Mak, R. White, and M. L. Rekart, "The unexpected impact of a chlamydia trachomatis infection control program on susceptibility to reinfection," *J Infect Dis*, 192(10), 1836–1844 (2005).

H. Buhaug, F. E. Skjeldestad, B. Backe, and A. Dalen, "Cost effectiveness of testing for chlamydial infections in asymptomatic women," *Med Care*, 27, 833–841 (1989).

H. Buhaug, F. E. Skjeldestad, L. E. Halvoersen, and A. Dalen, "Should asymptomatic patients be tested for *Chlamydia trachomatis* in general practice?" *Br J Gen Pract*, 40, 142–145 (1990).

Bureau of Labor Statistics. Databases, Tables & Calculators by Subject, CPI Inflation Calculator. United States Department of Labor, Washington, DC. Available at www.bls.gov/data/inflation_calculator.htm. Accessed August 11, 2017.

V. Cardinale, *1998 Drug Topics Red Book*. Medical Economics Co., Montvale, NJ, 1998.

C. Castillo-Chavez and Z. Feng, "Global stability of an age-structure model for TB and its applications to optimal vaccination strategies," *Math Biosci*, 151(2), 135–154 (1998).

W. Cates Jr., and J. N. Wasserheit, "Genital chlamydial infections: Epidemiology and reproductive sequelae," *Am J Obstet Gynecol*, 164(6 pt 2), 1771–1781 (1991).

Centers for Disease Control and Prevention (CDC), Tracking the Hidden Epidemics: Trends in STDs in the United States, 2000. Centers for Disease Control and Prevention, Atlanta, GA, 2001.

Centers for Disease Control and Prevention (CDC), "Sexually transmitted diseases treatment guidelines, 2010," *MMWR Recomm Rep*, 59(RR12), 1–110 (2010).

Centers for Disease Control and Prevention (CDC), Reported STDs in the United States: 2015 National Data for Chlamydia, Gonorrhea, and Syphilis. CDC Fact Sheet. Centers for Disease Control and Prevention (CDC), Atlanta, GA, October 2016. Retrieved from https://www.cdc.gov/nchhstp/newsroom/docs/factsheets/std-trends-508.pdf. Accessed on January 18, 2017.

Chlamydia Surveillance Data, 2010 Sexually Transmitted Disease Surveillance. Centers for Disease Control and Prevention (CDC), Atlanta, GA, November 2011. Retrieved from http://www.cdc.gov/std/stats10/chlamydia.htm. Accessed on April 26, 2012.

V. Colizza, A. Barrat, M. Barthelemy, and A. Vespignani, "The role of the airline transportation network in the prediction and predictability of global epidemics," *Proc Natl Acad Sci U S A*, 103(17), 2015–2020 (2006).

V. Colizza, A. Barrat, M. Barthelemy, A.-J. Valleron, and A. Vespignani, "Modeling the worldwide spread of pandemic influenza: Baseline case and containment interventions," *PLoS Med*, 4(1), e13 (2007a).

V. Colizza, A. Barrat, M. Barthelemy, and A. Vespignani, "Predictability and epidemic pathways in global outbreaks of infectious diseases: The SARS case study," *BMC Med*, 5, 34 (2007b).

V. Colizza, R. Pastor-Satorras, and A. Vespignani, "Reaction-diffusion processes and metapopulation models in heterogeneous network," *Nat Phys*, 3(4), 276–282 (2007c).

S. D. Datta, M. Sternberg, R. E. Johnson, S. Berman, J. R. Papp, G. McQuillan, and H. Weinstock, "Gonorrhea and chlamydia in the United States among persons 14 to 38 age, 1999 to 2002," *Ann Intern Med*, 147(2), 89–96 (2007).

D. Dean, D. Ferrero, and M. McCarthy, "Comparison of performance and cost-effectiveness of direct fluorescent-antibody, ligase chain reaction, and PCR assays for verification of chlamydial enzyme immunoassay results for populations with a low to moderate prevalence of *Chlamydia trachomatis* infection," *J Clin Microbiol*, 36(1), 94–99 (1998).

R. B. Deriso, "Harvesting strategies and parameter estimation for an age-structured model," *Can J Fish Aquat Sci*, 37(2), 268–282 (1980).

G. Dimitriu, "Parameter estimation in size/age structured population models using the moving finite element method." In *Numerical Methods and Applications*, vol. 2542 of Lecture Notes in Computer Science, pp. 420–429. Springer, Berlin/Heidelberg, Germany, 2003.

Z. Feng, C. Castillo-Chavez, and A. F. Capurro, "A model for tuberculosis with exogenous reinfection," *Theor Popul Biol*, 57(3), 235–247 (2000).

T. Gift, C. Walsh, A. Haddix, and K. L. Irwin, "A cost-effectiveness evaluation of testing and treatment of *Chlamydia trachomatis* infection among asymptomatic women infected with Neisseria gonorrhoeae," *Sex Transm Dis*, 29(9), 542–551 (2002).

J. Gmez-Gardenes, V. Latora, Y. Moreno, and E. Profumo, "Spreading of sexually transmitted diseases in heterosexual populations," *Proc Natl Acad Sci U S A*, 105(5), 1399–1404 (2008).

M. E. Halloran, N. M. Ferguson, S. Eubank, I. M. Longini, D. A. T. Cummings, B. Lewis, S. Xu, C. Fraser, A. Vullikanti, T. C. Germann, D. Wagener, R. Beckman, K. Kadau, C. Barrett, C. A. Macken, D. S. Burke, and P. Cooley, "Modeling targeted layered containment of an influenza pandemic in the United States," *Proc Natl Acad Sci U S A*, 105(12), 4639–4644 (2008).

L. E. Halvorsen, F. E. Skjeldestad, R. Mecsei, and A. Dalen, "*Chlamydia trachomatis* in cervix uteri specimens among patients in general practice," *Tidsskr Nor Laegeforen*, 108, 2706–2708 (1988).

Health Care Financing Administration, Medical Part B Reimbursement. Crompond, NY, 2000.

J. C. Heijne, C. L. Althaus, S. A. Herzog, M. Kretzschmar, and N. Low, "The role of reinfection and partner notification in the efficacy of chlamydia screening programs," *J Infect Dis*, 203(3), 372–377 (2010).

W. W. Holland and S. Steward (eds.), *Screening in Disease Prevention: What Works?* Radcliffe Publishing, Oxford, U.K., 2005.

H. Hooyberghs, B. V. Schaeybroeck, and J. O. Indekeu, "Percolation on bipartite scale-free networks," *Physica A*, 389(15), 2920–2929 (2010).

M. R. Howell, T. C. Quinn, and C. A. Gaydos, "Screening for *Chlamydia trachomatis* in asymptomatic women attending family planning clinics: A cost-effectiveness analysis of three strategies," *Ann Intern Med*, 128(4), 277–284 (1998).

D. Hu, E. W. Hook 3rd, and S. J. Goldie, "Screening for *Chlamydia trachomatis* in women 15 to 29 years of age: A cost-effectiveness analysis," *Ann Intern Med*, 141(7), 501–513 (2004).

D. Hu, E. W. Hook 3rd, and S. J. Goldie, "The impact of natural history parameters on the cost-effectiveness of chlamydia trachomatis screening strategies," *Sex Transm Dis*, 33(7), 428–436 (2006).

Y. Huang and P. Rohani, "Age-structured effects and disease interference in childhood infections," *Proc Biol Sci*, 273(1591), 1229–1237 (2006).

R. Huerta and L. S. Tsimring, "Contact tracing and epidemics control in social networks," *Phys Rev E Stat Nonlin Soft Matter Phys*, 66(5 Pt 2), 056115 (2002).

B. P. Katz, B. E. Batteiger, and R. B. Jones, "Effect of prior sexually transmitted disease on the isolation of *Chlamydia trachomatis*," *Sex Transm Dis*, 14(3), 160–164 (1987).

B. P. Katz, C. S. Danos, T. S. Quinn, V. Caine, and R. B. Jones, "Efficiency and cost-effectiveness of field follow-up for patients with *Chlamydia trachomatis* infection in a sexually transmitted diseases clinic," *Sex Transm Dis*, 15(1), 11–16 (1988).

E. L. Korenromp, M. K. Sudaryo, S. J. de Vlas, R. H. Gray, N. K. Sewankambo, D. Serwadda, M. J. Wawer, and J. D. Habbema, "What proportion of episodes of gonorrhoea and chlamydia becomes symptomatic?" *Int J STD AIDS*, 13(2), 91–101 (2002).

M. Kretzschmar, Y. T. van Duynhoven, and A. J. Severijnen, "Modeling prevention strategies for gonorrhea and *Chlamydia* using stochastic network simulations," *Am J Epidemiol*, 144(3), 306–317 (1996).

M. Kretzschmar, R. Welte, A. van den Hoek, and M. J. Postma "Comparative model-based analysis of screening programs for chlamydia trachomatis infections," *Am J Epidemiol*, 153(1), 90–101 (2001).

M. Kretzschmar, K. M. E. Turner, P. M. Barton, W. J. Edmunds, and N. Low, "Predicting the population impact of chlamydia screening programmes: Comparative mathematical modelling study," *Sex Transm Infect*, 85(5), 359–366 (2009).

C. Y. Lau and A. K. Qureshi, "Azithromycin versus doxycycline for genital chlamydial infections: A meta-analysis of randomized clinical trials," *Sex Transm Dis*, 29(9), 497–502 (2002).

E. F. Long, N. K. Vaidya, and M. L. Brandeau, "Controlling co-epidemics: Analysis of HIV and tuberculosis infection dynamics," *Oper Res*, 56(6), 1366–1381 (2008).

N. Low, "Screening programmes for chlamydial infection: When will we ever learn?" *BMJ*, 334(7596), 725–728 (2007).

N. Low, A. McCarthy, J. Macleod, C. Salisbury, R. Campbell, T. E. Roberts, P. Horner, S. Skidmore, J. A. C. Stern, E. Sanford, F. Ibrahim, A. Holloway, R. Patel, P. M. Barton, S. M. Robinson, N. Mills, A. Graham, A. Herring, E. O. Caul, G. Davey Smith, F. D. Hobbs, J. D. Ross, M. Egger, and Chlamydia Screening Studies (ClaSS) Group, "Epidemiological, social, diagnostic and economic evaluation of population screening for genital chlamydial infection," *Health Technol Assess*, 11(8), 1–165, iii–iv, ix–xii (2007).

N. Low, N. Bender, L. Nartey, A. Shang, and J. M. Stephenson, "Effectiveness of chlamydia screening: Systematic review," *Int J Epidemiol*, 38(2), 435–448 (2009).

D. Magid, J. M. Douglas Jr., and J. S. Schwartz, "Doxycycline compared with azithromycin for treating women with genital *Chlamydia trachomatis* infections: An incremental cost-effectiveness analysis," *Ann Intern Med*, 124(4), 389–399 (1996).

C. F. Martin, L. J. S. Allen, and M. S. Stamp, "An analysis of the transmission of chlamydia in a closed population," *J Differ Equ Appl*, 2(1), 1–29 (1996).

W. C. Miller, C. A. Ford, M. Morris, M. S. Handcock, J. L. Schmitz, M. M. Hobbs, M. S. Cohen, K. M. Harris, and J. R. Udry, "Prevalence of chlamydial and gonococcal infections among young adults in the United States," *JAMA*, 291(18), 2229–2236 (2004).

M. Molano, C. J. Meijer, E. Weiderpass, A. Aslan, H. Posso, S. Franceschi, M. Ronderos, N. Muñoz, and A. J. van den Brule, "The natural course of *Chlamydia trachomatis* infection in asymptomatic Colombian women: A 5-year follow-up study," *J Infect Dis*, 191(6), 907–916 (2005).

P. R. Monge and N. Contractor, *Theories of Communication Networks*. Oxford University Press, Oxford, U.K., 2003.

M. Morris and M. Kretzschmar, "Concurrent partnerships and the spread of HIV," *AIDS*, 11(5), 641–648 (1997).

J. Müller, M. Kretzschmar, and K. Dietz, "Contact tracing in stochastic and deterministic epidemic models," *Math Biosci*, 164(1), 39–64 (2000).

National Chlamydia Screening Steering Group (NCSSG). New Frontiers: Annual Report of the National Chlamydia Screening Programme in England 2005/06. HPA, London, U.K., 2006.

P. W. Nelson, M. Gilchrist, D. Coombs, J. Hyman, and A. S. Perelson, "An age-structured model of HIV infection that allows for variations in the production rate of viral particles and the death rate of productively infected cells," *Math Biosci Eng*, 1(2), 267–288 (2004).

R. B. Ness, D. E. Soper, R. L. Holley, J. Peipert, H. Randall, R. L. Sweet, S. J. Sondheimer, S. L. Hendrix, A. Amortegui, G. Trucco, T. Songer, J. R. Lave, S. L. Hiller, D. C. Bass, and S. F. Kelsey, "Effectiveness of inpatient and outpatient treatment strategies for women with pelvic inflammatory disease: Results from the Pelvic Inflammatory Disease Evaluation and Clinical Health (PEACH) Randomized Trial," *Am J Obstet Gynecol*, 186(5), 929–937 (2002).

J. Paavonen, N. Kiviat, R. C. Brunham, C. E. Stevens, C. C. Kuo, W. E. Stamm, A. Miettinen, M. Soules, D. A. Eschenbach, and K. K. Holmes, "Prevalence and manifestations of endometritis among women with cervicitis," *Am J Obstet Gynecol*, 152(3), 280–286 (1985).

T. C. Porco, P. M. Small, and S. M. Blower, "Amplification dynamics: Predicting the effect of HIV on tuberculosis outbreaks," *J Acquir Immune Defic Syndr*, 28(5), 437–444 (2001).

A. Ramezanpour, "Biology helps to construct weighted scale-free networks," *Europhys Lett*, 68(2), 316–322 (2004).

D. G. Regan, D. P. Wilson, and J. S. Hocking, "Coverage is the key for effective screening of *Chlamydia trachomatis* in Australia," *J Infect Dis*, 198(3), 349–395 (2010).

D. B. Rein, W. J. Kassler, K. L. Irwin, and L. Rabiee, "Direct medical cost of pelvic inflammatory disease and its sequelae: decreasing, but still substantial," *Obstet Gynecol*, 95(3), 397–402 (2000).

T. E. Roberts, S. Robinson, P. Barton, S. Bryan, N. Low, and Chlamydia Screening Studies (ClaSS) Group, "Screening for *Chlamydia trachomatis*: A systematic review of the economic evaluations and modeling," *Sex Transm Infect*, 82(3), 193–200 (2006).

C. Salisbury, J. Macleod, M. Egger, A. McCarthy, R. Patel, A. Holloway, F. Ibrahim, J. A. Sterne, P. Horner, and N. Low, "Opportunistic and systematic screening for chlamydia: A study of consultations by young adults in general practice," *Br J Gen Pract*, 56(523), 99–103 (2006).

D. Scholes, A. Stergachis, F. E. Heidrich, H. Andrilla, K. K. Holmes, and W. E. Stamm, "Prevention of pelvic inflammatory disease by screening for cervical chlamydial infection," *N Engl J Med*, 334, 1362–1366 (1996).

J. R. Schwebke, R. Sadler, J. M. Sutton, and E. W. Hook 3rd, "Positive screening tests for gonorrhea and chlamydial infection fail to lead consistently to treatment of patients attending a sexually transmitted disease clinic," *Sex Transm Dis*, 24(4), 181–184 (1997).

M. A. Shafer, R. H. Pantell, and J. Schachter, "Is the routine pelvic examination needed with the advent of urine-based screening for sexually transmitted diseases?" *Arch Pediatr Adolesc Med*, 153, 119–125 (1999).

O. Sharomi and A. B. Gumel, "Re-infection-induced backward bifurcation in the transmission dynamics of chlamydia trachomatis," *J Math Anal Appl*, 356(1), 96–118 (2009).

T. Sheldon, "Holland plans chlamydia screening in 300000 young people," *BMJ*, 335(7631), 1177 (2007).

SIG Health Care Information Netherlands, Medische Registratie Gepoolde Gegevens over 1993. Software Improvement Group (SIG), Utretcht, the Netherlands, 1994.

W. E. Stamm, M. E. Guinan, C. Johnson, T. Starcher, K. K. Holmes, and W. M. McCormack, "Effect of treatment regimens for *Neisseria gonorrhoeae* on simultaneous infection with *Chlamydia trachomatis*," *N Engl J Med*, 310, 545–549 (1984).

R. Steece, *National Pricing of Chlamydia Reagents*. Association of State and Territorial Public Health Laboratory Directors, Washington, DC, 1997.

K. R. Stratton, J. S. Durch, and R. S. Lawrence (eds.), "Appendix 2: Chlamydia." In: *Vaccines for the 21st Century: A Tool for Decisionmaking*, pp. 149–158. National Academies Press, Washington, DC (2000).

G. Tao, T. L. Gift, C. M. Walsh, K. L. Irwin, and W. J. Kassler, "Optimal resource allocation for curing *Chlamydia trachomatis* infection among asymptomatic women at clinics operating on a fixed budget," *Sex Transm Dis*, 29(11), 703–709 (2002).

K. Teisala, P. K. Heinonen, R. Aine, R. Punnonen, and J. Paavonen, "Second laparoscopy after treatment of acute pelvic inflammatory disease," *Obstet Gynecol*, 69(3 Pt 1), 343–346 (1987).

Y. Teng, Optimal Screening Strategy Design for Chlamydia Infection, PhD dissertation, Weldon School of Biomedical Engineering, Purdue University, West Lafayette, IN (2012).

Y. Teng, N. Kong, and W. Tu, "Estimating age-dependent per-encounter chlamydia trachomatis acquisition risk via a Markov-based state-transition model," *J Clin Bioinf*, 4(1), 7 (2014).

K. M. Turner, E. J. Adams, N. Gay, A. C. Ghani, C. Mercer, and W. J. Edmunds, "Developing a realistic sexual network model of chlamydia transmission in Britain," *Theor Biol Med Model*, 3, 3 (2006).

U.S. Department of Labor Bureau of Labor Statistics, Highlights of Womens Earnings in 2000. Report 952, p. 26. U.S. Department of Labor Bureau of Labor Statistics, Washington, DC, 2001. Available at https://www.bls.gov/opub/reports/womens-earnings/archive/womensearnings_2000.pdf. Accessed on August 11, 2017.

B. Van Der Pol, C. S. Kraft, and J. A. William, "Use of an adaptation of a commercially available PCR assay aimed at diagnosis of chlamydia and gonorrhea to detect *Trichomonas vaginalis* in urogenital specimens," *J Clin Microbiol*, 44(2), 366–373 (2006).

J. X. Velasco-Hernandez, F. Brauer, and C. Castillo-Chavez, "Effects of treatment and prevalence-dependent recruitment on the dynamics of a fatal disease," *IMA J Math Appl Med Biol*, 13(3), 175–192 (1996).

A. E. Washington and P. Katz, "Cost of and payment source for pelvic inflammatory disease. Trends and projections, 1983 through 2000," *JAMA*, 266(18), 2565–2569 (1991).

A. E. Washington, P. S. Arno, and M. A. Brooks, "The economic cost of pelvic inflammatory disease," *JAMA*, 255(13), 1735–1738 (1986).

E. J. Watson, A. Templeton, I. Russell, J. Paavonen, P. A. Mardh, and A. Stary, "The accuracy and efficacy of screening tests for *Chlamydia trachomatis*: A systematic review," *J Med Microbiol*, 51(12), 1021–1031 (2002).

R. Welte, M. Kretzschmar, R. Leidl, A. van den Hoek, J. C. Jager, and M. J. Postma "Cost-effectiveness of screening programs for *Chlamydia trachomatis*: A population-based dynamic approach," *Sex Transm Dis*, 27(9), 518–529 (2000).

L. Weström, "Incidence, prevalence, and trends of acute pelvic inflammatory disease and its consequences in industrialized countries," *Am J Obstet Gynecol*, 138(7 Pt 2), 880–892 (1980).

L. Weström, "Sexually transmitted diseases and infertility," *Sex Transm Dis*, 21(2 Suppl), S32–S37 (1994).

L. Weström, R. Joesoef, G. Reynolds, A. Hagdu, and S. E. Thompson, "Pelvic inflammatory disease and fertility. A cohort study of 1,844 women with laparoscopically verified disease and 657 control women with normal laparoscopic results," *Sex Transm Dis*, 19(4), 185–192 (1992).

P. Wølner-Hansen and L. Weström, "Second-look laparoscopy after acute salpingitis," *Obstet Gynecol*, 61(6), 702–704 (1983).

World Health Organization, Global Prevalence and Incidence of Selected Curable Sexually Transmitted Infections Overview and Estimates. Published in February 2001. Retrieved from http://www.who.int/hiv/pub/sti/who_hiv_aids_2001.02.pdf. Accessed on August 11, 2017.

J. M. Yeh, E. W. Hook 3rd, and S. J. Goldie, "A refined estimate of the average lifetime cost of pelvic inflammatory disease," *Sex Transm Dis*, 30(5), 369–378 (2003).

G. S. Zaric, "Resource allocation for control of infectious disease epidemics," *Comments Theor Biol*, 8(4/5), 475 (2003).

G. S. Zaric and M. L. Brandeau, "Resource allocation for epidemic control over short time horizons," *Math Biosci*, 171(1), 33–58 (2001).

G. S. Zaric and M. L. Brandeau, "Dynamic resource allocation for epidemic control in multiple populations," *IMA J Math Appl Med Biol*, 19(4), 235–255 (2002).

S. Zhao, Z. Xu, and Y. Lu, "A mathematical model of hepatitis B virus transmission and its application for vaccination strategy in China," *Int J Epidemiol*, 29(4), 744–752 (2000).

5

OPTIMAL SELECTION OF ASSAYS FOR DETECTING INFECTIOUS AGENTS IN DONATED BLOOD

Ebru K. Bish[1], Hadi El-Amine[2], Douglas R. Bish[1], Susan L. Stramer[3], and Anthony D. Slonim[4]

[1] Grado Department of Industrial and Systems Engineering, Virginia Tech, Blacksburg, VA, USA
[2] Systems Engineering and Operations Research Department, George Mason University, Fairfax, VA, USA
[3] Scientific Affairs, American Red Cross, Gaithersburg, MD, USA
[4] University of Nevada School of Medicine and Renown Health, Reno, NV, USA

5.1 INTRODUCTION AND CHALLENGES

5.1.1 Introduction

Blood products are vital healthcare commodities for the treatment of patients across all age groups and with a variety of treatment requirements. Patients undergoing major surgeries and cancer therapies need blood products, as well as trauma victims, certain premature infants, children with severe anemia, and pregnant women with complications. As a result, a large number of people need blood transfusion at some point in their lives (e.g., 40%–70% of the US population (Hay et al. 2006)). In the United States, the amount of blood collected in 2014 is about 16 million units, with around 14.5 million units transfused to about five million patients (American Red

Decision Analytics and Optimization in Disease Prevention and Treatment, First Edition.
Edited by Nan Kong and Shengfan Zhang.
© 2018 John Wiley & Sons, Inc. Published 2018 by John Wiley & Sons, Inc.

Cross 2014a). Worldwide, it is estimated that more than 108 million units of blood is collected annually (WHO 2014a). Moreover, the need for blood can increase significantly because of mass casualty disasters (e.g., hurricane, earthquake) or armed conflict (American Red Cross 2017).

Unfortunately various infections can be transmitted through the use of blood products. These "transfusion-transmittable infections" (TTIs) include the human immunodeficiency virus (HIV); hepatitis viruses, with the major ones being hepatitis viruses B and C (HBV and HCV); human T-cell lymphotropic virus (HTLV); syphilis; West Nile virus (WNV); *Babesia* parasite; Chagas' disease; and dengue virus; and new infections are continuously being discovered to be transmittable through blood transfusion (e.g., the dengue virus was discovered to be transmittable through transfusion only in 2002 (Katz 2010)). If transmitted, these infections can have dire consequences for the transfusion recipient. Consequently, post-donation screening of the blood for TTIs is essential for the safe use of blood products.

Today, there still remains a non-negligible risk of TTI even in developed countries where high efficacy tests are in use (American Red Cross 2014b). For example, babesiosis, a tick-borne disease caused by the *Babesia* parasite, can be deadly for vulnerable patients and is the leading cause of TTIs in the United States, with 162 reported cases of transfusion-transmitted babesiosis between 1979 and 2009 (Herwaldt et al. 2011). The number is on the rise, with 1128 babesiosis cases reported in 2011 and 937 cases reported in 2012 (CDC 2012). The safety of blood is far from ideal in other parts of the world, especially in some developing countries. For example, up to 150,000 pregnancy-related deaths worldwide could be avoided each year through access to safe blood (WHO 2014a). "Less than 30% of the countries have a well-organized blood collection service in place" (American Red Cross 2010). Limited resources and a lack of infrastructure dictate that only 88% of blood donations worldwide are screened as recommended by the World Health Organization (WHO), which includes testing for HIV, HBV, HCV, and syphilis; and this number is only 48% in developing countries (WHO 2014b). "For the blood donations collected in the remaining 41 countries, which account for 22% of the global donations reported to the WHO, the use of these basic quality assurance procedures is still unknown" (WHO 2014b). In Africa, with blood safety challenged by the HIV/AIDS and malaria epidemics, the situation is dire: the proportion of both existing and new HIV infections attributable to blood transfusion in the sub-Saharan Africa is estimated at 10%. With 11 million HIV infections having occurred on the continent to date, the cumulative total of transfusion-associated HIV infections in Africa may exceed 1 million. As many as 25% of HIV-infected women and children in some areas of Africa acquired their infection from a blood transfusion; and 42% of HIV-infected children over the age of 1 year in Kinshasa, Zaire, acquired infection from a blood transfusion (McFarland et al. 2003). These numbers underscore the importance of adequate post-donation testing of blood so that safe blood can be provided to those in need.

5.1.2 The Challenges

Major challenges to providing safe blood products can be summarized as follows:

1. Demand for blood products is high worldwide and blood products are highly perishable (e.g., the lifetime of red blood cells is 21 days). Therefore, a well-functioning healthcare system requires a high and constant flow of donations, leading to a high testing cost. However, healthcare resources are limited.

2. Multiple Food and Drug Administration (FDA)-licensed blood screening tests are available for blood collection centers to choose from, and the tests are imperfectly reliable and come with different costs and measure different markers in the body (e.g., antibodies, antigens, genetic material of the virus). Furthermore, new testing technologies are always being developed, offering new options of price and efficacy (Dzik 2003; Jackson et al. 2003). Thus, it is often the case that multiple tests, with varying degrees of efficacy and costs, are available for screening for the same infection.

3. The FDA requires blood collection centers to screen for a given set of infections and recommends screening for some other infections, but does not specify which particular tests should be used. Therefore, the blood collection center must design an effective and efficient blood screening scheme that reduces the risk of TTI in a resource-constrained environment. While doing so, the blood collection center needs to also determine whether to screen for infections recommended by the FDA as well as whether to screen for infections that are not in the FDA list. For example, current FDA guidelines recommend, but do not require, WNV screening and neither require nor recommend *Babesia* screening. Due to the high uncertainty around the dynamics, prevalence, and transmissibility of emerging infections, combined with the already high cost of donated blood testing, it may take a long time for the FDA to develop appropriate guidelines, especially for emerging infections. The American Association of Blood Banks currently has 68 emerging infections on their watch list (American Association of Blood Banks 2016).

4. Infection dynamics and prevalence rates in the donor population are highly uncertain. For emerging infections, such as babesiosis and WNV, not much is known other than that they are highly seasonal and endemic only in certain regions (Korves et al. 2006; Moritz et al. 2014; Stramer et al. 2005). The uncertainty around prevalence rates of well-established infections also remains high even in countries with good surveillance systems. This is because all surveillance methods (e.g., population-based studies, seroprevalence surveys, sentinel surveillances) are highly resource and time intensive and often study, due to data availability and resource limitations, subpopulations whose prevalence rates may significantly differ from the donor population (Arora et al. 2010; Busch et al. 2005; Chak et al. 2011; Grassly et al. 2004; Walker et al. 2001). In addition, many infections go undiagnosed or underreported. However, the

success of blood screening strategies is highly dependent on prevalence rates, and variations in prevalence rates and/or estimation errors may lead to an increase in the TTI risk. Furthermore, it is difficult to change the testing scheme in the short term (e.g., on a yearly basis) due to the huge setup involved with the new testing equipment, testing protocol, and contracts with testing laboratories.

5. Consequences of the various infections differ and may also depend on the characteristics of the transfusion recipient. For example, elderly patients and patients with underlying hypertension, cerebrovascular disease, and diabetes are at a higher risk of developing complications from a WNV infection (Hayes et al. 2005). Similarly, it is believed that complicated babesiosis is more likely to occur in patients with asplenia, malignancy, HIV, and chronic heart, lung, and liver diseases; in patients who are taking immunosuppressive medications; or in patients with a history of organ transplantation. However, not all risk factors are well understood in the medical literature (Vannier et al. 2008), and therefore it is practically impossible to reliably classify each patient as a "high-risk" versus "low-risk" patient for a certain infection prior to transfusion. This creates a huge challenge in formulating screening strategies based on risk characteristics of transfusion recipients.

6. Blood screening decisions have many other dimensions in addition to the test selection decision. For example, the blood collection center can utilize "universal" or "non-universal" testing schemes: the former refers to the practice of administering the same test set to each and every donated blood unit, while the latter allows for differential testing, that is, the blood center would administer multiple test sets, each applied to a fraction of the total blood units. The main motivation of non-universal testing is to make it feasible for the budget-constrained blood center to administer the expensive tests, which typically have a higher accuracy, to a portion of the donated blood. The differentiation can be random, or it can be targeted considering, for example, donation characteristics, such as the geographic region, donor demographics, and/or the donation season, which have all been shown to influence prevalence rates at statistically significant levels (Bish et al. 2014). Further, some tests can be administered on *pooled* blood units. In pooling, blood samples from multiple donors are combined into a single testing pool: if the pool tests positive, various retesting schemes are possible to identify the infected blood units (see, e.g., Aprahamian et al. 2016a,b). Pooling not only reduces the testing cost but also diminishes the test's efficacy (Behets et al. 1990; Burns and Mauro 1987; Hwang 1976; Jackson et al. 2003; Kline et al. 1989; Leiby 2001; Stramer et al. 2004; Weusten et al. 2002).

Currently, it is common practice for blood centers in the developed world, with well-organized blood collection systems in place, to use universal testing schemes. However, expensive testing technologies having higher accuracy are being developed continuously.

An example is the nucleic acid testing (NAT) technology for HIV, HBV, HCV, and WNV, which was recently approved by the FDA. NAT has significantly higher efficacy than current serological tests (which are based on antibody and antigen detection), and it also comes with pooling flexibility (in pool sizes of 6–24), which reduces the test's efficacy. This raises the question of whether the blood supply, as a whole, would be safer if the blood center were to use this expensive technology on a fraction of the donated blood, if they could not afford using it on all donated blood. For example, the American Red Cross routinely performs pooled NAT testing (in pool sizes of 16) for WNV but switches to the more reliable individual NAT testing in epidemic areas during epidemic time periods (American Red Cross 2014b). This can be seen as a form of non-universal testing, with donations received in different seasons and regions undergoing different testing. From the society's perspective, such a policy is equitable because it would reduce the risk for the whole blood supply, as a transfusion recipient could have blood screened by any of the test sets (the donor's identity is not attached to the blood donation, except for rare cases where a family member or a friend would donate blood for an emergency situation). Such non-universal testing schemes enable the decision maker to administer expensive, more reliable tests that would not have been budget feasible otherwise and have the potential to reduce the TTI risk over the current universal testing. However, these issues further complicate the testing decision.

In this setting, the resource-constrained blood collection center needs to devise a post-donation blood screening scheme so as to minimize the risk of an infectious donation being released into the blood supply. This decision is of utmost importance because of the dire consequences of transfusing infected blood units. A variety of tools have been applied to this decision problem, including standard cost-effectiveness analysis (e.g., Busch et al. 2009; Leiby 2001; Sendi et al. 2003; Simon et al. 2013), mathematical programming-based approaches (Aprahamian et al. 2016a; Bish et al. 2011, 2014; El-Amine et al. 2016, 2017; Xie et al. 2012), decision-theoretic approaches (e.g., Marshall et al. 2004), Markov process models (e.g., Jackson et al. 2003; Schwartz et al. 1990; Van Hulst et al. 2009), or simulation models (e.g., Custer et al. 2005; Lefrere et al. 1998). This chapter reviews a number of mathematical programming-based models and concludes with a discussion of promising areas for future research.

5.2   THE NOTATION AND DECISION PROBLEM

The decision maker faces the problem of selecting a set of screening tests, from a set of commercially available tests, to administer to each unit of donated blood to test for a set of TTIs (infections) that are required and/or recommended for screening by the FDA/WHO, so as to minimize the overall TTI risk in blood transfusion, that is, the conditional probability that a blood unit classified as "infection-free" is in fact infected.

Each screening test applies to a specific infection and provides binary results, with a "+" result indicating that the blood unit is infected and a "−" result indicating otherwise. Tests are imperfect and are characterized in terms of their *specificity* (the conditional probability that the test result is "−," given that the blood unit is not infected) and *sensitivity* (the conditional probability that the test result is "+," given that the blood unit is infected) (Pepe 2004). False-positive and false-negative test results are possible due to various reasons; see, for example, Dow (2000), Johnson (2010), and Moore et al. (2007). Due to the short shelf life of blood, all selected tests need to be administered concurrently (Hillyer 2001).

In practice the decision maker also needs to adopt a *decision rule*, which prescribes *when* to classify the blood unit as "infection-free" for a particular infection versus "infected," when the selected test set contains multiple tests for the same infection. The "believe the positive (BP)" rule is commonly used in blood screening due to its conservative nature and fits well with the objective of minimizing the TTI risk.[1] Under the BP rule, the blood unit is classified as "infected" for infection i if *at least* one test in the selected set for infection i returns a "+" result; equivalently, it is classified as "free" of infection i if *all* tests in the set come out "−." We use the BP rule in all blood screening schemes that we consider.

5.2.1   Notation

Throughout, $\vec{X} = (X_i)$ denotes a vector, $\bar{X}$ denotes the complement of event X, and ϕ and Φ, respectively, denote the empty set and the universal event. Let Ψ denote the set of infections required and/or recommended for screening; Ω_i denote the set of tests available to the decision maker for infection $i \in \Psi$, with $\Omega = \cup_{i \in \Psi} \Omega_i$; and $d(j)$ denote the infection test j, $j \in \Omega$, applies to. When we discuss non-universal testing schemes, we label all subsets of Ω as $S_0, S_1, \ldots, S_f$, where $f = 2^{|\Omega|} - 1$, $S_0 = \phi$, and $S_f = \Omega$, and denote this index set by $F = \{0, 1, \ldots, f\}$.

Decision variables:
Universal testing problem:
$S \subseteq \Omega$: set of tests to administer to each blood unit
Non-universal testing problem:
p_k: proportion of blood tested with test set S_k, $k \in F$

Consider a random blood unit to be tested. We define the following events and parameters:

Events:
A^i+, $i \in \Psi$: the event that the blood unit is infected by infection i, $(A^i - = \overline{A^i +})$
T_j+, $j \in \Omega$: the event that test j provides a "+" result for infection $d(j)$, $(T_j - = \overline{T_j +})$

---

[1] Bish et al. (2011) shows that under a universal testing scheme, the BP rule is the optimal decision rule for minimizing the TTI risk.

$T-(S) \equiv \bigcap_{j \in S} T_j-$, $S \subseteq \Omega$: the event that the blood unit is classified as infection-free based on the administered test set S and under the BP rule, $(T+(S) \equiv \overline{T-(S)} = \bigcup_{j \in S} T_j+)$.

We adopt the notation that when $S = \phi$, $T-(\phi) = \Phi$ and $\Pr(\bigcup_{j \in S} T_j+) = 0$.

Parameters:

Specificity (true-negative probability) of test $j = \Pr(T_j- \mid A^{d(j)}-)$, $j \in \Omega$

Sensitivity (true-positive probability) of test $j = \Pr(T_j+ \mid A^{d(j)}+)$, $j \in \Omega$

c_j, $j \in \Omega$: unit cost of administering test j

$C_k = \sum_{j \in S_k} c_j$, $k \in F$: cost, per blood unit, of administering all the tests in set S_k

B: total budget available per blood unit for administering the screening tests

α: maximum allowable fraction on waste (i.e., the fraction of infection-free blood falsely discarded)

5.2.2 Measures of Interest

Table 5.1 links the metrics of interest to the blood collection center to measures of accuracy, referred to as "classification probabilities" and "predictive values," used in the medical literature for tests with binary outcomes. Since in blood screening there are *multiple* TTIs that need to be detected via a *set* of tests, we first expand the classification probabilities and predictive values to the multi-infection multi-test setting under the BP decision rule and link them to our metrics.

TABLE 5.1   Measures of Accuracy for Binary Diagnostic Tests

Metrics	Universal Testing Schemes	
	Single-infection single-test setting (Pepe 2004)	Multi-infection multi-test setting under the BP rule
Classification Probabilities		
• False-positive probability	$\Pr\{T+ \mid A-\}$	$\Pr\left\{\bigcup_{j \in S} T_j+ \mid \bigcap_{i \in \Psi} A^i-\right\} \equiv \textbf{Waste}$
• True-positive probability	$\Pr\{T+ \mid A+\}$	$\Pr\left\{\bigcup_{j \in S} T_j+ \mid \bigcup_{i \in \Psi} A^i+\right\}$
Predictive Values		
• Positive predictive value[a]	$\Pr\{A+ \mid T+\}$	$\Pr\left\{\bigcup_{i \in \Psi} A^i+ \mid \bigcup_{j \in S} T_j+\right\}$
• Negative predictive value	$\Pr\{A- \mid T-\}$	$\Pr\left\{\bigcap_{i \in \Psi} A^i- \mid \bigcap_{j \in S} T_j-\right\} \equiv \textbf{1-risk}$

[a] For completeness, we define the positive predictive value as 0 when $S = \phi$.

Classification probabilities and predictive values are valuable in different contexts. Classification probabilities, namely, the false-positive probability $(\Pr\{T+\,|\,A-\})$ and true-positive probability $(\Pr\{T+\,|\,A+\})$, are useful in evaluating the diagnostic accuracy of a test and are commonly used in medical and biomedical research (e.g., Beutel 2000; Walter and Irwig 1988) as well as in engineering applications and statistical hypothesis testing (e.g., Ozekici and Pliska 1991; Raz and Kaspi 1991).[2] On the other hand, the positive predictive value $(\Pr\{A+\,|\,T+\})$ and negative predictive value $(\Pr\{A-\,|\,T-\})$ are valuable in clinical contexts, where the main focus is on how well the test outcome predicts the true infection or disease status. Unlike the classification probabilities, the predictive values depend not only on the test's efficacy but also on the infection's prevalence rate. As such, they cannot be used to describe the inherent accuracy of the test (which is where the classification probabilities are helpful), but they reflect the confidence on the test results. Obviously, there is a direct relationship between the classification probabilities and predictive values.

Thus, through focus on both *risk* and *waste*, the decision maker in the blood screening setting is concerned with both predictive metrics and classification metrics.

For non-universal testing, the TTI risk can be expressed as

$$Risk(nonuniv) = \frac{\sum_{k \in F} p_k \Pr\left\{\bigcup_{i \in \Psi} A^i+,\ T-(S_k)\right\}}{\sum_{k \in F} p_k \Pr\{T-(S_k)\}}.$$ [3]

Further, in practice, different infections have different impacts on the society and the individuals, in terms of costs of treatment, disability, loss of productivity, etc. These costs/burdens depend on the specific TTI as well as on the characteristics of the transfusion recipient. Measures such as quality-adjusted life year (QALY) and disability-adjusted life year (DALY) are commonly used in cost-effectiveness analysis to represent the overall burden of the infection (Marshall et al. 2004; Van Hulst et al. 2010), and one can expand the metrics in this section to incorporate the different impacts of the TTIs in the test selection decision; see Xie et al. (2012) for details.

---

[2] For example, in engineering applications, the true-positive and false-positive probabilities are referred to as the "hit rate" and "false alarm rate," respectively, while in statistical hypothesis testing, they are referred to as "statistical power" and "significance level," respectively; see Pepe (2004, chapter 2).

[3] Note the use of the expression $\dfrac{\sum_{k \in F} p_k \Pr\left\{\bigcup_{i \in \Psi} A_i+,\ T-(S_k)\right\}}{\sum_{k \in F} p_k \Pr\{T-(S_k)\}}$ for *Risk(nonuniv)* rather than the expression $\sum_{k \in F} p_k \Pr\left\{\bigcup_{i \in \Psi} A_i +\,|\,T-(S_k)\right\}$. The former expression is the one that corresponds to the TTI risk under the non-universal testing scheme, as it represents the proportion of infected blood within the blood pool classified as infection-free (Bish et al. 2014).

5.2.3 Model Formulation

In this setting, given a set of imperfectly reliable tests to select from to detect a set of infections, the primary objective of the decision maker is to minimize the TTI risk (or weighted risk), that is, the conditional probability that the blood unit classified as "infection-free" is in fact infected. The decision maker is resource constrained and may also be concerned about the amount of infection-free blood falsely discarded (*waste*). We model these constraints in the form of a budget constraint on the total test administration cost per unit blood and a waste constraint that limits the fraction of falsely discarded blood.

The mathematical formulations for the universal risk minimization problem (**U-RMP**) and the non-universal risk minimization problem (**N-RMP**) under budget and waste constraints are as follows:

U-RMP:

$$\text{Minimize}_{S \subseteq \Omega} \quad Risk(S) = \Pr\left(\bigcup_{i \in \Psi} A^i + \middle| T - (S) \right) \tag{5.1}$$

$$\text{subject to} \quad \sum_{j \in S} c_j \leq B \tag{5.2}$$

$$Waste = \Pr\left(T + (S) \middle| \bigcap_{i \in \Psi} A^i - \right) \leq \alpha. \tag{5.3}$$

The **U-RMP** model provides a universal testing scheme wherein the optimal test composition is administered to all donated blood units. In the non-universal setting, however, different test compositions can be administered to different proportions of the total blood.

Non-universal risk minimization problem (N-RMP):

$$\text{Minimize}_{\vec{p}} \quad Risk(nonuniv) = \frac{\sum_{k \in F} p_k \Pr\left\{ \bigcup_{i \in \Psi} A^i +, T - (S_k) \right\}}{\sum_{k \in F} p_k \Pr\{ T - (S_k) \}} \tag{5.4}$$

$$\text{subject to} \quad \sum_{k \in F} p_k C_k \leq B \tag{5.5}$$

$$\sum_{k \in F} p_k \Pr\left(T + (S_k) \middle| \bigcap_{i \in \Psi} A^i - \right) \leq \alpha \tag{5.6}$$

$$\sum_{k \in F} p_k = 1 \tag{5.7}$$

$$p_k \geq 0, \quad k \in F. \tag{5.8}$$

5.2.4   Relationship of the Proposed Mathematical Models to Cost-Effectiveness Analysis

Resource allocation problems have long been studied by operations researchers (see, for instance, Brandeau 2004 for excellent review and references). A commonly used formulation that is somewhat related to our problem is the traditional *knapsack* problem, which selects, from a set of candidates, each with a known reward and cost, the optimal set that is budget feasible and that maximizes the total reward (e.g., Brandeau 2004). The classical knapsack problem is as follows:

$$\text{Maximize}_{\bar{x}} \quad \sum_{j \in \Omega} R_j x_j \tag{5.9}$$

$$\text{subject to} \quad \sum_{j \in \Omega} c_j x_j \leq B \tag{5.10}$$

$$x_j \quad \text{binary,} \quad j \in \Omega, \tag{5.11}$$

where all notation is as defined in Section 5.2.1, with the addition that R_j denotes the reward of using intervention j, $j \in \Omega$. Decision variables include binary variables x_j, $j \in \Omega$, which equal 1 if intervention j is included in the optimal set and 0 otherwise. This formulation assumes that rewards of the different interventions have constant returns to scale and are independent (Brandeau 2004; Sendi et al. 2003; Van Hulst et al. 2010), which do not apply in the context of blood screening, as we elaborate in the succeeding text. However, even under these assumptions, the integer knapsack problem in (5.9)–(5.11) remains NP-hard and has been well researched in the literature, with pseudo-polynomial algorithms developed; see, for example, Andonov et al. (2000). Relaxing constraint (5.11), that is, assuming that the interventions are divisible, leads to the linear programming (LP) relaxation of the knapsack problem, whose optimal solution is to allocate the budget to the interventions in order of increasing cost-effectiveness ratios (c_j/R_j) (Dantzig 1957). This allocation rule will result with at most one intervention selected at a fractional level in the optimal set.

In the context of the post-donation test selection decision, interventions correspond to individual tests, and reward R_j may correspond to the measure the decision maker is seeking to minimize, such as the TTI risk (with the objective in Equation 5.9 changed to minimization), or the measure the decision maker is seeking to maximize, such as the number of infections averted or QALY or DALY gained as a result of intervention j. Then, the optimal solution to the LP relaxation of the knapsack problem corresponds to the cost-effectiveness solution, wherein tests are compared with each other in terms of their cost-effectiveness ratio (c_j/R_j); see, for example, Busch et al. 2009), Leiby 2001, Sendi et al. 2003, and Simon et al. (2013). However, as stated previously, the test selection problem for the donated blood setting has unique characteristics and exhibits major differences from the well-studied integer or linear knapsack problems.

Specifically, in the blood testing problem, candidate tests do *not* have constant returns to scale in the objective function (i.e., TTI risk or variations of it), that is, the test's contribution to the TTI risk depends not only on the efficacy of the test itself but also on the efficacy of the *entire* set of tests selected and the decision rule adopted, that is, $R_j(\vec{x})$, $\forall j \in \Omega$. There also exist other complications, as discussed in Section 5.1.2, such as the possibility of non-universal schemes, the need to determine a decision rule and a pooling strategy along with a test set, the need to consider other, possibly conflicting, objectives, such as reducing the amount of blood wasted, etc., under uncertainty in prevalence rates. Even with the test selection problem considered in its most basic form, with all decisions other than the test selection decision removed from the model, the test selection problem falls into the general class of nonlinear knapsack problems with a non-separable objective function, a problem considerably more difficult than other knapsack problems, which has received very limited attention in the literature (see Bretthauer and Shetty 2002 for a review). These characteristics complicate the problem considerably; problems **U-RMP** and **N-RMP** are NP-hard (Bish et al. 2011), and traditional knapsack results do not necessarily apply in this setting. In order to solve these test selection problems, Bish et al. (2011) develop an efficient algorithm for solving a special case of **U-RMP** and propose a near-optimal algorithm with a performance guarantee for the general **U-RMP** and **N-RMP**. We use these solution techniques to solve **U-RMP** and **N-RMP** in the remainder of this chapter.

In the remainder of this chapter, we discuss, through a case study, the implications of accurately modeling these dependencies among the tests and using mathematical programming-based algorithms to optimize the test selection decision.

5.3 THE CASE STUDY OF THE SUB-SAHARAN AFRICA REGION AND THE UNITED STATES

In this section, we summarize the findings from a case study and discuss the implications on the optimal test selection decision. All data sources, models, and algorithms are discussed in detail in Bish et al. (2011, 2014), El-Amine et al. (2016), and Xie et al. (2012).

In the case study, we use realistic data from two regions: sub-Saharan Africa and the United States. These two regions have very different characteristics in terms of infection prevalence rates, resource availability, and infrastructure (see, e.g., Busch et al. 2009; Owusu-Ofori et al. 2010; Van Hulst et al. 2010). Our purpose for considering these two very different regions is to also highlight the major role regional characteristics play in the optimal test selection decision.

In sub-Saharan Africa, an estimated 22.4 million people have HIV infections (around two-thirds of the global total), and the HIV prevalence in this region varies, by country, from 2% to 26% (UNAIDS 2008) (we use 11.25% in our study). HBV, HCV, and HTLV prevalence rates are also high for this region (Kiire 1996; Madhava et al. 2002; Proietti et al. 2005); see Table 5.2. In the United States the prevalence rates are much lower. However, the TTI risk is still non-negligible, as testing for

TABLE 5.2   Prevalence Rates (in %) in Sub-Saharan Africa and the United States (See Bish et al. (2011) for Data References)

	Sub-Saharan Africa	United States
HIV	11.250	0.008
HBV	8.200	0.067
HCV	0.450	0.291
HTLV	3.000	0.010
WNV	1.000	0.010

some emerging infections, such as babesiosis, the leading cause of TTIs in the United States, is not currently mandated by the FDA, but *Babesia* prevalence in the United States is on the rise; see Bish et al. (2015).

The WHO recommends screening for HIV, HBV, HCV, and syphilis (along with other infection based on local conditions) (WHO 2011), while the FDA adds HTLV and Chagas' disease to this list as infections required for screening and recommends screening for WNV (FDA 2014a). In our case study, we consider all infections that are currently required/recommended for screening by the WHO and FDA, except for syphilis and Chagas' disease, which we omit due to a lack of reliable data. Table 5.2 displays the prevalence rates of these infections for sub-Saharan Africa and the United States; see Bish et al. (2014) for data sources and details.

On the test side, we consider all FDA-licensed tests that screen for these infections whose sensitivity and specificity data are publicly available (FDA 2016), and we use the testing cost data in Jackson et al. (2003). The number of tests we consider for HBV, HIV, HCV, WNV, and HTLV are 6, 16, 7, 2, and 2, respectively. These tests represent a wide range of cost and efficacy.

As discussed in Section 5.1.2, WHO and FDA guidelines list the infections that are required/recommended for screening but leave it to the blood collection center to determine which screening tests and testing schemes to perform to be in compliance with these requirements. For all infections considered in the case study, multiple FDA-licensed tests, each with a different cost and efficacy, are available, leading to several test combinations that comply with WHO/FDA requirements. While checking for compliance, for the sub-Saharan Africa region, we consider compliance with the WHO guidelines, and for the United States we consider compliance with the FDA requirements. Specifically, for each region we construct two different testing schemes that comply with the FDA/WHO guidelines: for each infection recommended by the WHO (for the sub-Saharan Africa region) or required by the FDA (for the United States), the blood center selects the lowest cost test under the "min-cost" scheme and selects the risk-minimizing test for each infection under the "min-risk" scheme. These two extreme cases provide ranges for budget requirements and the TTI risk for test schemes that comply with the FDA/WHO guidelines.

Table 5.3 reports, for sub-Saharan Africa, the required budget and the corresponding TTI risk for the min-cost and min-risk test sets that satisfy the WHO

TABLE 5.3 Sub-Saharan Africa Region: *Risk* **Values for Test Sets That Meet the WHO Recommendations and for the Optimal Universal and Optimal Non-universal Test Sets**

	Budget ($)	WHO-Compliant Testing Risk (%)	U-RMP Solution Risk (%)	N-RMP Solution Risk (%)
WHO min-cost	9	5.640	5.640	5.640
WHO min-risk	14	5.320	2.069	1.469

Source: Bish et al. (2014). Reproduced with permission of Taylor & Francis.

TABLE 5.4 United States: *Risk* **Values for Test Sets That Meet the FDA Requirements and for the Optimal universal and Optimal Non-universal Test Sets**

	Budget ($)	FDA-Compliant Testing Risk (%)	U-RMP Solution Risk (%)	N-RMP Solution Risk (%)
FDA min-cost	17	0.0120	0.01148	0.00745
FDA min-risk	22	0.00194	0.00120	0.00120

Source: Bish et al. (2014). Reproduced with permission of Taylor & Francis.

guidelines and the TTI risk corresponding to the optimal universal and optimal non-universal test sets obtained, respectively, by the **U-RMP** and **N-RMP** models at those budget levels. Table 5.4 reports the corresponding results for the United States, with the difference that the required budgets for the min-cost and min-risk test sets are determined in accordance with the FDA requirements. (In the case study, we do not consider the waste constraint in (5.3). However, a constraint on the proportion of wasted blood can be easily added to the formulation; we refer the interested reader to Xie et al. (2012) for a detailed discussion on how *risk* and *waste* figures vary with parameter α.)

From Table 5.3, to follow the WHO guidelines in the sub-Saharan Africa region, the min-risk scheme would cost $14 with a TTI risk of 5.32%, but with this $14 budget **U-RMP** reduces the risk to 2.069% and **N-RMP** reduces it further to 1.469%. We did not impose WHO guidelines in **U-RMP** and **N-RMP**, but in this case, both optimal solutions meet WHO guidelines; they just use less expensive tests for these TTIs, which allows them to include tests for the other prevalent TTIs in this region.

For the United States, from Table 5.4, the FDA requirements can be satisfied with as little as $17 (the min-cost testing scheme), with a risk of 0.0120%, while at the same budget level, **U-RMP** can reduce the risk to 0.01148%, and **N-RMP** can further reduce it to 0.00745%, a considerable reduction. At the min-risk budget of $22, **N-RMP** and **U-RMP** solutions are identical, but their solution differs from the min-risk solution in that two tests for HCV are selected (the TTI having the highest prevalence rate), bringing the risk from 0.00194% down to 0.00120%. These results demonstrate the significant risk reduction that can be achieved through optimization-based models and through non-universal screening schemes.

In summary, this case study highlights the importance of generating region-specific test composition for blood screening that explicitly takes into account the prevalence rates of the TTIs. It also demonstrates that following the WHO and FDA guidelines is no guarantee of an optimal testing regime—sometimes it is better to deviate from the recommendations. Test selection is complex, and always choosing the risk-minimizing test for each infection does not ensure an overall risk-minimizing solution for a given budget level.

5.3.1 Uncertainty in Prevalence Rates

We next discuss the optimal test selection decision when infection prevalence rates are uncertain. In particular, we expand the **U-RMP** formulation by considering an uncertainty set around infection prevalence rates and formulating the test selection decision as a robust optimization problem (El-Amine et al. 2016). In particular, the robust optimization model determines an optimal set of tests to administer to each blood unit so as to minimize the maximum "*Regret*" incurred by committing to a test set without knowledge of the actual prevalence rate in a given year. The robust risk minimization problem (**R-U-RMP**) is as follows:

R-U-RMP:

$$\text{Minimize}_{S \subseteq \Omega} \quad \max_{\vec{\xi} \in \mathcal{U}} \{ Regret(S, \vec{\xi}) \} \tag{5.12}$$

$$\text{subject to} \quad \sum_{j \in S} c_j \leq B, \tag{5.13}$$

where $\vec{\xi} \equiv (\xi_i)_{i \in \Psi}$ denotes a possible realization of the prevalence rate vector for the infections in set Ψ and belongs to a convex uncertainty set $\mathcal{U}$; and $Regret(S, \vec{\xi}) \equiv Risk(S, \vec{\xi}) - Risk(S^*(\vec{\xi}), \vec{\xi})$, with $S^*(\vec{\xi})$ denoting the optimal test set (i.e., with minimum possible *Risk*) corresponding to prevalence vector $\vec{\xi}$, that is, it represents the additional *risk* incurred by committing to a test set S without knowledge of the actual prevalence rate vector, $\vec{\Xi}$. In El-Amine et al. (2016), we develop an exact algorithm to solve **R-U-RMP** for the special case where the uncertainty set, $\mathcal{U}$, has an interval structure, that is, $\mathcal{U} = \left(\left[l_i, u_i \right] \right)_{i \in \Psi}$.

Continuing with the US case study, we compare the robust optimization solution with the min-risk and min-cost testing schemes that comply with the FDA requirements using prevalence rate data on HIV, HBV, HCV, babesiosis, and WNV from the literature. For example, Figure 5.1 presents the variation in *regret* and *risk* for the **R-U-RMP** optimal solution and the FDA min-risk solution when the prevalence rate of each infection is varied over its range. Clearly, the ranges for both *risk* and *regret*

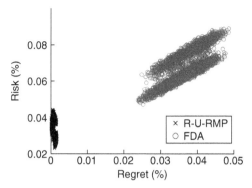

Figure 5.1   Joint distribution of *risk* and *regret*, in percent, between the robust scheme (**R-U-RMP**) and the FDA min-risk scheme.

in the robust testing solution are significantly smaller than those for FDA min-risk policies, underscoring the value of robust optimization in post-donation screening; see El-Amine et al. (2016) for details.

5.4   CONTRIBUTIONS AND FUTURE RESEARCH DIRECTIONS

In this chapter, we review mathematical models for an important problem faced by blood centers of selecting screening tests for donated blood. This decision has a significant impact on healthcare quality in both developed and developing countries. The work reviewed here generates insights on public policy on this important problem.

There are numerous avenues that are worthy of future research effort. An important direction is to expand the mathematical models to incorporate other important characteristics of this problem discussed in Section 5.1.2. There are also important decisions to be made on a broader, health policy, level. For example, no data are perfectly accurate, and the decision maker needs to allocate their limited resources among surveillance efforts (i.e., gathering more accurate data on infection prevalence rates and test reliability measures) and blood screening. While the former provides the decision maker with better information, possibly leading to a test set that better represents reality, the latter actually reduces risk in blood. As a future direction, it is worthwhile to explore this trade-off to devise effective resource allocation schemes among these efforts. Finally, it is important to incorporate the models and algorithms in decision support systems that can aid blood collection centers in their testing decision.

ACKNOWLEDGMENTS

We acknowledge the support of the National Science Foundation through NSF grant #1129688.

REFERENCES

American Association of Blood Banks (2016). "Emerging infectious disease agents and their potential threat to transfusion safety." http://www.aabb.org/tm/eid/Pages/default.aspx. Accessed on February 2016.

American Red Cross (2010). "*Arm to Arm.*" 2nd edition. http://www.redcrossblood.org/sites/arc/files/pdf/Arm_to_Arm_2010.pdf. Accessed on September 2017.

American Red Cross (2014a). "Blood facts and statistics." http://www.redcrossblood.org/learn-about-blood/blood-facts-and-statistics. Accessed on October 2014.

American Red Cross (2014b). "Blood testing." http://www.redcrossblood.org/learn-about-blood/what-happens-donated-blood/blood-testing. Accessed on October 2014.

American Red Cross (2017). "Emergency need for blood donations as Red Cross experiences critical blood shortage." http://www.redcross.org/news/press-release/Emergency-need-for-blood-donations-as-Red-Cross-experiences-critical-blood-shortage. Accessed on September 2017.

Andonov, R., Poirriez, V., and Rajopadhye, S. (2000). "Unbounded knapsack problem: Dynamic programming revisited." *European Journal of Operational Research*, 123 (2), pp. 394–407.

Aprahamian, H., Bish, D.R., and Bish, E.K. (2016). "Adaptive risk-based pooling in public health screening." Working paper. Department of Industrial and Systems Engineering, Virginia Tech, Blacksburg, VA.

Aprahamian, H., Bish, D.R., and Bish, E.K. (2016). "Residual risk and waste in donated blood with pooled nucleic acid testing." *Statistics in Medicine*, 35 (28), pp. 5283–5301.

Arora, D., Arora, B., and Khetarpal, A. (2010). "Seroprevalence of HIV, HBV, HCV and syphilis in blood donors in Southern Haryana." *Indian Journal of Pathology and Microbiology*, 53 (2), p. 308.

Behets, F., Bertozzi, S., Kasali, M., Kashamuka, M., Atikala, L., Brown, C., Ryder, R.W., and Quinn, C. (1990). "Successful use of pooled sera to determine HIV-1 seroprevalence in Zaire with development of cost-efficiency models." *AIDS*, 4, pp. 737–741.

Beutel, J. (2000). *Handbook of Medical Imaging: Medical Image Processing and Analysis.* SPIE Press, Bellingham, WA, 6th edition.

Bish, D.R., Bish, E.K., Xie, S.R., and Slonim, A.D. (2011). "Optimal selection of screening assays for infectious agents in donated blood." *IIE Transactions on Healthcare Systems Engineering*, 1 (2), pp. 67–90.

Bish, D.R., Bish, E.K., Xie, S.R., and Stramer, S.L. (2014). "Going beyond "same-for-all" testing of infectious agents in donated blood." *IIE Transactions*, 46 (11), pp. 1147–1168.

Bish, E.K., Moritz, M.K., El-Amine, H., Bish, D.R., and Stramer, S.L. (2015). "Cost effectiveness of *Babesia microti* antibody and nucleic acid blood donation screening using results from prospective investigational studies." *Transfusion*, 55 (9), pp. 2256–2271.

Brandeau, M.L. (2004). Allocating resources to control infectious diseases. *Operations Research and Health Care: A Handbook of Methods and Applications*, M.L. Brandeau, F. Sainfort, W.P. Pierskalla, eds. Kluwer's International Series, Boston, MA, pp. 443–464.

Bretthauer, K. and Shetty, B. (2002). "The nonlinear knapsack problem—Algorithms and applications." *European Journal of Operational Research*, 138, pp. 459–472.

Burns, K.C. and Mauro, C.A. (1987). "Group testing with test error as a function of concentration." *Communications in Statistics—Theory Methods*, 16, pp. 2821–2837.

Busch, M.P., Glynn, S.A., Stramer, S.L., Strong, D.M., Caglioti, S., Wright, D.J., Pappalardo, B., and Kleinman, S.H. (2005). "A new strategy for estimating risks of transfusion-transmitted viral infections based on rates of detection of recently infected donors." *Transfusion*, 45 (2), pp. 254–264.

Busch, M., Walderhaug, M., Custer, B., Allain, J.P., Reddy, R., and McDonough, B. (2009). "Risk assessment and cost-effectiveness/utility analysis." *Biologicals*, 37, pp. 78–87.

CDC (2012). "Babesiosis surveillance—18 states, 2011." *MMWR. Morbidity and Mortality Weekly Report*, 61 (27), p. 505.

Chak, E., Talal, A.H., Sherman, K.E., Schiff, E.R., and Saab, S. (2011). "Hepatitis C virus infection in the USA: An estimate of true prevalence." *Liver International*, 31 (8), pp. 1090–1101.

Custer, B., Busch, M., Marfin, A.A., and Petersen, L.R. (2005). "The cost-effectiveness of screening the U.S. blood supply for the West Nile Virus." *Annals of Internal Medicine*, 143, pp. 486–492.

Dantzig, G.B. (1957). "Discrete-variable extremum problems." *Operations Research*, 5 (2), pp. 266–288.

Dow, B.C. (2000). "Noise in microbiological screening assays." *Transfusion Medicine*, 10 (2), pp. 97–106.

Dzik, W.H. (2003). "Emily Cooley lecture 2002: Transfusion safety in the hospital." *Transfusion*, 43 (9), pp. 1190–1199.

El-Amine, H., Bish, E.K., and Bish, D.R. (2017). "Robust post-donation blood screening under prevalence rate uncertainty." *Operations Research*, DOI: http://pubsonline.informs.org/doi/10.1287/opre.2017.1658.

El-Amine, H., Bish, E.K., and Bish, D.R. (2017). "Optimal pooling strategies for nucleic acid testing of donated blood considering viral load growth curves and donor characteristics." *IIE Transactions on Healthcare Systems Engineering*, 7, pp. 15–28.

FDA (2014). "Infectious disease test." http://www.fda.gov/BiologicsBloodVaccines/Blood BloodProducts/ApprovedProducts/LicensedProductsBLAs/BloodDonorScreening/ InfectiousDisease/default.htm. Accessed on October 2014.

FDA (2016). "Complete list of donor screening assays for infectious agents and HIV diagnostic assays, 2016." https://www.fda.gov/biologicsbloodvaccines/bloodbloodproducts/ approvedproducts/licensedproductsblas/blooddonorscreening/infectiousdisease/ ucm080466.htm. Accessed on September 2017.

Grassly, N., Morgan, M., Walker, N., Garnett, G., Stanecki, K., Stover, J., Brown, T., and Ghys, P. (2004). "Uncertainty in estimates of HIV/AIDS: The estimation and application of plausibility bounds." *Sexually Transmitted Infections*, 80 (Suppl. 1), pp. i31–i38.

Hay, S.N., Scanga, L., and Brecher, M.E. (2006). "Life, death, and the risk of transfusion: A university hospital experience." *Transfusion*, 46 (9), pp. 1491–1493.

Hayes, E.B., Komar, N., Nasci, R.S., Montgomery, S.P., O'Leary, D.R., and Campbell, G.L. (2005). "Epidemiology and transmission dynamics of West Nile virus disease." *Emerging Infectious Diseases*, 11 (8), pp. 1167–1173.

Herwaldt, B.L., Linden, J.V., Bosserman, E., Young, C., Olkowska, D., and Wilson, M. (2011). "Transfusion-associated babesiosis in the United States: A description of cases." *Annals of Internal Medicine*, 155 (8), pp. 509–519.

Hillyer, C.D. (2001). *Handbook of Transfusion Medicine*. Academic Press, San Diego, CA.

Hwang, F.K. (1976). "Group testing with a dilution effect." *Biometrika*, 63, pp. 671–673.

Jackson, B.R., Busch, M.P., Stramer, S.L., and AuBuchon, J.P. (2003). "The cost-effectiveness of NAT for HIV, HCV, and HBV in whole-blood donations." *Transfusion*, 43, pp. 721–729.

Johnson, C. (2010). "Whose antibodies are they anyway? Factors known to cause false positive HIV antibody test results." http://www.virusmyth.com/aids/hiv/cjtestfp.htm. Accessed on April 2010.

Katz, L.M. (2010). "Joint statement before the blood products advisory committee—Risk of dengue virus infection in blood donors." From the Joint Statement of the AABB, American Red Cross, and America's Blood Centers, Gaithersburg, MD.

Kiire, C.F. (1996). "The epidemiology and prophylaxis of Hepatitis B in sub-Saharan Africa: A view from tropical and subtropical Africa." *Gut*, 38, pp. S5–12.

Kline, R.L., Brothers, T.A., Brookmeyer, R., Zegger, S., and Quinn, T.C. (1989). "Evaluation of Human Immunodeficiency Virus seroprevalence in population surveys using pooled sera." *Journal of Clinical Microbiology*, 27, pp. 1449–1452.

Korves, C.T., Goldie, S.J., and Murray, M.B. (2006). "Cost-effectiveness of alternative blood-screening strategies for West Nile virus in the United States." *PLoS Medicine*, 3 (2), p. e21.

Lefrere, J.J., Coste, J., Defer, C., Loiseau, P., Portelette, E., Mariotti, M., Lerable, J., Rouger, P., and Pawlotsky, J.M. (1998). "Screening blood donations for viral genomes: Multicenter study of real-time simulation using pooled samples on the model of Hepatitis C virus RNA detection." *Transfusion*, 38 (10), pp. 915–923.

Leiby, D.A. (2001). Parasites and other emergent infectious agents. *Blood Safety in the New Millennium*, S.L. Stramer, ed. American Association of Blood Banks, Bethesda, MD, pp. 55–78.

Madhava, V., Burgess, C., and Drucker, E. (2002). "Epidemiology of chronic Hepatitis C Virus infection in sub-Saharan Africa." *The Lancet Infectious Diseases*, 2, pp. 293–302.

Marshall, D.A., Kleinman, S.H., Wong, J.B., AuBuchon, J.P., Grima, D.T., Kulin, N.A., and Weinstein, M.C. (2004). "Cost-effectiveness of Nucleic Acid Test screening of volunteer blood donations for Hepatitis B, Hepatitis C and Human Immunodeficiency Virus in the United States." *Vox Sanguinis*, 86, pp. 28–40.

McFarland, W., Mvere, D., Shandera, W., and Reingold, A. (2003). "Epidemiology and prevention of transfusion-associated Human Immunodeficiency Virus transmission in sub-Saharan Africa." *Vox Sanguinis*, 72 (2), pp. 85–92.

Moore, M.C., Howell, D.R., and Barbara, J.A.J. (2007). "Donors whose blood reacts falsely positive in transfusion microbiology screening assays need not be lost to transfusion." *Transfusion Medicine*, 17 (1), pp. 55–59.

Moritz, E.D., Winton, C.S., Johnson, S.T., Krysztof, D.E., Townsend, R.L., Foster, G.A., Devine, P., Molloy, P., Brissette, E., Berardi, V.P., et al. (2014). "Investigational screening for *Babesia microti* in a large repository of blood donor samples from nonendemic and endemic areas of the United States." *Transfusion*, 54 (9), pp. 2226–2236.

Owusu-Ofori, S., Asenso-Mensah, K., Boateng, P., Sarkodie, F., and Allain, J.P. (2010). "Fostering repeat donations in Ghana." *Biologicals*, 38, pp. 47–52.

Ozekici, S. and Pliska, S. (1991). "Optimal scheduling of inspections: A delayed Markov model with false positive and negatives." *Operations Research*, 39 (2), pp. 261–273.

Pepe, M.S. (2004). *The Statistical Evaluation of Medical Tests for Classification and Prediction*. Oxford University Press, Oxford, U.K.

Proietti, F.A., Carneiro-Proietti, A.B.F., Catalan-Soares, B.C., and Murphy, E.L. (2005). "Global epidemiology of HTLV-I infection and associated diseases." *Oncogene*, 24, pp. 6058–6068.

Raz, T. and Kaspi, M. (1991). "Location and sequencing of imperfect inspection operations in serial multi-stage production systems." *International Journal of Production Research*, 29 (8), pp. 1645–1659.

Schwartz, J.S., Kinosian, B.P., Pierskalla, W.P., and Lee, H. (1990). "Strategies for screening blood for Human Immunodeficiency Virus antibody. Use of a decision support system." *Journal of the American Medical Association*, 264 (13), pp. 1704–1710.

Sendi, P., Al, M.J., Gafni, A., and Birch, S. (2003). "Optimizing a portfolio of healthcare programs in the presence of uncertainty and constrained resources." *Social Science & Medicine*, 57 (9), pp. 2207–2215.

Simon, M.S., Leff, J.A., Pandya, A., Cushing, M., Shaz, B.H., Calfee, D.P., Schackman, B.R., and Mushlin, A.I. (2013). "Cost-effectiveness of blood donor screening for *Babesia microti* in endemic regions of the United States." *Transfusion*, 54 (3 Pt 2), 889–899.

Stramer, S.L., Glynn, S.A., Kleinman, S.H., Strong, D.M., Caglioti, S., Wright, D.J., Dodd, R.Y., and Busch, M.P. (2004). "Detection of HIV-1 and HCV infections among antibody-negative blood donors by nucleic acid-amplification testing." *New England Journal of Medicine*, 351 (8), pp. 760–768.

Stramer, S.L., Fang, C.T., Foster, G.A., Wagner, A.G., Brodsky, J.P., and Dodd, R.Y. (2005). "West Nile virus among blood donors in the United States, 2003 and 2004." *New England Journal of Medicine*, 353 (5), pp. 451–459.

UNAIDS (2008). "Report on the global AIDS epidemic." Technical report. http://www.unaids. org/sites/default/files/media_asset/jc1510_2008globalreport_en_0.pdf. Accessed on September 2017

Van Hulst, M., Hubben, G.A.A., Kwamena, W.C.S., Promwong, C., Permpikul, P., Fongsatikul, L., Glynn, D.M., Sibinga, C.T.S., and Postma, M.J. (2009). "Web interface supported transmission risk assessment and cost-effectiveness analysis of postdonation screening: A global model applied to Ghana, Thailand, and the Netherlands." *Transfusion*, 49, pp. 2729–2742.

Van Hulst, M., Smit Sibinga, C.T., and Postma, M.J. (2010). "Health economics of blood transfusion safety—Focus on sub-Saharan Africa." *Biologicals*, 38 (1), pp. 53–58.

Vannier, E., Gewurz, B.E., and Krause, P.J. (2008). "Human babesiosis." *Infectious Disease Clinics of North America*, 22 (3), pp. 469–488.

Walker, N., Garcia-Calleja, J.M., Heaton, L., Asamoah-Odei, E., Poumerol, G., Lazzari, S., Ghys, P.D., Schwartländer, B., and Stanecki, K.A. (2001). "Epidemiological analysis of the quality of HIV sero-surveillance in the world: How well do we track the epidemic?" *AIDS*, 15 (12), pp. 1545–1554.

Walter, S.D. and Irwig, L.M. (1988). "Estimation of test error rates, disease prevalence, and relative risk from misclassified data: A review." *Journal of Clinical Epidemiology*, 41, pp. 923–937.

Weusten, J., van Drimmelen, H., and Lelie, P.N. (2002). "Mathematical modeling of the risk of HBV, HCV, and HIV transmission by window-phase donations not detected by NAT." *Transfusion*, 42, pp. 537–548.

WHO (2011). "Screening donated blood for transfusion transmissible infections—Recommendations." http://www.who.int/bloodsafety/ScreeningDonatedBloodforTransfusion.pdf. Accessed on January 2011.

WHO (2014). "10 facts on blood transfusion." http://www.who.int/features/factfiles/blood_transfusion/en/. Accessed on October 2014.

WHO (2014). "WHO global database on blood safety and blood safety indicators." World Health Organization, Geneva, Switzerland. http://www.who.int/bloodsafety/global_database/en/. Accessed on October 2014.

Xie, S.R., Bish, D.R., Bish, E.K., Slonim, A.D., and Stramer, S.L. (2012). "Safety and waste considerations in donated blood screening." *European Journal of Operational Research*, 217 (3), pp. 619–632.

6

MODELING CHRONIC HEPATITIS C DURING RAPID THERAPEUTIC ADVANCE: COST-EFFECTIVE SCREENING, MONITORING, AND TREATMENT STRATEGIES

SHAN LIU

Department of Industrial and Systems Engineering, University of Washington, Seattle, WA, USA

6.1 INTRODUCTION

Major infectious diseases such as HIV and viral hepatitis have long latency periods and may lead to adverse health outcomes and death to infected individuals several decades after infection acquisition. Recent advancements in the treatment of these diseases have led to potential cure, or transformed them into manageable lifelong chronic conditions (Ghany et al. 2009). However, treatment regimens for these diseases are often complicated, risky, costly, and/or nonreversible. In this chapter, we discuss relevant methods in decision-analytic modeling and highlight several recently published studies in the design and evaluation of screening, monitoring, and treatment strategies for chronic hepatitis C (HCV) care in the United States.

Chronic HCV is a liver disease affecting approximately 130–170 million people worldwide and 3–4 million Americans (Armstrong et al. 2006). Major HCV

Decision Analytics and Optimization in Disease Prevention and Treatment, First Edition.
Edited by Nan Kong and Shengfan Zhang.
© 2018 John Wiley & Sons, Inc. Published 2018 by John Wiley & Sons, Inc.

infection risk factors include blood transfusion before 1992, injection drug use, and lifestyle factors such as having greater than 20 lifetime sexual partners. More than half of HCV-positive Americans may be unaware of their infection (Armstrong et al. 2006). If untreated, chronic HCV is a slow progressing disease that causes liver fibrosis and end-stage liver diseases. Disease progression is often asymptomatic and can take up to 30 years to cause liver cirrhosis and hepatocellular carcinoma (HCC) (Salomon et al. 2003). The majority of HCV patients in the United States are infected with genotype 1 HCV, which has been historically difficult to treat (Ghany et al. 2011). The first FDA-approved drug, interferon monotherapy, appeared in 1991 with a cure rate below 10% (Alter and Liang 2012). Major breakthroughs in the past two decades have improved treatment effectiveness with additions of pegylated interferon and ribavirin as standard therapy, which required up to 48 weeks with an average 40% cure rate and substantial side effects (anemia, skin rash, depression, etc.). Recent advancements in years 2013–2016 include direct-acting antiviral (DAA) drugs, such as daclatasvir, elbasvir/grazoprevir, ledipasvir/sofosbuvir, ombitasvir/paritaprevir/ritonavir with dasabuvir, and simeprevir; up to 95% of patients with most genotypes of HCV infection going through treatment can now achieve sustained virologic response (SVR), with potential shorter treatment durations (as short as 8 weeks). After decades of brilliant advancement in antiviral drug development, many HCV experts are seeing the possibility of the "beginning of the end" in the battle against HCV (Alter and Liang 2012).

Chronic HCV care delivery, however, is more likely to be at the "end of the beginning" stage. In year 2013, the Centers for Disease Control and Prevention (CDC) and the US Preventive Services Task Force (USPSTF) both recommended a one-time HCV screening for all American adults born between 1945 and 1965 (Smith et al. 2012, Moyer 2013). The unrelenting pace of HCV drug development has caused considerable confusion in the delivery of care. The newest treatments come with substantially higher cost, reduced side effects, and potentially complex viral resistance and drug interaction challenges. The average wholesale price tag of the newer drugs can reach $1,000 per day ($60,000–$100,000 for a course of treatment). The scramble to increase the joint effort in screening and treatment has great potential to improve population health at significant societal cost.

To design and evaluate chronic HCV care policies, recent modeling efforts are mainly cost-effectiveness analysis (CEA) (Gold et al. 1996), which are economic studies comparing the long-term costs and health outcomes of alternative healthcare interventions (e.g., policies on screening and treatment) and new medical technologies (e.g., drugs, procedures, devices, etc.), often using decision-analytic methods (e.g., decision tree, Markov cohort model, Monte Carlo simulation, etc.). A growing literature on stochastic and dynamic models in medical decision making aims to optimize disease screening and treatment decisions over time, typically focusing on uncertainties in the disease process. Method such as Markov decision process (MDP) provides a framework for finding optimal solutions for sequential decision-making problems under uncertainty (Brandeau et al. 2004) and have been used in a variety of health applications including organ transplantation (Alagoz et al. 2004, 2005, 2007, 2010), breast cancer screening and treatment (Maillart et al. 2008, Ayer et al. 2012), HIV therapy sequencing (Shechter et al. 2008), and diabetes treatment (Mason et al. 2012).

This chapter discusses recent decision-analytic modeling research in developing policy guidelines and applied decision theory for the screening, monitoring, and treatment of chronic HCV during a time of rapid therapeutic advances in the United States. This chapter can be used as a guide to model similar research questions in other disease areas using decision-analytic approaches. In Section 6.2, we briefly review some of the modeling choices behind building disease natural history and intervention models and parameter estimation methods with examples on HCV disease progression and mortality rate estimation. Section 6.3 is organized into four sections. The first two sections highlight several CEA using decision-analytic Markov models to evaluate alternative HCV care interventions. The next two sections examine the optimal treatment adoption decisions from the patient's perspective and the optimal treatment delivery decisions under resource constraints from the health-care system's perspective. Concluding remarks are made in Section 6.4.

6.2 METHOD

CEA can be conducted under a decision-analytic modeling framework (Figure 6.1). It evaluates healthcare interventions by using mathematical models to simulate the disease natural history and interventions' effect to project the long-term outcomes of each strategy under consideration. Outcomes are typically expressed as expected number of events occurred (e.g., number of liver transplant, cases of liver cancer), lifetime costs, quality-adjusted life years (QALYs) gained, and incremental cost-effectiveness ratios (ICERs). These models are compact representations of reality

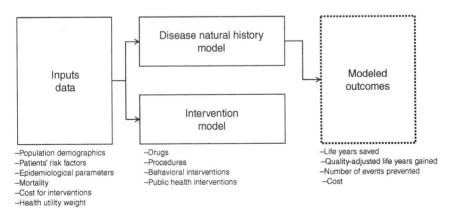

Figure 6.1 Decision-analytic modeling framework.

and are used to simulate infeasible experiments, explore a large number of alternative scenarios, extrapolate from intermediate endpoint to downstream health outcomes beyond clinical trials, compare different interventions using common measures, and inform decision in the absence of data (Buxton et al. 1997). They are most appropriate at early stages of designing new health interventions. Recently updated panel recommendations on conducting CEA in health and medicine can be found in Sanders et al. (2016).

The methods for conducting CEA studies include decision tree, Markov cohort model, and microsimulation. They appear to be deceptively simple at first glance; however, high-quality CEA studies are difficult to achieve due to the following methodological challenges (Caro et al. 2012):

1. Accurately capturing the heterogeneity in the target population by patient demographic and clinical characteristics, disease severity, and mortality that are appropriate to the decision problem. Additional stratification requires more data for parameter estimation and leads to increasingly complex model structure.

2. Accurately capturing sufficient details of the proposed interventions (i.e., prevention, screening, diagnostics, monitoring, treatment) to estimate their benefit and harm while preserving model transparency and computational efficiency. These details include frequency of service, treatment processes (drug dose, treatment duration, side effect, adherence), patients' flow throughout the care chain, medical personnel requirement, and effects on quality of life and cost.

3. Extrapolating beyond observed data to estimate long-term health outcomes (e.g., patient's lifetime) and estimating achievable treatment effectiveness in real-life practices as opposed to reported efficacy from controlled clinical trial settings.

4. Estimating disease natural history parameters given incomplete data.

5. Conducting systematic sensitivity analyses that include testing deterministic, probabilistic, and structural assumptions.

We encountered all of the aforementioned challenges in modeling chronic HCV interventions. We discuss several modeling choices and parameter estimation methods in the next section.

6.2.1 Modeling Disease Natural History and Intervention

Making the appropriate modeling choice to simulate the underlying disease natural history and intervention effect is a vital step before designing effective interventions. We provide a brief overview on several common modeling approaches here.

6.2.1.1 Discrete-Time Markov Chains (DTMC) Discrete-time Markov chain (DTMC) is the most common method used in decision-analytic models to simulate long-term outcomes of chronic diseases (Craig and Sendi 2002). It assumes that a patient is always in one of a finite number of discrete health states that are mutually

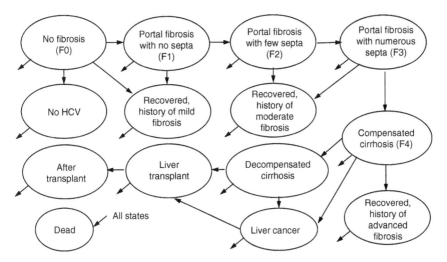

Figure 6.2 Markov model for chronic HCV.

exclusive and collectively exhaustive. All events are represented as transitions from one state to another. One key assumption of a Markov model is called the Markov property, which means that given the current state and the past states, the conditional probability of transiting to the next state is independent of past states and depends only on the current state.

For example, chronic HCV natural history can be modeled as a nonstationary (time-dependent) DTMC that simulates HCV disease progression (see Figure 6.2). The modeled cohort starts with a distribution of liver fibrosis stages characterized by the Metavir scoring system that represents the degree of liver damage from F0 (no fibrosis) to F4 (compensated cirrhosis). Successful treatment shifts people into recovered states that are stratified by their prior liver damage. Unsuccessfully treated patients continue to progress to end-stage liver diseases such as decompensated cirrhosis and liver cancer. Both patients with decompensated cirrhosis and liver cancer may receive liver transplants. Death can occur from any state. In Figure 6.2, each bubble represents a Markov state, and each arrow represents a transition probability.

6.2.1.2 Hidden Markov Model (HMM)   We often do not observe the true underlying disease transition dynamics. In a hidden Markov model (HMM), disease progression is assumed to be a Markov process with unobserved/hidden states. The sequence of health state transition is not directly observable, but the output of some screening/diagnostic tests that correlate with the health state is observable. Each state has a probability distribution over the possible test scores. Therefore the sequence/trajectory of test scores generated by an HMM provides the basis for inferring the true underlying disease transition. HMM makes an assumption that the system is Markovian, which means the probability of transitioning in the hidden state does not depend on the amount of time already spent in the current state. In cases that this assumption may not hold, a hidden semi-Markov model (HSMM) assumes the probability of there being a transition in the hidden state depends on the amount of time that has elapsed since entering into the current state. HSMM is Markovian only at the specified transition instants. The HSMM structure requires more advanced solution method (Titman and Sharples 2010).

6.2.1.3 Continuous-Time Markov Chain (CTMC)

A continuous-time Markov chain (CTMC) allows a patient to spend a continuous amount of time in any state, but in such a way as to retain the Markov property by assuming the length of time spent in a state (i.e., sojourn time) is exponentially distributed. There are some recent works on using CTMC and latent Markov models to estimate disease progression (Lange and Minin 2013). In Lang and Minin's study, the assumption of exponential sojourn time distributions of the Markov property is questioned, and multiple latent states mapping to each disease state are proposed. A successful application of a continuous-time progression model can be seen in estimating the progression of chronic obstructive pulmonary disease (COPD) (Wang et al. 2014).

6.2.1.4 Markov Decision Process (MDP)

MDP is a method used for sequential decision making in an uncertain environment. The goal is to find an optimal policy that tells the decision maker what to do in any situation when the outcomes of actions are uncertain over time. MDP consisted of the state transition dynamics (e.g., how the disease evolves over time), the state of the system (e.g., liver fibrosis stage), the action in each period (e.g., treatment or no treatment), the uncertainty or disturbance of the system (e.g., uncertain disease progression), and the reward associated with the state and action (e.g., QALYs). The policy consists of the action in each decision period, which is a function of the state (e.g., treatment decisions in all states and in all periods).

For example, if we are interested in finding the liver fibrosis stage-dependent optimal time to initiate HCV treatment, optimal treatment initiation can be modeled as an optimal stopping problem under the MDP framework. In a finite-horizon MDP, decisions are made in N period; these types of models are common in the technology adoption literature (Smith and McCardle 2002, Smith and Ulu 2012). Finite-horizon MDP can be solved by backward induction (i.e., solving the Bellman equations backward in time to obtain the optimal policy). Infinite-horizon MDP may require stricter assumptions on stationary transitions to be solved by value iteration and policy iteration (e.g., age-dependent mortality and disease progression rates may be problematic). Higher-dimensional MDP is also of interest and has been studied in liver transplantation (Sandikci et al. 2008).

6.2.2 Estimating Parameters for Disease Progression and Death

Estimating parameter values from observed data can be challenging due to limitations on the length and frequency of observation time, missing data, censored observations, and heterogeneity in the population. This topic has been extensively studied in statistics, machine learning, and medical informatics. We provide a brief discussion on several common approaches here.

6.2.2.1 *Markov Models* For DTMC, the transition probability matrix that describes disease progression is often estimated from observing a cohort of patients at common time intervals. When the cycle length of the model coincides with the observation interval and assuming the model is time-homogeneous, the observed transitions between different periods can be pooled to form a transition count matrix. The maximum likelihood estimate of the transition matrix is the row proportions of the count matrix. When the cycle length does not coincide with the observation interval, a matrix decomposition method can be used. If the observation intervals are unequal in length, the expectation–maximization (EM) algorithm can be applied to impute the missing data and obtain the maximum likelihood estimators (Craig and Sendi 2002). For HMM, the best set of state transition probabilities and output probability given a sequence of observations can be estimated using the Baum–Welch algorithm, which derives a local maximum likelihood estimate of the parameters of the HMM.

6.2.2.2 *Curving Fitting from Individual-Level Data* If only individual-level data are collected at irregular times, which are common in electronic health record outside of clinical trials and observational studies, one method to impute disease transitions is through curve fitting on individual observations (e.g., least-squares linear model, cubic smoothing spline, etc.) and then partition each curve into desired time intervals. Next we count the number of transitions from each disease state to the other state at each chosen time interval and create a transition probability matrix of movements between disease states (Shechter 2006). Successful applications of this method can be seen in modeling CD4 count decline in HIV patients (Shechter et al. 2008).

6.2.2.3 *Empirical Calibration* When population mean parameter values are not observable and both individual-level and cohort data are limited, we can use empirical calibration methods to reduce uncertainties. Calibration compares model outputs with empirical data as calibration targets (e.g., population disease prevalence and mortality rates). A number of different sets of plausible parameter estimates can be generated to fit the observed data, and these sets are selected by one or multiple goodness-of-fit metric (e.g., least squares, chi-squared, and the likelihood). Parameter search methods include grid search, random search (e.g., Latin hypercube), gradient method, Nelder–Mead, and simulated annealing, etc. (Vanni et al. 2011). Other Bayesian methods such as Markov chain Monte Carlo (MCMC) can also be used to generate a sample from the joint posterior density function of the model parameters (Vanni et al. 2011). Successful applications of empirical calibration can be seen in estimating the natural history of human papillomavirus (HPV) and cervical cancer (Goldhaber-Fiebert et al. 2010), as well as chronic HCV progression (Salomon et al. 2002).

Next, we show two parameter estimation examples in HCV modeling.

TABLE 6.1   Fibrosis Progression: Annual Probabilities; Mean (Ranges)

Salomon et al.		Thein et al.	
Age	Males	Fibrosis Stage	Random Effects Model Meta-Regression (All 111 Studies)
40–49	0.05 (0.03–0.09)	F0–F1	0.117 (0.107–0.127)
50–59	0.12 (0.07–0.14)	F1–F2	0.085 (0.078–0.093)
60–69	0.20 (0.12–0.30)	F2–F3	0.121 (0.112–0.130)
>70	0.26 (0.14–0.38)	F3–F4	0.115 (0.107–0.123)
Age	Females		
40–49	0.03 (0.01–0.06)		
50–59	0.06 (0.03–0.11)		
60–69	0.11 (0.04–0.21)		
70–79	0.14 (0.08–0.24)		
>80	0.20 (0.08–0.30)		

6.2.2.3.1   Estimating State Transition Probabilities   In the literature, two frequently cited chronic HCV disease progression parameters set are from studies done by Salomon et al. (2002) and Thein et al. (2011). Salomon et al. developed an epidemiologic model of HCV infection in the US population, which includes acquisition of infection, persistence, and progression (Salomon et al. 2002). Using empirical calibration, age- and sex-specific progression rates of liver fibrosis were obtained by matching model predictions with available data on infection prevalence and mortality from liver cancer. Thein et al. conducted a systematic review and meta-analysis of published prognostic studies and derived the annual stage-specific transition probabilities using Markov maximum likelihood estimation (Thein et al. 2011). The results of the two studies are shown in Table 6.1. The two parameter sets are similar after considering age and fibrosis stage differences in the two studies.

6.2.2.3.2   Estimating Mortality Rates   Quantifying mortality rates of HCV-positive individuals allows for more accurate estimates of the potential benefits of HCV interventions. CEA of expanded HCV screening and treatment require methods to appropriately quantify patients' differential mortality risks. No single study in the literature has provided sufficient data to estimate subgroup-specific prevalence of HCV, risk factor status, and mortality risks that a modeler would need for his/her desired study population. Therefore, we provided a combined modeling approach to infer risk-group-specific mortality rates for chronically HCV-infected US adults (Liu et al. 2013, Liu et al. 2014a). Estimates from public health data are incorporated into an alive–dead Markov model structure to infer the age-, sex-, race-, risk-, and HCV infection status-specific mortality rates that best fit the overall US age-specific population mortality rates. See Figure 6.3.

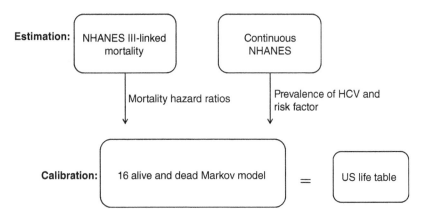

Figure 6.3 A method for creating 16 life tables by sex (male, female), race (white, black), HCV infection status (positive, negative), and risk status (high, low).

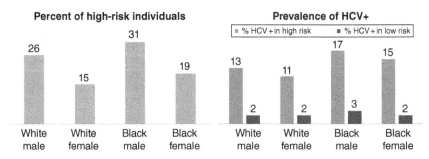

Figure 6.4 Risk factors and HCV prevalence in birth cohort 1952–1961 (birth year).

STATISTICAL ANALYSES ON HCV PREVALENCE AND RISK FACTORS   We estimated the prevalence of risk factors and the prevalence of HCV among high- and low-risk individuals stratified by age, sex, and race using data from the US National Health and Nutrition Examination Survey (NHANES) (2001–2008). We defined a high-risk person as someone having a history of injection drug use, transfusion prior to 1992, or greater than 20 lifetime sex partners. We combined all survey years to estimate prevalence for the 1952–1961 birth cohort in the base case using the 1962–1971 birth-cohort prevalence in sensitivity analyses ($n = 5654$). We used logistic regression to predict the prevalence of being high risk based on sex, race, and age accounting for sample weighting and NHANES complex sampling design. Similarly, we used logistic regression to predict the prevalence of individuals with HCV antibodies using sex, race, risk status, and age. We estimated HCV antibody prevalence for subgroups above age 40. Depending on subgroup, 15%–31% are high risk, and HCV antibody prevalence is higher for high-risk individuals (11%–17%) compared with low-risk individuals (2%–3%) (Liu et al. 2014a). See Figure 6.4.

STATISTICAL ANALYSES ON BACKGROUND MORTALITY   We developed a combined modeling approach to infer risk-group-specific mortality rates for chronically HCV-infected US adults. We analyzed the NHANES III-linked mortality data in which HCV status was assessed from 1988 to 1994 with mortality follow-up of the same persons through year 2006 ($n = 15,892$). We constructed Cox proportional hazard models to estimate the mortality hazard ratios for all-cause death by sex, race, HCV, risk status, interaction between HCV and risk status, age, and age-squared variables for people between ages 17 and 60, excluding cases with missing risk information. Controlling for age, we used four hazard ratios (male, black, HCV positive, and high risk) to calculate the 16 mortality hazard ratios. See Table 6.2. Result showed that all-cause mortality rates are higher in men (HR, 1.3 [1.1–1.7]); blacks (HR, 1.7 [1.5–2.1]); high-risk individuals (HR, 1.4 [1.0–1.9]); and HCV-infected individuals (HR, 3.5 [2.0–6.0]). To adjust for non-liver-related death, we adjusted the ratio for HCV infection down using a factor of 0.8 since it is estimated that for HCV-infected individuals, 20% of mortality is liver related (Liu et al. 2014a).

Using the 16 estimated hazard ratios, we calculated the population-weighted average mortality to match the 2006 US life table over ages 50–100 based on the prevalence of HCV and risk status by sex and race from NHANES (2001–2008) data analyses and the US 2009 census distribution for people aged 50–54 (non-black male 44%, non-black female 45%, black male 5%, and black female 6%). See Figure 6.3. To avoid overestimation of death in the older ages, we linearly attenuated the 16 hazard ratios starting from age 70 down to 1.0 by age 100. We inferred sixteen life tables by sex, race, risk, and HCV infection status. Result showed that within each subgroup, the life expectancy of high-risk individuals is up to 3 years shorter; similarly, the life expectancy of chronically HCV-infected individuals is up to 9 years shorter. The life expectancy of a 50-year-old individual is shown in Figure 6.5.

TABLE 6.2   Mortality Hazard Ratios

	Overall (95% CI)		
Male	1.32 (1.05–1.66)		
Black	1.74 (1.45–2.10)		
HCV positive	3.46 (2.00–5.97)		
High risk (≥20 sex partners)	1.41 (1.03–1.91)		
Males	**White**		**Black**	
	<20 sex partners	≥20 sex partners	<20 sex partners	≥20 sex partners
No HCV	1.32	1.85	2.29	3.23
HCV	3.64	5.12	6.34	8.92
Females	**White**		**Black**	
	<20 sex partners	≥20 sex partners	<20 sex partners	≥20 sex partners
No HCV	1	1.41	1.74	2.45
HCV	2.76	3.89	4.81	6.77

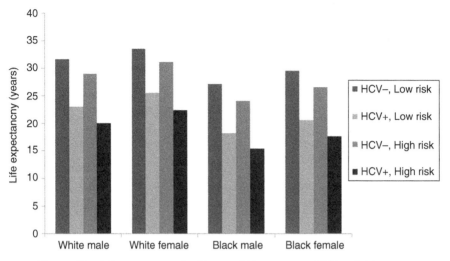

Figure 6.5   Life expectancy of a 50-year-old by sex, race, HCV, and risk status.

6.3   FOUR RESEARCH AREAS IN DESIGNING EFFECTIVE HCV INTERVENTIONS

In this section, we first discuss several CEAs that used decision-analytic models to provide policy guidance on the design of HCV care interventions (Liu 2013). Next, we highlight two optimization studies that modeled the HCV treatment adoption and delivery decisions from the patient's perspective and the healthcare system's perspective.

6.3.1   Cost-Effective Screening and Treatment Strategies

Back in year 2011, no consensus existed on a national HCV screening guideline to detect the estimated two million Americans who are unaware of their chronic HCV infections. Advisory groups differ, recommending birth-cohort screening for baby boomers, screening only high-risk individuals, or no screening. We evaluated risk-based versus birth-cohort HCV screening to identify previously undiagnosed 40–74-year-olds given newly available HCV treatments in Liu et al. (2013). The study aimed to inform health policy makers on whether the United States should be investing healthcare resources in large-scale population screening for HCV infection. Contemporary studies have shown that screening and treatment for chronic HCV are generally cost-effective, though the answer depends on treatment efficacy, drug costs, patients' initial disease stage, and adherence to treatment (Liu et al. 2011, 2012, 2013, Rein et al. 2011, Kabiri et al. 2014).

We assessed screening strategies in combination with treatment strategies (Figure 6.6). Screening strategies included (Liu et al. 2013):

(i) No screening: No systematic screening but HCV-infected individuals may receive treatment after chance identification.

(ii) Risk factor guided screening: HCV screening is only offered to individuals classified as "high risk" through an imperfect assessment of their risk history.

(iii) Birth-cohort screening: All individuals are offered HCV screening in the specified birth cohort.

Treatment-eligible, chronically infected individuals have their HCV infection genotyped. Three response-guided treatment strategies for HCV genotype 1 infected patients were:

(i) Standard therapy: Patients receive pegylated interferon with ribavirin.

(ii) Universal triple therapy: Patients receive pegylated interferon with ribavirin and a protease inhibitor.

(iii) IL-28B-guided triple therapy: Using IL-28B genotyping, non-CC-type patients receive triple therapy because they are less likely to respond on standard therapy, and CC-type patients receive standard therapy.

Standard and triple therapy treatments employ specific response-guided protocols (Liu et al. 2012). In all cases, patients diagnosed with genotype 2 and 3 receive

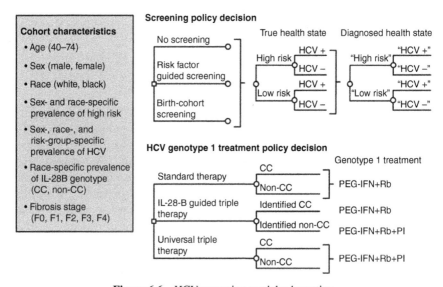

Figure 6.6 HCV screening model schematics.

24 weeks of standard therapy. Mortality rates were estimated using the method described in Section 6.2.2.3.2 for each sex, race, HCV status, and risk status subgroups.

For downstream treatment strategies, we also assessed the cost-effectiveness of protease inhibitors and an IL-28B genotyping assay to target treatment for chronic HCV patients in Liu et al. (2012). We found that both universal triple therapy and IL-28B-guided triple therapy are cost-effective with the least expensive protease inhibitor for patients with advanced fibrosis. After combining screening strategies with downstream treatment options, we found that screening all individuals aged 40–64 costs less than $100,000 per QALY gained (Liu et al. 2013). The cost-effectiveness of one-time birth-cohort HCV screening for 40–64-year-olds is comparable with that of other screening programs, provided that the healthcare system has sufficient capacity to deliver prompt treatment and appropriate follow-on care to many newly screen-detected individuals. Results from this study contributed to national guideline change. In year 2013, CDC and USPSTF both recommended a one-time HCV screening for all American adults born between 1945 and 1965 (Smith et al. 2012, Moyer 2013).

6.3.2   Cost-Effective Monitoring Guidelines

Previous HCV treatment guidelines recommended only initiating treatment when a patient has demonstrated significant liver fibrosis progression from a liver biopsy result. Liver biopsy is the gold standard for assessing liver fibrosis and is used as a benchmark for initiating chronic HCV treatment, though it is expensive and carries risks of complications. FibroTest, a noninvasive biomarker assay for fibrosis, has been proposed as a screening alternative to biopsy. We assessed whether a noninvasive biomarker could be used as a cost-effective alternative fibrosis assessment and monitoring tool and whether the recommended treatment delay is beneficial (Liu et al. 2011). We modeled six strategies of FibroTest and liver biopsy used alone or sequentially, with different interpretations on FibroTest cutoff thresholds and follow-up frequencies. See Figure 6.7.

Results from the decision-analytic model showed that treatment of chronic HCV without fibrosis screening is preferred for both men and women. In clinical settings where testing is required prior to treatment, FibroTest is more effective and less costly than liver biopsy. We concluded that early treatment of chronic HCV is superior to the other fibrosis monitoring strategies, especially with newly FDA-approved, highly effective HCV drugs (Liu et al. 2011).

6.3.3   Optimal Treatment Adoption Decisions

New medical interventions and technologies are frequently evaluated using CEA. However, the majority of such analyses ignore the influence of future technology improvement on the current treatment adoption decision. In this section, we discuss

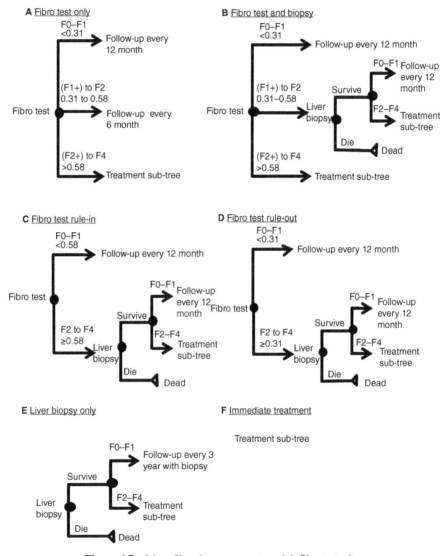

Figure 6.7   Liver fibrosis assessment model: Six strategies.

a modeling study that considers the question of how long a patient with a treatable chronic disease should wait for more effective treatments to emerge before accepting the best available treatment (Liu et al. 2017).

When an individual becomes ill, the action is usually immediate treatment. However, in situations where a slow progressing chronic disease that can take several decades to cause any major morbidity and mortality, and if the current treatment has low effectiveness or high risk of side effects, the decision on immediate treatment is less clear.

In the case of chronic HCV, only 5 years ago there was still a debate among physicians on limited evidence of long-term mortality benefits of treatment, and screening guidelines recommended no screening in the general US population. The previous treatment guidelines recommended patients with genotype 1 HCV to start treatment when there is evidence of significant fibrosis progression (F2+). With more effective drugs, early treatment has the benefit of halting disease progression, while late treatment at the F4 stage may show a decrease in treatment efficacy. Patients' baseline characteristics (sex, age, race, lifestyle factors, genetic difference, disease severity, likelihood of adherence to treatment, comorbidities, prior treatment failures) affect their rate of disease progression and likelihood of treatment success; thus they may receive differential benefits from waiting for better drugs. The study's objective is to find HCV patients' optimal treatment adoption decisions given uncertainty about future technological progress in a stylized decision theoretical model (Liu et al. 2017).

We modeled the patient-level treatment adoption decision problem as an optimal stopping problem using a discrete-time finite-horizon MDP. A patient with a given chronic disease visits a physician periodically to monitor disease progression and determine whether to start treatment during the visit or else to continue waiting. Treatment effectiveness is improving over time with some known probability distribution. At each visit the patient's current health and future expected health and the current best available treatment are known. If the patient decides to adopt treatment in any given period, a terminal reward (e.g., expected QALYs) is received and the process terminates. If the patient decides to wait, an immediate reward (e.g., quality-adjusted time until the next doctor visit) is accumulated for this period, and the patient reevaluates the treatment decision in the next period. The patient's disease progression is deterministic and fully observable, and the chronic disease alone does not substantially increase the patient's mortality rate during the decision horizon. If the patient fails treatment, retreatment is not considered (e.g., retreatment for HCV was less common due to low effectiveness among nonresponders and long treatment duration, especially with the older drugs). The objective is to maximize expected total health benefit for the patient. The notations are as follows:

- N: Number of time periods; decision horizon.
- k: Index for discrete time periods, $k = \{0, 1, \ldots, N-1\}$.
- T: A terminal state indicating that the patient has already been treated.
- p_k: State of the system; p_k denotes treatment effectiveness in period k when the patient has not been treated, expressed as the probability that the treatment will cure the patient's disease; $p_k \in [0,1]$. If the patient has been treated, $p_k = T$.
- w_k: Improvement in treatment effectiveness in period k; $w_k \sim U[0, \theta(1-p_k)]$, where θ can be considered as a variable to characterize the range of belief on the bound of future treatment improvement. $0 < \theta \le 1$.
- u_k: Decision variable for time k; $u_k = 1$ treat at time k, $u_k = 0$ wait.
- q_k: Reward in period k without treatment; this represents the patient's current health.

- H_k: Expected total future health reward if treatment accepted in period k is successful (e.g., expected quality-adjusted life expectancy).
- F_k: Expected total future health reward if treatment accepted in period k is unsuccessful (e.g., expected quality-adjusted life expectancy).
- $f_k(p_k, w_k, u_k)$: Function that describes the system dynamics; $p_{k+1} = f_k(p_k, w_k, u_k)$.
- $g_k(p_k, w_k, u_k)$: Reward function for period k, $k = \{0, 1, \ldots, N-1\}$.
- $g_N(p_N)$: Reward function for period N.
- $V_k(p_k)$: Value function for period k.

Using this notation, the system state dynamics are (see Figure 6.8)

$$p_{k+1} = f_k(p_k, w_k, u_k), \quad k = 0, 1, \ldots, N-1$$

where f_k is defined as

$$p_{k+1} = \begin{cases} T, & \text{if } p_k = T, \text{ or } \text{ if } p_k \neq T \text{ and } u_k = 1\,(\text{treat}) \\ p_k + w_k, & \text{otherwise} \end{cases}$$

The reward function to be maximized is

$$\mathrm{E}_{w_k} \left\{ g_N(p_N) + \sum_{k=0}^{N-1} g_k(p_k, w_k, u_k) \right\}, \quad k = 0, 1, \ldots, N-1$$

where

$$g_N(p_N) = \begin{cases} p_N H_N + (1 - p_N) F_N, & \text{if } p_N \neq T \\ 0, & \text{otherwise} \end{cases}$$

$$g_k(p_k, w_k, u_k) = \begin{cases} p_k H_k + (1 - p_k) F_k, & \text{if } p_k \neq T \text{ and } u_k = 1\,(\text{treat}) \\ q_k, & \text{if } p_k \neq T \text{ and } u_k = 0\,(\text{wait}) \\ 0, & \text{otherwise} \end{cases}$$

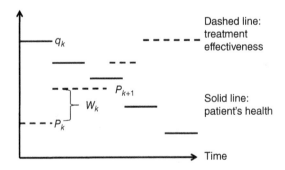

Figure 6.8 Patient's health and technology change over time.

We write the optimal value functions as

$$V_N\left(p_N\right)=\begin{cases}p_N H_N +\left(1-p_N\right)F_N, & \text{if } p_N \neq T \\ 0, & \text{if } p_N = T\end{cases}$$

$$V_k\left(p_k\right)=\begin{cases}\max\left[p_k H_k +\left(1-p_k\right)F_k, q_k + E\left\{V_{k+1}\left(p_{k+1}\right)\right\}\right], & \text{if } p_k \neq T \\ 0, & \text{if } p_k = T\end{cases} \quad (6.1)$$

We derived structural properties of the optimal solution and solved a three-period problem analytically using backward induction. We then applied the model to an example of chronic HCV treatment decisions for patients with various demographic characteristics (Liu et al. 2017). Results showed that HCV patients should be more willing to accept immediate treatment when they are older, sicker (i.e., higher fibrosis stage), or have high comorbidities, assuming non-decreasing future treatment effectiveness with a uniform distribution on the amount of treatment improvement in each period (e.g., no prior information on the new drug's effectiveness). This research demonstrates that analyses using non-dynamic models that find relatively ineffective treatments to be cost-effective for immediate use may suggest a suboptimal decision, especially for patients with minimal disease progression, and in situations where large increases in treatment effectiveness are expected based on current clinical trials' report. It also provides a framework for modeling optimal treatment decisions for a chronic disease when treatments are improving over time.

6.3.4   Optimal Treatment Delivery in Integrated Healthcare Systems

Management of HCV care delivery is particularly relevant to integrated healthcare systems that are under severe budget and/or capacity constraints. Two examples of such healthcare systems may come to mind, both of which address to the healthcare needs of vulnerable populations in the United States. The first example is the Veterans Health Administration (VHA)—the largest single provider of HCV cares in the nation. Over 189,000 veterans were diagnosed with chronic HCV from 2000 to 2008 (Goldhaber-Fiebert et al. 2013). The second example is incarcerated populations (Liu et al. 2014a). Over 500,000 estimated individuals living with chronic HCV infections are currently incarcerated in federal, state, and local correctional facilities (many are unidentified due to low screening rate). It is estimated that 12%–35% prisoners are infected with HCV—nearly 10 times the overall population prevalence (Chak et al. 2011, Spaulding and Thomas 2012, Larney et al. 2013). Recent research has shown that it is cost-effective to treat veterans and prisoners using the newest DAAs, but affordability is a significant issue (Liu et al. 2014b, 2016). Research on how to optimally allocate limited resources for screening and treatment in these integrated healthcare systems could shed some light on this major targeted public health opportunity. To date, few studies have examined the interaction and trade-offs between screening and treatment decisions of chronic HCV patients under budget/capacity constraints of an integrated healthcare system. An interesting research question is to design a general model framework to answer systematic care delivery questions in situations where basic science is close to finding a cure for a disease, and healthcare systems need to find the best care strategies to maximize both individuals and population health during the rapid ramp-up period of screening and treatment toward full control or eradication of the disease.

Resource allocation decisions in healthcare are often modeled using linear and nonlinear optimization method such as mixed-integer programming (MIP). Two relevant studies are done by Deo et al. In the first study, the authors explored the optimal fraction of patients to be screened and treated for HIV and the optimal staffing level in the Veterans Affairs (VA) healthcare chain under a one-year look-ahead budget planning horizon (Deo et al. 2015). The authors used a nonlinear MIP model to maximize patients' health. The study did not consider treatment priorities between patients. The second study combined healthcare operations and clinical disease progression to optimize and evaluate care pathways (Deo et al. 2013). The study aimed to improve access to community-based chronic care using a finite-horizon stochastic dynamic program, solved by a myopic heuristic. On the question of determining treatment priority, healthcare systems typically treat patients on a first-come-first-serve (FCFS) basis. In the organ transplantation literature, the equity–efficiency trade-off using simulation and priority queuing has been extensively studied (Su and Zenios 2006). One recent study also investigated setting HCV treatment priorities in the general US population (Cipriano et al. 2017).

The objective is to determine optimal implementation strategies for screening and treatment in HCV birth cohorts (born 1945–1975) to maximize population health during the next 10 years from the US healthcare payer's perspective under spending budget constraints (Li et al. 2017). Figure 6.9 illustrates the various components of the integrated HCV care management system.

The main components of the system are the target screening population with unknown HCV status; the HCV+ population who are the treatment candidates, which consist of both the treatment-naïve group (never previously treated for HCV infection) and the treatment-experienced group (previously failed HCV treatment); and the HCV– population who know they are either not infected through screening or cleared past infections through treatment or spontaneous viral clearance. Screening programs can identify additional HCV+ individuals who become treatment candidates. Patients from the treatment-naïve group who fail treatment will join the treatment-experienced group. Patients who are successfully treated will join the HCV-treated group. Individuals who are infection-free are susceptible to HCV reinfection; their risk of reinfection depends on age and lifestyle factors. Once reinfected or uncertain about HCV status, individuals again become targets for screening, though this process is often unobservable.

We developed a compartmental simulation model incorporating an MDP of chronic HCV natural history that mimics HCV transmission, progression, screening, treatment, and death in the healthcare system. The model can project the societal

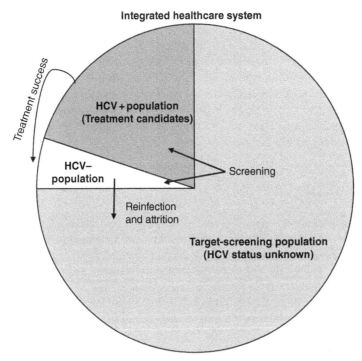

Figure 6.9 Model schematic of an integrated HCV care management system.

benefit measured by the total discounted QALYs of the targeted birth cohorts with given budget limits and optimized screening and treatment implementation scenarios. At the beginning of each time period (e.g., quarterly), a manager needs to decide on the targeted numbers to screen and treat, or a proportion of the budget allocated to screening versus treatment for the current period. Resource constraint ensures only a moderate proportion of treatment candidates will receive treatment per period. Any resource spent on screening is resource away from treatment. The goal is to maximize population lifetime health over a planning horizon (i.e., 10 years) under a budget/capacity constraint per period. Depending on the number of decision periods, it is methodologically challenging to solve this sequential decision-making problem. Advanced methods in simulation optimization were explored in developing novel solution algorithm to solve this problem (Huang et al. 2016).

We investigated a moderate budget ($5 billion/year) scenario and a low budget ($1 billion/year) scenario for three birth cohorts born between 1945 and 1975 (Li et al. 2017). Result showed that the best policy is to allocate a percentage of the budget to screening and then treat patients with the remaining budget and prioritize the sickest patients for treatment. When the budget is $1 billion/year, the best strategy is to allocate the entire budget to treatment. When the budget is $5 billion/year, it is optimal to allocate 60% of the budget to screening in the first 2 years and 0% thereafter for age cohort 40–49 and allocate 20% of the budget to screening starting in year 3 for age cohorts 50–59 and 60–69 under a 10-year planning horizon. We concluded that when budget is severely limited, all efforts should be focused on early treatment. With higher budget, better population health outcomes are achieved by reserving some budget for HCV screening while implementing a priority-based treatment strategy. This work has broad applicability to diverse healthcare systems and can help determine how much effort should be devoted to screening versus treatment under resource limitations.

6.4   CONCLUDING REMARKS

This chapter presents one central theme: designing cost-effective and optimal implementation of healthcare technologies and interventions for chronic disease care under uncertainty. We provide an overview on several published studies that modeled a set of screening, monitoring, and treatment strategies to improve chronic HCV patient care in the United States. Several CEAs highlighted in this chapter have made practical impact by being incorporated into major US guidelines discussions (Moyer 2013) and the decision-making process of large healthcare organizations such as the VA (Goldhaber-Fiebert et al. 2013). The application of MDP models to medical decision making is relatively recent. There are many exciting opportunities for future research in this area. One could extend the theoretical framework of optimal treatment adoption to incorporate additional uncertainties about costs, health effects, and technology improvements. Furthermore, finding the optimal treatment policy for heterogeneous populations based on personalized medicine is an area of interest for US healthcare providers. At the intersection of management science and medical decision making, decision analysts are in a unique position to help evaluate the benefits, harms, cost, and value of healthcare technology and interventions to improve patient care and healthcare policy design.

REFERENCES

Alagoz, O., C. L. Bryce, S. Shechter, A. Schaefer, C. C. Chang, D. C. Angus, and M. S. Roberts (2005). "Incorporating biological natural history in simulation models: Empirical estimates of the progression of end-stage liver disease." *Med Decis Making* 25(6): 620–632.

Alagoz, O., H. Hsu, A. J. Schaefer, and M. S. Roberts (2010). "Markov decision processes: A tool for sequential decision making under uncertainty." *Med Decis Making* 30(4): 474–483.

Alagoz, O., L. M. Maillart, A. J. Schaefer, and M. S. Roberts (2004). "The optimal timing of living-donor liver transplantation." *Manag Sci* 50(10): 1420–1430.

Alagoz, O., L. M. Maillart, A. J. Schaefer, and M. S. Roberts (2007). "Determining the acceptance of cadaveric livers using an implicit model of the waiting list." *Oper Res* 55(1): 24–36.

Alter, H. J. and T. J. Liang (2012). "Hepatitis C: The end of the beginning and possibly the beginning of the end." *Ann Intern Med* 156(4): 317–318.

Armstrong, G. L., A. Wasley, E. P. Simard, G. M. McQuillan, W. L. Kuhnert, and M. J. Alter (2006). "The prevalence of hepatitis C virus infection in the United States, 1999 through 2002." *Ann Intern Med* 144(10): 705–714.

Ayer, T., O. Alagoz, and N. K. Stout (2012). "OR Forum-A POMDP approach to personalize mammography screening decisions." *Oper Res* 60(5): 1019–1034.

Brandeau, M. L., F. Sainfort, and W. P. Pierskalla (2004). *Operations Research and Health Care: A Handbook of Methods and Applications.* Boston, MA: Kluwer Academic.

Buxton, M. J., M. F. Drummond, B. A. Van Hout, R. L. Prince, T. A. Sheldon, T. Szucs, and M. Vray (1997). "Modelling in economic evaluation: An unavoidable fact of life." *Health Econ* 6(3): 217–227.

Caro, J. J., A. H. Briggs, U. Siebert, K. M. Kuntz, and I.-S. M. G. R. P. T. Force (2012). "Modeling good research practices—Overview: A report of the ISPOR-SMDM Modeling Good Research Practices Task Force—1." *Value Health* 15(6): 796–803.

Chak, E., A. H. Talal, K. E. Sherman, E. R. Schiff, and S. Saab (2011). "Hepatitis C virus infection in USA: An estimate of true prevalence." *Liver Int* 31(8): 1090–1101.

Cipriano, L. E., S. Liu, K. S. Shahzada, M. Holodniy, and J. D. Goldhaber-Fiebert (August 2017). "Hepatitis C virus treatment prioritization improves population health outcomes." Under review.

Craig, B. A. and P. P. Sendi (2002). "Estimation of the transition matrix of a discrete-time Markov chain." *Health Econ* 11(1): 33–42.

Deo, S., S. Iranvani, T. Jiang, K. Smilowitz, and S. Samuelson (2013). "Improving health outcomes through better capacity allocation in a community-based chronic care model." *Oper Res* 61(6):1277–1294.

Deo, S., K. Rajaram, S. Rath, U. Karmarkar, and M. Goetz (2015). "Planning for HIV screening, testing and care at the Veterans Health Administration." *Oper Res* 63(2): 287–304.

Ghany, M. G., D. R. Nelson, D. B. Strader, D. L. Thomas, and L. B. Seeff (2011). "An update on treatment of genotype 1 chronic hepatitis C virus infection: 2011 practice guideline by the American Association for the Study of Liver Diseases." *Hepatology* 54(4): 1433–1444.

Ghany, M. G., D. B. Strader, D. L. Thomas, and L. B. Seeff (2009). "Diagnosis, management, and treatment of hepatitis C: An update." *Hepatology* 49(4): 1335–1374.

Gold, M. R., J. E. Siegel, L. B. Russell, and M. C. Weinstein (1996). *Cost-Effectiveness in Health and Medicine.* New York: Oxford University Press.

Goldhaber-Fiebert, J. D., P. G. Barnett, S. Dally, S. M. Asch, S. Liu, L. Cipriano, and D. K. Owens (2013). Assessment of alternative treatment strategies for chronic genotype 1 hepatitis C. Washington, DC: Department of Veterans Affairs. Available at http://www.hsrd. research.va.gov/publications/esp/hcv.cfm#.UXOBOqK86So. Accessed on April 15, 2013.

Goldhaber-Fiebert, J. D., N. K. Stout, and S. J. Goldie (2010). "Empirically evaluating decision-analytic models." *Value Health* 13(5): 667–674.

Huang, H., Z. Zabinsky, Y. Li, and S. Liu (2016). "Analyzing hepatitis C screening and treatment strategies using probabilistic branch and bound." *Proceedings of the 2016 Winter Simulation Conference*, T. M. K. Roeder, P. I. Frazier, R. Szechtman and E. Zhou, eds., December 11–14, 2016. Washington, DC.

Kabiri, M., A. B. Jazwinski, M. S. Roberts, A. J. Schaefer, and J. Chhatwal (2014). "The changing burden of hepatitis C virus infection in the United States: model-based predictions." *Ann Intern Med* 161(3): 170–180.

Lange, J. M. and V. N. Minin (2013). "Fitting and interpreting continuous-time latent Markov models for panel data." *Stat Med* 32(26): 4581–4595.

Larney, S., H. Kopinski, C. G. Beckwith, N. D. Zaller, D. D. Jarlais, H. Hagan, J. D. Rich, B. J. van den Bergh, and L. Degenhardt (2013). "Incidence and prevalence of hepatitis C in prisons and other closed settings: Results of a systematic review and meta-analysis." *Hepatology* 58(4): 1215–1224.

Li, Y., H. Huang, Z. B. Zabinsky, and S. Liu (2017). "Optimizing implementation of hepatitis C birth-cohort screening and treatment strategies: Model-based projections." *MDM Policy Pract* 2(1): 2381468316686795.

Liu, S. (2013). Optimizing hepatitis C treatment decisions in an era of rapid technological advances: Models and insights. PhD, Stanford University, Stanford, CA.

Liu, S., P. G. Barnett, M. Holodniy, J. J. Lo, V. R. Joyce, R. Gidwani, S. M. Asch, D. K. Owens, and J. D. Goldhaber-Fiebert (2016). "Cost-effectiveness of treatments for genotype 1 hepatitis C virus infection in non-VA and VA populations." *MDM Policy Pract* 1(1). DOI: https://doi.org/10.1177/2381468316671946

Liu, S., M. Brandeau, and J. D. Goldhaber-Fiebert (2017). Optimizing patient treatment decisions in an era of rapid technological advances. *Healthc Manag Sci* 20(1): 16–32. Published first online July 19, 2015.

Liu, S., L. E. Cipriano, and J. D. Goldhaber-Fiebert (2014a). Combining statistical analysis and Markov models with public health data to infer age-specific background mortality rates for hepatitis C infection in the U.S. (extended abstract). *International Conference on Smart Health*, Lecture Note in Computer Science Series, Beijing, China: Springer.

Liu, S., L. E. Cipriano, M. Holodniy, and J. D. Goldhaber-Fiebert (2013). "Cost-effectiveness analysis of risk-factor guided and birth-cohort screening for chronic hepatitis C infection in the United States." *PLoS One* 8(3): e58975.

Liu, S., L. E. Cipriano, M. Holodniy, D. K. Owens, and J. D. Goldhaber-Fiebert (2012). "New protease inhibitors for the treatment of chronic hepatitis C: A cost-effectiveness analysis." *Ann Intern Med* 156(4): 279–290.

Liu, S., M. Schwarzinger, F. Carrat, and J. D. Goldhaber-Fiebert (2011). "Cost effectiveness of fibrosis assessment prior to treatment for chronic hepatitis C patients." *PLoS One* 6(12): e26783.

Liu, S., D. Watcha, M. Holodniy, and J. D. Goldhaber-Fiebert (2014b). "Sofosbuvir-based treatment regimens for chronic, genotype 1 hepatitis C virus infection in U.S. Incarcerated populations: A cost-effectiveness analysis." *Ann Intern Med* 161(8): 546–553.

Maillart, L. M., J. S. Ivy, S. Ransom, and K. Diehl (2008). "Assessing dynamic breast cancer screening policies." *Oper Res* 56(6): 1411–1427.

Mason, J. E., D. A. England, B. T. Denton, S. A. Smith, M. Kurt, and N. D. Shah (2012). "Optimizing statin treatment decisions for diabetes patients in the presence of uncertain future adherence." *Med Decis Making* 32(1): 154–166.

Moyer, V. A. and on behalf of the U.S. Preventive Services Task Force (2013). "Screening for hepatitis C virus infection in adults: U.S. Preventive Services Task Force recommendation statement." *Ann Intern Med* 159(5): 349–357.

Rein, D. B., B. D. Smith, J. S. Wittenborn, S. B. Lesesne, L. D. Wagner, D. W. Roblin, N. Patel, J. W. Ward, and C. M. Weinbaum (2011). "The cost-effectiveness of birth-cohort screening for hepatitis C antibody in U.S. primary care settings." *Ann Intern Med* 156(4): 263–270.

Sanders, G. D., P. J. Neumann, A. Basu, D. W. Brock, D. Feeny, M. Krahn, K. M. Kuntz, D. O. Meltzer, D. K. Owens, L. A. Prosser, J. A. Salomon, M. J. Sculpher, T. A. Trikalinos, L. B. Russell, J. E. Siegel, and T. G. Ganiats (2016). "Recommendations for conduct, methodological practices, and reporting of cost-effectiveness analyses; second panel on cost-effectiveness in health and medicine." *JAMA* 316(10): 1093–1103.

Salomon, J. A., M. C. Weinstein, J. K. Hammitt, and S. J. Goldie (2002). "Empirically calibrated model of hepatitis C virus infection in the United States." *Am J Epidemiol* 156(8): 761–773.

Salomon, J. A., M. C. Weinstein, J. K. Hammitt, and S. J. Goldie (2003). "Cost-effectiveness of treatment for chronic hepatitis C infection in an evolving patient population." *JAMA* 290(2): 228–237.

Sandikci, B., L. M. Maillart, A. J. Shaefer, and O. Alagoz (2008). "Estimating the patient's price of privacy in liver transplantation." *Oper Res* 56(6): 1393–1410.

Shechter, S. (2006). When to initiate, when to switch, and how to sequence HIV therapies: A Markov decision process approach. PhD, University of Pittsburgh, Pittsburgh, PA.

Shechter, S. M., M. D. Bailey, A. J. Schaefer, and M. S. Roberts (2008). "The optimal time to initiate HIV therapy under ordered health states." *Oper Res* 56(1): 20–33.

Smith, B. D., R. L. Morgan, G. A. Beckett, Y. Falck-Ytter, D. Holtzman, and J. W. Ward (2012). "Hepatitis C virus testing of persons born during 1945–1965: Recommendations from the Centers for Disease Control and Prevention." *Ann Intern Med* 157(11): 817–822.

Smith, J. E. and K. F. McCardle (2002). "Structural properties of stochastic dynamic programs." *Oper Res* 50(5): 796–809.

Smith, J. E. and C. Ulu (2012). "Technology adoption with uncertain future costs and quality." *Oper Res* 60(2): 262–274.

Spaulding, A. C. and D. L. Thomas (2012). "Screening for HCV infection in jails." *JAMA* 307(12): 1259–1260.

Su, X. and S. Zenios (2006). "Recipient choice can address the efficiency-equity trade-off in kidney transplantation: A mechanism design model." *Manag Sci* 52(11): 1647–1660.

Thein, H. H., S. R. Walter, H. F. Gidding, J. Amin, M. G. Law, J. George, and G. J. Dore (2011). "Trends in incidence of hepatocellular carcinoma after diagnosis of hepatitis B or C infection: A population-based cohort study, 1992–2007." *J Viral Hepat* 18(7): E232–E241.

Titman, A. C. and L. D. Sharples (2010). "Semi-Markov models with phase-type Sojourn distributions." *Biometrics* 66: 742–752.

Vanni, T., J. Karnon, J. Madan, R. G. White, W. J. Edmunds, A. M. Foss, and R. Legood (2011). "Calibrating models in economic evaluation: A seven-step approach." *Pharmacoeconomics* 29(1): 35–49.

Wang, X., D. Sontag, and F. Wang (2014). "Unsupervised learning of disease progression models." *Proceedings of the 20th ACM SIGKDD International Conference on Knowledge Discovery and Data Mining*, New York.

PART 2

NONCOMMUNICABLE DISEASE PREVENTION

7

MODELING DISEASE PROGRESSION AND RISK-DIFFERENTIATED SCREENING FOR CERVICAL CANCER PREVENTION

ADRIANA LEY-CHAVEZ[1] AND JULIA L. HIGLE[2]

[1] *Department of Industrial and Mechanical Engineering, Universidad de las Américas Puebla, Puebla, Mexico*
[2] *Daniel J. Epstein Department of Industrial and Systems Engineering, University of Southern California, Los Angeles, CA, USA*

7.1 INTRODUCTION

This chapter presents the application of operations research methods to the development of models that are designed for the evaluation of the performance of screening policies. As such, this chapter will be of interest to operations research practitioners looking to make contributions to the field of healthcare by developing quantitative models that can be used to analyze public health decisions. We describe the quantitative methods used to model a representative population, the progression and regression of the disease, and the effects of screening interventions over time. We discuss the data commonly required to build each model component, as well as available data sources.

The model presented in this chapter is specific to cervical cancer (CC) prevention, but the methods used are generalizable to the study of other preventable diseases that progress over time. CC is a relevant public health problem: it is the second

Decision Analytics and Optimization in Disease Prevention and Treatment, First Edition.
Edited by Nan Kong and Shengfan Zhang.
© 2018 John Wiley & Sons, Inc. Published 2018 by John Wiley & Sons, Inc.

most common cancer in women worldwide (World Health Organization 2013). CC develops from persistent infection with some strains of human papillomavirus (HPV) (Muñoz 2000; Schiffman and Castle 2003). HPV is the most common sexually transmitted infection (STI) in the United States (Centers for Disease Control and Prevention 2017). Most HPV infections clear without treatment and without causing changes in the cervix. In some cases, a persistent infection can lead to precancerous cervical lesions. Left untreated, these lesions can progress to invasive cancer.

Screening for precancerous cervical lesions with cervical cytology has greatly reduced the incidence of CC. The primary screening tests include cervical cytology, HPV DNA testing, and colposcopy. These tests vary in both cost and accuracy. Cervical cytology screening, initiated with the Papanicolaou (Pap) test circa 1940, often fails to detect lesions due to its low sensitivity (Nanda et al. 2000). However, the lesions progress slowly, which permits detection over time with a program of regularly occurring screening. An HPV DNA test can indicate that a person is infected with oncogenic strains of HPV and is approved within recent screening guidelines (ACOG 2009; Saslow et al. 2012; Smith et al. 2010; Wright et al. 2007a). Colposcopy involves close examination of the cervix and is considered to be the gold-standard diagnostic test. When primary screening test results are inconclusive, "triage" screening is performed in an effort to resolve the ambiguity. There have been different screening approaches studied and recommended, varying by the test used and testing schedule. Current recommendations include annual screening when using the Pap test for primary screening or every 3 years when using the Pap test in combination with the HPV DNA test. Note that these recommendations do not vary with the screening test used as triage (i.e., a repeat Pap test, the HPV DNA test, or colposcopy). The most commonly used measures of performance for CC screening programs (as well as many other public health policies) are the costs and the number of quality-adjusted life years (QALYs) accumulated in the population with each alternative being evaluated. QALYs are a measure of health effectiveness and consist of weights that are assigned to health states. These weights range from zero to one, with one representing a state of perfect health.

In this chapter, we introduce various models used to represent the transition to CC, the outcomes of various screening tests, and the dynamics of risk factors within patients. Section 7.2 of this chapter includes a very brief introduction to the existing literature on applications of operations research to healthcare decisions related to disease prevention and treatment. This includes a brief overview of applications to screening and treatment decisions of various diseases, as well as applications specific to CC prevention.

In Section 7.3, we present the development of a simulation model of disease progression from infection with an oncogenic HPV strain to the development of precancerous lesions and invasive CC. Our model incorporates screening programs that consist of different screening tests and account for the imperfect accuracy of the tests. It also includes a representation of the patient population based on the changes in known behavioral and demographic risk factors for HPV infection and the manner in which these risk factors vary over a patient's lifetime. We describe our use of probability computations and nonlinear optimization to estimate the values of data that were not readily available in the literature.

In Section 7.4 we illustrate an application of our model toward the study of the cost-effectiveness of alternative screening strategies. We discuss the validation of the model output and a cost-effectiveness analysis performed to compare different screening strategies. We describe the methods used to adjust the model to perform a sensitivity analysis. We end with some concluding remarks in Section 7.5.

7.2 LITERATURE REVIEW

Markov processes are often used to model the progression of a disease through different stages over time. They have been used to evaluate screening strategies for breast cancer (Chen et al. 1998) and colorectal cancer (Delco and Sonnenberg 2000), as well as a variety of other progressive diseases. Monte Carlo simulations of Markov models are used when it is necessary to contain a state space explosion, such as when decisions depend on past states or individual patient characteristics. Examples of this can be found in the evaluation of the cost-effectiveness of intensified prevention programs for diabetic patients at different risks for foot ulcers and amputations (Ragnarson-Tennvall and Apelqvist 2001), the analysis of the effect of hormone replacement therapy in patients at different risk levels for affected diseases (Col et al. 1997; Perrault et al. 2005), the study of the effects of misclassification in randomized clinical trials of screening tests (Obuchowski and Lieber 2008), an evaluation of breast cancer screening strategies (Lee et al. 2008), a comparison of the cost-effectiveness of a one-time birth-cohort testing for hepatitis C infection with that of risk-based testing (McEwan et al. 2013), and a study of the healthcare cost savings of a community-based dementia screening program (Saito et al. 2014), among other applications.

Mathematical programming models are also used to represent diseases and the effect of healthcare interventions. Brandeau et al. (1991) constructed a model to evaluate screening programs for infection with human immunodeficiency virus (HIV). Long et al. (2009) used differential equations to develop a model of HIV transmission and progression to evaluate the cost-effectiveness of vaccination strategies in the United States.

Influence diagrams are compact graphical and mathematical representations useful for modeling decision problems with uncertainty and probabilistic dependence among variables and have been applied to prevention and treatment decisions. Examples of this include decisions about the treatment of neonatal jaundice (Gomez et al. 2007), the ranking of alternative radiation therapy plans for the treatment of prostate cancer (Meyer et al. 2004), and an estimation of the probability of incorrect breast cancer staging (Lee et al. 2006). In addition, Norman et al. (1998) used influence diagrams for patient-specific recommendations of prenatal testing strategies, Hazen (2004) analyzed joint replacement decisions, and van Gerven et al. (2007) defined treatment strategies for aggressive neuroendocrine tumors.

Markov decision processes (MDPs) and partially observable Markov decision processes (POMDPs) model the dynamic interaction between decisions and stochastic processes, such as screening or treatment decisions throughout the progression of a disease. MDPs assume the Markov property and contain a set of possible states, a set of possible actions, and a reward function. Magni et al. (2000) used an MDP to find the optimal time to treat mild hereditary spherocytosis and compared the results to those obtained using a static decision model. Abdollahian and Das (2014) used an MDP to identify optimal intervention strategies for women who carry gene mutations that put them at higher risk for breast and ovarian cancers. POMDPs are MDPs in which the current state can only be observed indirectly via imperfect observations, which often applies to the assessment of health states using screening and diagnostic tests. Hauskrecht and Fraser (2000) used a POMDP to model therapy planning for patients with ischemic heart disease. Ayer et al. (2012) used a POMDP to find mammography screening schedules that maximize QALYs based on the personal risk characteristics and prior screening history of each woman.

Within the specific context of CC, there have been numerous studies that use operations research methodologies. Goldie et al. (1999) developed a Markov model to represent the natural history of CC and the effects of screening, diagnosis, and treatment and used it to evaluate the cost-effectiveness of different CC screening strategies in HIV-infected women. Myers et al. (2000) constructed a Markov model that simulates the natural history of HPV and CC in a hypothetical cohort of women. Using an extended version of this simulation model, Kulasingam et al. (2006b) evaluated the cost-effectiveness of extending CC screening intervals among women with prior normal Pap tests. Goldie et al. (2004) evaluated the cost-effectiveness of using the HPV DNA test in combination with the Pap smear for primary screening in women over 30. Kulasingam et al. (2011) evaluated screening strategies with and without the HPV test and different ages at which to begin screening in terms of the number of colposcopies per life year gained associated with each alternative. This metric was chosen to represent the trade-off between the burden and benefits of screening. McLay et al. (2010) used a simulation-optimization model to design dynamic, age-based screening policies by varying how many lifetime screenings to perform and at what ages.

Similar approaches are used to analyze the cost-effectiveness of different triage strategies to follow up ambiguous primary screening test results (Johnson et al. 1993; Kim et al. 2002; Kulasingam et al. 2006a). Eggington et al. (2006) performed a cost-effectiveness analysis of different policies for referral to colposcopy after abnormal Pap results. Stout et al. (2008) used a simulation model to assess the benefits and potential risks to the patient with screening strategies that differ by primary, triage, and frequency approaches. They enumerate the health-related benefits and potential harms of different screening strategies to aid decision making by women and their primary care physicians.

Vaccination against HPV infection is expected to reduce the prevalence of precancerous cervical lesions, the necessary precursors to CC. With the introduction of vaccines to aid in the prevention of HPV infection, simulation models are being used to evaluate the cost-effectiveness of vaccination programs. For example, Sanders and Taira (2003) evaluated the cost-effectiveness of a potential vaccine that protects against infection with oncogenic HPV strains using a Markov model of the natural history of CC. Elbasha et al. (2007) evaluated alternative vaccination strategies with the quadrivalent HPV vaccine Gardasil. Kim et al. (2009) evaluated the cost-effectiveness of HPV vaccination in women aged 35–45 years, and Drolet et al. (2014) compared the cost-effectiveness of the more recent nonavalent vaccine with that of the quadrivalent vaccine. Franco et al. (2009) estimated the impact of HPV vaccination on the predictive value of the Pap test by simulating populations with different lesion prevalence rates.

Models to study CC prevention have also been developed and applied to low-resource settings (Goldie et al. 2001) and to other countries' screening and vaccination policies outside of the United States (Favato et al. 2007; Kohli et al. 2007; de Kok et al. 2012; Siebert et al. 2006; Vijayaraghavan et al. 2010; Westra et al. 2013).

7.3   MODELING CERVICAL CANCER SCREENING

Simulation is often used to evaluate healthcare alternatives when modeling diseases that are age dependent and/or involve healthcare decisions that depend on patient history. Additionally, it is a good method to use when it is necessary to track changes in patient attributes in order to capture disease progression and/or healthcare options, as when modeling personalized or risk-differentiated policies. The level of detail within a simulation model should be sufficient to accurately represent the population and disease under study and the alternatives under consideration. The simulation model should provide the outputs necessary to design and/or compare healthcare alternatives. The data necessary to populate a simulation model is often extensive and derived from various sources.

Our simulation model was designed to support comparative analyses of various CC screening strategies. It is a patient-based discrete-event simulation model constructed using Arena 12 (Rockwell Automation, Milwaukee, WI). It incorporates models of disease progression, screening, and life changes that impact the likelihood of acquiring an HPV infection. In the following sections, we describe the model components and the data used to populate them. Within the context of CC prevention, we describe how we model the natural history of the disease, screening interventions, and the changes in risk variables in a population of women. Models such as these are often a part of studies designed to evaluate public health guidelines, although the differentiated components needed depend on the decisions being considered in each case. The data commonly required for this type of model include disease prevalence and health state transition probabilities, accuracy and costs of screening tests, effects of known risk factors, and measures of outcomes. We describe the input data used, as well as the quantitative methods used to infer data that were not available in the literature.

7.3.1 Model Components

7.3.1.1 Natural History A model of the natural history of a disease is used to represent transitions between patient health states when the condition is left unattended. Health states relevant to the decisions being analyzed are included in the model. Note that as the types of decisions associated with a given disease vary from one study to the next, the models used may have different levels of detail and different endpoints. For a discrete-time model, the unit of time associated with transitions must be identified. For example, a disease that progresses very rapidly will require smaller time intervals than a disease that progresses more slowly. In cases where transitions between health states are probabilistically dependent on age or other conditions, age- or risk-dependent state transition probabilities should be used in the model. The data commonly used include disease prevalence (to assign initial health states to the population being modeled) and disease incidence and progression/regression rates. Prevalence is typically obtained from cross-sectional studies, while incidence and transition rates are typically from longitudinal cohort studies.

Our model examines the impact of a screening program for CC prevention. We model the disease progression from the point of infection with an oncogenic HPV strain through the various stages of precancerous lesions that lead to invasive CC. Our model of the natural history of the disease is depicted in Figure 7.1. Women who are not infected with oncogenic HPV are in the "noninfected" state, N. They can acquire an infection, which results in a transition to the infected state, I. Infections can clear or progress to precancerous lesions, known as cervical intraepithelial neoplasia (CIN). These lesions are graded by severity, from CIN^1 to CIN^3. Lesions can clear, progress to more serious lesions, regress to less serious lesions, or progress to invasive cancer, C. Women can remain in the lesion states for years before progressing to invasive cancer, and they may transition to death by other cause prior to that. In moving between health states, some transition probabilities are age dependent. Within the model, a woman's health state transitions are simulated over time until cancer is prevented (CP), cancer develops (C), or she dies by causes unrelated to CC (DO). When advanced precancerous lesions are identified and removed, the patient is placed under close monitoring and therefore removed from the preventive screening programs that are under consideration in this study. In our model, we consider this transition as a transition to "cancer prevented." These three states, CP, C, and DO, are represented as end states within our model of a screening program. In Figure 7.1, age increases from left to right and is reflected as a subscript on the health states that are non-end states. Thus, an infection that clears during the ith period is reflected as a transition from I_i to N_{i+1}.

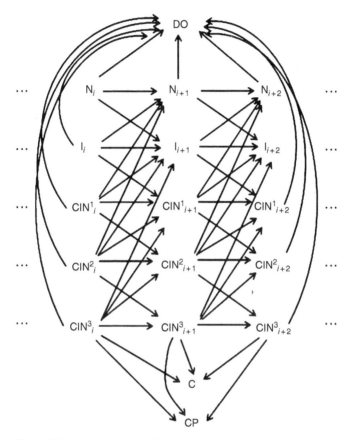

Figure 7.1   Markov model of natural history of disease progression.

With i denoting age, the health states are:

N_i: not infected, no lesion
I_i: infected, no lesion
$CIN_i^{\ell}, \ell \in \{1, 2, 3\}$
C: invasive cancer (end state)
CP: cancer prevented (end state)
DO: death by other cause (end state)

As the patient ages, it is possible to observe disease progression (e.g., a transition from I_i to CIN_{i+1}^1) and regression (e.g., a transition from I_i to N_{i+1}).

Our model adopts a discrete-time approach, and the issue of transition times must be resolved. Clinical studies have found the time between initial detection of infection with HPV and initial detection of CIN to be at least 2 years (Liaw et al. 1999; Trottier et al. 2009) and that women with invasive cancer tend to be more than 10 years older than women with CIN^3 (Moscicki et al. 2006; Schiffman and Kjaer 2003). Based on these studies, we considered 6-month interval between health transitions to be sufficiently small and record health state transitions every 6 months.

7.3.1.2 Patient Population   Representation of the patient population is necessary for most models designed to analyze public health decisions. In many cases, patients are initiated within a model at the same age and with no distinguishing characteristics. Other times, the population is initiated with an age distribution that represents that of the country or region being studied. If there are risk factors that influence the natural history of the disease or healthcare decisions, the population modeled may consist of patients with specific levels of the risk factors that are tracked over time and that collectively represent the distribution of the risk factors in the population being studied. Additionally, changes in risk factors over time should be consistent with the way they change in the population being studied. A model to quantify how each patient's risk factors influence disease progression and/or decisions may also be necessary. Common types of risk factors are demographic and behavioral variables, as well as genetic biomarkers. Data to model demographic variables can be obtained from the US Census Bureau, and data to model behavioral variables can be obtained from various Centers for Disease Control and Prevention (CDC) surveys.

A woman's risk for contracting an oncogenic HPV infection varies over the course of her lifetime. We define a woman's "risk" as the probability that she has an oncogenic HPV infection. In order to model the changes in this risk over time, we investigated the quantitative relationship between known risk factors for HPV infection and a woman's probability of being infected with an oncogenic HPV strain. These risk factors consist of behavioral and demographic characteristics. We performed a logistic regression analysis to quantify the associations between a patient's characteristics and her test results for an oncogenic HPV infection. This analysis yields a predictive multivariate logistic regression model that we use to calculate the probability of infection, given a set of characteristics.

We analyzed data from the National Health and Nutrition Examination Survey (NHANES), which includes patient demographic and behavioral data, as well as data on the presence or absence of oncogenic HPV infections. Details of the survey content and of the data collection and analysis methodologies are described by the National Center for Health Statistics (NCHS) (2014). Our analyses include data for 1120 women from the 2003 to 2004 NHANES cycle, aged 20–59. These women answered the demographic, smoking, and sexual behavior questionnaires and submitted a self-collected vaginal swab specimen for HPV testing. Forty-six women had missing values for one or more of the variables considered and were excluded from the multivariate analysis, resulting in a sample size of 1074 women for the multivariate analysis.

Independent variables were identified using "purposeful selection," as described in Hosmer et al. (2013), which begins with a univariate analysis and then moves to a multivariate analysis. We selected potential independent variables to be included in the model as predictors based on the existing literature about known risk factors for HPV infection (Dunne et al. 2007; Kahn et al. 2007; Moscicki et al. 2001; Sasagawa et al. 2005; Sellors et al. 2003; Winer et al. 2003; Wright et al. 2004). The demographic variables analyzed were *age, education level, country of birth, race, below poverty index*, and *marital status*. The sexual behavior variables were *age at first intercourse, number of lifetime sex partners, number of recent sex partners (in the past 12 months)*, and *history of chlamydia, genital herpes*, and *genital warts*. We combined two variables from the NHANES smoking questionnaire into one variable defined as *smoked at least 100 cigarettes in lifetime*; *if yes, current smoker*; *if no, former smoker*.

We used NCHS weights to account for the unequal probabilities of selection and to adjust for nonresponse. In the univariate analysis ($n = 1120$), the Wald χ^2 statistic was used to identify variables for inclusion in the multivariate analysis. Odds ratios were used to measure the magnitude of the associations, with each descriptor variable considered to be significantly associated with the dependent variable if the value 1 was not included in the 95% confidence interval of the odds ratio. Variables that were statistically significant at the $p < 0.20$ level in the univariate analysis were included in the preliminary multivariate model. For the multivariate analysis ($n = 1074$), the data for 834 women were randomly selected and used to develop the multivariate predictive model, and the remaining 240 were used for validation. There was no significant difference ($\alpha = 0.05$) found between the parameter estimates obtained using the sample size of 834 and those obtained using the full sample ($n = 1074$). This does not appear to depend on the specific sample that was selected, as it was observed in four different random samples of 834 women. All pairwise interactions of variables included in the multivariate model were evaluated. To validate the predictive model, we used the final multivariate model to estimate the probability of infection for the validation sample ($n = 240$). Goodness of fit was assessed using the Archer and Lemeshow F-adjusted mean residual goodness-of-fit test, which is designed to be used with survey data (Archer and Lemeshow 2006; Archer et al. 2007). All analyses were performed using Intercooled Stata 9.2 (StataCorp, College Station, TX).

The multivariate model excludes the variables that became nonsignificant in the multivariate analysis. Each variable that was not significant in the univariate analysis was added to the multivariate model to see if the parameter estimates or the goodness of fit of the model changed due to confounding. The variable below poverty index was included in the final multivariate model because it changed parameter estimates by more than 20% and resulted in an improved model fit. Interaction terms were not found to be significant at the 0.05 level. The Archer and Lemeshow F-adjusted mean residual goodness-of-fit test did not indicate a lack of fit between the NHANES data and the model. From these analyses we quantified a predictive relationship between demographic and behavioral characteristics and a woman's likelihood of having an oncogenic HPV infection at a given time. The final multivariate model included the following variables: *age, marital status, below poverty index*, and *number of lifetime partners*.

Within the simulation, the representation of a patient includes these characteristics, which change throughout her life, and a model of these changes over time was developed using probability distributions corresponding to changes within the US population. That is, a woman at time t is represented using risk characteristics: $w_t = \{$age, marital status, poverty status, number of lifetime sex partners$\}$. The predictive equation for the probability of an infection (i.e., $P_I(w_t)$) is calculated as

$$P_I\left(w_t\right) = \frac{1}{1 + e^{-w_t}} \qquad (7.1)$$

where $\quad w_t = -1.880 \quad + \left\{-1.094\left(\text{if age } 25-29\right); 1.029\left(\text{if age } 29-59\right)\right\}$

$$+0.541\left\{\left(\text{if not married and not living with partner}\right)\right\}$$

$$+0.621\left\{\left(\text{if below poverty index}\right)\right\}$$

$$+0.577\left\{\left(\text{if lifetime partners} \geq 5\right)\right\} \text{ at time } t$$

Our model of patient risk includes changes in marital status: first and second marriage, first and second divorce, and becoming widowed. We randomly assign an age of first marriage, marriage durations, and divorce durations (i.e., the number of years between the end of a first marriage and the start of a second) based on probability distributions corresponding to data from the US population (Bramlett and Mosher 2002; Centers for Disease Control and Prevention 2002; U.S. Census Bureau 2001). We used the NCHS age-specific all-cause mortality rates for men to model transitions to widowhood. We do not model third- and higher-order marriages, primarily because only 2.3% of women marry three or more times (Centers for Disease Control and Prevention 2002). We model changes in the number of lifetime partners using the probability distributions corresponding to the number of new partners women acquire each year (O'Dowd 2003). Within the simulation, unmarried women are randomly assigned to one of four quantities of new partners (i.e., $\{0, 1, 2, 3\}$) based on the probability distribution specific to their age group. We model the probability of transitioning in and out of poverty each year conditioned on marital status using data from the US Census Bureau (2001–2003) (U.S. Census Bureau 2003).

We assume that females under the age of 13 are not infected. Because the data available from NHANES are for women aged 20–59, our logistic regression model only applies to women within this age group. For women outside this age range, we use age-specific probabilities of infection (Kahn et al. 2007; Myers et al. 2000).

The logistic regression equation serves to calculate the probability that a woman has an oncogenic HPV infection (infection prevalence). To calculate the probability of infection incidence (i.e., acquiring a new infection) for use as a transition probability in our model from the state "not infected" to the state "infected," we use the epidemiologic relationship

$$\text{Prevalence} = \text{Incidence} * \text{Duration} \qquad (7.2)$$

as described by Ashengrau and Seage (2003). To estimate infection incidence, we use an infection duration of 8 months for women under age 20 and 15 months for women over age 20 based on clinical findings (Ho et al. 1998; Muñoz et al. 2004; Richardson et al. 2003).

7.3.1.3 Screening

Alternative screening and treatment strategies can be evaluated by including their effects in the model and comparing their outcomes. The effects of the screening and treatment strategies are modeled as changes in the transition probabilities to health states such as death and disease survival. They can also result in the possibility of transitioning into new states such as treatment and surveillance (close monitoring). The accuracy of a screening test is defined by its sensitivity (i.e., the probability that the test result will be positive given that the disease is present) and specificity (i.e., the probability that the test result will be negative given that the disease is absent). To represent this, it is necessary to distinguish between the health states and the test results in the model. For screening or treatment decisions that depend on several past test results and/or on other patient variables, the relevant history of each patient must be tracked in the model and used for decision making accordingly. The sensitivity and specificity of screening tests is typically found through clinical trials.

We modeled screening strategies consistent with the existing guidelines (e.g., ACOG 2009; Wright et al. 2007a) for primary screening and triage screening for inconclusive primary screening results. For primary screening, we simulated the use of the Papanicolaou (Pap) test at different frequencies and a combination of the Pap test and the HPV DNA test every 3 years. For triage screening, we simulated the use of a repeat Pap test at 6 months, the HPV DNA test, and colposcopy. Combinations of different primary and triage alternatives represent different screening strategies. We also designed and evaluated risk-differentiated screening strategies that screen each woman with the strategy deemed most appropriate for her particular risk for HPV infection.

We modeled the follow-up tests and treatment of detected lesions in accordance with the guidelines of the management of women with precancerous lesions (Wright et al. 2007b). Our model accounts for the fact that the screening tests have varying levels of precision (ALTS Group 2003; Kulasingam et al. 2006a; Nanda et al. 2000; Solomon et al. 2001). Additionally, the outcomes of screening tests are conditioned on the patient's current health state to reflect the fact that the tests have different probabilities of detection depending on the state of the disease.

Common performance measures of screening and treatment strategies include the costs and the number of QALYs accumulated with each alternative being evaluated. Costs can include the costs of screening (including test costs, fees of health professionals, and administrative costs), the costs of treatment (which can vary by disease stage), costs to the patient (including time spent attending screening, anxiety over screening, and consequences of overscreening and overtreating in the case of false-positive results), and costs of death (including the economic burden of life years lost and the burden to surviving family members). It is not always possible to capture all of the costs and consequences in a model due to limitations on the availability of data. However, in most cases the screening and treatment costs can be derived from average Medicare charges. QALYs were developed as a measure of health effectiveness for cost-effectiveness analysis (Weinstein et al. 2009) and consist of weights that are assigned to health states that range from zero to one, with one representing a state of perfect health. To determine how people value possible health states, preferences are elicited from a representative sample of the affected population (Weinstein et al. 2009). The Cost-Effectiveness Analysis Registry (CEAR) (2013) has collected data on QALY weights elicited and used that correspond to health states associated with many diseases and treatments.

To evaluate the cost-effectiveness of the various screening strategies, the total monetary costs and QALYs associated with each strategy were quantified. Data on the costs of screening tests were derived from average Medicare charges (Melnikow et al. 2010). The cost of an invasive CC case was estimated based on the cost of treatment and the economic burden per years of life lost for each person for whom the cancer resulted in death (estimated considering the average life expectancy). To evaluate the effectiveness of the strategies, the QALYs accumulated in the population were quantified; these were assigned to disease states using weights from the CEAR (2013).

7.3.2 Parameter Selection

Our model of the natural history of the disease requires data to represent transitions between the various health states. The probability of acquiring an HPV infection was calculated based on levels of risk factors associated with each patient using (7.1) and (7.2). This probability varies for each woman based on her levels of risk factors at a given point in time. The transition probabilities for infection clearance and lesion progression and regression have been inferred from clinical cohort studies (e.g., Insinga et al. 2007; Moscicki et al. 1998; Sherman et al. 2003; Trottier et al. 2009) and have been compiled to be used as transition probabilities in past cost-effectiveness analyses (Bergeron et al. 2008; Canfell et al. 2004; Goldie et al. 1999, 2001; Kohli et al. 2007; Myers et al. 2000; Sanders and Taira 2003). Rates of death from causes other than CC were estimated by subtracting age-specific CC mortality rates from age-specific all-cause mortality rates (NCHS 2010).

After conducting a thorough review of the literature, we found several data necessary to populate our model that are not reported in the current literature. For example, data on the true prevalence of lesions are not directly available in the literature. This is because the epidemiology studies only report the lesions that are detected, and the tests to detect lesions (i.e., Pap, colposcopy) have neither perfect sensitivity nor perfect specificity. We used probability computations and peripheral data within an optimization model to estimate the values of data that are not readily available in the literature.

Our study considers the following:

- Four lesion states, CIN^ℓ, $\ell \in \{0, 1, 2, 3\}$, where CIN^0 represents the absence of a lesion
- Three outcomes from a Papanicolaou test, P^r, $r \in \{+, -, 0\}$, indicating "positive," "negative," and "ambiguous," respectively
- Two outcomes from an HPV DNA test, H^r, $r \in \{+, -\}$, indicating "positive" or "negative" detection of high-risk HPV strains, respectively
- Relationships between test results and health states

For any combination of CIN^ℓ and P^r,

$$P\{P^r|CIN^\ell\}P\{CIN^\ell\} = P\{CIN^\ell|P^r\}P\{P^r\}$$
$$\Rightarrow P\{CIN^\ell\} = \frac{P\{CIN^\ell|P^0\}P\{P^0\}}{P\{P^0|CIN^\ell\}} \tag{7.3}$$

Estimates of $P\{CIN^\ell|P^0\}$, $P\{P^0\}$, $P\{P^+ \cup P^0|CIN^\ell\}$, and $P\{P^+|CIN^\ell\}$ have been observed in clinical studies (ALTS Group 2003; Kulasingam et al. 2002, 2006a; Manos et al. 1999). Additionally,

$$P\{P^-|CIN^\ell\} = 1 - P\{P^0|CIN^\ell\} - P\{P^+|CIN^\ell\} \tag{7.4}$$

and

$$P\{P^0|CIN^\ell\} = P\{P^+ \cup P^0|CIN^\ell\} - P\{P^+|CIN^\ell\}. \tag{7.5}$$

As such, Equations 7.3–7.5 represent $P\{CIN^\ell\}$ and $P\{P^r|CIN^\ell\}$ through related probabilities that have been estimated through clinical studies.

Our model also requires a relationship between HPV DNA test results and lesion status, $P\{CIN^\ell|H^r\}$. Estimates of $P\{H^r\}$ have been observed in clinical studies (Kulasingam et al. 2002; Manos et al. 1999). In order to obtain $P\{CIN^\ell|H^-\}$, note that

$$P\{CIN^\ell\} = P\{CIN^\ell H^-\} + P\{CIN^\ell H^+\}$$
$$\Rightarrow P\{CIN^\ell H^-\} = P\{CIN^\ell\} - P\{CIN^\ell H^+\} \tag{7.6}$$
$$= P\{CIN^\ell\} - P\{CIN^\ell|H^+\}P\{H^+\}$$

Given that

$$P\{CIN^\ell H^-\} = P\{CIN^\ell|H^-\}P\{H^-\} \tag{7.7}$$

we obtain

$$P\left\{CIN^\ell \,\middle|\, H^-\right\} = \frac{P\left\{CIN^\ell\right\} - P\left\{CIN^\ell \,\middle|\, H^+\right\} P\left\{H^+\right\}}{P\left\{H^-\right\}}. \tag{7.8}$$

In order to obtain $P\{CIN^\ell | H^+\}$, note that

$$P\left\{CIN^\ell \,\middle|\, H^+\right\} = \frac{P\left\{H^+ \,\middle|\, CIN^\ell\right\} P\left\{CIN^\ell\right\}}{P\left\{H^+\right\}}. \tag{7.9}$$

Estimates of $P\{H^+|CIN^\ell\}$ have been observed in clinical studies (ALTS Group 2003; Kulasingam et al. 2006a; Manos et al. 1999). Thus, given the representation of $P\{CIN^\ell\}$ in (7.3), we have mathematical descriptions of the remaining input parameters that are consistent with the laws of probability insofar as data observed through clinical studies are concerned.

Observation-based estimates of various probabilities that appear in (7.3)–(7.9) are drawn from multiple sources, and in some cases conflicts are present. Our goal is to select a set of values as input to our simulation model that are consistent with the laws of probability and exhibit minimal deviation from values observed in clinical studies. Our approach to selecting values of our input parameters involves an optimization model. The objective function incorporates the squared deviations of the parameters from values observed in clinical studies, while the constraints represent consequences drawn from the laws of probability. In presenting the optimization model used for parameter selection, we distinguish between values that will be used as input to our simulation and those that have been observed in clinical studies. For example,

- $P\{CIN^\ell|P^0\}$ represents the probability that a patient has CIN^ℓ given that a Papanicolaou test yielded an ambiguous result, an input parameter for the simulation model.
- $P\{CIN^\ell|P^0\}$ represents the fraction of patients with ambiguous results on their Papanicolaou tests that were observed with CIN^ℓ, as reported in the literature (e.g., Kulasingam et al. 2006a).

The parameter selection problem is as follows:

$$\text{Min} \quad \sum_{\ell=0}^{3} \left(P\left\{CIN^\ell \,\middle|\, P^0\right\} - \widehat{P\left\{CIN^\ell \,\middle|\, P^0\right\}} \right)^2 + \sum_{\ell=0}^{3} \left(P\left\{P^+ \,\middle|\, CIN^\ell\right\} - \widehat{P\left\{P^+ \,\middle|\, CIN^\ell\right\}} \right)^2$$

$$+ \sum_{\ell=0}^{3} \left(P\left\{H^+ \,\middle|\, CIN^\ell\right\} - \widehat{P\left\{H^+ \,\middle|\, CIN^\ell\right\}} \right)^2 + \left(P\left\{P^0\right\} - \widehat{P\left\{P^0\right\}} \right)^2 + \left(P\left\{H^+\right\} - \widehat{P\left\{H^+\right\}} \right)^2$$

$$+ \sum_{\ell=0}^{3} \left(P\left\{P^+ \cup P^0 \,\middle|\, CIN^\ell\right\} - \widehat{P\left\{P^+ \cup P^0 \,\middle|\, CIN^\ell\right\}} \right)^2$$

$$s.t. \quad P\left\{CIN^\ell\right\} = \frac{P\left\{CIN^\ell \,\middle|\, P^0\right\} P\left\{P^0\right\}}{P\left\{P^0 \,\middle|\, CIN^\ell\right\}} \quad \text{for } \ell \in \{0,1,2,3\}$$

$$\sum_{\ell=0}^{3} P\{CIN^{\ell}\} = 1$$

$$P\{H^+\} = \sum_{\ell=0}^{3} P\{H^+|CIN^{\ell}\} P\{CIN^{\ell}\}$$

$$P\{CIN^{\ell}|H^-\} = \frac{P\{CIN^{\ell}\} - P\{CIN^{\ell}|H^+\} P\{H^+\}}{P\{H^-\}} \quad \text{for } \ell \in \{0,1,2,3\}$$

$$\sum_{\ell=0}^{3} P\{CIN^{\ell}|H^-\} = 1$$

$$0 \le P\{P^0\} \le 1$$

$$0 \le P\{H^+\} \le 1$$

for $\ell = 0,1,2,3$: $\quad 0 \le P\{CIN^{\ell}\} \le 1$

$$0 \le P\{CIN^{\ell}|H^+\} \le 1$$

$$0 \le P\{CIN^{\ell}|H^-\} \le 1$$

$$0 \le P\{CIN^{\ell}|P^0\} \le 1$$

$$0 \le P\{P^+|CIN^{\ell}\} \le 1$$

$$0 \le P\{P^0 \cup P^+|CIN^{\ell}\} \le 1$$

$$0 \le P\{H^+|CIN^{\ell}\} \le 1$$

Input values for the simulation model were based on a solution to this optimization problem. This use of optimization models to infer data needed for disease modeling is a novel approach that can be useful when input data are not readily available in the literature. In this case, we used probability modeling to calculate the values of data required by the model that cannot be physically observed or measured due to the limitations of diagnostic tests. In those cases where data are available in the literature, our nonlinear programming model is designed to minimize the difference between the values that we use and the values reported in the literature while collectively satisfying the laws of probability. This approach can be especially useful when the data necessary to populate a simulation model are derived from multiple sources that do not coincide perfectly.

7.3.3   Implementation

We simulated theoretical cohorts of 100,000 women. The simulated populations were initialized in a manner consistent with the demographic distribution of the US population. The initial health states were randomly assigned using probability distributions from reports of the age-specific prevalence of oncogenic HPV infection (Kahn et al. 2007) and from our estimates of the prevalence of lesions. The women in each population were simulated sequentially, with disease progression, test results, and risk variables that evolved independently from woman to woman. Each woman in the simulation was followed through her screening years until she reached an end state, observing her health states and test results over time.

Each woman in the simulation is assigned an initial health state that is defined in terms of the existence or absence of oncogenic HPV infection and the various stages of precancerous cervical lesions; these are assigned according to our estimates of disease prevalence. The health state transitions are randomly generated using age-dependent transition probabilities consistent with available data regarding rates of disease progression and regression. Each woman is also assigned initial levels of the risk-related demographic and behavioral variables, and these are randomly updated over time according to probability distributions derived using data from each of the life changes in the US population.

The outcome of each test result is randomly generated using the corresponding probability distributions of test sensitivity and specificity, which are dependent on the true health state at the time of screening. The screening events simulated consist of different tests, at different frequencies, and different follow-up actions to resolve inconclusive results depending on the screening strategy being simulated and on each woman's past test results. In the case of the risk-differentiated screening strategies, these events also depend on each woman's specific risk level at a given time. Consequently, information on past test results for each woman was stored and used for decision making in the simulation model. Additionally, to simulate risk-differentiated strategies that use the infection probability of up to 25 years in the past to assign a risk category, the infection probability history of each individual was tracked and stored in the model. We evaluated screening alternatives based on the outcomes observed in the simulated populations.

We validated our simulation model by comparing the number of incident CC cases to the reported number of incident CC cases in the US population based on data from the Surveillance, Epidemiology, and End Results (SEER) Program. The incidence rate of CC reported by SEER for 2004–2008 was 8.1 cases per 100,000 women per year. Using the most commonly used screening strategy, our model reports 8.65 cases per 100,000 women. We also compared our results with SEER distribution of CC diagnoses by age at diagnosis by comparing the cumulative distribution of diagnoses by age as reported by SEER and as observed from our model and found a strong similarity between them. The precise cause of the discrepancies between our results and the SEER data is not known, but might be attributable to the parameter values that we estimated using optimization models and to the simplifying assumptions that we made. In addition to this, the higher CC incidence rate in our model may be due in part to the fact that SEER quantifies the number of cancer cases that are detected and reported, while our output reflects the total number of cancer cases that occur, because the simulation environment allows us to register all health states.

7.4   MODEL-BASED ANALYSES

A model such as the one described in this chapter can be used to support a variety of analyses. For example, we created a new risk-differentiated screening strategy that bases the screening protocols on the probability that the patient has an oncogenic HPV infection as indicated by the logistic regression equation presented in (7.1). This risk-differentiated strategy was developed by simulating risk-homogeneous populations with various probabilities of infection and determining the most cost-effective of the traditional screening strategies for each infection probability. The analysis indicated distinct screening strategies for each of three different risk levels, which we denoted as "low," "medium," and "high" risk levels. According to this classification, approximately 25% of a risk-heterogeneous population modeled after the US population was in the low risk category, 25% was in the high risk category, and the remainder was in the medium risk category. Each component of the risk-differentiated strategy refers to the combination of primary and triage screening approaches used. In all cases, the primary screening involved the Pap test with varying frequency and triage screening for ambiguous results using an HPV DNA test. For "low-risk" women, triennial screening is applied. For "medium-risk" women, biennial screening is applied. For high-risk women, annual screening is applied. In this manner, higher-risk women are screened more aggressively (i.e., more frequently) than lower-risk women.

We considered multiple ways to implement a risk-differentiated strategy. For example, one implementation would involve screening each woman as a function of her risk for infection at the time of screening. To account for the slow progression of the disease from infection to lesions and cancer, we also considered strategies that screen women as a function of their risk for infection in prior years. Thus, for a screening that takes place at time t, we investigated strategies based on the risk of infection i years prior to the time of screening, $P_I(w_{t-i})$, for $i \in \{5, 10, 15, 20, 25\}$.

7.4.1   Cost-Effectiveness Analysis

Within our comparative analyses, the performance of a screening strategy was assessed based on the total costs incurred and the total QALYs accumulated within simulated populations of 100,000 women. The strategies were compared using incremental cost-effectiveness ratios (ICER). Costs and QALYs are commonly used to calculate ICERs, which serve to compare the performance of alternatives in terms of both of these measures. The ICER for the more expensive and more effective of two strategies is the additional cost incurred divided by the additional QALYs gained. To calculate the ICERs, strategies are ordered by their total cost (from lowest to highest). Strategies that are both more costly and less effective in terms of QALYs than another strategy are considered dominated. The additional costs of a strategy are divided by the additional QALYs compared with the previous, less costly strategy. Following this approach, the strategy considered most cost-effective is the one that

TABLE 7.1   Cost-Effectiveness Analysis for Mixed-Risk Populations

| Strategy | Total | | Incremental | | | Comparison |
	Cost	QALYs	Cost	QALYs	ICER[a]	Strategy[a]
1. Triennial Pap+DNA triage	325,301,969	7,917,211				
2. R-D screen, $i=0$	351,032,712	7,923,237	25,730,744	6,026	4,270	1
3. R-D screen, $i=5$	360,775,487	7,923,945	9,742,775	708	13,761	2
4. R-D screen[b], $i=10$	374,357,420	7,924,414	13,581,933	469	28,959	3
5. R-D screen, $i=15$	380,750,526	7,924,423	6,393,106	9	710,345	4
6. Annual Pap+DNA triage	501,691,553	7,926,014	127,334,133	1,600	79,584	4

[a] Incremental cost effectiveness ratio.
[b] Indicates the most cost-effective strategy, based on a cost-effectiveness threshold of $50,000/QALY.
"R-D" indicates risk-differentiated strategy.
"i" corresponds to the age offset in risk calculation.

results in the highest number of QALYs while paying no more per QALY than an established threshold. In the United States, this threshold is typically $50,000/QALY (Eichler et al. 2004; Kulasingam and Myers 2003). In comparing two strategies, a more costly and more effective strategy is considered to be cost-effective if the incremental cost per QALY gained is at most $50,000. Others (Goldhaber-Fiebert et al. 2008; Kim et al. 2009) also considered strategies that fall within the range of $50,000–$100,000 per QALY gained to be cost-effective. In our analyses we considered a cost-effectiveness threshold of $50,000 per QALY gained.

The cost-effectiveness analysis performed is shown in Table 7.1. In this analysis, we considered 12 strategies that screened and triaged all women in the population in the same manner and six variations of the risk-differentiated strategy based on $P_I(w_{t-i})$ for $i \in \{0, 5, 10, 15, 20, 25\}$ described earlier in this section. Within the table, the six non-dominated strategies are presented in order of increasing costs.

As indicated in Table 7.1, the risk-differentiated strategy with a 10-year offset was found to be the most cost-effective strategy. This strategy uses $P_I(w_{t-10})$, the probability of infection of 10 years before the time of screening to determine a woman's risk level. To implement this screening strategy, the logistic regression equation would be used to estimate the $P_I(w_{t-10})$ for each woman based on her risk factors from 10 years prior to the screening date.

7.4.2   Sensitivity Analysis

In our initial analyses, we modeled 100% adherence to screening guidelines, so that all women attend all screening appointments. We also modeled a population that is not vaccinated against HPV infections. In this section we expand our model in order to evaluate the performance of screening strategies in vaccinated populations and populations with imperfect adherence to the screening guidelines. Risk-differentiated strategies are also found to be the most cost-effective under these conditions.

7.4.2.1 Modeling the Effect of Vaccination   To study the effect that a vaccinated population would have on the cost-effectiveness of screening strategies, we adjusted our model to simulate a population of women vaccinated with the quadrivalent HPV vaccine most widely available at the time of our study (Gardasil), which protects against infection with the oncogenic HPV types 16 and 18. HPV types 16 and 18 account for 14% of oncogenic HPV infections (Kahn et al. 2007) but are associated with 70% of CC cases (Clifford et al. 2006; Muñoz et al. 2004). The quadrivalent HPV vaccine also protects against HPV types 6 and 11, but these are non-oncogenic and therefore not relevant to our study.

We modified our population model by adjusting the probability of acquiring a new infection to reflect the fact that vaccinated women will not contract infections with HPV strains 16 and 18. Given that strain-specific disease progression rates are not readily available (Elbasha et al. 2007; McLay et al. 2010; Sanders and Taira 2003), we made adjustments to our model to approximately reflect a 14% reduction in the incidence of oncogenic HPV infections and a 70% reduction in CC cases within the vaccinated population. In particular, transition probabilities for lesion progression were reduced to simulate the effect of the subset of oncogenic HPV types other than 16 and 18, which are less likely to progress to precancerous lesions and CC (Clifford et al. 2006; Muñoz et al. 2004). While the number of cancer cases was reduced by approximately 70%, the percentages of cancer cases for each age group remained similar to the output of the model without vaccination, thereby maintaining a distribution of cancer cases similar to that of SEER (McLay et al. 2010). We performed this adjustment using the software system OptQuest (OptTek Systems, Boulder, CO) in combination with Arena to vary the lesion progression transition probabilities. OptQuest guides a series of simulations, searching for input values using scatter search, tabu search, and neural networks and evaluating whether the outputs satisfy the objectives and constraints defined (Glover et al. 1999).

We simulated a population in which all women are vaccinated and a population with the current vaccine coverage, which was approximately 33% (Centers for Disease Control and Prevention 2009). We assumed that vaccinated women have full immunity against the strains covered by the vaccine (Garland et al. 2007) and that immunity does not wane over time. The costs associated with the vaccine (Elbasha et al. 2007), which are incurred independent of the screening strategy used, were included in the analysis.

7.4.2.2 Modeling Imperfect Adherence   In our model we assume that all women attend all screening appointments, which is usually not the case. Paskett et al. 2010 found that approximately 68% of the population follows risk-appropriate screening guidelines. Additionally, it is well known that women at higher risk for HPV and CC are less likely to adhere to screening guidelines (Basen-Engquist et al. 2003; Eggleston et al. 2007; Marcus et al. 1992; Paskett et al. 2010).

To represent imperfect adherence in a way that reflects these findings, we would need data on the probability distribution of adherence, conditioned on different probabilities of infection. Since these data are not readily available, we made rough estimates of them that are consistent with the literature on adherence to CC screening in the following manner.

We classified the population by infection probability into low, medium, and high risk. We made estimates of probabilities of adherence conditioned on each risk level such that the probability of adherence of the overall population was approximately 70% and that the probability of adherence was inversely proportional to the probability of infection; we studied three different estimates of this probability distribution. In our model these probabilities of adherence represent the probability that each patient will attend screening, at each instance in which she has a screening event programmed.

Analyzing scenarios involving vaccination and imperfect adherence using our model permits evaluation of screening strategies in simulated populations of women that are representative of the US population. For example, in the case of imperfect adherence, we found that a risk-differentiated strategy that considers the risk level 10 years prior to the time of screening continues to be most cost-effective. In the case of vaccinated populations, we found that a screening strategy composed of risk-differentiated strategies for each of the vaccinated and non-vaccinated populations to be cost-effective. As such, models such as this can be applied to compare screening strategies in order to inform public health recommendations.

7.5 CONCLUDING REMARKS

Operations research methods can be applied to evaluate alternative screening strategies for disease prevention. In this chapter we have presented a series of models developed to represent the elements necessary to study risk-differentiated CC screening strategies.

The model of the natural history of the disease represents the disease progression and regression through infection and lesion states. The patient population model represents the changes in risk factors over time and uses a multivariate logistic regression equation to estimate each patient's infection probability conditioned on the levels of her risk variables. The model of primary and triage screening represents the tests that occur over time and their state-specific probabilities of accurately detecting disease. These models are interdependent and form part of a discrete-event simulation model that was used to evaluate alternative screening strategies in simulated populations of women. Probability modeling and nonlinear programming were used to estimate input data not directly available in the literature.

Markov models are often used in studies of preventive screening and treatment. However, Greenhalgh et al. (2013) noted that "in the case of diseases that are of lengthy duration with complex treatment pathways, patient-level simulations rather than the Markov approach better represents patient experience," given that "Markov models require the definition of essentially homogeneous health states in which patients share common risks, utility and treatment costs regardless of their prior history." We used a simulation model in order to represent the screening guidelines for CC (which consider several past test results in decision making). Additionally, the study of personalized risk-differentiated screening strategies requires patient-specific variables to be generated and tracked.

The methods described in this chapter can be applied to the development of quantitative models designed to evaluate screening or treatment alternatives for diseases that progress over time. Such studies require modeling of the progression (and regression, if applicable) of the disease. This includes the specification of state definitions and transition probabilities, such as described in this chapter. The effect of screening and/or treatment interventions (i.e., the costs and possible results) is another necessary aspect of such studies, and this should be represented accounting for the imperfect accuracy of the tests by using probability modeling, as shown here. The standard way of comparing healthcare alternatives is with a cost-effectiveness analysis using QALYs, as illustrated in this chapter. Not all diseases have known risk factors, but those that do can be studied using logistic regression to estimate the probability of disease occurrence given specific levels of risk factors. We describe this approach to incorporate risk in a study, as well as our approach to modeling the manner in which risk factors evolve over a patient's lifetime. For cases in which data cannot be obtained (e.g., because it is not physically possible to test, the diagnostic tests are imperfect, or the interventions or health transitions being evaluated have not been previously studied), we propose the use of optimization models to estimate these data. The sensitivity analyses that we performed included lack of adherence, which is a common issue in healthcare, and the use of vaccine, which may not be a factor that applies to other diseases.

This chapter illustrates an example of how operations research can be applied to study preventive screening alternatives. Studies such as this can be used to inform public health decisions at the population level, as well as to inform patient-specific decisions by the patient and physician.

REFERENCES

Abdollahian, M. and Das, T. (2014). A MDP model for breast and ovarian cancer intervention strategies for BRCA1/2 mutation carriers. *IEEE Journal of Biomedical and Health Informatics*, 19(2):720–727.

ACOG (2009). ACOG practice bulletin no. 109; cervical cytology screening. *Obstetrics and Gynecology*, 114(6):1409–1420.

ALTS Group (2003). Results of a randomized trial on the management of cytology interpretations of atypical squamous cells of undetermined significance. *American Journal of Obstetrics and Gynecology*, 188(6):1383–1392.

Archer, K. and Lemeshow, S. (2006). Goodness-of-fit test for a logistic regression model fitted using survey sample data. *The Stata Journal*, 6(1):97–105.

Archer, K., Lemeshow, S., and Hosmer, D. (2007). Goodness-of-fit tests for logistic regression models when data are collected using a complex sampling design. *Computational Statistics and Data Analysis*, 51(9):4450–4464.

Ashengrau, A. and Seage, G. (2003). *Essentials of Epidemiology in Public Health*. Jones and Bartlett Publishers, Sudbury, MA.

Ayer, T., Alagoz, O., and Stout, N. (2012). OR Forum-A POMDP approach to personalized mammography screening decisions. *Operations Research*, 60(5):1019–1034.

Basen-Engquist, K., Paskett, E., Buzaglo, J., Miller, S., Schover, L., Wenzel, L., and Bodurka, D. (2003). Cervical cancer. *Cancer*, 98(Suppl. 9):2009–2014.

Bergeron, C., Largeron, N., McAllister, R., Mathevet, P., and Remy, V. (2008). Cost-effectiveness analysis of the introduction of a quadrivalent Human Papillomavirus vaccine in France. *International Journal of Technology Assessment in Health Care*, 24(1):10–19.

Bramlett, M. and Mosher, W. (2002). Cohabitation, Marriage, Divorce, and Remarriage in the United States, National Center for Health Statistics. *Vital and Health Statistics*, 23(22). https://www.cdc.gov/nchs/data/series/sr_23/sr23_022.pdf. Accessed on August 22, 2017.

Brandeau, M., Lee, H., Owens, D., Sox, C., and Wachter, R. (1991). A policy model of human immunodeficiency virus screening and intervention. *Interfaces*, 21(3):5–25.

Canfell, K., Barnabas, R., Patnick, J., and Beral, V. (2004). The predicted effect of changes in cervical screening practice in the UK: Results from a modelling study. *British Journal of Cancer*, 91(3):530–536.

CEAR (2013). Cost Effectiveness Analysis Registry. Available at: http://healtheconomics.tuftsmedicalcenter.org/cear4/Home.aspx. Accessed on September 3, 2017.

Centers for Disease Control and Prevention (2002). National Survey of Family Growth, Cycle 6. Available at: https://www.cdc.gov/nchs/nsfg/nsfg_cycle6.htm. Accessed on September 3, 2017.

Centers for Disease Control and Prevention (2009). National Immunization Survey: Teen. Technical report. Available at: https://www.cdc.gov/mmwr/preview/mmwrhtml/mm5932a3.htm. Accessed on September 3, 2017.

Centers for Disease Control and Prevention (2017). Genital HPV Infection Fact Sheet. Available at: https://www.cdc.gov/std/hpv/stdfact-hpv.htm. Accessed on September 3, 2017.

Chen, H., Thurfjel, E., Dell, S., and Tabar, L. (1998). Evaluation by Markov chain models of a non-randomized breast cancer screening programme in women under 50 years in Sweden. *Journal of Epidemiology and Community Health*, 52(5):329–335.

Clifford, G., Franceschi, S., Dia, M., Muñoz, N., and Villa, L. (2006). Chapter 3: HPV type-distribution in women with and without cervical neoplastic diseases. *Vaccine*, 24(Supplement 3):S26–S34.

Col, N., Eckman, M., Karas, R., Pauker, S., Goldberg, R., Ross, E., Orr, R., and Wong, J. (1997). Patient-specific decisions about hormone replacement therapy in postmenopausal women. *Journal of the American Medical Association*, 277(14):1140–1147.

Delco, F. and Sonnenberg, A. (2000). A decision analysis of surveillance for colorectal cancer in ulcerative colitis. *Gut*, 46(4):500–506.

Drolet, M., Laprise, J., Boily, M., Franco, E., and Brisson, M. (2014). Potential cost-effectiveness of the nonavalent Human Papillomavirus (HPV) vaccine. *International Journal of Cancer*, 134(9):2264–2268.

Dunne, E., Unger, E., Sternberg, M., McQuillan, G., Swan, D., Patel, S., and Markowitz, L. (2007). Prevalence of HPV infection among females in the United States. *Journal of the American Medical Association*, 297:813–819.

Eggington, S., Hadwin, R., Brennan, A., and Walker, P. (2006). Modeling the Impact of Referral Guideline Changes for Mild Dyskaryosis on Colposcopy Services in England. Guidelines for the NHS Cervical Screening Programme. NHSCSP Publication 24. NHS Cancer Screening Programmes, Sheffield.

Eggleston, K., Coker, A., Das, I., Cordray, S., and Luchok, K. (2007). Understanding barriers for adherence to follow-up care for abnormal Pap tests. *Journal of Women's Health*, 16(3):311–330.

Eichler, H., Kong, S., Gerth, W., Mavros, P., and Jönsson, B. (2004). Use of cost-effectiveness analysis in health-care resource allocation decision-making: How are cost-effectiveness thresholds expected to emerge? *Value in Health*, 7:518–528.

Elbasha, E., Dasbach, E., and Insinga, R. P. (2007). Model for assessing Human Papillomavirus vaccination strategies. *Emerging Infectious Diseases*, 13(1):28–41.

Favato, G., Pieri, V., and Mills, R. (2007). Cost-Effective Analysis of Anti-HPV Vaccination Programme in Italy: A Multi-Cohort Markov Model. Social Science Research Network. Available at: http://ssrn.com/abstract=961847. Accessed on August 2014.

Franco, E., Mahmud, S., Tota, J., Ferenczy, A., and Coutlée, F. (2009). The expected impact of HPV vaccination on the accuracy of cervical cancer screening: The need for a paradigm change. *Archives of Medical Research*, 40(6):478–485.

Garland, S., Hernandez-Avila, M., Wheeler, C., Perez, G., Harper, D., Leodolter, S., Tank, G. W., Ferris, D. G., Steben, M., Bryan, J., Taddeo, F., Railkar, R., Esser, M., Sings, H., Nelson, M., Boslego, J., Sattler, C., Barr, E., and Koutsky, L. (2007). Quadrivalent vaccine against Human Papillomavirus to prevent anogenital diseases. *New England Journal of Medicine*, 356(19):1928–1943.

van Gerven, M., Díez, F., Taal, B., and Lucas, P. (2007). Selecting treatment strategies with dynamic limited-memory influence diagrams. *Artificial Intelligence in Medicine*, 40(7):171–186.

Glover, F., Kelly, J., and Laguna, M. (1999). New advances for wedding optimization and simulation. In Farrington, P., Nembhard, H., Sturrock, D., and Evans, G., editors, *Proceedings of the 31st Conference on Winter Simulation: Simulation—A Bridge to the Future*, volume 1, pp. 255–260. ACM Press, New York.

Goldhaber-Fiebert, J., Stout, N., Salomon, J., Kuntz, K., and Goldie, S. (2008). Cost-effectiveness of cervical cancer screening with Human Papillomavirus DNA testing and HPV-16,18 vaccination. *Journal of the National Cancer Institute*, 100(5):308–320.

Goldie, S., Weinstein, M., Kuntz, K., and Freedberg, K. (1999). The costs, clinical benefits, and cost-effectiveness of screening for cervical cancer in HIV-infected women. *Annals of Internal Medicine*, 130(2):97–107.

Goldie, S., Kuhn, L., Denny, L., Pollack, A., and Wright, T. (2001). Policy analysis of cervical cancer screening strategies in low resource settings: Clinical benefits and cost-effectiveness. *Journal of the American Medical Association*, 284(24):3107–3115.

Goldie, S., Kim, J., and Wright, T. (2004). Cost-effectiveness of Human Papillomavirus DNA testing for cervical cancer screening in women aged 30 years or more. *Obstetrics & Gynecology*, 103(4):619–631.

Gomez, M., Bielza, C., Fernandex, J., and Rios Insua, S. (2007). A graphical decision-theoretic model for neonatal jaundice. *Medical Decision Making*, 27(3):250–265.

Greenhalgh, J., Bagust, A., Boland, A., Blundell, M., Oyee, J., Beale, S., Dundar, Y., Hockenhull, J., Proudlove, C., and Chu, P. (2013). Rituximab for the first-line maintenance treatment of follicular non-Hodgkin's lymphoma. *PharmacoEconomics*, 31(5):403–413.

Hauskrecht, M. and Fraser, H. (2000). Planning treatment of ischemic heart disease with partially observable Markov-decision process. *Artificial Intelligence in Medicine*, 18(3):221–244.

Hazen, G. (2004). Dynamic influence diagrams: Applications to medical decision making. In Brandeau, M. L., Sainfort, F., and Pierskalla, W. P., editors, *Operations Research and Health Care*, pp. 613–638. Springer, Boston, MA.

Ho, G., Beardsley, R. B., Chang, C., and Burk, R. (1998). Natural history of cervicovaginal papillomavirus infection in young women. *The New England Journal of Medicine*, 338(7):423–438.

Hosmer, D. W., Lemeshow, S., and Sturdivant, R. X. (2013). *Applied Logistic Regression*, volume 398. John Wiley & Sons, Hoboken, NJ.

Insinga, R., Dasbach, E., Elbasha, E., Liaw, K., and Barr, E. (2007). Progression and regression of incident cervical HPV 6, 11, 16, and 18 infections in young women. *Infectious Agents and Cancer*, 2:15.

Johnson, N., Sutton, J., Thornton, J., Lilford, R., Johnson, V., and Peel, K. (1993). Decision analysis for best management of mildly dyskaryotic smear. *Lancet*, 342(8863):91–96.

Kahn, J., Lan, D., and Kahn, R. (2007). Sociodemographic factors associated with high-risk Human Papillomavirus infection. *Obstetrics and Gynecology*, 110(1):87–95.

Kim, J., Wright, T., and Goldie, S. (2002). Cost-effectiveness of alternative triage strategies for atypical squamous cells of undetermined significance. *Journal of the American Medical Association*, 287(18):2382–2390.

Kim, J., Ortendahl, J., and Goldie, S. (2009). Cost-effectiveness of Human Papillomavirus and cervical cancer screening in women older than 30 years in the United States. *Annals of Internal Medicine*, 151(8):538–545.

Kohli, M., Ferko, N., Martin, A., Franco, E., Jenkins, D., Gallivan, S., Sherla-Johnson, C., and Drummond, M. (2007). Estimating the long-term impact of a prophylactic Human Papillomavirus (HPV) 16/18 vaccine on the burden of cervical cancer in the UK. *British Journal of Cancer*, 96(1):143–150.

de Kok, I. M., van Rosmalen, J., Joost, D., Dillner, J., Arbyn, M., Sasieni, P., Iftner, T., and van Ballegooijen, M. (2012). Primary screening for Human Papillomavirus compared with cytology screening for cervical cancer in European settings: Cost effectiveness analysis based on a Dutch microsimulation model. *BMJ*, 344:e670.

Kulasingam, S. and Myers, E. (2003). Potential health and economic impact of adding a Human Papillomavirus vaccine to screening programs. *Journal of the American Medical Association*, 290:781–789.

Kulasingam, S., Hughes, J., Kiviat, N., Mao, C., Weiss, N., Kuypers, J., and Koutsky, L. (2002). Evaluation of Human Papillomavirus testing in primary screening for cervical abnormalities: Comparison of sensitivity, specificity, and frequency of referral. *Journal of the American Medical Association*, 288(14):1749–1757.

Kulasingam, S., Kim, J., Lawrence, W., Mandelblatt, J., Myers, E., Schiffman, M., Solomon, D., and Goldie, S. (2006a). Cost-effectiveness analysis based on the atypical squamous cells of undetermined significance/low-grade squamous intraepithelial lesion triage study ALTS. *Journal of the National Cancer Institute*, 98(2):92–100.

Kulasingam, S., Myers, E., Lawson, H., McConnell, K., Kerlikowske, K., Melnikow, J., Washington, A., and Sawaya, G. (2006b). Cost-effectiveness of extending cervical cancer screening intervals among women with prior normal pap tests. *Obstetrics & Gynecology*, 107(2):321–328.

Kulasingam, S., Havrilesky, L., Ghebre, R., and Myers, E. (2011). Screening for Cervical Cancer: A Decision Analysis for the US Preventive Services Task Force. AHRQ Publication No. 11-05157-EF-1. Agency for Healthcare Research and Quality, Rockville, MD.

Lee, R., Ekaette, E., Kelly, K., Craighead, P., Newcomb, C., and Dunscombe, P. (2006). Implications of cancer staging uncertainties in radiation therapy decisions. *Medical Decision Making*, 26(3):226–238.

Lee, J., Kopans, D., McMahon, P., Halpern, E., Ryan, P., Weinstein, M., and Gazelle, G. (2008). Breast cancer screening in BRCA1 mutation carriers: Effectiveness of MR imaging—Markov Monte-Carlo decision analysis. *Radiology*, 246(3):763–771.

Liaw, K., Glass, A., Manos, M., Greer, C., Scott, D., Sherman, M., Burk, R., Kurman, R., Wacholder, S., Rush, B., Cadell, D. M., Lawler, P., Tabor, D., and Schiffman, M. (1999). Detection of Human Papillomavirus DNA in cytologically normal women and subsequent cervical squamous intraepithelial lesions. *Journal of the National Cancer Institute*, 91:954–960.

Long, E., Brandeau, M., and Owens, D. (2009). Potential population health outcomes and expenditures of HIV vaccination strategies in the United States. *Vaccine*, 27(39): 5402–5410.

Magni, P., QUaglini, S., Marchetti, M., and Barosi, G. (2000). Deciding when to intervene: A Markov decision process approach. *International Journal of Medical Informatics*, 60(3):237–253.

Manos, M., Kinney, W., Hurley, L., Sherman, M., Shieh-Ngai, J., Kurman, R., Ransley, J., Fetterman, B., Hartinger, J., and McIntosh, K. (1999). Identifying women with cervical neoplasia using Human Papillomavirus DNA testing for equivocal Papanicolaou results. *Journal of the American Medical Association*, 281:1605–1610.

Marcus, A., Crane, L., Kaplan, C., Reading, A., Savage, E., Gunning, J., Bernstein, G., and Berek, J. (1992). Improving adherence to screening follow-up among women with abnormal pap smears: Results from a large clinic-based trial of three intervention strategies. *Medical Care*, 30(3):216–230.

McEwan, P., Ward, T., Yuan, Y., Kim, R., and L'Italien, G. (2013). The impact of timing and prioritization on the cost-effectiveness of birth cohort testing and treatment for hepatitis C virus in the United States. *Hepatology*, 58(1):54–64.

McLay, L. A., Foufoulides, C., and Merrick, J. (2010). Using simulation-optimization to construct screening strategies for cervical cancer. *Health Care Management Science*, 13(4):294–318.

Melnikow, J., Kulasingam, S., Slee, C., Helms, L., Kuppermann, M., Birch, S., McGahan, C., Coldman, A., Chan, B., and Sawaya, G. (2010). Surveillance after treatment of cervical intraepithelial neoplasia: Outcomes, costs, and cost-effectiveness. *Obstetrics & Gynecology*, 116:1158–1170.

Meyer, J., Phillips, M., Cho, P., Kalet, I., and Doctor, J. (2004). Application of influence diagrams to prostate intensity-modulated radiation theory plan selection. *Physics in Medicine and Biology*, 49(9):1637–1653.

Moscicki, A., Shiboski, S., Borering, J., Powell, K., Clayton, L., Jay, N., Darragh, T., Brescia, R., Kanowitz, S., Miller, S., Stone, J., Hanson, E., and Palefsky, J. (1998). The natural history of Human Papillomavirus infection as measured by repeated DNA testing in adolescent and young women. *Journal of Pediatrics*, 132(2):277–284.

Moscicki, A., Hills, N., Shiboski, S., Powell, K., Jay, J., Hanson, E., Miller, S., Clayton, L., Farhat, S., Broering, J., Darragh, T., and Palefsky, J. (2001). Risks for incident Human Papillomavirus infection and low-grade squamous intraepithelial lesion development in young females. *Journal of the American Medical Association*, 285:2995–3002.

Moscicki, A., Schiffman, M., Kjaer, S., and Villa, L. (2006). Chapter 5: Updating the natural history of HPV and anogenital cancer. *Vaccine*, 24:42–51.

Muñoz, N. (2000). Human Papillomavirus and cancer: the epidemiological evidence. *Journal of Clinical Virology*, 19:1–5.

Muñoz, N., Mendez, F., Posso, H., Molano, M., van den Brule, A., Ronderos, M., Meijer, C., Muñoz, A., and Instituo Nacional de Cancerologia HPV Study Group (2004). Incidence, duration, and determinants of cervical Human Papillomavirus infection in a cohort of Colombian women with normal cytological results. *The Journal of Infectious Diseases*, 190(12):2077–2087.

Myers, E., McCrory, D., Nanda, K., Bastian, L., and Matchar, D. (2000). Mathematical model for the natural history of Human Papillomavirus infection and cervical carcinogenesis. *American Journal of Epidemiology*, 151(12):1158–1171.

Nanda, K., McCrory, D., Myers, E., Bastian, L., Hasselblad, V., Hickey, J., and Matchar, D. (2000). Accuracy of the Papanicolaou test in screening for and follow-up of cervical cytologic abnormalities: A systematic review. *Annals of Internal Medicine*, 132(10):810–819.

NCHS (2010). National Center for Health Statistics: Mortality Data from the National Vital Statistics System. Available at: www.cdc.gov/nchs/deaths.htm. Accessed on June 2013.

NCHS (2014). National Center of Health Statistics. Available at: http://www.cdc.gov/nchs/nhanes/about_nhanes.htm. Accessed on November 2014.

Norman, J., Shahar, Y., Kupperman, M., and Gold, B. (1998). Decision-Theoretic Analysis of Prenatal Testing Strategies. Technical Report SMI-98-0711. Stanford Medical Informatics, Stanford University, Stanford, CA.

O'Dowd, K. (2003). Sexual risk status and behavior of New Jersey adults: Results from the New Jersey Behavioral Risk Factor Survey, 1998–1999. New Jersey Department of Health and Senior Services Topics in Health Statistics, Trenton, NJ.

Obuchowski, N. and Lieber, M. (2008). The effect of misclassification in screening trials: A simulation study. *Contemporary Clinical Trials*, 29(2):125–135.

Paskett, E., McLaughlin, J., Reiter, P., Lehman, A., Rhoda, D., Katz, M., Hade, E., Post, D., and Ruffin, M. (2010). Psychosocial predictors of adherence to risk appropriate cervical cancer screening guidelines: A cross-sectional study of women in Ohio Appalachia participating in the community awareness resources and education (CARE) project. *Preventive Medicine*, 50(1–2):74–80.

Perrault, S., Levington, C., Laurier, C., Moride, Y., Ste-Marie, L., and Crott, R. (2005). Validation of a decision model for preventive pharmacological strategies in postmenopausal women. *European Journal of Epidemiology*, 20(1):89–101.

Ragnarson-Tennvall, G. and Apelqvist, J. (2001). Prevention of diabetes-related foot ulcers and amputations: A cost-utility analysis based on Markov model simulation. *Diabetologia*, 44(11):2077–2087.

Richardson, H., Kelsall, G., Tellier, P., Voyer, H., Abramowicz, M., Ferenczy, A., Coutlée, F., and Franco, E. (2003). The natural history of type-specific Human Papillomavirus infections in female university students. *Cancer Epidemiology, Biomarkers & Prevention*, 12(6):485–490.

Saito, E., Nakamoto, B., Mendez, M., Mehta, B., and McMrtray, A. (2014). Cost effective community based dementia screening: A Markov model simulation. *International Journal of Alzheimer's Disease*, 2014:103138.

Sanders, G. and Taira, A. (2003). Cost effectiveness of a potential vaccine for Human Papillomavirus. *Emerging Infectious Diseases*, 9(1):37–48.

Sasagawa, T., Tani, M., and Yasuda, H. (2005). Sexual behavior and high risk Human Papillomavirus infections in Japanese women. *Sexually Transmitted Infections*, 81:280–282.

Saslow, D., Solomon, D., Lawson, H., Killackey, M., Kulasingam, S., Cain, J., Garcia, F., Moriarity, A., Waxman, A., Wentzensen, N., Jr, Downs, L., Spitzer, M., Moscicki, A.-B., Franco, E., Stoler, M., Schiffman, M., Castle, P., and Meyers, E. R. (2012). American Cancer Society, American Society for Colposcopy and Cervical Pathology, and American Society for Clinical Pathology screening guidelines for the prevention and early detection of cervical cancer. *CA: A Cancer Journal for Clinicians*, 63:147–172.

Schiffman, M. and Castle, P. (2003). Human Papillomavirus: Epidemiology and public health. *Archives of Pathology and Laboratory Medicine*, 127(8):930–934.

Schiffman, M. and Kjaer, S. (2003). Natural history of anogenital Human Papillomavirus infection and neoplasia. *JNCI Monographs*, 31:14–19.

Sellors, J., Karwalajtys, T., Kaczorowski, J., Mahony, J., Lytwyn, A., Chong, S., Sparro, J., and Lorincz, A. (2003). Incidence, clearance and predictors of Human Papillomavirus infection in women. *Canadian Medical Association Journal*, 168:421–425.

Sherman, M., Lorinca, A., Scott, D., Wacholder, S., Castle, P., Glass, A., Mielzynski-Lohnas, I., Rush, B., and Schiffman, M. (2003). Baseline cytology, Human Papillomavirus testing, and risk for cervical neoplasia: A 10-year cohort analysis. *Journal of the National Cancer Institute*, 95(1):46–52.

Siebert, U., Sroczynski, G., Hillemanns, P., Engel, J., Stabenow, R., Stegmaier, C., Voigt, K., Gibis, B., Holzel, D., and Goldie, S. (2006). The German cervical cancer screening model: Development and validation of a decision-analytic model for cervical cancer screening in Germany. *European Journal of Public Health*, 16(1):185–192.

Smith, R., Cokkinides, V., Brooks, D., Saslow, D., and Brawley, O. (2010). Cancer screening in the United States, 2010: A review of current American Cancer Society guidelines and issues in cancer screening. *CA: A Cancer Journal of Clinicians*, 60:99–119.

Solomon, D., Schiffman, M., and Tarone, R. (2001). Comparison of three management strategies for patients with atypical squamous cells of undetermined significance: Baseline results from a randomized trial. *Journal of the National Cancer Institute*, 93(4):293–299.

Stout, N., Goldhaber-Fiebert, J., Jeremy, D., Ortendahl, J., and Goldie, S. (2008). Trade-offs in cervical cancer prevention: balancing benefits and risks. *Archives in Internal Medicine*, 168(7):1881–1889.

Trottier, H., Mahmud, S. M., Lindsay, L., Jenkins, D., Quint, W., Wieting, S., Schuind, A., and Franco, E. (2009). Persistence of an incident Human Papillomavirus infection and timing of cervical lesions in previously unexposed young women. *Cancer Epidemiology, Biomarkers & Prevention*, 18(3):854–862.

U.S. Census Bureau (2001). Survey of Income and Program Participation, 2001 Panel. Wave 2 Topical Module. U.S. Department of Commerce, Economics and Statistics Administration, U.S. Census Bureau, Washington, DC.

U.S. Census Bureau (2003). Survey of Income and Program Participation. Available at: https://www.census.gov/sipp/. Accessed on September 2, 2017.

Vijayaraghavan, A., Efrusy, M., Mayrand, M., Santas, C., and Goggin, P. (2010). Cost-effectiveness of high-risk Human Papillomavirus testing for cervical cancer in Quebec, Canada. *Canadian Journal of Public Health/Revue Candienne de Sante'e Publique*, 101(3):220–225.

Weinstein, M., Torrance, G., and McGuire, A. (2009). QALYs: The basics. *Value in Health*, 12:S5–S9.

Westra, T., Stirbu-Wagner, I., Dorsman, S., Tutuhatunewa, E., de Vrij, E., Nijman, H., Daemen, T., Wilschut, J., and Postma, M. (2013). Inclusion of the benefits of enhanced cost-protection against cervical cancer and prevention of genital warts in the cost-effectiveness analysis of Human Papillomavirus in the Netherlands. *BMC Infectious Diseases*, 13(1):75.

Winer, R., Lee, S., Hughes, J., Adam, D., Kiviat, N., and Koutsky, L. (2003). Genital Human Papillomavirus infection: Incidence and risk factors in a cohort of female university students. *American Journal of Epidemiology*, 157:218–226.

World Health Organization (2013). Sexual and Reproductive Health. Available at: www.who.int/reproductivehealth/topics/cancers/en/. Accessed on June 2013.

Wright, T., Schiffman, M., Solomon, D., Cox, J., Garcia, F., Goldie, S., Hatch, K., Noller, K., Roach, N., Runowicz, C., and Saslow, D. (2004). Interim guidance for the use of Human Papillomavirus DNA testing as an adjunct to cervical cytology for screening. *Obstetrics and Gynecology*, 103:304–309.

Wright, Jr., T., Massad, L., Dunton, C., Spitzer, M., Wilkinson, E., and Solomon, D. (2007a). 2006 Consensus guidelines for the management of women with abnormal cervical cancer screening tests. *American Journal of Obstetrics and Gynecology*, 197(4):346–355. American Society for Colposcopy and Cervical Pathology-Sponsored Consensus Conference.

Wright, Jr., T., Massad, L., Dunton, C., Spitzer, M., Wilkinson, E., and Solomon, D. (2007b). 2006 consensus guidelines for the management of women with cervical intraepithelial neoplasia or adenocarcinoma in situ. *American Journal of Obstetrics and Gynecology*, 197:340–345.

8

USING FINITE-HORIZON MARKOV DECISION PROCESSES FOR OPTIMIZING POST-MAMMOGRAPHY DIAGNOSTIC DECISIONS

Sait Tunc[1], Oguzhan Alagoz[1], Jagpreet Chhatwal[2], and Elizabeth S. Burnside[3]

[1]*Department of Industrial and Systems Engineering, University of Wisconsin-Madison, Madison, WI, USA*
[2]*Institute for Technology Assessment, Massachusetts General Hospital, Harvard Medical School, Boston, MA, USA*
[3]*Department of Radiology, University of Wisconsin School of Medicine and Public Health, Madison, WI, USA*

8.1 INTRODUCTION

The American Cancer Society (ACS) estimates that approximately 231,840 women would be diagnosed with breast cancer in 2015, making breast cancer the most common non-skin cancer affecting women in the United States. Breast cancer also accounts for the second leading cause of cancer death in women, after lung cancer, with approximately 40,290 deaths (ACS 2015). The National Cancer Institute (NCI) estimates that one out of every eight women will develop breast cancer in their lifetime (Kootstra et al. 2010). All of these statistics indicate that breast cancer is an important disease that has significant impacts on the overall health of women.

Decision Analytics and Optimization in Disease Prevention and Treatment, First Edition.
Edited by Nan Kong and Shengfan Zhang.
© 2018 John Wiley & Sons, Inc. Published 2018 by John Wiley & Sons, Inc.

While various breast cancer treatment options such as radiation therapy, chemotherapy, and hormone therapy have become available in recent years, early diagnosis still remains as the keystone of successful treatment (Fryback et al. 2006; Alagoz et al. 2011). If the breast cancer is diagnosed at an early stage (stage I), the 5-year survival rate is about 100%; however if it is diagnosed in the more advanced metastatic stage, the 5-year survival rate drops to 21% (Hayat et al. 2007). There exist several breast cancer screening (or diagnostic) methods such as magnetic resonance imaging (MRI), X-ray mammography, and ultrasound. Among these techniques, mammography is the current standard practice for identifying cancer early in asymptomatic women (Smith et al. 2015; Siu and U.S. Preventive Services Task Force 2016).

While there have been many studies that focus on the optimal breast cancer screening strategies (Maillart et al. 2008; Ivy 2009; van Ravesteyn et al. 2012; Batina et al. 2013; Munoz et al. 2014; Sprague et al. 2014; Stout et al. 2014; Lee et al. 2015), there have been relatively fewer studies that focus on improving breast cancer diagnosis. On the other hand, an important decision problem arises when a mammogram is performed and viewed by a radiologist. Based on the mammography findings, first, the woman's risk of cancer needs to be accurately determined, and then appropriate management of the patients must be determined. There are three common options widely utilized by radiologists for managing patients: (i) immediate diagnostic actions including prompt biopsy, that is, examination of the breast tissue removed using a needle or surgical excision; (ii) routine follow-up mammography in a year; and (iii) short-term follow-up mammography in six months. During this decision-making process, radiologists face a trade-off between the early detection of cancer and avoiding the burden of unnecessary procedures.

Decisions regarding the recommendation of follow-up exams are not trivial as the mammography results include extensive amount of information that needs to be interpreted. The accuracy of mammography interpretation varies with the radiologist's skills and training (Beam et al. 1996; Barlow et al. 2004). There are several studies demonstrating the inefficiency of current clinical practice, suggesting that only 0.4% of mammograms requiring follow-up investigations result in breast cancer diagnosis (Sickles 1991; Varas et al. 1992, 2002; Vizcaíno et al. 2001). Another study of the Breast Cancer Surveillance Consortium (BCSC) shows that the cancer detection rate is 8.4 per 1000 among short-term follow-up recommendations (Sickles et al. 2005). In addition, there are several studies reporting significant variability among radiologists' interpretation of mammograms and diagnostic decisions (Elmore et al. 1994, 2015; Beam et al. 1996). While the rate of recommendation for short-term follow-up is reported around 40% in Geller et al. (2002), Monticciolo and Caplan (2004) found that the rate varied by site from 1.1% to 12.2% in a study investigating the use of follow-up recommendations in multiple sites.

To standardize mammography interpretation, the American College of Radiology (ACR) has developed a format called the Breast Imaging Reporting and Data System (BI-RADS) (BI-RADS 1998). BI-RADS format enables describing mammograms using standardized descriptors and classifying them into one of the six final assessment categories. However, BI-RADS assessment alone does not provide enough information to overcome the interpretation variability. An effort in that direction has been made by computer-aided diagnosis (CADx) models, which utilize BI-RADS features to estimate the probability of breast cancer (Burnside et al. 2006; Chhatwal et al. 2009; Ayer et al. 2010a, b). Recently, this effort was taken further by using finite-horizon Markov decision processes (MDPs) to determine the optimal probability thresholds for recommending biopsy or short-term follow-up for a given patient (Chhatwal et al. 2010; Ayvaci et al. 2012; Burnside et al. 2012; Alagoz et al. 2013). This chapter primarily focuses on the finite-horizon MDP models introduced in Chhatwal et al. (2010), Ayvaci et al. (2012), and Alagoz et al. (2013) and summarizes the problem formulations, structural and clinical findings, and results of these three articles.

The rest of this chapter is organized as follows. In Section 8.2, we describe the model formulations of a general finite-horizon MDP model for the optimal post-mammography diagnostic decision problem. In Section 8.3, we provide the structural properties of these MDP models. We then summarize the results of three MDP models in Section 8.4. We conclude with in Section 8.5.

8.2   MODEL FORMULATIONS

In this chapter, we will review three finite-horizon MDP models from the literature to address the optimal post-mammography diagnostic decision problem (Chhatwal et al. 2010; Ayvaci et al. 2012; Alagoz et al. 2013). While each model includes problem-specific assumptions and constraints, we will start with presenting a basic model formulation. For all these models, a woman undergoes a mammogram and a radiologist, who is the decision maker, examines the results. The radiologist makes a decision based on the woman's risk of cancer, which can be estimated heuristically or using a computer-aided prediction model. The objective of the decision maker is to maximize the woman's total expected quality-adjusted life years (QALYs). All of these studies assume that the radiologist is risk neutral so that they utilize total expected QALYs of the woman as the objective function. Finally, due to the lack of data on women with a history of biopsy, these models focus on women who did not have an earlier biopsy. In modeling terms, a woman is assumed to leave the decision process after a biopsy is performed. Next, we describe the formal definitions of these three MDP models.

Decision Epochs: $t = 0, 1, 2, \ldots, T, T < \infty$. Here, t is defined as the number of years in Chhatwal et al. (2010) and the number of 6-month periods in Ayvaci et al. (2012) and Alagoz et al. (2013), above the age of 40 years. The decision horizon ends at the age of 100 years, that is, $T = 60$ in Chhatwal et al. (2010) and $T = 120$ in Ayvaci et al. (2012) and Alagoz et al. (2013). While the total length of decision horizon differs, for all these models, the problem is formulated as a finite-horizon MDP.

States: s_t is defined as the system state at decision epoch t with $s_t \in S = \{0,1,\ldots,S,S+1,S+2\}$. Here, $\{0, 1, \ldots, S\}$ represents the risk score for which all three models use the discretized version of probability of breast cancer with $S = 100$. For instance, if the probability of cancer is 0.281, then the corresponding risk score is 28. $S+1$ represents the post-biopsy state and $S+2$ represents death.

Actions: Action space corresponding to decision epoch t and state s_t is defined as $A_t(s_t) = \{$Biopsy (Bx), Annual mammogram $(Am)\}$ in Chhatwal et al. (2010), for $t < T$ and $s_t \in S \setminus \{S+1, S+2\}$, and $A_t(s_t) = \varnothing$ for $t = T$ or $s_t \in \{S+1, S+2\}$. Ayvaci et al. (2012) and Alagoz et al. (2013) added a new action to their action space, namely, "short-term follow-up (Sf)."

Transition Probabilities: Transition probabilities follow a very similar structure for all three papers. Only a small difference occurs due to the inclusion of short-term follow-up. Here, we will provide a general transition probability structure. Let $p_t^a(s_{t+1} \mid s_t)$ denote the probability that the woman will be in state $s_{t+1} \in S$ at time $t+1$, given that the woman is in state s_t and the action is $a \in A$ at time t. Then,

$$p_t^{Bx}\left(s_{t+1} \mid s_t\right) = \begin{cases} 0 & \text{if } s_{t+1} \in S \setminus \{S+1\} \\ 1 & \text{if } s_{t+1} = S+1 \end{cases}$$

for $s_t \in S \setminus \{S+2\}$ and $p_t^{Bx}(S+2 \mid S+2) = 1$ for all $t < T$.

Similarly, if the action is Sf, we have $p_t^{Sf}(S+1 \mid S+1) = 1$, $p_t^{Sf}(S+2 \mid S+2) = 1$, $p_t^{Sf}(S+1 \mid s_t) = 0$ for all $s_t \in S \setminus \{S+1\}$ and $t < T$. And if the action is Am, the transition probabilities can be defined using

$$p_t^{Am}\left(s_{t+2} \mid s_t\right) = \sum_{s_{t+1} \in S} p_t^{Sf}\left(s_{t+1} \mid s_t\right) p_{t+1}^{Sf}\left(s_{t+2} \mid s_{t+1}\right).$$

Transitions to the death state $S+2$ require the analysis of different scenarios. Let $\rho_t^{nc}(S+2)$ represent the probability of death during decision epoch t when the woman has no cancer. Similarly, let $\rho_t^{nt}(S+2)$ represent the probability of death during decision epoch t when the woman has cancer but has not received any treatment. We can then define

$$p_t^{Sf}\left(S+2 \mid s_t\right) = w\left(s_t\right)\rho_t^{nc}(S+2) + \left(1 - w\left(s_t\right)\right)\rho_t^{nt}(S+2),$$

where $w(s_t) \triangleq s_t / 100$ represents the probability of cancer at time t. When the action is Am,

$$p_t^{Am}\left(S+2 \mid s_t\right) = \sum_{s_{t+1} \in S} p_t^{Sf}\left(s_{t+1} \mid s_t\right) p_{t+1}^{Sf}\left(S+2 \mid s_{t+1}\right)$$

$$= p_t^{Sf}\left(S+2 \mid s_t\right) + \sum_{s_{t+1} \in S \setminus \{S+2\}} p_t^{Sf}\left(s_{t+1} \mid s_t\right) p_{t+1}^{Sf}\left(S+2 \mid s_{t+1}\right).$$

For the model with only two actions, where Sf is ignored, p_t^{Am} will be defined the same as the p_t^{Sf} definition earlier.

Rewards: There are several alternative outcomes that can be used as reward. We will consider the most commonly used one in medical decision making, namely, expected QALYs (Pliskin et al. 1980; Drummond 2005). QALYs incorporate risk-neutral utilities of health states and measure both the quality and quantity of the expected life years. QALYs have been used extensively in the operations research applications in medical decision making (Sandikci et al. 2008; Shechter et al. 2008; Alagoz et al. 2010; Akan et al. 2012; Ayer et al. 2012, 2016; Zhang et al. 2012a, b; Erenay et al. 2014). All three MDP models use similar rewards defined as QALYs, and there is only a small difference in considering the disutility of the action. Let $r_t(s_t, Sf)$ represent the intermediate expected reward accrued between time t and $t+1$, when the woman is in state s_t and the action is Sf, and $r_t(s_t, Am)$ represent the intermediate expected reward accrued between time t and $t+2$, when the woman is in state s_t and the action is Am. If the action is Bx, then (Chhatwal et al. 2010) assumed that the woman leaves the decision process having a post-biopsy reward $r_t(s_t, Bx)$ corresponding to their risk score s_t. The definition of post-biopsy reward depends on whether the biopsy outcome is negative (benign), $r_t(s_t, Bx, NC)$, or positive (malignant), $r_t(s_t, Bx, C)$, and $r_t(s_t, Bx)$ can easily be calculated as

$$r_t\left(s_t,Bx\right) = r_t\left(s_t,Bx,NC\right)q_t\left(NC|s_t\right) + r_t\left(s_t,Bx,C\right)q_t\left(C|s_t\right) - dBx(t),$$

where $q_t(NC|s_t)$ and $q_t(C|s_t)$ represent the probability of positive and negative biopsy outcomes when the woman is in state s_t, respectively, and $dBx(t)$ represents the disutility of biopsy at time t. Ayvaci et al. (2012) and Alagoz et al. (2013) relaxed the assumption of leaving the decision process after a biopsy regardless of its outcome by assuming that a woman with benign biopsy outcome accrues an intermediate expected reward $r_t(s_t, Bx, NC)$ between time t and $t+1$ and moves to state 0.

Optimality Equations: Here, we will provide a general form of optimality equations that can account for the three-action scenario. Given the discount factor $\gamma \in [0, 1]$, the optimal policy for the aforementioned finite-horizon MDP can be calculated by dynamically solving the following Bellman equations (Puterman 1994):

$$\vartheta_t\left(s_t\right) = \max\left\{r_t\left(s_t,Bx\right), r_t\left(s_t,Sf\right) + \gamma\sum_{s'\in S}p_t^{Sf}\left(s'|s_t\right)\vartheta_{t+1}\left(s'\right),\right.$$
$$\left. r_t\left(s_t,Am\right) + \gamma^2\sum_{s'\in S}p_t^{Am}\left(s'|s_t\right)\vartheta_{t+2}\left(s'\right)\right\}, \quad s_t \in \mathcal{S}, t = 0,1,\ldots,T-2. \tag{8.1}$$

$$\vartheta_{T-1}\left(s_{T-1}\right) = \max\left\{r_{T-1}\left(s_{T-1},Bx\right), r_{T-1}\left(s_{T-1},Sf\right)\right.$$
$$\left. + \gamma\sum_{s'\in S}p_{T-1}^{Sf}\left(s'|s_{T-1}\right)\vartheta_T\left(s'\right)\right\}, \quad s_{T-1} \in \mathcal{S}. \tag{8.2}$$

For $t = T$, we add a boundary condition as follows:

$$\vartheta_T\left(s_T\right) = r_T\left(s_T,Sf\right) = r_T\left(s_T,Am\right) = r_T\left(s_T,Bx\right), \quad s_T \in \mathcal{S}. \tag{8.3}$$

Note that Ayvaci et al. (2012) also introduced an additional cost constraint that imposes an upper bound on the expected expenditures from follow-up imaging and biopsy under a policy π. Let $c_t(s_t, a_t(s_t))$ represent the total cost of action $a_t(s)t$ in state s_t at time t and define C^π as

$$C^\pi \triangleq \mathbb{E}^\pi \left[\sum_{t=0}^{T-1} \lambda^t c_t \left(s_t, a_t \left(s_t \right) \right) \right],$$

where λ is the discount factor for cost. Then the budget-constrained MDP model can be defined as follows:

$$\vartheta^{\pi, C_\sigma} \triangleq \sup \left\{ \vartheta^\pi \middle| C^\pi \leq C_\sigma \right\},$$

where C_σ represents the total budget allocation.

Note that the authors use finite-horizon MDP models for the post-mammography diagnostic decision problem to incorporate the woman's age into the models. As a woman gets older, her expected life years decrease, her history of biopsy or surgery may change, and her probability of death increases. To model the problem with an infinite-horizon MDP, one needs to incorporate age into the state space, which will noticeably increase the size of it and will necessitate the use of approximate dynamic programming to solve the resulting numerically intractable model.

8.3   STRUCTURAL PROPERTIES

In this section, we summarize the structural properties of the three MDP models with their clinical relevance. These properties are especially helpful in helping clinical decision makers to obtain insights and managerial intuition for the optimal diagnostic policy. We will provide the properties for the setup where the number of possible actions is three. We start with providing the necessary assumptions that will be used in this section.

Assumption 8.1
The reward functions $r_t(s_t, \text{Sf})$, $r_t(s_t, \text{Am})$, and $r_t(s_t, \text{Bx})$ are all nonincreasing in s_t for all t and in t.

Assumption 8.1 implies that the woman's resulting QALYs after each action do not increase with her risk of cancer or age.

Assumption 8.2
The transition probability matrices $\mathbb{P}_t^{Sf} = \left[p_t^{Sf}(.|.) \right]$ and $\mathbb{P}_t^{Am} = \left[p_t^{Am}(.|.) \right]$ satisfy the following:

$$\sum_{s'=j}^{S+1} p_t^{Sf}\left(s'|i \right) \leq \sum_{s'=j}^{S+1} p_{t+1}^{Sf}\left(s'|i \right)$$

$$\sum_{s'=j}^{S+1} p_t^{Am}\left(s'|i \right) \leq \sum_{s'=j}^{S+1} p_{t+1}^{Am}\left(s'|i \right)$$

for all $i, j \in \mathcal{S} \setminus \{S+1\}$.

Assumption 8.2 implies that the probability of woman moving to high-risk states, including death, increases with increasing age.

We start with showing the monotonicity of $\vartheta_t(s_t)$ in s and t, which enables proving more comprehensive results and making them clinically relevant. To show the monotonicity of $\vartheta_t(s_t)$, we need the following definition, which is commonly used in the MDP literature on optimal decision/treatment problems (Alagoz et al. 2004, 2007a, b; Shechter et al. 2008).

Definition 8.1

(Barlow and Proschan 1965) *A Markov chain is increasing failure rate (IFR) if its rows are in increasing stochastic order, that is, $q(i) = \sum_{j=m}^{S} P(j|i)$ is nondecreasing in i for all $m = 1, 2, \ldots, S$.*

Proposition 8.1 provides a set of sufficient conditions for $\vartheta_t(s_t)$ to be nonincreasing in s, which implies that the woman's total expected QALYs never increase with her risk score. Furthermore, Proposition 8.2 shows that $\vartheta_t(s_t)$ is nonincreasing in t, which similarly implies that the woman's total expected QALYs never increase with her age.

Proposition 8.1

If $\mathbb{P}_t^{Sf}$ and $\mathbb{P}_t^{Am}$ are IFR for $t = 1, 2, \ldots, T$, then $\vartheta_t(s)$ is nonincreasing in s, for $s = 1, \ldots, S$ and $t = 0, 1, \ldots, T-1$.

Proof: See the proof of Theorem 4.7.3 in Puterman (1994). ∎

Proposition 8.2

If Assumption 8.2 holds, then $\vartheta_t(s_t)$ is nonincreasing in t for all $s_t \in S \setminus \{S+1\}$.

Proof: See the proof of Proposition 2 in Chhatwal et al. (2010). ∎

Next we define a new type of structured policies proposed by Alagoz et al. (2013) for their problem context with three possible actions. The definition is an extension of control-limit policies and inspired by the double-threshold policies, which are used in the MDP literature on equipment maintenance problems. Similar to the control-limit policies, these structured policies reduce the complexity of the optimal policy search, and furthermore, they are easier to implement in clinical practice.

Definition 8.2

(Alagoz et al. 2013) *A policy $\pi = \left[a_t^*(s_t) \right]_{t=0,\ldots,T-1}$ is said to be a double-control-limit (DCL) policy if there exist thresholds $s_t^l, s_t^u \in S \setminus \{S+1\}$ such that*

$$a_t^*(s_t) = \begin{cases} Am & \text{if } s_t \leq s_t^l \\ Sf & \text{if } s_t^l < s_t < s_t^u \\ Bx & \text{if } s_t \geq s_t^u \end{cases}$$

for $t = 0, 1, \ldots, T-1$.

Figure 8.1 shows an example of a DCL policy. As can be seen from the figure, a DCL policy defines two thresholds for each state, divides the entire state space into three regions, and assigns an optimal action for each region.

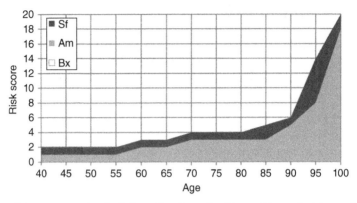

Figure 8.1 An example of a DCL policy for optimal breast biopsy decision problem.

Next, we provide Theorem 8.1 on sufficiency conditions under which there exists an optimal DCL policy. Before stating the theorem fully, we present several lemmas that are used in the proof of Theorem 8.1.

Lemma 8.1

Let $\mathbb{P} = \left[p_t\left(j|i\right) \right]$ *for* $i,\, j = 1,\, 2,\, \ldots,\, N$ *be an IFR transition probability matrix with* $\sum_{k=i+1}^{k^*} p_t\left(k|i+1\right) \geq \sum_{k=i+1}^{k^*} p_t\left(k|i\right)$ *for* $i < k^* \leq N$ *and* $t = 1,\, 2,\, \ldots,\, T-1$. *For any nonincreasing function* $f(i)$, *we have*

(a) $\displaystyle\sum_{k=1}^{i}\left\{p_t\left(k|i\right) - p_t\left(k|i+1\right)\right\} f(k) \geq \sum_{k=1}^{i}\left\{p_t\left(k|i\right) - p_t\left(k|i+1\right)\right\} f(i).$

(b) $\displaystyle\sum_{k=i+1}^{k^*}\left\{p_t\left(k|i\right) - p_t\left(k|i+1\right)\right\} f(k) \geq \sum_{k=i+1}^{k^*}\left\{p_t\left(k|i\right) - p\left(k|i+1\right)\right\} f(i+1).$

Proof: See the proof of Lemma 1 in Alagoz et al. (2004). ∎

The following lemma provides an upper bound on the difference in woman's total QALY between annual mammogram and short-term follow-up.

Lemma 8.2

$\vartheta_t(s_t, \text{Am}) - \vartheta_t(s_t, \text{Sf}) \leq 2d\text{Sf}(t) - d\text{Am}(t)$ *for all* $s_t \in \mathcal{S} \setminus \{S+2\}$ *and* t.

Proof: See the proof of Lemma 2 in Alagoz et al. (2013). ∎

In Lemma 8.2, $\vartheta_t(s_t, \text{Am})$ and $\vartheta_t(s_t, \text{Sf})$ represent the total expected QALYs, and $d\text{Am}(t)$ and $d\text{Sf}(t)$ represent the disutility corresponding to Am and Sf when the woman is in s_t at time t, respectively.

Lemma 8.3 provides an upper bound, $\tilde{r}_t(0)$, on $\vartheta_t(0, \text{Sf})$, where $\tilde{r}_t(0)$ represents the total expected QALYs of a woman if her risk score remains zero after time t and she never undergoes biopsy.

Lemma 8.3

Let $\tilde{r}_t(0)$ be defined as

$$\tilde{r}_t(0) \triangleq r_t(0, Sf) + \sum_{i=t}^{T-1} \gamma^{i+1-t} \left\{ \prod_{j=t}^{i} \left\{ 1 - p_j^{Sf}\left(S + 2 \middle| 0\right) \right\} \right\} r_{i+1}(0, Sf),$$

where $\tilde{r}_t(0) \geq r_t(0, Bx)$. Then $\vartheta_t(0) \leq \tilde{r}_t(0)$ for all $t = 1, 2, \ldots, T - 1$.

Proof: See the proof of Lemma 4 in Chhatwal et al. (2010). ∎

In the final lemma before the main result, Theorem 8.1, we provide an upper bound on the reward if the recommended action is Sf.

Lemma 8.4

Let $r_t^{max}(s_t, Sf)$ be defined as follows:

$$r_t^{max}\left(s_t, Sf\right) \triangleq r_t\left(s_t, Sf\right) + \gamma \sum_{s' < s_{t+1}^u} p_t^{Sf}\left(s' \middle| s_t\right) \tilde{r}_{t+1}(0) + \gamma \sum_{s' \geq s_{t+1}^u} p_t^{Sf}\left(s' \middle| s_t\right) r_{t+1}\left(s', Bx\right) \quad (8.4)$$

for all $s_t \in S \setminus \{S + 1\}$ and t, where $\tilde{r}_{t+1}(0)$ is as defined in Lemma 8.3 and s_t^u is defined as the optimal control-limit threshold at time t, that is, the optimal action for any $s_t \geq s_t^u$ at time t is Bx. Then $v_t(s_t, Sf) \leq r_t^{max}(s_t, Sf)$.

Proof: See the proof of Lemma 4 in Alagoz et al. (2013). ∎

Lemma 8.4 implies that if the recommended action is Sf, the maximum total reward is equal to the total reward attained by waiting for six months, plus either (i) the reward from biopsy if the risk of cancer increases beyond the biopsy threshold or (ii) the maximum reward she can attain if her risk score remains zero after time t and she never undergoes biopsy.

Finally, Theorem 8.1 shows the existence of an optimal DCL policy under some sufficiency conditions.

Theorem 8.1

(Alagoz et al. 2013) If $\mathbb{P}_t^{Sf}$ and $\mathbb{P}_t^{Am}$ are IFR and the following hold for all $s_t \in S \setminus \{S + 1\}$ and $t = 1, 2, \ldots, T - 1$:

$$\frac{r_t\left(s_t, Bx\right) - r_t\left(s_t + 1, Bx\right)}{\gamma^2 r_{t+2}\left(s_t + 1, Bx\right)} \leq p_t^{Sf}\left(S + 1 \middle| s_t + 1\right) - p_t^{Sf}\left(S + 1 \middle| s_t\right), \quad (8.5)$$

$$\sum_{s' = s_t + 1}^{S} p_t^{Am}\left(s' \middle| s_t + 1\right) \geq \sum_{s' = s_t + 1}^{S} p_t^{Am}\left(s' \middle| s_t\right), \quad (8.6)$$

$$p_t^{Sf}\left(i \middle| s_t\right) \geq p_t^{Sf}\left(i \middle| s_t + 1\right) \quad \text{if } i \leq s_t, \quad (8.7)$$

$$p_t^{Sf}\left(j \middle| s_t\right) \leq p_t\left(j \middle| s_t + 1\right) \quad \text{if } j > s_t, \quad (8.8)$$

and

$$\sum_{s'=s_t}^{S} \left\{ p_t^{Sf} \left(s' \big| s_t \right) - p_t^{Sf} \left(s' \big| s_t - 1 \right) \right\} \left\{ r_{t+1} \left(s', Bx \right) - \tilde{r}_{t+1} \left(s', Fu \right) \right\}$$

$$+ \left\{ p_t^{Sf} \left(S + 1 \big| s_t \right) - p_t^{Sf} \left(S + 1 \big| s_t - 1 \right) \right\} dSf \qquad (8.9)$$

$$\geq \sum_{s'=0}^{s_t - 1} \left\{ p_t^{Sf} \left(s' \big| s_t - 1 \right) - p_t^{Sf} \left(s' \big| s_t \right) \right\} \big| 2 dSf - dAm \big|,$$

and then there exists an optimal DCL policy.

Proof: See the proof of Theorem 1 in Alagoz et al. (2013).   ∎

In Theorem 8.1, inequality (8.5) implies that as the risk score increases, the percentage reduction in the post-biopsy reward is less than the increase in the risk of death related to waiting until next decision epoch. Inequality (8.6) implies that the transition rates to higher risk scores increase with the increasing current risk score, which is similar to IFR condition. Inequalities (8.7) and (8.8) imply that as the current risk score of the woman increases, the probability of transition to a lower risk score decreases, whereas the probability of transition to a higher risk score increases in the next decision epoch. Finally, (8.9) simply implies that as the current risk score of the woman increases, the relative benefit of the action Bx over Sf increases more than the relative benefit of action Sf over Am.

All of the structural analyses given earlier assume that there are three possible actions and no constraints on the budget. Note that the results can easily be applied to two-action scenario, with the only change that optimal DCL policies will be replaced by optimal control-limit policies (Chhatwal et al. 2010). Chhatwal et al. (2010) also presented an interesting theorem providing a set of sufficiency conditions that ensure that the optimal control threshold does not decrease with time in their problem context. This result is particularly interesting as, under certain conditions, it supports a clinical intuition that as the women get older, a higher probability threshold for biopsy should be set.

Theorem 8.2

(*Chhatwal et al.* 2010) *For a transition matrix* $\mathbb{P}_t^{Am}$ *satisfying IFR assumption, if an optimal control-limit threshold* s_t^u *exists for all t, then* s_t^u *is nondecreasing in t if*

$$r_t \left(s, Bx \right) \geq r_t \left(s, Am \right) + \gamma \sum_{s'<s} p_t^{Am} \left(s' \big| s \right) \tilde{r}_{t+1} (0) + \gamma \sum_{s' \geq s} p_t^{Am} \left(s' \big| s \right) r_{t+1} \left(s', Bx \right) \quad (8.10)$$

for all $s \in \mathcal{S} \setminus \{S + 1\}$

Proof: See the proof of Theorem 1 in Chhatwal et al. (2010).   ∎

In Theorem 8.2, inequality (8.10) implies that for any state, the expected post-biopsy reward is greater than the upper bound on the total reward attained by waiting another year and using the same risk score as the control-limit threshold. The clinical meaning of (8.10) is that benefit of delaying biopsy decreases with time due to a substantial reduction in potential benefits of biopsy.

An extension to these MDP models is proposed by Ayvaci et al. (2012) by adding budget constraint to the optimal biopsy decision-making problem. The addition of a budget constraint limits the expected expenditure under any policy. The expenditure of a policy is estimated by using the expected costs of short-term follow-up and biopsy following the suggestions of Poplack et al. (2005). Once the budget constraint is introduced, the new model can no longer be solved using the Bellman equations (8.1), (8.2), and (8.3). Ayvaci et al. (2012) proposed a mixed-integer program (MIP) formulation, named "constrained finite-horizon dual mixed-integer program (CFDMIP)," to solve the constrained MDP problem. Here, we present their main results and findings and refer the reader to that article for the details of their model formulation.

Ayvaci et al. (2012) first proposed an equivalent linear program (LP) formulation, constrained finite-horizon dual linear program (CFDLP), for the constrained MDP model. Note, however, that the existence of optimal deterministic policies will no longer be guaranteed by this model. In fact, an optimal policy will involve a randomized decision rule for some states. This brings a significant problem in the clinical interpretation of the optimal policy, as clinical decision making cannot involve any randomization. To enforce the existence of optimal deterministic policies, the authors introduce a set of constraints involving binary variables and propose their CFDMIP model.

In the next theorem, the relation between the optimal value function and the allocated budget is investigated. Since the marginal gains given in total expected QALYs decreases with the increasing budget, the optimal value function is concave in the available budget. The clinical explanation of this result is that increasing resources improves the health outcomes while diminishing the magnitude of these improvements.

Theorem 8.3

(*Ayvaci et al.* 2012) *For CFDLP model, the optimal total expected QALYs is a concave function of allocated budget on the feasible set.*

Proof: See the proof of Theorem 1 in Ayvaci et al. (2012).   ∎

Ayvaci et al. (2012) also provided the following lemma, which shows that the optimal value function of CFDMIP model also displays diminishing gains similar to CFDLP model.

Lemma 8.5

For CFDMIP model, the optimal total expected QALY is subadditive in allocated budgets that are binding.

Proof: See the proof of Lemma 2 in Ayvaci et al. (2012).   ∎

8.4 NUMERICAL RESULTS

In this section, we summarize some numerical results from Chhatwal et al. (2010), Ayvaci et al. (2012), and Alagoz et al. (2013) to illustrate the utilization of MDP models in post-mammography diagnostic decision-making problem. All of these

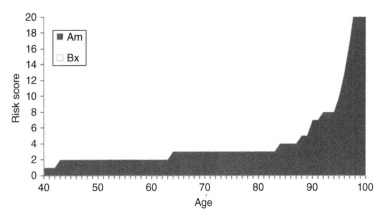

Figure 8.2 Optimal age-dependent biopsy thresholds obtained by a finite-horizon MDP model with two possible actions. Source: Chhatwal et al. (2010). Reproduced with permission of INFORMS.

models provide optimal policies that are easy to implement in clinical practice. We will skip the details of parameter estimation including states, state transition probabilities, and rewards and only summarize data sources for the model parameters and present some important results.

All three models use a clinical data set consisting of 65,892 consecutive mammographic findings from 18,269 patients collected at Medical College of Wisconsin, Milwaukee (MCS), between April 5, 1999, and February 9, 2004. They obtain the mammography outcomes through biopsy and also match them with the state cancer registries to include information about false-negative cases and malignant cases missed during the lecture of mammograms.

Next we present the optimal probability thresholds for biopsy decisions in different age groups from Chhatwal et al. (2010) in Figure 8.2. Chhatwal et al. (2010) used a discount factor $\gamma = 1$ over a year. Their optimal policy suggests to send a woman between the ages 40 and 42 for biopsy if the probability of cancer is 1% or higher. The threshold rises to 2% for a woman between the age of 43 and 63 and 3% for a woman between the ages of 64 and 82 and goes up to 20% for a 98-year-old woman. As Chhatwal et al. (2010) proved, under certain conditions, the optimal policy is of control-limit type and the threshold is nondecreasing with the woman's age.

In Figure 8.3, we present the optimal biopsy threshold from Alagoz et al. (2013). Note that there are three possible actions for this model, resulting in an optimal DCL policy with two thresholds. Their optimal policy suggests to send women between the ages 40 and 67 for biopsy if the probability of cancer is 2% or higher and recommend short-term follow-up if the probability of cancer is between 1% and 2% and routine annual mammogram if the probability of cancer is below 1%. The threshold for biopsy rises to 3% for women between the ages of 67 and 78, while the short-term follow-up threshold stays the same. Following a similar manner, optimal thresholds

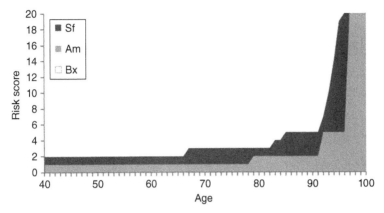

Figure 8.3 Optimal age-dependent biopsy thresholds obtained by a finite-horizon MDP model with three possible actions. Source: Alagoz et al. (2013). Reproduced with permission of INFORMS.

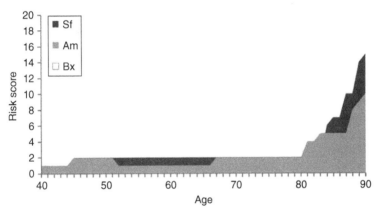

Figure 8.4 Optimal age-dependent biopsy thresholds obtained by a budget constrained finite-horizon MDP model. Source: Ayvaci et al. (2012). Reproduced with permission of INFORMS.

for all ages can be found using Figure 8.3. Again, as Alagoz et al. (2013) proved, under certain conditions, the optimal policy is of DCL type. Their results are particularly important to illustrate that by adding small changes to the model structure, one can obtain significant clinical benefits.

Finally, Figure 8.4 depicts an example of the optimal biopsy threshold from Alagoz et al. (2013) under moderate budget constraint. The optimal policy satisfying the budget constraint suggests that women between the ages 40 and 45 should get biopsy if the probability of cancer is 1% or higher and the biopsy threshold increases to 2% for women between the ages of 45 and 52. An interesting observation is that in the optimal scenario, no women between the ages 40 and 52 should get short-term follow-up. As expected, the budget constraint increases the biopsy threshold for almost all of the women, recommending fewer women to be biopsied. Furthermore, Figure 8.4 is a great example showing that adding budget constraint to the MDP formulation alters the property of optimal biopsy/short-term follow-up threshold being nondecreasing with age.

8.5 SUMMARY

The significant variability in mammography interpretation urges the development of mathematical models that provide radiologists with optimal thresholds over which to recommend biopsy and/or short-term follow-up. In this chapter, we consider optimal decision-making problems in the context of breast cancer screening. We focus on using finite-horizon discrete-time MDP models to address the optimal post-mammography diagnostic decision-making problem and present and compare the model formulations, structural properties, and findings of three models from the literature (Chhatwal et al. 2010; Ayvaci et al. 2012; Alagoz et al. 2013). These models specifically aim to avoid unnecessary biopsies, which lead to anxiety and overtreatment (Chhatwal et al. 2010); to limit the excessive use of short-term follow-up (Alagoz et al. 2013); and to reduce the overall cost without sacrificing QALYs (Ayvaci et al. 2012).

Chhatwal et al. (2010) found the optimal age-dependent biopsy threshold and showed that older women have a higher threshold than younger women. Alagoz et al. (2013) extended this model by adding short-term follow-up exam to the action space and provided an optimal policy that includes two thresholds, one for biopsy and the other for short-term follow-up. Finally, Ayvaci et al. (2012) introduced budget constraints to their setup and showed that using optimal thresholds obtained by a cost constrained model could save approximately 22% of total cost without sacrificing QALYs.

There are several limitations of these studies. As in the case of many medical studies, most of the limitations are related to the lack of relevant data. Ending the decision process after a biopsy, calculating transitions in between risk scores by ignoring age dependency, calculating the risk score solely based on mammography features, and having a limited action space are the examples of such limitations. Aside from these, radiologists are assumed to be risk neutral, and patient's preferences are ignored. Relaxing any of these assumptions or overcoming the limitations could lead to potential future research directions on optimal breast cancer diagnostic decisions.

ACKNOWLEDGMENTS

This research was supported in part by grant CMMI-0844423 from the National Science Foundation as well as grants R01CA165229 and R01LM010921 from the National Institutes of Health.

REFERENCES

ACS. 2015. Cancer facts and figures: 2015. American Cancer Society, Atlanta, GA.

Akan, M., O. Alagoz, B. Ata, F. S. Erenay, A. Said. 2012. A broader view of designing the liver allocation system. *Operations Research* 60(4), 757–770.

Alagoz, O., L. M. Maillart, A. J. Schaefer, M. S. Roberts. 2004. The optimal timing of living-donor liver transplantation. *Management Science* 50(10), 1420–1430.

Alagoz, O., L. M. Maillart, A. J. Schaefer, M. S. Roberts. 2007a. Choosing among living-donor and cadaveric livers. *Management Science* 53(11), 1702–1715.

Alagoz, O., L. M. Maillart, A. J. Schaefer, M. S. Roberts. 2007b. Determining the acceptance of cadaveric livers using an implicit model of the waiting list. *Operations Research* 55(1), 24–36.

Alagoz, O., H. Hsu, A. J. Schaefer, M. S. Roberts. 2010. Markov decision processes: A tool for sequential decision making under uncertainty. *Medical Decision Making* 30(4), 474–483.

Alagoz, O., T. Ayer, F. S. Erenay. 2011. Operations research models for cancer screening. In J. J. Cochran, ed., *Wiley Encyclopedia for Operations Research and Management Science*, vol. 1. John Wiley & Sons, Inc., Hoboken, NJ.

Alagoz, O., J. Chhatwal, E. S. Burnside. 2013. Optimal policies for reducing unnecessary follow-up mammography exams in breast cancer diagnosis. *Decision Analysis* 10(3), 200–224.

Ayer, T., O. Alagoz, J. Chhatwal, J. Shavlik, E. S. Burnside, C. E. Kahn. 2010a. Breast cancer risk estimation with artificial neural networks revisited: Discrimination and calibration. *Cancer* 116(14), 3310–3321.

Ayer, T., M. U. S. Ayvaci, Z. X. Liu, O. Alagoz, E. S. Burnside. 2010b. Computer-aided diagnostic models in breast cancer screening. *Imaging in Medicine* 2(3), 313–323.

Ayer, T., O. Alagoz, N. K. Stout. 2012. OR Forum-A POMDP approach to personalize mammography screening decisions. *Operations Research* 60(5), 1019–1034.

Ayer, T., O. Alagoz, N. K. Stout, E. S. Burnside. 2016. Heterogeneity in womens adherence and its role in optimal breast cancer screening policies. *Management Science* 62(5), 1339–1362.

Ayvaci, M., O. Alagoz, E. S. Burnside. 2012. The effect of budgetary restrictions on breast cancer diagnostic decisions. *Manufacturing & Service Operations Management* 14(4), 600–617.

Barlow, R. E., F. Proschan. 1965. *Mathematical Theory of Reliability*. Wiley, New York.

Barlow, W. E., C. Chi, P. A. Carney, S. H. Taplin, C. D'Orsi, G. Cutter, R. E. Hendrick, J. G. Elmore. 2004. Accuracy of screening mammography interpretation by characteristics of radiologists. *Journal of the National Cancer Institute* 96(24), 1840–1850.

Batina, N. G., A. Trentham-Dietz, R. E. Gangnon, B. L. Sprague, M. A. Rosenberg, N. K. Stout, D. G. Fryback, O. Alagoz. 2013. Variation in tumor natural history contributes to racial disparities in breast cancer stage at diagnosis. *Breast Cancer Research and Treatment* 138(2), 519–528.

Beam, C. A., P. M. Layde, D. C. Sullivan. 1996. Variability in the interpretation of screening mammograms by US radiologists. Findings from a national sample. *Archives of Internal Medicine* 156(2), 209–213.

BI-RADS. 1998. *Breast Imaging Reporting And Data System (BI-RADS)*. 3rd ed. American College of Radiology, Reston, VA.

Burnside, E. S., D. L. Rubin, J. P. Fine, R. D. Shachter, G. A. Sisney, W. K. Leung. 2006. Bayesian network to predict breast cancer risk of mammographic microcalcifications and reduce number of benign biopsy results: Initial experience. *Radiology* 240(3), 666–673.

Burnside, E. S., J. Chhatwal, O. Alagoz. 2012. What is the optimal threshold at which to recommend breast biopsy? *PLoS One* 7(11), e48820.

Chhatwal, J., O. Alagoz, M. J. Lindstrom, C. E. Kahn, K. A. Shaffer, E. S. Burnside. 2009. A logistic regression model to aid breast cancer diagnosis based on the national mammography database format. *American Journal of Roentgenology* 192(4), 1117–1127.

Chhatwal, J., O. Alagoz, E. S. Burnside. 2010. Optimal breast biopsy decision-making based on mammographic features and demographic factors. *Operations Research* 58(6), 1577–1591.

Drummond, M. F. 2005. *Methods for the Economic Evaluation of Health Care Programmes*. Oxford University Press, Oxford, UK.

Elmore, J. G., C. K. Wells, C. H. Lee, D. H. Howard, A. R. Feinstein. 1994. Variability in radiologists' interpretations of mammograms. *New England Journal of Medicine* 331(22), 1493–1499.

Elmore, J. G., G. M. Longton, P. A. Carney, B. M. Geller, T. Onega, A. N. A. Tosteson, H. D. Nelson, M. S. Pepe, K. H. Allison, S. J. Schnitt, et al. 2015. Diagnostic concordance among pathologists interpreting breast biopsy specimens. *JAMA* 313(11), 1122–1132.

Erenay, F. S., O. Alagoz, A. Said. 2014. Optimizing colonoscopy screening for colorectal cancer prevention and surveillance. *Manufacturing & Service Operations Management* 16(3), 381–400.

Fryback, D. G., N. K. Stout, M. A. Rosenberg, A. Trentham-Dietz, V. Kuruchittham, P. L. Remington. 2006. Chapter 7: The Wisconsin breast cancer epidemiology simulation model. *Journal of the National Cancer Institute. Monographs* 2006(36), 37–47.

Geller, B. M., W. E. Barlow, R. Ballard-Barbash, V. L. Ernster, B. C. Yankaskas, E. A. Sickles, P. A. Carney, M. B. Dignan, R. D. Rosenberg, N. Urban, Y. Zheng, S. H. Taplin. 2002. Use of the American College of Radiology BI-RADS to report on the mammographic evaluation of women with signs and symptoms of breast disease. *Radiology* 222(2), 536–542.

Hayat, M. J., N. Howlader, M. E. Reichman, B. K. Edwards. 2007. Cancer statistics, trends, and multiple primary cancer analyses from the Surveillance, Epidemiology, and End Results (SEER) Program. *The Oncologist* 12(1), 20–37.

Ivy, J. S. 2009. Can we do better? Optimization models for breast cancer screening. In P. M. Pardalos, H. Edwin Romeijn, eds., *Handbook of Optimization in Medicine*. Springer, Dordrecht, the Netherlands, pp. 1–28.

Kootstra, J. J., J. E. H. M. Hoekstra-Weebers, J. S. Rietman, J. de Vries, P. C. Baas, J. H. B. Geertzen, H. J. Hoekstra. 2010. A longitudinal comparison of arm morbidity in stage I–II breast cancer patients treated with sentinel lymph node biopsy, sentinel lymph node biopsy followed by completion lymph node dissection, or axillary lymph node dissection. *Annals of Surgical Oncology* 17(9), 2384–2394.

Lee, C. I., M. Cevik, O. Alagoz, B. L. Sprague, A. N. A. Tosteson, D. L. Miglioretti, K. Kerlikowske, N. K. Stout, J. G. Jarvik, S. D. Ramsey, C. D. Lehman. 2015. Comparative effectiveness of combined digital mammography and tomosynthesis screening for women with dense breasts. *Radiology* 274(3), 772–780.

Maillart, L. M., J. S. Ivy, S. Ransom, K. Diehl. 2008. Assessing dynamic breast cancer screening policies. *Operations Research* 56(6), 1411–1427.

Monticciolo, D. L., L. S. Caplan. 2004. The American College of Radiology's BI-RADS 3 classification in a nationwide screening program: Current assessment and comparison with earlier use. *The Breast Journal* 10(2), 106–110.

Munoz, D., A. M. Near, N. T. van Ravesteyn, S. J. Lee, C. B. Schechter, O. Alagoz, D. A. Berry, E. S. Burnside, Y. Chang, G. Chisholm, H. J. de Koning, M. A. Ergun, E. A. M. Heijnsdijk, H. Huang, N. K. Stout, B. L. Sprague, A. Trentham-Dietz, J. S. Mandelblatt, S. K. Plevritis. 2014. Effects of screening and systemic adjuvant therapy on ER-specific US breast cancer mortality. *Journal of the National Cancer Institute* 106(11), pii: dju289.

Pliskin, J. S., D. S. Shepard, M. C. Weinstein. 1980. Utility functions for life years and health status. *Operations Research* 28(1), 206–224.

Poplack, S. P., P. A. Carney, J. E. Weiss, L. Titus-Ernstoff, M. E. Goodrich, A. N. A. Tosteson. 2005. Screening mammography: Costs and use of screening-related services. *Radiology* 234(1), 79–85.

Puterman, M. L. 1994. *Markov Decision Processes: Discrete Stochastic Dynamic Programming*. John Wiley & Sons, Inc., New York.

van Ravesteyn, N. T., D. L. Miglioretti, N. K. Stout, S. J. Lee, C. B. Schechter, D. S. M. Buist, H. Huang, E. A. M. Heijnsdijk, A. Trentham-Dietz, O. Alagoz, A.M. Near, K. Kerlikowske, H. D. Nelson, J. S. Mandelblatt, H. J. de Koning. 2012. Tipping the balance of benefits and harms to favor screening mammography starting at age 40 years: A comparative modeling study of risk. *Annals of Internal Medicine* 156(9), 609–617.

Sandikci, B., L. M. Maillart, A. J. Schaefer, O. Alagoz, M. S. Roberts. 2008. Estimating the patient's price of privacy in liver transplantation. *Operations Research* 56(6), 1393–1410.

Shechter, S. M., M. D. Bailey, A. J. Schaefer, M. S. Roberts. 2008. The optimal time to initiate HIV therapy under ordered health states. *Operations Research* 56(1), 20–33.

Sickles, E. A. 1991. Periodic mammographic follow-up of probably benign lesions: Results in 3,184 consecutive cases. *Radiology* 179(2), 463–468.

Sickles, E. A., D. L. Miglioretti, R. Ballard-Barbash, B. M. Geller, J. W. T. Leung, R. D. Rosenberg, R. Smith-Bindman, B. C. Yankaskas. 2005. Performance benchmarks for diagnostic mammography. *Radiology* 235(3), 775–790.

Siu, A. L.; U.S. Preventive Services Task Force 2016. Screening for breast cancer: US Preventive Services Task Force recommendation statement. *Annals of Internal Medicine* 164(4), 279–296.

Smith, R. A., D. Manassaram-Baptiste, D. Brooks, M. Doroshenk, S. Fedewa, D. Saslow, O. W. Brawley, R. Wender. 2015. Cancer screening in the United States, 2015: A review of current American Cancer Society guidelines and current issues in cancer screening. *CA: A Cancer Journal for Clinicians* 65(1), 30–54.

Sprague, B. L., N. K. Stout, C. Schechter, N. T. van Ravesteyn, M. Cevik, O. Alagoz, C. I. Lee, J. J. van den Broek, D. L. Miglioretti, J. S. Mandelblatt, H. J. de Koning, K. Kerlikowske, C. D. Lehman, A. N. A. Tosteson. 2014. Benefits, harms, and cost-effectiveness of supplemental ultrasonography screening for women with dense breasts. *Annals of Internal Medicine* 162(3), 157–166.

Stout, N. K., S. J. Lee, C. B. Schechter, K. Kerlikowske, O. Alagoz, D. Berry, D. S. M. Buist, M. Cevik, G. Chisholm, H. J. de Koning, H. Huang, R. A. Hubbard, D. L. Miglioretti, M. F. Munsell, A. Trentham-Dietz, N. T. van Ravesteyn, A. N. A. Tosteson, J. S. Mandelblatt. 2014. Benefits, harms, and costs for breast cancer screening after US implementation of digital mammography. *Journal of the National Cancer Institute* 106(6), dju092.

Varas, X., F. Leborgne, J. H. Leborgne. 1992. Nonpalpable, probably benign lesions: Role of follow-up mammography. *Radiology* 184(2), 409–414.

Varas, X., J. H. Leborgne, F. Leborgne, J. Mezzera, S. Jaumandreu, F. Leborgne. 2002. Revisiting the mammographic follow-up of BI-RADS category 3 lesions. *American Journal of Roentgenology* 179(3), 691–695.

Vizcaíno, I., L. Gadea, L. Andreo, D. Salas, F. Ruiz-Perales, D. Cuevas, C. Herranz, F. Bueno. 2001. Short-term follow-up results in 795 nonpalpable probably benign lesions detected at screening mammography. *Radiology* 219(2), 475–483.

Zhang, J., B. T. Denton, H. Balasubramanian, N. D. Shah, B. A. Inman. 2012a. Optimization of prostate biopsy referral decisions. *Manufacturing & Service Operations Management* 14(4), 529–547.

Zhang, J., B. T. Denton, H. Balasubramanian, N. D. Shah, B. A. Inman. 2012b. Optimization of PSA screening policies a comparison of the patient and societal perspectives. *Medical Decision Making* 32(2), 337–349.

9

PARTIALLY OBSERVABLE MARKOV DECISION PROCESSES FOR PROSTATE CANCER SCREENING, SURVEILLANCE, AND TREATMENT: A BUDGETED SAMPLING APPROXIMATION METHOD

JINGYU ZHANG[1] AND BRIAN T. DENTON[2]

[1] *Enterprise Model Risk Management, Bank of America, Wilmington, DE, USA*
[2] *Department of Industrial and Operations Engineering, University of Michigan, Ann Arbor, MI, USA*

9.1 INTRODUCTION

Prostate cancer is the most common solid tumor in American men, with approximately one in six men being diagnosed during their lifetime (American Cancer Society 2012). While clinical tests and procedures such as the prostate-specific antigen (PSA) test and biopsy can help estimate the probability a patient has prostate cancer, the real cancer status cannot be known for certain until the prostate gland is pathologically examined following radical prostatectomy (RP), a surgery in which the prostate gland is removed. A PSA test is a simple blood test that can help detect initial signs of early asymptomatic prostate cancer for men under screening. PSA tests are also used to monitor cancer development or biochemical recurrence for prostate cancer patients under surveillance. A higher than normal PSA level is

Decision Analytics and Optimization in Disease Prevention and Treatment, First Edition.
Edited by Nan Kong and Shengfan Zhang.
© 2018 John Wiley & Sons, Inc. Published 2018 by John Wiley & Sons, Inc.

associated with higher than normal risk of having prostate cancer, but some patients with high PSA do not have prostate cancer; thus PSA testing can result in false positives. On the other hand, some patients with prostate cancer have low PSA; thus PSA testing can also result in false negatives.

Biopsy is recommended for patients who are at risk of having prostate cancer. It is a medical procedure that samples tissue from the prostate gland to see whether malignancy can be confirmed pathologically. If cancer is found, the pathologist reports a Gleason score, which is an estimate of aggressiveness of the cancer. Biopsy can have false-negative outcomes due to its sampling nature. Moreover, biopsies are also painful, cause anxiety for patients, and in rare cases can result in a serious infection.

For patients who have biopsy-detected prostate cancer, some form of treatment will be recommended. There are three common definitive treatment options for localized prostate cancer: RP, external beam radiation therapy, and brachytherapy (Hamilton et al. 2011). In this chapter, RP is the only definitive treatment option under consideration because it is (i) reported to be the best treatment in terms of survival rates for all the ages (Nepple et al. 2013; Sooriakumaran et al. 2014), (ii) historically the most common treatment (Burkhardt et al. 2002; Kawachi et al. 2010; Hamilton et al. 2011), and (iii) the only treatment after which the real cancer state can be confidently determined by pathologically examining the removed prostate gland; thus this treatment has the most reliable survival data.

Due to the potential side effects and complications of definitive treatments like RP and the relatively low mortality risk from localized prostate cancer compared with other competing risks, treatment of localized prostate cancer is controversial. To address the concerns of overdiagnosis and overtreatment, an alternative response to prostate cancer diagnosis, active surveillance (AS), has become popular for low-risk prostate cancer (Thompson et al. 2007; Klotz 2010; Mohler et al. 2010, 2012). AS involves monitoring the patient through PSA tests and biopsies in order to delay and potentially avoid unnecessary definitive treatments. If there is evidence of aggressive prostate cancer progression, then a definitive treatment such as RP is triggered; otherwise the patient continues surveillance as long as it is deemed beneficial given the competing risks.

AS protocols are defined by factors including PSA test frequency, biopsy frequency, and the trigger for initiating definitive treatment. Although various AS protocols have been proposed by Carter et al. (2002, 2007), Kakehi et al. (2008), Dall'Era et al. (2008), van den Bergh et al. (2009), Klotz et al. (2010), Soloway et al. (2010), and Lawrentschuk and Klotz (2011), the optimal strategy remains unknown. There is also a debate about the efficacy of RP versus AS for patients in different risk groups. Several groups of researchers compared the effectiveness of AS versus RP through randomized clinical trials (Steineck et al. 2002; Walsh 2005; Roemeling et al. 2007; Thompson et al. 2007; Hayes et al. 2010; Bill-Axelson et al. 2011; Wilt et al. 2012). However, clinical trials can test only a limited number of AS protocols and require a very long follow-up time to measure patient's quality-adjusted life expectancy.

The efficacy of AS is always underestimated unless the optimal AS protocol is identified and used. Additionally, nontrivial errors or inaccuracies due to the imperfect sensitivity of biopsy result in the patients' prostate cancer stage and grade not being completely observable.

From the aforementioned description, it is clear that there are many decisions to be made as part of screening, detection, and treatment of prostate cancer. Moreover, the optimal decisions must address the imperfect nature of information about the presence of cancer and the potential for unnecessary biopsies and treatments that could cause harm (Etzioni et al. 2002; Welch and Black 2010; Moyer 2012). The imperfect nature of information for making clinical decisions (e.g., PSA test results, biopsy results) makes this problem a natural candidate to be modeled as a partially observable Markov decision process (POMDP). A POMDP is a generalization of a Markov decision process (MDP) in which the states are not completely observable. In a POMDP the decision maker does not know exactly what state the process is in at each decision epoch; the probability of being in the states can be inferred based on observations of the system. Compared with MDPs, which are defined by a transition probability matrix and reward vector, POMDPs additionally require observations and an *information matrix* comprising the conditional probabilities of the observations given the underlying states, referred to as *core states*. Furthermore, the actions in a POMDP are defined on the *belief state*, which is a vector of probabilities of being in the core states.

POMDPs have been successfully applied in many industrial application areas. Machine maintenance and replacement (Eckles 1968; Ross 1971) and education (Karush and Dear 1967) were among the first areas of applications. Other industrial applications include structural inspection (Ellis et al. 1995), elevator control policies (Crites 1996), fisheries (Lane 1989), and autonomous robot navigation (Simmons and Koenig 1995). Some earlier examples of applications (Hu et al. 1993; Peek 1999; Hauskrecht and Fraser 2000; Tusch 2000) demonstrated that POMDP models also fit the context of medical decision making where a patient's true health state is not directly observable; instead, diagnostic tests provide imperfect information about a patient's true health state. In such situations, physicians rely on test results that provide estimates of the probability with which a patient is in a certain health state. In such cases, a POMDP describes the decision-making process more accurately than an MDP. Steimle and Denton (2017) provided a review of POMDPs in the medical context.

The remainder of this chapter is organized as follows. Section 9.2 introduces the basic concepts of a generic POMDP, provides its mathematical description, defines the notation used throughout this chapter, and reviews existing POMDP algorithms that have been proposed for solving POMDPs. In Section 9.3 a POMDP model is proposed specifically for prostate cancer screening, surveillance, and treatment. A new approximation method designed for solving finite-horizon POMDP problems is described in Section 9.4. In Section 9.5, the performance of the proposed approximation method is evaluated through computational experiments in terms of optimality gap and computation time compared with incremental pruning, a gold standard of POMDP exact algorithms. Discussions and conclusions are provided in Section 9.6.

9.2 REVIEW OF POMDP MODELS AND BENCHMARK ALGORITHMS

A POMDP is an MDP with states that are only partially observable. Core states define the true state of the system at a decision epoch, t, and are denoted by $s_t \in S$. Core state transitions are represented by a Markov chain with transition probabilities $p_t(s_{t+1}|s_t, a_t)$. Let $P(a_t)$ denote the matrix form of transition probabilities where $a_t \in A$ is the action in decision epoch t. At each decision epoch an observation is made by the decision maker. The core states are inferred from the observations through the conditional probabilities $q_t(\ell_t|s_t)$ where $\ell_t \in O$ denotes the observations. Q_t denotes the matrix form of $q_t(\ell_t|s_t)$ for all $s_t \in S$ and $\ell_t \in O$ known as the information matrix. Let $\pi_t(s_t) \in [0, 1]$ denote the probability (also referred to as the *belief*) of being in core state s_t at decision epoch t. Let $\pi_t = \{\pi_t(1), \pi_t(2), \ldots, \pi_t(|S|)\}$ denote the corresponding vector of beliefs for all $s_t \in S$. Bayesian updating is used to combine observations collected at each decision epoch with the prior belief to define the current belief state. The POMDP defined on the finite core state set, S, with finite action set, A, and finite observation set, O, can be transformed to a continuous and completely observable MDP defined on a continuous |S|-dimensional probability space of $\pi_t \in \Pi$, where $\Pi = [0, 1]^{|S|}$. After this transformation, the reward defined on the belief state

$$r_t(\pi_t, a_t(\pi_t)) = \sum_{s_t \in S} \pi_t(s_t) r_t(s_t, a_t(\pi_t))$$

is the expected reward over the core states in epoch t. The continuous belief state transition from π_t to π_{t+1} is defined by Bayesian updating as follows:

$$\pi_{t+1}(s_{t+1}) = \frac{q_{t+1}(\ell_{t+1}|s_{t+1}) \sum_{s_t \in S} p_t(s_{t+1}|s_t, a_t(\pi_t)) \pi_t(s_t)}{\sum_{s_{t+1} \in S} q_{t+1}(\ell_{t+1}|s_{t+1}) \sum_{s_t \in S} p_t(s_{t+1}|s_t, a_t(\pi_t)) \pi_t(s_t)} \tag{9.1}$$

Based on these definitions, the optimality conditions for the continuous state MDP can be written as

$$v_t(\pi_t) = \max_{a_t(\pi_t) \in A} \left\{ r_t(\pi_t, a_t(\pi_t)) + \lambda \sum_{\ell_{t+1} \in O} v_{t+1}(\pi_{t+1}) \tilde{p}_t(\ell_{t+1}|\pi_t, a_t(\pi_t)) \right\}, \quad \forall \pi_t \in \Pi \tag{9.2}$$

where

$$\tilde{p}_t(\ell_{t+1}|\pi_t, a_t(\pi_t)) = \sum_{s_{t+1} \in S} q_{t+1}(\ell_{t+1}|s_{t+1}) \sum_{s_t \in S} p_t(s_{t+1}|s_t, a_t(s_t)) \pi_t(s_t) \tag{9.3}$$

and λ is the discount factor. For finite-horizon POMDPs, the value function at the terminal decision epoch, $v_N(\pi_N)$, depends on a terminal reward, $r_N(s_N)$, as follows:

$$v_N\left(\pi_N\right)=\sum_{s\in S}\pi_N\left(s\right)r_N\left(s\right), \quad \forall \pi_N \in \Pi$$

POMDPs are often more difficult to solve than MDPs because they are defined on a continuous belief state. The number of possible policies increases super-exponentially as the decision horizon increases in POMDPs. For instance, a policy for a finite-horizon POMDP with horizon length N contains $\sum_{t=0}^{N}|O|^t = \dfrac{|O|^N - 1}{|O| - 1}$ possible observation histories. At each observation, $|A|$ actions can be chosen, which makes the total number of possible policies $|A|^{\frac{|O|^N - 1}{|O|-1}}$.

Many algorithms for solving POMDPs have been proposed in the operations research, computer science, and artificial intelligence communities since the 1970s. Sondik (1971) and Smallwood and Sondik (1973) first proved that the continuous belief state MDP obtained from a finite-horizon POMDP has a piecewise linear and convex value function at each decision epoch. Many subsequent algorithms solve the resulting continuous state MDP by taking advantage of this property. Each possible sequence of actions and observations, which defines a *policy*, corresponds to a hyperplane in the belief space, commonly referred to as an *α-vector*. The set of all the vectors corresponding to all the policies is called the *α-vector set*, and the optimal value function is constructed by the epigraph of the vectors of all possible policies. Since some vectors in the α-vector set may be dominated, the epigraph can often be represented by a smaller subset of α-vectors, called the minimal α-vector set, or parsimonious representation of the value function.

In the one-pass algorithm of Smallwood and Sondik (1973), an α-vector set is first generated for the final stage by enumerating all the possible action and observation combinations. In subsequent stages, in order to prune the α-vector set to a minimal α-vector set, each α-vector is checked for dominance with respect to other α-vectors by solving a linear program. The one-pass algorithm can require excessive computation since the number of constraints in each linear program is the total number of α-vectors and the number of α-vectors grows exponentially in the number of observation and decision epochs. This shortcoming became the target of later algorithmic improvements that try to find the minimal α-vector set more efficiently.

White (1991) proposed a more efficient routine to reduce the set of α-vectors to the minimal set. This routine generates the minimal α-vector set beginning with the null set. Thus, the linear program used to identify dominance of α-vectors has fewer constraints than the linear program in the one-pass algorithm, which enumerates all α-vectors. Littman (1994) proposed the *witness algorithm*, which divides the problem into smaller subproblems, according to different actions, in order to reduce the number of constraints in each linear program for identifying the minimal α-vector set. Each linear program finds a witness belief point at which another α-vector is found dominating all other α-vectors in the current minimal α-vectors set of an action and is subsequently added into this set.

Zhang and Liu (1996) developed an algorithm called *incremental pruning*. Rather than searching the entire state space, it constructs each possible α-vector in the minimal set in an incremental fashion by taking advantage of the decomposable nested structure of the value function of a POMDP. The minimal α-vector set associated with a specific action can be decomposed into the vector subsets according to the corresponding observations. The vector subsets are added one by one, and the dominated vectors are pruned each time a new subset is added. This algorithm was shown to be more efficient than other exact algorithms, such as the witness algorithm, in some cases.

Much of the recent literature on POMDPs has focused on methods for solving stationary infinite-horizon POMDPs. However, in the context of medical decision making, it is frequently the case that the underlying core state transitions are highly nonstationary and the horizon is most appropriately treated as a finite horizon. This is particularly true for chronic diseases such as cancer, cardiovascular disease, and diabetes, in which the risk of a patient having an adverse event increases with age. Finite-horizon POMDP models built for such purposes could have varying decision horizon, changing transition probabilities, actions, and information matrices for different decision epochs, which are some of the major differences when compared with prevailing stationary infinite-horizon POMDPs.

9.3 A POMDP MODEL FOR PROSTATE CANCER SCREENING, SURVEILLANCE, AND TREATMENT

In this model, prostate cancer testing, biopsy, and treatment decisions are performed at each decision epoch, t, within a nonstationary finite horizon ending at epoch T (an upper bound on the maximum age for screening, surveillance, and treatment). At each decision epoch, a patient is in one of seven partially observable prostate cancer states including no cancer (NC), organ-confined prostate cancer with Gleason score less than 7 (OCG1), organ-confined prostate cancer with Gleason score equal to 7 (OCG2), organ-confined prostate cancer with Gleason score greater than 7 (OCG3), extraprostatic or lymph node-positive prostate cancer (EPLN), no cancer recurrence following treatment (NRFT), possible cancer recurrence following treatment (PRFT), and two observable states, metastasis (M, also known as metastatic prostate cancer) and death (D). Note that NRFT and PRFT are not directly observable since there is no way to know if recurrence will be observed in the future. Let S denote the core state set and $s_t^{(i)} \in S$ index the state at epoch t and stage i. The possible transition between the core states is illustrated in Figure 9.1.

At each epoch there are three consecutive stages of actions: PSA testing, biopsy, and treatment. $a_t^{(1)} \in \{PSA, \overline{PSA}\}$ denotes the first-stage action at epoch t where PSA denotes the action to have a PSA test and $\overline{PSA}$ denotes no PSA test. $a_t^{(2)} \in \{B, \overline{B}\}$ denotes the second-stage action at epoch t where B means to have a biopsy and $\overline{B}$ denotes not to have a biopsy. $a_t^{(3)} \in \{RP, \overline{RP}\}$ denotes the third-stage action at epoch t

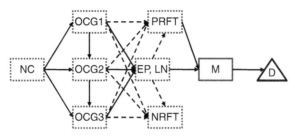

Figure 9.1 Markovian transitions among the prostate cancer states. Partially observable states are in the dotted box, completely observable states are in the solid box, and the triangle is the death from prostate cancer; transitions due to RP are represented by the dashed lines, and other transitions are represented using solid lines; death from other causes is possible from all states in the model but not shown in this figure.

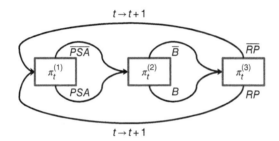

Figure 9.2 Recurring screening, surveillance, and treatment decision process for prostate cancer at decision epochs t, $t+1$, ..., T. The vector $\pi_t^{(i)}$ denotes the patient's belief state (probability of being in different health states) at decision stage i, PSA and $\overline{PSA}$ denote having or not having a PSA test, B and $\overline{B}$ denote having or not having a biopsy, and RP and $\overline{RP}$ denote performing or not performing RP, respectively. Death from any cause is possible but not shown in this figure.

where RP means to have an RP and $\overline{RP}$ denotes not to have an RP; then wait until the next epoch. While the first two stages, PSA testing and biopsy decisions, are assumed instantaneous and stay in the same epoch, it moves to the next epoch after the third stage, treatment decision. Due to the partially observable nature of some underlying cancer states, a belief state with probability distribution of being in each underlying cancer state represents patient's prostate cancer status at each decision epoch. Combinations of these three stages of actions for each belief state over the decision horizon define the policy for PSA testing, biopsy, and treatment for each belief state. The hierarchical nature of the decision process is illustrated in Figure 9.2.

The probability that the patient is in one of the core states at stage $i \in \{1, 2, 3\}$ of epoch t is denoted by

$$\pi_t^{(i)} = (\pi_t^{(i)}(NC), \pi_t^{(i)}(OCG1), \pi_t^{(i)}(OCG2), \pi_t^{(i)}(OCG3), \pi_t^{(i)}(EPLN)$$
$$\pi_t^{(i)}(M), \pi_t^{(i)}(NRFT), \pi_t^{(i)}(PRFT), \pi_t^{(i)}(D))$$

For the purpose of finding the optimal screening, surveillance, and treatment policy, the initial focus is on a population of men who have not been previously diagnosed with prostate cancer. Therefore patients are not in states NRFT, PRFT, M, or D at the beginning of the first decision epoch, and the belief state can be represented as

$$\pi_{t_0}^{(i)} = (\pi_{t_0}^{(i)}(NC), \pi_{t_0}^{(i)}(OCG1), \pi_{t_0}^{(i)}(OCG2), \pi_{t_0}^{(i)}(OCG3), \pi_{t_0}^{(i)}(EPLN), 0, 0, 0, 0)$$

which is a five-dimensional belief vector with four degrees of freedom because $\sum_{s_t^{(i)} \in S} \pi_t^{(i)}(s_t^{(i)}) = 1$ for any decision epoch t and stage i.

In addition to the observable core states (M and D), the first-stage observation set $O^{(1)}$ includes 5 PSA intervals: $[0, 2.5], [2.5, 4], [4, 7], [7, 10],$ and $[10, \infty)$. The second-stage observation set $O^{(2)}$ includes 4 biopsy results: negative biopsy result, Gleason score <7 (G1), $= 7$ (G2), and >7 (G3). The third-stage decision has no observations except for the observable core states. Each of the three decision stages has core state transition probabilities. In this model $p(s_t^{(2)} | s_t^{(1)}, a_t^{(1)})$ denotes the state transition probability from health state $s_t^{(1)}$ to $s_t^{(2)}$ at epoch t given action $a_t^{(1)}$, $p(s_t^{(3)} | s_t^{(2)}, a_t^{(2)})$ denotes the state transition probability from health state $s_t^{(2)}$ to $s_t^{(3)}$ at epoch t given action $a_t^{(2)}$, and $p(s_{t+1}^{(1)} | s_t^{(3)}, a_t^{(3)})$ denotes the state transition probability from health state $s_t^{(3)}$ to $s_{t+1}^{(1)}$ at epoch t given action $a_t^{(3)}$. $P(a_t^{(i)})$ is the matrix form of the core state transition probabilities. $Q(a_t^{(i)})$ is the information matrix of probabilities of observing a PSA interval or biopsy result conditional on the core states, where $q(o_t^{(i)} | s_t^{(i)}, a_t^{(i)})$ denotes the probability of observing $o_t^{(i)} \in O^{(i)}$ given that the patient is in health state $s_t^{(i)} \in S$ where $i \in \{1, 2\}$.

The overarching objective of screening, surveillance, and treatment is to maximize the expected quality-adjusted life years (QALYs), where QALYs are estimated by decrementing a normal life year based on (i) the occurrence of biopsy, (ii) short-term side effects of treatment, (iii) long-term complications of treatment, and (iv) the complications of metastases. Thus the optimal screening, surveillance, and treatment policy obtained from solving the POMDP trades off the slow progression of prostate cancer, side effects and complications of biopsy and treatment, increasing competing risks when aging, and potential longer life expectancy due to treatment. The objective of the model is represented by the reward function of the POMDP.

The rewards for stages 1 and 2 are denoted by $r(s_t^{(1)}, a_t^{(1)})$ and $r(s_t^{(2)}, a_t^{(2)})$ and are zero if no PSA test or biopsy is done, and otherwise they equal the negative disutilities of PSA tests or biopsy. The reward for stage 3, $r(s_t^{(3)}, a_t^{(3)})$, is the reward for living from epoch t to $t+1$ given the patient is in cancer state $s_t^{(3)}$ and action $a_t^{(3)}$ minus the disutility of treatment if treatment is done. The expected reward of a belief state $\pi_t^{(i)}$ is $r(\pi_t^{(i)}) = \sum_{s_t^{(i)} \in S} r(s_t^{(i)}, a_t^{(i)}) \pi_t^{(i)}(s_t^{(i)})$ for $i \in \{1, 2, 3\}$ at any epoch t. Interested readers should refer to Zhang (2011) for complete details about the sources and values of all model parameters.

9.4 BUDGETED SAMPLING APPROXIMATION

Exponential growth in the number of α-vectors is a limiting factor for solving POMDPs. The approximation method described in this section uses sampling to limit the number of α-vectors, and the number of sampled belief points, used to represent the value function at each decision epoch. It uses a combination of inner and outer linearization to estimate error bounds on the value function at each decision epoch. The lower and upper bounds are described in Section 9.4.1, and the complete algorithm is summarized in Section 9.4.2.

9.4.1 Lower and Upper Bounds

For a maximization problem, a subset of the minimal α-vector set results in a lower bound on the optimal value function for all $\pi \in \Pi$. Figure 9.3b illustrates the resulting lower bound for a two-core-state POMDP with the optimal value function in Figure 9.3a. Letting W_t denote the minimal α-vector set at epoch t, the value function can be written as

$$v_t(x) = \max_{w \in W_t} w \cdot x, \quad \forall x \in \Pi, \ \forall t \tag{9.4}$$

To control the size of the α-vector subset, let $L_t \subseteq W_t$ be a subset such that $|L_t| \le c$. The best subset of α-vectors, L_t^*, is defined as

$$L_t^* = \underset{L_t \subseteq W_t}{\arg\min} \int_{x \in \Pi} \left(\max_{w \in W_t} w \cdot x - \max_{\ell \in L_t} \ell \cdot x \right) f_t(x) dx$$

s.t. $\tag{9.5}$

$$|L_t| \le c$$

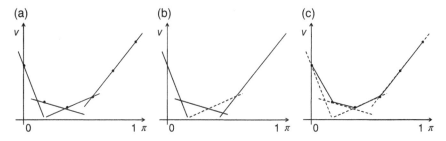

Figure 9.3 Illustration of the bounds of the approximation algorithm for a two-core-state POMDP with a scalar of fully represent the belief state. (a) The true value function represented by a minimal α-vector set. (b) A lower bound on the value function formed by an outer linearization represented by a subset of the minimal α-vector set. (c) An upper bound on the value function formed by an inner linearization represented by a set of sampled belief points and their values. Note that dots in (a) and (c) denote the sampled belief points and dashed lines in (b) and (c) denote the true value function.

where (9.5) minimizes the expected difference between the true value function and the lower bound over the entire belief state space, Π. Note that $f_t(x)$ is the probability density function for the belief state induced by the optimal policy. In other words, the belief points at epoch t are distributed according to $f_t(x)$ given the optimal policy and the belief points of interest at the initial epoch. Also note that L_t^* becomes the true minimal α-vector set W_t as $c \to \infty$. L_t^* provides an outer linearization of the value function and therefore a lower bound at each epoch, t, which can be written as

$$v_t^{LB}(x) = \max_{w \in L_t^*} w \cdot x, \quad \forall x \in \Pi, \; \forall t \tag{9.6}$$

In order to obtain an upper bound on the value function, inner linearization is utilized to describe a new value function representation based on a set of belief points. Letting Y_t be the set of sampled belief points on the convex epigraph of the value function, the value function can be written as

$$v_t(x) = \min_{g_y \in [0,1], \forall y \in Y_t} \left\{ \sum_{y \in Y_t} v_t(y) g_y \middle| \sum_{y \in Y_t} g_y y = x, \; \sum_{y \in Y_t} g_y = 1 \right\}, \quad \forall x \in \Pi, \; \forall t \tag{9.7}$$

The number of points that can be used to represent the upper bound on the value function can be large. Therefore a constraint is defined on the maximum number of points. Let U_t be a subset, $U_t \subseteq Y_t$, such that $|U_t| \le k$. The optimal subset for any epoch t, U_t^*, is defined as

$$U_t^* = \arg\min_{U_t \subseteq Y_t} \int_{x \in \Pi} \left(\min_{g_u \in [0,1], \forall u \in U_t} \left\{ \sum_{u \in U_t} v_t(u) g_u \middle| \sum_{u \in U_t} g_u u = x, \; \sum_{u \in U_t} g_u = 1 \right\} \right.$$
$$\left. - \min_{g_y \in [0,1], \forall y \in Y_t} \left\{ \sum_{y \in Y_t} v_t(y) g_y \middle| \sum_{y \in Y_t} g_y y = x, \; \sum_{y \in Y_t} g_y = 1 \right\} \right) f_t(x) dx \tag{9.8}$$

subject to
$$|U_t| \le k$$

where the objective sums the expected difference between the true value function and the upper bound. Figure 9.3c illustrates the upper bound for a two-core-state POMDP example. Note that the epigraph defined by U_t^* becomes the true value function when $k \to \infty$. U_t^* provides an inner linearization of the value function and therefore an upper bound at each epoch, t, which can be written as

$$v_t^{UB}(x) = \min_{g_y \in [0,1], \forall y \in U_t^*} \left\{ \sum_{y \in U_t^*} v_t(y) g_y \middle| \sum_{y \in U_t^*} g_y y = x, \; \sum_{y \in U_t^*} g_y = 1 \right\}, \quad \forall x \in \Pi, \; \forall t \tag{9.9}$$

Using (9.6) and (9.7) the following is a bound on the expected gap between the upper and lower bounds on the value function at decision epoch t:

$$\Delta_t = \int_{x \in \Pi} \left(v_t^{UB}(x) - v_t^{LB}(x) \right) f_t(x) dx. \tag{9.10}$$

Clearly (9.10) is optimistic since finding L_t^* and U_t^* is generally not possible for three reasons. First, in (9.5), (9.8), and (9.10), the minimal α-vector set W_t and point set Y_t at epoch t may be extremely large and computationally infeasible to enumerate. Second, due to the very large (possibly infinite in the continuous case) number of outcomes, it is generally not possible to compute the expectations in (9.5), (9.8), and (9.10) exactly. Third, the probability density function, $f_t(x)$, presumes the optimal policy for the POMDP is known.

In spite of the intractable nature of (9.5), (9.8), and (9.10), we show that suitably chosen subsets of W_t and Y_t can provide very good bounds. A budgeted sampling approximation that uses greedy sampling to select subsets of W_t and Y_t with the goal of finding near-optimal solutions and tight error bounds is described in the next subsection.

9.4.2 Summary of the Algorithm

This approach uses a sampled belief point set for inner linearization where the sampling proceeds as follows. The sampled belief point set at epoch t is denoted by N_t. Begin with one belief point of interest in the first decision epoch, $\bar{\pi}_1$, and let $N_1 = \{\bar{\pi}_1\}$. In each decision epoch, t, N_t is generated from N_{t-1} by sampling from all possible actions and observations. Observations are sampled based on the information matrix, $Q(a_t)$. Since the optimal action is unknown, a randomized policy is used to sample actions at each epoch. This policy is selected to trade off the competing needs for exploration and exploitation of the policy space (specific choices of the randomized policies used are provided in Section 9.5.2). The belief point sampling process is summarized in Algorithm 9.1.

The belief point sampling process results in at most k-sampled belief points at each epoch t. Using the sampled belief point set, N_t, the lower and upper bounds are computed as described in Algorithms 9.2 and 9.3, respectively.

In Algorithm 9.2, the lower-bound solution at epoch t is exact if the number of minimal α-vectors never reached the budget c in epochs $[t, T]$. Once the number of α-vectors in the true minimal α-vector set increases beyond c, step 3 proceeds with greedy selection of vectors using probability of dominance as a proxy for the importance of retaining the vector. Note that if a c is chosen not less than k, the number of α-vectors with nonzero probability of dominance cannot be more than c. In such a case it is not necessary to specify c, and k serves as the only tunable parameter in the lower-bound algorithm. Also note that Algorithm 9.2 avoids solving any linear program, which could significantly improve computation time compared with exact algorithms.

Algorithm 9.1   Belief Point Sampling

Set $N_1 = \{\bar{\pi}_1\}$, $t = 1$, and $\bar{\pi}_1 = 1$
repeat
  Find all the belief points with non-zero probability
  of being encountered at epoch $t+1$ from the belief point
  set and their probability of being encountered at epoch
  t and the randomized policy
  if The number of belief points with non-zero
  probability $\leq k$ **then**
    Add them to N_{t+1}
  else
    Add the k points with highest probability to N_{t+1}
  end if
  Let $t = t+1$
until $t = T$ **return** All the belief points in N_i, $\forall i \in [1,$
$T]$ and their probabilities of being encountered

Algorithm 9.2   Value Function Lower-Bound Algorithm

Initialize $\hat{L}_T$ as the true minimal α-vector set, L_T
Set $t = T-1$
repeat
  Find the dominating α-vector at each belief points in
  N_t using $\hat{L}_{t+1}$
  A probability of dominance for each α-vector is
  calculated as the sum of the probabilities of being
  encountered of the belief points for which this α-vector
  dominates
  if The number of dominating α-vectors $\leq c$
    Add all α-vectors to $\hat{L}_t$
  else
    Select c vectors with highest probability
  end if
  Let $t = t-1$
until $t = 1$ **return** α-vector set $\hat{L}_1$

Algorithm 9.3   Value Function Upper-Bound Algorithm

```
Let t̄ be the last epoch at which there are fewer than k
α-vectors in the true minimal α-vector set
Compute the value functions for all the points in N_t̄
using L̂_t̄ obtained from Value Function Lower-Bound
Algorithm
Let t = t̄ - 1
repeat
    Compute the value function for all belief points in N_t
    using Equation 9.2 in which all the needed value
    functions at epoch t+1 are estimated by inner
    linearization for the value functions for all the points
    in N_{t+1}
    Let t = t - 1
until t = 1 return Value functions for belief points in N_1
```

Note that Algorithm 9.3 starts from an intermediate result of Algorithm 9.2, $\hat{L}_{\bar{t}}$, at $\bar{t}$ because Algorithm 9.2 is still exact at $\bar{t}$ (i.e., $\hat{L}_{\bar{t}}$ is the minimal α-vector set at epoch $\bar{t}$). Also, note that when $k \to \infty$, N_t contains all the belief points that can be encountered for all t, and when $c \to \infty$, Algorithm 9.2 obtains all the dominant α-vectors. Therefore, as c and k tend to infinity, Algorithms 9.2 and 9.3 converge to the optimal solution.

9.5   COMPUTATIONAL EXPERIMENTS

The aforementioned approximation method was evaluated on a set of test instances based on the prostate cancer screening, surveillance, and treatment model presented in Section 9.3 and further described in Zhang (2011). In Section 9.5.1, details of the test instances are provided. Finally, in Section 9.5.2, results from solving the test instances are presented. All of the experiments were completed on a 64-bit Intel Xeon 2.5 GHz CPU with 6 MB cache. The solution methods were implemented using R version 2.12.1 and IBM ILOG CPLEX version 12.2.

9.5.1   Finite-Horizon Test Instances

Four finite-horizon test instances of the POMDP model for prostate cancer in Section 9.3 are solved. PSA testing, biopsy, and treatment decisions are made every three months until a maximum age of 100 in all these instances. Instance 1 uses the base-case parameter setting in the POMDP model provided by Zhang (2011).

Instance 2 uses a lower bound on the probability of death from all other causes. Instance 3 uses an upper bound on the probability of curing prostate cancer after treatment. Instance 4 uses the upper-bound value of the prostate cancer incidence rate. (The proposed test instances are available upon request from the authors.) Instances 2–4 provide some sensitivity analyses for some of the key parameters in instance 1. These four test instances are first solved for patients at age 40 with a prior belief of 1 of having no prostate cancer. The solutions imply that the optimal population-based prostate cancer screening policy is for all ages above 40 because prostate cancer incidence rate is essentially 0 for general men population younger than 40. The four test instances are also solved for patients of age 70 with a prior belief of 0.5 of having no cancer and 0.5 probability of having organ-confined prostate cancer.

9.5.2 Computational Experiments

The results of computational experiments are presented using the test instances and the budgeted sampling approximation method in Section 9.4.2 compared with using incremental pruning. Sensitivity analysis is conducted to evaluate sensitivity of the method to parameters that influence the performance of the approximation method, k, and the randomized policy. Note that c is not examined in the lower-bound algorithm because the constraint on c is never active when letting $c > k$. Therefore k serves as the only tunable parameter of the capacity constraints.

In the computational experiments, the base-case budget constraint parameter was set to $k = 3000$, and a uniformly randomized policy (equal probabilities for different actions) was used for sampling the belief space to generate N_t. Tables 9.1 and 9.2 illustrate the performance comparisons between the budgeted sampling approximation algorithm and incremental pruning in terms of optimality gap and computation time using the base-case budget constraint parameter settings. The objectives in Table 9.1 indicate the expected QALYs of healthy men at age 40 under optimal screening, surveillance, and treatment strategies, and the objectives in Table 9.2 correspond to the expected QALYs under the optimal strategies of 70-year-old men with 50% risk of having extraprostatic prostate cancer.

There are small optimality gaps resulting from the budget sampling approximation algorithm in Table 9.1 but no gap in Table 9.2 because the finite-horizon POMDP starting from age 40 leads to longer decision horizon than the finite-horizon POMDP starting from age 70. Table 9.2 presents cases in which the approximation algorithm can obtain the same solution quality as exact algorithms. It can be observed that the budgeted sampling approximation significantly reduced computation time compared with incremental pruning for the finite-horizon test instances. There are several reasons for this. First, the size of the linear program solved in the incremental pruning algorithm increases quickly with respect to the length of the decision horizon. The budgeted sampling approximation does not require the solution of linear programs in computing the lower bound and only requires the solution of small linear

TABLE 9.1 Performance Comparison of the Budgeted Sampling Approximation Method and Incremental Pruning (IP) via the Four Test Instances Starting from Prior Belief of 1 in No Cancer at Age 40

Instance 1	Method	IP	LBA	UBA	Gap
	Objective	37.774	37.618	37.787	0.169
	Time (minutes)	3136	871		
Instance 2	Method	IP	LBA	UBA	Gap
	Objective	38.474	38.441	38.621	0.179
	Time (minutes)	3108	926		
Instance 3	Method	IP	LBA	UBA	Gap
	Objective	37.661	37.623	37.806	0.183
	Time (minutes)	4010	927		
Instance 4	Method	IP	LBA	UBA	Gap
	Objective	37.411	37.399	37.578	0.179
	Time (minutes)	2974	906		

LBA denotes the lower-bound algorithm, UBA denotes the upper-bound algorithm, and gap denotes the optimality gap between the bounds.

TABLE 9.2 Performance Comparison of the Budgeted Sampling Approximation Method and Incremental Pruning (IP) via the Four Test Instances Starting from Prior Belief of 0.5 No Cancer and 0.5 Extraprostatic Prostate Cancer at Age 70

Instance 1	Method	IP	LBA	UBA	Gap
	Objective	12.439	12.439	12.439	0.000
	Time	46m22s	5m31s		
Instance 2	Method	IP	LBA	UBA	Gap
	Objective	12.939	12.939	12.939	0.000
	Time	95m43s	19m11s		
Instance 3	Method	IP	LBA	UBA	Gap
	Objective	12.571	12.571	12.571	0.000
	Time	127m50s	28m45s		
Instance 4	Method	IP	LBA	UBA	Gap
	Objective	12.409	12.409	12.409	0.000
	Time	39m21s	5m36s		

LBA denotes the lower-bound algorithm, UBA denotes the upper-bound algorithm, and gap denotes the optimality gap between the bounds. Time is reported in minutes (m) and seconds (s).

programs (the number of decision variables in the linear program of (9.9) is restricted by k) in computing the upper bound. Second, the budgeted sampling approximation estimates the optimal value function and policy at a specific belief point of interest at the starting epoch, while incremental pruning computes the entire belief space.

The one-way sensitivity analysis on algorithmic parameters of the budgeted sampling approximation is the focus in the remainder of this subsection. Table 9.3 illustrates how the results for instance 1 in Table 9.2 change with respect to k. Note that in the experiments, a c greater than k is used to guarantee that the number of α-vectors with nonzero probability of dominating will not exceed c, so that c will not influence the results. For the nine-dimensional POMDP problem, there must be at least 1 belief point of interest and nine belief points to compute the inner linearization for the upper bound on the value function, which makes it a total of at least 10 belief points to set up the upper-bound algorithm.

Table 9.3 illustrates that the budgeted sampling approximation can return tight error bounds within a short computation time compared with incremental pruning. Specifically, the optimality gap vanishes when $k \geq 12$ for this instance. As k increases, the computation time does not increase significantly. When k increases to the base-case value, 3000, the computation time increases to the number shown for instance 1 in Table 9.2. This suggests that the base-case parameter of k is conservatively selected for results in Table 9.2 in which the computation time of the budget sampling approximation algorithm can be shortened by reducing k without loss of accuracy.

Table 9.4 illustrates how the results change as the randomized policy used to initialize the budgeted sampling approximation changes for instance 1 in Table 9.2. In the POMDP, the randomized policy used for initialization can be determined by $Pr(B)$, the probability of taking the action of biopsy (B). The uniformly randomized

TABLE 9.3   The Performance of the Budgeted Sampling Approximation Method under Different Budget Constraints of $k = 11, 12, 13, 30, 300$, and 3000 Given $c \geq k$ Compared with Incremental Pruning (IP)

k		11		12		13	
Method	IP	LBA	UBA	LBA	UBA	LBA	UBA
Objective	12.439	12.439	12.453	12.439	12.439	12.439	12.439
Time	46m22s	1m45s		1m45s		1m45s	
k		30		300		3000	
Method	IP	LBA	UBA	LBA	UBA	LBA	UBA
Objective	12.439	12.439	12.439	12.439	12.439	12.439	12.439
Time	46m22s	1m50s		2m41s		5m31s	

LBA denotes the lower-bound algorithm, and UBA denotes the upper-bound algorithm. Time is reported in minutes (m) and seconds (s).

TABLE 9.4   The Performance of the Budgeted Sampling Approximation Method under Different Randomized Policies, Pr(B) = 0.1, 0.5, and 0.9 Compared with Incremental Pruning (IP)

k		11					
Pr(B)		0.1		0.5		0.9	
Method	IP	LBA	UBA	LBA	UBA	LBA	UBA
Objective	12.439	12.439	12.439	12.439	12.453	12.439	12.453
Time	46m22s	1m45s		1m45s		1m45s	
k		13					
Pr(B)		0.1		0.5		0.9	
Method	IP	LBA	UBA	LBA	UBA	LBA	UBA
Objective	12.439	12.439	12.439	12.439	12.439	12.439	12.453
Time	46m22s	1m45s		1m45s		1m46s	

LBA denotes the lower-bound algorithm, UBA denotes the upper-bound algorithm, LBACR denotes the lower-bound algorithm with core state reduction, and UBACR denotes the upper-bound algorithm with core state reduction. Time is reported in minutes (m) and seconds (s).

policy can be defined as Pr(B) = 0.5 where the two actions, biopsy and no biopsy, have equal probabilities. One-way sensitivity analysis was performed on the randomized policy by varying Pr(B) from 0.1 to 0.9, while the other parameter, k, is varied from $k = 11$ to $k = 13$, respectively, which are the low and high k values selected from Table 9.3.

Table 9.4 shows that the budgeted sampling approximation algorithm is quite robust with respect to variation in the randomized policies used to initialize the algorithm. Moreover, the different randomized policies result in a difference in computation time no more than 1 second. The optimality gap was slightly larger at the high values of Pr(B).

9.6   CONCLUSIONS

In this chapter, prostate cancer screening, surveillance, and treatment are collectively modeled as a finite-horizon POMDP with three stages in each decision epoch. This integrated formulation could potentially help the patients optimally decide when to have a PSA test, whether to follow up by a biopsy, and whether to subsequently initiate a definitive treatment at any age. The model took into account common risk factors such as age, PSA, and biopsy Gleason score, as well as disease- and age-specific survival expectations, QALY decrements because of surveillance and treatment, and other-cause mortality. The optimal strategy is not the same for all patients but individualized depending on patient's belief of being in different cancer states, which are Bayesian estimated by past observations of PSA and biopsy results.

The optimal prostate cancer screening and treatment policy obtained from the POMDP model has some characteristics that differ from other previous research (Zhang et al. 2012a, 2012b). First, the policy is based on the probability of being in one of several different cancer states, NC, OCG1, OCG2, OCG3, and EPLN, which is estimated from all of the patient's PSA and biopsy history using Bayesian updating. Second, there is no fixed PSA or biopsy frequency if AS is suggested; rather, PSA tests and biopsies are referred according to patient's age and the probabilities of being in different cancer states that maximizes the expected QALYs for the patient. Compared with the results under the assumption of treating the patients with RP immediately after diagnosis, the optimal surveillance and treatment strategy after including different cancer states and AS almost doubles the expected benefit of screening in terms of QALYs for the base-case parameter setting.

Results for the budgeted sampling approximation method, which uses budget constraints to restrict the numbers of sampled belief points and α-vectors at each decision epoch, suggest that the method may outperform incremental pruning on some non-stationary finite-horizon POMDPs. Specifically, the test instances in Table 9.3 demonstrated that the approximation method can generate solutions with zero optimality gap and significantly reduce the computation time compared with incremental pruning. The approximation methods are quite robust to the budge constraint, k, and the randomized policy used to initialize the budgeted sampling approximation method. Specifically for the test instances, $k \geq 12$ can guarantee the optimality gap obtained from the budgeted sampling approximation less than 0.001 QALYs, and the optimality gap and computation time are robust to a wide range of randomized policy. On the other hand, as one of the limitations, tuning parameter k cannot be automatically determined, and its optimal setting, which achieves the highest computational efficiency with no optimality gap, could vary from problem to problem. When problems scale up, it becomes more difficult to determine the tuning parameters of the approximation algorithm to keep a good balance between efficiency and accuracy, which could limit applicability of the algorithm especially when a user needs to guarantee zero optimality gap.

The three-stage POMDP formulation can be generalized to a multistage POMDP formulation for other medical decision-making problems. There are many examples of chronic diseases for which there are multiple tests with varying sensitivity and specificity for diagnosing a disease. For instance, bladder cancer has a similar surveillance process in which imperfect tests may be followed by biopsy and subsequent treatments. Examples of such tests include urine-based markers for bladder cancer (Lotan and Roehrborn (2002); Toma et al. (2004)). Thus, the model and methodologies described in this chapter are anticipated to be applicable to problems beyond the setting of prostate cancer.

REFERENCES

American Cancer Society. 2012. Cancer facts and figures 2012. Atlanta, GA.

van den Bergh, R. C. N., S. Roemeling, M. J. Roobol, G. Aus, J. Hugosson, A. S. Rannikko, T. L. Tammela, C. H. Bangma, F. H. Schrder. 2009. Outcomes of men with screen-detected prostate cancer eligible for active surveillance who were managed expectantly. *Eur. Urol.* 55(1): 1–8.

Bill-Axelson, A., L. Holmberg, M. Ruutu, H. Garmo, J. R. Stark, C. Busch, S. Nordling, M. Hggman, S.-O. Andersson, S. Bratell, A. Spngberg, J. Palmgren, G. Steineck, H.-O. Adami, J.-E. Johansson, S. P. C. G-4 Investigators. 2011. Radical prostatectomy versus watchful waiting in early prostate cancer. *N. Engl. J. Med.* 364(18): 1708–1717.

Burkhardt, J. H., M. S. Litwin, C. M. Rose, R. J. Correa, J. H. Sunshine, C. Hogan, J. A. Hayman. 2002. Comparing the costs of radiation therapy and radical prostatectomy for the initial treatment of early-stage prostate cancer. *J. Clin. Oncol.* 20(12): 2869–2875.

Carter, H. B., P. C. Walsh, P. Landis, J. I. Epstein. 2002. Expectant management of nonpalpable prostate cancer with curative intent: Preliminary results. *J. Urol.* 167(3): 1231–1234.

Carter, H. B., A. Kettermann, C. Warlick, E. J. Metter, P. Landis, P. C. Walsh, J. I. Epstein. 2007. Expectant management of prostate cancer with curative intent: An update of the Johns Hopkins experience. *J. Urol.* 178(6): 2359–2364; discussion 2364–2365.

Crites, R. H. 1996. Large-scale dynamic optimization using teams of reinforcement learning agents. Ph.D. thesis, University of Massachusetts, Amherst, MA.

Dall'Era, M. A., B. R. Konety, J. E. Cowan, K. Shinohara, F. Stauf, M. R. Cooperberg, M. V. Meng, C. J. Kane, N. Perez, V. A. Master, P. R. Carroll. 2008. Active surveillance for the management of prostate cancer in a contemporary cohort. *Cancer* 112(12): 2664–2670.

Eckles, J. E. 1968. Optimum maintenance with incomplete information. *Oper. Res.* 16(5): 1058–1067.

Ellis, H., M. Jiang, R. B. Corotis. 1995. Inspection, maintenance, and repair with partial observability. *J. Infrastruct. Syst.* 1(2): 92–99.

Etzioni, R., D. F. Penson, J. M. Legler, D. di Tommaso, R. Boer, P. H. Gann, E. J. Feuer. 2002. Overdiagnosis due to prostate-specific antigen screening: Lessons from U.S. prostate cancer incidence trends. *J. Natl. Cancer Inst.* 94(13): 981–990.

Hamilton, A. S., P. C. Albertsen, T. K. Johnson, R. Hoffman, D. Morrell, D. Deapen, D. F. Penson. 2011. Trends in the treatment of localized prostate cancer using supplemented cancer registry data. *BJU Int.* 107(4): 576–584.

Hauskrecht, M., H. Fraser. 2000. Planning treatment of ischemic heart disease with partially observable Markov decision processes. *Artif. Intell. Med.* 18: 221–244.

Hayes, J. H., D. A. Ollendorf, S. D. Pearson, M. J. Barry, P. W. Kantoff, S. T. Stewart, V. Bhatnagar, C. J. Sweeney, J. E. Stahl, P. M. McMahon. 2010. Active surveillance compared with initial treatment for men with low-risk prostate cancer: A decision analysis. *J. Am. Med. Assoc.* 304(21): 2373–2380.

Hu, C., W. S. Lovejoy, S. L. Shafer. 1993. Comparison of some suboptimal control policies in medical drug therapy. *Oper. Res.* 44: 696–709.

Kakehi, Y., T. Kamoto, T. Shiraishi, O. Ogawa, Y. Suzukamo, S. Fukuhara, Y. Saito, K.-I. Tobisu, T. Kakizoe, T. Shibata, H. Fukuda, K. Akakura, H. Suzuki, N. Shinohara, S. Egawa,

A. Irie, T. Sato, O. Maeda, N. Meguro, Y. Sumiyoshi, T. Suzuki, N. Shimizu, Y. Arai, A. Terai, T. Kato, T. Habuchi, H. Fujimoto, M. Niwakawa. 2008. Prospective evaluation of selection criteria for active surveillance in Japanese patients with stage t1cn0m0 prostate cancer. *Jpn. J. Clin. Oncol.* 38(2): 122–128.

Karush, W., R. Dear. 1967. Optimal strategy for item presentation in learning models. *Manage. Sci.* 13: 773–785.

Kawachi, M. H., R. R. Bahnson, M. Barry, J. E. Busby, P. R. Carroll, H. B. Carter, W. J. Catalona, M. S. Cookson, J. I. Epstein, R. B. Etzioni, V. N. Giri, G. P. Hemstreet, R. J. Howe, P. H. Lange, H. Lilja, K. R. Loughlin, J. Mohler, J. Moul, R. B. Nadler, S. G. Patterson, J. C. Presti, A. M. Stroup, R. Wake, J. T. Wei. 2010. NCCN clinical practice guidelines in oncology: Prostate cancer early detection. *J. Natl. Compr. Canc. Netw.* 8(2): 240–262.

Klotz, L. 2010. Active surveillance for prostate cancer: A review. *Curr. Urol. Rep.*11(3): 165–171.

Klotz, L., L. Zhang, A. Lam, R. Nam, A. Mamedov, A. Loblaw. 2010. Clinical results of long-term follow-up of a large, active surveillance cohort with localized prostate cancer. *J. Clin. Oncol.* 28(1): 126–131.

Lane, D. E. 1989. A partially observable model of decision making by fishermen. *Oper. Res.* 37(2): 240–254.

Lawrentschuk, N., L. Klotz. 2011. Active surveillance for low-risk prostate cancer: An update. *Nat. Rev. Urol.* 8(6): 312–320.

Littman, M. L. 1994. The witness algorithm: Solving partially observable Markov decision processes. Technical Report CS-94-40, Department of Computer Science, Brown University, Providence, RI.

Lotan, Y., C. G. Roehrborn. 2002. Cost-effectiveness of a modified care protocol substituting bladder tumor markers for cystoscopy for the followup of patients with transitional cell carcinoma of the bladder: A decision analytical approach. *J. Urol.* 167: 75–79.

Mohler, J., R. R. Bahnson, B. Boston, J. E. Busby, A. D'Amico, J. A. Eastham, C. A. Enke, D. George, E. M. Horwitz, R. P. Huben, P. Kantoff, M. Kawachi, M. Kuettel, P. H. Lange, G. Macvicar, E. R. Plimack, J. M. Pow-Sang, M. Roach, E. Rohren, B. J. Roth, D. C. Shrieve, M. R. Smith, S. Srinivas, P. Twardowski, P. C. Walsh. 2010. NCCN clinical practice guidelines in oncology: Prostate cancer. *J. Natl. Compr. Canc. Netw.* 8(2): 162–200.

Mohler, J. L., A. J. Armstrong, R. R. Bahnson, B. Boston, J. E. Busby, A. V. D'Amico, J. A. Eastham, C. A. Enke, T. Farrington, C. S. Higano, E. M. Horwitz, P. W. Kantoff, M. H. Kawachi, M. Kuettel, R. J. Lee, G. R. MacVicar, A. W. Malcolm, D. Miller, E. R. Plimack, J. M. Pow-Sang, M. Roach, 3rd, E. Rohren, S. Rosenfeld, S. Srinivas, S. A. Strope, J. Tward, P. Twardowski, P. C. Walsh, M. Ho, D. A. Shead. 2012. Prostate cancer, version 3.2012: Featured updates to the NCCN guidelines. *J. Natl. Compr. Canc. Netw.* 10(9): 1081–1087.

Moyer, V. A. 2012. Screening for prostate cancer: U.S. preventive services task force recommendation statement. *Ann. Intern. Med..* 157(2): 120–134.

Nepple, K. G., A. J. Stephenson, D. Kallogjeri, J. Michalski, R. L. Grubb, 3rd, S. A. Strope, J. Haslag-Minoff, J. F. Piccirillo, J. P. Ciezki, E. A. Klein, C. A. Reddy, C. Yu, M. W. Kattan, A. S. Kibel. 2013. Mortality after prostate cancer treatment with radical prostatectomy, external-beam radiation therapy, or brachytherapy in men without comorbidity. *Eur. Urol.* 64(3): 372–378.

Peek, N. B. 1999. Explicit temporal models for decision—Theoretic planning of clinical management. *Artif. Intell. Med.* 15: 135–154.

Roemeling, S., M. J. Roobol, S. H. de Vries, T. Wolters, C. Gosselaar, G. J. L. H. van Leenders, F. H. Schrder. 2007. Active surveillance for prostate cancers detected in three subsequent rounds of a screening trial: Characteristics, PSA doubling times, and outcome. *Eur. Urol.* 51(5): 1244–1250; discussion 1251.

Ross, S. M. 1971. Quality control under Markovian deterioration. *Manage. Sci.* 17(9): 587–596.

Simmons, R., S. Koenig. 1995. Probabilistic navigation in partially observable environments. In *Proceedings of the 14th International Joint Conference on Artificial Intelligence*, vol. 2. Morgan Kaufmann Publishers Inc., San Francisco, CA, pp. 1080–1087.

Smallwood, R. D., E. J. Sondik. 1973. The optimal control of partially observable Markov processes over a finite horizon. *Oper. Res.* 21(5): 1071–1088.

Soloway, M. S., C. T. Soloway, A. Eldefrawy, K. Acosta, B. Kava, M. Manoharan. 2010. Careful selection and close monitoring of low-risk prostate cancer patients on active surveillance minimizes the need for treatment. *Eur. Urol.* 58(6): 831–835.

Sondik, E. J. 1971. The optimal control of partially observable Markov processes. Ph.D. thesis, Stanford University, Stanford, CA.

Sooriakumaran, P., T. Nyberg, O. Akre, L. Haendler, I. Heus, M. Olsson, S. Carlsson, M. J. Roobol, G. Steineck, P. Wiklund. 2014. Comparative effectiveness of radical prostatectomy and radiotherapy in prostate cancer: Observational study of mortality outcomes. *BMJ* 348: g1502.

Steimle, L., B. Denton. 2017. Markov decision processes for screening and treatment of chronic diseases. In R. Boucherie, N. van Dijk, eds., *Markov Decision Processes in Practice*. Springer, Cham, Switzerland.

Steineck, G., F. Helgesen, J. Adolfsson, P. W. Dickman, J.-E. Johansson, B. J. Norln, L. Holmberg, Scandinavian Prostatic Cancer Group Study Number 4. 2002. Quality of life after radical prostatectomy or watchful waiting. *N. Engl. J. Med.* 347(11): 790–796.

Thompson, I., J. B. Thrasher, G. Aus, A. L. Burnett, E. D. Canby-Hagino, M. S. Cookson, A. V. D'Amico, R. R. Dmochowski, D. T. Eton, J. D. Forman, S. L. Goldenberg, J. Hernandez, C. S. Higano, S. R. Kraus, J. W. Moul, C. M. Tangen, A. U. A. P. C. C. G. U. Panel. 2007. Guideline for the management of clinically localized prostate cancer: 2007 update. *J. Urol.* 177(6): 2106–2131.

Toma, M. I., M. G. Friedrich, S. H. Hautmann, K. T. Jakel, A. Erbersdobler, A. Hellstern, H. Huland. 2004. Comparison of the immunocyt test and urinary cytology with other urine tests in the detection and surveillance of bladder cancer. *World J. Urol.* 22: 145–149.

Tusch, G. 2000. Optimal sequential decisions in liver transplantation based on a POMDP model. In *Proceedings of the 14th European Conference on Artificial Intelligence (ECAI 2000)*. IOS Press, Amsterdam, the Netherlands, pp. 186–190.

Walsh, P. C. 2005. Radical prostatectomy versus watchful waiting in early prostate cancer. *J. Urol.* 174(4 Pt 1): 1291–1292.

Welch, H. G., W. C. Black. 2010. Overdiagnosis in cancer. *J. Natl. Cancer Inst.* 102(9): 605–613.

White, C. C., III. 1991. A survey of solution techniques for the partially observed Markov decision process. *Ann. Oper. Res.* 32: 215–230.

Wilt, T. J., M. K. Brawer, K. M. Jones, M. J. Barry, W. J. Aronson, S. Fox, J. R. Gingrich, J. T. Wei, P. Gilhooly, B. M. Grob, I. Nsouli, P. Iyer, R. Cartagena, G. Snider, C. Roehrborn, R. Sharifi, W. Blank, P. Pandya, G. L. Andriole, D. Culkin, T. Wheeler, P. C. I. versus Observation Trial (PIVOT) Study Group. 2012. Radical prostatectomy versus observation for localized prostate cancer. *N. Engl. J. Med.* 367(3): 203–213.

Zhang, J. 2011. Partially observable Markov decision processes for prostate cancer screening. Ph.D. thesis, North Carolina State University, Raleigh, NC.

Zhang, N. L., W. Liu. 1996. Planning in stochastic domains: Problem characteristics and approximation. Technical Report HKUST-CS96-31, Department of Computer Science, Hong Kong University of Science and Technology, Hong Kong.

Zhang, J., B. T. Denton, H. Balasubramanian, N. D. Shah, B. A. Inman. 2012a. Optimization of prostate biopsy referral decisions. *Manuf. Serv. Oper. Manag.* 14(4): 529–547.

Zhang, J., B. T. Denton, H. Balasubramanian, N. D. Shah, B. A. Inman. 2012b. Optimization of PSA screening policies: A comparison of the patient and societal perspectives. *Med. Decis. Making* 32(2): 337–349.

10

COST-EFFECTIVENESS ANALYSIS OF BREAST CANCER MAMMOGRAPHY SCREENING POLICIES CONSIDERING UNCERTAINTY IN WOMEN'S ADHERENCE

MAHBOUBEH MADADI[1] AND SHENGFAN ZHANG[2]

[1] *Department of Industrial Engineering, Louisiana Tech University, Ruston, LA, USA*
[2] *Department of Industrial Engineering, University of Arkansas, Fayetteville, AR, USA*

10.1 INTRODUCTION

Imperfect adherence to medical screening tests and treatments is a well-recognized problem in the literature. Studies have shown that in the United States alone, nonadherence to medications accounts for 3%–10% of total US healthcare costs, which amounts to $100–$300 billion of avoidable healthcare costs (Benjamin 2012). Adherence to medications, in general, is estimated to be around 50% in developed countries, and this number is even lower in developing countries (O'Donohue and Levensky 2006). In the context of breast cancer screening, based on a recent report by the Centers for Disease Control and Prevention (CDC), only 66.8% of women 40 years of age and older had a mammogram between 2011 and 2013 (Center

Decision Analytics and Optimization in Disease Prevention and Treatment, First Edition.
Edited by Nan Kong and Shengfan Zhang.
© 2018 John Wiley & Sons, Inc. Published 2018 by John Wiley & Sons, Inc.

for Disease Control and Prevention 2016), and based on a study by Patrin et al., less than 10% of women undergo annual mammograms over a period of 9–10 years (Partin et al. 2005).

Studies on patient's adherence to screening and/or treatment can be categorized into two broad groups: (i) studies that aim to identify the adherence rate and the factors associated with it (Subramanian et al. 2004; Wu et al. 2007; Tejeda et al. 2009; Hassan et al. 2012; Madadi et al. 2014; Liang et al. 2016) and (ii) studies that characterize the effects of adherence on tests or treatment efficacy and/or optimize screening/treatment guidelines based on patients' adherence behaviors (Brailsford et al. 2012; Mason et al. 2012; Ayer et al. 2015; Madadi et al. 2015).

The focus of the first group of studies is on understanding the underlying factors that affect an individual's adherence to a screening test or medication. Different factors considered in these studies such as age, gender, race, insurance status, income, and family history of a specific disease. Understanding these factors assist the health providers in characterizing significant factors and predicting the adherence behavior of a patient. There are many studies in the literature addressing this issue for different chronic diseases, for example, breast cancer (Wu et al. 2007; Tejeda et al. 2009; Madadi et al. 2014) and colorectal cancer (Subramanian et al. 2004; Hassan et al. 2012; Liang et al. 2016).

The second group of studies aims at optimizing screening or treatment guidelines based on a patient's adherence to a screening or treatment strategy. This line of research tailors screening/treatment guidelines for each specific patient based on the factors that affect patient compliance. Unlike the first group of studies, there has been limited research in this area (Brailsford et al. 2012; Mason et al. 2012; Ayer et al. 2015; Madadi et al. 2015). Brailsford et al. (2012) used a three-phase discrete event simulation to model breast cancer and screening policies incorporating women's adherence factors in their model. They assigned behavioral attributes to each simulated woman to control her compliance with the prescribed mammograms in their model. They compared a limited number of screening policies, including the current UK policy, in terms of the number of screen-detected cancers and life years saved. Mason et al. (2012) developed a Markov decision process (MDP) model to optimize the treatment decision for patients with type 2 diabetes. Their model incorporates a Markov model linking adherence to treatment effectiveness and long-term health outcomes. In another study, Ayer et al. (2015) developed a partially observable MDP to analyze the role of behavioral heterogeneity in women's adherence on optimal mammography screening recommendations. Madadi et al. (2015) evaluated a wide range of static and dynamic mammography screening policies for different adherence groups with different characteristics. They characterized the most efficient in-practice and alternative screening policies for each adherence group in terms of quality-adjusted life years (QALYs) and lifetime breast cancer mortality risk.

This book chapter falls into the second category and focuses on the cost-effective analysis of different screening policies with consideration of interindividual adherence differences. More specifically, we aim to perform a cost-effectiveness analysis of mammography screening policies while incorporating the uncertainty in patients' adherence behaviors. There are a lot of controversies on the mammography screening recommendations, and there are varying guidelines from different health agencies on the best screening frequency and the age range that women should undergo mammography screenings. The US Preventive Services Task Force (USPSTF) issued a revised screening mammography guidelines in 2009 stating that the screening mammograms should be done every 2 years between ages 50 and 74 for women at average risk of breast cancer. In late 2015, the American Cancer Society (ACS) also revised its previous guideline of annual screenings starting at age 40 and issued a new guideline. In the new ACS guidelines, women aged 45–54 years should be screened annually, and women 55 years and older should transition to biennial screenings or have the opportunity to continue screening annually.

In this chapter, the objective is to characterize the most cost-effective mammography screening policies for different adherence cases. To the best of our knowledge, this is the first cost-effective analysis study incorporating uncertainty in adherence behaviors. In the following section, we will present a partially observable Markov chain to model and compute the expected remaining QALYs and the associated screening and treatment costs for different screening policies. We apply the model to breast cancer data to analyze different mammography screening policies for different adherence behaviors.

10.2   MODEL FORMULATION

A randomized discrete-time partially observable Markov chain is developed to calculate the associated expected remaining QALYs as well as the expected screening and treatment costs for different screening strategies. A partially observable rather than fully observable Markov chain is developed to take into account the possibility of receiving inaccurate results from the mammography screening tests (false negatives and false positives). The state transition diagram of the underlying Markov chain presenting the natural history of breast cancer is shown in Figure 10.1. We represent patient's health using the following five states: breast cancer-free (state 0), early breast cancer (state 1), advanced breast cancer (state 2), death from breast cancer (state 3), and death from other causes (state 4). We define cancer stages in our model based on the American Joint Committee on Cancer (AJCC) cancer stage classification. For more details about the breast cancer stage classification, please refer to Madadi et al. (2015). In our model, the first three states (states 0, 1, and 2) are partially observable since we cannot identify the true health status of a patient due to imperfect nature of mammography test. We assume that the transitions occur in 6-month intervals to capture the natural history of breast cancer, that is, to transition to the advanced breast cancer state, a patient should transition to the early breast cancer state first, which takes at least 6 months (Chen et al. 1996).

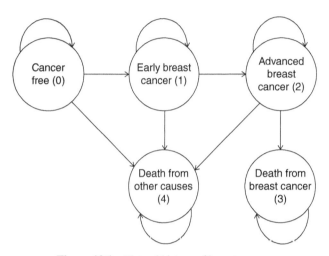

Figure 10.1   Natural history of breast cancer.

Two methods of detection are considered in the model: screening mammography and self-detection (SD), that is, breast self-examination. We also incorporate the possibility of interval cancer detection. Interval cancer and self-detected cancers are separated since their incidence rates and detection processes are different. Interval cancer occurs when a patient is detected with cancer within 1 year of receiving a negative mammogram result (Burhenne et al. 1994). However, in the case of an SD, the patient has not undergone a screening mammogram within the year prior to cancer diagnosis. Since it is very less likely to develop symptoms for a patient who received a negative mammogram result within the past year (interval cancer) compared with a patient whose last mammogram occurred more than 1 year prior to showing symptoms (SD), interval cancer detection and SD are distinguished.

At each epoch, there are two possible actions a patient can take: undergo a mammogram test or wait (do nothing). When the prescribed action is a mammogram, and the patient actually undergoes a mammogram test, she may receive a positive or a negative result. Since mammography is not a perfect test and has a relatively low sensitivity (the probability of receiving a true positive result), after a positive mammogram, a breast biopsy test is usually conducted to check if the result is true positive or not. Biopsy test is assumed to be perfect since it has a relatively high sensitivity and specificity (probability of receiving true negatives) rates. If the biopsy result is negative suggesting a false-positive mammogram, the patient proceeds to the next epoch. However, if the biopsy is also positive (confirms the mammographic findings), cancer is detected and the screening process terminates. After a cancer detection, we assume that the patient starts treatment. However, we do not model the treatment explicitly. Instead, we assume that when the patient is diagnosed with breast cancer, she receives a terminal (lump-sum) reward or cost (depending on the method of detection) and leaves the model. When a negative mammogram result is received, two events are possible afterward: some symptoms show up within 1 year (interval cancer), or the woman proceeds to the next epoch without developing any symptoms. If the patient shows symptoms and the interval cancer is detected, the patient receives a lump-sum reward or cost and leaves the model.

If the woman skips the recommended mammogram or the recommended action is to wait, she may develop some symptoms suggesting that there may be cancer present. In this case, depending on the action in the previous epoch (6 months ago), we either have an SD (if the previous action was a wait) or an interval cancer (if the previous action was a mammogram). Note that the interval between two decision epochs in the process is 6 months. Therefore, if the action in the previous epoch was a mammogram and symptoms occur after the current epoch, we have an interval cancer and not an SD. We assume that when the woman feels a lump in her breast (symptom), she will go for a mammogram and if the result of the mammogram is positive, she would have a biopsy test to confirm that the cancer is present. If both the mammography and biopsy tests are positive, similar to the previous case, the patient leaves the model. However, if the follow-up tests (i.e., mammogram or biopsy) are negative, the patient proceeds to the next epoch.

Let $q(t)$ denote the probability of patient adherence to a prescribed mammogram at time t. The value of $q(t)$ can be estimated based on the patient's characteristics using previous research on adherence, discussed earlier. Section 10.3 discusses the resources used to estimate a patient's adherence probability in more details. Let $q_1(t)$ and $q_2(t)$ be the lower and upper confidence bounds of the estimated adherence probability at time t ($q(t)$). The expected objective value (QALYs or cost) for policy d at time t when the current occupancy distribution is π can be calculated as follows:

$$V_t^a(\pi) = \begin{cases} \dfrac{1}{q_2(t) - q_1(t)} \displaystyle\int_{q_1(t)}^{q_2(t)} q(t)V_t^M(\pi) + (1 - q(t))V_t^W(\pi)dq(t), & \text{if } a_t = M, \\ V_t^W(\pi), & \text{if } a_t = W, \end{cases} \tag{10.1}$$

where $V_t^a(\pi)$ is the value function at time t when the occupancy distribution is π and action a is taken. Note that Equation 10.1 calculates the average value of the expected objective function over the interval $[q_1(t), q_2(t)]$.

In this section, we present the model formulation for the screening and treatment costs associated with screening policies. The formulation for the expected QALYs is similar and is omitted for the purpose of brevity. Interested readers can find the model for QALYs in Madadi et al. (2015).

Suppose $C_t^a(\pi)$ represents the cost associated with the screening policy under study when the belief state distribution is π and action a is taken at time t. The following are the formulations to estimate $C_t^a(\pi)$ when the prescribed action is to "undergo a mammogram test" (Equation 10.2) and to "wait and do nothing" (Equation 10.3). Note that in the following formulation, the time index of some notations such as occupancy distribution, states, actions, and observations are dropped for the brevity of notation.

If the prescribed action at time t is a mammogram, then the expected associated cost is

$$
\begin{aligned}
C_t^M(\pi) = &\ \pi(0)Q_t^M\left(M-|0\right)\left[SC_t(0,M,M-) + \lambda\sum_{s'=0}^{2}P_t^M\left(s'|0\right)C_{t+1}^{a_{t+1}}(v(\pi,M,M-))\right] \\
&+ \sum_{s=1,2}\pi(s)Q_t^M\left(M-|s\right)\left[Q_t^M\left(IC-|s\right)\left[SC_t\left(s,M,M-\&IC-\right)\right.\right. \\
&\left.\left.+\lambda\sum_{s'=0}^{2}P_t^M\left(s'|s\right)C_{t+1}^{a_{t+1}}\left(v\left(\pi,M,M-\right)\right)\right]+Q_t^M\left(IC+|s\right)LC_{1,t}\left(s\right)\right] \\
&+\pi(0)Q_t^M\left(M+|0\right)\left[SC_t(0,M,M+) + \lambda\sum_{s'=0}^{2}P_t^M\left(s'|0\right)C_{t+1}^{a_{t+1}}(v(\pi,M,M+))\right] \\
&+\sum_{s=1,2}\pi(s)Q_t^M\left(M+|s\right)LC_{2,t}(s),
\end{aligned}
$$

$$(10.2)$$

where $\pi(s)$ is the probability that the patient is currently in health state s and $Q_t^a\left(o|s\right)$ is the probability of observing observation o when action a is taken and the patient is in state s at time t. λ is the discount factor and $P_t^a\left(s'|s\right)$ is the probability of transitioning to state s' when the patient is currently in state s and action a is taken at time t. $LC_{1,t}(s)$ and $LC_{2,t}(s)$ are the lump-sum costs, or more specifically the total diagnostic costs and treatment cost upon cancer detection when the cancer is detected through symptoms and mammography screening tests at time t, respectively. The associated treatment costs include initial, continuing, and terminal care costs. Note that the treatment costs for screen-detected and symptomatic cancers are different due to the difference in the distribution of the stages at which the cancer would be detected under each diagnosis setting. $SC_t(s, a, o)$ is the associated screening costs when the patient is in state s and takes action a and observes o and is calculated in Equation 10.4.

The logic for Equation 10.2 is as follows. When a patient undergoes a mammogram, two outcomes are possible. She either receives a positive result or a negative result. The possible cases are discussed in the following.

If the patient is in the cancer-free state and she receives a negative result, the only cost occurs for the current period is the mammography cost. In this case, the patient remains in the model, and her occupancy distribution at time $t+1$ is updated. The updated occupancy distribution for epoch $t+1$ is represented by $v(\pi, a, o)$, and its formulation is presented later in this section (Equations 10.5 and 10.6).

If the patient is in the cancer states but receives a negative result, then she may develop some symptoms before the next time epoch with probability $Q_t^M\left(IC+|s\right), s=1,2$. In this case, interval cancer is identified, and the incurred cost includes the treatment costs as well as the screening and follow-up test costs to detect cancer $(LC_{1,t}(s))$.

In our model, we do not formulate the cancer post-diagnosis explicitly. Instead, we assume that after a cancer is detected a lump-sum cost (i.e., the expected total treatment and follow-up diagnostic costs) incurs to the system and the patient leaves the model. We assume that interval cancers can only occur in the cancer states since even the fastest-growing cancers cannot grow from a single cell to a symptomatic size within 6 months (Chen et al. 1996), which is the interval between two subsequent epochs in our model. If the patient is in one of the cancer states, receives a negative result, and does not develop any symptoms before the next time epoch, the only incurred cost is for the mammogram. In this case, she stays in the model and transits to the next time epoch.

If the patient is in the cancer-free state and receives a positive mammography test result, she will undergo a follow-up biopsy test. In this case, her actual health state is determined and she remains in the model. However, if she is in any of the two cancer states and receives a positive result, the costs incurred to the system are the associated treatment and follow-up costs, which are a function of her cancer state. In this case, the process is terminated and the patient leaves the model.

If the policy does not recommend a mammography test at time t ($a_t = W$), the expected screening and treatment cost is

$$
\begin{aligned}
C_t^W(\pi) = {} & \pi(0)Q_t^W\left(SD-|0\right)\left[SC_t(0,W,SD-) + \lambda\sum_{s'=0}^{2}P_t^W\left(s'|0\right)C_{t+1}^{a_{t+1}}\left(v(\pi,W,SD-)\right)\right] \\
& + \pi(0)Q_t^W\left(SD+|0\right)\left[SC_t(0,W,SD+) + \lambda\sum_{s'=0}^{2}P_t^W\left(s'|0\right)C_{t+1}^{a_{t+1}}\left(v(\pi,W,SD+)\right)\right] \\
& + (1-I(t))\left\{\sum_{s=1,2}\pi(s)Q_t^W\left(SD-|s\right)\left[SC_t\left(s,W,SD-\right)\right.\right. \\
& \left.+ \lambda\sum_{s'=0}^{2}P_t^W\left(s'|s\right)C_{t+1}^{a_{t+1}}\left(v(\pi,W,SD-)\right)\right] + \sum_{s=1,2}\pi(s)Q_t^W\left(SD+|s\right)LC_{2,t}(s)\right\} \\
& + I(t)\left\{\sum_{s=1,1}\pi(s)Q_t^W\left(IC-|s\right)\left[SC_t(s,W,IC-) + \lambda\sum_{s'=0}^{2}P_t^W\left(s'|s\right)C_{t+1}^{a_{t+1}}\left(v(\pi,W,IC-)\right)\right]\right. \\
& \left.+ \sum_{s=1,2}\pi(s)Q_t^W\left(IC+|s\right)LC_{2,t}(s)\right\},
\end{aligned}
$$

$$(10.3)$$

where $I(t)$ is an indicator function representing whether there was a mammogram scheduled within the last 12 months ($I(t) = 1$) or not ($I(t) = 0$) and $Q_t\left(IC+|s\right)$ is the probability of diagnosing interval cancer within 1 year of a negative mammogram test.

When the current action at time t is "to wait," for the cancer that develops symptoms, two separate cases need to be considered to distinguish between an SD and an interval cancer. If a cancer is diagnosed through symptoms and the patient did not undergo a mammogram test in the previous year, the diagnosis is considered as an SD. However, if there was a negative mammogram within the previous 12 months, the diagnosed cancer is an interval cancer.

The following discusses the logic behind Equation 10.3. If the patient is in the cancer-free state and does not show any symptoms, no cost incurs to the system for the current time epoch, and the patient remains in the model. However, if symptoms develop in a cancer-free patient, the follow-up test shows the true health state of the patient. In this case, the follow-up costs, including mammogram and possible biopsy costs, incurs to the system, and the patient proceeds to the next epoch. If the patient is in one of the cancer states and does not develop any symptoms, there is no cost incurred to the system. In this case, she proceeds to the next time epoch. However, if she is in cancer states and shows some symptoms that result in cancer detection, depending on the action in the previous time epoch, we have either SD (when $a_{t-1} = W$) or interval cancer (when $a_{t-1} = M$). In such case, the cancer is detected, and the expected follow-up test and future treatment costs are calculated, and the process is terminated. If the patient does not show any symptoms, she transits to the next epoch with no cost added to the system.

The associated costs of screening/diagnostic tests, $SC_t(s_t, a_t, o_t)$, are calculated as follows:

$$SC_t\left(s_t, a_t, o_t\right) = \begin{cases} C^M, & \text{if } a_t = M, o_t = M-\ \&\ IC-, \text{ or } o_t = M- \\ C^M + C^B, & \text{if } s_t = 0, a_t = M, o_t = M+, \\ 0, & \text{if } a_t = W, o_t = IC- \text{ or } SD-, \\ C^M + Q_t^M\left(M + |0\right)C^B, & \text{if } s_t = 0, a_t = W, o_t = SD+, \end{cases} \tag{10.4}$$

where C^M and C^B are the costs for mammography and biopsy test, respectively. Note that depending on the action taken and the observation received, this could include screening/diagnostic mammography costs and/or biopsy costs. More specifically, if the patient undergoes a mammogram, receives a negative result, and does not develop any symptoms until the next epoch, the associated screening cost is C^M. If the patient is in the cancer-free state and receives a positive result, she will be referred for biopsy. In such case, the associated screening cost is $C^M + C^B$. If the prescribed action is "to wait" and patient does not develop any symptoms until the next epoch, no screening cost is incurred. If the patient is in the cancer-free state, the prescribed action is "to wait" and the patient develops symptoms ($o_t = SD +$), she will be prescribed a mammogram and cost C^M will incur. However, it is possible that she receives a false-positive mammogram result (with probability $Q_t^M(M+|0)$) in which case she will be referred for biopsy and therefore biopsy cost of C^B will incur. Note that for the cases when the cancer is present and the test results are positive, the screening/diagnostic costs are added up to the lump-sum costs of $LC_{1,t}(s)$ or $LC_{2,t}(s)$. Note that $LC_{1,t}(s) \le LC_{2,t}(s)$ since it is more costly to treat a cancer in advanced stages.

As mentioned earlier, after each observation the patient occupancy distribution needs to be updated. Updates take place in two steps. In the first step, the occupancy distribution is updated based on the information gathered at time t after a "mammogram test" or "no symptom" outcome. Equation 10.5 presents the formulation to update the occupancy distribution π after taking action a_t and receiving observation o_t at time t. Note that the time indices in $\xi_{\pi,a,o}(s)$ are dropped for the clarity of notation:

$$
\xi_{\pi,a,o}(s) = \begin{cases}
\dfrac{\pi(s)Q_t^M\left(M-|s\right)Q_t^M\left(IC-|s\right)}{\displaystyle\sum_{j=0}^{2}\pi(j)Q_t^M\left(M-|j\right)Q_t^M\left(IC-|j\right)}, & \text{if } a_t = M,\ o_t = M-\ \&\ IC-, \\[3em]
\dfrac{\pi(s)Q_t^W\left(SD-|s\right)}{\displaystyle\sum_{j=0}^{2}\pi(j)Q_t^W\left(SD-|j\right)}, & \text{if } a_{t-1} = a_t = W,\ o_t = SD-, \\[3em]
\dfrac{\pi(s)Q_t^W\left(IC-|s\right)}{\displaystyle\sum_{j=0}^{2}\pi(j)Q_t^W\left(IC-|j\right)}, & \text{if } a_{t-1} = M,\ a_t = W,\ o_t = IC-, \\[3em]
1, & \text{if } s_t = 0,\ o_t = M+\ \text{or}\ SD+.
\end{cases}
$$

$$(10.5)$$

In the second step (Equation 10.6), we need to account for the possibility of transitioning from one health state to another during a time period (between time t and time $t+1$). Therefore, at time $t+1$ the updated occupancy distribution would be

$$
v(\pi,a,o)\left(s'\right) = \xi_{\pi,a,o}(s)\cdot P_t^a\left(s'|s\right). \qquad (10.6)
$$

10.3   NUMERICAL STUDIES

In this section, we examine the performance of different screening policies including in-practice guidelines and some alternative screening strategies. Estimations of parameters in the numerical analyses are adopted from the literature. Table 10.1 presents the input data sources used in the numerical analyses.

We consider two adherence cases in this section: (i) perfect adherence case and (ii) general population adherence case. In the first adherence case, we assume that the patient complies with the recommended policy completely and undergo mammography screenings at the prescribed ages. In the second case, however, we consider the US population adherence probabilities adopted from Madadi et al. (2014). These adherence probabilities (probability that the patient complies with a prescribed screening) are age dependent and are extracted using the Health Information National Trends Survey (HINTS) data (Nelson et al. 2004). For the immediate reward in calculating the QALYs, we used the age- and state-specific mammography and biopsy disutility

TABLE 10.1   Sources for Parameter Estimation

Parameter	References
Transition probabilities	Maillart et al. (2008) and Epstein et al. (2001)
BSE sensitivity and specificity	Baxter (2001)
Mammography sensitivity and specificity	Kerlikowske et al. (2000)
Initial risk of early and advanced breast cancer	Gail model (National Cancer Institute 2016; Gail et al. 1999)
Lump-sum rewards	SEER (Jemal et al. 2009), Arias et al. (2012), and Wishart et al. (2008)
Intermediate rewards	Sonnenberg and Beck (1993) and Stout et al. (2006)
Interval cancer rate	Croteau et al. (2005)
Screening and diagnostic mammograms, biopsy, and treatment costs	Tosteson et al.(2008), Bureau of Labor Statistics Consumer Price Index (2016)
Stage distribution of screen-detected breast cancer	Bleyer and Welch (2012)
Stage distribution of symptomatic breast cancer	Plevritis et al. (2007)
Adherence probabilities	Madadi et al. (2014) and HINTS (Nelson et al. 2004)
Discount factor	Gold et al. (1996)
Willingness to pay	Hirth et al. (2000)

values provided in Stout et al. (2006). Post-cancer life expectancies (the lump-sum rewards) are calculated using age-specific mortality rates for patients under cancer treatment from the SEER data based on the method described in Arias et al. (2012). Mammography and biopsy costs, as well as the expected treatment costs, are adopted from Tosteson et al. (2008). Note that all cost values in Tosteson et al. (2008) are in 2005 US dollars. These costs estimates are adjusted to the calendar year 2016 dollars by using the Bureau of Labor Statistics Consumer Price Index (2016).

The old and new ACS policies, the USPSTF policy, and biennial and triennial policies are among the in-practice policies investigated. Since the ACS does not specify a stopping age, two different stopping ages of 90 and 100 are considered. Stopping age of 100 is considered to be consistent with the US life tables reported by the CDC. We also considered stopping age of 90 since in the new ACS policy, it is stated that women should continue screening as long as they have a life expectancy of 10 years or more. As a result, there are two different alternatives for the old ACS policy. For the new ACS policy, as mentioned earlier, women are recommended to undergo either annual or biennial screening after 55. Considering the two different stopping ages, in total, there are four alternatives for the new ACS policy. We also examined the performance of several alternative policies in which screening interval changes in the patient lifetime to account for the dynamics of the breast cancer incidence and progression rate throughout the patient's lifetime. These dynamic alternative screening strategies are represented by a vector $(a_1, i_1, a_2, i_2, a_3)$ where the vector's elements represent the age at the first screening, first screening interval, switching age, second screening interval, and age at the last screening, respectively. For example, (45,1,50,2,90) presents a policy that recommends annual screenings between age 45 and 50 and biennial screenings afterward up to age 90.

Screening policies are compared in terms of the expected screening and treatment costs as well as the expected remaining QALYs. We calculate the cost-effectiveness ratio (CER) that represents additional costs per additional QALYs gained for choosing an intervention strategy (Gold et al. 1996):

$$CER_p = \frac{\Delta C_p}{\Delta Q_p} = \frac{C_p - C_o}{Q_p - Q_o}, \qquad (10.7)$$

where C_p, C_o, Q_p, and Q_o are the cost associated with policy p and "no screening" policies and QALYs associated with policy p and "no screening" policies, respectively.

Results are also interpreted using the net benefit framework, where net monetary benefit (NMB) is defined as

$$NMB_p = \gamma \cdot \Delta Q_p - \Delta C_p, \qquad (10.8)$$

where γ represents the cost-effectiveness threshold, or willingness to pay (WTP), in \$/QALY. We use a common value for γ of \$50,000 per additional QALY gained for an intervention provided in the literature (Hirth et al. 2000). Intervention programs inclusive of this CER threshold are considered cost-effective.

10.4   RESULTS

We present the results for two adherence cases (perfect adherence and population-average adherence) in Sections 10.4.1 and 10.4.2, separately.

10.4.1   Perfect Adherence Case

Table 10.2 shows the incremental costs, QALYs, CER, and NMB for different screening strategies under the assumption of perfect adherence. Note that for this case, we assume that a woman undergoes a prescribed screening mammogram with probability 1, that is, $q_1(t) = q_2(t) = 1$.

As the results show, all policies are cost-effective compared with "no screening" strategy using the WTP threshold of \$50,000. Policy (45,1,50,2,90) is the most cost-effective policy with an NMB value of \$20,715.83. Note that this policy is very similar to the new ACS policy with a slight difference in the screening frequency between age 50 and 55. Moreover, the two alternatives of the old ACS policy are the least cost-effective policies with CER value of 9730.09 and 9818.62 for the stopping ages of 90 and 100, respectively. Results also imply that the dynamic screening policies that alter screening intervals over the screening horizon are more effective than static policies such as the old ACS policies, every 2 years and every 3 years. The new

TABLE 10.2   Cost-Effectiveness Analysis of Different Screening Policies Relative to a No Screening Policy (Doing Nothing) – *perfect* **Adherence Case**

Policy	ΔCost ($)	ΔQALYs (years)	CER ($)	NMB($)
USPSTF	1093.89	0.4113	2659.59	17,905.41
(50,1,55,2,90)	1569.26	0.4645	3378.39	19,846.61
Every 3 years (stopping at age 90)	1718.86	0.4366	Dominated	17,893.08
Every 3 years (stopping at age 100)	1724.57	0.4372	Dominated	17,915.42
(45,1,50,2,90)	2262.99	0.5041	4489.17	20,715.83
Every 2 years (stopping at age 90)	2479.03	0.4968	Dominated	19,850.00
Every 2 years (stopping at age 100)	2484.94	0.4965	Dominated	19,820.09
New ACS (stopping at age 90)	2642.33	0.5003	Dominated	19,733.51
New ACS (stopping at age 100)	2650.36	0.5002	Dominated	19,711.40
New ACS (annual alt.- stop at age 90)	3340.93	0.5060	6602.63	18,697.37
New ACS (annual alt.- stop at age 100)	3353.89	0.5030	Dominated	18,482.23
(40,1,50,2,90)	3691.68	0.4883	Dominated	16,854.73
(40,1,55,2,90)	4071.04	0.4845	Dominated	15,822.44
Old ACS (stopping at age 90)	4769.69	0.4902	Dominated	14,779.91
Old ACS (stopping at age 100)	4782.65	0.4871	Dominated	14,536.38

ACS policies (biennial alternative) are dominated by the alternative screening policy (45,1,50,2,90). However, note that the QALYs for theses screening policies are very close (37.5183 years for (45,1,50,2,90) vs. 37.5145 and 37.5144 for the new ACS biennial alternative with stopping ages of 90 and 100, respectively). Note that the new ACS policies outperform the old ACS policies in terms of both the remaining expected QALYs and the expected costs.

Figure 10.2 shows the trade-off plot for different screening policies, that is, the incremental cost and QALYs compared to "no screening" policy. The USPSTF, (50,1,55,2,90), (45,1,50,2,90), and the annual alternative of the new ACS policy with stopping age of 90 are among the efficient frontier or dominant policies.

10.4.2   General Population Adherence Case

Table 10.3 presents the cost-effectiveness analysis results for the general population adherence case. For the general population case since the adherence is not perfect, it is expected that the most effective policy (with the highest QALYs) to be more invasive compared to the perfect adherence case. As the results suggest, the old ACS policy with stopping age of 90 has the highest QALYs. However, the most cost-effective policy for this case is the annual alternative of the new ACS policy with NMB value of $23,589.83.

Note that for both adherence cases, it is beneficial in terms of both QALYs and the expected cost to stop screening at age 90. In other words, the harms of screening at older ages outweigh the benefits. However, regarding the screening starting age, the results vary between the two adherence cases. For the general population case, due to non-perfect adherence, starting screenings at age 40 would be beneficial, while for

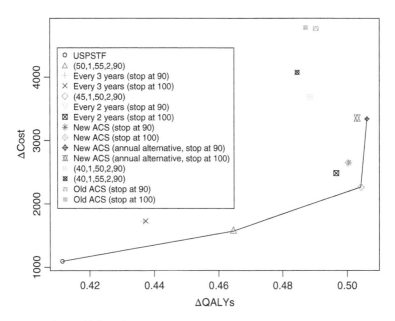

Figure 10.2 Efficient frontier policies – *perfect* adherence case.

TABLE 10.3   Cost-Effectiveness Analysis of Different Screening Policies Relative to a No Screening Policy (Doing Nothing) – *general population* **Adherence Case**

Policy	ΔCost ($)	ΔQALYs (years)	CER ($)	NMB($)
USPSTF	774.08	0.3748	2065.32	17,965.92
(50,1,55,2,90)	995.15	0.4250	2341.53	20,254.85
Every 3 years (stop at age 90)	1104.45	0.3941	Dominated	18,600.55
Every 3 years (stop at age 100)	1107.34	0.3949	Dominated	18,637.66
(45,1,50,2,90)	1368.54	0.4637	2951.35	21,816.46
New ACS (stop at age 90)	1544.08	0.4690	3292.28	21,905.92
New ACS (stop at age 100)	1548.37	0.4694	3298.61	21,921.63
Every 2 years (stop at age 90)	1609.82	0.4611	Dominated	21,445.18
Every 2 years (stop at age 100)	1612.98	0.4614	Dominated	21,457.02
New ACS (annual alt., stop at age 90)	1895.17	0.5097	3718.21	23,589.83
New ACS (annual alt., stop at age 100)	1900.86	0.5094	Dominated	23,569.14
(40,1,50,2,90)	2024.70	0.4704	Dominated	21,459.30
(40,1,55,2,90)	2200.42	0.4757	Dominated	21,584.58
Old ACS (stop at age 90)	2551.88	0.5164	4941.67	23,268.12
Old ACS (stop at age 100)	2557.58	0.5162	Dominated	23,252.42

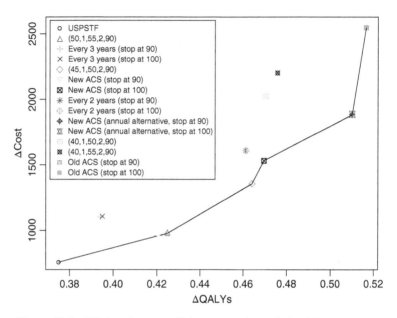

Figure 10.3   Efficient frontier policies – *general population adherence case.*

the perfect adherence case, the starting screening age of 45 is more effective. For both cases, static policies with fixed screening intervals are dominated by dynamic policies with a more invasive screening schedule in younger ages.

Figure 10.3 shows the trade-off plot for different screening policies for the general population. For this case, the USPSTF policy, all alternatives of the new ACS policy, and both alternatives of the old ACS policy are among the efficient frontier or dominant policies.

It is difficult to directly compare our results with those of previously published analyses because past results did not incorporate the uncertainty in adherence behavior, and also they varied considerably, in part because of differences in the analytic assumptions (including the age structure of the study population, screening methods included, screening scenarios evaluated, etc.). However, our results reiterate the overall conclusion from these previous analyses that, in general, a screening mammography program can be cost-effective compared with no screening (Mandelblatt et al. 2003; Stout et al. 2006).

10.5   SUMMARY

Current screening mammography guidelines assume that women's adherence to the guidelines is perfect, that is, women undergo their mammograms as prescribed by their physicians/health providers. However, as previously shown, this is not the case.

In this study, a randomized partially observable Markov chain is proposed to investigate the effectiveness and costs of various in-practice as well as alternative screening policies. Policies are evaluated concerning QALYs, and the associated screening and treatment costs while incorporating women' s adherence behavior to mammography guidelines. A cost-effective analysis of the policies is performed by estimating the CER and the NMB values.

Two different adherence cases are considered: perfect adherence and the general population adherence case. For the perfect adherence case, the most cost-effective screening policy is to perform annual screenings between 45 and 50 and then switch to biennial screening until age 90. This policy is very similar to the new ACS policy. For the general population case, the most cost-effective policy is the annual alternative of the new ACS policy with annual screenings between ages of 45 and 90. The model presented in this study can also be used for an individualized assessment of different screening policies (Madadi et al. 2015).

Our results also indicate that as the policies get more invasive (more frequent screenings with earlier starting age), the general population case obtains higher QALYs compared with the perfect adherence case, because of the disutilities associated with mammogram screening tests. The old ACS policy with stopping age of 100 is the most invasive policy considered in the analyses, which results in QALYs of 37.5044 and 37.5306 for the perfect adherence and the general population cases, respectively.

A set of efficient frontier policies with respect to incremental QALYs and incremental cost compared with "no screening" are extracted for different adherence cases. For the perfect adherence case, the USPSTF and the annual alternative of the ACS policy are among efficient frontier policies. For the general population, the USPSTF and all alternatives of the old and the new ACS policies are among efficient frontier policies.

The results of this study can help physicians/health providers tailor screening mammography recommendations based on their patients estimated adherence likelihood. In other words, based on the patient characteristics and estimated adherence level, physicians can decide if they should shorten or lengthen the interval between two subsequent mammograms and adjust the screening starting and stopping ages.

REFERENCES

Arias E, Heron M, Tejada-Vera B, "National vital statistics reports," United States Centers for Disease Control and Prevention, Atlanta, GA (2012).

Ayer T, Alagoz O, Stout NK, Burnside ES, "Heterogeneity in women's adherence and its role on optimal breast cancer screening policies," *Management Science* 62(5), pp. 1339–1362 (2015).

Baxter N, "Should women be routinely taught breast self-examination to screen for breast cancer?" *Canadian Medical Association Journal* 164(13), pp. 1837–1845 (2001).

Benjamin RM, "Medication adherence: Helping patients take their medicines as directed," *Public Health Reports* 127(1), pp. 2–3 (2012).

Bleyer A, Welch G, "Effect of three decades of screening mammography on breast-cancer incidence," *New England Journal of Medicine* 367(21), pp. 1998–2005 (2012).

Brailsford SC, Harper PR, Sykes J, "Incorporating human behavior in simulation models of screening for breast cancer," *European Journal of Operational Research* 219, pp. 491–507 (2012).

Bureau of Labor Statistics, http://www.bls.gov/data/inflation_calculator.htm. Accessed April 2016.

Burhenne HJ, Burhenne LW, Goldberg F, Hislop TG, Worth AJ, Rebbeck PM, Kan L, "Interval breast cancers in the Screening Mammography Program of British Columbia: Analysis and classification," *AJR. American Journal of Roentgenology* 162, pp. 1067–1071 (1994).

Center for Disease Control and Prevention, http://www.cdc.gov/nchs/data/hus/hus15.pdf#070. Accessed April 2016.

Chen HH, Duffy SW, Tabar L, "A Markov chain method to estimate the tumour progression rate from preclinical to clinical phase, sensitivity and positive predictive value for mammography in breast cancer screening," *Statistician* 45, pp. 307–317 (1996).

Croteau HN, Thberge I, Langlois A, Major D, Brisson J, direction systèmes de soins et services of Institut national de santé publique du Québec, 2005, "Interval cancer in women following a normal initial mammogram in the Quebec breast cancer screening program (PQDCS) in 1998–2000," Direction Systmes De Soins Et Services (2005), https://www.inspq.qc.ca/pdf/publications/535-IntervalCancer_Women.pdf. Accessed September 2017.

Epstein SS, Bertell R, Seaman B, "Dangers and unreliability of mammography: Breast examination is a safe, effective, and practical alternative," *International Journal of Health Services* 31(3), pp. 605–615 (2001).

Gail MH, Costantino JP, Bryant J, Croyle R, Freedman L, Heizlsouer K, Vogel K, "Weighing the risks and benefits of tamoxifen treatment for preventing breast cancer," *Journal of the National Cancer Institute* 91(21), pp. 1829–1846 (1999).

Gold MR, Siegel JE, Russell LB, Weinstein MC, *"Cost-Effectiveness in Health and Medicine,"* Oxford University Press, New York (1996).

Hassan C, Rossi PG, Camilloni L, Rex DK, Jimenez-Cendales B, Ferroni E, Borgia P, Zullo A, Guasticchi G, HTA Group, "Meta-analysis: Adherence to colorectal cancer screening and the detection rate for advanced neoplasia, according to the type of screening test," *Alimentary Pharmacology & Therapeutics* 36(10), pp. 929–940 (2012).

Hirth RA, Chernew ME, Miller E, Fendrick AM, Weissert WG, "Willingness to pay for a quality-adjusted life year: In search of a standard," *Medical Decision Making* 20(3), pp. 332–342 (2000).

Jemal A, Siegel R, Ward E, Hao Y, Xu J, Thun MJ, "Cancer statistics, 2009," *CA: A Cancer Journal for Clinicians* 59(4), pp. 225–249 (2009).

Kerlikowske K, Carney PA, Geller B, Mandelson MT, Taplin SH, Malvin K, Ernster V, Urban N, Cutter G, Rosenberg R, Ballard-Barbash R, "Performance of screening mammography among women with and without a first-degree relative with breast cancer," *Annals of Internal Medicine* 133(11), pp. 855–863 (2000).

Liang PS, Wheat CL, Abhat A, Brenner AT, Fagerlin A, Hayward RA, Thomas JP, Vijan S, Inadomi JM, "Adherence to competing strategies for colorectal cancer screening over 3 years," *American Journal of Gastroenterology* 111(1), pp. 105–114 (2016).

Madadi M, Zhang S, Yeary KHK, Henderson LM, "Analyzing factors associated with womens attitudes and behaviors toward screening mammography using design-based logistic regression," *Breast Cancer Research and Treatment* 144(1), pp. 193–204 (2014).

Madadi M, Zhang S, Henderson LM, "Evaluation of breast cancer mammography screening policies considering adherence behavior," *European Journal of Operational Research* 247(2), pp. 630–640 (2015).

Maillart LM, Ivy JS, Ransom S, Diehl K, "Assessing dynamic breast cancer screening policies," *Operations Research* 56(6), pp. 1411–1427 (2008).

Mandelblatt J, Saha S, Teutsch S, Hoerger T, Siu AL, Atkins D, Klein J, Helfand M, "The cost-effectiveness of screening mammography beyond age 65 years: A systematic review for the U.S. Preventive Services Task Force," *Annals of Internal Medicine* 139, pp. 835–842 (2003).

Mason JE, England DA, Denton BT, Smith SA, Kurt M, Shah ND, "Optimizing statin treatment decisions for diabetes patients in the presence of uncertain future adherence," *Medical Decision Making* 32(1), pp. 154–166 (2012).

National Cancer Institute, http://www.cancer.gov/bcrisktool/. Accessed April 2016.

Nelson D, Kreps G, Hesse B, Croyle RT, Willis G, Arora NK, Rimer BK, Viswanath KV, Weinstein N, Alden S, "The Health Information National Trends Survey (HINTS): Development, design, and dissemination," *Journal of Health Communication* 9, pp. 443–460 (2004).

O'Donohue WT, Levensky ER, "*Promoting Treatment Adherence: A Practical Handbook for Health Care Providers*," Sage Publications, New York (2006).

Partin MR, Slater JS, Caplan L, "Randomized controlled trial of a repeat mammography intervention: Effect of adherence definitions on results," *Preventive Medicine* 41(34), pp. 734–740 (2005).

Plevritis SK, Salzman P, Sigal BM, "A natural history model of stage progression applied to breast cancer," *Statistics in Medicine* 26, pp. 581–595 (2007).

Sonnenberg FA, Beck, JR, "Markov models in medical decision making: A practical guide," *Medical Decision Making* 13(4), pp. 322–338 (1993).

Stout NK, Rosenberg MA, Trentham-Dietz A, Smith MA, Robinson SM, Fryback DG, "Retrospective cost effectiveness analysis of screening mammography," *Journal of the National Cancer Institute* 98(11), pp. 774–782 (2006).

Subramanian S, Klosterman M, Amonkar MM, Hunt TL, "Adherence with colorectal cancer screening guidelines: A review," *Preventive Medicine* 38, pp. 536–550 (2004).

Tejeda S, Thompson B, Coronado GD, Martin DP, Heagerty PJ, "Predisposing and enabling factors associated with mammography use among hispanic and non-hispanic white women living in a rural area," *Journal of Rural Health* 25(1), pp. 85–92 (2009).

Tosteson ANA, Stout NK, Fryback DG, Acharyya S, Herman B, Hannah L, Pisano E, on behalf of the DMIST Investigators. "Cost-effectiveness of digital mammography breast cancer screening: Results from ACRIN DMIST," *Annals of Internal Medicine* 148(1), pp. 1–10 (2008).

Wishart GC, Greenberg DC, Britton PD, Chou P, Brown CH, Purushotham AD, Duffy SW, "Screen-detected vs symptomatic breast cancer: Is improved survival due to stage migration alone?" *British Journal of Cancer* 98(11), pp. 1741–1744 (2008).

Wu H, Zhu K, Jatoi I, Shah M, Shriver CD, Potter J, "Factors associated with the incompliance with mammogram screening among individuals with a family history of breast cancer or ovarian cancer," *Breast Cancer Research and Treatment* 101(3), pp. 317–324 (2007).

11

AN AGENT-BASED MODEL FOR IDEAL CARDIOVASCULAR HEALTH

YAN LI[1,2], NAN KONG[3], MARK A. LAWLEY[4,5], AND JOSÉ A. PAGÁN[1,6,7]

[1] Center for Health Innovation, The New York Academy of Medicine, New York, NY, USA
[2] Department of Population Health Science and Policy, Icahn School of Medicine at Mount Sinai, New York, NY, USA
[3] Weldon School of Biomedical Engineering, Purdue University, West Lafayette, IN, USA
[4] Department of Industrial and Systems Engineering, Texas A&M University, College Station, TX, USA
[5] Department of Biomedical Engineering, Texas A&M University, College Station, TX, USA
[6] Department of Public Health Policy and Management, College of Global Public Health, New York University, New York, NY, USA
[7] Leonard Davis Institute of Health Economics, University of Pennsylvania, Philadelphia, PA, USA

11.1 INTRODUCTION

Cardiovascular disease (CVD) is the leading cause of death in the United States and the world (Alwan 2011). More than 2150 people die of CVD in the United States each day, and the annual direct and indirect costs associated with CVD have been estimated to be more than $300 billion in recent years (Go et al. 2013). Although myocardial infarction (MI) and stroke events are serious and deadly, CVD is generally preventable if people maintain desirable cardiovascular health and reduce risk factors.

To better measure and improve cardiovascular health, the American Heart Association (AHA) developed the concept of ideal cardiovascular health, which is

Decision Analytics and Optimization in Disease Prevention and Treatment, First Edition.
Edited by Nan Kong and Shengfan Zhang.
© 2018 John Wiley & Sons, Inc. Published 2018 by John Wiley & Sons, Inc.

also called "Life's Simple 7" (Lloyd-Jones et al. 2010). In particular, this definition means that a person is considered to have ideal cardiovascular health if he/she does not have CVD while also achieving optimal levels in seven health behaviors and factors, including not smoking, being physically active, eating a healthy diet, having a normal body weight, and maintaining optimal levels for blood glucose, blood pressure, and cholesterol. Table 11.1 presents a summary of how to measure Life's Simple 7. Research has shown that the selected seven health behaviors and factors are important predictors of the prevalence of CVD and mortality due to CVD (Ford et al. 2012a). Specifically, people with healthy lifestyle behaviors (e.g., those who do not smoke, follow a healthy diet, and are physically active) have reduced mortality from all causes and CVD (Ford and Capewell 2011; Ford et al. 2012b). Based on the definition of ideal cardiovascular health, the AHA developed an impact goal that aims to improve the cardiovascular health of all Americans by 20% while reducing deaths from CVD by 20% by 2020 (Lloyd-Jones et al. 2010). Despite the importance of having ideal cardiovascular health in CVD prevention, recent studies found that only about 3% of American adults have ideal cardiovascular health as defined by the AHA (Fang et al. 2012).

The low level of health behaviors associated with ideal cardiovascular health in the United States calls for the development of systems strategies to optimize the prevention and management of CVD. Computer simulation models and systems science methodologies provide clinicians, community-based organizations, and policy makers with the possibility of testing interventions and policies in a virtual and low-cost environment; thus, simulation-based approaches to understanding health progression and behaviors have attracted a great amount of attention in both research and practice. Unal et al. (2006) conducted a systematic literature review of coronary heart disease policy models and discussed their strengths and limitations. However, among the 42 policy models they reviewed, most were Markov-based

TABLE 11.1   Levels of Ideal Cardiovascular Health Based on Life's Simple 7

Life's Simple 7	Poor	Intermediate	Ideal
Blood pressure	SBP ≥ 140 or DBP ≥ 90 mmHg	SBP 120–139 or DBP 80–90 mmHg	SBP < 120 or DBP < 80 mmHg
Physical activity	None	1–149 minutes/week moderate	≥ 150 minutes/week moderate
Cholesterol	≥ 240 mg/dL	200–239 mg/dL	< 170 mg/dL
Healthy diet	0–1 components	2–3 components	4–5 components
Healthy weight	BMI ≥ 30 kg/m²	BMI 25–29.9 kg/m²	BMI < 25 kg/m²
Smoking status	Current smoker	Former ≤ 12 months	Never/quit ≥ 12 months
Blood glucose	≥ 126 mg/dL	100–125 mg/dL	< 100 mg/dL

Source: Adapted from Lloyd-Jones et al. (2010).
BMI, body mass index; DBP, diastolic blood pressure; SBP, systolic blood pressure.
1 component indicates a healthy dietary component such as fruits and vegetables, fish, and nuts.

models that have limited capability in capturing non-Markov disease progression, human behaviors, and population heterogeneity. Recently, Hirsch et al. (2010) developed a system dynamics (SD) model that incorporates the complex causal pathways associated with CVD progression and used the model to evaluate the effectiveness of different interventions. Although SD is a promising and coherent modeling approach, a major limitation is that findings from the model are hard to generalize to populations with different characteristics (as individuals are homogeneous within the model).

In this chapter, we present an agent-based model (ABM) based on the concept of ideal cardiovascular health developed by the AHA. This model allows us to track population cardiovascular health and the progression of CVD over time (years) and study the impact of interventions (especially lifestyle interventions) on population health outcomes. In particular, our model can generate a user-specified population, capture each individual's growth and dynamic changes of health behaviors and factors, simulate the implementation of several lifestyle interventions, and report a set of health outcomes and mortality over a time horizon of interest. The model structure, data sources, and some of the simulation results have been reported in our previous studies (Li et al. 2014a, b). This chapter provides readers with a detailed description of the ABM and combines results from our previous studies to show how the model could be used to inform public health decision making. The chapter also includes an in-depth discussion of potential model extensions and points out future directions for the application of agent-based modeling in studying other chronic health conditions.

11.2 METHODOLOGY

11.2.1 Agent-Based Modeling

Agent-based modeling is a class of computational models for simulating the behaviors and interactions of agents and how agents' behaviors give rise to system-level phenomenon over time. While standard statistical models strive to explore causal relationships based on observations from data, an ABM is more suitable to capture complex health problems (e.g., progression of chronic health conditions) given that it allows the integration of data and theories from many different sources and at many levels of analysis. Moreover, agent-based modeling has been shown to be more advantageous than other systems science methodologies, such as discrete-event simulation and SD, when it comes to modeling the behaviors of individuals in a diverse population (Rahmandad and Sterman 2008; Siebers et al. 2010). The advantages of agent-based modeling can be summarized as follows:

- The capability to capture demographic diversity by generating a population of agents with different attributes
- Detailed individual-level modeling of behaviors and health outcomes

- Flexibility of aggregating and disaggregating populations based on certain criteria to inform decision making for different groups of interest (e.g., by age, geographic location)
- Capability of representing stochastic variability due to uncertainties in demographic inputs and parameter estimation
- Incorporation of history dependence in state transitions
- Flexibility to incorporate agent interactions

By using simple rules of behavior and action, agent-based modeling can be used to model complex social and health problems in an intuitive way that is appealing to policy makers (Macal and North 2010). For example, agent-based modeling has been applied to solve complex problems in many fields, such as economics, political science, and other empirical social sciences (Cederman 2002; Fagiolo et al. 2007; Bruch and Atwell 2015). In addition, Barnes et al. (2013) provided a literature review that summarizes the applications of agent-based modeling in the context of healthcare operations management. However, to the best of our knowledge, agent-based modeling has not been used to model cardiovascular health using a comprehensive evidence-based framework such as Life's Simple 7. This study aims to fill this research gap and provide a framework for future similar modeling efforts.

11.2.2   Model Structure

In our model, agents (persons) are defined by the factors in Life's Simple 7 (i.e., smoking, physical activity, diet, body weight, cholesterol, blood pressure, blood glucose) as well as by age, by gender, and by whether or not having a history of MI or stroke. Age and gender are intrinsic factors (i.e., not affected by other factors). The basic time unit is 1 year, so each agent becomes 1 year older at each simulation time step. Each agent's behaviors and health factors change simultaneously and interactively based on the predefined rules during simulation. Figure 11.1 presents the state charts in the model to capture behavior changes (e.g., transitions between "healthy diet" and "unhealthy diet"), health factor changes (e.g., transitions between "normal blood pressure" and "hypertension"), and CVD-related health outcome changes (e.g., transitions from "no CVD history" to "history of MI," "history of stroke," or "death") at each time step (Li et al. 2014a). Note that the health states defined in our ABM are a simplified version of the health states defined by the AHA as shown in Table 11.1. In particular, in Figure 11.1, "not smoking" means a person never smoked or did not smoke for more than one year, "had a healthy diet" means a person ate five or more fruits or vegetables per day, "physically active" means a person had more than 150 minutes moderate physical activity per week, and "normal weight" means a person had a body mass index (BMI) lower than 25 kg/m².

Our model allows correlation among health factors. For example, changes in body weight are correlated with the changes in the diet and physical activity status. These correlations among health factors, along with the normal progression of the disease,

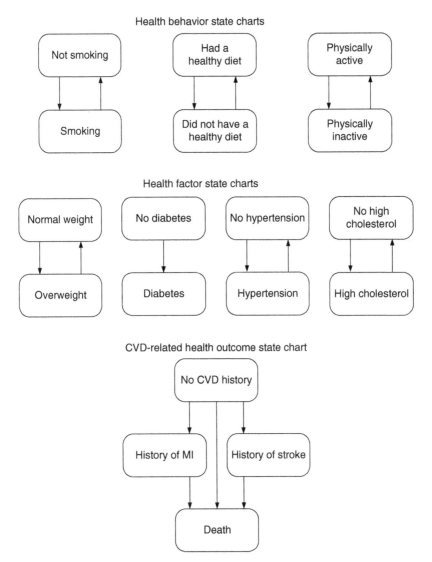

Figure 11.1 Eight parallel state charts capturing individual health progression. Source: Li et al. (2014a). Reproduced with permission of IEEE.

will produce nonlinear emergent outcomes (e.g., incidences of CVD across different populations) that are difficult to capture with traditional statistical methods. In addition, we developed an intuitive user interface that allows users to define the population size, the simulated time horizon, and a set of basic demographic and health characteristics of the population of their interest. The user interface also includes an output window where users can observe time series of prevalence of several key risk factors and CVDs. We also developed a population health animation from which users can easily track and visualize population health outcomes and mortality. Finally, users can select different lifestyle interventions or combinations of different interventions to evaluate the effectiveness of different interventions over a specified time length.

11.2.3   Parameter Estimation

Model parameters determine the dynamics of health factors and the disease progression. Most parameters, such as transition probabilities among different states and the correlations among different health factors, are estimated from the best available evidence published in clinical or behavioral studies. We follow several commonly used standards to estimate parameters. For example, when age-specific transition probabilities are available, they are preferred than static transition probabilities. In addition, when there are two or more sources for estimating a specific transition probability, the more recent source is adopted. Table 11.2, also presented in Li et al. (2014a), summarizes major parameters and the corresponding data sources.

For the smoking state chart, we estimate transition probabilities based on age-specific smoking initiation and cessation rates. Figure 11.2 shows the age-specific smoking initiation probabilities estimated from Escobedo et al. (1990). Note that smoking initiation probabilities are negligible for people younger than age 7 or older than age 35 and, thus, are assumed to be 0. Smoking cessation probabilities are estimated to be 0.054 for people of age 20–34 and 0.01 for people ages 35 or over based on Gilpin and Pierce (2002). For the healthy diet state chart, the annual transition probability from "did not have a healthy diet" to "had a healthy diet" is

TABLE 11.2   Data Sources for Major Parameters

Parameters	Data Sources
Smoking initiation and cessation	Escobedo et al. (1990) and Gilpin and Pierce (2002)
Change of diet status	Dalziel and Segal (2007)
Change of physical activity status	Dalziel et al. (2006)
Body weight progression	Ogden et al. (2007), Kaukua et al. (2003), and Pan et al. (2011)
Effect of diet status on body weight	He et al. (2004)
Effect of physical activity status on body weight	Hu et al. (2003)
Blood glucose progression	Bonora et al. (2004)
Blood pressure progression	Vasan et al. (2002)
Cholesterol progression	Panagiotakos et al. (2008)
Risks of CVD	Anderson et al. (1991)
Mortality rates	Heron et al. (2009)

Source: Li et al. (2014a). Reproduced with permission of IEEE.

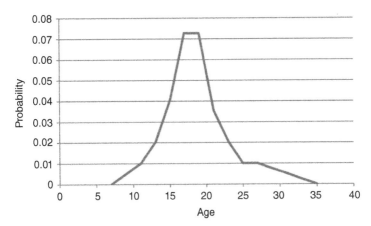

Figure 11.2   Annual smoking initiation probability. Source: Estimated from Escobedo et al. (1990).

estimated to be 0.03 for people of all ages based on Dalziel and Segal (2007). We assume that the transition probabilities for both directions between the two states are equal. For the physical activity state chart, we also assume that the transition probabilities for both directions between the states physically active and physically inactive are equal, which is estimated to be 0.049 for people of all the ages according to Dalziel et al. (2006).

Due to lack of age-specific data in the literature, annual transition probabilities for the body weight state chart are assumed to be age independent and are estimated based on three recent studies (Kaukua et al. 2003; Ogden et al. 2007; Pan et al. 2011). We also assume that the transition from normal weight to overweight is affected by diet and physical activity since it has been shown that both ideal diet and ideal physical activity reduce the risk of becoming obese (Pan et al. 2011). We capture this effect by multiplying the annual transition probability by the corresponding relative risks associated with having a healthy diet and being physically active (Hu et al. 2003; He et al. 2004).

We estimate the transition probabilities for the state charts for cholesterol, blood pressure, and blood glucose based on the age-specific annual incidence rates for high cholesterol, hypertension, and diabetes estimated from the relevant literature (Vasan et al. 2002; Bonora et al. 2004; Panagiotakos et al. 2008). Figure 11.3 presents these incidence rates. It is clear that a person being overweight or obese has a higher risk of high cholesterol, hypertension, and diabetes. Thus, we estimate relative risks associated with being overweight from published studies and adjust the transition probabilities accordingly (Thompson et al. 1999).

We estimate transition probabilities from "no CVD history" to "history of MI" or "history of stroke" using the Framingham CVD risk calculator (Anderson et al. 1991), a parametric model that has been widely used to predict probabilities of CVD outcomes based on several important risk factors such as age, gender, smoking, blood

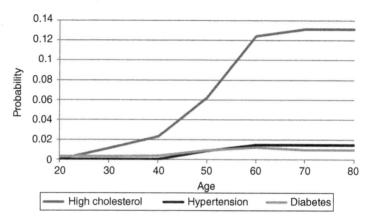

Figure 11.3   Annual incidence rates for high cholesterol, hypertension, and diabetes. Source: Estimated from Bonora et al. (2004), Vasan et al. (2002), and Panagiotakos et al. (2008).

pressure, blood glucose, and cholesterol level. Since risk factors change dynamically during simulation, the transition probabilities in the CVD state chart are also dynamic and updated at each time step.

Finally, mortality rates are based on cause of death, due to either CVD or other causes. We estimate the overall mortality rates based on the age- and gender-specific data obtained from the US vital statistics report (Heron et al. 2009). The mortality rate due to CVD is a function of risk factors estimated dynamically using the Framingham risk calculator (Anderson et al. 1991). Then, the mortality rate due to other causes is estimated as the difference between the overall mortality rate and the mortality rate due to CVD.

11.2.4   User Interface

Figure 11.4 shows the user interface of our ABM model for ideal cardiovascular health. The input interface contains fields for users to define the population characteristics and health profiles of the population of interest. Specifically, these input variables include population size, age and gender distributions, and proportions of people who are not currently smoking are physically active (more than 150 minutes/week of moderate physical activity), eat a healthy diet (five or more fruits/vegetables per day), have a normal body weight (BMI < 25), do not have diabetes, do not have hypertension, do not have high cholesterol, have a history of MI, and have a history of stroke.

In addition, the user interface allows users to select the lifestyle interventions of their interest and specify the time horizon of policy relevance. The animation helps users visualize population health outcome dynamics and, thus, may prove useful to engage decision makers in different sectors that may find the model results relevant to their work. The output interface presents the yearly prevalence dynamics for

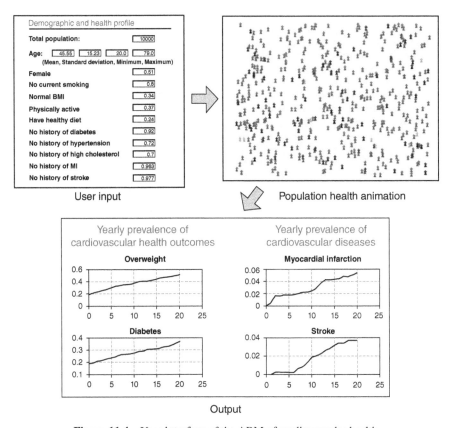

Figure 11.4   User interface of the ABM of cardiovascular health.

cardiovascular health outcomes, diseases, and mortality. This presentation of simulation results with respect to time may help decision makers evaluate both short-term and long-term outcomes of a certain intervention or program.

11.2.5   Model Validation

We have conducted internal validation and face validation by examining model structure and mathematical equations and consulting with CVD experts. Our model is a reasonable simplified representation of cardiovascular health progression with consideration of several important risk factors. In addition, we have conducted preliminary predictive validation by comparing simulated results with real population statistics using multi-year cross-sectional dataset (Li et al. 2014a). As the development of an ABM is an iterative process, we will continue to improve model validity by incorporating more recent epidemiological evidence and high-quality longitudinal data when they are available.

11.3 RESULTS

11.3.1 Simulating American Adults

In this numerical study, we estimated population characteristics and health profiles for American adults from the Behavioral Risk Factor Surveillance System (BRFSS) (Centers for Disease Control and Prevention 2007, 2012), which is a large-scale telephone-based national survey targeting adults living in households. We drew data from the 2007 BRFSS for all American adults between ages 20 and 79. Table 11.3, adapted from Li et al. (2014a), presents these population characteristics.

Using the simulated population, we assessed the effectiveness of five hypothetical lifestyle interventions (i.e., "quit smoking," "promote a healthy diet," "improve physical activity," "reduce obesity," and "comprehensive") in terms of incidence reductions for people with diabetes, a history of MI, and a history of stroke in 5, 10, 15, and 20 years. Among these interventions, "quit smoking," "promote a healthy diet," "improve physical activity," and "reduce obesity" are the lifestyle programs implemented to reduce by half the proportion of the population who smokes, eats less than five fruits and vegetables/day, exercises less than 150 minutes/week, and has a BMI of 25 or more, respectively. The "comprehensive" lifestyle program is the combination of the aforementioned four programs. We assume that the hypothetical interventions only work at the beginning of the simulation, which means some people may return to their unhealthy behaviors as the simulation continues. It is worth noting that although the interventions we simulated are hypothetical, the model can simulate real-world lifestyle interventions if relevant information (e.g., relative risk, adherence rate) about the intervention is available.

We generated 10,000 adults based on the relevant characteristics of BRFSS respondents and simulated the progression of the three health conditions with no intervention and with different lifestyle programs over different years. Figure 11.5 reports the reduced number of people with these chronic conditions by implementing the lifestyle programs as opposed to not implementing any interventions.

The first chart in Figure 11.5 shows the most effective program for preventing diabetes is "comprehensive" and the least effective is "promote a healthy diet." More

TABLE 11.3 Population Characteristics of American Adults

Age (Mean)	Age (Standard Deviation)	Female (%)	No Smoking (%)	BMI < 25 (%)	Physically Active (%)
45.5	15.2	51.1	80.0	34.2	36.9

Have healthy Diet (%)	No Diabetes (%)	No Hypertension (%)	No High Cholesterol (%)	History of MI (%)	History of Stroke (%)
24.4	91.7	73.1	70.5	3.7	2.3

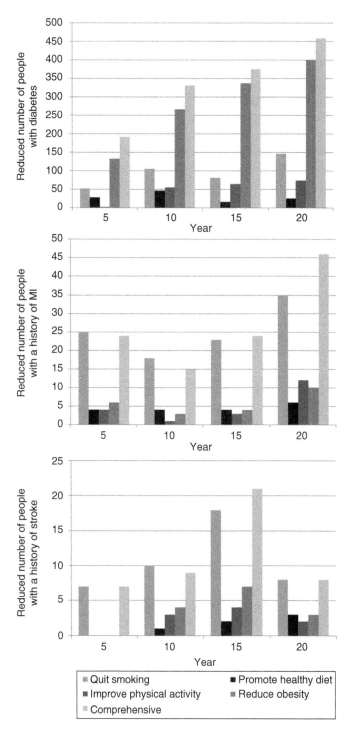

Figure 11.5 Prevention effects of five alternative lifestyle interventions in different time horizons. Source: Li et al. (2014a). Reproduced with permission of IEEE.

specifically, among the simulated 10,000 persons, the "comprehensive" lifestyle program may reduce diabetes incidence by 200 in 5 years and by more than 450 in 20 years. Given that the lifetime direct cost of treating diabetes is nearly $85,200 per person as given in Zhuo et al. (2013), implementing a "comprehensive" lifestyle program may lead to substantial healthcare cost savings resulting from lifestyle changes. Although healthcare cost savings can be estimated from these expected differences in diabetes incidence over 5 and 20 years, a precise economic evaluation would require consideration of intervention cost as well as a model with more predictive accuracy.

The other two charts focus on the prevention effect on MI and stroke. The "comprehensive" program may reduce the incidence of MI by 46 and the incidence of stroke by 8 in 20 years. The smaller reduction in incidence of MI and stroke compared with diabetes may be due to the facts that the prevalence of diabetes is higher and incidence of diabetes is more sensitive to improvement in lifestyle. In addition, the reduction in disease incidence from interventions does not increase monotonically over years, which is likely caused by a reduced population size due to early mortality. Among all the non-comprehensive interventions, "quit smoking" is the most effective program, whereas the other three lifestyle programs have a less significant effect in preventing MI and stroke.

11.4   SIMULATING THE MEDICARE-AGE POPULATION AND THE DISEASE-SPECIFIC SUBPOPULATIONS

In this numerical study, we simulated the US Medicare-age population (i.e., insured adults 65 years old and over) because agent-based modeling may prove particularly useful for assessing interventions within populations that tend to be targeted for careful management such as adults with Medicare Advantage insurance coverage or Medicare beneficiaries belonging to an accountable care organization. This population also has a much higher prevalence of CVD compared with other age groups. To study this population with more granularity, we further divided this population into three disease-specific subpopulations, which are the US Medicare-age populations with diabetes, hypertension, and high cholesterol. Using the 2007 BRFSS data, we estimated the population characteristics and health profiles of adults between the ages of 65 and 94 (inclusive) (Table 11.4). We studied this population in a previous study in which we demonstrated the potential of using agent-based modeling to improve population health management in primary care settings (Li et al. 2014b).

Diabetes, hypertension, and high cholesterol are the health outcomes of interest because they are prevalent and are important risk factors for CVDs. We simulated health progression of these populations with implementation of the "comprehensive" lifestyle program for 1, 3, and 5 years. Table 11.5, also presented in Li et al. (2014b), compares the simulated health outcomes for normal health progression and a

TABLE 11.4   Characteristics of the Medicare-Age Population and Three Disease-Specific Subpopulations

	All	Subpopulation Diabetes	Subpopulation Hypertension	Subpopulation High Cholesterol
Mean age (SD)	74.31 (6.64)	73.79 (6.29)	74.56 (6.57)	73.71 (6.29)
Female (%)	57.29	52.49	58.12	58.25
No currently smoking (%)	91.06	92.45	91.84	91.14
BMI < 25 (%)	35.97	20.63	29.72	32.25
Physically active (%)	33.05	25.65	30.08	32.73
Have healthy diet (%)	28.87	26.52	27.59	27.57
No diabetes (%)	80.39		74.74	76.67
No hypertension (%)	41.82	25.07		32.05
No high cholesterol (%)	49.41	39.82	40.92	
History of MI (%)	13.26	21.10	16.17	16.90
History of stroke (%)	8.41	12.89	10.73	9.74

Source: Li et al. (2014b). Reproduced with permission of SAGE Journals.

TABLE 11.5   Simulated Population Health Outcomes for Normal Health Progression and Comprehensive Lifestyle Program

	Diabetes (%)			Hypertension (%)			High Cholesterol (%)		
	NHP	CLP	p	NHP	CLP	p	NHP	CLP	p
All									
Year 1	21.3	20.8	0.193	58.8	58.5	0.333	58.1	57.7	0.283
Year 3	24.3	23.1	0.023	60.9	60.2	0.155	68.9	67.9	0.064
Year 5	27.0	25.3	0.003	62.9	61.9	0.072	76.7	75.7	0.048
Subpopulation with Diabetes									
Year 1				75.6	75.3	0.311	66.5	66.1	0.275
Year 3				76.9	76.3	0.158	75.4	74.5	0.071
Year 5				77.8	77.2	0.155	81.9	80.6	0.009
Subpopulation with Hypertension									
Year 1	26.6	26.2	0.260				65.3	65.0	0.328
Year 3	29.6	28.4	0.031				73.9	73.1	0.100
Year 5	32.2	30.7	0.011				80.2	79.1	0.027
Subpopulation with High Cholesterol									
Year 1	24.7	24.3	0.255	68.4	68.2	0.381			
Year 3	28.0	26.8	0.029	70.0	69.4	0.178			
Year 5	30.5	28.9	0.007	71.3	70.6	0.138			

Source: Li et al. (2014b). Reproduced with permission of SAGE Journals.
CLP, comprehensive lifestyle program; NHP, normal health progression.

comprehensive lifestyle program. We conducted one-tailed two-proportion z-tests to assess the significance of the population health improvement with implementation of the comprehensive lifestyle program.

There would be a significant reduction ($p < 0.05$) in the proportion of the population with diabetes after the lifestyle program is implemented for 3 or 5 years for the Medicare-age population and the two subpopulations with hypertension or high cholesterol. Also, the lifestyle program would be effective in reducing the proportion of the population with high cholesterol after it is implemented for 5 years. In contrast, the lifestyle program might not be significantly effective in preventing hypertension over a time period less than 5 years. These simulation results can be useful to policy makers interested in the better allocation of resources to improve cardiovascular health of a population based on its specific characteristics.

11.5 FUTURE RESEARCH

Although our previous studies have demonstrated that an ABM of cardiovascular health has the potential of enhancing population health management (Li et al. 2014b), our current model structure still has limited capability in capturing the complex progression of CVD, which may impair the credibility of our model in informing public health decision making. We plan to extend and improve our model in the following three directions.

First, we will expand each of the eight behavior and health factor state charts to capture individual cardiovascular health progression with more realism. In the current model, most health behaviors and factors are captured by simple two-state transitions. We will evaluate additional clinical evidence and design more realistic mechanisms that will guide the dynamic change and progression of health behaviors and factors. For example, smoking status could be modeled by three discrete states based on the "poor," "intermediate," and "ideal" definition of cardiovascular health (Lloyd-Jones et al. 2010). Other factors could be modeled as continuous variables that will rely on differential equations to capture changes in values. The refined state change mechanisms are expected to improve the predictive validity of the model and also allow us to study the health outcomes that have not been included in the current model (e.g., overweight, complications from diabetes).

Second, we will incorporate social influence in modeling health behaviors and factors. Christakis and Fowler (2008) showed how social influences and social networks can influence smoking behavior dynamics. Recently, Hammond and Ornstein (2014) developed an ABM of social influence on body weight by drawing evidence and theories from physiology and social psychology and examined how body weight norms can affect the development and progression of obesity. These studies showed that social influences may have a significant impact on human behaviors and health and, thus, should not be ignored in modeling cardiovascular health. Incorporating social influences will help us capture the spillover effect of certain lifestyle interventions and further increase the predictive validity of the model.

Finally, we will incorporate cost and quality of life parameters in our model so that it can be used for cost-effectiveness analysis (CEA) of alternative lifestyle intervention programs. Most model-based CEA studies are based on Markov chains, which use aggregated health states and transition probabilities to capture the progression of the studied disease. The ABM-based CEA is expected to outperform the traditional Markov-based CEA in not only capturing the disease progression with more granularity but also incorporating patient preferences (compliance), healthcare-seeking behaviors, population interactions, and heterogeneous characteristics across populations. In addition, ABMs can be built based on individual-level data, which could result in a simulated population cohort that has a better representation of the real population. With the successful application of ABM-based CEA for colorectal cancer screening policies as shown in Subramanian et al. (2009), we believe our potential application of ABM-based CEA for CVD prevention strategies will be promising and appealing to decision makers.

11.6 SUMMARY

In this chapter, we present a detailed overview of an ABM for ideal cardiovascular health and demonstrate the potential use of the model by assessing the impact of a set of hypothetical lifestyle programs on several CVD-related health outcomes for different populations. We point out the limitations of the current model and discuss specific research directions to address these limitations and improve the model. Although we are still in the process of extending the model, the modeling framework presented here could be easily adapted to model other chronic diseases (e.g., diabetes, obesity, cancer) and capture the interplay among health behaviors, health factors, and disease progression. Nevertheless, the model provides a convenient tool for policy makers to gain new insights about the comparative effectiveness of alternative lifestyle interventions for a variety of populations without the need to spend substantial resources testing and implementing the programs in the field.

REFERENCES

Alwan, "Global status report on noncommunicable diseases 2010," World Health Organization, Geneva, Switzerland, 2011. Available at: http://www.cabdirect.org/abstracts/20113168808. html. Accessed on August 22, 2017.

K. M. Anderson, P. M. Odell, P. W. Wilson, and W. B. Kannel, "Cardiovascular disease risk profiles," *American Heart Journal*, 121(1), 293–298, 1991.

S. Barnes, B. Golden, and S. Price, "Applications of agent-based modeling and simulation to healthcare operations management," in B. T. Denton, *Handbook of Healthcare Operations Management*, pp. 45–74, Springer, New York, 2013.

E. Bonora, S. Kiechl, J. Willeit, F. Oberhollenzer, G. Egger, J. B. Meigs, R. C. Bonadonna, and M. Muggeo, "Population-based incidence rates and risk factors for type 2 diabetes in white individuals: The Bruneck study," *Diabetes*, 53(7), 1782–1789, 2004.

E. Bruch and J. Atwell, "Agent-based models in empirical social research," *Sociological Methods & Research*, 44(2), 186–221, 2015.

L. E. Cederman, "Endogenizing geopolitical boundaries with agent-based modeling," *Proceedings of the National Academy of Sciences*, 99(3), 7296–7303, 2002.

Centers for Disease Control and Prevention, "Behavioral Risk Factor Surveillance System: Overview BRFSS 2007," 2007. Available at: https://www.cdc.gov/brfss/annual_data/annual_2007.htm. Accessed on September 3, 2017.

Centers for Disease Control and Prevention, "Behavioral Risk Factor Surveillance System: Overview BRFSS 2012," 2012. Available at: https://www.cdc.gov/brfss/annual_data/annual_2012.html. Accessed on September 3, 2017.

N. A. Christakis and J. H. Fowler, "The collective dynamics of smoking in a large social network," *New England Journal of Medicine*, 358(21), 2249–2258, 2008.

K. Dalziel and L. Segal, "Time to give nutrition interventions a higher profile: Cost-effectiveness of 10 nutrition interventions," *Health Promotion International*, 22(4), 271–283, 2007.

K. Dalziel, L. Segal, and C. R. Elley, "Cost utility analysis of physical activity counselling in general practice," *Australian and New Zealand Journal of Public Health*, 30(1), 57–63, 2006.

L. G. Escobedo, R. F. Anda, P. F. Smith, P. L. Remington, and E. E. Mast, "Sociodemographic characteristics of cigarette smoking initiation in the United States: Implications for smoking prevention policy," *JAMA*, 264(12), 1550–1555, 1990.

G. Fagiolo, A. Moneta, and P. Windrum, "A critical guide to empirical validation of agent-based models in economics: Methodologies, procedures, and open problems," *Computational Economics*, 30(3), 195–226, 2007.

J. Fang, Q. Yang, Y. Hong, and F. Loustalot, "Status of cardiovascular health among adult Americans in the 50 states and the District of Columbia, 2009," *Journal of the American Heart Association*, 1(6), e005371, 2012.

E. S. Ford and S. Capewell, "Proportion of the decline in cardiovascular mortality disease due to prevention versus treatment: Public health versus clinical care," *Annual Review of Public Health*, 32, 5–22, 2011.

E. S. Ford, K. J. Greenlund, and Y. Hong, "Ideal cardiovascular health and mortality from all causes and diseases of the circulatory system among adults in the United States," *Circulation*, 125(8), 987–995, 2012.

E. S. Ford, M. M. Bergmann, H. Boeing, C. Li, and S. Capewell, "Healthy lifestyle behaviors and all-cause mortality among adults in the United States," *Preventive Medicine*, 55(1), 23–27, 2012.

A. Gilpin and J. P. Pierce, "Demographic differences in patterns in the incidence of smoking cessation: United States 1950–1990," *Annals of Epidemiology*, 12(3), 141–150, 2002.

S. Go, D. Mozaffarian, V. L. Roger, E. J. Benjamin, J. D. Berry, W. B. Borden, D. M. Bravata, D. Shifan, E. S. Ford, C. S. Fox et al., "Executive summary: Heart disease and stroke statistics: 2013 update: A report from the American Heart Association," *Circulation*, 127(1), 143–146, 2013.

R. A. Hammond and J. T. Ornstein, "A model of social influence on body mass index," *Annals of the New York Academy of Sciences*, 1331, 34–42, 2014.

K. He, F. B. Hu, G. A. Colditz, J. E. Manson, W. C. Willett, and S. Liu, "Changes in intake of fruits and vegetables in relation to risk of obesity and weight gain among middle-aged women," *International Journal of Obesity*, 28(12), 1569–1574, 2004.

M. Heron, D. L. Hoyert, S. L. Murphy, J. Xu, K. D. Kochanek, and B. Tejada-Vera, "Deaths: Final data for 2006," *National Vital Statistics Reports*, 57(14), 2009.

G. Hirsch, J. Homer, E. Evans, and A. Zielinski "A system dynamics model for planning cardiovascular disease interventions," *American Journal of Public Health*, 100(4), 616–622, 2010.

B. Hu, T. Y. Li, G. A. Colditz, W. C. Willett, and J. E. Manson, "Television watching and other sedentary behaviors in relation to risk of obesity and type 2 diabetes mellitus in women," *JAMA*, 289(14), 1785–1791, 2003.

J. Kaukua, T. Pekkarinen, T. Sane, and P. Mustajoki, "Health-related quality of life in obese outpatients losing weight with very-low-energy diet and behaviour modification: A 2-year follow-up study," *International Journal of Obesity*, 27(9), 1072–1080, 2003.

Y. Li, N. Kong, M. A. Lawley, and J. A. Pagán, "Assessing lifestyle interventions to improve cardiovascular health using an agent-based model," in *Proceedings of the 2014 Winter Simulation Conference*, IEEE Press, Piscataway, NJ. pp. 1221–1232, 2014.

Y. Li, N. Kong, M. A. Lawley, and J. A. Pagán "Using systems science for population health management in primary care," *Journal of Primary Care & Community Health*, 5(4), 242–246, 2014.

D. M. Lloyd-Jones, Y. Hong, D. Labarthe, D. Mozaffarian, L. J. Appel, L. Van Horn, K. Greenlund, S. Daniels, G. Nichol, G. F. Tomaselli et al., "Defining and setting national goals for cardiovascular health promotion and disease reduction: The American Heart Association's strategic Impact Goal through 2020 and beyond," *Circulation*, 121(4), 586–613, 2010.

M. Macal and M. J. North, "Tutorial on agent-based modelling and simulation," *Journal of Simulation*, 4(3), 151–162, 2010.

L. Ogden, M. D. Carroll, M. A. McDowell, and K. M. Flegal, "Obesity among adults in the United States—No statistically significant change since 2003–2004," *NCHS Data Brief*, 1, 1–8, 2007.

L. Pan, D. S. Freedman, C. Gillespie, S. Park, and B. Sherry, "Incidences of obesity and extreme obesity among us adults: Findings from the 2009 Behavioral Risk Factor Surveillance System," *Population Health Metrics*, 9(2), 56, 2011.

B. Panagiotakos, C. Pitsavos, Y. Skoumas, Y. Lentzas, and C. Stefanadis, "Five-year incidence of type 2 diabetes mellitus among cardiovascular disease-free Greek adults: Findings from the ATTICA study," *Vascular Health and Risk Management*, 4(3), 691–698, 2008.

H. Rahmandad and J. Sterman, "Heterogeneity and network structure in the dynamics of diffusion: Comparing agent-based and differential equation models," *Management Science*, 54(5), 998–1014, 2008.

P.-O. Siebers, C. M. Macal, J. Garnett, D. Buxton, and M. Pidd, "Discrete-event simulation is dead, long live agent-based simulation!" *Journal of Simulation*, 4(3), 204–210, 2010.

S. Subramanian, G. Bobashev, and R. J. Morris, "Modeling the cost-effectiveness of colorectal cancer screening: policy guidance based on patient preferences and compliance," *Cancer Epidemiology, Biomarkers & Prevention*, 18(7), 1971–1978, 2009.

D. Thompson, J. Edelsberg, G. A. Colditz, A. P. Bird, and G. Oster, "Lifetime health and economic consequences of obesity," *Archives of Internal Medicine*, 159(18), 2177–2183, 1999.

B. Unal, S. Capewell, and Critchley, J. A., "Coronary heart disease policy models: A systematic review," *BMC Public Health*, 6, 213, 2006.

R. S. Vasan, A. Beiser, S. Seshadri, M. G. Larson, W. B. Kannel, R. B. D'Agostino, and D. Levy, "Residual lifetime risk for developing hypertension in middle-aged women and men: The Framingham Heart Study," *JAMA*, 287(8), 1003–1010, 2002.

X. Zhuo, P. Zhang, and T. J. Hoerger, "Lifetime direct medical costs of treating type 2 diabetes and diabetic complications," *American Journal of Preventive Medicine*, 45(3), 253–261, 2013.

PART 3

TREATMENT TECHNOLOGY AND SYSTEM

12

BIOLOGICAL PLANNING OPTIMIZATION FOR HIGH-DOSE-RATE BRACHYTHERAPY AND ITS APPLICATION TO CERVICAL CANCER TREATMENT

Eva K. Lee[1], Fan Yuan[1], Alistair Templeton[2], Rui Yao[2], Krystyna Kiel[2], and James C.H. Chu[2]

[1] *NSF-Whitaker Center for Operations Research in Medicine and HealthCare, Georgia Institute of Technology, Atlanta, GA, USA*
School of Industrial and Systems Engineering, Georgia Institute of Technology, Atlanta, GA, USA
NSF I/UCRC Center for Health Organization Transformation, Arlington, VA, USA
[2] *Department of Radiation Oncology Rush University Medical Center, Chicago, IL, USA*

12.1   INTRODUCTION

Almost a million cancer patients in the United States receive some form of radiation therapy each year (American Cancer Society 2017). Radiation is delivered using either external beam technology or a procedure known as brachytherapy. Brachytherapy uses a radioactive substance sealed in needles, seeds, wires, or catheters, which are placed directly (permanently or temporarily) into or near the cancer. This allows a full tumoricidal effect to eradicate the tumor from within the cancer site while ensuring that minimal radiation reaches the healthy surrounding tissues. For high-dose-rate (HDR) brachytherapy, patients receive treatment through catheters during 3–10 outpatient sessions over a period of 5 days to 2 weeks. Brachytherapy preserves organs, usually with no loss of functionality; thus, it is rapidly becoming the choice of treatment for prostate, breast, cervix, and uterus cancer.

Decision Analytics and Optimization in Disease Prevention and Treatment, First Edition.
Edited by Nan Kong and Shengfan Zhang.
© 2018 John Wiley & Sons, Inc. Published 2018 by John Wiley & Sons, Inc.

Operations research (OR) has brought breakthrough advances in treatment-planning optimization, as evidenced by the 2007 Franz Edelman Award work by Memorial Sloan Kettering Cancer Center (MSKCC), which saves half a billion dollars in yearly operations and delivery costs via intelligent real-time OR-based treatment-planning approaches, while the tumor control probability (TCP) (i.e., the probability of extinction of clonogenic tumor cells by the end of treatment) improves from 65% to 95% (Lee and Zaider 2008).

The content of this chapter, starting from the next paragraph, is mostly excerpted from the *Interfaces* Wagner Prize published article (Lee et al. 2013).

Specifically this chapter summarizes our work on two first-of-its-kind advances to HDR brachytherapy treatment design. First, TCP, which depends upon a highly complex function that models the responses of cancer cells and normal cells to radiation, is incorporated into the planning objective. This is distinct from the dose-based planning that is commonly employed in current treatment design. Second, positron emission tomography (PET) information, which relates cancer cell proliferation and distribution, is incorporated within the constraints, facilitating targeted, escalated dose delivery to improve the overall clinical outcome of HDR treatments.

This work is distinct from the MSKCC in three ways: (i) HDR brachytherapy uses temporary implants that require multiple sessions; in addition to determining seed positions, the dwell time also has to be optimized. (ii) This is the first time that TCP, an important measure of desired outcome, has been successfully incorporated in a treatment-planning analytical model; we determine the TCP function from a complex biological model and place it in the objective. (iii) This is the first time that PET tumor cell proliferation and distribution are incorporated within radiation therapy (external beam or brachytherapy) for dose-escalation planning.

The optimization models we develop, which are TCP driven and PET image guided and permit HDR with dose escalation, initially prove to be intractable. The intractability arises from three sources. First, our models share the denseness properties of previous treatment-planning models (Lee and Zaider 2008). We found that even without the complications that nonlinear TCP functions and PET-based dose escalation introduce, we could not solve the associated treatment-planning instances using competitive optimization software, even after we ran this software for several months of CPU time. Second, the extreme nonlinearity of the TCP functions increases the difficulties. Third, the competing PET-based dose-escalation constraints that seek to go between cancer pockets and critical normal tissues offer only a tight solution space.

The methodologies we develop are applicable to most types of cancer. In our discussion, we focus on treatment of cervical cancer. Cervical cancer ranks as the second most common cancer in women worldwide, with about 500,000 new cases and 270,000 deaths annually. Almost 85% of cervical cancer cases are in less developed countries (American Cancer Society 2017). The majority of cervical cancer cases (75%) are caused by the human papillomavirus (National Cancer Institute 2013). The cancer grows slowly and in its early stages may not have any symptoms.

Thus, the mortality rate remains high at about 35%. In the United States in 2017, an estimated 12,820 women will be diagnosed with cervical cancer, and about 4,120 women will die from it (American Cancer Society 2017). About 0.68% of women born today will be diagnosed with cervical cancer at some time during their lifetimes (Howlader et al. 2013).

When detected at an early stage, the 5-year survival rate for women with invasive cervical cancer is 92%. If cervical cancer has spread to surrounding tissues or organs and/or the regional lymph nodes, the 5-year survival rate is 57%. If the cancer has spread to a distant part of the body, the 5-year survival rate is 17%. The choice of treatment depends on the stage of the cancer, the size of the tumor, the patient's desire to have children, and the patient's age. Standard treatments include surgery, chemotherapy, and radiation therapy. With advances in radiation therapy modalities and their organ-preserving characteristics, it is rapidly becoming the treatment of choice for cervical cancer (Nag et al. 1999).

This chapter is mostly excerpted from *the Interfaces* Wagner Prize published article (Lee et al. 2013). We first describe our original treatment-planning models as we applied them to cervical cancer. Next we describe our computational breakthroughs that permit rapid, accurate solutions. Our planning methods were implemented by Rush University Medical Center. To the best of our knowledge, Rush University conducted the first and only clinical trial in the United States in 2011 for HDR brachytherapy with PET-based dose escalation applied to cervical cancer. We report on how, with modeling assistance, the Medical Center was able to increase its treatment success and improve its quality of care, thus reducing both mortality and personal and financial burdens for cervical cancer patients.

12.2   CHALLENGES AND OBJECTIVES

With advances in computed tomography (CT) and magnetic resonance (MR) imaging technology, it is possible to produce contours of gross tumor volume, clinical target volume (CTV), planning target volume (PTV), and organs at risk (OARs) and to view the radiation dose within these contours as radionuclide implant locations and dwell times are adjusted. This in turn enables the use of optimization technology to derive custom treatment plans that best achieve the clinical goals of delivering a full tumoricidal dose to eliminate the cancers while minimizing the doses to OARs (Gallagher and Lee 1997, Lee et al. 1999, Kirisits et al. 2005, Duan et al. 2008, Holloway et al. 2009, Kang et al. 2010, Tanderup et al. 2010). Inverse planning and multi-objective optimization with penalty costs have become more commonly used to address the trade-off between treating the tumor and sparing the OARs, while the optimization solution process remains a major challenge (Lahanas et al. 2003, Alterovitz et al. 2006, Morton et al. 2008, Kim et al. 2009, Ruotsalainen et al. 2010, Holm et al. 2012). Because treatment planning is intrinsically combinatorial in nature, relaxation and heuristic algorithms (e.g., linear programming or simulated annealing) have been typically employed (Alterovitz et al. 2006, Morton et al. 2008, Beliën et al. 2009, Karabis et al. 2009, Kim et al. 2009, Holm et al. 2012).

PET imaging is an important advance for cervical cancer brachytherapy treatment planning (Bailey et al. 2005, Wachter-Gerstner et al. 2003). The ability of PET imaging to accurately define the primary lesion by including positive lymph nodes in the PTV facilitates treatment planning. The use of FDG-PET (i.e., PET with fluoro-deoxyglucose as a radiopharmaceutical tracer) offers a unique method for visualizing tumors, which permits treatment optimization (Malyapa et al. 2002). Integrated PET and CT for treatment planning for three-dimensional conformal radiation therapy improves the standardization of volume delineation (Ciernik et al. 2003). MR spectroscopy (MRS)-guided dose escalation for prostate cancer indicates that the TCP can be dramatically improved if biological information can be included within a personalized treatment design (Zaider et al. 2000, Lee and Zaider 2008). This work differs from the dose-escalation work of Zaider et al. (2000) in that, in addition to incorporating dose-escalation constraints within the treatment constraints, our model incorporates, within the objective function, data on the radioresistance and sensitivity of both tumor and normal cells to drive the optimization process.

The crux and challenges of HDR brachytherapy treatment planning include the following: (i) The seed type, spatial configuration, and dwell time per treatment must be determined. (ii) Tumor control, a very complex biological relationship, depends on the time of the treatment, radioactive decay of the radioisotope, dose received, volume and density of tumor cells, and biological radiosensitivity and radioresistancy of the normal and tumor cells. (iii) Current therapies treat the diseased organ as a homogeneous mass; however, advances in PET imaging can now distinguish cell populations based on cell density, and the metabolic activities of tumor cells, clearly differentiating them from the normal healthy cells. Such capability demands advances in treatment-planning optimization where tumor biological knowledge is incorporated, if true personalized targeted treatment is to be realized and result in improvements in local TCPs.

This work reports complex biological treatment planning via an OR approach, as we describe in the following:

- We derive novel OR-based TCP-driven PET-image-guided dose-escalation treatment plans via multi-objective nonlinear mixed-integer programming (NMIP). This marks the first time that TCP is incorporated both within the treatment optimization and as a plan objective; this is also the first time in which PET-image cell-proliferation knowledge is coupled within the treatment-plan solution space.

- We derive generalized conflict hypergraphs and uncover new polyhedral theory and facial structures for these NMIP instances.

- We design a rapid branch-and-cut and local-search solution engine that couples novel cutting planes, matrix reduction, and intelligent geometric heuristics, along with a local hybrid genetic algorithm, to arrive at good solutions to these intrinsically *NP-hard* and intractable treatment-planning instances.

We test the robustness of the resulting plans. The clinicians evaluate the quality of the plans based on the TCP, dose distribution, and other clinical metrics that are important indicators of treatment outcomes.

12.3 MATERIALS AND METHODS

12.3.1 High-Dose-Rate Brachytherapy

HDR brachytherapy treatment is given in 3–10 sessions, depending on the type of cancer being treated. The HDR system uses a single tiny highly radioactive source of Iridium-192, which is laser welded to the end of a thin, flexible stainless steel cable. The source is housed in an afterloader, a remote control device that mechanically places the radioactive source at predetermined positions within the applicator and stores the source between treatments. The computer-guided afterloader directs the source into the treatment catheters or applicator, which has been placed in the patient. The source travels through each catheter in predefined steps, called "dwell" positions. The distribution of radiation and dose is determined by the dwell positions at which the source stops and the length of time it dwell there. This ability to vary the dwell times is similar to having an unlimited choice of source strengths. This level of dose control is possible only with HDR brachytherapy.

A major advantage of HDR is that the final doses are known before any radiation treatment is given. Because the patient and implant position is the same as when the treatment plan is devised, the doses are accurate. Further, because of the high radioactivity of the Iridium-192 source, the treatment time takes only minutes, rendering little opportunity for the implant to move and deposit radiation dose where it is not intended.

The gynecological HDR procedure can be briefly summarized as follows. First, in the operating room, catheters are inserted into a patient who is under local, general, or spinal anesthesia. Interstitial catheters are inserted through the body tissue to encompass the tumor. For cervical treatment, a template is sutured to the skin to hold the treatment catheters in position. A CT scan is taken to determine the exact location of the catheters in relationship to the diseased organ and normal tissues. The CT images are used for treatment-planning optimization. The dosimetrist (i.e., a specialist who has the expertise necessary to generate radiation dose distributions and dose calculations), in collaboration with a medical physicist and a radiation oncologist, designs the plan on a computer and customizes the radiation dose to conform to the target volume while minimizing the dose to the nearby normal tissues. After the physician has approved the treatment plan, the computer transfers the treatment-plan instructions to the HDR remote afterloader. On the day of the treatment, the patient is moved into the brachytherapy treatment room. The ends of the treatment catheters that protrude outside the body are connected to "transfer" tubes, which are then connected to the afterloader. The programmed instructions guide the afterloader on where to direct the source and how long to leave the source in each dwell position.

The patient is alone in the treatment room as the treatment is being given, and the therapists and nurses continually monitor the treatment through an intercom and closed-circuit TV cameras. The entire treatment process takes approximately 30–90 minutes, depending on the size and complexity of the implant and the activity of the source. Upon treatment completion, the sutures holding the catheters in place are clipped and the implant is gently removed. Figure 12.1 depicts the delivery of HDR brachytherapy for cervical cancer.

12.3.2   PET Image

For our study of a group of cervical cancer patients, we obtained both PET images and CT scans. The biological PET image is first fused onto the treatment CT image (see Figure 12.2). PTVs, critical structures, and OARs are delineated from CT images. The enhanced PET signal allows the identification of dense pockets of cancer cells, which define the boost target volume (BTV). HDR plans are optimized to deliver a prescribed dose of 35 Gy Ir^{192} to the PTV and 37–40 Gy to the BTV, following 45 Gy of external beam radiotherapy.

12.3.3   Novel OR-Based Treatment-Planning Model

The OR challenges we faced are the following:

  i. Effectively modeling the TCP within the treatment-planning objective
 ii. Incorporating the PET-image information for biological targeted dose escalation
iii. Advancing computational strategies to solve the associated intractable nonlinear combinatorial instances

12.3.3.1 Dose Calculation   Dose calculation is based on guidelines from the American Association of Physicists in Medicine (AAPM) task groups for brachytherapy (Rivard et al. 2004). Briefly, let $\dot{D}(r)$ denote the dose contribution per minute of a seed to a voxel that is r units away. The two-dimensional dose-rate calculation can be represented as $\dot{D}(r,\theta)$, which is calculated based on the AAPM task groups for brachytherapy TG43U1 and U2 (Rivard et al. 2004):

$$2D: \quad \dot{D}(r,\theta) = S_K \cdot \Lambda \cdot \frac{G(r,\theta)}{G(r_0,\theta_0)} \cdot g(r) \cdot F(r,\theta), \qquad (12.1)$$

where S_k is the air-kerma strength (U, $1U = 1\,cGy\,cm^2/hour$); $\Lambda = \dot{D}(r_0,\theta_0)/S_k$ represents the dose-rate constant (cGy/hr-U); $g(r)$ is a radial dose function; $G(r, \theta)$ represents a geometry function, with $G(r_0, \theta_0)$ as the geometry function at the reference point (r_0, θ_0), where $r_0 = 1$ cm and $\theta_0 = 90°$; and $F(r, \theta)$ is a two-dimensional anisotropy function. The values for the geometry function $G(r,\theta)$ are obtained from tabulated data.

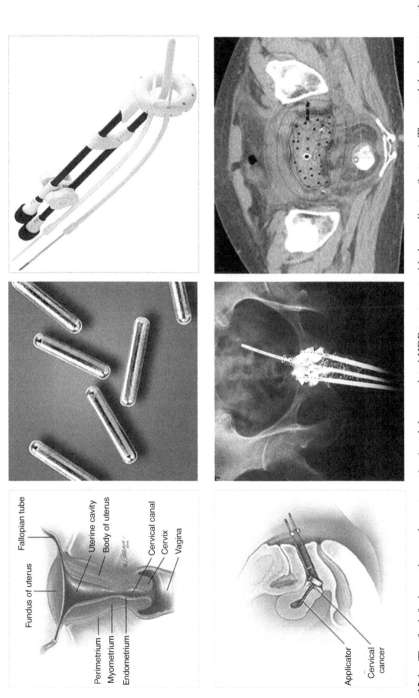

Figure 12.1 The far left shows the cervix anatomy (top) and the associated HDR treatment with the applicator (bottom). The remaining images on the top show the Ir[192] radioactive seeds and the Vienna ring CT-MR applicator. The bottom middle shows the CT image of the catheters and seed positions with respect to the diseased cervix. The bottom right shows a transverse view with isodose curves overlaid.

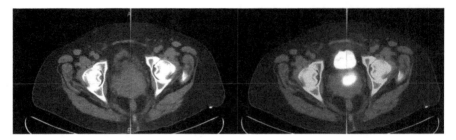

Figure 12.2   This figure shows a CT treatment image for the cervix (left) and the resulting image with an overlay of the PET image for plan design and optimization (right). We can clearly see the PET tumor pockets (bright spots) inside the cervix.

12.3.3.2   Incorporating the TCP within the Treatment-Planning Objective   To the extent that PET can be taken to indicate the presence of faster-proliferating and (or) a higher density of tumor cells, recognizing such regions in the organ could be consequential in terms of tumor control. We incorporate the TCP within our treatment-planning process. Specifically, we are interested in (i) the maximal TCP gain obtainable by incorporating PET information in treatment planning and (ii) the largest fractional tumor pocket volume for which PET-guided planning remains useful. Clearly, if tumor cells are uniformly spread throughout most of the cervix volume, the gain would be insignificant.

We generalize the TCP based on a reliable biological model developed by Zaider and Minerbo (2000). The formulas are derived using the birth and death processes. For brachytherapy, the TCP equation is

$$
\text{TCP}(t) = \left[1 - \frac{S(t)e^{(b-d)t}}{1 + bS(t)e^{(b-d)t} \displaystyle\int_0^t \frac{dt'}{S(t')e^{(b-d)t'}}} \right]^n ,
\tag{12.2}
$$

where n is the initial number (at time $t = 0$) of tumor cells, $S(t)$ is the survival probability of tumor cells at time t, and b and d are the birth and death rates of these cells, respectively.

The birth rate b and the death rate d relate to two parameters: potential doubling time T_{pot} and tumor cell loss factor ϕ, where $b = 0.693/T_{pot}$ and $\phi = d/b$. In the TCP calculation, the time t in Equation 12.2 is typically taken to be the duration of the treatment period or the expected remaining life span of the patient.

For simplicity and convenience in Equation 12.2, we use the linear quadratic expression for the survival function $S(D) = e^{-\alpha D - \beta q(t) D^2}$, where D is the dose delivered over the time interval t and $q(t)$ makes explicit the repair of sublethal damage. In the case in which the dose rate decreases exponentially,

$$q(t) = \frac{2(\lambda t)^2}{(\mu t)^2 (1 - \lambda^2/\mu^2)(1 - e^{-\lambda t})^2} \left[e^{-(\lambda + \mu)t} + \mu t \left(\frac{1 - e^{-2\lambda t}}{2\lambda t} \right) - \frac{1 + e^{-2\lambda t}}{2} \right],$$

where λ is the radioactive decay constant of the radioisotope ($\lambda = 0.0094$ d^{-1} for ^{192}Ir), and $\mu = 1/t_0$, where t_0 is the average time for the sublethal damage repair, typically in the order of 1 hour.

To complete the TCP calculation, we give numerical values to the parameters n, T_{pot}, ϕ, α, β, and t_0 to represent the response of the rapidly proliferating and (or) radioresistant segment of tumor cells.

The TCP value is sensitive to the volume and density of cells. We take the volume and density of cells in the cervical tumor ranges from $\rho = 10^8$ to $\rho = 10^{10}$ cells / cm^3. The potential doubling time is taken as $T_{pot} = 15$ or $T_{pot} = 20$ days, and the cell loss factor is taken as $\phi = 0.5$ or $\phi = 0.75$. In addition, $\alpha = 0.487$ Gy^{-1}, $\beta = 0.055$ Gy^{-2} for radiosensitive cells, and $\alpha = 0.155$ Gy^{-1}, $\beta = 0.052$ Gy^{-2} for radioresistant cells, whose values are determined from *in vitro* cell-survival measurements. For the sublethal damage repair constant, we take $t_0 = 1$ hour.

12.3.3.3 Novel TCP-Driven PET-Image-Guided Treatment-Planning Model

We design a multi-objective mixed-integer programming (MIP) model for HDR brachytherapy treatment planning. The model incorporates the TCP as the objective function, in addition to the rapid dose falloff function to ensure dose conformity to the tumor region.

In our treatment-planning model, we represent each anatomical structure by a collection of discretized voxels (three-dimensional volumetric pixels) and choose sizes such that they are conducive for modeling. Each dwell location is modeled via two variables: a binary decision variable to indicate whether a radioactive seed will be deposited and a continuous variable to denote the associated dwell time.

Mathematically, let x_j be a 0/1 indicator variable for recording placement or nonplacement of a seed in grid position j and t_j be the continuous variable for the dwell time of the seed in this grid position. The total radiation dose at voxel P is given by

$$\sum_j \dot{D}(\|P - X_j\|)t_j, \tag{12.3}$$

where X_j is a vector corresponding to the coordinates of grid point j, $\|\cdot\|$ denotes the Euclidean norm, and $\dot{D}(r)$ denotes the dose contribution per minute of a seed to a voxel that is r units away.

The target lower and upper bounds, L_P and U_P, for the radiation dose at voxel P are represented by the following dose constraints:

$$\sum_j \dot{D}(\|P - X_j\|)t_j \geq L_P \tag{12.4a}$$

$$\sum_j \dot{D}(\|P - X_j\|)t_j \leq U_P. \tag{12.4b}$$

For each voxel P in each anatomical structure, a binary variable is used to capture whether or not the desired dose level is achieved. For simplicity, we use the BTV to represent the set of tumor voxels identified by the PET images.

The TCP-driven PET-image-guided dose-escalated multi-objective treatment model is given by the following formulation:

Minimize $\max_{j} t_j$

Maximize $\sum_{P} \left(\eta_P v_P^L + \mu_P v_P^U \right)$

Maximize TCP

subject to

$$\sum_{j} \dot{D}\left(\left\| P - X_j \right\| \right) t_j \geq \text{PrDose} \cdot \lambda \quad P \text{ in BTV} \tag{12.5}$$

$$\sum_{j} \dot{D}\left(\left\| P - X_j \right\| \right) t_j + M_P \left(1 - v_P^L \right) \geq L_P \quad P \text{ in PTV} - \text{BTV} \tag{12.6}$$

$$P \text{ in OARs}$$

$$\sum_{j} \dot{D}\left(\left\| P - X_j \right\| \right) t_j - N_P \left(1 - v_P^U \right) \leq U_P, \quad P \text{ in PTV} - \text{BTV} \tag{12.7}$$

$$P \text{ in OARs,}$$

$$\left| \text{BTV} \right| + \sum_{p \in (\text{PTV} - \text{BTV})} v_P^L \geq \alpha \left| \text{PTV} \right|, \tag{12.8}$$

$$t_j \leq T_j x_j \tag{12.9}$$

$$\sum_{j} x_j \leq MaxSeeds \tag{12.10}$$

$$v_P^L, v_P^U, x_j \in \{0,1\}, t_j \geq 0$$

The first objective deals with temporal delivery that governs the dwell times. The second objective is to find a treatment plan that satisfies as many bound constraints as possible; this is surrogate to rapid dose falloff, ensuring conformity of the prescribed dose to the tumor. The parameters η_P and μ_P allow us to prioritize the importance of various anatomical structures. Using a weighted sum is important for the cervical cancer cases to balance the volume of the cervix versus the nearby OARs (e.g., bladder, rectum, and bowel). The third objective function incorporates the TCP function, which depends on the duration of the treatment, radioactive decay of the radioisotope, dose received, volume and density of tumor cells, and the biological radiosensitivity and radioresistancy of the normal and tumor cells.

PrDose represents the clinical prescribed dose to the tumor, and λ ($\lambda > 1$) represents the dose-escalation factor. This factor is guided by clinicians as well as its effect on normal tissue complication. Constraint (12.5) ensures that the PET-identified tumor voxels receive escalated doses. In Constraints (12.6) and (12.7), v_P^L and v_P^U are 0/1 variables. If a solution is found such that $v_P^L = 1$, then the lower bound for the dose level at point P is satisfied. Similarly, if $v_P^U = 1$, the upper bound at point P is satisfied (see Constraint 12.7).

The constants M_P and N_P are chosen appropriately for the PTV and for various OARS. For PTV, M_P corresponds to the underdose limit, whereas N_P corresponds to overdose limit, and $L_P = PrDose$ corresponds to the prescription dose. M_P and N_P are strategically chosen so that the overall PTV dose remains relatively homogeneous (e.g., setting $(N_P + PrDose)/(PrDose - M_P) < 1.2$), as the clinicians desire. For the OARs, N_P represents the maximum dose tolerance that the organs can sustain, without inflicting severe and permanent harm. These values are determined from clinical findings and are part of the planning procedures and guidelines. For cervical cancer treatment, Constraint (12.6) does not apply to any OAR.

In Constraint (12.8), α corresponds to the minimum percentage of tumor coverage required (e.g., $\alpha = 0.95$). Because all the PET-identified tumor voxels satisfy the prescribed dose bound (and beyond), we count those in PTV-BTV and these BTV voxels to ensure that overall it satisfies α percent of the tumor volume. Here, $|PTV|$ represents the total number of voxels used to represent the PTV of the cervix. Constraint (12.8) thus corresponds to the coverage level that the clinician desires. In Constraint (12.9), the duration t_j in grid position j is positive only when this position is selected. Its value is bounded by the maximum time limit T_j. The time usually is bounded by the length of the treatment session, which is usually between 20 and 30 minutes, depending on the tumor stage and prognosis condition. Constraint (12.10) limits the number of seeds used to *MaxSeeds*. The constant can be omitted; however, in some cases, clinicians know their desired numbers, which they tell the planner.

Note that BTV voxels are excluded in Constraint (12.7) because there is no reason to place an upper bound on the dose to these tumor voxels. Constraint (12.5) ensures that no underdose for PET-identified voxels exists; thus, Constraint (12.6) is unnecessary for these voxels.

12.3.4   Computational Challenges and Solution Strategies

The treatment model has three objectives: (i) the temporal delivery objective that governs the dwell times; (ii) the dose volume-based objective that, along with the temporal objective, guides the optimization engine to a solution that best satisfies the imposed dosimetric and volumetric constraints for conformal treatment; and (iii) the biological and clinical TCP objective.

To apply our multiple-objective MIP solution strategies, we begin by first solving the MIP instance that requires the minimum PTV coverage while minimizing the maximum dwell time across all the possible seed locations.

For the dose volume-based objective, these MIP instances inherit the dense dose matrix properties as in the MSKCC brachytherapy instances (Lee and Zaider 2008). Using a competitive commercial solver, the solver does not return a feasible solution, even after running for a month of CPU time on an Intel Xeon E5430 Quad Core Xeon Processors at 2.66 GHz, 1333 MHz FSB, and 12 MB cache per processor.

We employ hypergraphic polyhedral cuts to accelerate the solution process. In particular, Easton et al. (2003) introduced the notion of uniform hypergraph and derived facial structures of uniform hypercliques. In their work, they showed that these hyperclique inequalities can help to solve the small, yet 100% dense, previously intractable market-share instances successfully. Lee and Zaider (2008) showed that hypercliques, along with novel matrix-reduction approaches and clever geometric-based heuristics, can help solve these intractable MIP instances to optimality. Furthermore, the solution process can be achieved within seconds; thus, the real-time treatment-planning process, which has since become standard across the United States for prostate permanent implants, was realized.

In our work, the challenges are more complex; these challenges include the multi-objective nature of our problem, the highly nonlinear TCP objective, and the competing dose escalation and OAR dose distribution within the solution space.

We advance the polyhedral theory work of Easton et al. (2003) and introduce the concept of generalized conflict hypergraphs. Within this high-dimensional construct, we derive new polyhedral theories, including generalized hyperclique, hyper-oddholes, hyper-antioddholes, hyper-webs, hyper-antiwebs, and hyper-star facial structures and their associated Chvátal–Gomory (CG) ranks (Lee, Maheshwary and Wei 2016).

Computationally, we tackle the dose volume-based and the biological tumor control objectives simultaneously using a branch-and-cut and local-search approach. We caution that because TCP is highly nonlinear, it is difficult to convexify or linearize it for actual branch-and-cut solution exploration. Specifically, we solve the MIP instance with the dose volume-based objective via a branch-and-cut algorithm that couples new polyhedral cuts, along with matrix reduction and intelligent geometric heuristics algorithms. When we obtain an integer solution or when a heuristic within the branch-and-cut setting returns a feasible solution, we perform a local search to examine the TCP values across the entire neighborhood. Given a seed configuration with dwell times, we calculate the associated TCP based on the resulting PTV and PET-pocket dose–volume histograms. We then keep the best solution (i.e., the solution with the maximum TCP value) as the incumbent solution. The local search involves swapping and a hybrid genetic algorithm, where one can rapidly examine the neighborhood space to identify the best TCP-value solutions. Such an approach guarantees the return of a feasible solution while exploiting the best possible TCP values within the neighborhood feasible space.

We examine multiple model variations to determine the one with the best performance in terms of dose distribution to various organs and the associated TCP. The variations include minimizing the overdose and underdose to the PTV and (or) a combination of these. The overdose and underdose can be obtained by transforming the binary variables v_P^L and v_P^U in Constraints (12.6) and (12.7) into continuous variables to capture the dose differences. The weights in the objective function can be nonlinear to the overdose or underdose amount (e.g., it can be piecewise linear or quadratic penalties). Other variations include maximizing the dose falloff from the prescribed PTV dose. In Lee et al. (2016), we report further advances in directly addressing the TCP objective via the solution of successive MIP approximations.

12.4   VALIDATION AND RESULTS

To gauge the feasibility, characteristics, and potential benefit of PET-image-guided dose escalation, our initial validation consists of 15 cases of cervical cancer. Each patient had previously received a 45 Gy dose of external radiation. The PTV ranges from 82.8 to 137.47 cm^3 and the BTV ranges from 10% to 41%. For each case, we contrast three alternative strategies: (i) a standard HDR plan with no dose escalation, (ii) a BTV escalation with the same PTV prescription dose, and (iii) a BTV escalation with a reduced PTV prescription dose. For both escalation strategies, we consider two variations (a 37 Gy increase and a 40 Gy increase to the BTV) and observe the effects on PTV and OAR dose profiles and TCP quality.

Figure 12.3a illustrates the dose–volume histogram and dose profiles for a patient with a BTV that is 20.1% of the cervix. The y-axis is the cumulative volume, and the x-axis is the radiation dose received. In this figure, the standard plan is labeled by a square, escalated PET ≥ 37 Gy with 35 Gy PTV prescribed dose is labeled by circles, escalated PET ≥ 37 Gy with 33 Gy reduced PTV dose is labeled by an x, escalated PET ≥ 40 Gy with 35 Gy PTV prescribed dose is labeled by triangles, and escalated PET ≥ 40 Gy and 33 Gy reduced PTV dose is labeled by rhombuses. We can observe the escalated dose of the BTV versus the PTV. Further, compared with the standard plan, dose reduction occurs in the rectum and bladder in the escalated plans with a BTV ≥ 37 Gy. We observe a larger reduction when we increase the BTV to ≥ 40 Gy. This translates to a reduction in normal tissue toxicity and complications. Figure 12.3b illustrates similar trends for a small BTV volume (i.e., 10.4% of the PTV).

To contrast the dose distributions of the standard versus escalated plans, Figure 12.4 illustrates clear hot spots (i.e., high-dose, 150% isodose curves) around the PET-identified voxels in the escalated plan; however, they are absent in the standard plan.

For the 15 cases, the TCPs for standard plans range from 48% to 63%. For dose escalation with 35 Gy PTV prescribed dose, when an escalated dose of ≥ 37 Gy is placed in the PET-identified tumor pockets, all escalated plans show a slight reduction of 0.5%–12.4% in the rectum and bladder dose, while 99% of the BTV receives over 40 Gy. The resulting TCP values range from 82% to 99%. When the BTV is less than 15% of the PTV, dose escalation can be delivered with a virtually identical PTV dose, as in the standard plan. When the BTV is over 20% of the PTV, dose escalation to PET-identified voxels intrinsically increases the PTV dose by 1%. Boosting the BTV to 40 Gy results in no dose increase to the PTV in all plans.

When the PTV is prescribed as a reduced dose of 33 Gy, independent of the size of the BTV, escalation can be achieved, while the dose to the PTV, bladder, and

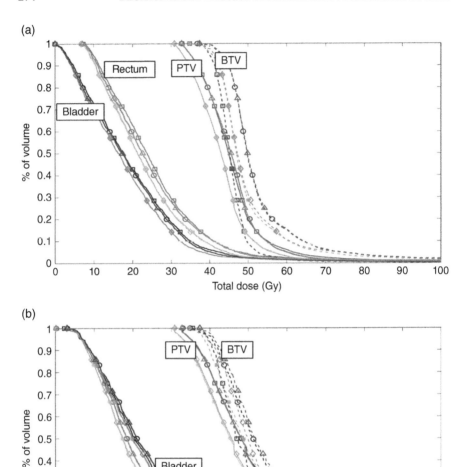

Figure 12.3 (a) This figure shows the dose–volume histogram for a cervical cancer patient with a PET pocket that is 20.1% of the PTV. □: Standard HDR plan (PTV prescribed dose = 35 Gy); there is no separate curve for the PET. ○: Escalated PET (PTV prescribed dose = 35 Gy, PET ≥ 37 Gy). *: Escalated PET and reduced PTV dose (PTV prescribed dose = 33 Gy, PET ≥ 37 Gy). Δ: Escalated PET (PTV prescribed dose = 35 Gy, PET ≥ 40 Gy). ❖ : Escalated PET and reduced PTV dose (PTV prescribed dose = 33 Gy, PET ≥ 40 Gy). (b) This figure illustrates the dose–volume histogram for a cervical cancer patient with a PET pocket that is 10.4% of the PTV.

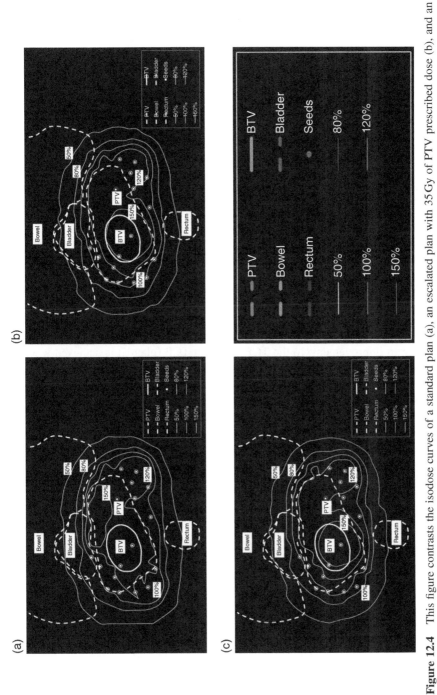

Figure 12.4 This figure contrasts the isodose curves of a standard plan (a), an escalated plan with 35 Gy of PTV prescribed dose (b), and an escalated plan with 33 Gy of PTV prescribed dose (c). We can observe the very conformed 100% isodose curves to the PTV contour. The 150% isodose curves in both escalated plans around the PET-identified pockets are clearly absent from the standard plan. The 120% isodose curve is tighter in the bottom escalated plan, reflecting the lower dose to PTV because of the lower prescribed value (33 Gy vs. 35 Gy).

TABLE 12.1   TCPs in Various Plans

PET/PTV Ratio Category	Small	Medium	Large
Planning target volume (PTV in cc)	82.80	137.47	92.47
PET-identified volume (BTV in cc)	8.60	27.63	29.74
Ratio: BVT/PTV	10.4%	20.1%	32.2%
Treatment-planning model	**Tumor control probability (TCP)**		
A. Standard HDR plan (PTV dose = 35 Gy)	0.48	0.53	0.63
B. BTV ≥ 37 Gy, PTV = 35Gy	**0.86**	**0.82**	**0.85**
C. BTV ≥ 37 Gy, PTV = 33Gy	**0.94**	**0.86**	**0.90**
D. BTV ≥ 40 Gy, PTV = 33Gy	**0.97**	**0.89**	**0.93**
E. BTV ≥ 40 Gy, PTV = 35Gy	**0.99**	**0.91**	**0.95**

The boldface values represent the TCP associated with escalated plans.

rectum are reduced simultaneously. All plans can be generated within minutes. This allows for real-time OR-based treatment planning and on-the-fly dynamic reconfiguration.

Table 12.1 highlights the TCP for three representative patients: BTV ≤ 11% of PTV (small), 11%–25% (medium), and ≥25% (large). On all patients, the TCP of all escalated plans is over 82%. Specifically, when the BTV is boosted to over 40 Gy, the resulting TCP is uniformly high (≥89%). We list the plans A–E according to improvements to the TCP. The best TCP (plan E) is achieved when we boost the PET-identified pockets to over 40 Gy while maintaining the PTV dose at 35 Gy. This can be partially explained by the fact that there remain cancer cells loosely populated outside the PET-identified pockets. Hence, a prescribed dose of 35 Gy is able to eliminate these cancer cells, but a prescribed dose of 33 Gy may not be as effective. Table 12.2 contrasts the dose received by the OARs. For brevity, we focus on the plans where the PTV all receives 35 Gy prescribed dose (i.e., plans A, B, and E).

12.5   FINDINGS, IMPLEMENTATION, AND CHALLENGES

With the precision of the HDR brachytherapy delivery, a TCP improvement in treatment plans can be readily realized in the outcomes of actual treatments. TCP offers biological information about tumor and normal cells and their radiosensitivity and radioresistancy to radiation doses; thus, incorporating such information in optimized personalized treatment plans is invaluable. Coupled with TCP knowledge, advances in biological and functional imaging offer new opportunities to incorporate radiobiological parameters within the planning process. The OR-based treatment-planning algorithm we describe herein allows for TCP-driven PET-enhanced personalized treatment, which facilitates the targeted delivery of escalated doses and improvements in overall clinical outcomes.

TABLE 12.2 Dose Distribution in Standard Plans versus Escalated Plans (Using the Same Prescribed PTV Dose)

Patient	Plans	D90 (cGy)		D 2cc (cGy)		Mean Dose (cGy)	
		PTV	PET Pockets	Bladder	Rectum	Bladder	Rectum
Small	Standard	3735.8	4091.3	2650.37	2400.57	2272.5	2006.5
	B: BTV ≥ 37 Gy, PTV = 35 Gy	−0.7%	+3.2%	−6.5%	−0.2%	−0.5%	−0.9%
	E: BTV ≥ 40 Gy, PTV = 35 Gy	−0.6%	+4.6%	−6.1%	−0.2%	−0.5%	−0.8%
Medium	Standard	3675.4	4135	2602.77	2654.15	1782.2	2006.1
	B: BTV ≥ 37 Gy, PTV = 35 Gy	+0.8%	+3.8%	+3.1%	−3.2%	−1.0%	−0.9%
	E: BTV ≥ 40 Gy, PTV = 35 Gy	+0.4%	+6.5%	+2.3%	−2.0%	−1.8%	−2.6%
Large	Standard	3666.2	4046	2791.26	2881.11	1189.3	3042.2
	B: BTV ≥ 37 Gy, PTV = 35 Gy	−0.7%	+3.1%	−8.5%	−7.5%	−6.4%	−6.9%
	E: BTV ≥ 40 Gy, PTV = 35 Gy	+0.1%	+7.1%	−5.0%	−8.5%	−1.7%	−12.4%

D90 (cGy) represents the dose received by 90% of the organ and D 2 cc is the minimum dose to the most exposed 2 cm³ of OARs.

Our study reveals improvements both in local tumor control and OAR toxicity, two competing and desirable goals that were previously thought to be unachievable simultaneously. The work herein showcases the importance of novel modeling and breakthrough optimization solution strategies in personalized treatment-planning advances. The dose escalation is sensitive to the size of the PET volume. In addition, we have demonstrated that it is possible to reduce the PTV dose while escalating doses to the PET pockets, as plans C and D, in which the PTV receives only 33 Gy, show.

This work addresses three unique challenges:

- The TCP function is complex and highly parametric and is sensitive to the density of cancer cells and the radiobiological characteristics of normal and tumor cells.

- The biological-driven MIP treatment models are intractable using existing methodologies and competitive solvers. They would require breakthroughs in polyhedral theory and computational advances. This is the first time that TCP is being incorporated within a treatment-planning optimization modeling and solution process. This is also the first time that PET-image-guided dose escalation is being performed.

- The actual gain in local tumor control must be validated through clinical trials to quantify the associated treatment outcome improvements that are realized through PET-guided dose escalation.

In practice, the sophisticated modeling and novel and fast optimization algorithm ensures that there is no increase in solution time for escalated dose planning. The radiation oncologists must guide us regarding the proper escalated dose values.

Rush University Medical Center began a clinical trial for PET hot HDR dose resteering in July 2011. All patients enrolled were diagnosed as having International Federation of Gynecology and Obstetrics (FIGO) IIB or IIIB cervical cancer. In a FIGO IIB cancer, the tumor has spread to the parametrial area (i.e., tissue surrounding the uterus); in a FIGO IIIB cancer, the tumor has grown into the pelvic wall and (or) causes hydronephrosis or nonfunctioning kidneys (American Joint Committee on Cancer 2009). The patient's treatment included whole pelvic radiation therapy with concurrent chemotherapy. The radiation therapy treatment schemes included external beam treatments for the cervix and parametrium, along with HDR to the cervix with boosted PET-positive doses. The HDR CTVs were delineated based on CT and MR imaging positive volumes. The PET-positive volumes were boosted to 50% higher doses than those delivered to CTVs. Some cases were treated with the Syed applicator; others were treated with the tandem–ring applicator, in conjunction with three or four parametrial interstitial needles.

All patients who entered the study received two treatment plans: one using the in-house treatment-planning algorithm for dose escalation and another using a commercial algorithm (currently used in the clinic) with options for manual fine-tuning.

The attending physician was responsible for selecting the final plan. Acceptable boost plans were achieved for all patients. These boosted plans were then successfully delivered to all patients. For the boosted plans, the PET pockets received elevated doses compared to the standard plans, while doses to the bladder and rectum were reduced. The clinician was pleased with the performance of the PET-image-guided targeted dose escalation and the successful completion of the clinical study. The hospital is planning to continue the study by enrolling additional patients. The results thus far indicate that such dose escalation is feasible to deliver and is beneficial to the cancer patients. The techniques are applicable to the treatment of other types of cancer, including breast, lung, prostate, and esophagus cancer.

12.6   IMPACT AND SIGNIFICANCE

As we state previously, cervical cancer is the second most common cancer in women worldwide; approximately 500,000 new cases are diagnosed each year (World Health Organization 2013). In developing nations, it is often the most common cause of cancer-related death among women and a leading cause of death overall (National Cancer Institute 2013). In this section, we discuss the significance of our work.

12.6.1   Quality of Care and Quality of Life for Patients

- Compared to standard HDR plans, PET-guided dose-escalation plans improve tumor control consistently across all patients. This translates to improvements in cure rates and reductions in mortality.
- Clinical evidence shows a reduction of the radiation dose to the bowel, bladder, and rectum. Thus, our system reduces side effects and complications. This has a profound impact on both healthcare costs and the patient's quality of life.
- The planning process requires only seconds to return good treatment plans. This offers quality assurance in treatment delivery (image guided or not), independent of the training and experience of the operators. It helps to ensure a uniform quality of care among patients and across all hospital sites.

12.6.2   Advancing the Cancer Treatment Frontier

- The work marks the first time that complex TCP is incorporated within treatment planning and as an objective in driving high-quality treatment plans.
- This work also marks the first time that PET images are incorporated within the treatment-planning environment for targeted dose-escalation planning optimization.
- The fast solution engine and the seamless incorporation of functional imaging information allows treatment-plan optimization and re-optimization in real time

based on new images as the patients receive daily treatments. This opens up the potential for next-generation adaptive real-time image-guided HDR brachytherapy.

- With advances in biological imaging, such as PET and MRS, incorporation of such knowledge within treatment modalities will soon become a standard for personalized treatment planning. To the best of our knowledge, Rush University's radiation therapy clinical trial is the first and only one in the country that delivers PET-based dose-escalation HDR brachytherapy for patients with cervical cancer. Our work has the potential to set the national standards and guidelines for biological image-guided brachytherapy treatment.

- Observing the clinical trend, brachytherapy is rapidly becoming the treatment of choice, because its side effects are generally less severe when compared with external beam radiation therapy and surgery and because of its effectiveness for early-stage treatment. Further, brachytherapy preserves the organ and its functionality. The latter is of special concern to younger early-stage cancer patients who still look forward to bearing children.

- The methodologies are applicable to brachytherapy (both high dose rate and low dose rate) for other types of cancer, including prostate, breast, bile duct, lung, and sarcoma, and for external beam radiation.

12.6.3   Advances in Operations Research Methodologies

- This study marks the first use of sophisticated combinatorial optimization approaches to tackle the complexities inherent in incorporating TCP as a clinical objective within HDR brachytherapy. The resulting treatment plans offer superior TCPs with simultaneous toxicity reduction to OARs. This can be a precursor to subsequent clinical trials.

- This study is the first in which PET images are incorporated within the planning optimization model, giving rise to the competing goals of escalating the dose to the tumor, while simultaneously not increasing (or reducing) the dose to the OARs.

- The highly nonlinear multi-objective MIP environment offers a powerful modeling paradigm. However, the resulting intractable instances demand theoretical and computational breakthroughs to solve these instances for actual clinical delivery.

- We introduce a new concept of generalized conflict hypergraphs and derive polyhedral results, including hypercliques, hyper-oddholes, hyper-antiodholes, hyper-webs, hyper-antiwebs, and hyper-star facial structures and their associated CG ranks.

- The branch-and-cut and local-search approach described herein couples new polyhedral cuts, along with matrix reduction and intelligent geometric heuristics. This approach can successfully address the highly complex and nonlinear

TCP function and the dose-based objective. It can rapidly return good, feasible solutions.

- Independently, this work motivates our polyhedral investigation on MIP convexification of posynomial and signomial functions (Shapoval and Lee 2012a, b), an area that deserves advances in its own right, because many real-world problems can be modeled as complex NMIPs that demand theoretical and computational advances.

Within the medical community, there is an urgent push to incorporate the radiobiological characteristics of normal and tumor cells, and biological and functional imaging advances, within treatment delivery to realize and improve clinical outcomes and tumor control. Our work provides proof of concept of the feasibility and potential clinical benefits of such personalized, targeted treatment-planning design and delivery. Moreover, the resulting plans offer improvements in tumor control and reduce the radiation to the OARs, two competing and desirable characteristics that were previously thought to be unachievable simultaneously.

Our rapid operator-independent biological treatment-planning system provides the groundwork for advancing the technological frontier of image-guided brachytherapy. It opens up opportunities to conduct complex clinical investigations that may otherwise be impossible, as evidenced in MRS-guided dose-escalation studies (Zaider et al. 2000, Zaider and Lee 2005, Lee and Zaider 2001, 2003a, 2003b, 2006). The sophisticated OR modeling paradigm provides great flexibility in realistically modeling the clinical problem, and the novel rapid solution engine objectively returns the best possible plans.

ACKNOWLEDGMENT

This work is partially supported by a grant from the National Science Foundation.

REFERENCES

Alterovitz R, Lessard E, Pouliot J, Hsu IC, O'Brien JF, Goldberg K (2006) Optimization of HDR brachytherapy dose distributions using linear programming with penalty costs. *Med. Phys.* 33(11):4012–4019.

American Cancer Society (2017) Cancer facts & figures 2017. https://www.cancer.org/research/cancer-facts-statistics/all-cancer-facts-figures/cancer-facts-figures-2017.html. Accessed December 13, 2017.

American Joint Committee on Cancer (2009) Cervix uteri cancer staging. https://cancerstaging.org/references-tools/quickreferences/Documents/CervixMedium.pdf. Accessed July 1, 2013.

Bailey DL, Townsend DW, Valk PE, Maisey MN (2005) *Positron Emission Tomography: Basic Sciences* (Springer-Verlag, Secaucus, NJ).

Beliën J, Colpaert J, De Boeck L, Demeulemeester E (2009) A hybrid simulated annealing linear programming approach for treatment planning in HDR brachytherapy with dose volume constraints. https://www.researchgate.net/publication/228982165. Accessed July 1, 2013.

Ciernik IF, Dizendorf E, Baumert BG, Reiner B, Burger C, Davis JB, Lütolf UM, Steinert HC, Von Schulthess GK (2003) Radiation treatment planning with an integrated positron emission and computer tomography (PET/CT): A feasibility study. *Int. J. Radiat. Oncol. Biol. Phys.* 57(3):853–863.

Duan J, Kim RY, Elassal S, Lin HY, Shen S (2008) Conventional high-dose-rate brachytherapy with concomitant complementary IMRT boost: A novel approach for improving cervical tumor dose coverage. *Int. J. Radiat. Oncol. Biol. Phys.* 71(3):765–771.

Easton T, Hooker K, Lee EK (2003) Facets of the independent set polytope. *Math. Program. Ser. B* 98(1–3):177–199.

Gallagher RJ, Lee EK (1997) Mixed integer programming optimization models for brachytherapy treatment planning. http://www.ncbi.nlm.nih.gov/pmc/articles/PMC2233571/pdf/procamiaafs00001-0316.pdf. Accessed July 1, 2013.

Holloway CL, Racine M, Cormack RA, O'Farrell DA, Viswanathan AN (2009) Sigmoid dose using 3D imaging in cervical-cancer brachytherapy. *Radiother. Oncol.* 93(2):307–310.

Holm A, Larsson T, Carlsson TA (2012) Impact of using linear optimization models in dose planning for HDR brachytherapy. *Med. Phys.* 39(2):1021.

Howlader N, Noone AM, Krapcho M, Garshell J, Neyman N, Altekruse SF, Kosary CL, et al., eds. (2013) SEER cancer statistics review, 1975–2010. http://seer.cancer.gov/csr/1975_2010/. Accessed July 1, 2013.

Kang HC, Shin KH, Park SY, Kim JY (2010) 3D CT-based high-dose-rate brachytherapy for cervical cancer: Clinical impact on late rectal bleeding and local control. *Radiother. Oncol.* 97(3):507–513.

Karabis A, Belotti P, Baltas D (2009) Optimization of catheter position and dwell time in prostate HDR brachytherapy using HIPO and linear programming. http://www.pi-medical.gr/sites/default/files/OptimizationCatheterPositionHIPOandMILP.pdf. Accessed July 1, 2013.

Kim DH, Wang-Chesebro A, Weinberg V, Pouliot J, Chen LM, Speight J, Littell R, Hsu IC (2009) High-dose rate brachytherapy using inverse planning simulated annealing for locoregionally advanced cervical cancer: A clinical report with 2-year follow-up. *Int. J. Radiat. Oncol. Biol. Phys.* 75(5):1329–1334.

Kirisits C, Pötter R, Lang S, Dimopoulos J, Wachter-Gerstner N, Georg D (2005) Dose and volume parameters for MRI-based treatment planning in intracavitary brachytherapy for cervical cancer. *Int. J. Radiat. Oncol. Biol. Phys.* 62(3):901–911.

Lahanas M, Baltas D, Giannouli S (2003) Global convergence analysis of fast multiobjective gradient based dose optimization algorithms for high dose rate brachytherapy. *Phys. Med. Biol.* 48(5):599–617.

Lee EK, Gallagher RJ, Silvern D, Wuu CS, Zaider M (1999) Treatment planning for brachytherapy: An integer programming model, two computational approaches and experiments with permanent prostate implant planning. *Phys. Med. Biol.* 44(1):145–165.

Lee EK, Zaider M (2001) On the determination of an effective planning volume for permanent prostate implants. *Int. J. Radiat. Oncol. Biol. Phys.* 49(4):1197–1206.

Lee EK, Zaider M (2003a) Intraoperative dynamic dose optimization in permanent prostate implants. *Int. J. Radiat. Oncol. Biol. Phys.* 56(3):854–861.

Lee EK, Zaider M (2003b) Mixed integer programming approaches to treatment planning for brachytherapy: Application to permanent prostate implants. *Ann. Oper. Res. Optim. Med.* 119(1–4):147–163.

Lee EK, Zaider M (2006) Incorporating biological metabolite information within treatment of prostate carcinoma and analysis of dose escalation effect. *Int. J. Radiat. Oncol. Biol. Phys.* 66(3):S572–S573. Supplement (Proceedings of the 48th Annual ASTRO Meeting), S572–S573.

Lee EK, Zaider M (2008) Operations research advances cancer therapeutics. *Interfaces* 38(1):5–25 (The Franz Edelman Award Achievement in Operations Research 2008).

Lee EK, Yuan F, Templeton A, Yao R, Kiel K, Chu JCH (2013) Biological planning for high-dose rate brachytherapy: Application to cervical cancer treatment. *Interfaces* 43(5):462–467 (The Daniel H Wagner Prize for Excellence in Operations Research Practice 2013).

Lee EK, Maheshwary S, Wei X (2016) Facets of conflict hypergraph. *SIAM J. Optim.* Submitted.

Lee EK, Yuan F, Templeton A, Yao R, Kiel K, Chu JCH (2016) Optimizing tumor control probability in radiation therapy treatment—Application to HDR cervical cancer. *Med. Phys.* 43(6):3806

Malyapa RS, Mutic S, Low DA, Zoberi I, Bosch WR, Laforest R, Miller TR, Grigsby PW (2002) Physiologic FDG-PET three-dimensional brachytherapy treatment planning for cervical cancer. *Int. J. Radiat. Oncol. Biol. Phys.* 54(4):1140–1146.

Morton GC, Sankreacha R, Halina PA, Loblaw A (2008) A comparison of anatomy-based inverse planning with simulated annealing and graphical optimization for high-dose-rate prostate brachytherapy. *Brachytherapy* 7(1):12–16.

Nag S, Orton C, Young D (1999) The American Brachytherapy Society survey of brachytherapy practice for carcinoma of the cervix in the United States. *Gynecol. Oncol.* 73(1):111–118.

National Institutes of Health (2013) NIH research portfolio online reporting tools. http://report.nih.gov/nihfactsheets/viewfactsheet.aspx?csid=76. Accessed July 1, 2013.

Rivard MJ, Coursey BM, DeWerd LA, Hanson WF, Huq MS, Ibbott GS, Mitch MG, Nath R, Williamson JF (2004) Update of AAPM task group no. 43 report: A revised AAPM protocol for brachytherapy dose calculations. *Med. Phys.* 31(12):633–674.

Ruotsalainen H, Miettinen K, Palmgren J, Lahtinen T (2010) Interactive multiobjective optimization for anatomy-based three-dimensional HDR brachytherapy. *Phys. Med. Biol.* 55(16):4703–4719.

Shapoval R, Lee EK (2015a) Mixed integer programming convexification of posynomial functions. Submitted.

Shapoval R, Lee EK (2015b) Mixed integer programming convexification. II. Extension from posynomial to signomial functions. Submitted.

Tanderup K, Nielsen SK, Nyvang GB, Pedersen EM, Røhl L, Aagaard T, Fokdal L, Lindegaard JC (2010) From point A to the sculpted pear: MR image guidance significantly improves tumour dose and sparing of organs at risk in brachytherapy of cervical cancer. *Radiother. Oncol.* 94(2):173–180.

Wachter-Gerstner N, Wachter S, Reinstadler E, Fellner C, Knocke TH, Pötter R (2003) The impact of sectional imaging on dose escalation in endocavitary HDR-brachytherapy of cervical cancer: Results of a prospective comparative trial. *Radiother. Oncol.* 68(1):51–59.

World Health Organization (2013) Comprehensive cervical cancer prevention and control: A healthier future for girls and women. http://www.who.int/reproductivehealth/topics/cancers/en/. Accessed July 1, 2013.

Zaider M, Lee EK (2005) Treatment planning for low dose rate and high dose rate brachytherapy. In *Basic and Advanced Techniques in Prostate Brachytherapy.* Editors: Dicker A, Merrick GS, Gomella LG, Valicenti RK, Waterman F, Gomella L (Taylor & Francis, London, U.K.), pp. 142–156.

Zaider M, Minerbo GN (2000) Tumour control probability: A formulation applicable to any temporal protocol of dose delivery. *Phys. Med. Biol.* 45(2):279–293.

Zaider M, Zelefsky MJ, Lee EK, Zakian KL, Amols HI, Dyke J, Cohen G, Hu Y, Endi AK, Chui C, Koutcher JA (2000) Treatment planning for prostate implants using MR spectroscopy imaging. *Int. J. Radiat. Oncol. Biol. Phys.* 47(4):1085–1096.

13

FLUENCE MAP OPTIMIZATION IN INTENSITY-MODULATED RADIATION THERAPY TREATMENT PLANNING

DIONNE M. ALEMAN

Department of Mechanical & Industrial Engineering and Institute for Health Policy, Management & Evaluation, University of Toronto, Toronto, ON, Canada
Guided Therapeutics Core, Techna Institute, Toronto, ON, Canada

13.1 INTRODUCTION

Cancer is among the leading causes of death worldwide, with annual cancer rates expected to increase from 14 million in 2012 to 22 million by 2032 (World Health Organization 2015). Radiation therapy is one of the most widely used approaches to treat cancer (American Cancer Society 2017); however, depending on the treatment site, long-term side effects including infertility, bladder and kidney problems, dry mouth, and even paralysis can occur if treatments are not carefully designed to avoid healthy tissues (American Cancer Society 2017). While there are several forms of radiation therapy, for example, stereotactic radiosurgery and brachytherapy, the most common form of radiation therapy is intensity-modulated radiation therapy (IMRT), wherein radiation is delivered to the patient via external beams. Unlike conformal radiation therapy, in IMRT, the radiation distribution of each beam can be finely controlled, allowing for very accurate treatments to target cancerous tissue while avoiding healthy cells.

Decision Analytics and Optimization in Disease Prevention and Treatment, First Edition.
Edited by Nan Kong and Shengfan Zhang.
© 2018 John Wiley & Sons, Inc. Published 2018 by John Wiley & Sons, Inc.

Prior to delivering radiation, a CT image is taken of the patient and the cancerous structures (called targets) and healthy structures (called organs at risk (OARs)) are contoured by hand. Using the CT image and the contours, the patient is discretized into 3D pixels called *voxels* (volume pixels), and each voxel belongs to a single structure. A desired amount of radiation is designated for each structure, and a dosimetrist uses a commercial treatment planning software to design a treatment that meets the desired treatment guidelines as best as possible. The treatment is then reviewed by a clinical team and may be sent back to the dosimetrist for improvement. This process is repeated until a satisfactory treatment is obtained. IMRT optimization seeks to eliminate the iterative nature of treatment planning by improving the planning engine in the commercial treatment planning software so that a high-quality treatment that meets or exceeds clinical guidelines is obtained on the first attempt.

Radiation in IMRT is delivered using a device called a linear accelerator (Figure 13.1a). To achieve unique radiation distributions for each beam, a multileaf collimator (MLC) is positioned in the linear accelerator, and the "leaves" (Figure 13.1b) move in and out to block or unblock radiation in parts of the beam, resulting in customizable beam shapes (Figure 13.1c). The MLC moves as radiation is delivered, and leaving some areas of the beam blocked or unblocked longer than other areas results in nearly infinitely customizable radiation distributions. Typically, the MLC leaves can move in increments of 0.5 cm, and the leaves are also about 0.5 cm wide. Thus, the MLC allows us to effectively treat each beam, which is generally about 40 cm × 40 cm in size, as hundreds of small 0.5 cm × 0.5 cm *beamlets*, the radiation intensities of which (called *fluences*) can be independently controlled. Depending on the specific linear accelerator and MLC make and model, there may exist rules governing the relative positions of adjacent leaves, but these restrictions do not limit the ultimate fluences that can be delivered.

In delivering the treatment to the patient, the treatment is divided into 25–35 smaller *fractions*, which are administered daily to the patient. IMRT treatments are delivered by positioning the linear accelerator for a single beam orientation, delivering the appropriate fluence map, stopping the radiation, and then moving to the next beam and repeating for each beam. This process is called step-and-shoot delivery. An alternative approach is to continuously deliver radiation while the linear accelerator and MLC move in a process called volumetric modulated arc therapy (VMAT) (Otto 2008). VMAT is gaining in popularity for some treatment sites (most notably, prostate) (see, e.g., Craft et al. 2012; Men et al. 2010b), but step-and-shoot IMRT is currently more common in general.

To design an IMRT treatment, first, the beam orientations are selected. Generally, these beams are obtained solely from rotating the linear accelerator gantry (shown slightly rotated in Figure 13.1a), which sweeps out a disc of potential beam orientations; such beam orientations are called coplanar. However, other components of the linear accelerator can also move, for example, the couch can be rotated translated in all dimensions, which would result a much larger set of candidate beam orientations called non-coplanar beams. Clinically, most treatments use an odd number of

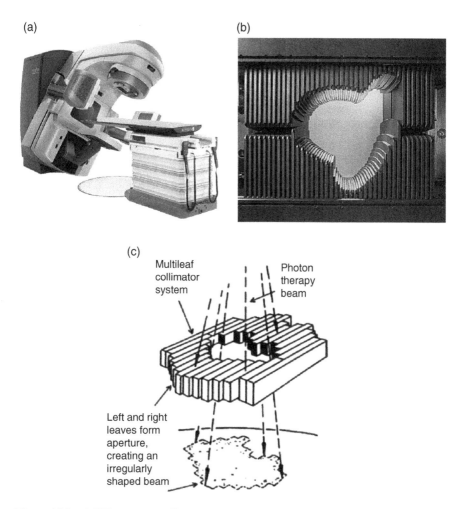

Figure 13.1   IMRT treatment delivery devices. (a) Linear accelerator and (b) MLC (c) MLC impact on beam shape. Source: (a and b) Reproduced with permission of Varian Systems, Inc. (c) Romeijn and Dempsey (2008). Reproduced with permission of Springer.

equi-spaced coplanar beams, usually 5–11 beams, depending on the treatment site. Odd numbers are chosen to avoid parallel-opposed beams, which conventionally are undesirable for most treatment sites (one notable exception is breast treatments). Once the beam orientations are selected, the fluences of each beam, called *fluence maps*, are obtained by selecting beamlet intensities and then identifying leaf positions to achieve these fluence maps or by selecting whole apertures (shapes) of the MLC directly. If beamlet-based fluence maps are obtained, then the last step of planning is to identify a sequence of MLC movements to achieve the fluence maps.

While multiple valid leaf sequences may exist, leaf sequences that result in shorter treatment times (i.e., sequences with fewer movements) are preferred.

IMRT treatment planning optimization is therefore typically divided into three consecutively solved decision-making problems: (i) beam orientation optimization (BOO), (ii) fluence map optimization (FMO), and (iii) leaf sequencing optimization (LSO). Alternatively, FMO and LSO can be combined into direct aperture optimization (DAO). While BOO, FMO, and LSO problems, and DAO to a lesser extent, are all well studied in the literature (see, e.g., the IMRT review paper by Romeijn and Dempsey (2008)), FMO has received the most attention by far, likely because it is the most computationally tractable and because the quality of the fluence maps usually has a much larger impact on overall clinical treatment quality than the beams or the leaf sequences. The fractionation problem to optimally divide the treatment into fractions is not well studied, with few previous studies focusing on the problem from a rigorous mathematical optimization framework (Aleman et al. 2014).

An important consideration during the planning and delivery stages of IMRT treatment is uncertainty. Organs can shift and move due to breathing or setup errors during each individual treatment (called *intrafraction motion*) or can shift as time goes by from fraction to fraction (called *interfraction motion*). While most IMRT literature assumes a deterministic treatment scenario, attempts to predict and plan for intra- and interfraction motion are becoming more common, particularly robust optimization formulations to control worst-case scenario treatment quality. Adaptive treatments (see, e.g., Chan and Mišić 2013; Men et al. 2009; Wu et al. 2008), where a new treatment is planned (or an existing treatment is updated) for each fraction, are also gaining popularity, though such multi-plan modeling approaches will not be presented in this chapter.

This chapter focuses on computationally tractable single-plan FMO modeling and optimization approaches for step-and-shoot delivery in deterministic and robust scenarios and is organized as follows. Section 13.2 explains the criteria used to evaluate treatment plans. Sections 13.3 and 13.4 elaborate how FMO models are posed and optimized, respectively. Finally, conclusions and future directions are presented in Section 13.5.

13.2 TREATMENT PLAN EVALUATION

While objective function values, optimality gaps, and computation times are the sole criteria for evaluating most optimization approaches regardless of application, in IMRT, solutions are evaluated almost exclusively on clinical treatment quality. Computation time is important to maintain real-world usefulness (FMO should not take more than a few minutes), and optimality is important only insofar as it ensures consistent quality and standardization across treatment planners.

Clinical treatment metrics for IMRT broadly fall into two categories: physical dose measures and biological measures. The difference between these measures is that the former captures measurable delivered dose, while the latter infers tissue responses to radiation (Bortfeld 1999). It is important to note that different clinics will use different treatment criteria, and criteria may vary with multimodal treatments (e.g., surgery and/or chemotherapy in conjunction with radiation).

13.2.1 Physical Dose Measures

Physical dose measures include dose–volume histograms (DVHs), isodose lines, and D_x and V_x specifications. The notation D_x for a particular structure means "the minimum dose received by $\geq x\%$ of the structure volume," while V_x means "the percentage of the structure volume receiving $\geq x\%$ of the prescribed dose." Note that minimum, maximum, and mean doses received by a structure can be expressed as D_{100}, D_0, and D_{50}, respectively. For the targets, which are generally the *gross tumor volume* (GTV) (the visible cancerous region in the CT) and the *planning tumor volume* (PTV) (the GTV plus some margin to account for microscopic tumor extension and potential uncertainty), D_x and V_x are given in terms of percentage of the prescription dose. For OARs, they are given in terms of absolute dose.

Table 13.1 illustrates some common dose measures for common treatment sites in terms of Gy ("gray," a common unit of radiation for therapeutic radiation delivery). As can be seen in the table, some OARs are constrained by maximum amount of dose (e.g., spinal cord), while others are constrained by dose to partial volumes (e.g., saliva glands). Organs that can receive high dose to partial volumes and still survive are called *parallel* structures (e.g., saliva glands), while organs that cannot survive after high dose to any portion are called *serial* structures (e.g., spinal cord).

Unlike D_x and V_x, DVHs and isodose lines are visual representations of dose. As the name implies, DVHs are plots of dose vs. volume for each structure. Figure 13.2a illustrates

TABLE 13.1   Common Physical Dose Criteria for Some Treatment Sites

Site	Organ	Prescription Dose	Dose Criteria
Head and neck	GTV	70 Gy	$D_{95} \geq 100\%$, $V_{95} \geq 100\%$, $V_{110} \leq 5\%$
	PTV	50 Gy	$D_{95} \geq 100\%$, $V_{120} \leq 10\%$
	Saliva glands	—	$V_{35Gy} \leq 50\%$
	Spinal cord	—	$V_{45Gy} \leq 0\%$
	Mandible	—	$V_{70Gy} \leq 0\%$
Prostate	PTV	74 Gy	$V_{95} \geq 98\%$, $V_{107} \leq 0\%$
	Bladder	—	$V_{40Gy} \leq 25\%$, $V_{20Gy} \leq 50\%$
	Rectum	—	$V_{70Gy} \leq 5\%$, $V_{40Gy} \leq 25\%$, $V_{20Gy} \leq 50\%$
	Femoral heads	—	$V_{40Gy} \leq 5\%$
Lung	PTV	66 Gy	$V_{100} \geq 95\%$, $V_{113} \leq 3\%$
	Lung	—	$V_{20Gy} \leq 30\%$, $V_{30Gy} \leq 20\%$, $D_{50} \leq 20$ Gy
	Spinal cord	—	$V_{45Gy} \leq 0\%$
	Heart	—	$V_{40Gy} \leq 50\%$
	Esophagus	—	$V_{55Gy} \leq 30\%$

(a)

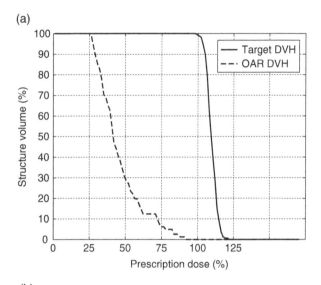

(b)

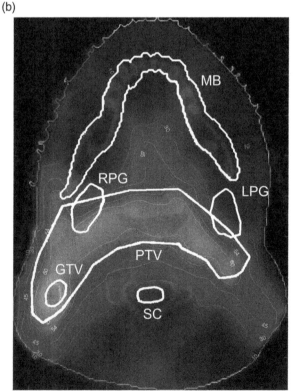

Figure 13.2   Visual evaluation measures of physical dose. (a) Example DVH and (b) CT slice with isodose lines and structure contours. LPG, left parotid gland; MB, mandible; RPG, right parotid gland; SC, spinal cord.

sample DVHs of a target structure and an OAR. Ideally, target DVH curves should be flat at 100% volume up to 100% of the prescription dose (indicating that 100% of the structure receives 100% of the prescription dose) and then fall steeply to 0% (indicating that very little of the structure receives more than 100% of the prescription dose). Conversely, DVH curves for OARs should fall quickly to zero, indicating that very little of the structure receives significant dose. Isodose lines (Figure 13.2b) are contour lines of the dose overlaid on slices of the CT image and are often colored according to dose intensity. Isodose lines should be evaluated for each CT slice and should show tight conformity of the prescription isodose line to the targets, as well as homogeneity of dose in the target (no hotspots or coldspots) and acceptable dose to OARs.

13.2.2 Biological Dose Measures

Although physical criteria dominate IMRT optimization models and radiotherapy treatment evaluation, a few biological criteria should be discussed due to their clinical relevance. These criteria are the tumor control probability (TCP), normal tissue complication probability (NTCP), and equivalent uniform dose (EUD), which has several variants, the most common of which is the generalized EUD (gEUD). The functions to express TCP and NTCP (see, e.g., Mohan et al. 1992) are mathematically intractable for rigorous optimization (and, hence, very infrequently incorporated into IMRT optimization (Alber and Nusslin 1999; Levin-Plotnik and Hamilton 2004)) and thus will not be discussed. We specifically note that most papers claiming to optimize TCP and NTCP are in fact using commercial treatment planning systems to obtain treatments (see, e.g., Semenenko et al. 2008; Witte et al. 2007), so the validity of the actual optimization process is unknown. EUD, on the other hand, can be formulated in an optimization-friendly convex expression, though EUD formulations are still more complex than those based on physical criteria. It is worth noting that TCP and NTCP can be calculated from EUD (Romeijn et al. 2004; Wu et al. 2002), and TCP and NTCP are sometimes calculated after optimization to compare treatments.

EUD is meant to approximate dose response more closely than the dose–volume parameters used in physical criteria. We will focus on gEUD due to its prevalence and flexibility in IMRT optimization (Romeijn et al. 2004). Given dose z_{js} to voxel j in structure s containing a set of $\mathcal{V}_s$ voxels, gEUD for structure s is defined by the following expression (Niemierko 1997; Wu et al. 2002):

$$\text{gEUD}_s = \left(\frac{1}{|\mathcal{V}_s|} \sum_{j \in \mathcal{V}_s} z_{js}^{a_s} \right)^{1/a_s} \tag{gEUD}$$

where a_s is a parameter specific to structure s describing the tumor or OAR-specific dose–volume effect. As shown by the a value interpretations in Table 13.2, tumors are usually assigned large negative a values to control minimum dose, while OARs are usually assigned either small positive values or ∞ if the OAR is parallel or

TABLE 13.2   Interpretations of a Values in gEUD Equation

a	gEUD Meaning
∞	Maximum dose
$-\infty$	Minimum dose
1	Arithmetic mean dose
0	Geometric mean dose

Source: Wu et al. (2002). Reproduced with permission of Elsevier.

serial in structure, respectively. Because of its flexibility to capture dose preferences and its convex nature, gEUD is commonly used in IMRT optimization approaches (see, e.g., Craft et al. 2007; Romeijn et al. 2004; Wu et al. 2002; Zinchenko et al. 2008).

13.3   FMO OPTIMIZATION MODELS

FMO formulations are varied and include linear programming (LP)-based multicriteria optimization (Breedveld et al. 2007; Craft et al. 2007; Hamacher and Küfer 2002; Thieke et al. 2007) and mixed-integer linear programming (MILP) (Bednarz et al. 2002; Ferris et al. 2006; Langer et al. 1990, 1996, Lee et al. 2003, 2006; Shepard et al. 1999). The vast majority of FMO literature is based on the optimization of physical dose criteria, but some approaches based on biological criteria have been explored (Alber and Nusslin 1999; Craft et al. 2007; Das 2009; Jones and Hoban 2000; Kallman et al. 1992; Mavroidis et al. 2001; Niemierko 1997; Niemierko et al. 1992; Romeijn et al. 2004; Wu et al. 2002, 2003; Zinchenko et al. 2008). We will focus on modern techniques for modeling FMO in computationally tractable ways using physical criteria. We first present a generic FMO model and then possible objective functions and constraints.

Defining the set of OARs as $\mathcal{O}$ and the set of targets as $\mathcal{T}$, the set of structures in a treatment is $\mathcal{S} = \mathcal{O} \cup \mathcal{T}$. Each structure $s \in \mathcal{S}$ has a set $\mathcal{V}_s$ of voxels. Since FMO is performed given a fixed set of beams, the set of beamlets, B, is fixed. The decision variables in FMO are the fluences of each beamlet, defined as x_i, $i \in \mathcal{B}$. Dose z_{js} to voxel j in structure s from beamlet intensities $\mathbf{x}$ is calculated using a linear sum:

$$z_{js} = \sum_{i \in \mathcal{B}} D_{ijs} x_i \quad \forall s \in \mathcal{S}, j \in \mathcal{V}_s \tag{13.1}$$

where D_{ijs}, called a dose deposition coefficient, is the fraction of dose from beamlet i reaching voxel j in structure s at unit intensity. A description of how to calculate dose deposition coefficients can be found in, for example, Aleman et al. (2008c).

Say, a function $F(\mathbf{z})$ exists to quantify the quality of voxel doses $\mathbf{z}$, where smaller values of $F(\mathbf{z})$ indicate better treatments. A generic FMO model to optimize voxel doses $\mathbf{z}$ arising from beamlet intensities $\mathbf{x}$ is then

$$\text{Minimize} \qquad F(\mathbf{z}) \qquad\qquad\qquad \text{(FMO)}$$
$$\text{Subject to} \quad z_{js} = \sum_{i\in\mathcal{B}} D_{ijs} x_i \quad \forall s \in \mathcal{S}, j \in \mathcal{V}_s$$
$$x_i \geq 0 \quad \forall i \in \mathcal{B}$$

Note that the constraint on z_{js} is used for notational convenience and is generally not considered a constraint. Since $\mathbf{z}$ is a function of $\mathbf{x}$, any instance of $\mathbf{z}$ can be replaced by $\mathbf{Dx}$ as defined in Equation 13.1.

13.3.1   Objective Functions

Objective functions can optimize either physical (dose-based) or biological (effect-based) measures. Common formulations for each approach are presented in this section.

13.3.1.1   Physical Objective Functions   In 2004, Romeijn et al. showed that convex penalty function criteria capture the vast majority of plan evaluation criteria in the medical physics literature. Since then, the most common approach to FMO objective function formulation is the following convex penalty approach that uniquely penalizes the over- and underdose of each voxel:

$$F(\mathbf{z}) = \sum_{s \in \mathcal{S}} \sum_{j \in \mathcal{V}_s} \frac{1}{|\mathcal{V}_s|} \left(\overline{w}_s \left(z_{js} - \overline{T}_s \right)_+^p + \underline{w}_s \left(\underline{T}_s - z_{js} \right)_+^p \right) \qquad (13.2)$$

where $(\cdot)_+$ indicates $\max\{\cdot,0\}$; $\overline{T}_s$ and $\underline{T}_s$ are thresholds above and below which dose in structure s is penalized, respectively; and $\overline{w}_s$ and $\underline{w}_s$ are weights on over- and underdose for structure s, respectively. The penalty for each voxel is divided by the size of the structure to prevent large (but potentially unimportant) structures dominating small structures.

For OARs, $\underline{T}_s$ and $\underline{w}_s$ are typically zero, though either may be set to a positive value in recognition of the fact that a particular OAR may inevitably have to receive some dose. Commonly, $\overline{T}_s = \underline{T}_s$, though some new radiation optimization studies use unique values for each (see, e.g., Ghobadi et al. 2012). If $\overline{T}_s = \underline{T}_s$ and $\overline{w}_s = \underline{w}_s$, this function is a continuously differentiable quadratic function. Otherwise, it is a non-smooth function with non-differentiable points where $z_{js} \in \left[\underline{T}_s, \overline{T}_s \right]$. Experimentally, these non-differentiable points do not affect optimization performance (Aleman et al. 2010).

Quadratic variations of this penalty function with $p=2$ are most common (Aleman et al. 2008a, 2008b, 2013; Men et al. 2009; Mišić et al. 2009, 2010; Romeijn et al. 2003, 2006), though linear approaches with $p=1$ have also been used for improved computational performance (Cao and Lim 2010; Lim and Cao 2012; Lim et al. 2008, 2014).

Experimentally, the quadratic variation of this convex penalty function is often powerful enough to not require hard constraints on any voxel doses; however, significant effort in tuning the threshold and weight parameters may be necessary.

In some robust FMO formulations to account for uncertainty in organ positions, the objective is often to simply minimize total dose to OARs (Bortfeld et al. 2008; Chan et al. 2006),

$$F(\mathbf{z}) = \sum_{s \in \mathcal{O}} \sum_{j \in V_s} z_{js}$$

or weighted total dose to OARs (Chan et al. 2014b; Mahmoudzadeh et al. 2015):

$$F(\mathbf{z}) = \sum_{s \in \mathcal{O}} \sum_{j \in V_s} \frac{1}{|V_s|} w_s z_{js}$$

Both these formulations are special instances of the convex penalty function in Equation 13.2. Other robust formulations, however, use a more standard version of the convex penalty approach in Equation 13.2 with $p = 1$ (Chu et al. 2005; Ólafsson and Wright 2006).

Despite the popularity of these objective functions, all but the simple minimization of total OAR dose rely on parameters to dictate the importance over- and underdosing and the importance of one structure compared with another. Tuning these parameters often requires significant effort and should be done across a large set of patients to ensure broad applicability of the final parameter values. It may be appropriate to generate unique parameter sets based on treatment site, target size, target proximity to OARs, or other measures that can be determined a priori. While there are no formal approaches to the parameter-tuning process, graphical user interface (GUI) approaches to assist planners in selecting parameters and comparing plans generated by different parameters are growing in popularity (Ripsman et al. 2015b).

13.3.1.2 Biological Objective Functions As stated in Section 13.2.2, EUD and its variants are the only commonly used biological measures in radiotherapy optimization due their convex formulations. To use gEUD to optimize dose to targets ($\mathcal{T}$), simply sum the gEUD values for each target $s \in \mathcal{T}$ ($\text{gEUD}_a(s)$) according to Equation gEUD:

$$F(\mathbf{z}) = -\sum_{s \in \mathcal{T}} \text{gEUD}_s$$

Note that the negative sum of the gEUD values is taken since the general FMO model is a minimization, and, for targets, gEUDs are most commonly maximized. Values for a_s should be chosen from Table 13.2 according to the desired metric to optimize (e.g., $a_s = \infty$ to maximize maximum dose or $a_s = -\infty$ to maximize minimum dose). With any gEUD target objective, it is likely that a constraint will be required to limit the maximum dose to the target voxels (see Section 13.3.2.1) to prevent overdose.

To use gEUD to optimize OAR ($\mathcal{O}$) doses, again select appropriate a_s values for each $s \in \mathcal{O}$ and sum the OAR gEUD values:

$$F(\mathbf{z}) = \sum_{s \in \mathcal{O}} \text{gEUD}_s$$

Because it is desirable to keep OARs doses low, the gEUDs are directly minimized, unlike the case of optimizing target gEUDs. When minimizing dose to OARs using gEUD, it is unlikely that any constraints will be required to explicitly control OAR dose; however, such constraints can be added if needed to guide the optimization to clinically acceptable solutions.

As with physical dose objectives, it may be necessary to weigh the importance of structures in the objective function. For example, to weigh the gEUDs when minimizing OARs to place more emphasis on select organs, simply add penalty weights to each structure's gEUD (Romeijn et al. 2004):

$$F\left(\mathbf{z}\right) = \sum_{s \in \mathcal{O}} w_s \text{gEUD}_s$$

where larger w_s values indicate more importance. As with the penalty parameters in physical dose objectives, w_s will have to be tuned to values that consistently yield quality treatments and may be specific to different sites and patient geometries.

13.3.2   Constraints

As with objective functions, constraints can control either physical or biological measures. Common formulations for each approach are presented in this section.

13.3.2.1   *Full-Volume Physical Dose Constraints*   Full-volume constraints require that the dose in every voxel of a structure be within predetermined upper and lower bounds (Bednarz et al. 2002; Hamacher and Küfer 2002; Lee et al. 2003, 2006; Romeijn et al. 2003) and can be simply formulated as

$$z_{js} \geq \underline{Z}_s \quad \forall j \in \mathcal{V}_s$$
$$z_{js} \leq \overline{Z}_s \quad \forall j \in \mathcal{V}_s$$

where $\underline{Z}_s$ and $\overline{Z}_s$ are lower and upper bounds on dose to any voxel in structure s, respectively. These constraints are often useful for ensuring target dose homogeneity. For serial OARs, where a maximum dose must be observed in order for the organ to continue functioning after treatment, the full-volume upper bound constraint may be useful.

13.3.2.2   *Partial-Volume Physical Dose Constraints*   Partial-volume constraints, also called DVH constraints, require that dose in only a subset of voxels be within

predetermined upper and/or lower bounds (Chan et al. 2014b; Lee et al. 2003, 2006; Mahmoudzadeh et al. 2015; Romeijn et al. 2003, 2005, 2006; Shepard et al. 1999). Approaches to add partial-volume constraints generally included the introduction of a binary variable for every voxel and partial-volume constraint, rendering the inclusion of these constraints computationally challenging until Romeijn et al. (2006) proposed a linear formulation for partial-volume constraints using the financial engineering concept of conditional value at risk (CVaR), which constrains the mean upper and lower tails of a distribution. Since the CVaR approach is linear and does not cause an explosion of variables, it will be presented in detail here.

Romeijn et al. (2006) define two types of partial-volume constraints that may be applied to a structure:

1. Mean dose to the $(1 - \alpha)\%$ of voxels receiving the lowest amount of dose must be $\geq L^{\alpha}$ CVaR-L

2. Mean dose to the $(1 - \alpha)\%$ of voxels receiving the highest amount of dose must be $\leq U^{\alpha}$ CVaR-U

Note that CVaR-L applies to target structures, while CVaR-U applies to OARs. We present CVaR-U first. Define the upper mean tail dose at level α as

$$\bar{\phi}_s^{\alpha}(\mathbf{z}) = \underbrace{\bar{\zeta}_s^{\alpha}(\mathbf{z})}_{\text{Start of upper tail}} + \underbrace{\frac{1}{(1-\alpha)|\mathcal{V}_s|}\sum_{j\in\mathcal{V}_s}\left(z_{js}-\bar{\zeta}_s^{\alpha}(\mathbf{z})\right)_{+}}_{\text{Mean dose of all voxels in the upper tail}},$$

where $\bar{\zeta}_s^{\alpha}(\mathbf{z})$ is equal to the lowest dose value among the $(1-\alpha)|\mathcal{V}_s|$ voxels receiving the highest dose. This expression can be written as

$$\bar{\phi}_s^{\alpha}(\mathbf{z}) = \min_{\bar{\zeta}_s^{\alpha}\in\mathbb{R}}\left\{\bar{\zeta}_s^{\alpha} + \frac{1}{(1-\alpha)|\mathcal{V}_s|}\sum_{j\in\mathcal{V}_s}\left(z_{js}-\bar{\zeta}_s^{\alpha}\right)_{+}\right\}$$

Similarly, for CVaR-L, the lower mean tail dose at level α is defined as

$$\underline{\phi}_s^{\alpha}(\mathbf{z}) = \max_{\underline{\zeta}_s^{\alpha}\in\mathbb{R}}\left\{\underline{\zeta}_s^{\alpha} + \frac{1}{(1-\alpha)|\mathcal{V}_s|}\sum_{j\in\mathcal{V}_s}\left(\underline{\zeta}_s^{\alpha}-z_{js}\right)_{+}\right\}$$

Then, the following constraints are added to the FMO model:

$$-\underline{\phi}_s^{\alpha}(\mathbf{z}) \geq L_s^{\alpha} \quad \forall s\in\mathcal{T}, \alpha\in\underline{A}_s$$

$$\underline{\phi}_s^{\alpha}(\mathbf{z}) \leq U_s^{\alpha} \quad \forall s\in\mathcal{O}, \alpha\in\bar{A}_s$$

$$\underline{\zeta}_s^{\alpha} \text{ free} \quad \forall s\in\mathcal{T}, \alpha\in\bar{A}_s$$

$$\bar{\zeta}_s^{\alpha} \text{ free} \quad \forall s\in\mathcal{O}, \alpha\in\bar{A}_s$$

where $\underline{A}_s$ and $\bar{A}_s$ are the sets of desired α levels for constraints of types CVaR-L and CVaR-U, respectively. Full-volume constraints are often used in conjunction with partial-volume constraints to ensure that the tails of the dose distributions do not become overly long.

As presented by Romeijn et al. (2006), the CVaR formulation has interesting properties relevant to radiation therapy optimization. When $\alpha = 0$, both $\bar{\phi}_s^{\alpha}(\mathbf{z})$ and $\underline{\phi}_s^{\alpha}(\mathbf{z})$ are equal to the mean dose of the structure; for serial OARs, it is often important to constrain mean dose, and such a constraint can then be easily represented using CVaR notation. Further,

$$\lim_{\alpha \uparrow 1} \underline{\phi}_s^{\alpha}(\mathbf{z}) = \min_{j \in V_s} \left\{ z_{js} \right\}$$
$$\lim_{\alpha \uparrow 1} \bar{\phi}_s^{\alpha}(\mathbf{z}) = \max_{j \in V_s} \left\{ z_{js} \right\}$$

so minimum and maximum dose constraints can also be captured by CVaR formulations.

13.3.2.3 Biological Dose Constraints

While biological constraints are more commonly present in objectives than in constraints, they can easily be placed in constraints to explicitly restrict biological dose effects. Lower and upper limits on gEUD can be simply applied to each structure s:

$$\text{gEUD}_s \geq \underline{E}_s \quad \forall s \in \mathcal{S}$$
$$\text{gEUD}_s \leq \bar{E}_s \quad \forall s \in \mathcal{S}$$

where $\underline{E}_s$ and $\bar{E}_s$ are lower and upper bounds on gEUD in structure s, respectively. The parameter a_s in Equation gEUD for each structure s should be chosen according to the clinical opinion on each structure's response to dose (Table 13.2). For OARs in particular, it may be appropriate to constrain gEUD for several values of a_s, for example, constrain both the maximum dose ($a_s = \infty$) and the arithmetic mean dose ($a = 1$). Given that there are usually only a small number of OARs, additional constraints for multiple values of a_s are unlikely to significantly affect computation time.

13.3.3   Robust Formulation

Robust FMO formulations to capture intrafraction uncertainty in organ positions are gaining in popularity (see, e.g., Bertsimas et al. 2010; Chan et al. 2006; Chu et al. 2005; Ólafsson and Wright 2006; Vrančić et al. 2009). The goal of robust formulations is to design a treatment plan that, unlike stochastic recourse formulations, hedges against worst-case motion outcomes that may not have been predicted a priori. Here, we present the formulation in Chan et al. (2006), as it based on physical criteria, is fully linear (and therefore computationally tractable) and has spawned many of the more recent robust investigations in IMRT.

This formulation seeks to capture motion caused by breathing, which can be considered a cyclical motion comprised of several phases. To this end, a motion probability density function (pdf) is created from 4D CT images to define the proportion of time the target spends in each breathing phase. The discretized pdf is called a *probability mass function* (pmf). Bounds that are on the uncertainty of the motion distribution are provided, but the distribution itself is undefined, and thus the formulation is distribution-free. The formulation will return a solution that is feasible for all breathing motions produced within the defined pmf uncertainty set.

An assumption is made that any realized pmf during treatment will be wholly contained within the mean (nominal) pmf p plus or minus upper ($\bar{p}$) and lower ($\underline{p}$) error bars, respectively, yielding the largest realizable pmf domain $\mathcal{P} = \{[p + \bar{p}, p - \underline{p}] : \bar{p} \neq 0, \underline{p} \neq 0\}$. An uncertainty region $\mathcal{U} \subseteq \mathcal{P}$ is defined as the locations where the realized pmf may deviate from the nominal pmf; in other words, $\mathcal{U}$ is the domain of breathing patterns that are expected. High irregularity in patient breathing results in $\mathcal{U}$ being equal or nearly equal to $\mathcal{P}$, while regular breathing results in $\mathcal{U}$ being much smaller than $\mathcal{P}$. Asymmetric adjustments to $\mathcal{U}$ can be made to address irregularities in inhale versus exhale breathing phases. The pmf uncertainty set $P_{\mathcal{U}}$ is then

$$P_{\mathcal{U}} = \{\tilde{p} : \tilde{p}(u) \in \left[p(u) + \bar{p}(u), p(u) - \underline{p}(u)\right], \forall u \in \mathcal{U}$$
$$\tilde{p}(u) \geq 0, \forall u \in \mathcal{P}; \sum_{u \in \mathcal{P}} \tilde{p}(u) = 1; \tilde{p}(u) = p(u), \forall u = \mathcal{P} \setminus \mathcal{U}\}$$

Note that the uncertainty set addresses breathing patterns that are possible ($\mathcal{P}$), but not explicitly planned for ($\mathcal{U}$).

To transform the deterministic FMO formulation to a robust formulation, we replace the dose deposition coefficients D_{ijs} with motion-adjusted coefficients $\tilde{D}_{ijs}$ and incorporate the breathing pmfs into the dose calculation:

$$z_{js}^{\text{robust}} = \sum_{i \in \mathcal{B}} \sum_{u \in \mathcal{P}} \tilde{D}_{ijs} \tilde{p}(u) x_i \quad \forall \tilde{p} \in P_{\mathcal{U}}, s \in \mathcal{S}, j \in \mathcal{V}_s \tag{13.3}$$

The robust model is then to minimize z_{js}^{robust} for all OARs with full-volume constraints on z_{js}^{robust} for target voxels. However, the dose calculation in Equation 13.3 yields infinitely many constraints since there are infinitely many elements in $P_{\mathcal{U}}$. We therefore instead reformulate the constraints on target voxel dose to instead limit the dose in the worst-case realization, which can be thought of as the nominal dose plus an adjustment. Because it controls the worst-case dose outcome, the model is said to be robust. The robust model is thus defined as

$$\underset{\mathbf{x}}{\text{Minimize}} \quad \sum_{i \in \mathcal{B}} \sum_{s \in \mathcal{O}} \sum_{j \in \mathcal{V}_s} \sum_{u \in \mathcal{P}} \tilde{D}_{ijs} p(u) x_i \qquad \text{(Robust FMO)}$$

$$\text{Subject to} \quad \underbrace{\sum_{i \in \mathcal{B}} \sum_{u \in \mathcal{P}} \tilde{D}_{ijs} p(u) x_i}_{\text{Nominal dose}} + \underbrace{\beta_{js}(\mathbf{x})}_{\text{Worst-case dose adjustment}} \geq \underline{Z}_s \quad \forall s \in \mathcal{T}, j \in \mathcal{V}_s$$

$$x_i \geq 0 \qquad\qquad\qquad \forall i \in \mathcal{B}$$

where $\beta_{js}(\mathbf{x})$, the additional (negative) dose realized by a worst-case variation, is the result of the following optimization model per voxel:

$$\beta_{js}(\mathbf{x}) = \underset{\hat{p}}{\text{Minimize}} \quad \sum_{i \in B} \sum_{u \in \mathcal{U}} \tilde{D}_{ijs} \, \hat{p}(u) x_i$$

$$\text{Subject to} \quad \sum_{u \in \mathcal{U}} \hat{p}(u) = 0$$

$$-\underline{p}(u) \leq \hat{p}(u) \leq \overline{p}(u) \quad \forall u \in \mathcal{U}$$

Note that $\beta_{js}(\mathbf{x})$ is typically negative, since in the worst case, the target will be underdosed, not overdosed. A robust FMO variation that incorporates the CVaR approach to implement partial-volume constraints can be found in Chan et al. (2014b).

13.4 OPTIMIZATION APPROACHES

Approaches to solve FMO models depend on the tractability of the model formulation and are as varied as the model formulations. We focus on approaches that are applicable to the computationally tractable model formulations presented in Section 13.3.

For linear and mixed-integer linear FMO models, which include the CVaR and robust formulations presented, the most popular approach is commercial optimization software, including CPLEX (IBM, Armonk, NY) and Gurobi Optimizer (Gurobi Optimization, Inc., Houston, TX) (see, e.g., Chan et al. 2006; Craft et al. 2007; Lim et al. 2008; Romeijn et al. 2006; Wu et al. 2008). While commercial software is capable of solving these problems to optimality quickly, a practical drawback is that clinics might not have access to commercial software to implement the proposed FMO approaches, and commercial treatment planning system vendors may not be willing to incorporate other commercial software into their own platforms. Thus, custom-built optimization approaches are popular in IMRT, even for relatively simple model formulations.

For linearly constrained FMO models with quadratic objectives, projected gradient methods, are predominately used for their speed, lack of dependence on the Hessian calculations, and ease of implementation (see, e.g., Aleman et al. 2008a, 2008b, 2013; Lahanas et al. 2003; Men et al. 2009; Mišić et al. 2010). Projected gradient approaches are widespread enough to have resulted in a review of their speed for IMRT optimization (Zhang et al. 2004). However, projected gradient methods have no guarantee of optimality, and, while mathematical optimality is unimportant from a clinical perspective, the lack of guarantee on solution quality means that treatment plans may be inconsistent and non-standardized and may depend on how long a particular dosimetrist is willing to allow the algorithm to run, not to mention the specifics of algorithm implementation. Notably, Aleman et al. (2013) found that different line search strategies within the projected gradient routine yield drastic performance differences in IMRT (with quadratic interpolation performing the fastest, but a customized nonuniform backtracking method yielding the best objective function values). They also found that a warm start (as opposed to the traditional near-zero start) can significantly improve both final objective function value and total computation time by as much as an order of magnitude for very large treatment sites.

Custom interior point methods have been shown to be as fast as projected gradient approaches for linearly constrained quadratic FMO models, but with the benefit of guaranteed optimality gaps (see, e.g., Aleman et al. 2010, 2014). Reformulation of these quadratic FMOs to conic problems solved via commercial software (Chu et al. 2005; Kim et al. 2012, 2013) or novel constraint-generation interior point methods (Oskoorouchi et al. 2011) has also been shown to yield ε-optimal solutions. While these approaches are empirically better than projected gradient approaches, and potentially similar or better in computation time, practical challenges may exist in real-world implementation using commercial software or in gaining acceptance of complex, potentially non-intuitive optimization approaches from clinicians.

Despite the rise in availability of multiprocessor and multi-thread computing systems, very little IMRT optimization studies, let alone research focused on just FMO, have made systematic investigations into the use of parallel, distributed, and GPU computing. Among the first attempts at harnessing modern computing infrastructure for IMRT is that by Men et al. (2009), who developed a GPU-based approach for projected gradient methods for FMO; this group also developed similar methods for DAO for adaptive radiation therapy (Men et al. 2010a) and dose calculation (Gu et al. 2009; Jia et al. 2011). Ziegenhein et al. (2013) later developed a GPU-based approach to IMRT optimization. Aleman et al. (2013) used parallelization to speed up dose calculation and gradient calculation in a projected gradient algorithm for FMO, finding almost linear time increase with the number of processors used; a complete algorithm description of the parallelized components is presented in their study. Earlier work from this group applied parallelization to neighborhood search approaches for beam orientation optimization in IMRT (Mišić et al. 2010).

13.5 CONCLUSIONS

FMO in IMRT has been widely studied, and a variety of computationally tractable linear and quadratic model formulations exist for both deterministic and robust scenarios. As speed in FMO computations is paramount, especially as the medical physics field looks more toward adaptive radiotherapy that requires re-optimization of plans each day, future effort in the area of FMO should focus on fast optimization techniques that do not rely on commercial software. Specifically, incorporation of modern computing infrastructure including parallel, distributed, and GPU computing should be at the forefront of future FMO research. Additionally, reliance on time-intensive manual parameter tuning in FMO objectives is an important practical area needing more investigation, whether from an inverse planning perspective (Chan et al. 2014a) or from a human factors interface perspective (Ripsman et al. 2015a).

REFERENCES

M. Alber and F. Nusslin. An objective function for radiation treatment optimization based on local biological measures. *Physics in Medicine and Biology*, 44:479–493, 1999.

D. M. Aleman, A. Kumar, R. K. Ahuja, H. E. Romeijn, and J. F. Dempsey. Neighborhood search approaches to beam orientation optimization in intensity modulated radiation therapy treatment planning. *Journal of Global Optimization*, 42:587–607, 2008.

D. M. Aleman, H. E. Romeijn, and J. F. Dempsey. A response surface approach to beam orientation optimization in intensity modulated radiation therapy treatment planning. *INFORMS Journal on Computing: Computational Biology and Medical Applications*, 20(3):1–15, 2008.

D. M. Aleman, H. E. Romeijn, and J. F. Dempsey. Beam orientation optimization methods in intensity modulated radiation therapy treatment planning. In G. J. Lim and E. K. Lee, editors, *Optimization in Medicine and Biology*, volume 3. CRC Press, Boca Raton, FL, 2008.

D. M. Aleman, D. Glaser, H. E. Romeijn, and J. F. Dempsey. Interior point algorithms: Guaranteed optimality for fluence map optimization in IMRT. *Physics in Medicine and Biology*, 55(18):5467, 2010.

D. M. Aleman, V. V. Mišić, and M. B. Sharpe. Computational enhancements to fluence map optimization for total marrow irradiation using IMRT. *Computers & Operations Research*, 40(9):2167–2177, 2013.

D. M. Aleman, J. Wallgren, H. E. Romeijn, and J. F. Dempsey. A fluence map optimization model for restoring traditional fractionation in IMRT treatment planning. *Optimization Letters*, 8(4):1453–1473, 2014.

American Cancer Society. Cancer treatment & survivorship facts and figures 2016–2017. https://www.cancer.org/content/dam/cancer-org/research/cancer-facts-and-statistics/cancer-treatment-and-survivorship-facts-and-figures/cancer-treatment-and-survivorship-facts-and-figures-2016-2017.pdf, 2017. Accessed September 8, 2017.

G. Bednarz, D. Michalski, C. Houser, M. S. Huq, Y. Xiao, P. R. Anne, and J. M. Galvin. The use of mixed-integer programming for inverse treatment planning with pre-defined field segments. *Physics in Medicine and Biology*, 47:2235–2245, 2002.

D. Bertsimas, O. Nohadani, and K. M. Teo. Nonconvex robust optimization for problems with constraints. *INFORMS Journal on Computing*, 22(1):44–58, 2010.

T. Bortfeld. Optimized planning using physical objectives and constraints. *Seminars in Radiation Oncology*, 9(1):20–34, 1999.

T. Bortfeld, T. C. Y. Chan, A. Trofimov, and J. N. Tsitsiklis. Robust management of motion uncertainty in intensity-modulated radiation therapy. *Operations Research*, 56(6): 1461–1473, 2008.

S. Breedveld, P.R. Storchi, M. Keijzer, A.W. Heemink, and B.J. Heijmen. A novel approach to multi-criteria inverse planning for IMRT. *Physics in Medicine and Biology*, 52:6339–6353, 2007.

W. Cao and G. J. Lim. Optimization models for cancer treatment planning. In J. J. Cochran, L. A. Cox, P. Keskinocak, J. P. Kharoufeh, and J. Cole Smith, editors, *Wiley Encyclopedia of Operations Research and Management Science*. John Wiley & Sons, Inc., Hoboken, NJ, 2010.

T. C. Y. Chan and V. V. Mišić. Adaptive and robust radiation therapy optimization for lung cancer. *European Journal of Operational Research*, 231(3):745–756, 2013.

T. C. Y. Chan, T. Bortfeld, and J. N. Tsitsiklis. A robust approach to IMRT optimization. *Physics in Medicine and Biology*, 51(10):2567, 2006.

T. C. Y. Chan, T. Craig, T. Lee, and M. B. Sharpe. Generalized inverse multiobjective optimization with application to cancer therapy. *Operations Research*, 62(3):680–695, 2014.

T. C. Y. Chan, H. Mahmoudzadeh, and T. G. Purdie. A robust-CVaR optimization approach with application to breast cancer therapy. *European Journal of Operational Research*, 238(3):876–885, 2014.

M. Chu, Y. Zinchenko, S. G. Henderson, and M. B. Sharpe. Robust optimization for intensity modulated radiation therapy treatment planning under uncertainty. *Physics in Medicine and Biology*, 50(23):5463, 2005.

D. Craft, T. Halabi, H.A. Shih, and T. Bortfeld. An approach for practical multiobjective IMRT treatment planning. *International Journal of Radiation Oncology, Biology, Physics*, 69:1600–1607, 2007.

D. Craft, D. McQuaid, J. Wala, W. Chen, E. Salari, and T. Bortfeld. Multicriteria VMAT optimization. *Medical Physics*, 39(2):686–696, 2012.

S. Das. A role for biological optimization within the current treatment planning paradigm. *Medical Physics*, 36(10):4672–4682, 2009.

H.E. Romeijn, J. F. Dempsey, and J. G. Li. A unifying framework for multi-criteria fluence map optimization models. *Physics in Medicine and Biology*, 49:1991–2003, 2004.

M. C. Ferris, R. R. Meyer, and W. D'Souza. Radiation treatment planning: Mixed integer programming formulations and approaches. In G. Appa, L. Pitsoulis, and H. P. Williams, editors, *Handbook on Modelling for Discrete Optimization*, pp. 317–340. Springer-Verlag, New York, 2006.

K. Ghobadi, H. R. Ghaffari, D. M. Aleman, D. A. Jaffray, and M. Ruschin. Automated treatment planning for a dedicated multi-source intracranial radiosurgery treatment unit using projected gradient and grassfire algorithms. *Medical Physics*, 39(6):3134–3141, 2012.

X. Gu, D. Choi, C. Men, H. Pan, A. Majumdar, and S. B. Jiang. GPU-based ultra-fast dose calculation using a finite size pencil beam model. *Physics in Medicine and Biology*, 54(20):6287, 2009.

H. W. Hamacher and K.-H. Küfer. Inverse radiation therapy planning a multiple objective optimization approach. *Discrete Applied Mathematics*, 118:145–161, 2002.

X. Jia, X. Gu, Y. Jiang Graves, M. Folkerts, and S. B. Jiang. GPU-based fast Monte Carlo simulation for radiotherapy dose calculation. *Physics in Medicine and Biology*, 56(22): 7017, 2011.

L. C. Jones and P. W. Hoban. Treatment plan comparison using equivalent uniform biologically effective dose (eubed). *Physics in Medicine and Biology*, 45:159–170, 2000.

P. Kallman, B. K. Lind, and A. Brahme. An algorithm for maximizing the probability of complication–free tumor–control in radiation-therapy. *Physics in Medicine and Biology*, 37:871–890, 1992.

H. Kim, T.-S. Suh, R. Lee, L. Xing, and R. Li. Efficient IMRT inverse planning with a new L1-solver: Template for first-order conic solver. *Physics in Medicine and Biology*, 57(13):4139, 2012.

H. Kim, S. Becker, R. Lee, S. Lee, S. Shin, E. Candès, L. Xing, and R. Li. Improving IMRT delivery efficiency with reweighted L1-minimization for inverse planning. *Medical Physics*, 40(7):071719, 2013.

M. Lahanas, E. Schreibmann, and D. Baltas. Multiobjective inverse planning for intensity modulated radiotherapy with constraint-free gradient-based optimization algorithms. *Physics in Medicine and Biology*, 48(17):2843, 2003.

M. Langer, R. Brown, M. Urie, J. Leong, M. Stracher, and J. Shapiro. Large-scale optimization of beam weights under dose-volume restrictions. *International Journal of Radiation Oncology, Biology, Physics*, 18:887–893, 1990.

M. Langer, S. Morrill, R. Brown, O. Lee, and R. Lane. A comparison of mixed integer programming and fast simulated annealing for optimizing beam weights in radiation therapy. *Medical Physics*, 23:957–964, 1996.

E. K. Lee, T. Fox, and I. Crocker. Simultaneous beam geometry and intensity map optimization in intensity-modulated radiation therapy treatment planning. *Annals of Operations Research*, 119:165–181, 2003.

E. K. Lee, T. Fox, and I. Crocker. Integer programming applied to intensity-modulated radiation therapy treatment planning. *International Journal of Radiation Oncology, Biology, Physics*, 64:301–320, 2006.

D. Levin-Plotnik and R. J. Hamilton. Optimization of tumour control probability for heterogeneous tumours in fractionated radiotherapy treatment protocols. *Physics in Medicine and Biology*, 49(3):407, 2004.

G. J. Lim and W. Cao. A two-phase method for selecting {IMRT} treatment beam angles: Branch-and-prune and local neighborhood search. *European Journal of Operational Research*, 217(3):609–618, 2012.

G. J. Lim, J. Choi, and R. Mohan. Iterative solution methods for beam angle and fluence map optimization in intensity modulated radiation therapy planning. *OR Spectrum*, 30(2):289–309, 2008.

G. J. Lim, L. Kardar, and W. Cao. A hybrid framework for optimizing beam angles in radiation therapy planning. *Annals of Operations Research*, 217(1):357–383, 2014.

H. Mahmoudzadeh, J. Lee, T. C. Y. Chan, and T. G. Purdie. Robust optimization methods for cardiac sparing in tangential breast IMRT. *Medical Physics*, 42(5):2212–2222, 2015.

P. Mavroidis, B. K. Lind, and A. Brahme. Biologically effective uniform dose for specification, report and comparison of dose response relations and treatment plans. *Physics in Medicine and Biology*, 46:2607–2630, 2001.

C. Men, X. Jia, and S. B. Jiang. GPU-based ultra-fast direct aperture optimization for online adaptive radiation therapy. *Physics in Medicine and Biology*, 55(15):4309, 2010.

C. Men, X. Gu, D. Choi, A. Majumdar, Z. Zheng, K. Mueller, and S. B. Jiang. GPU-based ultrafast IMRT plan optimization. *Physics in Medicine and Biology*, 54(21): 6565, 2009.

C. Men, H. E. Romeijn, X. Jia, and S. B. Jiang. Ultrafast treatment plan optimization for volumetric modulated arc therapy (VMAT). *Medical Physics*, 37(11):5787–5791, 2010.

V. V. Mišić, D. M. Aleman, and M. B. Sharpe. Total marrow irradiation using intensity modulated radiation therapy optimization. In *Proceedings of the IERC Annual Conference*. IERC, Miami, FL, 2009.

V. V. Mišić, D. M. Aleman, and M. B. Sharpe. Neighborhood search approaches to noncoplanar beam orientation optimization for total marrow irradiation using IMRT. *European Journal of Operational Research*, 205(3):522–527, 2010.

R. Mohan, G. S. Mageras, B. Baldwin, L. J. Brewster, G. J. Kutcher, S. Leibel, C. M. Burman, C. C. Ling, and Z. Fuks. Clinically relevant optimization of 3d conformal treatments. *Medical Physics*, 19(4):933–944, 1992.

A. Niemierko. Reporting and analyzing dose distributions: A concept of equivalent uniform dose. *Medical Physics*, 24(1):103–110, 1997.

A. Niemierko, M. Urie, and M. Goitein. Optimization of 3d radiation-therapy with both physical and biological end-points and constraints. *International Journal of Radiation Oncology, Biology, Physics*, 23:99–108, 1992.

A. Ólafsson and S. J. Wright. Efficient schemes for robust IMRT treatment planning. *Physics in Medicine and Biology*, 51(21):5621, 2006.

M. R. Oskoorouchi, H. R. Ghaffari, T. Terlaky, and D. M. Aleman. An interior point constraint generation algorithm for semi-infinite optimization with health-care application. *Operations Research*, 59(5):1184–1197, 2011.

K. Otto. Volumetric modulated arc therapy: IMRT in a single gantry arc. *Medical Physics*, 35(1):310–317, 2008.

D. Ripsman, K. Ghobadi, D. M. Aleman, and D. A. Jaffray. A graphical interface for interactive parameter selection in radiation therapy treatment planning. In *Proceedings of the 13th Imaging Network of Ontario Symposium*, p. 61. Imaging Network of Ontario, Toronto, ON, 2015.

D. A. Ripsman, D. M. Aleman, and K. Ghobadi. Interactive visual guidance for automated stereotactic radiosurgery treatment planning. *Expert Systems with Applications*, 42(21): 8337–8348, 2015.

H. E. Romeijn and J. F. Dempsey. Intensity modulated radiation therapy treatment plan optimization. *TOP*, 16(2):215–243, 2008.

H. E. Romeijn, R. K. Ahuja, J. F. Dempsey, A. Kumar, and J. G. Li. A novel linear programming approach to fluence map optimization for intensity modulated radiation therapy treatment planning. *Physics in Medicine and Biology*, 38:3521–3542, 2003.

H. E. Romeijn, R. K. Ahuja, J. F. Dempsey, A. Kumar, and J. G. Li. A column generation approach to radiation therapy treatment planning using aperture modulation. *SIAM Journal on Optimization*, 15:838–862, 2005.

H. E. Romeijn, R. K. Ahuja, J. F. Dempsey, and A. Kumar. A new linear programming approach to radiation therapy treatment planning problems. *Operations Research*, 54(2):201–216, 2006.

V. A. Semenenko, B. Reitz, E. Day, X. S. Qi, M. Miften, and X. A. Li. Evaluation of a commercial biologically based IMRT treatment planning system. *Medical Physics*, 35(12):5851–5860, 2008.

D. M. Shepard, M. C. Ferris, G. H. Olivera, and T. R. Mackie. Optimizing the delivery of radiation therapy to cancer patients. *SIAM Review*, 41:721–744, 1999.

C. Thieke, K.H. Küfer, M. Monz, A. Scherrer, F. Alonso, U. Oelfke, P. E. Huber, J. Debus, and T. Bortfeld. A new concept for interactive radiotherapy planning with multicriteria optimization: first clinical evaluation. *Radiotherapy Oncology*, 85:292–298, 2007.

C. Vrančić, A. Trofimov, T. C. Y. Chan, G. C. Sharp, and T. Bortfeld. Experimental evaluation of a robust optimization method for IMRT of moving targets. *Physics in Medicine and Biology*, 54(9):2901, 2009.

M. G. Witte, J. van der Geer, C. Schneider, J. V. Lebesque, M. Alber, and M. van Herk. IMRT optimization including random and systematic geometric errors based on the expectation of TCP and NTCP. *Medical Physics*, 34(9):3544–3555, 2007.

World Health Organization. Cancer. http://www.who.int/mediacentre/factsheets/fs297/en/, February 2015. Accessed June 7, 2015.

Q. Wu, R. Mohan, A. Niemierko, and R. Schmidt-Ullrich. Optimization of intensity-modulated radiotherapy plans based on the equivalent uniform dose. *International Journal of Radiation Oncology, Biology, Physics*, 52(1):224–235, 2002.

Q. W. Wu, D. Djajaputra, Y. Wu, J. N. Zhou, H. H. Liu, and R. Mohan. Intensity-modulated radiotherapy optimization with gEUD-guided dose-volume objectives. *Physics in Medicine and Biology*, 48:279–291, 2003.

Q. J. Wu, D. Thongphiew, Z. Wang, B. Mathayomchan, V. Chankong, S. Yoo, W. R. Lee, and F.-F. Yin. On-line re-optimization of prostate IMRT plans for adaptive radiation therapy. *Physics in Medicine and Biology*, 53(3):673, 2008.

X. Zhang, H. Liu, X. Wang, L. Dong, Q. Wu, and R. Mohan. Speed and convergence properties of gradient algorithms for optimization of IMRT. *Medical Physics*, 31(5):1141–1152, 2004.

P. Ziegenhein, C. Ph. Kamerling, M. Bangert, J. Kunkel, and U. Oelfke. Performance-optimized clinical IMRT planning on modern CPUs. *Physics in Medicine and Biology*, 58(11):3705, 2013.

Y. Zinchenko, T. Craig, H. Keller, T. Terlaky, and M. B. Sharpe. Controlling the dose distribution with gEUD-type constraints within the convex radiotherapy optimization framework. *Physics in Medicine and Biology*, 53(12):3231, 2008.

14

SLIDING WINDOW IMRT AND VMAT OPTIMIZATION

DAVID CRAFT AND TAREK HALABI

Radiation Oncology, Department of Physics, Harvard Medical School, Boston, MA, USA

14.1 INTRODUCTION

Intensity-modulated radiation therapy (IMRT) is a treatment technique for X-ray irradiation of tumors that involves blocking the radiation beams—which come in from several angles around the patient—in order to create modulated, as opposed to uniform, fields of radiation. This allows the dose that is deposited within the patient to be sculpted to conform to the tumor and to avoid, as much as physically possible, large amounts of dose to normal tissues (Bortfeld 2006; Webb 2003).

The modulation of the X-ray fluence is accomplished by a multi-leaf collimator (MLC), which is a large bank of paired, parallel thick metal leaves that slide in and out of the radiation field. There are two techniques for using the MLC to create modulated fields: static and dynamic. In static IMRT, the leaves are first moved to a position to create a desired aperture shape, and then the beam is turned on and exposed for a certain duration of time. After this the beam is turned off, the leaves are repositioned to form the next aperture shape, and the beam is exposed again while the leaves are stationary (Galvin et al. 1993; Xia and Verhey 1998). This process is repeated as necessary to build up the desired fluence profile. This process is also called step-and-shoot IMRT.

In dynamic IMRT, the leaves are moved continuously while the beam is on; thus the fluence profile is dynamically generated. In one form of dynamic IMRT, the

Decision Analytics and Optimization in Disease Prevention and Treatment, First Edition.
Edited by Nan Kong and Shengfan Zhang.
© 2018 John Wiley & Sons, Inc. Published 2018 by John Wiley & Sons, Inc.

MLC leaves are swept unidirectionally across the field (Convery and Rosenbloom 1992), which is called sliding window delivery. "Sliding window" refers to the (usually narrow) opening that "slides" across the field as the leaves move across. Converting a fluence map to a sliding window leaf trajectory that recreates that map is an efficiently solvable problem (Spirou and Chui 1994; Stein et al. 1994; Svensson et al. 1994) (indeed, it can be posed as a small linear or convex quadratic program). The unidirectional sweep idea can also be used for step-and-shoot delivery, as was proposed by Bortfeld et al. (1994).

The delivery time for an IMRT field using a unidirectional leaf sweep is the sum of the time it takes the leaves to move across the entire field plus a term that reflects how much modulation there is across the field (i.e., a quantification of how many bumps there are in the fluence map). This latter term, which is called sum-of-positive gradients (SPG), adds up for each row all of the positive jumps in the discretized fluence map across the leaf row in the direction of the leaf motion. The maximum value of this across all the leaf rows is the SPG of the field. Thus, for continuous unidirectional leaf sweep, the following equation gives the delivery time T for an IMRT field:

$$T = \frac{W_F}{v_{\max}} + \frac{\max_{\text{rows}}\left(\sum \frac{df(p)^+}{dp}\right)}{r} \tag{14.1}$$

where W_F is the field width and $v_{\max}$ is the maximum leaf speed. $\frac{df(p)}{dp}$ is the local fluence gradient (this can be from a continuously represented fluence profile $f(x)$ or, more commonly, a discrete one, in which case it is just the discrete difference between neighboring bixels). p measures the position across the leaf row, and r is the (constant) dose rate. The $(\cdot)^+$ operator is shorthand for $\max(\cdot, 0)$.

Many clinics prefer static IMRT delivery due to concerns about safety: static fields can more easily be monitored and tested. However, with modern real-time dose verification techniques (Fuangrod et al. 2013) and improved control systems, dynamic delivery is likely to gain additional traction. Dynamic delivery using the sweep technique offers the chance to deliver arbitrarily shaped fluence maps in reasonable times, whereas for step-and-shoot delivery, planners try to keep the total number of apertures low since time to move from one aperture to the next and verify the collimator leaf positions adds to the total delivery time. Since the number of apertures is kept low, there is a greater discrepancy between the desired fluence map and the fluence map that you actually achieve, a discrepancy that need not occur in dynamic (sliding window) delivery (Xia et al. 2007). Dynamic delivery (in particular, unidirectional sliding window with constant dose rate) allows for achieving exactly the desired fluence map and also permits convex optimization-based approaches to controlling the delivery time by adding fluence profile smoothing to the planning optimization problem (Alber and Nüsslin 2000; Craft et al. 2007b; Webb et al. 1998), thus allowing planners to have control between dose plan quality and delivery efficiency, which is fundamental to IMRT plan design although difficult to assess with current commercial planning systems. Sliding window delivery has also been exploited for its natural ability to compensate for organ motion during treatment (McMahon et al. 2008; Papiez and Rangaraj 2005; Xu et al. 2009). Finally, for a given fluence map, sliding window delivery with infinite leaf speed (vendors are always increasing the max leaf speed v_{max}) gives the theoretical most efficient delivery time as per Equation 14.1. For these reasons, in this chapter we cover dynamic IMRT.

14.2   TWO-STEP IMRT PLANNING

A common approximation used in IMRT optimization research is to first model the problem without explicitly including the MLC shapes. This is done by subdividing each treatment field into a discrete grid of "beamlets," which are typically $1 \times 1 \, cm^2$ or smaller. The beamlet approximation uses the concept of a dose-influence matrix D. The patient's CT scan is discretized into an even grid of volume elements, called voxels, that are on the order of $3 \times 3 \times 3 \, mm^3$. The dose-influence matrix has the dimensions of number of voxels (order of 10^6) by number of beamlets (order of 10^4). The element D_{vb} is the dose delivered to voxel v from a unit amount of beamlet b.

Using the dose-influence approximation and assuming a predecided set of beam angles (so that the D matrix is able to be computed), we have the following basic radiotherapy optimization problem:

$$\begin{aligned} \text{Minimize} \quad & g(d) \\ & Dx = d \\ & d \in C \\ & x \geq 0, \end{aligned} \tag{14.2}$$

where g is a function that judges the quality of the dose distribution d, written as a vector; x are the individual beamlet fluence values to be optimized, also concatenated into a vector; and C is a constraint set on the dose vector. Note that due to the linear mapping from x to d, provided that the function g is convex and the set C is convex, this leads to a convex optimization problem that can in theory be solved efficiently. Smoothing terms can be added as constraints or an objective function on the x vector and still keep the problem convex; see, for example, Craft et al. (2007b).

After formulation (14.2) is solved, the optimal solution x needs to be converted into a set of linear accelerator (linac) machine instructions in order to form the fluence maps with the MLCs. This step is called the leaf sequencing step or the segmentation step. The full procedure—first solving the optimization problem (14.2) and then sequencing the MLC leaves—is dubbed two-step IMRT planning.

14.3   ONE-STEP IMRT PLANNING

The issue with the two-step approach is that there is often a discrepancy between the idealized optimal fluence maps that you get from formulation (14.2) and the fluence maps you get after MLC sequencing. This has been addressed by many researchers in order to improve the two-step approach; see, for example, Jelen et al. (2005), but one-step approaches have become popular as well (called direct aperture optimization (DAO)) (Hårdemark et al. 2003; Shepard et al. 2002; Siebers et al. 2002). In these, the MLC leaf patterns are directly optimized. For step-and-shoot IMRT, this leads to a nonconvex optimization problem since the mapping between leaf position and dose to a voxel is a nonconvex function (it is sigmoidal). Nonconvex formulations—while potentially yielding good treatment plans—suffer from not being able to be solved to provable optimality: one never knows if a better solution exists when using a descent method for a problem like DAO.

For sliding window approaches, the fluence maps can be swept out exactly, although there may still be some discrepancy between the ideal fluence map and the achieved fluence map because aspects including leaf transmission, the tongue and groove effect, and MLC scatter are not taken into account in a two-step sliding window approach. This motivates a one-step method for sliding window delivery, where the unidirectionality of leaf motion is taken advantage of to keep the problem convex and MCL hardware properties are taken into account as well.

14.3.1   One-Step Sliding Window Optimization

Several effects specific to MLC delivery are absent from the initial optimization of the two-step approach. Beamlets, for example, are idealized narrow pencil-like fluences with sharp lateral falloff that cannot be realized near aperture edges. The aperture edge of most leaf designs is round to maintain relatively constant penumbra across different position offsets from the central axis of the beam. Leakage radiation through the leaves is another example. Also, beyond exponential attenuation of primary X-rays, secondary radiation scattered from the MLC itself is initially ignored. Both workflow and plan quality would benefit from inclusion of these and other effects in the initial fluence map optimization.

The continuous and unidirectional motion of sliding window delivery facilitates convex methods for modeling these effects and others. In fact the full two-step procedure can be consolidated into a single convex optimization for this technique (Papp and Unkelbach 2014). The unidirectional leaf motion across each field is critical for this to be modeled in a convex way, since with that assumption, the fluence delivered at a beamlet is proportional to the difference of the leaf passage times for the right and left leaves that expose that beamlet. Arbitrary leaf motion would necessitate much more intricate (nonconvex) modeling. Our model that we present next extends the basic method of Papp and Unkelbach (2014) (where the time a beamlet is exposed is the difference of the leaf passing times for that beamlet) by modeling leaf transmission and, to first order, leaf scatter.

While it is clear (see Spirou and Chui 1994) that intra-leaf transmission can be included in one-step convex formulations such as Papp and Unkelbach (2014), this is not so obvious for other effects such as leaf-end penumbra and first-order collimator scatter. The formulation given in the succeeding text demonstrates that these effects can in fact be modeled in a one-step convex formulation of the unidirectional sliding window problem.

We model the leaves directly (leaf modeling is almost totally absent in the plan optimization step of most two-step approaches). We begin with the observation that the dose to a voxel for a treatment field exposed for u_T monitor units (constant dose rate is assumed throughout this section, which is a good assumption for sliding window delivery (Craft et al. 2014b; Papp and Unkelbach 2014) and makes the monitor units time proportional, which allows us to use them interchangeably) is equal to the dose delivered by the open field minus any dose that is blocked by the MLC leaves. We make the assumption that the blocking of the different leaves in different positions is additive. We compute the dose to voxel v (for one IMRT field) as the total dose if the field was fully exposed (leaves retracted) and subtract off the dose that is blocked by the left and right leaves in all of the positions they occupy throughout the delivery of that field:

$$d_v = u_T R_v - \sum_{l,p} \left(B_{vlp}^L u_{lp}^L + B_{vlp}^R u_{lp}^R \right) \quad \forall v, \tag{14.3}$$

where u_T is the total MU for the entire field exposure, R_v is the dose delivered per unit MU to voxel v with an open rectangular field, B_{vlp}^L is the dose blocked per unit MU to voxel v by left (L) leaf l in position p, and u_{lp}^L is the number of MUs for which the leaf is in that position. Similarly for the right leaf R. Here note that we are representing a continuous leaf trajectory by a series of discrete points. This can be enhanced to model linear interpolation between the discrete points (Papp and Unkelbach 2014), which is how such trajectories are handled by hardware control systems, but for simplicity we leave that out.

In practice, dose computation would be performed in two steps: (i) The computation of primary fluence that is allowed through open fields as well as fluence blocked by leaves. The latter is computed as primary fluence lost in the collimating leaf minus fluence that is scattered by the leaf. Fluence that may be further scattered by other leaves (for any allowable positioning of these other leaves) is ignored (to preserve additivity), which means that we also forgo modeling the tongue and groove effect (although we still permit the modeling of the individual tongues and grooves, just not their geometric interactions). (ii) The computation of dose deposited in voxels from the fluence computed in (i), which can be handled by standard fluence map to dose conversion algorithms. This produces the B matrices in formulation (14.3). While (ii) would have to be computed per patient, (i) is performed only once for the machine and MLC being modeled, and the results are stored for future use. This computation is long—computations need to be made for every individual leaf as it takes on its various allowable positions and for a large set of jaw positions—but it is done in the initial software dose computation commissioning phase only and is fully parallelizable.

The following constraint enforces that the opposing leaves in a leaf pair l do not collide by making sure the time spent in each discretized leaf position p is such that the left leaf always trails the right leaf (in a left to right sweep):

$$\sum_{q \leq p} u_{lq}^{L} \geq \sum_{q \leq p} u_{lq}^{R} \quad \forall l, p \tag{14.4}$$

If we enforce a nonzero minimum gap between moving leaves, which is a typical machine requirement, we can modify this such that the inequality is strict:

$$\sum_{q \leq p} u_{lq}^{L} \geq \sum_{q \leq p} u_{lq}^{R} + \epsilon \quad \forall l, p \tag{14.5}$$

where ϵ is a small positive number.

We assume each leaf sweeps entirely across the field. For example, we can assume that the leaves start parked under one jaw and move all the way to the other jaw. The next constraints relate the total field time to the time for each pair to sweep across the fields:

$$\sum_{p} u_{lp}^{L} = \sum_{p} u_{lp}^{R} = u_{T} \quad \forall l \tag{14.6}$$

Finally, since leaves have a maximum velocity, they have to spend at least some amount of time at each p location along the leaf sweep trajectory. Therefore we also enforce the constraints

$$
\begin{aligned}
u_{lp}^{L} &\geq \delta \quad \forall l, p \\
u_{lp}^{R} &\geq \delta \quad \forall l, p
\end{aligned}
\tag{14.7}
$$

This modeling allows a fully convex formulation of the deliverable sliding window radiotherapy problem, where the B matrices account for some of the physics of MLC fluence creation that normally gets ignored in beamlet-based dose deposition matrix approaches:

$$
\begin{aligned}
\text{Minimize} \quad & f(d) \\
& d_{v} = u_{T} R_{v} - \sum_{l,p} \left(B_{vlp}^{L} u_{lp}^{L} + B_{vlp}^{R} u_{lp}^{R} \right) \quad \forall v \\
& \sum_{q \leq p} u_{lq}^{L} \geq \sum_{q \leq p} u_{lq}^{R} + \epsilon \quad \forall l, p \\
& \sum_{p} u_{lp}^{L} = \sum_{p} u_{lp}^{R} = uT \quad \forall l \\
& u_{lp}^{L} \geq \delta \quad \forall l, p \\
& u_{lp}^{R} \geq \delta \quad \forall l, p
\end{aligned}
\tag{14.8}
$$

This formulation is written for one field only. To extend it to multiple fields would require another index (the d_{v} equality would be a summation over fields), but we have suppressed this for readability. This formulation and extensions are currently being tested by our group.

14.4 VOLUMETRIC MODULATED ARC THERAPY

Volumetric modulated arc therapy (VMAT) is gaining in popularity as a version of IMRT that is quicker to deliver than standard IMRT. In VMAT, the beam is kept on as the gantry rotates around the patient. The literature on VMAT and IMRT comparisons generally inflates the time savings the VMAT offers. In reality, the time savings of VMAT should be just the time it takes the gantry to rotate around the patient, which is about 1 minute, since this is the "dead time" during which an IMRT treatment is not treating but the clock is running. In practice, however, individual IMRT field gantry angle verifications and step-and-shoot delivery, with significant pauses in between each aperture exposure, cause IMRT delivery times to be much more than 1 minute longer than VMAT treatment times for the same patient. Nevertheless, VMAT does offer a potential time speedup over IMRT. In addition to the treatment time consideration, there is also the potential for higher-quality treatment plans since dose can be delivered through any angles desired—there is no need to prespecify a limited number of gantry angles as is done in standard IMRT. However, the optimization problem is larger since dose-influence matrices need to be precomputed at a fine angular resolution around the patients (typically $2°$–$4°$).

In addition to the larger size of the optimization problem, VMAT is typically considered a fundamentally harder optimization problem than fixed field IMRT since leaf positions are coupled as the beam rotates around the patient. However, when viewed from the perspective of sliding window (or dynamic delivery in general) IMRT, where leaf positions are also coupled through time, the VMAT problem seems not harder. The issue is that most existing VMAT algorithms are based on step-and-shoot treatment optimization techniques (Otto 2008), where each aperture shape is independent of the previous and next aperture shape. Thus, step-and-shoot approaches, when applied to VMAT, need to be greatly modified. For example, at the most basic level, a set of step-and-shoot apertures needs to be ordered such that the time taken to transition from one to the next is minimized. In addition, if the apertures are determined independently, then presumably they will be quite distinct. Therefore, when transitioning from one to the next, much extra fluence will be delivered, thus altering the desired fluence profile. This is typically handled in a post-optimization step that further tweaks leaf positions and the dose rate. Attacking the VMAT problem therefore from first principles rather than trying to modify an unsuitable algorithm (step and shoot) is prudent.

The initial approaches to sliding window VMAT optimization involved optimizing fluence maps at about every $10°$ around the patient followed by sequencing those fluence maps. In Luan et al. (2008), each of the fluence maps is sequenced into k sliding window apertures (discrete unidirectional positions). Then, using these k apertures at each fluence map, k arcs around the patient (either full arcs or partial arcs) are defined, and during each of these k gantry sweeps, one of the apertures from each map is delivered. Graph algorithms are used to figure out the best choice for which apertures to use for each of the arcs. This method leads to prolonged delivery time since k gantry sweeps are done rather than one. To overcome this, Chen et al.

(2011) and Wang et al. (2008) enforced that each fluence map is swept out entirely across the arc sector it is assigned to (i.e., the 10°) during a single gantry sweep. Graph algorithms are again used to compute how to do this in a time efficient manner, given that the leaf ending positions from one sector become the starting positions for another sector.

A newer approach to sliding window VMAT begins with a very fine gantry spacing (2°) and optimizes fluence maps at those positions (Craft et al. 2012b; Gaddy and Papp 2016; Salari et al. 2012; Wala et al. 2012). Similar neighboring fluence maps are then successively merged. Merged maps are delivered as one fluence map, which is the sum of the two fluence maps that were merged; this decreases the total delivery time. After each merging step the plan is evaluated for dosimetric quality. Merging continues until dosimetric quality degrades too much. This plan can then be refined by local leaf refinement to compensate for both dose computation approximations and the small angle approximation, which is used implicitly (Papp and Unkelbach 2014); see Figure 14.1. Solving the VMAT problem using the sliding

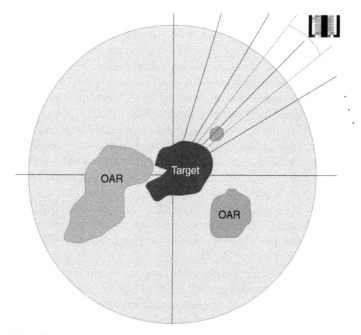

Figure 14.1   Sliding window VMAT optimization. Fluence maps are optimized at the angles represented by the solid lines around the patient. The fluence maps are delivered by sweeping them out with left to right sweeps and then right to left sweeps over the angular sectors as depicted by the dotted lines. Provided the resolution of the angular spacing is fine enough, the discrepancy between the dose delivered by the fluence map at the solid line and the dose delivered when the fluence map is swept out by a moving gantry over the angular sector shown by the dotted curve will be tolerable.

technique with formulation (14.8) would be a useful extension as well, as would exploring a hybrid approach between sliding window delivery and larger/open field delivery characteristic of non-sliding window VMAT approaches (discussed further in the succeeding text).

A full review of VMAT optimization techniques is given in Unkelbach et al. (2015).

14.5 FUTURE WORK FOR RADIOTHERAPY OPTIMIZATION

14.5.1 Custom Solver for Radiotherapy

While much work has gone on over the past 20 years to build custom solvers for IMRT (Breedveld et al. 2012; Men et al. 2009; Meng et al. 2010; Zhu and Xing 2009), the large majority of the algorithms are not designed to find a provable optimal solution to the problem. There is a need for convex formulations and accompanying solvers that are tailored to the radiotherapy problem given in formulation (14.2), particularly to handle very large-scale instances that arise in both noncoplanar beam angle optimization and VMAT, as well as intensity-modulated proton therapy (IMPT), which has more decision variables than IMRT due to multiple energy layers. It is still not clear which of gradient-based methods (Llacer et al. 2003; Spirou and Chui 1998), interior point methods (Aleman et al. 2010) including barrier methods (Alber and Reemtsen 2007), projection methods (Xiao et al. 2004), or simplex methods (Ólafsson and Wright 2006) is the best choice for solving (14.2). Robust optimization for IMPT, to deal with the uncertainties that arise from the sensitivity of the proton dose deposition to patient setup and internal geometry changes, leads to an even larger-scale optimization problem, making the choice of a good solver all the more pertinent. The CORT dataset has been released to promote testing of algorithms on a common dataset (Craft et al. 2014a), and a Matlab radiation planning research software called matRad, written in Matlab and integrating the large-scale interior point solver Ipopt, has been released (Cisternas et al. 2015).

14.5.2 Incorporating Additional Hardware Considerations into Sliding Window VMAT Planning

The treatment heads of the main linac vendors (Varian, Elekta, and Siemens) are different regarding jaw configurations and MLC leaf characteristics, and as such specialized information needs to be taken into account depending on which MLC is being modeled. The MLC unit, with the jaws, can be rotated during the treatment as well. Such collimator angle optimization has barely been considered to this point in the literature. Collimator angle choices can have a sizeable impact on delivery efficiency however due to the fact that, for example, a single bimodal field to block the patient's spine can be delivered in one shot if the collimator leaves are aligned with the spine, but if the leaves are perpendicular to the spine, the delivery takes twice as long (Chen et al. 2015).

14.5.3   Trade-Off between Delivery Time and Plan Quality

Formulation (14.8) allows for controlling total treatment MU (which is proportional to treatment time for a fixed dose rate) by putting the u_T term, the total number of MU for a field, into the objective function or as a constraint. Radiation delivery naturally involves a trade-off between plan quality and treatment delivery time: the more sculpted a dose distribution, the more time it takes to deliver it. Even though this trade-off is fundamental to day-to-day treatment planning, the trade-off is not explicitly considered in commercial planning systems. Planners end up guessing, for example, how many beams to use, and they often do not have time to explore other options.

One way to speed up a sliding window delivery is to not enforce that leaves slide all the way across the field. This idea has been explored in Chen et al. (2011), but extending this to allow for hybrid-type deliveries—for example, VMAT deliveries where open fields are used over some angular sections or close in/open out leaf motions are used to efficiently create unimodal fluence humps—has yet to be explored. This would be promising in light of Equation 14.1, which has the nontrivial first term, which is the time for the leaves to cross the entire field: if we can eliminate or reduce this term for some of the fields around the patient, we can get more efficient deliveries.

Linacs come installed with a flattening filter, upstream of the MLC, which produces a relatively flat beam fluence profile for creating uniform fields across entire targets. But such filters reduce the efficiency of the treatment machine, and with IMRT they are not needed since the MLC leaves can be used to create the desired fluence profile (Georg et al. 2011). Most clinics, for historical reasons and because they perform both IMRT and non-IMRT treatments, use the flattening filter. But from a treatment delivery efficiency standpoint, it is worth considering removing the flattening filter and doing only IMRT in a clinic. Moving to only IMRT can also be beneficial from a workflow and safety point of view since fewer systems/modalities need to be supported if all plans are IMRT. Limited segment IMRT can take the place of more traditional 3D conformal therapy (Khan and Craft 2014).

This paper has not covered the issue of noncoplanar VMAT arcs or beam angle optimization/selection for IMRT in general, but these are difficult (nonconvex) optimization problems. Although much work has been done on them (see, e.g., Bangert et al. 2013; Papp et al. 2015), none of these strategies have yet to enter mainstream clinical software.

14.5.4   What Do We Optimize?

While out of scope for the topic of this paper, it bears mentioning that exactly what should be optimized in a radiation therapy plan is not clear. The conflicting desires to get a large dose to the targets and small doses to nearby healthy organs motivates the use of multicriteria optimization methods (Craft et al. 2006, 2007a; Hong et al. 2008; Pardo-Montero and Fenwick 2010; Romeijn et al. 2004), including prioritized optimization approaches (Breedveld et al. 2007; Clark et al. 2008; Falkinger et al. 2012; Jee et al. 2007; Wilkens et al. 2007), but deciding the underlying objective functions and constraint functions to use is still problematic. One of the reasons for this is that treatment planners and physicians often care about the physical location of the dose in the organs and the targets, and they judge that by observing the dose distribution in 3D. Functions used in optimization formulations almost never account for the spatial location of the doses (e.g., this information is not in the formulations given in this paper). Even if such spatial information could be incorporated (and it could be; it is just not clear exactly how it should be), one is still left with the fundamental trade-off aspects of how to model and capture trade-offs that physicians rarely make explicitly in their prescriptions. If a disease site has eight regions of interest, there are $(8 \times 7)/2 = 28$ pairs of structures to potentially have to say something like "an $x\%$ drop in the maximum dose to organ A is worth the same as a $y\%$ drop in the mean dose to organ B," and this is already a vast simplification because x and y will themselves depend on the absolute dose levels and fractionation schemes involved. Since such detailed information cannot possibly be conveyed for every patient case, some groups have adopted a multicriteria Pareto surface approach to allow physicians and planners to interactively navigate through treatment plan space (see e.g. Craft et al. (2012a); Monz et al. (2008); Wala et al. 2013)). Nevertheless this feels like an intermediate solution, and much discussion in the field is toward more automated approaches such as Breedveld et al. (2012), but fundamental to automated planning is the question of what should the goal of radiation therapy be. The idea of "maximizing the probability of uncomplicated tumor control" was put forth over two decades ago (Ågren et al. 1990) but has not entered wide clinical usage. Additionally, this concept, called $p+$, ignores the subtleties in managing toxicity risk versus potential tumor cure: it might be worth a certain type of complication if it means a greatly improved chance of survival. It also obfuscates the idea that patients differ in their risk preferences (van Tol-Geerdink et al. 2006), some opting for more aggressive treatments and some opting for milder ones.

Shared databases that shed light on the complex relationship between radiotherapy doses and delivery timing (fractionation), concomitant therapies such as chemotherapy, patient-specific genetic profile, and health status, and patient outcomes will be a vital contribution to this (Efstathiou et al. 2013; McNutt et al. 2010; Roelofs et al. 2014; Westberg et al. 2014).

14.6 CONCLUDING THOUGHTS

Since the treatment delivery time can be handled exactly for sliding window delivery, either by using the SPG approach as in Equation 14.1 or by directly controlling the total MU parameter in formulation (14.8), sliding window IMRT optimization allows the planners to have complete control over the trade-off between dose quality and treatment time. Also, due to the convexity of the formulations, sliding window delivery allows treatment plans to be averaged in order to mix plans of different strengths and weaknesses to get the right trade-off plan, which is a very desirable property for Pareto surface navigation (Craft et al. 2014b). Sliding window delivery allows one to get plans of the highest-quality possible given the beam angles (IMRT) or gantry arc definition (VMAT) selected.

Dual arc VMAT (sending the gantry around the patient twice) is commonly done in clinical settings since it leads to higher plan quality, but in theory, one should be able to go around just one and slow the beam down (to modulate the fields) as much as necessary for a high-quality plan. Thus, the prevalence of dual arc usage must be due to the fact that either (i) commercial VMAT solvers are not doing a good enough job in their single rotation treatments or (ii) linac VMAT control systems restrict the number of control points (leaf positions, gantry angles, and monitor unit information are passed to the control system in terms of discrete data points called control points), thus restricting the amount of modulation that a single arc can provide. As clinics upgrade to new hardware and control systems, where the number of control points restriction have been greatly relaxed, we should see dual arc treatments being less common, provided the commercial VMAT optimization algorithms are good.

REFERENCES

A. Ågren, A. Brahme, and I. Turesson. Optimization of uncomplicated control for head and neck tumors. *International Journal of Radiation Oncology, Biology, Physics*, 19(4): 1077–1085, 1990.

M. Alber and F. Nüsslin. Intensity modulated photon beams subject to a minimal surface smoothing constraint. *Physics in Medicine and Biology*, 45:N49–N52, 2000.

M. Alber and R. Reemtsen. Intensity modulated radiotherapy treatment planning by use of a barrier-penalty multiplier method. *Optimisation Methods and Software*, 22(3):391–411, 2007.

D. Aleman, D. Glaser, H.E. Romeijn, and J. Dempsey. Interior point algorithms: Guaranteed optimality for fluence map optimization in IMRT. *Physics in Medicine and Biology*, 55(18):5467, 2010.

M. Bangert, P. Ziegenhein, and U. Oelfke. Comparison of beam angle selection strategies for intracranial IMRT. *Medical Physics*, 40(1):011716, 2013.

T. Bortfeld. IMRT: A review and preview. *Physics in Medicine and Biology*, 51(13):R363, 2006.

T. Bortfeld, A.L. Boyer, W. Schlegel, D.L. Kahler, and T.J. Waldron. Realization and verification of three-dimensional conformal radiotherapy with modulated fields. *International Journal of Radiation Oncology, Biology, Physics*, 30(4):899–908, 1994.

S. Breedveld, P. Storchi, P. Voet, and B. Heijmen. iCycle: Integrated, multicriterial beam angle, and profile optimization for generation of coplanar and noncoplanar IMRT plans. *Medical Physics*, 39:951, 2012.

S. Breedveld, P.R.M. Storchi, M. Keijzer, A.W. Heemink, and B.J.M. Heijmen. A novel approach to multi-criteria inverse planning for IMRT. *Physics in Medicine and Biology*, 52:6339, 2007.

D. Chen, S. Luan, and C. Wang. Coupled path planning, region optimization, and applications in intensity-modulated radiation therapy. *Algorithmica*, 60(1):152–174, 2011.

H. Chen, B. Winey, J. Daartz, K. Oh, J. Shin, and D. Gierga. Efficiency gains for spinal radiosurgery using multicriteria optimization intensity modulated radiation therapy guided volumetric modulated arc therapy planning. *Practical Radiation Oncology*, 5(1):49–55, 2015.

E. Cisternas, A. Mairani, P. Ziegenhein, O. Jäkel, and M. Bangert. matRad—A multi-modality open source 3D treatment planning toolkit. In *World Congress on Medical Physics and Biomedical Engineering, June 7–12, 2015, Toronto, Canada*, pp. 1608–1611. Cham, Switzerland: Springer, 2015.

V. Clark, Y. Chen, J. Wilkens, J. Alaly, K. Zakaryan, and J. Deasy. IMRT treatment planning for prostate cancer using prioritized prescription optimization and mean-tail-dose functions. *Linear Algebra and Its Applications*, 428(5):1345–1364, 2008.

D.J. Convery and M.E. Rosenbloom. The generation of intensity-modulated fields for conformal radiotherapy by dynamic collimation. *Physics in Medicine and Biology*, 37(6):1359–1374, 1992.

D. Craft, M. Bangert, T. Long, D. Papp, and J. Unkelbach. Shared data for intensity modulated radiation therapy (IMRT) optimization research: The CORT dataset. *GigaScience*, 3(1):1, 2014.

D. Craft, T. Halabi, H. Shih, and T. Bortfeld. Approximating convex Pareto surfaces in multi-objective radiotherapy planning. *Medical Physics*, 33(9):3399–3407, 2006.

D. Craft, T. Halabi, H. Shih, and T. Bortfeld. An approach for practical multi-objective IMRT treatment planning. *International Journal of Radiation Oncology, Biology, Physics*, 69(5):1600–1607, 2007.

D. Craft, T. Hong, H. Shih, and T. Bortfeld. Improved planning time and plan quality through multicriteria optimization for intensity-modulated radiotherapy. *International Journal of Radiation Oncology, Biology, Physics*, 82(1):e83–e90, 2012.

D. Craft, D. McQuaid, J. Wala, W. Chen, E. Salari, and T. Bortfeld. Multicriteria VMAT optimization. *Medical Physics*, 39:686, 2012.

D. Craft, D. Papp, and J. Unkelbach. Plan averaging for multicriteria navigation of sliding window IMRT and VMAT. *Medical Physics*, 41(2):021709, 2014.

D. Craft, P. Süss, and T. Bortfeld. The tradeoff between treatment plan quality and required number of monitor units in IMRT. *International Journal of Radiation Oncology, Biology, Physics*, 67(5):1596–1605, 2007.

J. Efstathiou, D. Nassif, T. McNutt, C. Bogardus, W. Bosch, J. Carlin, R. Chen, H. Chou, D. Eggert, B. Fraass, et al. Practice-based evidence to evidence-based practice: Building the national radiation oncology registry. *Journal of Oncology Practice*, 9(3):e90–e95, 2013.

M. Falkinger, S. Schell, J. Müller, and J. Wilkens. Prioritized optimization in intensity modulated proton therapy. *Zeitschrift für Medizinische Physik*, 22(1):21–28, 2012.

T. Fuangrod, H. Woodruff, E. van Uytven, B. McCurdy, Z. Kuncic, D. O'Connor, and P. Greer. A system for EPID-based real-time treatment delivery verification during dynamic IMRT treatment. *Medical Physics*, 40(9):091907, 2013.

M. Gaddy and D. Papp. Technical note: Improving the VMERGE treatment planning algorithm for rotational radiotherapy. *Medical Physics*, 43(7):4093–4097, 2016.

J. Galvin, X. Chen, and R. Smith. Combining multileaf fields to modulate fluence distributions. *International Journal of Radiation Oncology, Biology, Physics*, 27:697–705, 1993.

D. Georg, T. Knöös, and B. McClean. Current status and future perspective of flattening filter free photon beams. *Medical Physics*, 38(3):1280–1293, 2011.

B. Hårdemark, A. Liander, H. Rehbinder, and J. Löf. Direct machine parameter optimization with RayMachine® in Pinnacle3®. RaySearch White Paper. Stockholm, Sweden: RaySearch Laboratories AB, 2003.

T. Hong, D. Craft, F. Carlsson, and T. Bortfeld. Multicriteria optimization in intensity-modulated radiation therapy treatment planning for locally advanced cancer of the pancreatic head. *International Journal of Radiation Oncology, Biology, Physics*, 72(4):1208–1214, 2008.

K.W. Jee, D. McShan, and B. Fraass. Lexicographic ordering: Intuitive multicriteria optimization for IMRT. *Physics in Medicine and Biology*, 52:1845, 2007.

U. Jelen, M. Sohn, and M. Alber. A finite size pencil beam for IMRT dose optimization. *Physics in Medicine and Biology*, 50(8):1747–1766, 2005.

F. Khan and D. Craft. Three-dimensional conformal planning with low-segment multicriteria intensity modulated radiation therapy optimization. *Practical Radiation Oncology*, 5(2): e103–e111, 2014.

J. Llacer, J. Deasy, T. Bortfeld, T. Solberg, and C. Promberger. Absence of multiple local minima effects in intensity modulated optimization with dose-volume constraints. *Physics in Medicine and Biology*, 48(2):183–210, 2003.

S. Luan, C. Wang, D. Cao, D. Chen, D. Shepard, and C. Yu. Leaf-sequencing for intensity-modulated arc therapy using graph algorithms. *Medical Physics*, 35:61, 2008.

R. McMahon, R. Berbeco, S. Nishioka, M. Ishikawa, and L. Papiez. A real-time dynamic-MLC control algorithm for delivering IMRT to targets undergoing 2d rigid motion in the beams eye view. *Medical Physics*, 35(9):3875–3888, 2008.

T. McNutt, J. Wong, J. Purdy, R. Valicenti, and T. DeWeese. OncoSpace: A new paradigm for clinical research and decision support in radiation oncology. In *10th International Conference on Computers in Radiotherapy*, Amsterdam, the Netherlands, 2010.

C. Men, X. Gu, D. Choi, A. Majumdar, Z. Zheng, K. Mueller, and S. Jiang. GPU-based ultra-fast IMRT plan optimization. *Physics in Medicine and Biology*, 54(21):6565–6573, 2009.

B. Meng, L. Zhu, B. Widrow, S. Boyd, and L. Xing. A unified framework for 3D radiation therapy and IMRT planning: Plan optimization in the beamlet domain by constraining or regularizing the fluence map variations. *Physics in Medicine and Biology*, 55(22):N521, 2010.

M. Monz, K.-H. Küfer, T. Bortfeld, and C. Thieke. Pareto navigation—Algorithmic foundation of interactive multi-criteria IMRT planning. *Physics in Medicine and Biology*, 53(4): 985–998, 2008.

A. Ólafsson and S. Wright. Linear programing formulations and algorithms for radiotherapy treatment planning. *Optimization Methods and Software*, 21(2):201–231, 2006.

K. Otto. Volumetric modulated arc therapy: IMRT in a single gantry arc. *Medical Physics*, 35(1):310–317, 2008.

L. Papiez and D. Rangaraj. DMLC leaf-pair optimal control for mobile, deforming target. *Medical Physics*, 32(1):275–285, 2005.

D. Papp, T. Bortfeld, and J. Unkelbach. A modular approach to intensity-modulated arc therapy optimization with noncoplanar trajectories. *Physics in Medicine and Biology*, 60(13):5179, 2015.

D. Papp and J. Unkelbach. Direct leaf trajectory optimization for volumetric modulated arc therapy planning with sliding window delivery. *Medical Physics*, 41(1):011701, 2014.

J. Pardo-Montero and J. Fenwick. An approach to multiobjective optimization of rotational therapy. II. Pareto optimal surfaces and linear combinations of modulated blocked arcs for a prostate geometry. *Medical Physics*, 37:2606, 2010.

E. Roelofs, A. Dekker, E. Meldolesi, R. van Stiphout, V. Valentini, and P. Lambin. International data-sharing for radiotherapy research: An open-source based infrastructure for multicentric clinical data mining. *Radiotherapy and Oncology*, 110(2):370–374, 2014.

H. Romeijn, J. Dempsey, and J. Li. A unifying framework for multi-criteria fluence map optimization models. *Physics in Medicine and Biology*, 49:1991–2013, 2004.

E. Salari, J. Wala, and D. Craft. Exploring trade-offs between VMAT dose quality and delivery efficiency using a network optimization approach. *Physics in Medicine and Biology*, 57(17):5587, 2012.

D. Shepard, M. Earl, X. Li, S. Naqvi, and C. Yu. Direct aperture optimization: A turnkey solution for step-and-shoot IMRT. *Medical Physics*, 29:1007–1018, 2002.

J. Siebers, M. Lauterbach, P. Keall, and R. Mohan. Incorporating multi-leaf collimator leaf sequencing into iterative IMRT optimization. *Medical Physics*, 29(6):952–959, 2002.

S. Spirou and C. Chui. Generation of arbitrary intensity profiles by dynamic jaws or multileaf collimators. *Medical Physics*, 21(7):1031–1041, 1994.

S.V. Spirou and C.-S. Chui. A gradient inverse planning algorithm with dose-volume constraints. *Medical Physics*, 25(3):321–333, 1998.

J. Stein, T. Bortfeld, B. Dörschel, and W. Schlegel. Dynamic x-ray compensation for conformal radiotherapy by means of multi-leaf collimation. *Radiotherapy and Oncology*, 32:163–173, 1994.

R. Svensson, P. Källman, and A. Brahme. An analytical solution for the dynamic control of multileaf collimators. *Physics in Medicine and Biology*, 39:37–61, 1994.

J. Unkelbach, T. Bortfeld, D. Craft, M. Alber, M. Bangert, R. Bokrantz, D. Chen, R. Li, L. Xing, C. Men, S. Nill, D. Papp, E. Romeijn, and E. Salari. Optimization approaches to volumetric modulated arc therapy planning. *Medical Physics*, 42(3):1367–1377, 2015.

J.J. van Tol-Geerdink, P.F. Stalmeier, E.N. van Lin, E.C. Schimmel, H. Huizenga, W.A. van Daal, and J.-W. Leer. Do prostate cancer patients want to choose their own radiation treatment? *International Journal of Radiation Oncology, Biology, Physics*, 66(4):1105–1111, 2006.

J. Wala, D. Craft, J. Paly, A. Zietman, and J. Efstathiou. Maximizing dosimetric benefits of imrt in the treatment of localized prostate cancer through multicriteria optimization planning. *Medical Dosimetry*, 38(3):298–303, 2013.

J. Wala, E. Salari, W. Chen, and D. Craft. Optimal partial-arcs in VMAT treatment planning. *Physics in Medicine and Biology*, 57(18):5861, 2012.

C. Wang, S. Luan, G. Tang, D. Chen, M. Earl, and C. Yu. Arc-modulated radiation therapy (AMRT): A single-arc form of intensity-modulated arc therapy. *Physics in Medicine and Biology*, 53(22):6291–6303, 2008.

S. Webb. The physical basis of IMRT and inverse planning. *British Journal of Radiology*, 76:678–689, 2003.

S. Webb, D. Convery, and P. Evans. Inverse planning with constraints to generate smoothed intensity-modulated beams. *Physics in Medicine and Biology*, 43:2785–2794, 1998.

J. Westberg, S. Krogh, C. Brink, and I. Vogelius. A DICOM based radiotherapy plan database for research collaboration and reporting. *Journal of Physics: Conference Series*, 489: 012100, 2014.

J. Wilkens, J. Alaly, K. Zakarian, W. Thorstad, and J. Deasy. IMRT treatment planning based on prioritizing prescription goals. *Physics in Medicine and Biology*, 52(6):1675–1692, 2007.

P. Xia and L. Verhey. Multileaf collimator leaf sequencing algorithm for intensity modulated beams with multiple static segments. *Medical Physics*, 25:1424–1434, 1998.

P. Xia, J.Y. Ting, C.G. Orton. Segmental MLC is superior to dynamic MLC for IMRT delivery. *Medical Physics*, 34(7):2673–2675, 2007.

Y. Xiao, D. Michalski, Y. Censor, and J. Galvin. Inherent smoothness of intensity patterns for intensity modulated radiation therapy generated by simultaneous projection algorithms. *Physics in Medicine and Biology*, 49(14):3227, 2004.

J. Xu, N. Papanikolaou, C. Shi, and S. Jiang. Synchronized moving aperture radiation therapy (SMART): Superimposing tumor motion on IMRT MLC leaf sequences under realistic delivery conditions. *Physics in Medicine and Biology*, 54(16):4993, 2009.

L. Zhu and L. Xing. Search for IMRT inverse plans with piecewise constant fluence maps using compressed sensing techniques. *Medical Physics*, 36(5):1895, 2009.

15

MODELING THE CARDIOVASCULAR DISEASE PREVENTION–TREATMENT TRADE-OFF

GEORGE MILLER

Center for Value in Health Care, Altarum, Ann Arbor, MI, USA

15.1 INTRODUCTION

It is frequently claimed that spending on prevention in the United States accounts for only 3% of national health expenditures, representing an inappropriate emphasis on treatment over prevention. In reality, the 3% figure appears to understate prevention spending: depending on what is counted as prevention, prevention spending approaches nearly 9% of national health expenditures (Miller et al. 2011a). But is this enough? Would we as a nation be healthier if we shifted some spending from treatment of existing disease to prevention?

As has been noted by Cohen, Neumann, and Weinstein (2008), this question ignores the fact that there are opportunities to improve the health of the nation by shifting resources from less cost-effective interventions to more cost-effective ones both within and between prevention and treatment. However, our intention is to investigate conditions under which shifting spending between treatment interventions (TI) with "typical" cost-effectiveness and prevention interventions (PI) with "typical" cost-effectiveness would improve health. We make this concept more precise in what follows.

Decision Analytics and Optimization in Disease Prevention and Treatment, First Edition.
Edited by Nan Kong and Shengfan Zhang.
© 2018 John Wiley & Sons, Inc. Published 2018 by John Wiley & Sons, Inc.

To address this question, we have developed a model to estimate the cost-effectiveness of alternative spending streams for disease treatment and prevention and for research into new TI and PI. We have exercised the model to develop insights into the optimal spending mix for prevention and treatment of cardiovascular disease (CVD) and into the ways in which investments in prevention and treatment interact. We consider CVD prevention to include both primary and secondary prevention, using standard definitions (as presented, e.g., by Miller et al. (2011a)): primary prevention consists of interventions to prevent the occurrence of disease or disability, while secondary prevention consists of interventions to detect and arrest disease or disability in its early asymptomatic stages. This means, for example, that spending to control hypertension and hyperlipidemia in patients without diagnosed CVD is considered prevention, while similar spending on CVD patients is treatment.

A number of models have been developed to investigate the prevention and treatment of CVD. In a systematic review of such models, Unal, Capewell, and Critchley (2006) identify 42 models employing methods such as simulation, Markov or cell-based structures, and life table analysis. These models and other methods have been used in numerous studies of the effectiveness of alternative CVD TI and PI. For example, Maciosek et al. (2006) used the results of previous cost-effectiveness studies to prioritize clinical preventive services for a variety of diseases, including CVD. Among their conclusions was that aspirin use and smoking cessation efforts are two of the highest-priority preventive measures in terms of their cost-effectiveness and reduction of clinically preventable burden. Ford et al. (2007) used the IMPACT mortality model to identify the relative impact of alternative treatments and changes in risk factors (total cholesterol, systolic blood pressure, smoking prevalence, physical activity, body mass index, and diabetes prevalence) on the observed decline in US deaths from coronary heart disease between 1980 and 2000. They conclude that risk factor reduction accounted for approximately half of the decline, with the other half attributable to medical therapies. Unal, Critchley, and Capewell (2004) describe a similar study of the reduction in coronary heart disease in the United Kingdom. Among their conclusions is that nearly half of the observed decline in deaths could be attributed to smoking cessation. Kahn et al. (2008) conducted simulations with the Archimedes model to establish the effects of 11 preventive measures (involving aspirin administration, cholesterol reduction, blood pressure reduction, control of glucose levels in diabetics, smoking cessation, and weight reduction) on the morbidity, mortality, and costs associated with CVD.

These and other studies contribute to an improved understanding of the relative merits of currently available alternatives for treating and preventing CVD. Our work is designed to complement these contributions by investigating two areas (and their interactions) that these studies do not explicitly address: (i) the trade-offs between emphasis on treatment and on prevention of CVD in order to establish an ideal prevention–treatment mix and (ii) the effects of research into new and improved CVD PI and TI on downstream costs and effectiveness and on the ideal prevention–treatment mix. Our model was developed to generate insights to help educate the intuition of policy analysts regarding these interactions and trade-offs. It was therefore deliberately designed with a simple structure that allows interpretation and understanding of the dynamics that drive its results. Unlike the earlier models, it was not designed with the detail necessary to explore the effects of specific interventions, nor was it designed to generate precise recommendations regarding an optimal mix of prevention and treatment spending.

Some simple models have previously been developed to address the trade-offs between treatment and prevention. Our model is in this latter category of more aggregate models that provide some general insights not easily gleaned from more detailed models such as those discussed earlier. Russell (2000) describes a simple relationship to show how the cost-effectiveness of prevention changes with the introduction of a new treatment therapy. Her analysis shows that a new, more expensive, and more effective treatment can cause the cost-effectiveness of a PI to either improve or become worse, and it suggests that a highly cost-effective PI is likely to become more cost-effective when a new treatment is introduced. Homer and Hirsch (2006) develop a simple systems dynamics model of chronic disease prevention, which they use to illustrate the effects of different levels of investment in "onset prevention" versus "complications prevention." Heffley (1982) uses a simple Markov model and optimization theory to identify the optimal allocation of resources between treatment and prevention. Heffley's model is most similar to ours, but its structure differs from ours in important ways (e.g., his model allows for cures, while ours represents chronic conditions that can be controlled but not cured; his model does not capture deaths, whereas ours includes deaths from CVD and from other causes). However, his use of a Markov structure and the form of his equations representing the impact of prevention and treatment expenditures on transitions among disease states within this structure are very similar to our approach. All of these simple trade-off models were developed for illustrative purposes rather than detailed research, none of them have been used to study prevention and treatment of CVD, and none of them explicitly address the allocation of resources to research into new treatment and prevention alternatives. However, they provide a useful starting point for the research described here.

15.2 METHODS

15.2.1 Model Overview

We use a simple Markov model to represent the flow of a homogeneous population from birth to a healthy state, a single diseased state, and death (Figure 15.1). Population flows are represented with equations that relate spending on PI, TI, prevention research (PR), and treatment research (TR) to transition rates from the healthy state to the diseased state and from the diseased state to death from CVD. (Non-CVD deaths are represented with constant input mortality rates.) The impact of these equations on spending for TI and TR is illustrated in Figure 15.2. (The equations and data used to produce this graph are described in the following.) For a given research investment level, intervention spending produces diminishing returns as it

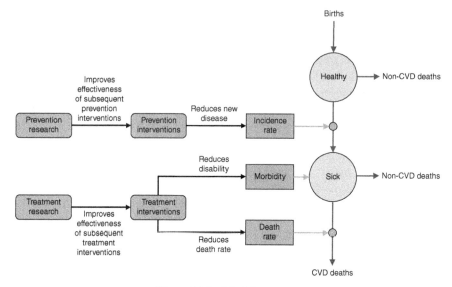

Figure 15.1   Model structure.

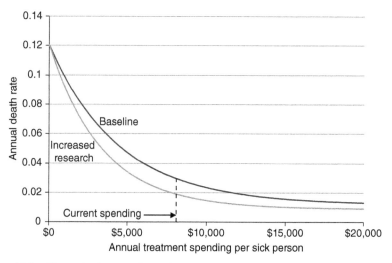

Figure 15.2   Illustrative impact of equations—death rate as a function of treatment spending.

increases, and the impact of additional spending is assessed with respect to current spending levels. Thus, a 10% increase in treatment spending from its current level will cause the death rate to decline from 0.030 to 0.027. Though not shown in the exhibit, treatment spending also affects the average morbidity level of the sick population (again, with diminishing returns), measured as the annual fraction of a quality-adjusted life year (QALY) accrued by the average sick patient (where a healthy individual accrues 1.0 QALY per year). As shown in the figure, a specific level of research spending causes the intervention spending curve to shift down and to the left (for intervention spending greater than 0). The magnitude of this shift also exhibits diminishing returns as this research spending level increases. For given investment streams, the model produces time histories of the sizes of the healthy and diseased populations, total discounted QALYs associated with the investments, total discounted expenditures associated with the investments, and the resultant cost-effectiveness of the investments (the discounted cost associated with an investment per discounted QALY saved). The next section describes the model structure, including the forms of the equations, in detail.

The model, which is implemented in an Excel spreadsheet, can be run with input investment streams or can find the optimal mix of prevention and treatment spending. In the descriptive mode, updates to the investment streams (or other inputs) result in automatic recomputation of the simulated time history of spending, annual population in the healthy and sick states, annual deaths of each type, and average morbidity of the sick population. Optimization of the spending mix begins with a fixed total amount of per capita spending per year and repeats these computations in an iterative search (using the bisection method) until the model finds the fixed annual fraction of the resultant total spending to be applied to prevention in order to maximize total discounted QALYs accrued over an input time horizon.

The model was designed with a relatively simple structure in order to promote qualitative understanding of the complex interactions of spending on prevention, treatment, and research. This simple structure does not, however, allow for accurate quantitative predictions about the magnitude of changes in morbidity and mortality associated with specific changes in the allocation of spending. Results described in Section 15.3 should be interpreted with this limitation in mind.

15.2.2 Model Structure

The generic mathematical model used in this analysis was developed for investigating the impacts of healthcare spending changes on multiple output measures related to the effects of disease. The disease of interest may be single and specific (e.g., diabetes), encompass a group of several related diseases (e.g., CVD including stroke, myocardial infarction, etc.), or may be entirely generic (as in the case of modeling all chronic disease). Examples of output measures include number of deaths per year, number of QALYs gained, and cost-effectiveness measures. The model may be used to maximize or minimize one or more output measures and, therefore, may also be used to design a spending plan that is optimal in some sense.

The model tracks an infinitely divisible population as its constituents, subpopulations (SPs) whose size need not be integer; these transition between three health states—healthy, sick, and dead—from year to year. It is deterministic in that the rates of transition are not randomly generated, but rather are precisely determined though mathematical functions taking spending and health state populations as inputs.

The model can also be considered Markovian since the state transition history of an SP is ignored; only the SP's current health state is considered in calculating transition rates to other states. Unlike many Markov processes, however, this one is not time-homogeneous: the rates assigned to various states may change over time as spending fluctuates and SPs within states grow or shrink in size. (Note that we use the short-hand terminology "rate" to mean the yearly probability of transition, not the expected number of transitions per time unit.)

Many simplifying assumptions are made in this model, not because they are necessary to make its construction possible, but because of unexpected subtleties and complexities encountered in the output analyses of even this "simple" formulation. Adding extra complexity could potentially obfuscate the roles played by the more basic elements of the model and make determining a realistic set of input data more challenging while adding little value to the analysis. Chief among these simplifications are a single sickness state, no transitions back to healthy once sick (corresponding approximately to many chronic diseases), and no explicit effects of aging (i.e., each SP has groupwise transition rates independent of its age-demographic makeup). This latter simplification should have a small effect on our results given that the age mix of each SP will likely change only modestly over time. Once the model's output is better understood, each of these simplifications could be addressed in turn to examine its contributory effects.

Both prevention and treatment of disease are considered. Prevention spending affects the rate of transition from the healthy state to the sick state, while treatment spending affects the transition rate from the sick state to the death state. Spending is further divided into two additional categories: intervention and research. Intervention directly controls transition rates, while research affects the extent to which intervention dollars have an impact.

Spending per capita is used to calculate intervention effects on transition rates and total spending for research effects. Intervention spending is transient in the sense that it must continually occur to have a continued effect, whereas research spending is cumulative over time (once research occurs, it is "remembered" from that point forward). Additionally, all four types of spending—PR, PI, TR, and TI—are subject to user-defined lags that indicate the time interval between commitment of funds and their ultimate effects on transition rates. (A lag of zero would indicate instantaneous effects.) Figure 15.1 (presented in the previous section) shows the basic flow of the model.

Clearly, the heart of the model lies in the functions that assign transition rates. Without loss of generality, we will discuss some properties of these functions by referring to the function that sets the rate of transition from healthy to sick (i.e., the sickness rate). There are several properties that one would wish to guarantee, including:

1. Monotonicity: As intervention spending per capita increases, the sickness rate should only decrease.

2. Diminishing returns: As intervention spending per capita increases, the change in sickness rate per dollar spent should lessen.

3. The sickness rate should approach a nonnegative asymptote. A strictly positive asymptote would indicate a disease that cannot be eradicated even with infinite spending, given current research levels. A disease that could be eradicated would require a zero rate at some non-infinite spending; however, for model simplicity, this is approximated by a zero asymptote.

4. Research spending should increase the purchasing power of each intervention dollar as well as decrease the asymptote mentioned earlier (while keeping it above zero). For simplicity, a single research factor (defined in the following) is used for both purposes.

A simple function that satisfies properties 1 to 3 is based on an exponential form:

$$r^s(t) = r_0^s \left[\left(1 - \frac{r_\infty^s}{r_0^s} \right) \exp\left(-b^s \, \frac{x^{PI}(t - L_{PI})}{h(t - L_{PI})} \right) + \frac{r_\infty^s}{r_0^s} \right] = r_0^s \, f^s\left(y^{PI}(t) \right)$$

where $r^s(t)$ is the sickness rate at time (year) t, r_0^s is the estimated sickness rate with no intervention spending, r_∞^s is the estimated sickness rate with infinite spending (the asymptotic rate), $x^{PI}(t - L_{PI})$ is PI spending incurred L_{PI} years before time t (the PI lag interval), $h(t - L_{PI})$ is the size of the healthy population in the year funds were committed, f^s represents the term in square brackets as a function of t, $y^{PI}(t) = x^{PI}(t - L_{PI})/h(t - L_{PI})$, and $b^s = -\left(\frac{1}{y_c^{PI}} \right) \ln\left(\frac{r_\infty^s - r_c^s}{r_\infty^s - r_0^s} \right)$ where c-subscripted parameters represent current "real-world" values. A similar function governs the death rate, with suitable modifications to superscripts (d replacing s), using the sick population in the denominator of the exponential term rather than the healthy population. For the rest of this discussion, the s superscripts will be omitted to reduce clutter, with the understanding that we are referring to the sickness rate equation.

The aforementioned defines an exponential function that passes through two particular points, namely, the sickness rate at zero spending r_0 and the rate at current spending r_c, and approaches the asymptotic rate r_∞. In a typical scenario, r_c is known and r_∞ is assigned a value derived from expert opinion. r_0 is usually unknown because it requires knowledge of the rate under no spending. However, r_0 can be estimated from either the average or the marginal cost per QALY, the latter providing information concerning the derivative of the rate function at the current spending level and thus by extension the intercept value at zero spending (one can use the "Goal Seek" functionality of Excel to determine the value of r_0 necessary to achieve known marginal costs). Thus, while this exponential form is not itself derived from empirical observation, it possesses properties that reflect real-world dynamics, and it can be fully specified by fitting its parameter values to data describing the impact of interventions on incidence or mortality rates. It is also the form previously used by Heffley (1982) to describe the impact of prevention spending on sickness rates.

To address property 4, we introduce a PR factor that will be inserted into the rate function previously given. Let g_{inc}^{PR} denote an increment value for this factor and let x_{inc}^{PR} be an accompanying spending amount. Together, these determine the effect of research spending on the value of the research factor through the relation

$$g^{PR}(t) = 1 + \left(\frac{g_{\text{inc}}^{PR}}{x_{\text{inc}}^{PR}} \right) \left(x_{\text{base}}^{PR} + \sum_{i=0}^{t} x^{PR}(i - L_{PR} - L_{PI}) \right)$$

where x_{base}^{PR} is the baseline amount of research funding assumed to have taken effect by the beginning of the modeling period (often assumed for simplicity to be zero). The interpretation of this relation is that for every x_{inc}^{PR} dollars spent on research, the factor is increased by g_{inc}^{PR} after the appropriate lag period. Note that lags for both research and intervention must be taken into account, since the effects of research spending do not manifest themselves until (i) the research lag is completed, allowing intervention money spent from that point forward to take advantage of the new technology, and (ii) the intervention spending itself takes effect, only after its own additional lag. The research factor is inserted into the rate equation thus

$$r(t) = r_0 \left[\left(1 - \frac{r_\infty / r_0}{g^{PR}(t)} \right) \exp\left(-g^{PR}(t) b y^{PI}(t) \right) + \frac{r_\infty / r_0}{g^{PR}(t)} \right]$$

$$= r_0 f\left(y^{PI}(t), x^{PR}(t - L_{PR} - L_{PI}), x^{PR}(t - 1 - L_{PR} - L_{PI}), \ldots, x^{PR} \right.$$
$$\left. (0 - L_{PR} - L_{PI}), x_{\text{base}}^{PR} \right)$$

where $g^{PR}(t)$ follows the research spending relation given earlier. Note that the requirements of property 4 are met by this formulation. Also note that the f multiplier of r_0 becomes a function of not just intervention spending at one time period but also a function of an accumulation of research spending over multiple time periods. Furthermore, increased research expenditures produce diminishing returns in their impact on the effectiveness of a fixed level of intervention spending. Cases of $t - L_{PR} - L_{PI} < 0$ may indicate a research commitment made previous to the start of the model timeframe coming to fruition or may be simply ignored or given a value of zero if dictated by the scenario under investigation. Again, a similar construction holds for the death rate formulation. Figure 15.2 (presented in the previous section) illustrates the effects of these equations.

In determining the number of QALYs generated by a spending stream, it is necessary to specify the number of QALYs each sick person generates in 1 year (a healthy person generates 1.0 QALY). It seems reasonable that as spending per sick person increases, the number of QALYs per sick person (QPS) would also increase, from some base level corresponding to no treatment at all to some upper level corresponding to unlimited spending. Furthermore, it seems plausible that the QPS value would approach this upper bound asymptotically. In addition, the QPS upper bound should be allowed to increase as TR money is spent (while never being allowed to exceed 1). To satisfy these requirements, the following function is used in the model to determine the QPS value in a given year:

$$QPS(t) = QPS_L + \left[\left(1 - \frac{(1 - QPS_U)}{g^{PR}(t)} \right) - QPS_L \right] \left(\frac{r_t^d - r_0^d}{\dfrac{r_\infty^d}{g^{PR}(t)} - r_0^d} \right)$$

where $QPS(t)$ is the QPS measure at time (year) t and QPS_L and QPS_U are the lower bound and the unadjusted upper bound, respectively.

As mentioned earlier, a useful capability of the model is to determine an optimal mix of spending between prevention and treatment. One obvious optimization goal is to maximize the number of discounted QALYs generated by a fixed spending stream. In the baseline for this study, the total amount of per capita spending is fixed at $2118 per person per year with 28% of that dedicated to prevention—the current observed real-world values for CVD spending (Miller, Hughes-Cromwick, and Roehrig 2011b). For the purposes of optimization, however, we are free to divide that amount between prevention and treatment. Each year, some proportion p of all intervention spending is allocated to PI, and $1 - p$ to TI. The value of p remains fixed from year to year, and the goal of the optimization is to find its best value. The model is able to perform an iterative search over all possible values of p to determine the QALY-maximizing optimum. Through an extension of the iterative search into a higher-dimensional search space, the model can also determine the optimal apportioning of PI, TI, PR, and TR spending.

15.2.3 Model Inputs

We have populated the model with data representing prevention and treatment of CVD (Table 15.1). Within CVD, we include coronary heart disease, stroke, heart failure, peripheral artery disease, and arterial embolisms and thromboses (ICD-10 I20-25, I50, I60-70, I73-74). Starting in the base year of 2009 (year 0 in the model), we track the US population over the age of 45 years, including annual "births" of new, healthy (i.e., free of CVD) 45-year-olds, transitions from this healthy state to sick (with CVD), and deaths from either the healthy or the sick state. Baseline incidence and death rates, per capita spending levels, parameters representing the effectiveness of spending on prevention and treatment, and time lags representing the delay between research expenditures and the time at which the results of research are realized in improved effectiveness of prevention or treatment are set to represent as closely as possible recent history in the United States. We produce model results over a 100-year horizon, and we discount future expenditures and QALYs at 3% per year.

Our methods for estimating baseline CVD spending are described by Miller, Hughes-Cromwick, and Roehrig (2011b) and Miller et al. (2012a). (Spending on prevention of CVD is considerably higher than for most conditions because it

TABLE 15.1   Baseline Parameter Values

Parameter	Value	Source
"Births"/year (age 45)	4.5 million	US Census Bureau (2008)
Initial non-CVD population (age 45+)	96.3 million	National Center for Health Statistics (2010) and US Census Bureau (2008)
Initial CVD population (age 45+)	22.7 million	Minino (2011) and US Census Bureau (2008)
CVD death rate	3.0%	Minino (2011) and US Census Bureau (2008)
Death rate from other causes for CVD population	1.8%	Minino (2011) and US Census Bureau (2008)
Death rate for non-CVD population	1.2%	Minino (2011) and US Census Bureau (2008)
CVD incidence rate with current prevention spending	2.0%	Roger et al. (2011)
Time horizon	100 years	—
Discount rate for money	3.0%	Gold et al. (1996)
Discount rate for QALYs	3.0%	Gold et al. (1996)
Prevention lag	10 years	—
Annual CVD prevention and treatment spending per capita	$2,118	Authors' analysis using methods and data from Miller, Hughes-Cromwick, and Roehrig (2011a)
Fraction of annual spending devoted to CVD prevention	28.1%	Authors' analysis using methods and data from Miller, Hughes-Cromwick, and Roehrig (2011a)
Marginal cost/QALY for current prevention spending	$16,918	Center for the Evaluation of Value and Risk in Health (2014)
Marginal cost/QALY for current treatment spending	$20,550	Center for the Evaluation of Value and Risk in Health (2014)
QALY/sick person-year (lower bound)	0.45	Dyer et al. (2010)
QALY/sick person-year (upper bound)	0.85	Dyer et al. (2010)
Impact of prevention research breakthrough[a]	100 million QALYs	—
Impact of treatment research breakthrough[a]	100 million QALYs	—
Research lag	23 years	Authors' analysis using methods and data from US Government Accountability Office (2006), Congressional Budget Office (2006), and Skinner and Staiger (2009)

[a] Several parameters combine to achieve this effect, which is applied only in model runs investigating the impacts of research.

includes significant spending on hypertension and hyperlipidemia in patients without diagnosed CVD.) Note that spending is input as an annual per capita value, so that total spending will vary with the size of the population. Prevention expenditures are assumed to take effect after a 10-year lag, representing the time between initial application of a PI and the time at which the prevented condition might have occurred in the absence of the preventive measure. A 10-year lag might correspond, for example, to the delay associated with the use of drugs to control hypertension by 50-year-olds. Because the magnitude of this lag varies by type of prevention, our analysis includes varying its value parametrically.

The effectiveness of spending on prevention and treatment is based on our analysis (Miller, Cohen, and Roehrig 2012b, Miller et al. 2012a) of CVD-specific data from the Tufts Cost-Effectiveness Analysis Registry (Center for the Evaluation of Value and Risk in Health 2014). The previous section describes our method for converting these values to parameters of the equations that describe the impact of spending on CVD sickness and death rates.

The bounds on QALYs per sick person-year, which were inferred from the work of Dyer et al. (2010), represent average morbidity levels in the presence of no treatment spending (lower bound) and unlimited spending (upper bound). These bounds were not approached in any of our model runs; in the base case described in the following, QALYs per sick person-year after 100 years was 0.75. While we recognize that some individuals in our "healthy" population will have some level of morbidity due to conditions other than CVD, we represent their average morbidity level with a QALY value of 1.0. This overstatement has little impact on our overall results, because all reported cost-effectiveness results are presented as differences from a reference case, where the result of interest is the difference in QALYs achieved between the two cases.

Although there is substantial evidence that past medical research has had a significant impact on morbidity and mortality (e.g., Congressional Budget Office 2007, Lichtenberg 2006, 2010), we could find no reliable data describing the magnitude of the relationship between research spending and subsequent effectiveness of CVD prevention and treatment. For this reason (and for other reasons briefly discussed in Section 15.4), model runs that include either PR or TR are assumed to generate 100 million additional (discounted) QALYs over a 100-year horizon. These values were selected merely to demonstrate the impact of a successful research program on the cost-effectiveness of prevention and treatment of CVD. However, our analysis suggests that they are lower than the impact of cholesterol reduction as a risk factor on CVD mortality that is reported by Ford et al. (2007), which is largely the result of the introduction of statins. They also appear to be consistent with the impact of new laboratory procedures introduced between 1990 and 1998 on subsequent life years saved (though not associated only with CVD), as reported by Lichtenberg (2006). The magnitude of the lag between initiation of an ultimately successful research program and broad clinical use of its results is discussed further in Section 15.3.8; its derivation is described by Miller et al. (2012a).

Results in the following section are produced by varying these parameter values selectively.

15.3   RESULTS

15.3.1   Base Case

Running the model with the data described in Table 15.1, but with no research spending, produces a set of baseline results with which we compare various other model runs. This model run produces the input values of 28.1% of spending allocated to prevention, a marginal treatment cost-effectiveness of $20,550 per QALY, and a marginal prevention cost-effectiveness of $16,918 per QALY. Figure 15.3 illustrates the resultant time history of the healthy, sick, and total population over the model's 100-year time horizon.

We do not expect the model, with its many simplifications, to produce highly accurate population, morbidity, and mortality forecasts: as noted earlier, the model was developed to explore the dynamics of alternative spending streams, rather than to predict the effects of this spending precisely. As shown in Figure 15.3, the model's projection of overall growth in the 45+ population is slightly higher than projections by the US Census Bureau (2008) until 2025 (corresponding to year 16 in the figure), when the two forecasts are equal. For subsequent years until 2050 (the last year of the Census forecast, which corresponds to year 41 in the figure), the model projects a slightly slower growth in the population and will be 8.7% lower than the Census projection by 2050 (170.7 million vs. 187.0 million). Among the reasons for this latter discrepancy are that our model does not represent net internal migration and uses a constant annual "birth" rate of 4.5 million 45-year-olds in order to retain our model's simplicity (this rate grows to 5.3 million in the Census projections). When we use the model to find an optimal spending mix, we distribute per capita spending (rather than total spending) between prevention and treatment. As a result, the impact of any understatement of population size on the optimal spending mix is small, though the optimal value of the objective function is understated somewhat.

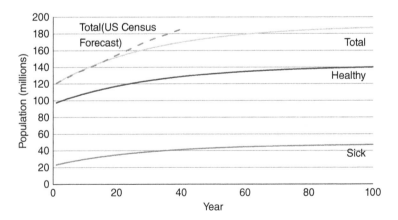

Figure 15.3   Population growth in base case.

The model forecasts a growth rate in deaths from CVD of 82% between 2010 and 2050; this compares favorably with the forecast by Foot et al. (2005) of the growth in the heart disease death rate of 83%. (However, this latter forecast excludes stroke, which is included in the model.) Heidenreich et al. (2011) forecast a growth from 2010 to 2030 in the prevalence of coronary heart disease, heart failure, and stroke of 16.6%, 25% and 24.9%, respectively. Their numbers correspond to an overall growth in prevalence of all three diseases between 16.6% and 19.1%, depending on the degree to which more than one of these conditions is present in an individual. In comparison, the model forecasts that overall CVD prevalence will grow by 25.5% over the same period. Thus, while the model does not replicate other forecasts, it is somewhat consistent with them.

15.3.2   Interaction between Prevention and Treatment Spending

To investigate the interaction between the cost-effectiveness of prevention and of treatment spending, we made a number of model runs in which we varied the treatment spending per sick person, while holding prevention spending per capita constant, and computed the marginal cost-effectiveness of prevention using the standard definition of cost-effectiveness, as described by Gold et al. (1996). By marginal cost-effectiveness, we mean the slope of the cost-effectiveness curve with respect to a change in treatment spending. We estimate this slope by adding a very small amount of annual prevention spending and computing the cost-effectiveness of this spending as $(C_1 - C_0)/(Q_1 - Q_0)$, where $C_1 - C_0$ is the small incremental change in discounted prevention spending and $Q_1 - Q_0$ is the resultant change in discounted QALYs realized over the model's 100-year time horizon. Results are summarized in Figure 15.4.

As treatment spending grows, the figure shows that the marginal cost-effectiveness of prevention first increases (becomes worse), because improved treatment results in a smaller benefit (in terms of avoiding lost QALYs) associated with prevention. However, as treatment spending becomes larger, the marginal cost-effectiveness of prevention decreases (improves) for two reasons. Firstly, diminishing returns from the higher treatment spending result in high treatment costs with little additional treatment effectiveness. Secondly, because increasing treatment expenditures causes the CVD death rate to decline, the increasing size of the sick population leads to higher total treatment spending. The improved marginal cost-effectiveness of prevention in this situation is associated with avoiding these higher treatment costs. Note that if treatment spending per sick person is held constant, increased prevention spending per capita has no effect on the marginal cost-effectiveness of treatment spending: the effects of treatment spending are not affected by prevention spending once an individual enters the sick population.

These results illustrate that the cost-effectiveness of additional spending on prevention depends on current treatment spending levels. As will be shown in Section 15.3.8, the cost-effectiveness of prevention spending also depends on treatment capabilities. These two effects complicate efforts to measure the value of prevention.

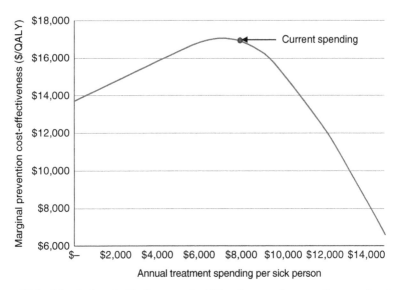

Figure 15.4 Marginal cost-effectiveness of additional prevention spending as a function of treatment spending level.

15.3.3 Impact of Discount Rate on Cost-Effectiveness

It is sometimes argued that the generally accepted practice (Gold et al. 1996) of discounting both cost and QALYs in cost-effectiveness analysis at the same discount rate tends to bias such analyses in favor of TI over prevention (Menzel 2011). This is because prevention expenditures tend to produce results after a longer time delay (and the resultant effectiveness is therefore more heavily discounted) than with treatment spending. This effect grows as the discount rate increases. However, recent discount rate guidelines from the federal government recommend the use of discount rates that are lower than the commonly used value of 3% (Office of Management and Budget 2011). To illustrate the effect of changing the discount rate, Figure 15.5 shows its impact on the marginal cost-effectiveness of treatment and prevention for our CVD example, in which we assume that treatment effects occur immediately after the expenditure is made, whereas the impact of prevention spending is realized after a 10-year delay.

As the exhibit shows, lowering the discount rate causes the marginal cost-effectiveness of both prevention and treatment to decrease (because either type of spending has downstream benefits that are discounted less as the discount rate decreases), but it decreases more rapidly for prevention. As a result, spending to prevent CVD appears more cost-effective than treatment only if the discount rate does not exceed roughly 4%. Future use in cost-effectiveness analyses of discount rates lower than 3% should cause PI to fare more favorably when compared with TI.

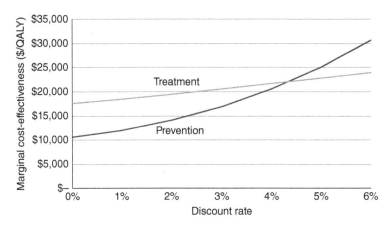

Figure 15.5 Impact of discount rate on marginal cost-effectiveness.

TABLE 15.2 Optimization of Spending Mix (Percent of Annual Expenditures to Prevention)

Variable	Value	
	Base	Optimized
Percent of expenditures to prevention	28.1%	37.7%
Healthy population at 100 years (million)	140.2	146.8
Sick population at 100 years (million)	47.2	43.8
Total population at 100 years (million)	187.4	190.7
Average QALYs/sick person at 100 years	0.75	0.74
Marginal treatment cost-effectiveness ($/QALY)	$20,550	$19,001
Marginal prevention cost-effectiveness ($/QALY)	$16,918	$18,782

15.3.4 Optimal Spending Mix

To investigate the extent to which the current mix of expenditures between prevention and treatment is appropriate from a societal perspective, we used the model to identify the percent of annual per capita spending that should be allocated to prevention to maximize the overall effectiveness of prevention and treatment expenditures. More precisely, we fixed per capita annual CVD spending on prevention and treatment combined to current levels and found the fixed percentage annual split between prevention and treatment of the resultant total funding that maximizes the total number of (discounted) QALYs realized during the model's 100-year time horizon. Results associated with this optimal allocation of expenditures are compared with base-case values in Table 15.2.

The table indicates that it would be optimal (in the sense of our computations) to increase annual spending on prevention from 28.1% to 37.7% of total spending, possibly helping to validate the concern of some that prevention is underfunded compared with treatment. (Note, however, that the limited empirical basis for some aspects of the model's equations means that this precise optimal amount should not be taken as a recommendation.) Such a shift would increase the size of the healthy population at 100 years by 6.6 million and the size of the total population by 3.3 million. The size of the sick population would decline by 3.4 million for two reasons: the increased spending on prevention would reduce the CVD incidence rate, and the diversion of expenditures from treatment to prevention would cause the CVD death rate to increase. The average morbidity level of the sick population after 100 years would be 0.74 QALYs per person-year, slightly lower than the base-case value of 0.75. Because of diminishing returns, the increased spending on prevention would cause the marginal cost-effectiveness for prevention to increase (worsen), while decreased spending on treatment would cause the marginal cost-effectiveness of treatment to decrease (improve), so that the two types of investments would have nearly equal cost-effectiveness. (Note that optimal allocation of a fixed budget between prevention and treatment would result in the marginal cost-effectiveness of prevention to exactly equal that of treatment. However, our optimization scheme allocates fixed per capita spending between prevention and treatment. Because the size of the population, and therefore the total expenditures being allocated, varies as the spending mix varies, our formulation does not produce equal marginal cost-effectiveness values at the optimal mix.)

Figure 15.6 shows how the discounted total QALYs (accrued over the model's 100-year horizon), the prevention marginal cost-effectiveness, and the treatment marginal cost-effectiveness vary as the spending mix deviates from optimal. As indicated in Table 15.2, total discounted QALYs are maximized when prevention expenditures increase from 28.1% to 37.7% of expenditures, at which point the two marginal cost-effectiveness values are nearly equal. Because of diminishing returns, the marginal cost-effectiveness of prevention increases (worsens) as the prevention share of expenditures increases, while the marginal cost-effectiveness of treatment decreases (improves).

15.3.5   Impact of Prevention Lag on Optimal Mix

Unlike treatment of existing disease, the effectiveness of prevention spending is usually realized after a significant lag following the investment in prevention. (In contrast, our analysis assumes that no lag is associated with realizing the effectiveness associated with treatment spending.) The duration of this lag depends on the nature of the preventive intervention. For example, the reduction in incidence of CVD associated with a program to discourage smoking among teenagers will occur with a much greater lag than the reduction associated with the use of statins by a population of 50-year-olds. The impact of the duration of this lag on the optimal mix of spending between treatment and prevention is shown in Figure 15.7.

With a 3% discount rate, the optimal percent of spending on prevention ranges from 50% if there is no lag to 0% as the lag approaches 35 years. For comparison,

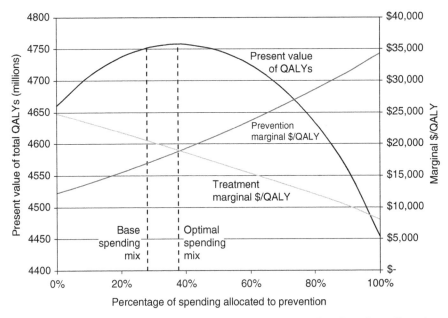

Figure 15.6 Total QALYs and marginal cost-effectiveness as a function of spending mix.

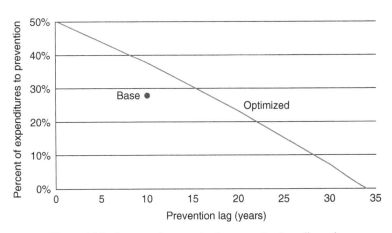

Figure 15.7 Impact of prevention lag on optimal sending mix.

our base-case (un-optimized) spending mix assumes a 10-year lag before it has an impact and allocates 28.1% of annual spending to prevention; as noted in the previous section, the optimal mix with a 10-year lag is 37.7%. It can be argued that identifying near-term benefits of prevention (such as the impact of smoking cessation on reducing the incidence of low birth weight in addition to its longer-term

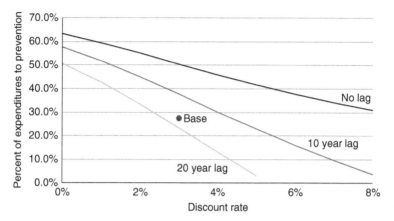

Figure 15.8   Impact of discount rate on optimal spending mix for alternative prevention lags.

benefits in reducing CVD and other conditions) will help reinforce prevention's value. This analysis illustrates a reason for this argument.

15.3.6   Impact of Discount Rate on Optimal Mix

For reasons noted earlier, the impact of the prevention lag depends on the rate used to discount future costs and effectiveness. Figure 15.8 illustrates the extent of this impact. The figure indicates the optimal mix of spending between prevention and treatment as a function of the discount rate for three alternative lags in the time until prevention expenditures have an impact. In general, the optimal percent of spending allocated to prevention declines as either the discount rate or the lag increases (although, as noted earlier, the precise magnitude of this effect might differ somewhat from that predicted by the model). Thus, the relative value of PI with near-term benefits (discussed in the previous section) declines with a reduction in the discount rate.

15.3.7   Impact of Time Horizon on Optimal Mix

A significant issue in cost-effectiveness analysis involves establishing the time horizon over which a new intervention is assumed to have an impact (sometimes referred to as the analytic horizon). On the one hand, a long time horizon ignores the possibility that future technology will make current interventions obsolete or that future population changes will make projections of the costs and benefits of current interventions inaccurate. On the other hand, a short horizon neglects downstream costs and benefits that will accrue from near-term application of a currently available intervention. For example, the Congressional Budget Office's current cost projection

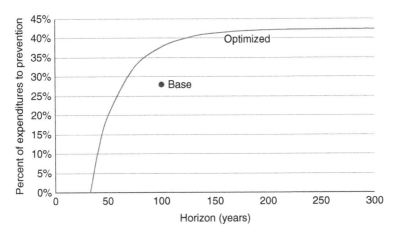

Figure 15.9 Impact of time horizon on optimal spending mix.

methods have been criticized for their mandated use of a 10-year horizon, which captures near-term intervention costs but not their effects on long-term costs (Huang et al. 2009). Figure 15.9 indicates the effect of the time horizon on the optimal allocation of spending to prevention for our scenario and illustrates that adoption of a relatively short horizon tends to favor treatment over prevention, largely because of the time lag before which prevention expenditures become effective.

15.3.8 Impacts of Research

A research breakthrough in either prevention or treatment can have an impact on the cost-effectiveness of additional expenditures in either type of intervention and can change the optimal mix of spending between the two. To investigate this impact, we hypothesize a successful prevention (or treatment) research program that begins at the start of our model run. Based on our analysis of data in the literature (US Government Accountability Office 2006, Congressional Budget Office 2006, Skinner and Staiger 2009), we assume that it will take 23 years for newly initiated research to become active in clinical use. This includes a 5-year preclinical phase, a 7-year clinical phase, a 2-year licensing phase, and 9 years for diffusion of the new intervention into common practice. (In reality, of course, each of these phases has a time distribution, resulting in a random time from initiation of research until adoption of its results; for simplicity, we assume this lag has a fixed duration.) In the absence of more specific data, we assume that either type of research breakthrough generates 100 million additional discounted QALYs over our model's 100-year horizon. Table 15.3 presents the results of this exercise both for our current (un-optimized) spending pattern and for the optimal allocation of spending between treatment and prevention. Note that these results exclude any expenditure to fund the research itself.

TABLE 15.3 Impacts of Research Spending

Variable	Not Optimized			Optimized		
	Base	Treatment Research	Prevention Research	Base	Treatment Research	Prevention Research
Percent of expenditures to prevention	28.1%	28.1%	28.1%	37.7%	30.7%	47.0%
Healthy population at 100 years (millions)	140.2	141.0	163.9	146.8	142.8	184.8
Sick population at 100 years (millions)	47.2	54.8	43.8	43.8	53.7	35.4
Total population at 100 years (millions)	187.4	195.7	207.6	190.7	196.5	220.2
Marginal treatment cost-effectiveness ($/QALY)	$20,550	$18,820	$21,442	$19,001	$18,433	$18,584
Marginal prevention cost-effectiveness ($/QALY)	$16,918	$17,758	$13,683	$18,782	$18,254	$18,348

Before optimization (where 28.1% of expenditures are allocated to prevention each year), TR causes both the healthy and the sick populations to increase over the base case, resulting in 4.4% growth of the total population at year 100. Growth in the sick population results from the reduced CVD death rate caused by the TR; the small growth in the healthy population results from the increase in per capita prevention expenditures (and resultant decrease in the sickness rate) associated with the additional total expenditures generated by the larger overall population. (Recall that annual per capita expenditures for the entire population—both healthy and sick—are fixed in the model.) The marginal cost-effectiveness of treatment improves (a direct effect of the TR effort), while the marginal cost-effectiveness of prevention becomes somewhat worse. This latter effect is similar to that observed in Section 15.3.2 and illustrates that the cost-effectiveness of additional spending on prevention depends on current capabilities to treat. Because these capabilities change over time, decision makers should be aware that published estimates of the cost-effectiveness of a PI do not necessarily reflect the intervention's future value.

Before optimization, PR also causes the healthy population to increase and the sick population to decline (both primarily because of a reduction in the sickness rate caused by the research), resulting in a net 10.8% increase in the total population at year 100. The marginal cost-effectiveness of prevention improves (primarily a direct effect of the PR breakthrough), while the marginal cost-effectiveness of treatment worsens (because the larger total population and smaller sick population result in increased per capita spending on the sick population, producing diminishing returns).

Thus, while our two research examples produce the same overall effectiveness (as measured in additional QALYs achieved), they have substantially different impacts on the healthy and sick populations: each class of research causes the size of the target population (healthy or sick) and the total population to increase, but PR has the advantage of causing the sick population to decline, while TR decreases the severity of the illness for a larger sick population.

Maximizing total QALYs is achieved at a lower allocation of resources to prevention in the presence of TR (30.7% rather than 37.7%) and at a higher allocation to prevention in the presence of PR (47.0%). With TR, the shift to more treatment spending in the presence of greater treatment effectiveness causes a decline in the size of the healthy population at 100 years, but the size of the sick population grows significantly (by 22.6%) because treatment spending is both higher and more effective at reducing the CVD death rate. With PR, the greater effectiveness and magnitude of prevention spending causes a 25.9% increase in the healthy population, a drop in the sick population, and a net increase in the total population of 15.5%. As with our earlier optimization runs, optimization in the presence of either type of research causes the marginal cost-effectiveness of treatment and of prevention to approach each other in value.

It is interesting to compare the population trajectories over time for these cases. Figure 15.10 shows the time history for the total population for the non-optimized research runs. (The curves have very similar shapes for the optimized runs.)

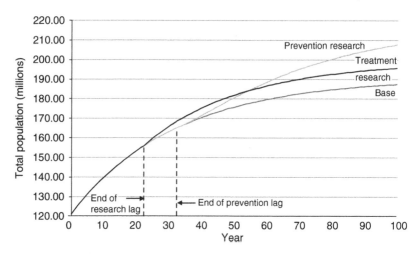

Figure 15.10   Impact of research spending on population (not optimized).

Note that all three runs produce identical populations until the end of the 23-year research lag, after which the TR case begins to show an increase in the population. After the additional 10-year prevention lag, the PR case begins to diverge from the base case, with its population eventually exceeding that of the treatment case. These time trajectories illustrate the importance of considering time delays in assessing the impact of research expenditures, especially for PR, with its typical additional delay after the results of research have begun to be used.

15.4   DISCUSSION

Our model of the impacts of CVD prevention and treatment spending contains many simplifications: homogeneous healthy and sick populations, a constant annual "birth" rate, no explicit representation of aging, generic treatment of multiple CVD as a single condition, no distinction among specific PI or TI, deterministic treatment of lags, and no growth of per capita spending over time (which is inconsistent with historical CVD spending (Miller, Hughes-Cromwick, and Roehrig 2011b)). The model shows the directions of various effects that result primarily from diminishing returns assumptions. We are comfortable with these assumptions and therefore are comfortable with the directions of the effects. However, we did not conduct empirical research into the rates at which returns diminish, so the sizes of these effects are not empirically based.

Although our model incorporates the impact of research spending on the effectiveness of subsequent spending on prevention and treatment, lack of data describing such impact, as well as other technical issues, precluded including this impact in our analysis. (Instead, we hypothesized a research breakthrough of a specific magnitude and explored its effects.) Among the other technical issues is the need to characterize research spending over time in a way that appropriately captures its downstream effects. Another technical issue relates to the model's use of a fixed production function for research findings that incorporates diminishing returns. Over time, as the cumulative amount of research spending increases, this function specifies that returns to an additional dollar of research decrease. Using this function, we discovered that it is optimal to front-load research spending until the value of an additional dollar falls so low that it is better used elsewhere (e.g., for direct PI or TI). Once this point has been reached, research spending essentially ceases altogether, because the value of an additional dollar of research has reached a permanent point where it is outcompeted by other uses. In order to justify the regular annual spending on research that generally occurs in practice, it is necessary to change the model. For example, one could specify that the production function for healthcare research findings is not fixed but, instead, shifts upward each year due to continued investments elsewhere in pure research. In this way, the value of an additional dollar of healthcare research spent this year will be greater than that if spent last year because it will make use of new knowledge gained from ongoing pure research. (See, e.g., the disaggregated research production function proposed by Tassey (2005).) There are other ways to modify the research production function that justify regular annual spending, but this is a very complex area, and more study is needed in order to determine the best specification for our model.

In spite of these limitations, the model produces results that are reasonably consistent with other projections of population growth and growth in CVD prevalence and death rates. At the same time, the model's simplicity supports its use in describing and understanding the complex interactions associated with alternative spending streams for prevention and treatment of CVD and the impacts of advances in research to improve the efficacy of such spending. We have found that:

- Spending on prevention and on treatment has interacting effects—the marginal cost-effectiveness of prevention spending depends on both the level and effectiveness of treatment spending.
- The optimal mix of CVD spending (i.e., the spending mix that maximizes the overall QALYs achieved) requires a shift in spending from treatment to prevention.
- The estimated cost-effectiveness and optimal mix of prevention depend significantly on assumptions used in the underlying analysis, including the discount rate used, the analysis time horizon, and the lag before preventive measures take effect.
- A research breakthrough in prevention (or treatment) causes overall effectiveness and the marginal cost-effectiveness of prevention (treatment) to improve as expected, but the marginal cost-effectiveness of treatment (prevention) tends to decline. While each class of research results in an increase in the size of the total population, PR causes the sick population to decrease, while TR decreases the severity of the illness for a larger sick population.

These results have implications for the allocation of spending between prevention and treatment of CVD, the funding of CVD research, and the methods used to assess the cost-effectiveness of specific interventions.

ACKNOWLEDGMENT

This research was supported by Award Number R21HL098874 from the National Heart, Lung, and Blood Institute (NHLBI). The content is solely the responsibility of the author and does not necessarily represent the official views of the NHLBI or the National Institutes of Health. The author would like to thank co-investigators Matthew Daly and Charles Roehrig of Altarum for their substantial contributions to this research.

REFERENCES

Center for the Evaluation of Value and Risk in Health, Institute for Clinical Research and Health Policy Studies, Tufts Medical Center. 2014. Cost-Effectiveness Analysis Registry. http://www.cearegistry.org. Accessed August 3, 2014.

Cohen, J., P. Neumann, M. Weinstein. 2008. Does preventive care save money? Health economics and the presidential candidates. *The New England Journal of Medicine* 358, 661–663.

Congressional Budget Office. 2006. Research and Development in the Pharmaceutical Industry. October. United States Congress. CBO, Washington, DC.

Congressional Budget Office. 2007. Federal Support for Research and Development. June. CBO, Washington, DC.

Dyer, M.T.D., K.A. Goldsmith, L.S. Sharples, M.J. Buxton. 2010. A review of health utilities using the EQ-5D in studies of cardiovascular disease. *Health and Quality of Life Outcomes* 8, 13.

Foot, D.K., R.P. Lewis, T.A. Pearson, G.A. Beller. 2005. Demographics and cardiology, 1950–2050. *Journal of the American College of Cardiology* 35, 1067–1081.

Ford, E.S., U.A. Ajani, J.B. Croft, J.A. Critchley, D.R. Labarthe, T.E. Kottke, W.H. Giles, S. Capewell. 2007. Explaining the decrease in US deaths from coronary disease, 1980–2000. *The New England Journal of Medicine* 356, 2388–2398.

Gold, M., L. Russell, J. Siegel, M. Weinstein. 1996. *Cost-Effectiveness in Health and Medicine*. Oxford University Press, New York.

Heffley, D.R. 1982. Allocating health expenditures to treatment and prevention. *Journal of Health Economics* 1, 265–290.

Heidenreich, P.A., J.G. Trogdon, O.A. Khavjou, J. Butler, K. Dracup, M.D. Ezekowitz, E.A. Finkelstein, Y. Hong, S.C. Johnston, A. Khera, D.M. Lloyd-Jones, S.A. Nelson, G. Nichol, D. Orenstein, P.W.F. Wilson, Y.J. Woo. 2011. Forecasting the future of cardiovascular disease in the United States: A policy statement from the American Heart Association. *Circulation* 123, 933–944.

Homer, J.B., G.B. Hirsch. 2006. System dynamics modeling for public health: Background and opportunities. *American Journal of Public Health* 96, 452–458.

Huang, E.S., A. Basu, M.J. O'Grady, J.C. Capretta. 2009. Using clinical information to project federal health care spending. *Health Affairs* 28, w978–w990.

Kahn, R., R.M. Robertson, R. Smith, D. Eddy. 2008. The impact of prevention on reducing the burden of cardiovascular disease. *Circulation* 118, 576–585.

Lichtenberg, F. 2006. The Impact of New Laboratory Procedures and Other Medical Innovations on the Health of Americans, 1990–2003: Evidence from Longitudinal, Disease-Level Data. Working Paper No. 12120, March. National Bureau of Economic Research, Cambridge, MA.

Lichtenberg, F. 2010. Has Medical Innovation Reduced Cancer Mortality? Working Paper No. 15880, April. National Bureau of Economic Research, Cambridge, MA.

Maciosek, M.V., A.B. Coffield, N.M. Edwards, T.J. Flottemesch, M.J. Goodman, L.I. Solberg. 2006. Priorities among effective clinical preventive services: Results of a systematic review and analysis. *American Journal of Preventive Medicine* 31, 52–61.

Menzel, P.T. 2011. Should the value of future health benefits be time-discounted? In: H.S. Faust, P.T. Menzel (eds), *Prevention vs. Treatment: What's the Right Balance?* Oxford University Press, New York, pp. 245–276.

Miller, G., P. Hughes-Cromwick, C. Roehrig. 2011a. National spending on cardiovascular disease, 1996–2008. *Journal of the American College of Cardiology* 58, 2017–2019.

Miller, G., C. Roehrig, P. Hughes-Cromwick, P.A. Turner. 2011b. What is currently spent on prevention as compared to treatment? In: H.S. Faust, P.T. Menzel (eds), *Prevention vs. Treatment: What's the Right Balance?* Oxford University Press, New York, pp. 37–55.

Miller, G., J. Cohen, C. Roehrig. 2012a. Cost-effectiveness of cardiovascular disease spending. *Journal of the American College of Cardiology* 60, 2123–2124.

Miller, G., C. Roehrig, M. Daly, P. Hughes-Cromwick, A. Turner. 2012b. Systems Science Methods for Addressing the Cardiovascular Disease Prevention–Treatment Tradeoff. Final report of grant number 1R21HL098874-01. National Heart, Lung, and Blood Institute, Bethesda, MD. Altarum (available from author).

Minino, A.M. 2011. Death in the United States, 2009. NCHS Data Brief No. 64, July. National Center for Health Statistics, Bethesda, MD.

National Center for Health Statistics. 2010. Summary Health Statistics for US Adults: National Health Interview Survey, 2009. Vital and Health Statistics, Series 10, Number 249, December. US Department of Health and Human Services, Hyattsville, MD.

Office of Management and Budget. 2011. Discount Rates for Cost-Effectiveness, Lease Purchase, and Related Analyses. OMB Circular No. A-94, Appendix C, December. Executive Office of the President of the United States, Washington, DC.

Roger, V.L., A.S. Go, D.M. Lloyd-Jones, R.J. Adams, J.D. Berry, T.M. Brown, M.R. Carnethon, S. Dai, G. de Simone, E.S. Ford, C.S. Fox, H.J. Fullerton, C. Gillespie, K.J. Greenlund, S.M. Hailpern, J.A. Heit, P.M. Ho, V.J. Howard, B.M. Kissela, S.J. Kittner, D.T. Lackland, J.H. Lichtman, L.D. Lisabeth, D.M. Makuc, G.M. Marcus, A. Marelli, D.B. Matchar, M.M. McDermott, J.B. Meigs, C.S. Moy, D. Mozaffarian, M.E. Mussolino, G. Nichol, N.P. Paynter, W.D. Rosamond, P.D. Sorlie, R.S. Stafford, T.N. Turan, M.B. Turner, N.D. Wong, J. Wylie-Rosett. 2011. Heart disease and stroke statistics—2011 update: A report from the American Heart Association. *Circulation* 123, e18–e209.

Russell, L.B. 2000. How treatment advances affect prevention's cost-effectiveness: Implications for the funding of medical research. *Medical Decision Making* 20, 352–354.

Skinner, J., D. Staiger. 2009. Technology Diffusion and Productivity Growth in Health Care. Working Paper No. 14865, April. National Bureau of Economic Research, Cambridge, MA.

Tassey, G. 2005. The disaggregated technology production function: A new model of university and corporate research. *Research Policy* 34, 287–303.

Unal, B., J.A. Critchley, S. Capewell. 2004. Explaining the decline in coronary heart disease mortality in England and Wales between 1981 and 2000. *Circulation* 109, 1101–1107.

Unal, B., S. Capewell, J.A. Critchley. 2006. Coronary heart disease policy models: A systematic review. *BMC Public Health* 6, 213.

US Census Bureau, Population Division. 2008. US Population Projections. https://www.census.gov/data/tables/2008/demo/popproj/2008-summary-tables.html. Accessed August 31, 2017.

US Government Accountability Office. 2006. New Drug Development: Science, Business, Regulatory, and Intellectual Property Issues Cited as Hampering Drug Development Efforts. GAO-07-49, November. GAO, Washington, DC.

16

TREATMENT OPTIMIZATION FOR PATIENTS WITH TYPE 2 DIABETES

JENNIFER MASON LOBO

Department of Public Health Sciences, University of Virginia, Charlottesville, VA, USA

16.1 INTRODUCTION

Diabetes is a chronic disease that affects over 29 million people in the United States (CDC 2014). The majority of these patients have type 2 diabetes. Risk factors for developing type 2 diabetes include being overweight, inactivity, family history of diabetes, and being 45 years old or older. Patients with type 2 diabetes are unable to effectively use insulin, a hormone produced by the pancreas that allows glucose to enter cells and be used for energy. When glucose builds up in the blood, there is an increased risk of stroke, coronary heart disease (CHD) events (e.g., heart attack), blindness, kidney damage, and nerve damage. Among adults with diagnosed diabetes, 71% have high blood pressure or use blood pressure medication, and 65% have high cholesterol or use cholesterol medication (CDC 2014). Adults with diabetes are also at a greater risk of death compared with adults without diabetes, mainly due to increased rates of stroke and CHD events, including heart attacks (CDC 2014). Blood pressure and cholesterol medications can be used to reduce a patient's risk for these adverse health events.

Patients with chronic diseases often take multiple medications to manage their conditions. Multiple medication use, also referred to as polypharmacy or

Decision Analytics and Optimization in Disease Prevention and Treatment, First Edition.
Edited by Nan Kong and Shengfan Zhang.
© 2018 John Wiley & Sons, Inc. Published 2018 by John Wiley & Sons, Inc.

hyperpharmacotherapy, is common for diabetes patients in particular, given that these patients typically take medications to manage blood glucose, blood pressure, and cholesterol. The US guidelines for managing blood pressure and cholesterol can result in six or more medications being initiated over a patient's lifetime to manage these two risk factors alone (Antonopoulos 2002; Chobanian et al. 2003). Forty percent of diabetes patients have at least three comorbid conditions that are often also managed through the use of medications (Piette and Kerr 2006). While medications help a patient manage his or her disease, multiple medication use can put a patient at risk for adverse effects, drug–drug interactions, and drug–disease interactions (Hilmer and Gnjidic 2009). Along with these potential side effects of treatment, patients may incur excessive costs or the burden of managing treatment regimens that goes along with taking multiple medications. For example, polypharmacy is a risk factor for poor adherence to medication (Richter et al. 2003). The burden of taking multiple medications is particularly high for patients with chronic conditions since often the clinical intent is to continue taking medications throughout a patient's lifetime (Chobanian et al. 2003; Snow et al. 2004; Vijan and Hayward 2004).

In this chapter we describe a Markov decision process (MDP) model to optimize the order and timing of blood pressure and cholesterol medications for patients with type 2 diabetes. We include constraints on the action space to reduce the total number of medications initiated over a patient's lifetime, thus reducing polypharmacy. Outcomes of interest include effects on quality of life from medication use, stroke, and CHD events and overall costs of medication and treatment of events. Through this work we will answer the following research questions: What are the quality of life and cost effects of limiting the total number of blood pressure and cholesterol medications a patient can take over his or her lifetime? While taking fewer medications reduces the cost of medication, what effect does this have on the expected cost of treating events? We will investigate optimal treatment plans where the number of total blood pressure and cholesterol medications a patient can initiate is constrained by a *medication budget*, the maximum number of medications a patient is allowed to initiate over his or her life.

The remainder of this chapter is outlined as follows: In Section 16.2 we present a brief literature review of related optimal treatment models for patients with type 2 diabetes. In Section 16.3 we present the MDP model formulation. In Section 16.4 we present the results of the numerical experiments. Finally, in Section 16.5 we present conclusions and potential future directions for the model.

16.2   LITERATURE REVIEW

Several models have been developed to evaluate and optimize treatment decisions for patients with diabetes. Denton et al. (2009) developed a nonstationary MDP model to determine the optimal start time of statins, a commonly used cholesterol-lowering medication, for patients with type 2 diabetes. The authors explored the use of three different cardiovascular risk models to estimate the annual risk of stroke and CHD events. The objective was to maximize the monetary rewards multiplied by quality-adjusted life years (QALYs) minus costs of treatment over the patient's lifetime. A QALY is a number between 0 and 1 for 1 year of life where 1 equates to a year of perfectly healthy life and reductions from 1 represent reductions in quality of life due to factors such as medication use and adverse health events. While it is difficult to estimate QALY values, several methods have been developed to elicit QALY values from patients, including time trade-off (Attema et al. 2013) and standard gamble (van Osch and Stiggelbout 2008). Denton et al. (2009) found that it was optimal for patients to start statins as early as age 40, though the optimal timing of statin therapy was dependent not only on the risk model used but also on patient factors including age and gender. In related work, Kurt et al. (2011) formulated an infinite-horizon MDP to determine the optimal start time of statins with an objective to maximize QALYs before a patient's first major diabetes complication or death. The authors proved structural properties for the model including the sufficient conditions for an optimal control-limit policy with respect to a patient's cholesterol level (ratio of total cholesterol (TC) to high-density lipoprotein (HDL)) and age. The numerical study highlighted the importance of individualizing treatment guidelines based on cholesterol values, patient preferences, and response to statins.

Mason et al. (2012) extended the work of Denton et al. (2009) by determining the optimal time to initiate statins while also considering a patient's adherence to the treatment, as this was not explicitly considered by Denton et al. (2009). Four adherence states were defined to describe the percentage of days covered (PDC) (Bryson et al. 2007) by medication over a year (nonadherent, $PDC \leq 10\%$; low adherence, $10\% < PDC \leq 40\%$; medium adherence, $40\% < PDC \leq 80\%$; high adherence, $PDC > 80\%$). A Markov model was developed to describe the adherence behavior and the corresponding effect on cholesterol levels. While 49% of patients were highly adherent ($PDC > 80\%$) in the first year after initiating statins, this percentage decreased to 27% after 10 years. In addition, over 45% of patients were nonadherent to therapy ($PDC \leq 10\%$) in the long term (20 years after initiation). Mason et al. (2012) found that it was optimal to delay initiation of statins given less than perfect adherence to treatment, although improving adherence to statins would provide a greater increase in QALYs. Mason et al. (2014) also extended the work of Denton et al. (2009) by developing an MDP model to optimize treatment for multiple medications to treat two risk factors—blood pressure and cholesterol. Treatment decisions were optimized over a patient's lifetime by maximizing monetary rewards multiplied by QALYs minus costs for health services and medication. Optimal treatment plans were compared to US and international guidelines for managing blood pressure and cholesterol levels for patients with type 2 diabetes. Optimal treatment plans resulted in reduced costs and equal or greater life years and QALYs compared with the guidelines, primarily due to waiting longer between medication initiations than recommended by the guidelines. This work highlighted the need for coordination of treatment for risk factors that both affect a patient's risk of stroke and CHD events.

Many models have also been developed to optimize glycemic control for patients with diabetes. A non-exhaustive survey of this literature is provided. Zhang et al. (2014) developed a population-based Markov model for glycemic control for patients with type 2 diabetes. Zhang et al. (2014) provided a comparison of alternative treatment intensification strategies following first-line treatment of blood glucose with metformin with the primary prevention goal of delaying a patient's first major complication due to diabetes. Strategies were compared using outcomes including treatment costs, life years, QALYs, and mean time to insulin dependence. Zhang et al. (2014) found that the second-line therapy sulfonylurea provided comparable health outcomes with other strategies while being less costly. McEwan et al. (2015) used the Cardiff Diabetes Model, a stochastic simulation model (McEwan et al. 2006), to assess the cost-effectiveness of varying blood glucose thresholds for therapy intensification. In the model, cohorts of 1000 patients are simulated for as long as 40 years with age and clinical factors updated every 6 months. McEwan et al. (2015) found that a lower blood glucose threshold for initiation of secondary medications led to reduced time on monotherapy (an average of 1.1 years), increased lifetime cost of therapy, and reduced overall complications. Higher thresholds minimized treatment-related disutility due to delayed initiation of insulin. Basu et al. (2016) developed a microsimulation model to compare cost-effectiveness and clinical outcomes for a treat-to-target strategy for blood pressure, cholesterol, and blood glucose and a risk-based strategy for managing the risk of macrovascular and microvascular events. The model was used to guide treatment decisions for diabetes patients in low- and middle-income countries with resource constraints. Basu et al. (2016) found that the risk-based strategy was more cost-effective and would avoid 24.4–30.5% more complications than the treat-to-target strategy. When insulin was not an available treatment option, the treat-to-target strategy was preferred for preventing microvascular events. Other computer simulation models for predicting outcomes for patients with type 2 diabetes have been presented and refined through the regular Mount Hood Challenge meetings held since 2000. Palmer and the Mount Hood 5 Modeling Group (2013) describe the findings of the Fifth Mount Hood Challenge Meeting in which eight modeling groups tested the ability of their models to simulate outcomes of four clinical trials for patients with type 2 diabetes. Overall, the models were generally able to predict the relative risk of events for interventions compared with controls; however, the models did not perform as well in estimating the absolute risk of events. Palmer and the Mount Hood 5 Modeling Group (2013) describe lessons learned from the meeting, including understanding the importance of assumptions for updating patient risk factors over time and correctly matching risk factors of the trial patients.

Other MDP models have been built to optimize treatment decisions for patients with other chronic conditions. Overviews of MDP models used to optimize treatment of other conditions, including HIV, hepatitis C, and ischemic heart disease, have been presented elsewhere (Alagoz et al. 2010; Zhang et al. 2013; Ayer et al. 2014). While previous MDP models have been used to optimize treatment decisions for patients with chronic diseases, to our knowledge none of these studies have considered a limited action space to determine the effect of controlling medication use on outcomes. In light of the potential for negative effects from polypharmacy, we build on previous work by Mason et al. (2014) to study outcomes associated with reducing the total number of medications a patient initiates. The base model from Mason et al. (2014) is extended to include a medication budget, and new results are included in this chapter to analyze the incremental cost-effectiveness between policies with different medication budgets.

16.3   MODEL FORMULATION

We use an MDP to model the health status of a population of individuals from diagnosis of diabetes (with no medications) until the end of life. In the model we define patient health status (TC, HDL, and systolic blood pressure (SBP)), medication status, and the number of stroke and CHD events that have occurred. The objective of this model is to determine the optimal order and timing of blood pressure and cholesterol medications to effectively manage the risk of adverse events subject to polypharmacy constraints.

Figure 16.1 displays a simplified state transition diagram for the model. The bold arrows represent potential actions for initiating medications. As shown in the

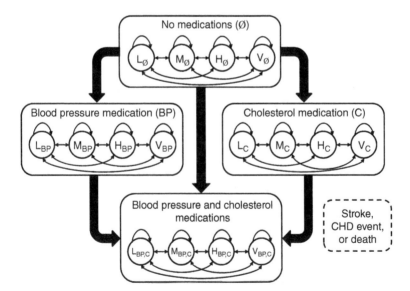

Figure 16.1   Simplified state transition diagram for the case of two medications, one blood pressure medication and one cholesterol medication. The occurrence of a stroke, a CHD event, or death can occur from any health state. When medications are initiated (actions denoted by the bold arrows), the risk factor values improve and the risk of adverse events is reduced.

diagram, treatment decisions are irreversible; once a patient initiates treatment, he or she remains on that medication. Patients may incur a stroke, CHD event, or death from other causes from any state. The health states, represented by L (low), M (medium), H (high), and V (very high), are altered once medication is initiated to reflect the improvement in the risk factor value and the reduced risk of adverse events. Regardless of the medication state, patients move stochastically among health states over time. The following subsections outline the elements of our MDP model.

16.3.1   Decision Epochs

The decision process takes place over a finite decision horizon represented by a discrete set of decision epochs indexed by $t = 1,\ldots, T$. The length of the decision epoch represents the time between doctor visits (e.g., yearly or every 6 months). Patients still alive at the end of the decision horizon do not initiate any new medications, and rewards are accrued based on their medication status at time T. The value of T is chosen to correspond to an age after which no new medications for managing blood pressure and cholesterol would be initiated.

16.3.2   States

We define a patient's health state in each decision epoch by the patient's TC, HDL, and SBP levels and history of adverse events. The metabolic states are defined by the following: $\mathcal{L}_{TC} = \{L, M, H, V\}$, $\mathcal{L}_{HDL} = \{L, M, H, V\}$, and $\mathcal{L}_{SBP} = \{L, M, H, V\}$. The threshold values used to define these states are based on clinically relevant cut points informed by treatment guidelines (Cleeman et al. 2001). The history of adverse events is defined by the current number of each type of event the patient has incurred up to a maximum of k events of each type: $\mathcal{L}_S = \{0,1,\ldots,k\}$ and $\mathcal{L}_{CHD} = \{0,1,\ldots,k\}$. The complete set of health states is given by $\mathcal{L} = \mathcal{L}_{TC} \times \mathcal{L}_{HDL} \times \mathcal{L}_{SBP} \times \mathcal{L}_S \times \mathcal{L}_{CHD}$. Elements of $\mathcal{L}$ are indexed by ℓ. The death states are represented by the following: $\mathcal{D} = \{\mathcal{D}_S, \mathcal{D}_{CHD}, \mathcal{D}_O\}$ where $\mathcal{D}_S$ represents death from a stroke, $\mathcal{D}_{CHD}$ represents death from a CHD event, and $\mathcal{D}_O$ represents death from other causes.

Medication states are denoted by $\mathcal{M} = \{\boldsymbol{m} = (m_1, m_2,\ldots,m_n) : m_i \in \{0,1\}, \forall i = 1, 2,\ldots,n\}$ where n denotes the number of medications. If medication i is not currently being taken, $m_i = 0$. If the patient is taking medication i, then $m_i = 1$ and the patient remains on that medication, that is, $m_i = 1$, for all future time periods. A proportional reduction in SBP occurs when a blood pressure medication is started. Likewise, a proportional decrease in TC and a proportional increase in HDL occur when a cholesterol medication is started. The entire state space is given by $\mathcal{L} \times \mathcal{M} \cup \mathcal{D}$, and there are a total of $4^3 \times (k+1)^2 \times 2^n + 3$ states.

16.3.3 Actions

The recurring decision at each decision epoch is to determine if it is optimal to initiate a medication (I) or to do nothing (W). The constraint on the total number of medications that might be initiated is incorporated into the action definition. Given n total potential medications and a medication budget of $\bar{n}$, where $\bar{n} \le n$, we define the set of possible actions in the following way:

$$A_{(\ell, m_i)} = \begin{cases} \{I_i, W_i\} & \text{if } m_i = 0, \\ \{W_i\} & \text{if } m_i = 1 \text{ or } \sum_{j=1}^{n} m_j = \bar{n}, \end{cases} \tag{16.1}$$

where $A_{(\ell, m)} = \left\{ A_{(\ell, m_1)} \times A_{(\ell, m_2)} \times \cdots \times A_{(\ell, m_n)} \right\}$ and action $a \in A_{(\ell, m)}$ denotes the action taken in state (ℓ, m). For a patient in state (ℓ, m) that takes action a, the subsequent medication state is given by m', where m_i' is defined as 1 for any medications i that are newly initiated by action a; the medication status remains the same for all other medications.

16.3.4 Probabilities

We include three types of probabilities in the model: probability of death from other causes, probability of fatal and nonfatal stroke and CHD events, and probabilities among health states. The nonstationary, age-dependent (i.e., epoch-dependent) probability of death from other causes is denoted by π_t^O. For patients in state (ℓ, m), a nonfatal stroke occurs with probability $\pi_t^S(\ell, m)$, a fatal stroke occurs with probability $\tilde{\pi}_t^S(\ell, m)$, a nonfatal CHD event occurs with probability $\pi_t^{CHD}(\ell, m)$, and a fatal CHD event occurs with probability $\tilde{\pi}_t^{CHD}(\ell, m)$. The event histories, ℓ_S and ℓ_{CHD}, are incremented when stroke and CHD events occur, respectively. For a patient in state (ℓ, m) during epoch t, the probability of moving into one of the death states $d \in \mathcal{D}$ at the beginning of epoch $t+1$ is denoted by $\bar{p}_t(d|\ell, m)$, where

$$\bar{p}_t(d|\ell, m) = \begin{cases} \pi_t^O & \text{if } d = \mathcal{D}_O, \\ \tilde{\pi}_t^{CHD}(\ell, m) & \text{if } d = \mathcal{D}_{CHD}, \\ \tilde{\pi}_t^S(\ell, m) & \text{if } d = \mathcal{D}_S, \end{cases} \tag{16.2}$$

for $(\ell, m) \in \mathcal{L} \times \mathcal{M}$. The death states are absorbing states: $\bar{p}_t(d|d) = 1$ for all $t \in 1, \ldots, T$.

Transitions among health states are denoted by $q_t(\ell'|\ell)$. These probabilities are independent of medication status since they are computed from the natural history model that tracks health status in the absence of medication. While the probabilities among health states are independent from the medication status, the TC, HDL, and

SBP values themselves are altered based on medication status and the associated proportional changes. In other words, the values associated with the L, M, H, and V states are shifted by medication use. These altered medication values are used in the risk equations to calculate the risk of fatal and nonfatal events. The probabilities among health states are defined by the following:

$$p_t\left(j\middle|\ell,m\right) = \left[1 - \sum_{d \in \mathcal{D}} \overline{p}_t\left(d\middle|\ell,m\right)\right] q_t\left(j\middle|\ell\right) \quad \text{for } \ell, j \in \mathcal{L}. \tag{16.3}$$

16.3.5   Rewards

We combine QALY and cost outcomes by multiplying the expected QALYs in the reward function by a willingness-to-pay (WTP) factor. This WTP factor represents the value society places on one QALY. The reward function is able to express the trade-offs of treatment by incorporating the downside of medication use through reduction in quality of life and increases in cost and the positive consequences of treatment through improvements to expected quality of life and cost from reduced risk of adverse events. The reward function is defined by the following equation:

$$r_t\left(\ell,m\right) = R\left(\ell,m\right) - \left(C^{\mathrm{S}}\left(\ell\right) + C^{\mathrm{CHD}}\left(\ell\right)\right) - \left(\mathrm{CF}^{\mathrm{S}}\left(\ell\right) + \mathrm{CF}^{\mathrm{CHD}}\left(\ell\right)\right) - C^{\mathrm{MED}}\left(m\right) - C^{\mathrm{O}}, \tag{16.4}$$

for $t = 1, \dots, T$, where $R(\ell, m) = R^{\mathrm{WTP}}(1 - d^{\mathrm{S}}(\ell))(1 - d^{\mathrm{CHD}}(\ell))(1 - d^{\mathrm{MED}}(m))$ is the monetary reward for one QALY. R^{WTP} is the WTP factor, and $d^{\mathrm{S}}(\ell)$, $d^{\mathrm{CHD}}(\ell)$, and $d^{\mathrm{MED}}(m)$ are the decrements in quality of life from stroke, CHD events, and medication use, respectively. The costs in the reward function include the cost of initial treatment for stroke ($C^{\mathrm{S}}(\ell)$) and CHD ($C^{\mathrm{CHD}}(\ell)$), the follow-up costs for stroke ($\mathrm{CF}^{\mathrm{S}}(\ell)$) and CHD ($\mathrm{CF}^{\mathrm{CHD}}(\ell)$), the medication costs ($C^{\mathrm{MED}}(m)$), and the costs of all other treatment for diabetes patients (C^{O}).

16.3.6   Value Function

The objective of the MDP is to maximize expected total rewards over a patient's lifetime. The value function that maximizes rewards in each state for $t = 1, \dots, T-1$ is defined by the following recursive equation:

$$v_t\left(\ell,m\right) = \max_{\mathbf{a} \in A_{(\ell,m)}} \left\{ r_t\left(\ell,m'(\mathbf{a})\right) + \lambda \sum_{\forall j \in \mathcal{L} \cup \mathcal{D}} p_t\left(j\middle|\ell,m'(\mathbf{a})\right) v_{t+1}\left(j,m'(\mathbf{a})\right) \right\}, \tag{16.5}$$

where j is an index over the living and death states, $m'(\mathbf{a})$ is defined as the medication state m that has been updated according to action $\mathbf{a}$ as described in Subsection 16.3.3, and $\lambda \in [0, 1)$ is the discount factor. The value function boundary condition is defined by the following:

$$v_T\left(\ell,m\right) = r_T\left(\ell,m\right) + E\left[\mathrm{Rewards}\middle|\ell,m\right], \tag{16.6}$$

where $E[\text{Rewards}|\ell, m]$ is the expected rewards accrued after the end of the decision horizon. During this period no new medications are initiated; all rewards are based on the treatment status at time T.

16.4   NUMERICAL RESULTS

In this section we present the findings from the numerical experiments. Subsection 16.4.1 provides an overview of the model development and inputs, and Subsection 16.4.2 provides a summary and discussion of the results.

16.4.1   Model Inputs

The model was developed using an observational dataset created from the Mayo Clinic Electronic Medical Records and Diabetes Electronic Management System (DEMS) from patients seen at Mayo Clinic in Rochester, MN (Gorman et al. 2000). Data elements included in the dataset include SBP, TC, HDL, HbA1c, age, gender, and medication use. This cohort of patients has been fully described previously (Mason et al. 2014).

We use yearly decision epochs with a time horizon that spans from age 40 to age 100. Patients are newly diagnosed and on no blood pressure or cholesterol medications at age 40. Transition probabilities among the health states were estimated using SBP, TC, and HDL values from the Mayo Clinic dataset. The threshold values for defining the states L, M, H, and V are the following: 120, 140, and 160 mmHg for SBP; 160, 200, and 240 mg/dL for TC; and 40, 50, and 60 mg/dL for HDL. The probabilities of fatal and nonfatal stroke and CHD events were calculated using the UK Prospective Diabetes Study (UKPDS) risk equations (Stevens et al. 2001, 2004; Kothari et al. 2002). These equations provide risk estimates for diabetes patients based on metabolic values, age, and gender. In the numerical experiments, $k = 1$. The probabilities of death from other causes were estimated from the CDC mortality tables (Xu et al. 2010).

The cost inputs are found in Table 16.1, including the WTP factor for QALYs and the discount factor for discounting costs in the value function. The utility decrements for stroke and CHD events are also found in Table 16.1, and the utility decrements and costs for the medications are provided in Table 16.2. Statins were assumed to reduce TC by 14% and increase HDL by 7.3%, while fibrates reduced TC by 3.9% and increased HDL by 4.7%; the blood pressure medications each reduced SBP by the following amounts: 3.7% reduction from ACE inhibitors/ARBs, 5% reduction from thiazides, 4.6% reduction from beta blockers, and 2.5% reduction from calcium channel blockers (Mason et al. 2014). The medication effect percentage changes are assumed to be additive for patients taking multiple medications affecting the same risk factor.

TABLE 16.1   Summary of the Cost and Utility Inputs for the Model

Parameter Type	Parameter	Value	Source
Cost inputs	Initial cost for stroke (C^S)	$13,204	AHRQ (2006)
	Initial cost for CHD (C^{CHD})	$18,590	AHRQ (2006)
	Follow-up for stroke (CF^S)	$1,664	Thom et al. (2006)
	Follow-up for CHD (CF^{CHD})	$2,576	Thom et al. (2006)
	WTP factor (R^{WTP})	$100,000	Rascati (2006)
	Discount factor (λ)	0.97	Gold et al. (1996)
Utility inputs	CHD decrement (d^{CHD})	0.07	Tsevat et al. (1993)
	Stroke decrement (d^S)	0.21	Tengs and Lin (2003)

TABLE 16.2   Summary of Medication Costs that Represent the Lower Bound on Treatment Costs in the United States (Red Book 2009) and Medication Disutility Values (Tengs and Wallace 2000; Pignone et al. 2006; Mason et al. 2014)

Medication Type	Medication	Cost ($)	Utility Decrement
Cholesterol medication	Statins	212	0.003
	Fibrates	652	0.003
Blood pressure medication	ACE inhibitors/ARBs	48	0.005
	Thiazides	48	0.005
	Beta blockers	48	0.005
	Calcium channel blockers	866	0.005

16.4.2   Optimal Treatment Policies to Reduce Polypharmacy

In this subsection we explore the trade-offs involved with reducing polypharmacy. We compare policies obtained via solving the model in Section 16.3, hereafter referred to as *optimal treatment*, to the US guidelines when restricting the number of total medications that may be used. Comparisons are made for males and females, averaged over all combinations of TC, HDL, and SBP, for $\bar{n} = 2,...,6$. To provide baseline expected QALYs and costs for patients, we also consider the case of no treatment ($\bar{n} = 0$). The case of a medication budget of one medication ($\bar{n} = 1$) is not considered since it is not clinical practice for diabetes patients to be limited to one medication to control both blood pressure and cholesterol. Under the guidelines, blood pressure treatment is initiated when SBP > 130 (Antonopoulos 2002), and cholesterol treatment is initiated when low-density lipoprotein (LDL) ≥ 100 (Chobanian et al. 2003). Consistent with these guidelines, statins were the first-line cholesterol treatment, and blood pressure medications were initiated in the following order: thiazides, ACE inhibitors/ARBs, beta blockers, and calcium channel blockers. The medication budget reduces the number of medications available to use when following the guidelines. When the guidelines called for two medications to be initiated in the same year and the medication budget only allowed for one additional medication, a cholesterol medication was chosen.

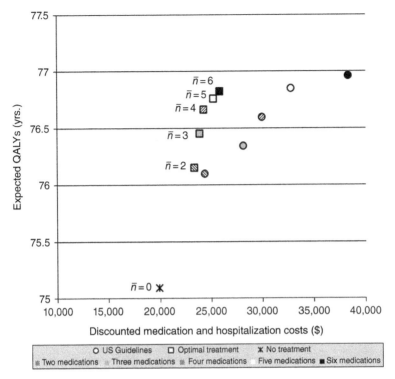

Figure 16.2 Expected QALYs and expected costs for male patients when varying treatment policies—US guidelines or optimal treatment—and the maximum number of medications a patient can initiate over his or her lifetime.

From Figure 16.2 we see that as the number of available medications increases under optimal treatment, the expected QALYs increase with minimal increase in costs. The increase in QALYs is due to the reduced occurrence of stroke and CHD events, and small decreases in quality of life due to increased medication use; the small increase in costs is due to a decrease in costs from avoided events and an increase in costs from increased medication use. When more than four medications are allowed, the marginal benefit in QALYs is decreased, and the costs increase at a higher rate compared with the previous cost increases. The final medications initiated have less effect on preventing adverse events. The US guidelines have nearly identical expected costs and QALYs when the medication budget is two ($\bar{n} = 2$). However, as more medications are allowed, the expected costs increase at a greater rate than the costs under optimal treatment. This is primarily due to the earlier timing of additional treatments under the US guidelines and the suboptimal order in which medications are initiated. The results are very similar for female patients, as shown in Figure 16.3, though there is an even greater difference in costs between optimal treatment and the US guidelines.

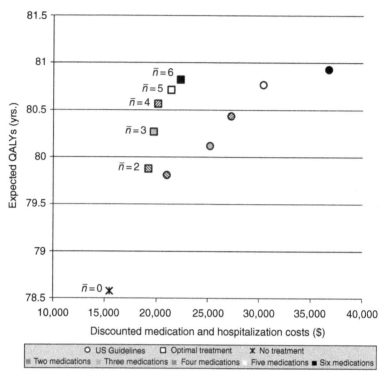

Figure 16.3 Expected QALYs and expected costs for female patients when varying treatment policies—US guidelines or optimal treatment—and the maximum number of medications a patient can initiate over his or her lifetime.

With both the male and female results, the expected QALYs are higher for the US guidelines. This is due to the WTP factor used in the reward function (Equation 16.4). The WTP factor used in the numerical experiments, $R^{WTP} = \$100,000$, is a commonly used value in the health economics literature to determine cost-effectiveness of a new healthcare intervention (Rascati 2006). Varying this value also allows for trade-off between maximizing QALYs and minimizing costs, leading to different policies for medication initiation. If we set $R^{WTP} = 0$, the objective of the value function would be to minimize costs. Alternatively, if we allow $R^{WTP} \to \infty$, the objective of the value function would be to maximize QALYs. Under this scenario the optimal treatment expected QALYs would be greater than those for the US guidelines.

While this is a population-level model, individual treatment recommendations can be gleaned from the model. The optimal order and timing of medical treatments is dependent on gender and blood pressure and cholesterol values over time. For a male patient with very high TC, low HDL, and very high SBP at age 40, one health trajectory would lead to the following optimal treatment recommendations with $\bar{n} = 6$:

begin statins at age 40, thiazides at age 46, beta blockers at age 49, ACE inhibitors/ARBs at age 53, fibrates at age 60, and calcium channel blockers at age 77. An alternative health trajectory would lead to recommendations of delayed initiation of medications. As $\bar{n}$ is reduced, the order and timing of medications remains the same with the medication budget removing the medications initiated latest in life. For female patients, the order of medication initiation is the same. Given the same TC, HDL, and SBP values as male patients, female patients will initiate treatments at the same age or older ages. For a female patient with very high TC, low HDL, and very high SBP at age 40, the same health trajectory as the example male patient would lead to the following optimal treatment recommendations with $\bar{n} = 6$: begin statins at age 40, thiazides at age 52, beta blockers at age 57, ACE inhibitors/ARBs at age 61, fibrates at age 64, and calcium channel blockers at age 80.

We calculate the incremental cost-effectiveness ratio (ICER) (Gold et al. 1996) using the following formula to compare two alternative treatments T_A and T_B:

$$\text{ICER} = \frac{\text{Cost}(T_B) - \text{Cost}(T_A)}{\text{QALY}(T_B) - \text{QALY}(T_A)} \tag{16.7}$$

This calculation computes the rate of increase in cost per additional QALY between the treatments being compared.

As shown in Tables 16.3 and 16.4, the ICERs are similar for males and females for each comparison, with females having slightly lower (more favorable) ICERs overall. For optimal treatment, the cost of increased QALYs received through additional medication use is much higher for $\bar{n} > 4$. The ICERs for $\bar{n} > 4$ are between five and seven times greater for optimal treatment than the ICER for $\bar{n} = 4$.

Comparisons of the optimal treatment ICERs with the US guideline ICERs further reveal the suboptimality of the guidelines. Under the guidelines, patients who choose to take fewer medications will pay greater amounts for increases in QALYs than patients under optimal treatment for incremental comparisons. The ICER for optimal treatment is also more favorable when considering the comparison of no medication budget restriction ($\bar{n} = 6$) relative to no medication ($\bar{n} = 0$) even though the US guidelines have greater increases in QALYs. For males, the optimal treatment ICER is

TABLE 16.3 Comparison of QALYs, Costs ($), and ICERs ($/QALY) for Male Patients

Scenario	Optimal Treatment			US Guidelines		
	QALYs	Costs ($)	ICER	QALYs	Costs ($)	ICER
$\bar{n} = 0$	75.09	19,896	—	75.09	19,896	—
$\bar{n} = 2$	76.15	23,333	3,240	76.1	24,347	4,412
$\bar{n} = 3$	76.45	23,859	1,753	76.35	28,131	15,455
$\bar{n} = 4$	76.67	24,250	1,831	76.6	29,964	7,260
$\bar{n} = 5$	76.76	25,213	10,112	76.85	32,787	11,133
$\bar{n} = 6$	76.83	25,834	9,837	76.96	38,318	49,086

TABLE 16.4   Comparison of QALYs, Costs ($), and ICERs ($/QALY) for Female Patients

Scenario	Optimal Treatment			US Guidelines		
	QALYs	Costs ($)	ICER	QALYs	Costs ($)	ICER
$\bar{n} = 0$	78.58	15,498	—	78.58	15,498	—
$\bar{n} = 2$	79.88	19,176	2,827	79.81	20,974	4,433
$\bar{n} = 3$	80.27	19,694	1,321	80.12	25,172	13,705
$\bar{n} = 4$	80.58	20,076	1,280	80.44	27,232	6,433
$\bar{n} = 5$	80.71	21,373	8,840	80.77	30,389	9,578
$\bar{n} = 6$	80.82	22,267	8,425	80.93	36,691	38,902

$3413/QALY compared with the guideline ICER of $9851/QALY. For females, the optimal treatment ICER is $3022/QALY compared with the guideline ICER of $9018/QALY.

16.5   CONCLUSIONS

The results show the cost and QALY trade-offs for patients interested in reducing polypharmacy. The ICERs are most favorable when considering medication budgets of up to four medications. Patients who are concerned about the negative effects of polypharmacy would benefit from using the optimal guidelines to inform both the order of medications and the timing of treatment initiation. The results from this model serve as an additional piece of information for diabetes patients making blood pressure and cholesterol treatment decisions in consultation with their doctors. With this additional information, patients have more confidence in treatment decisions by understanding the trade-offs that are involved.

This analysis provides a summary of the potential harms and benefits of limiting the number of medications to manage blood pressure and cholesterol for patients with type 2 diabetes. While medication disutilities and costs do capture some downsides of treatment, it is important to model the effects of reducing the total number of medications; the objective function may not sufficiently capture the negative effects of multiple medication use, including drug–drug interactions, drug–disease interactions, and complex medication regimens.

There are several natural extensions for this work. For example, future work to optimize treatment decisions for patients with type 2 diabetes could include treatment decisions for glycemic control medications or consideration of medication use for other comorbid conditions. While this work used constraints on the action space to reduce polypharmacy, another approach would be to use constrained MDPs to incorporate medication budget constraints or restrictions in the amount of disutility a patient was willing to give up for medication use. In addition, given sufficient data for model calibration, more explicit modeling of the poor effects of polypharmacy could be incorporated, including modeling the percentage of patients that stop medications due to interactions or poor adherence. Finally, while the example presented in this chapter is specific to managing blood pressure and cholesterol for patients with diabetes, the methods can be applied more generally to problems related to managing multiple risk factors for patients with chronic diseases.

REFERENCES

AHRQ. 2006. Nationwide Inpatient Sample. Tech. rep., Healthcare Cost and Utilization Project. Healthcare Research and Quality, Rockville, MD.

Alagoz, O., H. Hsu, A.J. Schaefer, M.S. Roberts. 2010. Markov decision processes: A tool for sequential decision making under uncertainty. *Medical Decision Making* 30(4): 474–483.

Antonopoulos, S. 2002. Third Report of the National Cholesterol Education Program (NCEP) Expert Panel on Detection, Evaluation, and Treatment of High Blood Cholesterol in Adults (Adult Treatment Panel III) final report. *Circulation* 106: 3143–3421.

Attema, A.E., Y. Edelaar-Peeters, M.M. Versteegh, E.A. Stolk. 2013. Time trade-off: One methodology, different methods. *The European Journal of Health Economics* 14: 53–64.

Ayer, T., P. Keskinocak, J. Swann. 2014. Research in public health for efficient, effective, and equitable outcomes. In J.C. Smith, ed., *INFORMS Tutorials in Operations Research*. INFORMS, Catonsville, MD.

Basu, S., V. Shankar, J.S. Yudkin. 2016. Comparative effectiveness and cost-effectiveness of treat-to-target versus benefit-based tailored treatment of type 2 diabetes in low-income and middle-income countries: A modelling analysis. *The Lancet Diabetes and Endocrinology* 4(11): 922–932.

Bryson, C.L., D.H. Au, B. Young, M.B. McDonell, S.D. Fihn. 2007. A refill adherence algorithm for multiple short intervals to estimate refill compliance (ReComp). *Medical Care* 45(6): 187–194.

CDC. 2014. National Diabetes Statistics Report: Estimates of Diabetes and Its Burden in the United States, 2014. Tech. rep., U.S. Department of Health and Human Services, Atlanta, GA.

Chobanian, A.V., G.L. Bakris, H.R. Black, W.C. Cushman, L.A. Green, et al. 2003. The seventh report of the Joint National Committee on prevention, detection, evaluation, and treatment of high blood pressure. *Hypertension* 42: 1206–1252.

Cleeman, J.I., S.M. Grundy, D. Becker, L.T. Clark, R.S. Cooper, M.A. Denke, W.J. Howard, D.B. Hunninghake, D.R. Illingworth, R.V. Luepker, P. McBride, J.M. McKenney, R.C. Pasternak, N.J. Stone, L. Van Horn, H.B. Brewer, N.D. Ernst, D. Gordon, D. Levy, B. Rifkind, J.E. Rossouw, P. Savage, S.M. Haffner, D.G. Orloff, M.A. Proschan, J.S. Schwartz, C.T. Sempos, S.T. Shero, E.Z. Murray. 2001. Executive summary of the Third Report of the National Cholesterol Education Program (NCEP) expert panel on detection, evaluation, and treatment of high blood cholesterol in adults (Adult Treatment Panel III). *JAMA* 285(19): 2486–2497.

Denton, B.T., M. Kurt, N.D. Shah, S.C. Bryant, S.A. Smith. 2009. Optimizing the start time of statin therapy for patients with diabetes. *Medical Decision Making* 29: 351–367.

Gold, M.R., J.E. Siegel, L.B. Russell, M.C. Weinstein, eds. 1996. *Cost-Effectiveness in Health and Medicine*. Oxford University Press, New York.

Gorman, C.A., B.R. Zimmerman, S.A. Smith, S.F. Dinneen, J.B. Knudsen, D. Holm, B. Jorgensen, S. Bjornsen, K. Planet, P. Hanson, R.A. Rizza. 2000. DEMS—A second generation diabetes electronic management system. *Computer Methods and Programs in Biomedicine* 62(2): 127–140.

Hilmer, S.N., D. Gnjidic. 2009. The effects of polypharmacy in older adults. *Clinical Pharmacology and Therapeutics* 85(1): 86–88.

Kothari, V., R.J. Stevens, A.I. Adler, I.M. Stratton, S.E. Manley, H.A. Neil, R.R. Holman. 2002. UKPDS 60—Risk of stroke in type 2 diabetes estimated by the United Kingdom Prospective Diabetes Study risk engine. *Stroke* 33(7): 1776–1781.

Kurt, M., B.T. Denton, A. Schaefer, N. Shah, S. Smith. 2011. The structure of optimal statin initiation policies for patients with type 2 diabetes. *IIE Transactions on Healthcare* 1(1): 49–65.

Mason, J.E., D.A. England, B.T. Denton, S.A. Smith, M. Kurt, N.D. Shah. 2012. Optimizing statin treatment decisions for diabetes patients in the presence of uncertain future adherence. *Medical Decision Making* 32(1): 154–166.

Mason, J.E., B.T. Denton, N.D. Shah, S.A. Smith. 2014. Optimizing the simultaneous management of blood pressure and cholesterol for type 2 diabetes patients. *European Journal of Operational Research* 233: 727–738.

McEwan, P., J.R. Peters, K. Bergenheim, C.J. Currie. 2006. Evaluation of the costs and outcomes from changes in risk factors in type 2 diabetes using the Cardiff stochastic simulation cost-utility model (DiabForecaster). *Current Medical Research and Opinion* 22(1): 121–129.

McEwan, P., J. Gordon, M. Evans, T. Ward, H. Bennett, K. Bergenheim. 2015. Estimating cost-effectiveness in type 2 diabetes: the impact of treatment guidelines and therapy duration. *Medical Decision Making* 35(5): 660–670.

van Osch, S.M.C., A.M. Stiggelbout. 2008. The construction of standard gamble utilities. *Health Economics* 17(1): 31–40.

Palmer, A.J., The Mount Hood 5 Modeling Group. 2013. Computer modeling of diabetes and its complications: A report on the Fifth Mount Hood Challenge Meeting. *Value in Health* 16(4): 670–685.

Piette, J.D., E.A. Kerr. 2006. The impact of comorbid chronic conditions on diabetes care. *Diabetes Care* 29(3): 725–731.

Pignone, M., S. Earnshaw, J.A. Tice, M.J. Pletcher. 2006. Aspirin, statins, or both drugs for the primary prevention of coronary heart disease events in men: A cost-utility analysis. *Annals of Internal Medicine* 144: 326–336.

Rascati, K.L. 2006. The $64,000 question—What is a quality-adjusted life-year worth? *Clinical Therapeutics* 28(7): 1042–1043.

Red Book. 2009. Red Book: 2009 Edition. Tech. rep., Thomson Healthcare, Inc., Montvale, NJ.

Richter, A., S.E. Anton, P. Koch, S.L. Dennett. 2003. The impact of reducing dose frequency on health outcomes. *Clinical Therapeutics* 25(8): 2307–2335.

Snow, V., M.D. Aronson, E.R. Hornbake, C. Mottur-Pilson, K.B. Weiss. 2004. Lipid control in the management of type 2 diabetes mellitus: A clinical practice guideline from the American College of Physicians. *Annals of Internal Medicine* 140(8): 644–649.

Stevens, R.J., V. Kothari, A.I. Adler, I.M. Stratton, R.R. Holman. 2001. The UKPDS risk engine: A model for the risk of coronary heart disease in type 2 diabetes (UKPDS 56). *Clinical Science* 101(6): 671–679.

Stevens, R.J., R.L. Coleman, A.I. Adler, I.M. Stratton, D.R. Matthews, R.R. Holman. 2004. Risk factors for myocardial infarction case fatality and stroke case fatality in type 2 diabetes (UKPDS 66). *Diabetes Care* 27(1): 201–207.

Tengs, T.O., T.H. Lin. 2003. A meta-analysis of quality-of-life estimates for stroke. *Pharmoeconomics* 21(3): 191–200.

Tengs, T.O., A. Wallace. 2000. One thousand health-related quality-of-life estimates. *Medical Care* 38(6): 583–637.

Thom, T., N. Haase, W. Rosamond, V.J. Howard, J. Rumsfeld, T. Manolio, Z.J. Zheng, K. Flegal, C. O'Donnell, S. Kittner, D. Lloyd-Jones, D.C. Goff, Y.L. Hong, R. Adams, G. Friday, K. Furie, P. Gorelick, B. Kissela, J. Marler, J. Meigs, V. Roger, S. Sidney, P. Sorlie, J. Steinberger, S. Wasserthiel-Smoller, M. Wilson, P. Wolf. 2006. Heart disease and stroke statistics—2006 update—A report from the American Heart Association Statistics Committee and Stroke Statistics Subcommittee. *Circulation* 113(6): E85–E151.

Tsevat, J., L. Goldman, J.R. Soukup, G.A. Lamas, K.F. Connors, C.C. Chapin, T.H. Lee. 1993. Stability of time-tradeoff utilities in survivors of myocardial infarction. *Medical Decision Making* 13(2): 161–165.

Vijan, S., R.A. Hayward. 2004. Pharmacologic lipid-lowering therapy in type 2 diabetes mellitus: Background paper for the American College of Physicians. *Annals of Internal Medicine* 140: 650–658.

Xu, J.Q., K.D. Kochanek, S.L. Murphy, B. Tejada-Vera. 2010. Deaths: Final data for 2007. National vital statistics reports; vol. 58 no. 19, National Center for Health Statistics, Hyattsville, MD.

Zhang, J., J.E. Mason, B.T. Denton, W.P. Pierskalla. 2013. Disease prevention, detection, and treatment. In Gass, S.I. and Fu, M., eds., *Encyclopedia of Operations Research and Management Science*, 3rd Edition. Springer, New York.

Zhang, Y., R.G. McCoy, J.E. Mason, S.A. Smith, N.D. Shah, B.T. Denton. 2014. Second-line agents for glycemic control for type 2 diabetes: Are newer agents better? *Diabetes Care* 37(5): 1338–1345.

17

MACHINE LEARNING FOR EARLY DETECTION AND TREATMENT OUTCOME PREDICTION

EVA K. LEE

NSF-Whitaker Center for Operations Research in Medicine and HealthCare, Georgia Institute of Technology, Atlanta, GA, USA
School of Industrial and Systems Engineering, Georgia Institute of Technology, Atlanta, GA, USA
NSF I/UCRC Center for Health Organization Transformation, Arlington, VA, USA

17.1 INTRODUCTION

Classification is a fundamental machine learning task whereby rules are developed for the allocation of independent entities to groups. Classic examples of applications include medical diagnosis (the allocation of patients to disease classes based on symptoms and laboratory tests) and credit screening (the acceptance or rejection of credit applications based on applicant data). Data are collected concerning entities with known group membership. This *training data* is used to develop rules for the classification of future entities with unknown group membership.

Cognitive science is the science of learning, knowing, and reasoning. *Pattern recognition* is a broad field within cognitive science that is concerned with the process of recognizing, identifying, and categorizing input information. These areas intersect with computer science, particularly in the closely related areas of *artificial intelligence*, *machine learning*, and *statistical pattern recognition*. Artificial intelligence is associated with constructing machines and systems that reflect human abilities in cognition.

Decision Analytics and Optimization in Disease Prevention and Treatment, First Edition.
Edited by Nan Kong and Shengfan Zhang.
© 2018 John Wiley & Sons, Inc. Published 2018 by John Wiley & Sons, Inc.

Machine learning refers to how these machines and systems replicate the learning process, which is often achieved by seeking and discovering patterns in data, or statistical pattern recognition.

Discriminant analysis is the process of discriminating between categories or populations. Associated with discriminant analysis as a statistical tool are the tasks of determining the features that best discriminate between populations and the process of classifying new entities based on these features. The former is often called *feature selection* and the latter is referred to as *statistical pattern classification*.

Supervised learning is the process of developing classification rules based on entities for which the classification is already known. Note that the process implies that the populations are already well defined. *Unsupervised learning* is the process of discovering patterns from unlabeled entities and therefore discovering and describing the underlying populations. *Semi-supervised learning* falls between supervised and unsupervised learning that uses a large collection of unlabeled entities jointly with a few labeled entities for improving classification performance. Models derived using supervised learning can be used for both functions of discriminant analysis—feature selection and classification. The model that we consider in Section 17.3 is a method for supervised learning, so we assume that populations are previously defined.

A fundamental problem in discriminant analysis, or supervised learning, concerns the classification of an entity into one of several *a priori*, mutually exclusive groups based upon k-specific measurable features of the entity. Typically, a discriminant (predictive) rule is formed from data collected on a sample of entities for which the group classifications are known. New entities, whose classifications are unknown, will then be classified based on this rule. Such an approach has been applied in a variety of domains, and a large body of literature on both the theory and applications of discriminant analysis exists (e.g., see early work from the bibliography in McLachlan (1992)).

In experimental biological and medical research, very often, experiments or tests are performed, and measurements are recorded under different conditions. A critical analysis involves the discrimination of different features under different conditions that will reveal potential predictors for biological and medical phenomena. Hence, classification techniques play an extremely important role in biological analysis as they facilitate systematic correlation and classification of different biological and medical phenomena. A resulting predictive rule can assist in early health risk and disease prediction and diagnosis, identifying new target therapeutic sites (genomic, cellular, and molecular) for drug delivery, disease prevention and early intervention, optimal treatment design, and treatment outcome prediction.

There are five fundamental steps in discriminant analysis:

1. Determine the data for input and the predictive output classes.
2. Gather a training set of data (including output class) from human experts or from laboratory experiments. Each element in the training set is an entity with corresponding known output class.
3. Determine the input attributes to represent each entity.

4. Identify discriminatory attributes and establish the predictive rule(s).
5. Validate the performance of the predictive rule(s).

In our Center for Operations Research in Medicine and Healthcare, we have developed a general-purpose machine learning framework that incorporates an optimization-based discriminant analysis model and a rapid solution engine for large-scale complex biological and biomedical informatics analyses. Our classification model, the first discrete support vector machine, offers these distinct features simultaneously:

1. It can classify any number of distinct groups.
2. It allows incorporation of heterogeneous, continuous, and temporal features as input.
3. It utilizes a high-dimensional data transformation to reduce attribute dimension and minimize noise and errors.
4. It incorporates a reserved-judgment region that provides a safeguard against overtraining.
5. It enables successive multistage classification capability (Brooks and Lee 2010, 2014; Gallagher et al. 1996, 1997; Lee 2007, 2008, 2009; Lee et al. 2003).

Studies involving vaccine immunogenicity prediction, early detection of mild cognitive impairment (MCI) and Alzheimer's disease (AD), CpG island aberrant methylation in human cancer, ultrasonic cell disruption in drug delivery, tumor volume identification, predicting early atherosclerosis using biomarkers, and finger-printing native and angiogenic microvascular networks using functional perfusion data demonstrate that our approach is adaptable and can produce effective and reliable predictive rules for a broad varieties of biomedical applications (Cao et al. 2013; Feltus et al. 2003, 2006; Kazmin et al. 2017; Koczor et al. 2013; Lee 2007, 2008, 2009; Lee et al. 2002, 2004, 2012, 2016; McCabe et al. 2009; Nakaya et al. 2011, 2015; Querec et al. 2009).

Section 17.2 briefly describes the background of discriminant analysis. Section 17.3 describes the optimization-based multistage discriminant analysis predictive models for classification. The use of the predictive models on various biological and medical applications is presented in Section 17.4. This is followed by a brief summary in Section 17.5.

17.2 BACKGROUND

The main objective in discriminant analysis is to derive rules that can be used to classify entities into groups. Discriminant rules are typically expressed in terms of variables representing a set of measurable attributes of the entities in question.

Data on a sample of entities for which the group classifications are known (perhaps determined by extraordinary means) are collected and used to derive rules that can be used to classify new yet-to-be-classified entities. Often there is a trade-off between the discriminating ability of the selected attributes and the expense of obtaining measurements on these attributes. Indeed, the measurement of a relatively definitive discriminating feature may be prohibitively expensive to obtain on a routine basis or perhaps impossible to obtain at the time that classification is needed.

Thus, a discriminant rule based on a selected set of feature attributes will typically be an imperfect discriminator, sometimes misclassifying entities. Depending on the application, the consequences of misclassifying an entity may be substantial. In such a case, it may be desirable to form a discrimination rule that allows less specific classification decisions or even non-classification of some entities to reduce the probability of misclassification.

To address this concern, a number of researchers have suggested methods for deriving *partial discrimination rules* (Broffit et al. 1976; Gessaman and Gessaman 1972; Habbema et al. 1974; Ng and Randles 1986; Quesenberry and Gessaman 1968). A partial discrimination rule allows an entity to be classified into some subset of the groups (i.e., rule out membership in the remaining groups) or be placed in a "reserved-judgment" category. An entity is considered misclassified only when it is assigned to a nonempty subset of groups not containing the true group of the entity. Typically, methods for deriving partial discrimination rules attempt to constrain the misclassification probabilities (e.g., by enforcing an upper bound on the proportion of misclassified training sample entities). For this reason, the resulting rules are also sometimes called *constrained discrimination rules.*

Partial (or constrained) discrimination rules are intuitively appealing. A partial discrimination rule based on relatively inexpensive measurements can be tried first. If the rule classifies the entity satisfactorily according to the needs of the application, then nothing further needs to be done. Otherwise, additional measurements—albeit more expensive—can be taken on other, more definitive discriminating attributes of the entity.

One disadvantage of partial discrimination methods is that there is no obvious definition of optimality among any set of rules satisfying the constraints on the misclassification probabilities. For example, since some correct classifications are certainly more valuable than others (e.g., classification into a small subset containing the true group vs. a large subset), it does not make sense simply to maximize the probability of correct classification. In fact, to maximize the probability of correct classification, one would simply classify every entity into the subset consisting of all the groups—clearly this is not an acceptable rule.

A simplified model, whereby one incorporates only the reserved-judgment region (i.e., an entity is either classified as belonging to exactly one of the given a priori groups or it is placed in the reserved-judgment category), is amenable to reasonable notions of optimality. For example, in this case, maximizing the probability of correct classification is meaningful. For the two-group case, the simplified model and the more general model are equivalent. Research on the two-group case is summarized in McLachlan (1992). For three or more groups, the two models are not equivalent, and most work has been directed toward the development of heuristic methods for the more general model (e.g., see Beckman and Johnson 1981; Broffit et al. 1976; Gessaman and Gessaman 1972; Ng and Randles 1986; Quesenberry and Gessaman 1968).

Assuming that the group density functions and prior probabilities are known, Anderson (1969) showed that an optimal rule for the problem of maximizing the probability of correct classification subject to constraints on the misclassification probabilities must be of a specific form when discriminating among multiple groups with a simplified model. The formulas in Anderson's result depend on a set of parameters satisfying a complex relationship between the density functions, the prior probabilities, and the bounds on the misclassification probabilities. Anderson's model is appealing since it can handle any number of groups. However, establishing a viable mathematical model to describe Anderson's result and finding values for these parameters that yield an optimal rule are challenging tasks. Gallagher et al. (1997) presented the first computational model for Anderson's results. And Brooks and Lee (2010, 2014) showed that the resulting decision model is *NP-complete*.

A variety of mathematical programming models have been proposed for the discriminant analysis problem (Bajgier and Hill 1982; Bal and Örkcü 2011; Bennett and Bredensteiner 1997; Bennett and Mangasarian 1993; Cavalier et al. 1989; Freed and Glover 1981, 1986; Gehrlein 1986; Glen 1999; Glover 1990; Glover et al. 1988; Gochet et al. 1997; Koehler and Erenguc 1990; Liittschwager and Wang 1978; Mangasarian 1993; Mangasarian et al. 1995; Nakayama and Kagaku 1998; Pavur and Loucopoulos 1995; Stam and Joachimsthaler 1989; Stam and Ragsdale 1992). None of these studies deal formally with measuring the performance of discriminant rules specifically designed to allow allocation to a reserved-judgment region. There is also no mechanism employed to explicitly constrain the level of misclassifications for each group, although some researchers manage to include it within their objective functions.

Many different techniques and methodologies have contributed to advances in classification, including artificial neural networks, decision trees, kernel-based learning, machine learning, mathematical programming, statistical analysis, boosting, and support vector machines (Bishop 1995; Breiman et al. 1984, Cristianini and Taylor 2000, Duda et al. 2001; Dreiseitl and Ohno-Machado 2002; Freund et al. 1999; Lim et al. 2000; Müller et al. 2001; Vapnik 1999). There are some review papers for classification problems with mathematical programming techniques. Stam (1997) summarized basic concepts and ideas and discussed potential research directions on classification methods that optimize a function of the L_p-norm distances. The paper focuses on continuous models and includes normalization schemes, computational aspects, weighted formulations, secondary criteria, and extensions from two-group to multi-group classifications. Wilson (1996) presented a series of integer programming formulations for statistical classification problems and compared their performance on sample data. Zopounidis and Doumpos (2002) reviewed the research conducted on the framework of the multi-criteria decision aiding, covering different classification models. Mangasarian (1997) and Bradley et al. (1999) gave an overview of using mathematical programming approaches to solve data mining problems. Byvatov and Schneider (2002) provided an overview on the theory and basic principles of support vector machine and their application to bioinformatics. Lee and Wu (2007, 2009) provided a comprehensive overview of continuous and discrete mathematical programming models for classification problems and their usage within medicine.

17.3   MACHINE LEARNING WITH DISCRETE SUPPORT VECTOR MACHINE PREDICTIVE MODELS

In our computational center, we have been developing and advancing a general-purpose machine learning framework for classification in medicine and biology. The system consists of a pattern recognition module, a feature selection module, and a classification modeler and rapid solver module. The pattern recognition module involves automatic image analysis, "omic" pattern recognition, spectrum pattern extractions, and unstructured text mining capabilities. The feature selection module consists of a combinatorial selection algorithm where discriminatory patterns are extracted from among a large set of pattern attributes. These modules are wrapped around the classification modeler and solver into a machine learning framework. Our system is applicable to a wide variety of applications, including biological, biomedical, and logistics problems. Utilizing the technology of large-scale discrete optimization and support vector machines, our classification model includes the following features within a single modeling framework:

1. The ability to classify any number of distinct groups
2. The ability to incorporate heterogeneous and temporal type of attributes as input
3. A high-dimensional data transformation that reduces attribute dimension, noise and errors
4. Constraints to limit the rate of misclassification and a reserved-judgment region that provides a safeguard against overtraining (which tends to lead to high misclassification rates from the resulting predictive rule)
5. Successive multistage classification capability to handle data points placed in the reserved-judgment region

Based on the description in Gallagher et al. (1996, 1997); Lee et al. (2003); Lee (2007, 2008, 2009), we summarize in the following text some of the classification models that we have developed.

17.3.1   Modeling of Reserved-Judgment Region for General Groups

When the population densities and prior probabilities are known, the constrained rules with a reject option (reserved judgment), based on Anderson's results, call for finding a partition $\{R_0, \ldots, R_G\}$ of $\Re^k$ that maximizes the probability of correct allocation subject to constraints on the misclassification probabilities; that is,

$$\text{maximize} \quad \sum_{g=1}^{G} \pi_g \int_{R_g} f_g(w)\,dw \tag{17.1}$$

$$\text{subject to} \quad \int_{R_g} f_h(w)\,dw \le \alpha_{hg}, \quad h,g = 1,\ldots,G, h \ne g, \tag{17.2}$$

where f_h, $h=1, \ldots, G$, are the group conditional density functions, π_g denotes the prior probability that a randomly selected entity is from group g, $g=1, \ldots, G$, and α_{hg}, $h \ne g$, are constants between zero and one. Under quite general assumptions, it was shown that there exist unique (up to a set of measure zero) nonnegative constants λ_{ih}, $i,h \in \{1,\ldots,G\}$, $i \ne h$, such that the optimal rule is given by

$$R_g = \left\{ x \in \Re^k : L_g(x) = \max_{h \in \{0,1,\ldots,G\}} L_h(x) \right\}, \quad g = 0,\ldots,G \tag{17.3}$$

where

$$L_0(x) = 0 \tag{17.4}$$

$$L_h(x) = \pi_h f_h(x) - \sum_{\substack{i=1 \\ i \ne h}}^{G} \lambda_{ih} f_i(x), \quad h = 1,\ldots,G \tag{17.5}$$

For $G=2$ the optimal solution can be modeled rather straightforward. However, finding optimal λ_{ih} s for the general case, $G \ge 3$, is a difficult problem, with the difficulty increasing as G increases. Our model offers an avenue for modeling and finding the optimal solution in the general case. It is the first such model to be computationally viable (Gallagher et al. 1996, 1997).

Before proceeding, we note that R_g can be written as $R_g = \left\{ x \in \Re^k : L_g(x) \ge L_h(x) \text{ for all } h=0,\ldots,G \right\}$. So, since $L_g(x) \ge L_h(x)$ if and only if $\left(1/\sum_{t=1}^{G} f_t(x) \right) L_g(x) \ge \left(1/\sum_{t=1}^{G} f_t(x) \right) L_h(x)$, the functions L_h, $h=1,\ldots,G$, can be redefined as

$$L_h(x) = \pi_h p_h(x) - \sum_{\substack{i=1 \\ i \ne h}}^{G} \lambda_{ih} p_i(x), \quad h = 1,\ldots,G \tag{17.6}$$

where $p_i(x) = f_i(x)\big/\sum_{t=1}^{G} f_t(x)$. We assume that L_h is defined as in Equation 17.6 in our model.

17.3.2 Discriminant Analysis via Mixed-Integer Programming

Assume that we are given a training sample of N entities whose group classifications are known; say, n_g entities are in group g, where $\sum_{g=1}^{G} n_g = N$. Let the k-dimensional vectors x^{gj}, $g = 1, \ldots, G, j = 1, \ldots, n_g$, contain the measurements on k available characteristics of the entities. Our procedure for deriving a discriminant rule proceeds in two stages. The first stage is to use the training sample to compute estimates $\hat{f}_h$, either parametrically or nonparametrically, of the density functions f_h (e.g., see McLachlan 1992) and estimates $\hat{\pi}_h$ of the prior probabilities π_h, $h = 1, \ldots, G$. The second stage is to determine the optimal λ_{ih}'s given these estimates. This stage requires being able to estimate the probabilities of correct classification and misclassification for any candidate set of λ_{ih} s. One could, in theory, substitute the estimated densities and prior probabilities into Equation 17.5 and directly use the resulting regions R_g in the integral expressions given in (17.1) and (17.2). This would involve, even in simple cases such as normally distributed groups, the numerical evaluation of k-dimensional integrals at each step of a search for the optimal λ_{ih} s.

Computationally, we have designed an alternative approach. After substituting the $\hat{f}_h$'s and $\hat{\pi}_h$'s into Equation 17.5, we simply calculate the proportion of training sample points that fall in each of the regions $R_1, \ldots, R_G$. The mixed-integer programming (MIP) models discussed herein attempt to maximize the proportion of training sample points correctly classified while satisfying constraints on the proportions of training sample points misclassified. This approach has two advantages. First, it avoids having to evaluate the potentially difficult integrals in Equations 17.1 and 17.2. Second, it is nonparametric in controlling the training sample misclassification probabilities. That is, even if the densities are poorly estimated (by assuming, e.g., normal densities for non-normal data), the constraints are still satisfied for the training sample. Better estimates of the densities may allow a higher correct classification rate to be achieved, but the constraints will be satisfied even if poor estimates are used. Unlike most support vector machine models that minimize the sum of errors, our objective is driven by the number of correct classifications and will not be biased by the distance of the entities from the supporting hyperplane. Hence, our model returns a robust classifier.

A word of caution is in order. In traditional unconstrained discriminant analysis, the true probability of correct classification of a given discriminant rule tends to be smaller than the rate of correct classification for the training sample from which it was derived. One would expect to observe such an effect for the method described herein as well. In addition, one would expect to observe an analogous effect with regard to constraints on misclassification probabilities—the true probabilities are likely to be greater than any limits imposed on the proportions of training sample misclassifications. Hence, the α_{hg} parameters should be carefully chosen for the application in hand.

Our first model is a nonlinear 0/1 MIP model with the nonlinearity appearing in the constraints. Model 1 maximizes the number of correct classifications of the given N training entities. Similarly, the constraints on the misclassification probabilities are modeled by ensuring that the number of group g training entities in region R_h is less than or equal to a prespecified percentage, α_{hg} $(0 < \alpha_{hg} < 1)$, of the total number, n_g, of group g entities, $h, g \in \{1, \ldots, G\}, h \neq g$.

For notational convenience, let $\mathbf{G} = \{1, \ldots, G\}$ and $\mathbf{N}_g = \{1, \ldots, n_g\}$, for $g \in \mathbf{G}$. Also, analogous to the definition of p_i, define $\hat{p}_i$ by $\hat{p}_i(x) = \hat{f}_i(x) / \sum_{t=1}^{G} \hat{f}_t(x)$. In our model, we use binary indicator variables to denote the group classification of entities. Mathematically, let u_{hgj} be a binary variable indicating whether or not x^{gj} lies in region R_h, that is, whether or not the jth entity from group g is allocated to group h. Then model 1 can be written as follows:

DAMIP (model 1):

$$\text{Maximize} \sum_{g \in G} \sum_{j \in N_g} u_{ggj}$$

subject to

$$L_{hgj} = \hat{\pi}_h \hat{p}_h \left(x^{gj} \right) - \sum_{i \in G \backslash h} \lambda_{ih} \hat{p}_i \left(x^{gj} \right), \qquad h, g \in \mathbf{G}, j \in \mathbf{N}_g \qquad (17.7)$$

$$y_{gj} = \max \left\{ 0, L_{hgj} : h = 1, \ldots, G \right\}, \qquad g \in \mathbf{G}, j \in \mathbf{N}_g \qquad (17.8)$$

$$y_{gj} - L_{ggj} \leq M \left(1 - u_{ggj} \right), \qquad g \in \mathbf{G}, j \in \mathbf{N}_g \qquad (17.9)$$

$$y_{gj} - L_{hgj} \geq \varepsilon \left(1 - u_{hgj} \right), \qquad h, g \in \mathbf{G}, j \in \mathbf{N}_g, h \neq g \quad (17.10)$$

$$\sum_{j \in N_g} u_{hgj} \leq \lfloor \alpha_{hg} n_g \rfloor, \qquad h, g \in \mathbf{G}, h \neq g \qquad (17.11)$$

$$-\infty < L_{hgj} < \infty, \; y_{gj} \geq 0, \; \lambda_{ih} \geq 0, \quad u_{hgj} \in \{0,1\}$$

Constraint (17.7) defines the variable L_{hgj} as the value of the function L_h evaluated at x^{gj}. Therefore, the continuous variable y_{gj}, defined in constraint (17.8), represents $\max\{L_h(x^{gj}): h = 0, \ldots, G\}$, and consequently, x^{gj} lies in region R_h if and only if $y_{gj} = L_{hgj}$. The binary variable u_{hgj} indicates whether or not x^{gj} lies in region R_h, that is, whether or not the jth entity from group g is allocated to group h. In particular, constraint (17.9), together with the objective, forces u_{ggj} to be 1 if and only if the jth entity from group g is correctly allocated to group g. Constraints (17.10) and (17.11) ensure that at most $\lfloor \alpha_{hg} n_g \rfloor$ (i.e., the greatest integer less than or equal to $\alpha_{hg} n_g$), group g entities are allocated to group $h, h \neq g$. One caveat regarding the indicator variables u_{hgj} is that although the condition $u_{hgj} = 0$, $h \neq g$, implies (by constraint (17.10)) that $x^{gj} \notin R_h$, the converse need not hold. As a consequence, the number of misclassifications may be over-counted. However, in our preliminary numerical study, we found that the actual amount of over-counting is minimal. One could force the converse (thus,

$u_{hgj} = 1$ if and only if $x^{gj} \in R_h$) by adding constraints $y_{gj} - L_{hgj} \leq M(1 - u_{hgj})$, for example. Finally, we note that the parameters M and ε are extraneous to the discriminant analysis problem itself but are needed in the model to control the indicator variables u_{hgj}. The intention is for M and ε to be, respectively, large and small positive constants.

17.3.3 Model Variations

We explore different variations in the model to grasp the quality of the solution and the associated computational effort.

A first variation involves transforming model 1 to an equivalent linear mixed-integer model. In particular, model 2 replaces the N constraints defined in (17.8) with the following system of $3GN + 2N$ constraints:

$$y_{gj} \geq L_{hgj}, \qquad h, g \in \mathbf{G}, \ j \in \mathbf{N}_g \qquad (17.12)$$

$$\tilde{y}_{hgj} - L_{hgj} \leq M\left(1 - v_{hgj}\right), \qquad h, g \in \mathbf{G}, \ j \in \mathbf{N}_g \qquad (17.13)$$

$$\tilde{y}_{hgj} \leq \hat{\pi}_h \hat{p}_h \left(x^{gj}\right) v_{hgj}, \qquad h, g \in \mathbf{G}, \ j \in \mathbf{N}_g \qquad (17.14)$$

$$\sum_{h \in G} v_{hgj} \leq 1, \qquad g \in \mathbf{G}, \ j \in \mathbf{N}_g \qquad (17.15)$$

$$\sum_{h \in G} \tilde{y}_{hgj} = y_{gj}, \qquad g \in \mathbf{G}, \ j \in \mathbf{N}_g \qquad (17.16)$$

where $\tilde{y}_{hgj} \geq 0$ and $v_{hgj} \in \{0,1\}, h, g \in \mathbf{G}, j \in \mathbf{N}_g$. These constraints, together with the nonnegativity of y_{gj}, force $y_{gj} = \max\{0, L_{hgj} : h = 1, \ldots, G\}$.

The second variation involves transforming model 1 to a heuristic linear MIP model. This is done by replacing the nonlinear constraint (17.8) with $y_{gj} \geq L_{hgj}, h, g \in \mathbf{G}, j \in \mathbf{N}_g$ and including penalty terms in the objective function. In particular, model 3 has the objective

$$\text{Maximize} \sum_{g \in G} \sum_{j \in \mathcal{N}_g} \beta u_{ggj} - \sum_{g \in G} \sum_{j \in \mathcal{N}_g} \gamma y_{gj},$$

where β and γ are positive constants. This model is heuristic in that there is nothing to force $y_{gj} = \max\{0, L_{hgj} : h = 1, \ldots, G\}$. However, since in addition to trying to force as many u_{ggj}'s to one as possible, the objective in model 3 also tries to make the y_{gj}'s as small as possible; hence the optimizer tends to drive y_{gj} toward $\max\{0, L_{hgj} : h = 1, \ldots, G\}$. We remark that β and γ could be stratified by group (i.e., introduce possibly distinct $\beta_g, \gamma_g, g \in \mathbf{G}$) to prioritize the relative importance of certain groups to be correctly classified.

A reasonable modification to models 1, 2, and 3 involves relaxing the constraints specified by (17.11). Rather than placing restrictions on the number of type g training entities classified into group h, for all $h, g \in \mathbf{G}, h \neq g$, one could simply place an upper bound on the *total* number of misclassified training entities. In this case, the $G(G-1)$ constraints specified by (17.11) would be replaced by a single constraint:

$$\sum_{g \in G} \sum_{h \in G \backslash \{g\}} \sum_{j \in N_g} u_{hgj} \leq \lfloor \alpha N \rfloor \qquad (17.17)$$

where α is a constant between 0 and 1. We will refer to models 1, 2, and 3, modified in this way, as models 1T, 2T, and 3T, respectively. Of course, other modifications are also possible. For instance, one could place restrictions on the total number of type g points misclassified for each $g \in \mathbf{G}$. Thus, in place of the constraints specified in (17.17), one would include the constraints $\sum_{h \in G \backslash \{g\}} \sum_{j \in N_g} u_{hgj} \leq \lfloor \alpha_g N \rfloor$, $g \in \mathbf{G}$, where $0 < \alpha_g < 1$.

We also explore a heuristic linear model of model 1. In particular, consider the linear program (DALP):

DALP:

$$\text{Minimize} \quad \sum_{g \in G} \sum_{j \in N_g} \left(c_1 w_{gj} + c_2 y_{gj} \right) \qquad (17.18)$$

subject to

$$L_{hgj} = \hat{\pi}_h \hat{p}_h \left(x^{gj} \right) - \sum_{i \in G \backslash h} \lambda_{ih} \hat{p}_i \left(x^{gj} \right), \quad h, g \in \mathbf{G}, j \in \mathbf{N_g} \qquad (17.19)$$

$$L_{ggj} - L_{hgj} + w_{gj} \geq 0, \qquad\qquad h, g \in \mathbf{G}, h \neq g, j \in \mathbf{N_g} \quad (17.20)$$

$$L_{ggj} + w_{gj} \geq 0, \qquad\qquad\qquad g \in \mathbf{G}, j \in \mathbf{N_g} \qquad (17.21)$$

$$-L_{hgj} + y_{gj} \geq 0, \qquad\qquad\quad h, g \in \mathbf{G}, j \in \mathbf{N_g} \qquad (17.22)$$

$$-\infty < L_{hgj} < \infty, \ w_{gj}, y_{gj}, \lambda_{ih} \geq 0$$

Constraint (17.19) defines the variable L_{hgj} as the value of the function L_h evaluated at x^{gj}. As the optimization solver searches through the set of feasible solutions, the λ_{ih} variables will vary, causing the L_{hgj} variables to assume different values. Constraints (17.20), (17.21), and (17.22) link the objective function variables with the L_{hgj} variables in such a way that correct classification of training entities and allocation of training entities into the reserved-judgment region are captured by the objective function variables. In particular, if the optimization solver drives w_{gj} to zero for some g, j pair, then constraints (17.20) and (17.21) imply that $L_{ggj} = \max\{0, L_{hgj}: h \in \mathbf{G}\}$.

Hence, the jth entity from group g is correctly classified. If, on the other hand, the optimal solution yields $y_{gj}=0$ for some g, j pair, then constraint (17.22) implies that $\max\{0, L_{hgj}: h \in \mathbf{G}\}=0$. Thus, the jth entity from group g is placed in the reserved-judgment region. (Of course, it is possible for both w_{gj} and y_{gj} to be zero. One should decide prior to solving the linear program how to interpret the classification in such cases.) If both w_{gj} and y_{gj} are positive, the jth entity from group g is misclassified.

The optimal solution yields a set of λ_{ih} s that best allocates the training entities (i.e., "best" in terms of minimizing the penalty objective function). The optimal λ_{ih} s can then be used to define the functions L_h, $h \in \mathbf{G}$, which in turn can be used to classify a new entity with feature vector $x \in \mathfrak{R}^k$ by simply computing the index at which $\max\{L_h(x): h \in \{0, 1, ..., G\}\}$ is achieved.

Note that model DALP places no a priori bound on the number of misclassified training entities. However, since the objective is to minimize a weighted combination of the variables w_{gj} and y_{gj}, the optimizer will attempt to drive these variables to zero. Thus, the optimizer is, in essence, attempting either to correctly classify training entities ($w_{gj}=0$) or to place them in the reserved-judgment region ($y_{gj}=0$). By varying the weights c_1 and c_2, one has a means of controlling the optimizer's emphasis for correctly classifying training entities versus placing them in the reserved-judgment region. If $c_2/c_1 < 1$, the optimizer will tend to place a greater emphasis on driving the w_{gj} variables to zero than driving the y_{gj} variables to zero (conversely, if $c_2/c_1 > 1$). Hence, when $c_2/c_1 < 1$, one should expect to get relatively more entities correctly classified, fewer placed in the reserved-judgment region, and more misclassified than when $c_2/c_1 > 1$. An extreme case is when $c_2=0$. In this case, there is no emphasis on driving y_{gj} to zero (the reserved-judgment region is thus ignored), and the full emphasis of the optimizer is to drive w_{gj} to zero.

Table 17.1 summarizes the number of constraints, the total number of variables, and the number of 0/1 variables in each of the discrete support vector machine models and in the heuristic LP model (DALP). Clearly, even for moderately sized discriminant analysis problems, the MIP instances are relatively large. Also, note that model 2 is larger than model 3, both in terms of the number of constraints and the number of variables. However, it is important to keep in mind that the difficulty of solving an MIP problem cannot, in general, be predicted solely by its size; problem structure has

TABLE 17.1 Model Size

Model	Type	Constraints	Total Variables	0/1 Variables
1	Nonlinear MIP	$2GN+N+G(G-1)$	$2GN+N+G(G-1)$	GN
2	Linear MIP	$5GN + 2N+G(G-1)$	$4GN+N+G(G-1)$	$2GN$
3	Linear MIP	$3GN+G(G-1)$	$2GN+N+G(G-1)$	GN
1T	Nonlinear MIP	$2GN+N + 1$	$2GN+N+G(G-1)$	GN
2T	Linear MIP	$5GN + 2N + 1$	$4GN+N+G(G-1)$	$2GN$
3T	Linear MIP	$3GN + 1$	$2GN+N+G(G-1)$	GN
DALP	Linear program	$3GN$	$NG+N+G(G-1)$	0

a direct and substantial bearing on the effort required to find optimal solutions. The LP relaxation of these MIP models poses computational challenges as commercial LP solvers return (optimal) LP solutions that are infeasible. This is due to the equality constraints (17.7) linking very small-magnitude and dense coefficients together and the use of big M and small ε in the formulation (constraints (17.9) and (17.10)).

It is interesting to note that the set of feasible solutions for model 2 is "tighter" than that for model 3. In particular, if F_i denotes the set of feasible solutions of model i, then

$$F_1 = \left\{ (L, \lambda, u, y) : \text{there exists } \tilde{y}, v \text{ such that } (L, \lambda, u, y, \tilde{y}, v) \in F_2 \right\} \subsetneq F_3 \qquad (17.23)$$

The novelties of the classification models developed herein include the following:

1. They are suitable for discriminant analysis given any number of groups.
2. They accept heterogeneous types of attributes as input.
3. They use a parametric approach to reduce high-dimensional attribute spaces.
4. They allow constraints on the number of misclassifications and utilize a reserved judgment to facilitate the reduction of misclassifications. The latter point opens the possibility of performing multistage analysis.

Clearly, the advantage of an LP model over an MIP model is that the associated problem instances are computationally much easier to solve. However, the most important criterion in judging a method for obtaining discriminant rules is how the rules perform in correctly classifying and predicting new unseen entities. Once the rule is developed, applying it to a new entity to determine its group is trivial. Extensive computational experiments have been performed to gauge the qualities of solutions of different models (Gallagher et al. 1997; Lee 2007, 2008, 2009; Lee et al. 2003).

17.3.4 Theoretical Properties and Computational Strategies

Theoretically and empirically, DAMIP has many appealing characteristics including that:

1. The resulting classification rule is *strongly universally consistent*, given that the Bayes optimal rule for classification is known (Brooks and Lee 2010, 2014).
2. The misclassification rates using the DAMIP method are consistently lower than other classification approaches in both simulated data and real-world data.
3. The classification rules from DAMIP appear to be insensitive to the specification of prior probabilities yet capable of reducing misclassification rates when the number of training entities from each group is different.
4. The DAMIP model generates stable classification rules regardless of the proportions of training entities from each group.

The DAMIP model and its variations described herein offer a computational avenue for numerically estimating optimal values for the λ_{ih} parameters in Anderson's formulas. However, it should be emphasized that MIP problems are themselves difficult to solve. Anderson himself noted the extreme difficulty of finding an optimal set of λ_{ih}'s (Anderson 1969). Indeed, DAMIP is proven to be *NP-complete* when the number of groups is greater than 2 (Brooks and Lee 2010, 2014). Nevertheless integer programming—and in particular those with 0/1 variables—is a powerful modeling tool, and a wide variety of real-world problems have been modeled as mixed-integer programs. Numerically, much effort has been invested in advancing computational strategies for solving difficult MIP problem instances.

The numerical work reported in Section 17.4 is based on an MIP solver that is built on top of a general-purpose in-house mixed-integer programming solver, MIPSOL, which integrates state-of-the-art MIP computational devices such as problem preprocessing, primal heuristics, global and local reduced-cost fixing, and cutting planes within a branch-and-bound framework (Mitchell 2002; Savelsbergh 1994). The solver has been shown to be effective in solving a wide variety of large-scale real-world instances (Lee and Zaider 2008; Lee et al. 2013). For our DAMIP MIP instances, special techniques including variable aggregation, a heuristic branching scheme, and hypergraphic cut generation are employed (Brooks and Lee 2010, 2014; Easton et al. 2003; Gallagher et al. 1997).

17.4   APPLYING DAMIP TO REAL-WORLD APPLICATIONS

The main objective in discriminant analysis is to derive rules that can be used to classify entities into groups. Computationally, the challenge lies in the effort expended to develop such a rule. Feasible solutions obtained from our classification models correspond to predictive rules. Empirical results (Brooks and Lee 2010, 2014; Gallagher et al. 1997; Lee et al. 2003) indicate that the resulting classification model instances are computationally very challenging and even intractable by competitive commercial MIP solvers. However, the resulting predictive rules prove to be very promising, offering correct predictive accuracy on new unknown data ranging from 80% to 100% on various types of biomedical problems. Our results indicate that the general-purpose classification framework that we have designed has the potential to be a very powerful predictive decision tool for clinical setting.

The choice of MIP as the underlying modeling and optimization technology for our support vector machine classification model is guided by the desire to simultaneously incorporate a variety of important and desirable properties of predictive models within a general framework. MIP itself allows for the incorporation of continuous and discrete variables and linear and nonlinear constraints, providing a flexible and powerful modeling environment.

17.4.1 Validation of Model and Computational Effort

We performed 10-fold cross-validation and designed simulation and comparison studies on our preliminary models. The results, reported in Gallagher et al. (1997) and Lee et al. (2003), show that the methods are promising, based on applications to both simulated data and real-application datasets from the machine learning database repository (Murphy and Aha 1994). Furthermore, our methods compare well with existing methods, often producing better results when compared with other approaches such as artificial neural networks, quadratic discriminant analysis, tree classification, and other support vector machines.

17.4.2 Applications to Biological and Medical Problems

Our mathematical modeling and computational algorithmic design shows great promise. Compared with well- known and competitive classifiers, the DAMIP predictive rules result in higher blind prediction accuracy on new data (with unknown group status). The rules are also robust and are insensitive to imbalance in sample size. This is partly due to the transformation of raw data via the set of constraints in (17.7) and the distinct features that occur simultaneously in a single modeling framework. While most support vector machines (summarized in Lee and Wu 2007, 2009) directly determine the hyperplanes of separation using raw data, our approach transforms the raw data via a probabilistic model before the determination of the supporting hyperplanes. Further, the separation is driven by maximizing the total number of correctly classified entities, instead of minimizing the sum of errors (representing distances of entities from the hyperplanes) as in other support vector machines. The combination of these two strategies offers better and more robust classification capability. Noise in the transformed data is not as profound as in the raw data. And the magnitudes of errors do not skew the determination of the separating hyperplanes, since all entities have "equal" importance when correct classification is being counted.

To highlight the broad applicability of our approach, we briefly summarize the application of our predictive models and solution algorithms to seven different biological and medical problems. These projects were closely collaborated with experimental biologists and clinical investigators. We also include multi-group classification using the UCI Repository of machine learning databases. Applications to finance and other industry applications are described elsewhere (Brooks and Lee 2006, 2007; Gallagher et al. 1997; Lee et al. 2003).

17.4.2.1 *Quick Test to Predict Immune Responses to Flu Shots*   The text herein is a summary of our work in Lee et al. (2016); Nakaya et al. (2011, 2015); Querec et al. (2009). Vaccines have drastically reduced the mortality and morbidity of many diseases. However, they have historically been developed empirically, and recent development of vaccines against current pandemics such as HIV and malaria has been met with difficulty. The path to licensure of candidate vaccines involves very

lengthy and expensive clinical trials to assess their efficacy and safety. These trials involve thousands of subjects and can cost hundreds of millions of dollars to complete. As a result, very few vaccine concepts are tested.

A major challenge in vaccinology is that the effectiveness of vaccination can only be ascertained after vaccinated individuals have been exposed to infection. The ability to identify early predictive signatures of vaccine responses and novel and robust correlates of protection from infection will play an instrumental role in developing next-generation rationally designed vaccines. It will facilitate rapid design and evaluation of new and emerging vaccines and the identification of individuals who are unlikely to be protected by a vaccine. This work focuses on predicting the immunity of a vaccine without exposing individuals to infection. The study addresses a long-standing challenge in the development of vaccines—that of only being able to determine immunity or effectiveness long after vaccination and, often, only after being exposed to infection.

Three studies involving nine trials of patient subjects were carried out. The first study aims to predict the body's ability (shortly after immunization) to stimulate a strong and enduring immunity against yellow fever. Healthy individuals were vaccinated with YF-17D and T-cell and antibody responses in their blood were captured for 30 days. These blood samples were studied with genomic signatures characterized. There was a striking variation in the responses between individuals. Analysis of gene expression patterns in white blood cells revealed that in the majority of the individuals, the vaccine induced a network of genes involved in the early innate immune response against the viruses. DAMIP takes in these gene expression data and uses it to uncover discriminatory gene signatures to establish the classification rule that can classify the magnitude of induced T-cell and antibody responses. To validate its predictive accuracy, and whether these gene signatures could actually predict immune response, a second group of individuals were vaccinated for independent blind predication.

To analyze the generalizability of this approach, we apply DAMIP to predict the effectiveness of other vaccines, including flu vaccines. The second study is based on a series of clinical studies during the annual flu seasons in 2007, 2008, and 2009. Healthy young adults were vaccinated with a standard flu shot (trivalent inactive vaccine). Others were given live attenuated vaccine nasally. Comprehensively surveyed, the activity levels of all human genes in blood samples from the volunteers revealed that the activity of many genes involved in innate immunity and interferon and reactive oxygen species signaling were changing after flu vaccination. Biological analysis also identified genes in the "unfolded protein response," necessary for cells to adapt to the stress of producing high levels of antibodies. These genomic expression data are then input into our DAMIP model to identify discriminatory gene signatures that can classify patients who respond positively to the vaccine versus those who do not.

The yellow fever study offered a groundbreaking work in vaccine immunogenicity. DAMIP identified signatures of gene expression in the blood of healthy humans a few days after vaccination that could predict with up to 90% accuracy the strength of the immune response, weeks or months after yellow fever vaccination. In the flu analysis, being named 2011 Paper of the Year by the International Society of Vaccine, we extended this approach to the seasonal influenza vaccines over the course of three influenza seasons. By studying gene expression patterns in the blood a few days after vaccination, we were able to identify "signatures" that were capable of predicting the magnitude of the later immune response, with >90% accuracy. More importantly one of the genes in the signature, CAMK4, was negatively correlated with antibody titers; our results revealed an unappreciated role for CAMK4 in B-cell responses. This landmark study demonstrates the use of DAMIP in predicting vaccine efficacy and highlights one of the ways for the future of vaccinology—use of systems biology tools to perform sophisticated human studies that in turn returns specific hypothesis to be tested experimentally. This work was named the winner of the 2015 INFORMS Daniel H. Wagner Prize for Excellence in Operations Research Practice (Lee et al. 2016).

Encouragingly, some of the genes identified in the seasonal flu study were also predictors of the antibody response to vaccination against yellow fever. Further, DAMIP facilitates discovery of new functions for genes, even when scientists previously did not suspect their involvement in antibody responses (Ravindran et al. 2014, 2016). We have subsequently applied DAMIP in a malaria study that will assist with the first widely tested of the vaccine in Africa in 2018 (Kazmin et al. 2017; Christensen 2017).

17.4.2.2 Predictive Model for Early Detection of Mild Cognitive Impairment and Alzheimer's Disease

The text is an excerpt of our work in Lee et al. (2012). The number of people affected by AD is growing at a rapid rate, and the subsequent increase in costs will have significant impacts on the world's economies and healthcare systems. Alzheimer's Disease (AD), the sixth leading cause of death in the United States, is a progressive and irreversible brain disease, causing memory loss and other cognitive dysfunction severe enough to affect daily life. It is estimated that one in eight elderly Americans suffer from AD. The number of AD victims is briskly rising, with an estimated 35 million people worldwide currently living with AD or some forms of dementia. AD is currently incurable. Drugs are used to manage the symptoms, but no treatments to prevent or meaningfully slow the disease's progression are known to exist.

Since changes in the brain triggered by AD develop slowly over many years and symptom onset coincides with advanced neurodegeneration, the need to identify new and noninvasive diagnostics before any symptoms occur has become a public health imperative. Creating new opportunities for early intervention is vital. Systems predictive analyses on noninvasive tests that can identify people who are at risk but currently have no symptoms are critical to curtail the rapid rise of this illness.

Neuropsychological tests are inexpensive and noninvasive and can be incorporated within an annual physical examination. Thus they can serve as a baseline for early cognitive impairment or AD risk prediction. We apply the DAMIP machine learning framework for early detection of mild cognitive impairment (MCI) and AD. Anonymous data of neuropsychological tests from 35 subjects were collected at Emory Alzheimer's Disease Research Center from 2004 to 2007. Eighteen types of neuropsychological tests were applied to the subjects, but only four of them were applied to all subjects, thus being used in our predictive model. These tests included Mini–Mental State Examination (MMSE), clock drawing test, word list memory tasks by the Consortium to Establish a Registry for Alzheimer's Disease (CERAD), and Geriatric Depression Scale (GDS).

The MMSE is a brief screening tool for cognitive impairment. It covers five areas of cognitive function, including orientation, registration, attention and calculation, recall, and language. The clock drawing test assesses cognitive functions, particularly visuospatial abilities and executive control functions. The CERAD word list memory tasks assess the learning ability for new verbal information. The tasks include word list memory with repetition, word list recall, and word list recognition. The GDS is a screening tool to assess depression in older population.

There were 153 features, including raw data from the four neuropsychological tests as well as subjects' age. Raw data from tests contained answers to individual questions in the tests. Discarding features that contained missing values or that were nondiscriminating (i.e., features that contained almost the same value among all subjects), 100 features were used for feature selection and classification. The clinicians also summarize performance of subtotal scores in different tests, resulting in 9 scores for each patient.

Using two trials of patients with AD, MCI, and control groups, we show that one can successfully develop a classification rule based on data from neuropsychological tests to predict AD, MCI, and normal subjects where the blind prediction accuracy exceeds 90%. Table 17.2 illustrates one predictive rule obtained for this study. Further, our study strongly suggests that raw data of neuropsychological tests have higher potential to predict subjects from AD, MCI, and control groups than preprocessed subtotal score-like features, as contrasted in Table 17.3. When applying our predictive rule to a third trial of 200 patients, over 88% blind prediction accuracy is

TABLE 17.2   Classification Results of Emory Data, 10-Fold Cross-Validation, and Blind Prediction

	AD	MCI	Ctl	AD	MCI	Ctl		AD	MCI	Ctl	AD	MCI	Ctl
	10-Fold Cross-Validation							Blind Prediction					
AD	4	1	0	0.80	0.20	0.00	AD	2	0	0	1.00	0.00	0.00
MCI	0	11	0	0.00	1.00	0.00	MCI	1	4	0	0.20	0.80	0.00
Ctl	0	0	8	0.00	0.00	1.00	Ctl	0	0	4	0.00	0.00	1.00
Unbiased estimate accuracy: 96%							Blind prediction accuracy: 91%						

Five discriminatory features were selected (among the 100 features): MMSE:cMMtotal; WordList:cWL2Butter; WordList:cWL2Queen; WordList:cWL2Ticket; GDS:GDS13.

TABLE 17.3   Classification Results of the Same Emory Data, 10-Fold Cross-Validation, and Blind Prediction from 9 Score-Type Features Instead of Raw Data

10-Fold Cross-Validation						Blind Prediction					
	AD	MCI	Ctl	AD	MCI	Ctl	AD	MCI	Ctl	AD	MCI	Ctl
AD	4	1	0	0.80	0.20	0.00	AD	1	1	0	0.50	0.50	0.00
MCI	1	9	1	0.09	0.82	0.09	MCI	0	5	0	0.00	1.00	0.00
Ctl	0	2	6	0.00	0.25	0.75	Ctl	0	1	3	0.00	0.25	0.75
Unbiased estimate accuracy: 79%						Blind prediction accuracy: 82%					

Two discriminatory features were selected: MMSE:cMMtotal; Word List:cWLcorTotal.

achieved. The classification approach and the results offer the potential for development of a clinical decision-making tool for early detection. Further study must be conducted to validate its clinical significance and its predictive accuracy among various demographic groups and across multiple sites.

17.4.2.3 Predicting Aberrant CpG Island Methylation in Human Cancer

We summarize our findings from Feltus, Lee et al. (2003, 2006); McCabe et al. (2009) herein. Epigenetic silencing associated with aberrant methylation of promoter region CpG islands is one mechanism leading to loss of tumor suppressor function in human cancer. Profiling of CpG island methylation indicates that some genes are more frequently methylated than others and that each tumor type is associated with a unique set of methylated genes. However, little is known about why certain genes succumb to this aberrant event. To address this question, restriction landmark genomic scanning (RLGS) is used to analyze the susceptibility of 1749 unselected CpG islands to de novo methylation driven by overexpression of DNMT1. We found that whereas the overall incidence of CpG island methylation was increased in cells overexpressing DNMT1, not all loci were equally affected. The majority of CpG islands (69.9%) were resistant to de novo methylation, regardless of DNMT1 overexpression. In contrast, we identified a subset of methylation-prone CpG islands (3.8%) that were consistently hypermethylated in multiple DNMT1-overexpressing clones. Methylation-prone and methylation-resistant CpG islands were not significantly different with respect to size, C+G content, CpG frequency, chromosomal location, or gene or promoter association. To discriminate methylation-prone from methylation-resistant CpG islands, we developed a novel DNA pattern recognition model and algorithm (Lee et al. 2006) and coupled our DAMIP predictive model described herein with the patterns found. The feature selection uncovered seven novel sequence patterns and their frequency of occurrence. The resulting rule was capable of discriminating methylation-prone from methylation-resistant CpG islands with 90% correctness upon cross-validation. It could blind predict new CpG islands (methylation status unknown to us) with 85% accuracy. The findings indicate that CpG islands differ in their intrinsic susceptibility to de novo methylation and suggest that the propensity for a CpG island to become aberrantly methylated can be predicted based on its sequence context.

The significance of this research is twofold. Firstly, the identification of sequence pattern/attributes that can discriminate methylation-prone CpG islands will lead to a better understanding of the basic mechanisms underlying aberrant CpG island methylation. Because genes that are silenced by methylation are otherwise structurally sound, the potential for reactivating these genes by blocking or reversing the methylation process represents an exciting new molecular target for chemotherapeutic intervention. A better understanding of the factors that contribute to aberrant methylation, including the identification of sequence elements that may act to target aberrant methylation, will be an important step in achieving this long-term goal. Secondly, the classification of the more than 29,000 known (but as yet unclassified) CpG islands in human chromosomes will provide an important resource for the identification of novel gene targets for further study as potential molecular markers that could impact on both cancer prevention and treatment. Extensive RLGS fingerprint information (and thus potential training sets of methylated CpG islands) already exists for a number of human tumor types, including breast, brain, lung, leukemias, hepatocellular carcinomas, and PNET (Costello et al. 2000a, b; Fruhwald et al. 2000; Rush et al. 2001). Thus, the methods and tools developed are directly applicable to CpG island methylation data derived from human tumors. Moreover, new microarray-based techniques capable of "profiling" more than 7000 CpG islands have been developed and applied to human breast cancers (Brock et al. 2001; Yan et al. 2000, 2001). Indeed, we have shown that using the predictive rule established from the breast cancer cell line and applying it to lung cancer cells, the blind prediction accuracy reaches over 80% (McCabe et al. 2009). We are uniquely poised to take advantage of the tumor CpG island methylation profile information that will likely be generated using these techniques over the next several years. Thus, our general-purpose predictive modeling framework has the potential to lead to improved diagnosis and prognosis and treatment design for cancer patients.

17.4.2.4 *Ultrasonic Assisted Cell Disruption for Drug Delivery* Although biological effects of ultrasound must be avoided for safe diagnostic applications, ultrasound's ability to disrupt cell membranes has attracted interest as a method to facilitate drug and gene delivery. Our study in Lee et al. (2004) seeks to develop rules for predicting the degree of cell membrane disruption based on specified ultrasound parameters and measured acoustic signals. Too much ultrasound destroys cells, while cell membranes will not open up for absorption of macromolecules when too little ultrasound is applied. The key is to increase cell permeability to allow absorption of macromolecules and to apply ultrasound transiently to disrupt viable cells so as to enable exogenous material to enter without cell damage. Thus our task is to uncover a "predictive rule" of ultrasound-mediated disruption of red blood cells using acoustic spectrums and measurements of cell permeability recorded in experiments.

DAMIP is applied to data obtained from a sequence of experiments on bovine red blood cells. For each experiment, the attributes consist of four ultrasound parameters, acoustic measurements at 400 frequencies, and a measure of cell membrane disruption. To avoid overtraining, various feature combinations of the 404 predictor variables are selected when developing the classification rule. The results indicate that the variable combination consisting of ultrasound exposure time and acoustic signals measured at the driving frequency and its higher harmonics yields the best rule. Further, our method compares favorably with classification tree and other ad hoc approaches, with correct classification rate of 80% upon cross-validation and 85% blind prediction accuracy when classifying new unknown entities. Our methods used for deriving the prediction rules are broadly applicable and could be used to develop prediction rules in other scenarios involving different cell types or tissues. These rules and the methods used to derive them could be used for real-time feedback about ultrasound's biological effects. For example, it could assist clinicians during a drug delivery process or could be imported into an implantable device inside the body for automatic drug delivery and monitoring.

17.4.2.5 Identification of Tumor Shape and Volume in Treatment of Sarcoma

This project involves the determination of tumor shape for adjuvant brachytherapy treatment of sarcoma, based on catheter images taken after surgery (Lee et al. 2002). In this application, the entities are overlapping consecutive triplets of catheter markings, each of which is used to determine the shape of the tumor contour. The triplets are to be classified into one of two groups: group 1 = [triplets for which the middle catheter marking should be bypassed] and group 2 = [triplets for which the middle marking should not be bypassed]. To develop and validate the classification rule, we used clinical data collected from fifteen soft tissue sarcoma (STS) patients. Cumulatively, this comprised 620 triplets of catheter markings. By careful (and tedious) clinical analysis of the geometry of these triplets, 65 were determined to belong to group 1, the "bypass" group, and 555 were determined to belong to group 2, the "do-not-bypass" group.

A set of attributes associated with each triplet is then determined. The choice of what attributes to measure to best distinguish triplets as belonging to group 1 or group 2 is nontrivial. The attributes involved distance between each pair of markings, angles, and curvature formed by the three triplet markings. Based on the selected attributes, DAMIP was used to develop a classification rule. The resulting rule provides 98% correct classification on cross-validation and was capable of correctly predicting 95% of the shape of the tumor on new patients' data. We remark that the current clinical procedure requires manual outline based on markers in films of the tumor volume. Our study was the first to automate the construction of tumor shape for sarcoma adjuvant brachytherapy (Lee et al. 2002).

17.4.2.6 Discriminant Analysis of Biomarkers for Prediction of Early Atherosclerosis

Oxidative stress is an important etiologic factor in the pathogenesis of vascular disease (Lee 2007). This stress results from an imbalance between injurious oxidant and protective antioxidant events in which the former predominate (McCord 2000;

Sies 1985). This results in the modification of proteins and DNA, alteration in gene expression, promotion of inflammation, and deterioration in endothelial function in the vessel wall, all processes that ultimately trigger or exacerbate the atherosclerotic process (Chevion et al. 2000; Tahara et al. 2001). It was hypothesized that novel biomarkers of oxidative stress could predict early atherosclerosis in a relatively healthy nonsmoking population who are free from cardiovascular disease. One hundred and twenty-seven healthy nonsmokers without known clinical atherosclerosis had carotid intima-media thickness (IMT) measured using ultrasound. Plasma oxidative stress was estimated by measuring plasma lipid hydroperoxides using the determination of reactive oxygen metabolites (d-ROMs) test. Clinical measurements include traditional risk factors including age, sex, low-density lipoprotein (LDL), high-density lipoprotein (HDL), triglycerides, cholesterol, body mass index (BMI), hypertension, diabetes mellitus, smoking history, family history of CAD, Framingham risk score, and Hs-CRP.

For this prediction, the patients are first clustered into two groups: (group 1: IMT≥0.68, group 2: IMT<0.68). Based on this separator 30 patients belong to group 1, and 97 belong to group 2. Randomly selecting 90 patients from these two groups as a training set, DAMIP trains and learns and returns the most discriminatory patterns among the 14 clinical measurements, ultimately resulting in a prediction rule based on age, sex, BMI, HDLc, Fhx CAD<60, hs-CRP, and d-ROM as discriminatory attributes. The resulting rule provides 80% and 89% blind prediction accuracy on the remaining 37 patients classifying into group 1 and group 2, respectively. In particular, the importance of d-ROM as a discriminatory predictor for IMT status was confirmed during the machine learning process. This biomarker was selected at each iteration as the "machine" learned and trained to develop a predictive rule to correctly classify patients in the training set. We also performed predictive analysis using Framingham risk score and d-ROM; in this case the unbiased correct classification rates for groups 1 and 2 are 77% and 84%, respectively. This is the first study to illustrate that the measures of oxidative stress can be effectively used along with traditional risk factors to generate a predictive rule that can potentially serve as an inexpensive clinical diagnostic tool for predicting early atherosclerosis.

17.4.2.7   Fingerprinting Native and Angiogenic Microvascular Networks through Pattern Recognition and Discriminant Analysis of Functional Perfusion Data

The cardiovascular system provides oxygen and nutrients to the entire body (Lee 2007). Pathological conditions that impair normal microvascular perfusion can result in tissue ischemia, with potentially serious clinical effects. Conversely, development of new vascular structures fuels the progression of cancer, macular degeneration, and atherosclerosis. Fluorescence microangiography offers superb imaging of the functional perfusion of new and existent microvasculature, but quantitative analysis of the complex capillary patterns is challenging.

In Lee 2007, we developed an automated pattern recognition algorithm to systematically analyze the microvascular networks and then applied DAMIP to generate a predictive rule. The pattern recognition algorithm identifies the complex vascular branching patterns, and the predictive rule demonstrates 100% and 91% correct classification on perturbed (diseased) and normal tissue perfusion, respectively. We confirmed that transplantation of normal bone marrow to mice in which genetic deficiency resulted in impaired angiogenesis eliminated predicted differences and restored normal tissue perfusion patterns (with 100% correctness). The pattern recognition and DAMIP offers an elegant solution for the automated fingerprinting of microvascular networks that could contribute to better understanding of angiogenic mechanisms and be utilized to diagnose and monitor microvascular deficiencies. Such information would be valuable for early detection and monitoring of functional abnormalities before they produce obvious and lasting effects, which may include improper perfusion of tissue, or support of tumor development.

The algorithm can be used to discriminate between the angiogenic response in a native healthy specimen compared with groups with impairment due to age or chemical or other genetic deficiency. Similarly, it can be applied to analyze angiogenic responses as a result of various treatments. This will serve two important goals. First, the identification of discriminatory attributes that distinguish angiogenesis status will lead to a better understanding of the basic mechanisms underlying this process. Because therapeutic control of angiogenesis could influence physiological and pathological processes such as wound and tissue repairing, cancer progression and metastasis, or macular degeneration, the ability to understand it under different conditions will offer new insight in developing novel therapeutic interventions, monitoring, and treatment, especially in aging and heart disease. Thus, our study and the results form the foundation of a valuable diagnostic tool for changes in the functionality of the microvasculature and for discovery of drugs that alter the angiogenic response. The methods can be applied to tumor diagnosis, monitoring, and prognosis. In particular, it will be possible to derive microangiographic fingerprints to acquire specific microvascular patterns associated with early stages of tumor development. Such "angioprinting" could become an extremely helpful early diagnostic modality, especially for easily accessible tumors such as skin cancer.

17.4.3 Applying DAMIP to UCI Repository of Machine Learning Databases

UCI Machine Learning Repository maintains 404 data sets as a service to the machine learning community (Murphy and Aha 1994). We demonstrate the multi-group and multi-stage classification capabilities of DAMIP using some of these instances.

17.4.3.1 Determining the Type of Erythemato-squamous Disease   The differential diagnosis of erythemato-squamous diseases is an important problem in dermatology. They all share the clinical features of erythema and scaling, with very little differences. The six groups are psoriasis, seborrheic dermatitis, lichen planus, pityriasis rosea, chronic dermatitis, and pityriasis rubra pilaris. Usually a biopsy is necessary for the diagnosis, but unfortunately these diseases share many histopathological features as well. Another difficulty for the differential diagnosis is that a disease may show the features of another disease at the beginning stage and may have the characteristic features at later stages.

The six groups consist of 366 subjects (112, 61, 72, 49, 52, 20, respectively) with 34 clinical attributes. Patients were first evaluated clinically with 12 features. Afterward, skin samples were taken for evaluation of 22 histopathological features. The values of these histopathological features are determined by an analysis of the samples under a microscope. The 34 attributes include:

1. Clinical attributes: Erythema, scaling, definite borders, itching, Koebner phenomenon, polygonal papules, follicular papules, oral mucosal involvement, knee and elbow involvement, scalp involvement, family history, and age
2. Histopathological attributes: Melanin incontinence, eosinophils in the infiltrate, PNL infiltrate, fibrosis of the papillary dermis, exocytosis, acanthosis, hyperkeratosis, parakeratosis, clubbing of the rete ridges, elongation of the rete ridges, thinning of the suprapapillary epidermis, spongiform pustule, Munro microabscess, focal hypergranulosis, disappearance of the granular layer, vacuolization and damage of basal layer, spongiosis, sawtooth appearance of retes, follicular horn plug, perifollicular parakeratosis, inflammatory mononuclear infiltrate, and band-like infiltrate

Using 250 randomly selected subjects to develop the rule, our multi-group DAMIP model selected 27 discriminatory attributes and successfully classified the patients into six groups, each with an unbiased estimate of greater than 93% accuracy (with 100% correct rate for groups 1, 3, 5, 6) and an average overall accuracy of 98%. Blind prediction on the remaining 116 patients yields a prediction accuracy of 91% for each group.

17.4.3.2 Predicting Presence/Absence of Heart Disease   The four databases concerning heart disease diagnosis were collected by Dr. Janosi of Hungarian Institute of Cardiology, Budapest; Dr. Steinbrunn of University Hospital, Zurich; Dr. Pfisterer of University Hospital, Basel, Switzerland; and Dr. Detrano of V.A. Medical Center, Long Beach and Cleveland Clinic Foundation. Each database contains the same 76 attributes. The "goal" field refers to the presence of heart disease in the patient. The classification attempts to discriminate *presence* (values 1, 2, 3, 4, involving a total of 509 subjects) from *absence* (value 0, involving 411 subjects). The attributes include demographics, physio-cardiovascular conditions, traditional risk factors, family history, personal lifestyle, and cardiovascular exercise measurements. This dataset has posed some challenges to past analysis via various classification approaches, resulting in less than 80% unbiased classification accuracy. Applying our classification model without reserved judgment, we obtain 79% and 85% correct classification for each group, respectively.

To gauge the usefulness of multistage analysis, we apply two-stage classification. In the first stage, 14 attributes were selected as discriminatory. Specifically, 235 (out of 276) *absence* subjects were classified correctly into group *absence*, and 203 (out of 223) *presence* subjects were classified into group *presence*. This yields an

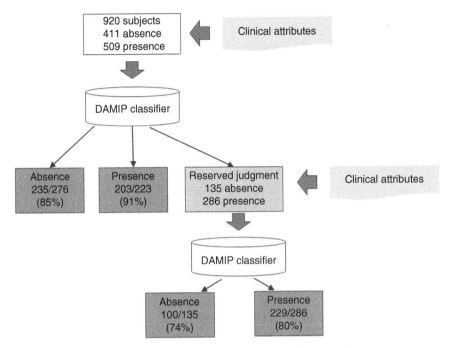

Figure 17.1 A tree diagram for two-stage DAMIP classification and prediction of heart disease.

accuracy of 85% and 91%, respectively, for each group. The reserved judgment comprises the remaining 135 *absence* subjects and 286 *presence* subjects. In the second stage, 11 attributes were selected in which 100 *absence* subjects, and 229 *presence* subjects were classified correctly into respective groups. Combining the two stages, we obtained a correct classification of 82% and 85%, respectively, for diagnosis of absence or presence of heart disease. Figure 17.1 illustrates the two-stage classification.

To gauge the predictive power, 600 subjects used for training via multistage DAMIP classification result in 85% and 84% accuracy for 10-fold cross-validation. Blind prediction on the remaining 320 subjects results in 85% and 83% prediction accuracy.

17.4.3.3 Prediction of Protein Localization Sites The protein localization data-base consists of eight groups with a total of 336 instances (143, 77, 52, 35, 20, 5, 2, 2, respectively) each with seven attributes. The eight groups are eight localization sites of protein, including cp (cytoplasm), im (inner membrane without signal sequence), pp (periplasm), imU (inner membrane, uncleavable signal sequence), om (outer membrane), omL (outer membrane lipoprotein), imL (inner membrane lipo-protein), and imS (inner membrane, cleavable signal sequence). However, the last four groups are taken out from our classification experiment since the population sizes are too small to ensure significance.

The seven attributes include mcg (McGeoch's method for signal sequence recognition), gvh (von Heijne's method for signal sequence recognition), lip (von Heijne's signal peptidase II consensus sequence score), chg (presence of charge on N-terminus of predicted lipoproteins), aac (score of discriminant analysis of the amino acid content of outer membrane and periplasmic proteins), alm1 (score of the ALOM membrane-spanning region prediction program), and alm2 (score of ALOM program after excluding putative cleavable signal regions from the sequence).

In the classification there are four groups, 307 instances, each with seven attributes. Our classification model selected the discriminatory patterns mcg, gvh, alm1, and alm2 to form the predictive rule with unbiased correct classification rates of 89%, compared with the results of 81% by other classification models (Horton and Nakai 1996). Using only 200 instances to train, the blind prediction accuracy on the remaining 107 instances reaches over 90% for each of the four groups.

17.4.3.4 Pattern Recognition in Satellite Images for Determining Types of Soil The Satellite Database consists of the multispectral values of pixels in 3×3 neighborhoods in a satellite image and the classification associated with the central pixel in each neighborhood. The goal is to predict this classification given the multispectral values. In the sample database, the class of a pixel is coded as a number. There are six groups with 4435 samples in the training dataset and 2000 samples in testing dataset; and each sample entity has 36 attributes describing the spectral bands of the image.

The original Landsat Multispectral Scanner (MSS) image data for this database was generated from data purchased from NASA by the Australian Centre for Remote Sensing. The Landsat satellite data is one of the many sources of information available for a scene. The interpretation of a scene by integrating spatial data of diverse types and resolutions including multispectral and radar data, maps indicating topography, land use, etc. is expected to assume significant importance with the onset of an era characterized by integrative approaches to remote sensing (e.g., NASA's Earth Observing System commencing this decade).

One frame of Landsat MSS imagery consists of four digital images of the same scene in different spectral bands. Two of these are in the visible region (corresponding approximately to green and red regions of the visible spectrum) and two are in the (near) infrared. Each pixel is an 8-bit binary word, with 0 corresponding to black and 255 to white. The spatial resolution of a pixel is about $80\,m \times 80\,m$. Each image contains 2340×3380 such pixels.

The database is a (tiny) subarea of a scene consisting of 82×100 pixels. Each line of data corresponds to a 3×3 square neighborhood of pixels completely contained within the 82×100 subarea. Each line contains the pixel values in the four spectral bands (converted to ASCII) of each of the 9 pixels in the 3×3 neighborhood and a number indicating the classification label of the central pixel. The number is a code for the following six groups: red soil, cotton crop, gray soil, damp gray soil, soil with vegetation stubble, and very damp gray soil. Running the DAMIP model, 17 discriminatory attributes were selected to form the classification rule, producing a blind prediction accuracy of 85%.

17.5 SUMMARY AND CONCLUSION

In the chapter, we summarize a class of general-purpose predictive models that we have developed based on the technology of large-scale optimization and support vector machines (Gallagher et al. 1997; Lee 2007, 2008, 2009; Lee et al. 2003; Brooks and Lee 2010, 2014). Our models seek to maximize the correct classification rate while constraining the number of misclassifications in each group. The models incorporate the following features simultaneously:

1. The ability to classify any number of distinct groups.
2. The ability to allow the incorporation of heterogeneous and temporal types of attributes as input.
3. A high-dimensional data transformation that reduces dimension, noise, and errors in biological data.
4. Constraining the misclassification in each group and a reserved-judgment region that provides a safeguard against overtraining (which tends to lead to high misclassification rates from the resulting predictive rule).
5. Successive multistage classification capability to handle data points placed in the reserved-judgment region. The performance and predictive power of the classification models is validated through a broad class of biological and medical applications.

Classification models are critical to medical advances as they can be used in genomic, cell, molecular, and system-level analyses to assist in early risk prediction, diagnosis and detection of disease, intervention and monitoring, and treatment outcome prediction. As shown in the vaccine immunogenicity prediction, the predictive signatures can guide the rapid development of vaccines against emerging infections and aid in the monitoring of suboptimal immune responses in the elderly, infants, or people with weakened immune systems. Neuropsychological tests are inexpensive and noninvasive, and it can be incorporated within an annual physical examination for baseline record. Our study on AD shows that neuropsychological tests can offer predictive capability for earliest diagnosis. Identifying individuals who are at risk but currently have no symptoms is critical to curtail the rapid rise of this illness. In the CpG island study for human cancer, such prediction and diagnosis opens up novel therapeutic sites for early intervention. The ultrasound application illustrates its application to a novel drug delivery mechanism, assisting clinicians during a drug delivery process, or in devising implantable devices into the body for automated drug delivery and monitoring. Prediction of the shape of a cancer tumor bed provides a personalized treatment design, replacing tedious and subjective manual estimates by sophisticated automated computer predictive models. Prediction of early atherosclerosis through inexpensive biomarker measurements and traditional risk factors can serve as a potential clinical diagnostic tool for routine physical and health maintenance, alerting doctors and patients the need for early intervention to prevent serious vascular disease. Fingerprinting of microvascular networks opens up the possibility for early diagnosis of perturbed systems in the body that may trigger disease (e.g., genetic deficiency, diabetes, aging, obesity, macular degeneracy, tumor formation), identifying target sites for treatment and monitoring prognosis and success of treatment. Determining the type of erythemato-squamous disease and the presence/ absence of heart disease helps clinicians to correctly diagnose and effectively treat patients. Thus classification models can serve as a basis for predictive health and precision medicine where the desire is to diagnose early and provide timely and personalized target intervention. This has the potential to reduce healthcare costs, improve success of treatment, and improve quality of life of patients.

The modeling framework of the discrete support vector machines, DAMIP, offers great flexibility, enabling one to simultaneously incorporate the features as listed here in this section, as well as many other features. Further theoretical study will be performed on these models to understand their characteristics and the sensitivity of the predictive patterns to model and parameter variations. We note that deriving the predictive rules for such problems can be computationally demanding due to the *NP-hard* nature of MIP. However, blind prediction can be achieved in seconds, opening up real-time predictive tools for routine usage. We continue to work on improving optimization algorithms utilizing novel cutting plane and branch-and-bound strategies, fast heuristic algorithms, parallel algorithms, and in-data computing in the cloud.

ACKNOWLEDGMENT

This research was partially supported by the National Institutes of Health and the National Science Foundation.

REFERENCES

Anderson, J. A. (1969). "Constrained discrimination between k populations." *Journal of the Royal Statistical Society, Series B*, 31, 123–139.

Bajgier, S. M. and A. V. Hill (1982). "An experimental comparison of statistical and linear programming approaches to the discriminant problems." *Decision Sciences*, 13, 604–618.

Bal, H. and H. H. Örkcü (2011). "A new mathematical programming approach to multi-group classification problems." *Computers & Operations Research*, 38(1), 105–111.

Beckman, R. J. and M. E. Johnson (1981). "A ranking procedure for partial discriminant analysis." *Journal of the American Statistical Association*, 76(375), 671–675.

Bennett, K. P. and E. J. Bredensteiner (1997). "A parametric optimization method for machine learning." *INFORMS Journal on Computing*, 9, 311–318.

Bennett, K. P. and O. L. Mangasarian (1993). "Multicategory discrimination via linear programming." *Optimization Methods and Software*, 3, 27–39.

Bishop, C. M. (1995). *Neural Networks for Pattern Recognition*. Oxford, U.K.: Oxford University Press.

Bradley, P. S., U. M. Fayyad, and O. L. Mangasarian (1999). "Mathematical programming for data mining: Formulations and challenges." *INFORMS Journal on Computing*, 11, 217–238.

Breiman, J., R. Friedman, A. Olshen, and C. J. Stone (1984). *Classification and Regression Trees*. Monterey, CA: Wadsworth.

Brock, G. J., T. H. Huang, C. M. Chen, and K. J. Johnson (2001). "A novel technique for the identification of CpG islands exhibiting altered methylation patterns (ICEAMP)." *Nucleic Acids Research*, 29, E123.

Broffit, J. D., R. H. Randles, and R. V. Hogg (1976). "Distribution-free partial discriminant analysis." *Journal of the American Statistical Association*, 71, 934–939.

Brooks, J. P. and E. K. Lee (2006). "Solving a mixed-integer programming formulation of a multi-category constrained discrimination model." In *Proceedings of the 2006 INFORMS Workshop on Artificial Intelligence and Data Mining INFORMS*, 1–6.

Brooks, J. P. and E. K. Lee (2007). "Mixed integer programming constrained discrimination model for credit screening." *Proceedings of the 2007 Spring Simulation Multiconference–3*, 127–132. Norfolk, Virginia — March 25–29, 2007. Society for Computer Simulation International San Diego, CA, USA.

Brooks, J. P. and E. K. Lee (2010). "Analysis of the consistency of a mixed integer programming-based multi-category constrained discriminant model." *Annals of Operations Research*, 174(1), 147–168.

Brooks, J. P. and E. K. Lee (2014). "Solving a multigroup mixed-integer programming-based constrained discrimination model." *INFORMS Journal on Computing*, 26(3), 567–585.

Byvatov, E. and G. Schneider (2002). "Support vector machine applications in bioinformatics." *Applied Bioinformatics*, 2(2), 67–77.

Cao, K., N. Lailler, Y. Zhang, A. Kumar, K. Uppal, Z. Liu, E. K. Lee, H. Wu, M. Medrzycki, C. Pan, P.-Y. Ho, G. P. Cooper, Jr., X. Dong, C. Bock, E. E. Bouhassira and Y. Fan (2013). "High-resolution mapping of h1 linker histone variants in embryonic stem cells." *PLoS Genetics*, 9(4), e1003417.

Cavalier, T. M., J. P. Ignizio, and A. L. Soyster (1989). "Discriminant analysis via mathematical programming: certain problems and their causes." *Computers and Operations Research*, 16, 353–362.

Chevion, M., E. Berenshtein, and E. R. Stadtman (2000). "Human studies related to protein oxidation: Protein carbonyl content as a marker of damage." *Free Radical Research*, 33(Suppl), S99–S108.

Christensen, J. (2017). First malaria vaccine to be widely tested in Africa next year. http://www.cnn.com/2017/04/24/health/malaria-vaccine-trial-who/index.html. Accessed on April 26, 2017

Conway, K. E., B. B. McConnell, C. E. Bowring, C. D. Donald, S. T. Warren, and P. M. Vertino (2000). "TMS1, a novel proapoptotic caspase recruitment domain protein, is a target of methylation-induced gene silencing in human breast cancers." *Cancer Research*, 60, 6236–6242.

Costello, J. F., M. C. Fruhwald, D. J. Smiraglia, L. J. Rush, G. P. Robertson, X. Gao, F. A. Wright, J. D. Feramisco, P. Peltomaki, J. C. Lang, D. E. Schuller, L. Yu, C. D. Bloomfield, M. A. Caligiuri, A. Yates, R. Nishikawa, H. H. Su, N. J. Petrelli, X. Zhang, M. S. O'Dorisio, W. A. Held, W. K. Cavenee, and C. Plass (2000a). "Aberrant CpG-island methylation has non-random and tumour-type-specific patterns." *Nature Genetics*, 24, 132–138.

Costello, J. F., C. Plass, and W. K. Cavenee (2000b). "Aberrant methylation of genes in low-grade astrocytomas." *Brain Tumor Pathology*, 17, 49–56.

Cristianini, N. and J. Shawe-Taylor (2000). *An Introduction to Support Vector Machines and Other Kernel-Based Learning Methods*. Cambridge, U.K.: Cambridge University Press.

Duarte Silva, A. P. and A. Stam (1994). "Second order mathematical programming formulations for discriminant analysis." *European Journal of Operational Research*, 72, 4–22.

Duda, R. O., P. E. Hart, and D. G. Stork (2001). *Pattern Classification* (2nd edition). New York. John Wiley & Sons, Inc..

Dreiseitl, S. and L. Ohno-Machado (2002). "Logistic regression and artificial neural network classification models: A methodology review." *Journal of Biomedical Informatics*, 35(5), 352–359.

Easton, T., K. Hooker, and E. K. Lee (2003)."Facets of the independent set polytope." *Mathematical Programming B*, 98, 177–199.

Feltus, F. A., E. K. Lee, J. F. Costello, C. Plass, and P. M. Vertino (2003). "Predicting aberrant CpG island methylation." *Proceedings of the National Academy of Sciences*, 100(21), 12253–12258.

Feltus, F. A., E. K. Lee, J. F. Costello, C. Plass, and P. M. Vertino (2006). "DNA signatures associated with CpG island methylation states." *Genomics*, 87, 572–579.

Fisher, R. A. (1936). "The use of multiple measurements in taxonomic problems." *Annals of Eugenics*, 7, 179–188.

Freed, N. and F. Glover (1981). "A linear programming approach to the discriminant problem." *Decision Sciences*, 12, 68–74.

Freed, N. and F. Glover (1986). "Evaluating alternative linear programming models to solve the two-group discriminant problem." *Decision Sciences*, 17, 151–162.

Freund, Y., R. Schapire, and N. Abe (1999). "A short introduction to boosting." *Journal of Japanese Society for Artificial Intelligence*, 14(771–780), 1612.

Frommer, M., L. E. McDonald, D. S. Millar, C. M. Collis, F. Watt, G. W. Grigg, P. L. Molloy, and C. L. Paul (1992). "A genomic sequencing protocol that yields a positive display of 5-ethylcytosine residues in individual DNA strands." *Proceedings of the National Academy of Sciences of the United States of America*, 89, 1827–1831.

Fruhwald, M. C., M. S. O'Dorisio, L. J. Rush, J. L. Reiter, D. J. Smiraglia, G. Wenger, J. F. Costello, P. S. White, R. Krahe, G. M. Brodeur, and C. Plass (2000). "Gene amplification in NETs/medulloblastomas: Mapping of a novel amplified gene within the MYCN amplicon." *Journal of Medical Genetics*, 37, 501–509.

Gallagher, R. J., E. K. Lee, and D. Patterson (1996). "An optimization model for constrained discriminant analysis and numerical experiments with iris, thyroid, and heart disease datasets."

Proc AMIA Annu Fall Symp. 1996:209–13. Publisher: Oxford University Press. United Kingdom.

Gallagher, R. J., E. K. Lee, and D. A. Patterson (1997). "Constrained discriminant analysis via 0/1 mixed integer programming." *Annals of Operations Research*, 74, 65–88, Special Issue on Non-Traditional Approaches to Statistical Classification and Regression.

Gardiner-Garden, M. and M. Frommer (1987). "CpG islands in vertebrate genomes." *Journal of Molecular Biology*, 196, 261–282.

Gehrlein, W. V. (1986). "General mathematical programming formulations for the statistical classification problem." *Operations Research Letters*, 5, 299–304.

Gessaman, M. P. and P. H. Gessaman (1972). "A comparison of some multivariate discrimination procedures." *Journal of the American Statistical Association*, 67, 468–472.

Glen, J. J. (1999). "Integer programming methods for normalisation and variable selection in mathematical programming discriminant analysis models." *Journal of the Operational Research Society*, 50, 1043–1053.

Glover, F. (1990). "Improved linear programming models for discriminant analysis." *Decision Sciences*, 21, 771–785.

Glover, F., S. Keene, and B. Duea (1988). "A new class of models for the discriminant problem." *Decision Sciences*, 19, 269–280.

Gochet, W., A. Stam, V. Srinivasan, and S. Chen (1997). "Multigroup discriminant analysis using linear programming." *Operations Research*, 45, 213–225.

Habbema, J. D. F., J. Hermans, and A. T. Van Der Burgt (1974). "Cases of doubt in allocation problems." *Biometrika*, 61, 313–324.

Herman, J. G., J. R. Graff, S. Myohanen, B. D. Nelkin, and S. B. Baylin (1996). "Methylation-specific PCR: A novel PCR assay for methylation status of CpG islands." *Proceedings of the National Academy of Sciences of the United States of America*, 93, 9821–9826.

Horton, P. and K. Nakai (1996). "A probabilistic classification system for predicting the cellular localization sites of proteins." *Intelligent Systems in Molecular Biology* (pp. 109–115). St. Louis, MO, June 12–15, 1996. Menlo Park, CA: The AAAI Press.

Kazmin, D., H. I. Nakaya, E. K. Lee, M. J. Johnson, R. van der Most, R. A. van den Berg, W. R. Ballou, E. Jongert, U. Wille-Reece, C. Ockenhouse, A. Aderem, D. E. Zak, J. Sadoff, J. Hendriks, J. Wrammert, R. Ahmed, and B. Pulendran (2017). "Systems analysis of protective immune responses to RTS,S malaria vaccination in humans." *Proceedings of the National Academy of Science*, 114(9), 2425–2430.

Koczor, C. A., E. K. Lee, R. A. Torres, A. Boyd, J. D. Vega, K. Uppal, F. Yuan, E. J. Fields, A. M. Samarel, and W. Lewis (2013). "Detection of differentially methylated gene promoters in failing and nonfailing human left ventricle myocardium using computation analysis." *Physiological Genomics*, 45(14), 597–605.

Koehler, G. J. and S. S. Erenguc (1990). "Minimizing misclassifications in linear discriminant analysis." *Decision Sciences*, 21, 63–85.

Lee, E. K. (2007). "Large-scale optimization-based classification models in medicine and biology." *Annals of Biomedical Engineering*, 35(6), 1095–1109.

Lee, E. K. (2008). "Optimization-based predictive models in medicine and biology." In *Optimization in Medicine* (pp. 127–151). Editors: C. J. S. Alves, P. M. Pardalos, L. N. Vicente. New York: Springer.

Lee, E. K. (2009). "Machine learning framework for classification in medicine and biology." In *Integration of AI and OR Techniques in Constraint Programming for Combinatorial Optimization Problems* (pp. 1–7). Editors: W. J. van Hoeve, E. Coban. Berlin/Heidelberg, Germany: Springer.

Lee, E. K., T. Easton, and K. Gupta (2006). "Novel evolutionary models and applications to sequence alignment problems." *Operations Research in Medicine—Computing and Optimization in Medicine and Life Sciences*, 148, 167–187.

Lee, E. K., A. Y. C. Fung, J. P. Brooks, and M. Zaider (2002). "Automated tumor volume contouring in soft-tissue sarcoma adjuvant brachytherapy treatment." *International Journal of Radiation Oncology, Biology, and Physics*, 47(11), 1891–1910.

Lee, E. K., R. Gallagher, A. Campbell, and M. Prausnitz (2004). "Prediction of ultrasound-mediated disruption of cell membranes using machine learning techniques and statistical analysis of acoustic spectra." *IEEE Transactions on Biomedical Engineering*, 51(1), 1–9.

Lee, E. K., R. J. Gallagher, and D. Patterson (2003). "A linear programming approach to discriminant analysis with a reserved judgment region." *INFORMS Journal on Computing*, 15(1), 23–41.

Lee, E. K., H. Nakaya, F. Yuan, T. Querec, F. Pietz, B. A. Benecke, G. Burel, and B. Pulendra (2016). "Machine learning framework for predicting vaccine immunogenicity." *Interfaces*, 46(5), 368–390, The Daniel H. Wagner Prize for Excellence in Operations Research Practice.

Lee, E. K. and T. L. Wu (November 2007). "Classification and disease prediction via mathematical programming." In *Data Mining, Systems Analysis and Optimization in Biomedicine* (Vol. 953, No. 1, pp. 1–42). Editors: O. Seref, O. Erhun Kundakcioglu, P. M. Pardalos. Melville, NY: AIP Publishing.

Lee, E. K., T. L. Wu, and J. P. Brooks (2008). "Classification and disease prediction via mathematical programming." *Optimization in Medicine and Biology* (Chapter 1, pp. 3–60). Editors: G. J. Lim, E. K. Lee. Boca Raton, FL: Auerbach Publications/Taylor & Francis Group.

Lee, E. K. and T. L. Wu (2009) Classification and disease prediction via mathematical programming. In: PM Pardalos, HE Romeijn, eds. Handbook of Optimization in Medicine, Chapter 12. Springer Optimization and Its Applications. The Netherlands: Springer 2009:26:381–430.

Lee, E. K., T. L. Wu, F. Goldstein, and A. Levey (2012). "Predictive model for early detection of mild cognitive impairment and Alzheimer's disease." In *Optimization and Data Analysis in Biomedical Informatics* (pp. 83–97). Editors: P. M. Pardalos, T. F. Coleman, and P. Xanthopoulos. New York: Springer.

Lee, E. K., F. Yuan, A. Templeton, R. Yao, K. Kiel, and J. C. H. Chu (2013). "Biological planning for high-dose rate brachytherapy: Application to cervical cancer treatment." *Interfaces*, 43(5), 462–476, The Daniel H. Wagner Prize for Excellence in Operations Research Practice.

Lee, E. K. and M. Zaider (February 2008). "Operations research advances cancer therapeutics." *Interfaces*, 38(1), 5–25, Franz Edelman Award Achievement in Operations Research.

Liittschwager, J. M. and C. Wang (1978). "Integer programming solution of a classification problem." *Management Science*, 24, 1515–1525.

Lim, T. S. W., Y. Loh, and Y. S. Shih (2000). "A comparison of prediction accuracy, complexity, and training time of thirty-three old and new classification algorithms." *Machine Learning*, 40, 203–228.

Mangasarian, O. L. (1993). "Mathematical programming in neural networks." *ORSA Journal on Computing*, 5, 349–360.

Mangasarian, O. L., W. N. Street, and W. H. Wolberg (1995). "Breast cancer diagnosis and prognosis via linear programming." *Operations Research*, 43, 570–577.

Mangasarian, O. L. (1997). "Mathematical programming in data mining." *Data Mining and Knowledge Discovery*, 1(2), 183–201.

McCabe, M. T., E. K. Lee, and P. M. Vertino (2009). "A multifactorial signature of DNA sequence and polycomb binding predicts aberrant CpG island methylation." *Cancer Research*, 69(1), 282–291.

McCord, J. M. (2000). "The evolution of free radicals and oxidative stress." *American Journal of Medicine*, 108, 652–659.

McLachlan, G. J. (1992). *Discriminant Analysis and Statistical Pattern Recognition*. New York: Wiley.

Mitchell, J. E. (2002). "Branch-and-cut algorithms for combinatorial optimization problems." *Handbook of Applied Optimization*. Editors: P. M. Pardalos, M. G. C. Resende (pp. 65–77). Oxford, U.K.: Oxford University Press.

Müller, K. R., S. Mika, G. Rätsch, K. Tsuda, and B. Schölkopf (2001). "An introduction to kernel-based learning algorithms." *IEEE Transactions on Neural Networks*, 12(2), 181–201.

Murphy, P. M. and D. W. Aha (1994). "UCI Repository of machine learning databases." Department of Information and Computer Science, University of California, Irvine, CA.

Nakaya, H. I., J. Wrammert, E. K. Lee, L. Racioppi, S. Marie-Kunze, W. N. Haining, L. Racioppi, S. Marie-Kunze, W. Nicholas Haining, A. R. Means, S. P. Kasturi, N. Khan, G.-M. Li, M. McCausland, V. Kanchan, K. E. Kokko, S. Li, R. Elbein, A. K. Mehta, A. Aderem, K. Subbarao, R. Ahmed, and B. Pulendran (2011). "Systems biology of seasonal influenza vaccination in humans." *Nature Immunology*, 12(8), 786.

Nakaya, H. I., T. Hagan, M. Kwissad, E. K. Lee, M. Kwissa, N. Rouphael, D. Frasca, M. Gersten, A. K. Mehta, R. Gaujoux, G.-M. Li, S. Gupta, R. Ahmed, M. J. Mulligan, S. Shen-Orr, B. B. Blomberg, S. Subramaniam, and B. Pulendran (December 15, 2015). "Systems analysis of immunity to influenza vaccination across multiple years and in diverse populations reveals shared molecular signatures." *Immunity*, 43(6), 1186–1198.

Nakayama, H. and N. Kagaku (1998). "Pattern classification by linear goal programming and its extensions." *Journal of Global Optimization*, 12(2), 111–126.

Nath R., W. M. Jackson, and T. W. Jones (1992). "A comparison of the classical and the linear programming approaches to the classification problem in discriminant analysis." *Journal of Statistical Computation and Simulation*, 41, 73–93.

Ng, T.-H. and R. H. Randles (1986). "Distribution-free partial discrimination procedures." *Computers and Mathematics with Applications*, 12A, 225–234.

Patterson, D. A. (1996). "Three population constrained discrimination." Technical Report. Department of Mathematical Sciences, University of Montana, Missoula, MT.

Pavur, R. and C. Loucopoulos (1995). "Examining optimal criterion weights in mixed integer programming approaches to the multiple-group classification problem." *Journal of the Operational Research Society*, 46, 626–640.

Querec, T. D., R. S. Akondy, E. K. Lee, W. Cao, H. I. Nakaya, D. Teuwen, A. Pirani, K. Gernert, J. Deng, B. Marzolf, K. Kennedy, H. Wu, S. Bennouna, H. Oluoch, J. Miller, R. Z. Vencio,

M. Mulligan, A. Aderem, R. Ahmed, and B. Pulendran (2009). "Systems biology approach predicts immunogenicity of the yellow fever vaccine in humans." *Nature Immunology*, 10(1), 116–125.

Quesenberry, C. P. and M. P. Gessaman (1968). "Nonparametric discrimination using tolerance regions." *Annals of Mathematical Statistics*, 39, 664–673.

Ravindran, R., N. Khan, H. I. Nakaya, S. Li, J. Loebbermann, M. S. Maddur, Y. Park, D. P. Jones, P. Chappert, J. Davoust, D. S. Weiss, H. W. Virgin, D. Ron, and B. Pulendran (2014). "Vaccine activation of the nutrient sensor GCN2 in dendritic cells enhances antigen presentation." *Science*, 343(6168), 313–317

Ravindran, R., J. Loebbermann, H. I. Nakaya, N. Khan, H. Ma, L. Gama, D. K. Machiah, B. Lawson, P. Hakimpour, Y.-C. Wang, S. Li, P. Sharma, R. J. Kaufman, J. Martinez, and B. Pulendran (2016). "The amino acid sensor GCN2 controls gut inflammation by inhibiting inflammasome activation." *Nature*, 531 (7595), 523–527.

Rush, L. J., Z. Dai, D. J. Smiraglia, X. Gao, F. A. Wright, M. Fruhwald, J. F. Costello, W. A. Held, I. Yu, R. Krahe, J. E. Kolitz, C. D. Bloomfield, M. A. Caligiuri, and C. Plass (2001). "Novel methylation targets in de novo acute myeloid leukemia with prevalence of chromosome 11 loci." *Blood*, 97, 3226–3233.

Savelsbergh, M. W. (1994). "Preprocessing and probing techniques for mixed integer programming problems." *ORSA Journal on Computing*, 6(4), 445–454.

Sies, H. (1985). "Oxidative stress: Introductory comments." In: *Oxidative Stress* (pp. 1–8). Editor: H. Sies. London, U.K.: Academic Press, Inc.

Stam, A. (1997). "Nontraditional approaches to statistical classification: Some perspectives on *Lp*-norm methods." *Annals of Operations Research*, 74, 1–36.

Stam, A. and E. A. Joachimsthaler (1989). "Solving the classification problem in discriminant analysis via linear and nonlinear programming." *Decision Sciences*, 20, 285–293.

Stam, A. and E. A. Joachimsthaler (1990). "A comparison of a robust mixed-integer approach to existing methods for establishing classification rules for the discriminant problem." *European Journal of Operational Research*, 46, 113–122.

Stam, A. and C. T. Ragsdale (1992). "On the classification gap in mathematical-programming-based approaches to the discriminant problem." *Naval Research Logistics*, 39, 545–559.

Tahara, S., M. Matsuo, and T. Kaneko (2001). "Age-related changes in oxidative damage to lipids and DNA in rat skin." *Mechanisms of Ageing and Development*, 122, 415–426.

Vapnik, V. (1999). *The Nature of Statistical Learning Theory*. New York: Springer-Verlag.

Wilson, J. M. (1996). "Integer programming formulations of statistical classification problems." *Omega*, 24(6), 681–688.

Yan, P. S., C. M. Chen, H. Shi, F. Rahmatpanah, S. H. Wei, C. W. Caldwell, and T. H. Huang (2001). "Dissecting complex epigenetic alterations in breast cancer using CpG island microarrays." *Cancer Research*, 61, 8375–8380.

Yan, P. S., M. R. Perry, D. E. Laux, A. L. Asare, C. W. Caldwell, and T. H. Huang (2000). "CpG island arrays: An application toward deciphering epigenetic signatures of breast cancer." *Clinical Cancer Research*, 6, 1432–1438.

Zimmermann, A. and H. U. Keller (1987). "Locomotion of tumor cells as an element of invasion and metastasis." *Biomedicine & Pharmacotherapy*, 41, 337–344.

Zopounidis, C. and M. Doumpos (2002). "Multicriteria classification and sorting methods: A literature review." *European Journal of Operational Research*, 138, 229–246.

INDEX

Decision Analytics and Optimization in Disease Prevention and Treatment, First Edition.
Edited by Nan Kong and Shengfan Zhang.
© 2018 John Wiley & Sons, Inc. Published 2018 by John Wiley & Sons, Inc.

Wiley Series in
Operations Research and Management Science

Operations Research and Management Science (ORMS) is a broad, interdisciplinary branch of applied mathematics concerned with improving the quality of decisions and processes and is a major component of the global modern movement towards the use of advanced analytics in industry and scientific research. The *Wiley Series in Operations Research and Management Science* features a broad collection of books that meet the varied needs of researchers, practitioners, policymakers, and students who use or need to improve their use of analytics. Reflecting the wide range of current research within the ORMS community, the series encompasses application, methodology, and theory and provides coverage of both classical and cutting-edge ORMS concepts and developments. Written by recognized international experts in the field, this collection is appropriate for students and professionals from private and public sectors, including industry, government, and nonprofit organizations that are interested in ORMS at a technical level. The series comprises four sections: Analytics, Decision and Risk Analysis, Optimization Models, and Stochastic Models.

Advisory Editors • Analytics
Jennifer Bachner, Johns Hopkins University
Khim Yong Goh, National University of Singapore

Founding Series Editor
James J. Cochran, University of Alabama

Analytics
Yang and Lee • *Healthcare Analytics: From Data to Knowledge to Healthcare Improvement*
Attoh-Okine • *Big Data and Differential Privacy: Analysis Strategies for Railway Track Engineering*
Kong and Zhang • *Decision Analytics and Optimization in Disease Prevention and Treatment*

Decision and Risk Analysis
Barron • *Game Theory: An Introduction*, Second Edition
Brailsford, Churilov, and Dangerfield • *Discrete-Event Simulation and System Dynamics for Management Decision Making*
Johnson, Keisler, Solak, Turcotte, Bayram, and Drew • *Decision Science for Housing and Community Development: Localized and Evidence-Based Responses to Distressed Housing and Blighted Communities*
Mislick and Nussbaum • *Cost Estimation: Methods and Tools*

Forthcoming Titles
Aleman and Carter • *Healthcare Engineering*

Optimization Models
Ghiani, Laporte, and Musmanno • *Introduction to Logistics Systems Management, Second Edition*
Tone • *Advances in DEA Theory and Applications: With Examples in Forecasting Models*

Forthcoming Titles
Smith • *Learning Operations Research Through Puzzles and Games*

Stochastic Models
Ibe • Random Walk and Diffusion Processes

Forthcoming Titles
Donohue, Katok, and Leider • *The Handbook of Behavioral Operations*
Matis • *Applied Markov Based Modelling of Random Processes*